Renwise

See inside for an illustration of

Criminal Justice in America 7e

George F. Cole
University of Connecticut

Christopher E. Smith
Michigan State University

Christina DeJong
Michigan State University

WADSWORTH
CENGAGE Learning·

Australia • Brazil • Japan • Korea • Mexico • Singapore • Spain • United Kingdom • United States

Criminal Justice in America, **Seventh Edition**
George F. Cole, Christopher E. Smith,
Christina DeJong

Editor-in-Chief: Linda Ganster

Senior Acquisitions Editor:
Carolyn Henderson Meier

Senior Developmental Editor: Shelley Murphy

Assistant Editor: Rachel McDonald

Editorial Assistant: Casey Lozier

Media Editor: Ting Jian Yap

Market Development Manager:
Michelle Williams

Brand Manager: Melissa Larmon

Senior Content Project Manager:
Christy A. Frame

Senior Art Director: Maria Epes

Senior Manufacturing Planner: Judy Inouye

Rights Acquisitions Specialist: Roberta Broyer

Production Service: Greg Hubit Bookworks

Photo Researcher: Sarah Evertson

Text Researcher: Pablo D'Stair

Copy Editor: Marne Evans

Proofreader: Debra Nichols

Text Designer: Jeanne Calabrese

Interior Design Images: crime scene tape:
© Mark Wineman/iStockphoto; green
graphic: © Ali Mazraie Shadi/iStockphoto;
prison cell: © Marina Nezhinkay/iStockphoto;
U.S. flag: © Liudmila Chernova/iStockphoto;
globe and gears: © DNY59/iStockphoto;
spotlight: © Yarygin/iStockphoto; purple
graphic: © Momcilo Grujic/iStockphoto;
compass: © DNY59/iStockphoto; talk bubbles
chat: © hh5800/iStockphoto.com

Cover Designer: Riezebos Holzbaur/
Tae Hatayama

Cover Images: statue: Alan Schein Photography/
Corbis; policeman on motorcycle: Steve Allen/
Getty Images; handcuffed inmate: David
R. Frazier/Photo Researchers, Inc; eagle
illustration: Mike Quon/Quon Design

Compositor: MPS Limited

Library of Congress Control Number: 2012941552

ISBN-13: 978-1-285-06766-7

ISBN-10: 1-285-06766-5

Wadsworth
20 Davis Drive
Belmont, CA 94002-3098
USA

Cengage Learning is a leading provider of customized learning solutions with
office locations around the globe, including Singapore, the United Kingdom,
Australia, Mexico, Brazil, and Japan. Locate your local office at
www.cengage.com/global

Cengage Learning products are represented in Canada by Nelson Education, Ltd.

To learn more about Wadsworth, visit **www.cengage.com/wadsworth**

Purchase any of our products at your local college store or at our preferred
online store **www.cengagebrain.com**

Unless otherwise noted, all content is © Cengage Learning.

Printed in the United States of America
1 2 3 4 5 6 7 16 15 14 13 12

Brief Contents

part one   Crime and the Criminal Justice System

1   The Criminal Justice System   3

2   Crime and Crime Causation   39

3   Criminal Justice and the Rule of Law   73

part two   Police

4   Police   107

5   Policing: Contemporary Issues and Challenges   141

6   Police and Law   179

part three   Courts

7   Courts and Adjudication   209

8   Pretrial Procedures, Plea Bargaining, and the Criminal Trial   243

9   Punishment and Sentencing   275

part four   Corrections

10   Corrections   309

11   Incarceration and Prison Society   343

12   Probation and Intermediate Sanctions   379

part five   Special Issues in Criminal Justice

13   Reentry into the Community   401

14   Technology and Criminal Justice   429

15   Juvenile Justice   467

Contents

Preface xv

---

part one   Crime and the Criminal Justice System

1   The Criminal Justice System 3

The Goals of Criminal Justice 5
   Doing Justice 5
   Controlling Crime 6
   Preventing Crime 6

Criminal Justice in a Federal System 7
   Two Justice Systems 8
   Expansion of Federal Involvement 8

Criminal Justice as a Social System 11

Characteristics of the Criminal Justice System 12
   Discretion 12
   Resource Dependence 13
   Sequential Tasks 14
   Filtering 14

Operations of Criminal Justice Agencies 15
   Police 15
   Courts 16
   Corrections 16

The Flow of Decision Making
in the Criminal Justice System 17
   Steps in the Decision-Making Process 19
   The Criminal Justice Wedding Cake 22
   Crime Control versus Due Process 23

Crime and Justice in a Multicultural Society 25
   Disparity and Discrimination 25

Explaining Disparities 27

---

the criminal justice process: The State
of Michigan versus Christopher Jones 34

2   Crime and Crime Causation 39

Types of Crime 41
   Visible Crime 41
   Occupational Crime 42

Organized Crime 42
Victimless Crimes 43
Political Crime 43
Cyber Crime 44

How Much Crime Is There? 45
   The Uniform Crime Reports 46
   The National Crime Victimization Surveys 49
   Trends in Crime 50

Crime Victimization 52
   Who Is Victimized? 52
   Acquaintances and Strangers 55
   The Impact of Crime 56
   The Experience of Victims in the Criminal Justice
System 58
   The Role of Victims in Crime 59

Causes of Crime 59
   Classical and Positivist Theories 60
   Biological Explanations 61
   Psychological Explanations 62
   Sociological Explanations 63
   Life Course Theories 65
   Integrated Theories 66
   Women and Crime 66
   Assessing Theories of Criminality 67

**3   Criminal Justice
and the Rule of Law** 73

Foundations of Criminal Law 75

Substantive Criminal Law 76
   Definitions and Classifications of Criminal Laws 76
   Elements of a Crime 79
   Seven Principles of Criminal Law 80
   Defenses against Criminal Charges 81
   Justification Defenses 84
   Excuse Defenses 84

Procedural Criminal Law **88**

The Bill of Rights and the Fourteenth Amendment   89

The Fourteenth Amendment and Due Process   92

The Due Process Revolution   92

The Fourth Amendment: Protection against Unreasonable Searches and Seizures   93

The Fifth Amendment: Protection against Self-Incrimination and Double Jeopardy   94

The Sixth Amendment: The Right to Counsel and a Fair Trial   95

The Eighth Amendment: Protection against Excessive Bail, Excessive Fines, and Cruel and Unusual Punishments   97

Constitutional Rights and Criminal Justice Professionals   **100**

inside the criminal justice system & beyond: One Man's Journey—My Affair with Heroin   **104**

part two   Police

4   **Police**   **107**

The Development of Police in the United States   **108**

The English Roots of the American Police   108

Policing in the United States   110

The Next Era: Homeland Security? Scarce Resources?   114

Law Enforcement Agencies   **116**

Federal Agencies   116

State Agencies   118

County Agencies   118

Native American Tribal Police   118

Municipal Agencies   119

Special Jurisdiction Agencies   119

Who Are the Police?   **120**

Recruitment   120

The Changing Profile of the Police   123

Training   125

The Police Subculture   **126**

The Working Personality   126

Police Morality   127

Police Isolation   128

Job Stress   128

Police Functions   **130**

Order Maintenance   130

Law Enforcement   130

Service   131

Implementing the Mandate   131

Organization of the Police   **132**

Bureaucratic Elements   132

Operational Units   134

The Police Bureaucracy and the Criminal Justice System   134

Police Policy   **135**

Police Discretion   143

Police Abuse of Power   **145**

Use of Force   145

Corruption   147

Civic Accountability   **148**

Internal Affairs Units   149

Civilian Review Boards   149

Standards and Accreditation   149

Civil Liability Lawsuits   150

Delivery of Police Services   **151**

Police Response   151

Productivity   152

Patrol Functions   **154**

Investigation   155

Special Operations   156

Issues in Patrolling   **158**

Assignment of Patrol Personnel   158

The Future of Patrol   161

Police and the Community   **162**

Special Populations   162

Policing in a Multicultural Society   162

Community Crime Prevention   163

Homeland Security   **166**

Preparing for Threats   166

New Laws and Controversies   169

Security Management and Private Policing   **170**

Functions of Security Management and Private Policing   171

Private Police and Homeland Security   172

Private Employment of Public Police   172

The Public–Private Interface   173

Recruitment and Training   173

5   **Policing: Contemporary Issues and Challenges**   **141**

Everyday Action of Police   **143**

Encounters between Police and Citizens   143

6   **Police and Law**   **179**

Legal Limitations on Police Investigations   **180**

Search and Seizure Concepts   181

Use of Force and the Fourth Amendment   182

The Concept of Arrest 183

Warrants and Probable Cause 183

Warrantless Searches 186

Special Needs beyond the Normal Purposes
of Law Enforcement 186

Stop and Frisk on the Streets 187

Search Incident to a Lawful Arrest 189

Exigent Circumstances 189

Consent 190

Automobile Searches 191

Questioning Suspects 193

Miranda Rules 193

The Consequences of Miranda 195

The Exclusionary Rule 197

The Application of the Exclusionary Rule to the States 198

Exceptions to the Exclusionary Rule 198

inside the criminal justice system
& beyond: One Man's Journey—Stepping into
a New World: Arrested, Booked, Charged, Jailed,
and Investigated 206

part three | Courts

7 Courts and Adjudication 209

The Functions and Structure of American Courts 211

The Functions of Courts 211

The Structure of Courts 212

To Be a Judge 215

Who Becomes a Judge? 215

Functions of the Judge 216

How to Become a Judge 218

The Prosecutorial System 221

Politics and Prosecution 221

The Prosecutor's Influence 223

The Prosecutor's Roles 223

Discretion of the Prosecutor 225

Key Relationships of the Prosecutor 226

Decision-Making Policies 227

The Defense Attorney: Image and Reality 229

The Role of the Defense Attorney 229

Realities of the Defense Attorney's Job 230

The Environment of Criminal Practice 232

Counsel for Indigents 232

The Courtroom: How It Functions 237

8 Pretrial Procedures, Plea Bargaining, and the Criminal Trial 243

From Arrest to Trial or Plea 244

Bail: Pretrial Release 247

The Reality of the Bail System 247

Bail Agents 249

Setting Bail 250

Reforming the Bail System 250

Pretrial Detention 252

Plea Bargaining 255

Exchange Relationships in Plea Bargaining 256

Tactics of Prosecutor and Defense 256

Pleas without Bargaining 257

Legal Issues in Plea Bargaining 257

Criticisms of Plea Bargaining 258

Trial: The Exceptional Case 259

Jury Trial 260

The Trial Process 261

Evaluating the Jury System 267

Appeals 268

Habeas Corpus 269

Evaluating the Appellate Process 270

9 Punishment and Sentencing 275

The Goals of Punishment 277

Retribution—Deserved Punishment 277

Deterrence 277

Incapacitation 279

Rehabilitation 280

A New Approach to Punishment: Restorative Justice 281

Forms of the Criminal Sanction 282

Incarceration 283

Intermediate Sanctions 286

Probation 287

Death 287

The Sentencing Process 296

The Administrative Context of the Courts 296

Attitudes and Values of Judges   297

Presentence Report   298

Sentencing Guidelines   299

Who Gets the Harshest Punishment?   301

inside the criminal justice system &
beyond: One Man's Journey—Prosecution, Adjudication,
and Sentencing   306

part four | Corrections

10 Corrections   309

Development of Corrections   310

Invention of the Penitentiary   310

Reform in the United States   312

Reformatory Movement   315

Improving Prison Conditions for Women   316

Rehabilitation Model   316

Community Model   317

Crime Control Model   317

Organization of Corrections
in the United States   319

Federal Corrections System   319

State Corrections Systems   319

Private Prisons   322

Jails: Detention and Short-Term Incarceration   324

The Law of Corrections   327

Constitutional Rights of Prisoners   327

Law and Community Corrections   331

Law and Correctional Personnel   332

Correctional Policy Trends   333

Community Corrections   335

Incarceration   336

11 Incarceration and Prison Society   343

The Modern Prison: Legacy of the Past   344

Goals of Incarceration   347

Prison Organization   348

Governing a Society of Captives   349

The Defects of Total Power   350

Rewards and Punishments   350

Gaining Cooperation: Exchange Relationships   351

Inmate Leadership   351

The Challenge of Governing Prisons   352

Correctional Officers: The Linchpins of Management   352

The Officer's Role   352

Recruitment of Officers   353

Use of Force   354

Who Is in Prison?   355

Elderly Prisoners   355

Prisoners with HIV/AIDS   357

Mentally Ill Prisoners   357

Long-Term Prisoners   358

The Convict World   358

Adaptive Roles   359

The Prison Economy   361

Women in Prison   362

The Subculture of Women's Prisons   363

Male versus Female Subcultures   364

Issues in the Incarceration of Women   365

Prison Programs   367

Classification of Prisoners   367

Educational Programs   368

Vocational Education   368

Prison Industries   369

Rehabilitative Programs   369

Medical Services   370

Violence in Prison   371

Assaultive Behavior and Inmate Characteristics   372

Prisoner–Prisoner Violence   373

Prisoner–Officer Violence   374

Officer–Prisoner Violence   374

Decreasing Prison Violence   375

12 Probation and Intermediate Sanctions   379

Community Corrections: Assumptions   380

Probation: Correction without Incarceration   381

Origins and Evolution of Probation   382

Organization of Probation   383

Probation Services   384

Revocation and Termination of Probation   385

Assessing Probation   387

Intermediate Sanctions in the Community **388**

Intermediate Sanctions Administered Primarily
by the Judiciary 389

Intermediate Sanctions Administered in the Community 391

Intermediate Sanctions Administered in Institutions
and the Community 395

Implementing Intermediate Sanctions 396

The Future of Community Corrections **398**

part five Special Issues in Criminal Justice

13 Reentry into the Community 401

Prisoner Reentry **402**

Contemporary Budget Cuts and Prisoner Release 403

Institutional Reentry Preparation Programs 404

Release and Supervision **406**

The Origins of Parole 406

The Development of Parole in the United States **407**

Release Mechanisms **407**

Expiration Release 408

Mandatory Release 408

Other Conditional Release 408

Discretionary Release 409

The Parole Board Process 409

Impact of Release Mechanisms 414

Parole Supervision in the Community **415**

Community Programs following Release 416

Parole Officer: Cop or Social Worker? 418

The Parole Bureaucracy 419

Adjustment to Life Outside Prison 419

Revocation of Parole 421

The Future of Prisoner Reentry **422**

inside the criminal justice system
& beyond: One Man's Journey—Prison **426**

14 Technology and Criminal Justice 429

Technological Development and Criminal Justice **431**

Competition and Adaptation 431

Science and the Presumption of Progress 432

Crime and Technology **434**

Cyber Crime 434

Counterfeiting 437

Policing and New Technology **440**

Communications and Computer Technology 441

DNA Analysis 445

Surveillance and Identification 451

Weapons Technology 453

Technology in Courts and Corrections **455**

Courts 455

Corrections 459

Current Questions and Challenges for the Future **462**

15 Juvenile Justice 467

Youth Crime in the United States **468**

The Development of Juvenile Justice **470**

The Puritan Period (1646–1824) 472

The Refuge Period (1824–1899) 472

The Juvenile Court Period (1899–1960) 472

The Juvenile Rights Period (1960–1980) 473

The Crime Control Period (1980–2005) 475

The "Kids Are Different" Period (2005–Present) 475

The Juvenile Justice System **479**

Age of Clients 479

Categories of Cases under Juvenile Court Jurisdiction 479

The Juvenile Justice Process **481**

Police Interface 481

Intake Screening at the Court 483

Pretrial Procedures 484

Transfer (Waiver) to Adult Court 485

Adjudication 486

Disposition 488

Corrections 488

Problems and Perspectives **492**

inside the criminal justice system &
beyond: One Man's Journey—Reflections **496**

Glossary **498**

References **504**

Name Index **520**

Subject Index **526**

Boxed Features

careers in criminal justice

Mark Bridge, Crime Analyst	Chapter 2	p. 47
Abraham V. Hutt, Criminal Defense Attorney	Chapter 3	p. 82
Mary Peterson, Police Officer	Chapter 4	p. 121
Erin Goff, Intelligence Analyst	Chapter 5	p. 168
Karl Huether, U.S. Border Patrol Agent	Chapter 6	p. 188
Kym Worthy, Prosecuting Attorney	Chapter 7	p. 222
Kirk Daily, District Associate Judge	Chapter 9	p. 302
Scott Yokom, Assistant Resident Unit Supervisor	Chapter 10	p. 322
Lisa Zimmer, Assistant Clinical Director	Chapter 11	p. 370
Scott Lopofsky, U.S. Probation Officer Assistant	Chapter 12	p. 384
Richard Rosales, Reentry Specialist	Chapter 13	p. 405
Lindsey Murray, Forensic DNA Analyst	Chapter 14	p. 450
Kia Loggins, Intake Referee	Chapter 15	p. 484

close up

Racial Profiling	Chapter 1	p. 29
Hate Crimes: A New Category of Personal Violence	Chapter 2	p. 45
Criminal Intent and the Appropriateness of Punishment	Chapter 3	p. 83
The Use of Volunteers in Law Enforcement	Chapter 4	p. 136
Living under Suspicion	Chapter 5	p. 164
Herring v. United States, 555 U.S. 135 (2009)	Chapter 6	p. 202
The Accountability of Prosecutors	Chapter 7	p. 224
The "*CSI* Effect" and Jurors' Expectations about Scientific Evidence	Chapter 8	p. 265
Judges and Sentencing	Chapter 9	p. 299
Free Exercise of Religion Inside Prisons	Chapter 10	p. 329
One Man's Walk through Atlanta's Jungle	Chapter 11	p. 345
Survival Tips for Beginners	Chapter 11	p. 360
Life under Home Confinement	Chapter 12	p. 393
A Personal Encounter with the Parole Process in Michigan	Chapter 13	p. 412
Cell Phones in Prisons	Chapter 14	p. 461
J. D. B. v. North Carolina (2011)	Chapter 15	p. 477

the policy debate

Have Tough Crime-Control Policies Caused a Decline in Crime?	Chapter 2	p. 52
Should Ex-Felons' Gun-Ownership Rights Be Restored?	Chapter 3	p. 91
Should Terrorism Suspects in the United States Enjoy the Protections of the Bill of Rights?	Chapter 6	p. 184

Should the Death Penalty Be Abolished?   Chapter 9   p. 294
Should Prison Populations Be Reduced through the
Accelerated Release of Offenders?   Chapter 13   p. 410
Should Juvenile Offenders Be Tried as Adults?   Chapter 15   p. 486

comparative perspective

Procedural Criminal Law in Russia   Chapter 3   p. 97
The Exclusionary Rule in Canada and Europe   Chapter 6   p. 199
Pretrial Detention in the Philippines   Chapter 8   p. 254
Behind Bars in North America and Europe   Chapter 10   p. 334
The Day Fine: Questions and Challenges from a European Punishment   Chapter 12   p. 390
Gang Behavior and the Criminal Justice Response in Europe: Eurogang   Chapter 15   p. 493

Cases Cited

Adams v. Williams, 189, 192
Argersinger v. Hamlin, 233
Arizona v. Gant, 189
Atkins v. Virginia, 290
Austin v. United States, 98

Batson v. Kentucky, 263
Baze v. Rees, 291
Beard v. Banks, 328
Bell v. Wolfish, 329
Berghuis v. Thompkins, 194
Blackledge v. Allison, 255
Blakely v. Washington, 301
Board of Education v. Earls, 475
Bordenkircher v. Hayes, 258
Boykin v. Alabama, 257
Brady v. Maryland, 224
Breed v. Jones, 474
Brendlin v. California, 182
Brewer v. Williams, 200
Brigham City, Utah v. Stuart, 190
Brown v. Mississippi, 194
Brown v. Plata, 330, 371, 409
Bumper v. North Carolina, 190, 192
Burch v. Louisiana, 261

California v. Acevedo, 191, 192
Carroll v. United States, 191, 192
Chandler v. Miller, 475
Chimel v. California, 189, 192
City of Indianapolis v. Edmond, 187, 192
Clark v. Arizona, 86
Connick v. Thompson, 224
Coolidge v. New Hampshire, 181
Cooper v. Pate, 327
Couch v. Jabe, 329
Cupp v. Murphy, 190, 192

Dakota v. Opperman, 192
Delaware v. Prouse, 187
Dickerson v. United States, 194
District Attorney's Office v. Osborne, 303, 449
District of Columbia v. Heller, 91
Douglas v. California, 233

Eddings v. Oklahoma, 474
Escobedo v. Illinois, 194

Florida v. J. L., 189
Florida v. Powell, 194
Ford v. Wainwright, 292
Furman v. Georgia, 290

Georgia v. Randolph, 191
Gideon v. Wainwright, 95, 233
Glover v. Johnson, 330
Gragnon v. Scarpelli, 332
Graham v. Connor, 183
Graham v. Florida, 99, 474, 476
Gregg v. Georgia, 290
Griffin v. Wisconsin, 331

Hamdi v. Rumsfeld, 75, 169
Heath v. Alabama, 94
Herring v. United States, 201, 202–203
Hudson v. Palmer, 328

Illinois v. Caballes, 93
Illinois v. Gates, 185
Illinois v. Lidster, 187
Illinois v. Rodriguez, 191
Illinois v. Wardlow, 189, 192
In re Gault, 473, 474
In re Kemmler, 432
In re Winship, 474
Indiana v. Edwards, 95
Irizarry v. United States, 301

J. D. B. v. North Carolina, 194, 476, 477–478
Johnson v. California, 330
Johnson v. Zerbst, 233

Kansas v. Hendricks, 420
Kennedy v. Louisiana, 291
Kent v. United States, 473, 474
Kentucky v. King, 190
Knowles v. Iowa, 191, 192
Kyllo v. United States, 452

Lafler v. Cooper, 257
Lee v. Washington, 330
Lewis v. United States, 96
Lockhart v. McCree, 292
Lockyer v. Andrade, 99

Mapp v. Ohio, 198, 200
Maryland v. Wilson, 191, 192
Massiah v. United States, 194
McCleskey v. Kemp, 290
McDonald v. Chicago, 91, 213
McKeiver v. Pennsylvania, 474
Melendez-Diaz v. Massachusetts, 449
Michigan Department of State Police v. Sitz, 187, 192
Michigan v. Long, 191
Miller v. Alabama, 476

Miranda v. Arizona, 193, 233
Missouri v. Frye, 257
Missouri v. Seibert, 196
M'Naghten Case, 86
Monell v. Department of Social Services of the
    City of New York, 150, 332
Montana v. Egelhoff, 86
Morrissey v. Brewer, 331, 421
Murray v. Giarratano, 233

New York v. Class, 191, 192
New York v. Quarles, 194
Nix v. Williams, 200
North Carolina v. Alford, 258

Oklahoma Publishing Co. v. District Court, 474

Pennsylvania Board of Pardons and
    Parole v. Scott, 331
Pepper v. United States, 301
Powell v. Alabama, 92, 233
Procunier v. Martinez, 328

R. v. Grant, 199
Ricketts v. Adamson, 258
Robinson v. California, 80
Roper v. Simmons, 291, 474, 475, 494
Ross v. Moffitt, 95, 233
Rothgery v. Gillespie, 95

Safford Unified School District #1 v. Redding, 475
Samson v. California, 331
Santobello v. New York, 255, 258
Schall v. Martin, 474, 475
Skinner v. Oklahoma, 61

Smith v. Daily Mail Publishing Co., 474
Stanford v. Kentucky, 474
Strickland v. Washington, 233, 292

Tennessee v. Garner, 182
Terry v. Ohio, 164, 187, 192
Thompson v. Oklahoma, 474
Trop v. Dulles, 98
Turner v. Safley, 328

United States v. Bajakajian, 98
United States v. Booker, 301
United States v. Brawner, 87
United States v. Drayton, 190, 192
United States v. Jacobson, 85
United States v. Jones, 452
United States v. Leon, 199, 200
United States v. Robinson, 189, 192
United States v. Salerno and Cafero, 98, 252
United States v. Wade, 233

Vernonia School District v. Acton, 475
Virginia v. Black, 45
Virginia v. Moore, 189

Warden v. Hayden, 189, 192
Weeks v. United States, 197, 198
Wiggins v. Smith, 292
Williams v. Florida, 261
Wilson v. Seiter, 329
Wisconsin v. Mitchell, 45
Witherspoon v. Illinois, 292
Wolf v. Colorado, 198
Wolff v. McDonnell, 330
Wyoming v. Houghton, 191

Preface

Criminal Justice in America, Seventh Edition, is designed for instructors seeking a textbook that provides students a thorough introduction to the dynamics of the American system of criminal justice without overwhelming them. The text is an offspring of *The American System of Criminal Justice*, which has been used by more than half a million students over the course of its 13 editions. But much has changed in the 30 years since the first edition of *The American System of Criminal Justice* was published. And that is exactly why we created *Criminal Justice in America*—a briefer, more applied, student-centered introduction to the American system of criminal justice. In creating this text, we did not merely drop a few chapters, combine others, and limit the graphic elements to reduce page count, however. We started from scratch. So, while *Criminal Justice in America* relies on the research and conceptual framework of the larger text, it is not overly theoretical; throughout the book, examples from today's headlines are used to link the concepts and information to real-life criminal justice situations. And while the focus of *Criminal Justice in America* is just as interdisciplinary as the comprehensive book's focus is, it is less encyclopedic and benefits from added career-based material; international and comparative coverage; skill-building writing exercises; and up-to-the-minute coverage of technology, terrorism, homeland security, cyber crime, and other current topics.

The Approach of This Text

Three key assumptions about the nature of American criminal justice as a discipline and the way the introductory course should be taught run throughout the book.

1. *Criminal justice involves public policies* that are developed within the political framework of the democratic process.
2. *The concept of social system is an essential tool* for explaining and analyzing the way criminal justice is administered and practiced.
3. *American values provide the foundation on which criminal justice is based.*

With concerns about terrorism and civil liberties at the forefront of the national agenda, basic American values—individual liberty, equality, fairness, and the rule of law—need to be emphasized.

This book's approach has met with a high degree of acceptance and might be called the dominant paradigm in criminal justice education. Criminal justice is interdisciplinary, with criminology, sociology, law, history, psychology, and political science contributing to the field. The three themes of public policy, social system, and American values help place the research contributions of these disciplines in a context that allows students to better understand the dynamics of criminal justice.

Organization

The Seventh Edition is organized to introduce important fundamental concepts, use those concepts in presenting the important institutional segments of the justice system (police, courts, corrections), and then highlight important contemporary issues concerning reentry from prison, the use of technology, and juvenile justice. The organization of the book is designed to provide comprehensive coverage of the criminal justice system that follows an appropriate sequence, stimulates student interest, and illuminates contemporary issues and problems. The 15-chapter structure of the book creates an opportunity for instructors to move at a steady pace of approximately one chapter per week in the typical length of an academic semester.

Part One of the Seventh Edition presents three chapters that introduce core concepts of the criminal justice system, describe the nature and extent of crime, and supply a framework for understanding the role of law in defining crime and protecting individuals' rights.

Three chapters on police compose Part Two. Here the Seventh Edition builds upon the core concepts in Part One to describe and examine the history, functions, and organization of policing. One chapter examines contemporary issues affecting police, including choices about patrol strategies and delivery of services, the challenges of homeland security, and the increasing importance of private security. The legal issues surrounding police authority to conduct searches and question suspects are covered in a separate chapter. Part Two also examines issues concerning civic accountability and the abuse of police authority.

The focus of the chapters in Part Three is on the courts, plea bargaining, and adjudication. One chapter discusses the important roles of judges, prosecutors, and defense attorneys. Other chapters examine the bail process, plea bargaining, and trials. The final chapter in Part Three describes the sentencing process, including the forms and purposes of punishment.

Part Four concerns corrections, and includes material on corrections history and prisoners' rights. One chapter covers detailed aspects of incarceration and prison society. A separate chapter presents probation and intermediate sanctions.

Part Five covers special issues in criminal justice, and the chapter on reentry and parole completes the community corrections coverage introduced in the final chapter of Part Four. Separate chapters examine the rapid changes in use of technology by all institutions within the criminal justice system. The final chapter examines juvenile justice and contemporary debates about appropriate punishment and treatment for youthful offenders.

New to the Seventh Edition

For this Seventh Edition, we are very pleased to welcome a new coauthor, Christina DeJong, Ph.D., Associate Professor of Criminal Justice and Director of the Center for Integrative Studies in Social Science at Michigan State University. Dr. DeJong, a criminologist who earned her doctorate at the University of Maryland, has published extensively on such topics as domestic violence, women offenders, juvenile justice, and policing. Her expertise on the foregoing topics, as well as criminology and corrections, has made significant contributions to chapters throughout the book.

This edition encompasses important revisions in content and presentation. Users of the Seventh Edition will find many significant changes. In particular, we present ethics issues at the end of each chapter based on actual events in the news, which will challenge students to confront real dilemmas and problems. Amid significant budget cuts affecting criminal justice agencies at all levels of government, we have integrated discussions of the impacts of these budget reductions into topics concerning actors and agencies across the justice system. Throughout the book, we have increased our coverage of technology, homeland security, and cyber crime, reflecting the growing importance of these subjects in the study of criminal justice. In addition, new topics are covered in "Close Up," "The Policy Debate," and "Comparative Perspective" boxes that focus on such contemporary issues as restoration of rights for ex-felons; reliance on volunteers for justice system functions; the purported "*CSI* effect" and its influence on jurors; implications of cell phones being smuggled to offenders inside prisons; as well as a first-person account of a parole board hearing.

The remainder of this section outlines the major content changes in the book and then examines the elements in each chapter that are new to this Seventh Edition.

Enhanced Coverage

Focus on the Effects of Budget Cuts on Criminal Justice Agencies Integrated within the chapters are discussions and examples of the impact of budget cuts on police, courts, and corrections. Attention is directed toward police departments that must make difficult choices when personnel cutbacks reduce their ability to provide services. Similar issues affect other segments of the justice system as, for example, financial considerations drive efforts to reduce prison populations at a time when states are less able to fund beneficial reentry programs. By emphasizing the current budgetary environment, the material helps students to understand the connections between criminal justice agencies and broader government issues, and to appreciate the specific problems currently facing police chiefs and other administrators who must make tough choices about how to use limited resources.

Expanded Coverage of Cyber Crime Rapidly expanding methods of cyber crime are imposing extraordinarily significant costs on governments, businesses, and individuals worldwide. To fully understand the ramifications of this misuse of technology, criminal justice students need to be aware of the challenges in addressing forms of criminal behavior that are continuously shifting and adapting with each technological innovation. This edition presents information on new aspects of international cyber crime activities, financial scams, and law enforcement's efforts to stay ahead of these issues.

Expanded Coverage of Prison Population Reduction, Parole, and Reentry Reconsideration of sentencing practices as well as financial pressures have led to state and federal efforts to reduce prison populations. The reasons and ramifications of these policy decisions are addressed in several chapters. New material discusses the different parole processes and reentry programs used by various state governments. This subject is one of the most important issues facing legislatures around the country and is essential knowledge for contemporary students of criminal justice.

Real Ethical Problems and Dilemmas Facing Officials in Each Segment of the Criminal Justice System "A Question of Ethics: Think, Discuss, Write" is a newly designed feature that concludes each chapter. This contemplative exercise dispenses with the prior edition's use of hypothetical scenarios and provides real situations drawn from recent news reports. Students are asked to consider real cases concerning police use of force, probation officers' acceptance of bribes, officials' respect for citizens' constitutional rights, and other situations that actually arise in the criminal justice system. Students are challenged to place themselves in the position of administrators who must think about how to organize or reform training, supervision, and other elements that are essential for addressing ethical lapses by justice system officials.

Chapter-by-Chapter Changes

- **Chapter 1,** "The Criminal Justice System," opens with a new vignette concerning the highly publicized trial and acquittal of Casey Anthony, the Florida woman accused of killing her own daughter. The case illustrates the various stages of the justice process. The chapter discusses the impact of budget cuts on the criminal justice system and adds new material on such subjects as the definition of crimes and racial disparities in the system. There is a new, updated figure, "Criminal Justice as a Filtering Process," which graphically illustrates the "filtering" of cases from the system, beginning with the number of crimes committed and following through to the number of offenders who are eventually convicted and sentenced to jail or prison. The new "Question of Ethics" feature compares the light sentence imposed on boxing champion Floyd Mayweather with the severe sentence imposed on another man convicted of a similar offense. Students are asked to consider whether prosecutors have an ethical obligation to pursue equivalent charges and punishments for similar offenders and offenses.

- **Chapter 2,** "Crime and Crime Causation," begins with a new vignette concerning the shooting of Congresswoman Gabrielle Giffords in Tucson, Arizona. Such examples challenge students to consider the causes of crime and whether different kinds of causes may be at work for different crimes, situations, and offenders. The chapter contains new material on medical marijuana laws, presents explanations for the nation's reduced crime rate, addresses the lack of connection between fear of crime and actual crime rates, and offers theories about the use of neighborhood programs to reduce gang violence. The "Question of Ethics" feature examines government compensation funds for crime victims and the issues surrounding disparities in what different programs provide for victims.
- **Chapter 3,** "Criminal Justice and the Rule of Law," opens with a new vignette describing the 2011 trial in Maine of a former college lacrosse player who used the insanity defense after committing the gruesome murder of his girlfriend. The issue was complicated by permanent neurological damage he had suffered years earlier in a traffic collision. Because the insanity defense was raised, the case illuminates issues of criminal responsibility and legal defense. New to this edition are "The Policy Debate" feature that centers on whether ex-felons should regain gun rights, and the "Comparative Perspective" box that addresses procedural criminal law in Russia. The chapter includes an illustrative comparison of murder statutes from selected states, and ends with "A Question of Ethics" that examines police use of a GPS device to monitor the movements of a suspect's car. Ultimately, the student is asked to weigh in on *United States v. Jones,* the U.S. Supreme Court's 2012 decision on this issue.
- **Chapter 4,** "Police," opens with a description of the events leading to the 2012 shootings of six Ogden, Utah, police officers. This vignette effectively illustrates the unexpected dangers that law enforcement officers face every day. The chapter contains new material on the impact of police budget cuts, including the extreme situations in Flint, Michigan, and Camden, New Jersey. A simplified police department organizational chart for Odessa, Texas, has been included. There is also new material on special jurisdiction police agencies. A new "Close Up" examines the use of volunteer auxiliary officers. The "Question of Ethics" feature asks the student to contemplate the recent problem of undercover police officers in New York City arresting innocent people in an effort to meet arrest quotas. There is also an expanded number of key terms relating to policing.
- **Chapter 5,** "Policing: Contemporary Issues and Challenges," presents a new opening vignette concerning the attempted car bombing in New York City's Times Square. There is new, reorganized coverage of police misconduct to more effectively connect this subject with the risks posed by police discretion. In addition to an expanded number of key terms, the chapter presents new material on a variety of topics, including evidence-based policing, task forces, and School Resource Officers (SROs). A new figure shows licensing requirements for private security officers in various states. A new "Close Up" examines police stops and searches of minority group members. The "Question of Ethics" feature concerns excessive use of force by police caught on a video camera mounted in the police cruiser.
- **Chapter 6,** "Police and Law," opens with the story of a warrantless automobile search based on an arrest unrelated to the automobile. The case eventually reached the U.S. Supreme Court and produced a controversial decision that limited police officers' authority (*Arizona v. Gant,* 2006). A new "Close Up" feature examines Supreme Court justices' divided opinions and reasoning in a controversial case concerning the exclusionary rule (*Herring v. United States, 2009*). There is also new material on a recent Supreme Court search and seizure case (*Kentucky v. King,* 2011) and several recent *Miranda* rights cases (*Berguis v. Thompson,* 2010, *Florida v. Powell,* 2010, and *J. D. B. v. North Carolina,* 2011. A new "Comparative Perspective" examines the exclusionary rule in Canada and several European countries. "A Question of Ethics" concerns police officers attempting to persuade suspects to waive their *Miranda* rights.

- **Chapter 7,** "Courts and Adjudication," has a new opening vignette about the highly publicized murder of a Yale University student, and the eventual 2011 guilty plea by the accused university employee. There is new material on problem-solving courts as well as discussion of the impact of budget cuts on courts and prosecutors. A new "Close Up" examines the Supreme Court's 2011 decision that shielded prosecutors from liability for misconduct (*Connick v. Thompson*). A new "Criminal Justice: Myth & Reality" box explores plea bargaining and its connection to the courtroom workgroup. The "Question of Ethics" feature concerns a Montana federal judge's admission in 2012 that he used a courthouse computer to send a highly offensive, racist email joke about President Barack Obama.

- **Chapter 8,** "Pretrial Procedures, Plea Bargaining, and the Criminal Trial," uses an opening scenario that focuses on the 2010 trial of Hollywood actor Shelley Malil and the plea bargain conviction of actor Mel Gibson for domestic violence. Prosecutors' efforts to abolish plea bargaining are examined in "Criminal Justice: Myth and Reality." There is new material on the Bronx Bail Fund and about Americans' views on the fairness of juries. A new "Close Up" examines the purported "*CSI* effect" and the impact of television shows on jurors' expectations about scientific evidence. The "Question of Ethics" feature highlights concerns pertaining to the use of technology and social media by jurors during trials.

- **Chapter 9,** "Punishment and Sentencing," begins with a new opening vignette on the 2011 sentences imposed in the high-profile cases of Rod Blagojevich, the former governor of Illinois; Raj Rajaratnam, a Wall Street multimillionaire; and Dr. Conrad Murray, whose drug prescriptions contributed to the death of singer Michael Jackson. New material is presented concerning the impact of budget cuts on sentencing and corrections, the use of "earned time" credits to reduce sentences, and the public's view on specific deterrence. New tables present material on such matters as Florida's estimated cost savings from reliance on intermediate sanctions and the decline in death sentences and executions. A new "Close Up" examines the differing sentences imposed by judges' rulings in similar cases. The "Question of Ethics" feature concerns the 2012 conviction of a former Rutgers University student for a hate crime committed when he secretly broadcasted, via computer, his gay dorm roommate's intimate encounter with an older man—an action that apparently contributed to the roommate's subsequent suicide.

- **Chapter 10,** "Corrections," opens with a discussion of the 2010 Pew Center report documenting the continued growth of the nation's prison population, despite actions by individual states to reduce their inmate counts. The report starkly illustrates major debates in criminal justice: "Do we overuse incarceration as a sanction?" "Can state and local governments afford the high costs associated with running prisons and jails?—What are the alternatives?" There is new material on the impact of budget problems for state and local corrections officials. A new "Close Up" examines a prisoner's right to free exercise of religion. There is new material concerning the Supreme Court's controversial decision (*Brown v. Plata*, 2011) on California prison overcrowding and inadequate medical services. The new "Question of Ethics" focuses on two Pennsylvania judges' illegal behavior in accepting payments from a private corrections company.

- **Chapter 11,** "Incarceration and Prison Society," reflects a reordering of chapters, thus allowing the discussion of all institutional corrections topics to take place before subsequently examining aspects of community corrections in now-consecutive chapters. New information has been added to the discussion on elderly prisoners, and there is a broader examination of issues facing women in prison, with particular attention directed toward incarcerated mothers. New material has been added about the Prison Rape Elimination Act and its implications. There is also expanded coverage of mental illness among prisoners and the impact of violence against women prisoners. The new "Question of Ethics" feature examines the problem of corrections officers smuggling contraband into secure institutions.

- **Chapter 12,** "Probation and Intermediate Sanctions," reflects the new chapter order to place community corrections topics together in consecutive chapters.

The new opening vignette focuses on singer Chris Brown and the intermediate sanctions he received for assaulting his girlfriend, the singer Rhianna. The chapter presents updated information concerning the impact of budget cuts and the cost differences between probation and imprisonment. New topics introduced include the use of volunteers to assist in probation programs and Colorado's efforts to recover restitution money from offenders. A new table uses state of New York data to illustrate the reasons for probation revocation. The "Close Up" in this chapter examines home confinement as an intermediate sanction. In addition, a new "Comparative Perspective" explores the use of day fines as sanctions in European countries. The "Question of Ethics" feature looks at actual cases of probation officers accepting bribes and stealing money from the court.

- **Chapter 13,** "Reentry into the Community," opens with a vignette that highlights several examples of media coverage of horrific crimes committed by parolees. These examples illuminate the challenges of reentry, and help the student consider factors relevant to the individual offender. The public's perception of ex-prisoners and the potential risks they pose to society are also examined. This issue will become more important as budget deficits increasingly spur governors and legislators to find ways to reduce the size and costs of state corrections systems. There is additional material on institutional reentry programs and release mechanisms that are employed in different states. An expanded examination of parole compares the actual parole board processes in various states, including a new "Close Up" presenting coauthor Christopher Smith's first-person account of serving as a prisoner's representative in a Michigan parole hearing. Related to the new material on the effect of budget cuts on reentry programs, there is a new "Policy Debate" box that examines the accelerated release of offenders from prison. The "Question of Ethics" feature views the conflicts that arise when parole officers exceed their authority in searching homes within the community to look for parolees and/or evidence of parole violations or crimes.

- **Chapter 14,** "Technology and Criminal Justice," presents a new opening vignette concerning the criminal conviction for online-based sex crimes of Scott Ritter, well-known United Nations weapons inspector who was a central figure in the events leading to the Iraq War. The chapter contains discussion of how technology is used both by offenders, to commit new kinds of crimes or to increase their efficiency and success in traditional crimes, and by law enforcement officials, who seek their own improvements in fighting crime. There is expanded coverage related to identity theft and other cyber crimes, with a new table that illuminates the frequency of identity theft and the resulting financial losses. The chapter "Close Up" examines the current problem of cell phones being smuggled into prisons. The impact of recent and continued budget cuts on the operation of crime labs and the testing of criminal evidence essential to police and prosecutors is examined in depth. The "Question of Ethics" feature scrutinizes the police use of electronic devices to extract information from drivers' cell phones during traffic stops.

- **Chapter 15,** "Juvenile Justice," provides a new opening vignette concerning an 11-year-old boy who shot his pregnant stepmother, raising the issue of appropriate punishment for children who commit crimes. There is increased coverage of the problem of gangs, including a new "Comparative Perspective" on the EuroGang project, which provides differing perspectives on youth gangs in the United States and Europe. There is an updated discussion on the issue of life-without-parole sentences for juvenile offenders. There is also a new "Close Up" on the Supreme Court's recent decision concerning police officers' new responsibility for considering a suspect's age in determining if and when to provide *Miranda* warnings. The "Question of Ethics" feature considers the increased use of pepper spray as a control mechanism at a juvenile detention facility in Texas.

Study and Review Aids

To help students identify and master core concepts, *Criminal Justice in America* provides several study and review aids in each chapter:

- *Chapter outlines* preview the structure of each chapter.
- *Opening vignettes* introduce the chapter topic with a high-interest, real-life case or illustrative discussion of a major policy issue, enhancing the book's relevancy for today's student.
- *Learning Objectives* highlight the chapter's key topics and themes and serve as a road map for readers.
- *Checkpoints* throughout each chapter allow students to test themselves on content and get immediate feedback to help them assess their understanding of concepts as they progress through the chapter.
- End-of-chapter *Summaries* and *Questions for Review* reinforce key concepts and provide further checks on learning.
- *Key Terms and Cases* are listed at the end of each chapter; these are defined throughout the text in the margins and included in the Glossary.

Promoting Understanding

Aided by the features just described, diligent students can master the essential content of the introductory course. While such mastery is no small achievement, most instructors aim higher. They want students to complete this course with the ability to take a more thoughtful and critical approach to issues of crime and justice. *Criminal Justice in America*, Seventh Edition, provides several features that help students learn how to think about the field.

- **Stop & Analyze** This feature follows each set of Checkpoint critical-thinking questions and asks students to concretely articulate arguments and analytical conclusions about issues relevant to the preceding section of the text.
- **Close Ups and Other Real-Life Examples** Understanding criminal justice in a purely theoretical way does not give students a balanced understanding of the field. The wealth of examples in this book shows how theory plays out in practice and what the human implications of policies and procedures are. In addition to the many illustrations in the text, the "Close Up" features in each chapter draw on newspaper articles, court decisions, first-person accounts, and other current sources.
- **A Question of Ethics: Think, Discuss, Write** In the criminal justice system, decisions must be made within the framework of law but also be consistent with the ethical norms of American society. At the end of each chapter, completely revamped boxes entitled "A Question of Ethics: Think, Discuss, Write" use actual news reports on the justice system to place students in the context of decision makers faced with a problem involving ethics. Students become aware of the many ethical dilemmas that criminal justice personnel must deal with and the types of questions they may have to answer if they assume a role in the system. Moreover, they are challenged to offer solutions that administrators might employ in using training, supervision, or other approaches to reduce behavior problems by justice system employees.
- **What Americans Think** Public opinion plays an important role in the policy-making process in a democracy. As such, we present the opinions of Americans on controversial criminal justice issues, as collected through surveys.
- **The Policy Debate** This edition includes boxes presenting important policy issues for student discussion and debate. In each, we describe an issue such as aggressive policing or the death penalty, outline its pros and cons, and then ask students to decide which policy they think the United States should adopt.
- **Careers in Criminal Justice** The topical focus on career opportunities is primarily intended to help students think about the wide range of occupational possibilities in criminal justice. As they examine the qualifications and career

path of an actual criminal justice professional, students gain insights about who plays what role in the criminal justice system. Each professional featured provides an insightful comment on the challenges of his or her particular occupation.

- **Criminal Justice: Myth & Reality** Through the examination of widely held beliefs about criminal justice, students can look critically at the actual complexity or unexpected consequences of various policies and practices. By addressing viewpoints that many students themselves hold, students are encouraged to question assumptions and seek information before drawing conclusions.
- **Comparative Perspective** The globalization of crime and the need for international cooperation in criminal justice require that students be aware of criminal justice issues and institutions in other countries. Moreover, American students can gain additional perspective on their own system by contrasting the United States with other countries. The "Comparative Perspective" feature, included in each section of the text, presents such diverse topics as the role of the defense attorney in Russia, pretrial detention in the Philippines, and the use of day fines in Europe.
- **Inside the Criminal Justice System & Beyond** Many students have limited firsthand knowledge of what it is like to be "processed" by the criminal justice system. A hallmark of *Criminal Justice in America* is this serialized essay by Chuck Terry. Each part of the book concludes with a segment of Terry's moving story, providing a rare insider's look at the steps in the criminal justice process.

Supplements

An extensive package of supplemental aids accompanies this edition of *Criminal Justice in America*. They are available to qualified adopters. Please consult your local sales representative for details.

For the Instructor

Instructor's Manual with Test Bank Fully updated and revised by Cheryn Rowell of Stanly Community College, the manual includes learning objectives, key terms, a detailed chapter outline, a chapter summary, discussion topics, student activities, media tools, and a newly expanded Test Bank. The learning objectives are correlated with the discussion topics, student activities, and media tools. Each chapter's Test Bank contains questions in multiple-choice, true–false, completion, and essay formats, with a full answer key. The Test Bank has almost 60 percent more questions than the prior edition and features new scenario-based questions to test student's critical-thinking skills. The Test Bank is coded to the learning objectives that appear in the main text, and includes the page numbers in the main text where the answers can be found. Finally, each question in the Test Bank has been carefully reviewed by experienced criminal justice instructors for quality, accuracy, and content coverage. Our Instructor Approved seal, which appears on the front cover, is our assurance that you are working with an assessment and grading resource of the highest caliber. The manual is available for download on the password-protected website and can also be obtained by emailing your local Cengage Learning representative.

ExamView® Computerized Testing The comprehensive Instructor's Manual with Test Bank is backed up by ExamView, a computerized test bank available for PC and Mac computers. With ExamView you can create, deliver, and customize tests and study guides (both print and online) in minutes. You can easily edit and import your own questions and graphics, change test layouts, and reorganize questions. And using ExamView's complete word-processing capabilities, you can enter an unlimited number of new questions or edit existing questions.

PowerLecture™ with ExamView The fastest, easiest way to build customized, media-rich lectures, PowerLecture™ provides a collection of book-specific Microsoft® PowerPoint® lecture and class tools to enhance the educational experience.

PowerLecture includes lesson plans, lecture outlines linked to the learning objectives for each chapter, art from the text, new videos, animations, and more. The DVD-ROM also contains electronic copies of the Instructor's Manual, Test Bank, and Lesson Plans; it also includes ExamView testing software, which allows you to create customized tests in minutes using items from the test bank in computerized format.

Lesson Plans   Fully updated and revised by John Hazy of Youngstown State University, the Lesson Plans bring accessible, masterful suggestions to every lesson. This supplement includes a sample syllabus, learning objectives, lecture notes, discussion topics and in-class activities, a detailed lecture outline, assignments, media tools, and "What if . . ." scenarios. The learning objectives are integrated throughout the Lesson Plans, and current events and real-life examples in the form of articles, websites, and video links are incorporated into the class discussion topics, activities, and assignments. The lecture outlines are correlated with PowerPoint slides for ease of classroom use. Lesson Plans are available on the PowerLecture resource and the instructor website.

Real World Resources: Tools to Enhance Relevancy   The media tools from across all of the book supplements are gathered into one location and organized by chapter and Learning Objective. Each item has a description of the resource and a directed learning activity. Available on the companion website, WebTutor, and CourseMate, these can be used as resources for additional learning or as assignments.

PowerPoints   Helping you make your lectures more engaging while effectively reaching your visually oriented students, these handy Microsoft® PowerPoint® slides outline the chapters of the main text in a classroom-ready presentation. The PowerPoint slides are updated to reflect the content and organization of the new edition of the text and feature some additional examples and real-world cases for application and discussion. Available for download on the password-protected instructor book companion website, the presentations can also be obtained by emailing your local Cengage Learning representative. Fully updated and revised by James Chapman of Wake Technical Community College.

Video Library   So many exciting new videos—so many great ways to enrich your lectures and spark discussion of the material in this text. Your Cengage Learning representative will be happy to provide details on our video policy by adoption size. The library includes these selections and many others.

- *ABC® Videos* feature short, high-interest clips from current news events as well as historic raw footage going back 40 years. Perfect for discussion starters or to enrich your lectures and spark interest in the material in the text, these brief videos provide students with a new lens through which to view the past and present, one that will greatly enhance their knowledge and understanding of significant events and open up to them new dimensions in learning. Clips are drawn from such programs as *World News Tonight, Good Morning America, This Week, PrimeTime Live, 20/20*, and *Nightline*, as well as numerous ABC News specials and material from the Associated Press Television News and British Movietone News collections.
- *Cengage Learning's "Introduction to Criminal Justice Video Series"* features videos supplied by the BBC Motion Gallery. These short, high-interest clips from CBS and BBC news programs—everything from nightly news broadcasts and specials to *CBS News Special Reports, CBS Sunday Morning, 60 Minutes*, and more—are perfect classroom discussion starters. Designed to enrich your lectures and spark interest in the material in the text, these brief videos provide students with a new lens through which to view the past and present, one that will greatly enhance their knowledge and understanding of significant events and open up to them new dimensions in learning. Clips are drawn from BBC Motion Gallery.

Criminal Justice Media Library   Cengage Learning's Criminal Justice Media Library includes nearly 300 media assets on the topics you cover in your courses. Available to stream from any computer, the Criminal Justice Media Library's assets include such valuable resources as Career Profile Videos featuring interviews with criminal justice professionals from a range of roles and locations, simulations that allow students to step into various roles and practice their decision-making skills, video clips on current topics from ABC® and other sources, animations that illustrate key concepts, interactive learning modules that help students check their knowledge of important topics, and Reality Check exercises that compare expectations and preconceived notions against the real-life thoughts and experiences of criminal justice professionals. The Criminal Justice Media Library can be uploaded and used within many popular Learning Management Systems (LMS), and all video assets include assessment questions that can be delivered straight to the grade book in your LMS. You can also customize it with your own course material. Please contact your Cengage Learning representative for ordering and pricing information.

WebTutor™ on Blackboard® and WebCT® Jump-start your course with customizable, rich, text-specific content within your Course Management System. Whether you want to Web-enable your class or put an entire course online, WebTutor delivers. WebTutor offers a wide array of resources, including media assets, Test Bank, practice quizzes linked to chapter learning objectives, and additional study aids. Visit www .cengage.com/webtutor to learn more.

For the Student

Study Guide An extensive student guide has been developed for this edition by Christine Stymus of Bryant & Stratton College. Because students learn in different ways, the guide includes a variety of pedagogical aids to help them. Each chapter is outlined and summarized, major terms and figures are defined, plus media tools for directed learning and self-tests are provided.

CourseMate Cengage Learning's Criminal Justice CourseMate brings course concepts to life with interactive learning, study, and exam-preparation tools that support the printed textbook. CourseMate includes an integrated eBook, quizzes mapped to chapter learning objectives, flash cards, videos, and more, and EngagementTracker, a first-of-its-kind tool that monitors student engagement in the course. The accompanying instructor website offers access to password-protected resources such as an electronic version of the instructor's manual and PowerPoint slides.

Careers in Criminal Justice Website *Can be bundled with this text at no additional charge.* Featuring plenty of self-exploration and profiling activities, the interactive Careers in Criminal Justice Website helps students investigate and focus on the criminal justice career choices that are right for them. Includes interest assessment, video testimonials from career professionals, resume and interview tips, links for reference, and a wealth of information on "soft skills" such as health and fitness, stress management, and effective communication. Ask your Cengage representative about state-specific versions of the website that provide statutes, employment opportunities, etc., for individual states.

CLeBook Cengage Learning's Criminal Justice eBooks allow students to access our textbooks in an easy-to-use online format. Highlight, take notes, bookmark, search your text, and, for most texts, link directly into multimedia. In short, CLeBooks combine the best features of paper books and eBooks in one package.

Current Perspectives: Readings from InfoTrac® College Edition These readers, designed to give students a closer look at special topics in criminal justice, include free access to InfoTrac College Edition. The timely articles are selected by experts in each topic from within InfoTrac College Edition. They are available free when bundled with the text and include the following titles:

- Introduction to Criminal Justice
- Community Corrections
- Cyber Crime
- Victimology
- Juvenile Justice
- Racial Profiling
- White-Collar Crime
- Terrorism and Homeland Security
- Public Policy and Criminal Justice
- Technology and Criminal Justice
- Ethics in Criminal Justice
- Forensics
- Corrections
- Law and Courts
- Policy in Criminal Justice

A Group Effort

No one can be an expert on every aspect of the criminal justice system. Authors need help in covering new developments and ensuring that research findings are correctly interpreted. The many criminal justice students and instructors who have used previous editions of *Criminal Justice in America* have contributed abundantly to this edition. Their comments provided crucial practical feedback. Others gave us their comments personally when we lectured in criminal justice classes around the country.

Many others have helped us as well. Chief among them was Senior Acquisitions Editor Carolyn Henderson Meier, who is very supportive of our efforts. Senior Developmental Editor Shelley Murphy contributed invaluable ideas and tremendous organizational skills as we revised the book. The project has benefited much from the attention of Senior Content Project Managers Christy Frame and Jennifer Risden. As copy editor, Marne Evans made valuable contributions to improving the effectiveness of our presentation. Debra Nichols made useful suggestions in her role as proofreader. As always, Greg Hubit used his managerial skills to oversee the project from manuscript submission to the bound book. Jeanne Calabrese designed the interior of the book. Finally, the following reviewers for this edition contributed valuable comments:

Lorna Alvarez-Rivera, *Ohio University*
C. Nana Derby, *Virginia State University*
Peter W. Fenton, *Kennesaw State University*
J. Price Foster, *University of Louisville*
Natasha A. Frost, *Northeastern University*
Kelly Gould, *Sacramento City College*
Marvin Krohn, *University of Florida*
Jacqueline M. Mullany, *Triton College*
Althea E. Seaborn, *Norwalk Community College*
Gary A. Sokolow, *College of the Redwoods*
Edward G. Walker, *Harrison College*

We would also like to thank all those who reviewed the previous editions of this book:

Jerry Armor, *Calhoun Community College*
Lee Ayers-Schlosser, *Southern Oregon University*
Allan R. Barnes, *University of Alaska, Anchorage*
Lee Boggess, *Fairmont State University*
Paula M. Broussard, *University of Southwestern Louisiana*
Michael P. Brown, *Ball State University*
Avon Burns, *Charles S. Mott Community College*

Damon D. Camp, *Georgia State University*
Steven Cherman, *Indiana University*
W. H. Copley, *College of Denver*
Mark E. Correia, *University of Nevada, Reno*
Matthew S. Crow, *University of West Florida*
Beverly Curl, *Long Beach City College*
John Dempsey, *Suffolk Community College*
Rhonda R. Dobbs, *University of Texas at Arlington*
Daniel Doyle, *University of Montana*
Larry Farnsworth, *Unity College*
Arnett Gaston, *University of Maryland, College Park*
James N. Gilbert, *University of Nebraska, Kearney*
Pamela Hart, *Iowa Western Community College*
Kim Hassell, *University of Wisconsin, Milwaukee*
Jacqueline B. Helfgott, *Seattle University*
Robert M. Hurley, *Sacramento State University*
Mark Jones, *East Carolina University*
Tim Jones, *Athens State College*
Judy Hails Kaci, *California State University, Long Beach*
John Kavanaugh, *Scottsdale Community College*
William E. Kelly, *Auburn University*
Deborah L. Lauferweiler-Dwyer, *University of Arkansas at Little Rock*
Walter Lewis, *St. Louis Community College at Meramec*
Lee Libby, *Shoreline Community College*
James Madden, *Lake Superior State University*
Don Mason, *Rio Hondo Community College*
Michael O. Maume, *University of North Carolina at Wilmington*
William McCarney, *Western Illinois University*
Thomas D. McDonald, *North Dakota State University*
Nicholas Meier, *Kalamazoo Valley Community College*
Linda M. Merola, *George Mason University*
Eric Moore, *Texas A&M University, Corpus Christi*
Dale T. Mooso, *San Antonio College*
Frank Morgan, *Richard Bland College*
Patrick Patterson, *Mohawk Valley Community College*
Patricia Payne, *Middlesex County College*
Tim Perry, *Shoreline Community College*
Rudy K. Prine, *Valdosta State University*
Richard Ramos, *Contra Costa College*
Melody L. Rayl, *Johnson County Community College*
Walter F. Ruger, *Nassau Community College*
Gregory D. Russell, *Washington State University*
Amy Thistlethwaite, *Northern Kentucky College*
Angelo Triniti, *Passaic County Community College*
Melvin Wallace, *McHenry County College*
Bob Walsh, *University of Houston, Downtown*
Chief John H. Ward, Ret., *Cape Fear Community College*
Vincent J. Webb, *University of Nebraska, Omaha*
Richard G. Wright, *Bridgewater State College*

Ultimately, however, the full responsibility for the book is ours alone. We hope you
will benefit from it, and we welcome your comments.

George F. Cole   georgefrasercole@gmail.com

Christopher E. Smith   smithc28@msu.edu

Christina DeJong   dejongc@msu.edu

About the Authors

George F. Cole is Professor Emeritus of Political Science at the University of Connecticut. A specialist in the administration of criminal justice, he has published extensively on such topics as prosecution, courts, and corrections. George Cole is also coauthor with Christopher Smith and Christina DeJong of *The American System of Criminal Justice*, coauthor with Todd Clear and Michael Reisig of *American Corrections*, and coauthor with Marc Gertz and Amy Bunger of *The Criminal Justice System: Politics and Policies*. He developed and directed the graduate corrections program at the University of Connecticut and was a Fellow at the National Institute of Justice (1988). Among his other accomplishments, he has been granted two awards under the Fulbright-Hays Program to conduct criminal justice research in England and the former Yugoslavia. In 1995 he was named a Fellow of the Academy of Criminal Justice Sciences for distinguished teaching and research.

Trained as a lawyer and social scientist, **Christopher E. Smith**, J.D., Ph.D., is Professor of Criminal Justice at Michigan State University, where he teaches courses on criminal justice policy, courts, corrections, and law. He was named as the recipient of the "Outstanding Teaching Award" for the Michigan State University College of Social Science in 2012. In addition to writing more than 100 scholarly articles, he is the author of more than 20 books, including several other titles with Wadsworth: *Criminal Procedure*; *Law and Contemporary Corrections*; *Courts, Politics, and the Judicial Process*; *The Changing Supreme Court: Constitutional Rights and Liberties* with Thomas R. Hensley and Joyce A. Baugh; *Courts and Public Policy*; *Politics in Constitutional Law*; and *Courts and the Poor*.

Christina DeJong, Ph.D., is Associate Professor of Criminal Justice and Director of the Center for Integrative Studies in Social Science at Michigan State University. She earned her degrees at the University of Texas and the University of Maryland. At Michigan State, she is a noted researcher and award-winning teacher for a variety of criminology topics, including recidivism, violence against women, and police–community relations. She is the coauthor of *The Supreme Court, Crime, and the Ideal of Equal Justice*, and numerous articles in such journals as *Justice Quarterly, Criminology, Women and Criminal Justice,* and *Violence and Victims*.

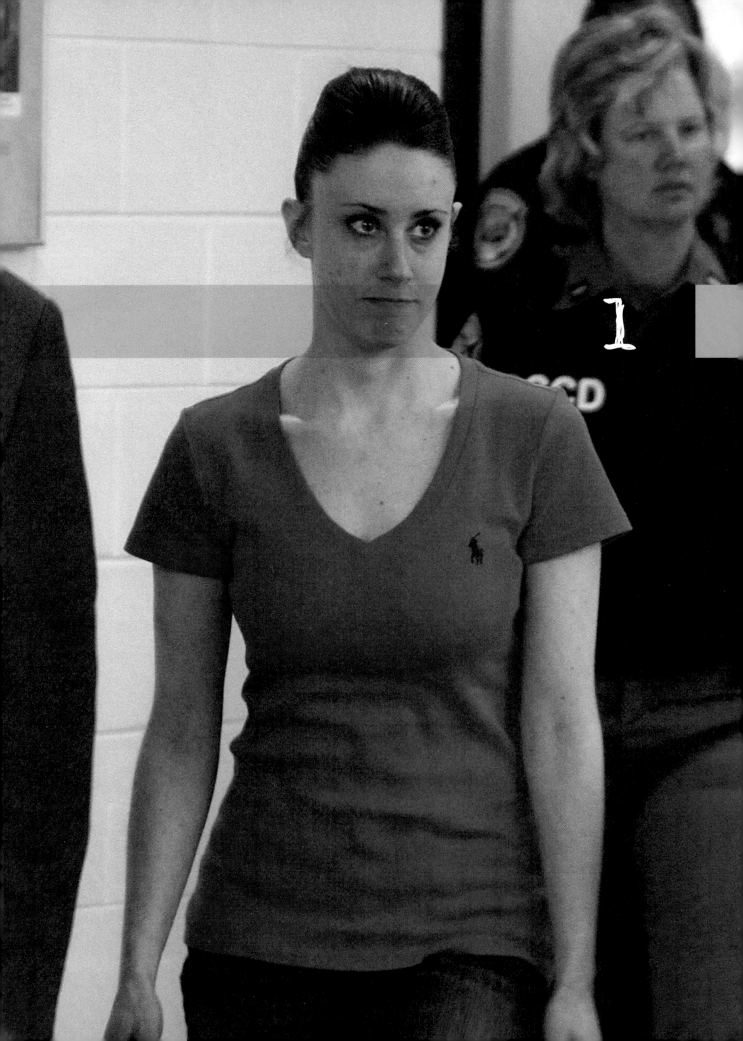

The Criminal Justice System

Learning Objectives

- ⮕ Understand the goals of the criminal justice system
- ⮕ Recognize the different responsibilities of federal and state criminal justice operations
- ⮕ Analyze criminal justice from a systems perspective
- ⮕ Identify the authority and relationships of the main criminal justice agencies, and understand the steps in the decision-making process for criminal cases
- ⮕ Understand the criminal justice "wedding cake" concept as well as the due process and crime control models
- ⮕ Recognize the possible causes of racial disparities in criminal justice

A nationwide television audience waited in anticipation on July 5, 2011, when news reports announced that a Florida jury would issue its verdict in the Casey Anthony murder trial. In a case that transfixed the nation and generated thousands of hours of coverage on news and talk shows, Anthony was charged with murdering her own two-year-old daughter, Caylee. When the "not guilty"

verdict was announced on television, many Americans were shocked. Indeed, a *USA Today*/Gallup Poll found that 64 percent of Americans believed that Anthony was guilty of murder (Dorell, 2011). Legal analyst and television host Nancy Grace stated that "there is no way this verdict speaks the truth" (T. Stanley, 2011).

The surprise and disappointment expressed by many observers stemmed

3

Thousands of St. Louis residents participated in a unity march against crime in June 2008. Their theme of a "Call to Oneness" was intended to make people think about social problems and crime in their communities. How can the interest and energy generated by such public events be translated into concrete actions to prevent crime?

Doing justice successfully is a tall order. We can easily identify situations in which criminal justice agencies and processes fall short of this ideal. In authoritarian political systems, criminal justice primarily serves the interests of those in power, but in a democracy people can try to improve the capacity of their institutions to do justice. Thus, however imperfect they may be, criminal justice institutions and processes can enjoy public support. In a democracy, a system that makes doing justice a key goal is viewed as legitimate and can therefore pursue the secondary goals of controlling and preventing crime.

Controlling Crime

The criminal justice system is designed to control crime by arresting, prosecuting, convicting, and punishing those who disobey the law. A major constraint on the system, however, is that efforts to control crime must be carried out within the framework of law. Criminal law not only defines what is illegal but also outlines the rights of citizens and the procedures officials must use to achieve the system's goals. Police officers and prosecutors must follow the law when investigating crimes. They cannot use unrestrained methods of their own choosing in conducting searches and questioning suspects.

In every city and town, the goal of crime control is actively pursued: Police officers walk a beat, patrol cars race down dark streets, lawyers speak before a judge, probation officers visit clients, and guards patrol the grounds of a prison. Taking action against wrongdoers helps control crime, but the system must also attempt to prevent crimes from happening.

Preventing Crime

Crime can be prevented in various ways. Perhaps most important is the deterrent effect of the actions of police, courts, and corrections. These actions not only punish those who violate the law, they also provide examples that will likely keep others from committing wrongful acts. For example, a racing patrol car responding to a crime scene also serves as a warning that law enforcement is at hand. Technological advances also can deter crime with new kinds of surveillance and searches, but sometimes at a cost to privacy and personal liberty.

Crime prevention depends on the actions of criminal justice officials and citizens. Unfortunately, many people do not take the simple steps necessary to protect themselves and their property. For example, they leave their homes and cars unlocked, forgo alarm systems, and walk in dangerous areas.

Citizens do not have the authority to enforce the law; society has assigned that responsibility to the criminal justice system. Thus, citizens must rely on the police to stop criminals; they cannot take the law into their own hands. Still, they can and must be actively engaged in preventing crime.

The ways in which American institutions have evolved to achieve the goals of doing justice, controlling crime, and preventing crime lead to a series of choices. Decisions must be made that reflect legal, political, social, and moral values. As we study the system, we need to be aware of the possible conflicts among these values and the implications of choosing one value over another. The tasks assigned to the criminal justice system could be much easier to perform if they were clearly defined so that citizens and officials could act with precise knowledge of their duties.

check point

1. **What is the difference between *mala in se* and *mala prohibita* crimes?**
   Legislatures define punishable, harmful behaviors that are wrongs in themselves, such as murder (*mala in se*), and other actions that they simply choose to prohibit as too harmful to be permitted (*mala prohibita*).

2. **What are the three goals of the criminal justice system?**
   Doing justice, controlling crime, preventing crime.

3. **What is meant by "doing justice"?**
   The pursuit of fairness and equity as offenders are held fully accountable for their actions, the rights of persons who have contact with the system are protected, like offenses are treated alike, and officials take into account relevant differences among offenders and offenses.

stop& analyze

What is the role of the individual citizen in crime prevention? List two things that you do right now that contribute to crime prevention. What are two additional things that you could easily incorporate into your daily life that would also contribute to crime prevention?

Criminal Justice in a Federal System

Criminal justice, like other aspects of American government, is based on the concept of **federalism**, in which power is divided between a central (national) government and regional (state) governments. States have a great deal of authority over their own affairs, but the federal government handles matters of national concern. Because of federalism, no single level of government is solely responsible for the administration of criminal justice.

The U.S. government's structure was created in 1789 with the ratification of the U.S. Constitution. The Constitution gave the national government certain powers, including raising an army, coining money, and making treaties with foreign countries. But the states retained all other powers, including police power. No national police force with broad powers may be established in the United States.

The Constitution does not include criminal justice among the federal government's specific powers. However, the United States government is involved in criminal justice in many ways. For example, the Federal Bureau of Investigation (FBI) is a national law enforcement agency. Federal criminal cases are tried in U.S. district courts, which are federal courts, and there are federal prisons throughout the nation. Most criminal justice activity, however, occurs at the state level. The vast majority

federalism A system of government in which power is divided between a central (national) government and regional (state) governments.

© GARY WILLIAMS/epa/Corbis

Federal law enforcement agencies bear special responsibility for certain crimes, such as antiterrorism investigations, bank robberies, and drug trafficking. Federal agencies also provide expert assistance for the investigation of crimes that rely on scientific evidence, such as arson. Local agencies may request assistance from federal experts. Would law enforcement nationwide be more effective if all police officers worked under a single federal agency rather than thousands of different state and local agencies?

of crimes are defined by state laws rather than federal law. Thus laws are enforced and offenders are brought to justice mainly in the states, counties, and cities. As a result, local traditions, values, and practices shape the way criminal justice agencies operate. Local leaders, whether members of the city council or influential citizens, can help set law enforcement priorities by putting pressure on the police. Will the city's police officers crack down on illegal gambling? Will juvenile offenders be turned over to their parents with stern warnings, or will they be sent to state institutions? The answers to these and other important questions vary from city to city.

Two Justice Systems

Both the national and state systems of criminal justice enforce laws, try criminal cases, and punish offenders, but their activities differ in scope and purpose. While most crimes are defined by state laws, a variety of national criminal laws have been enacted by Congress and are enforced by the FBI, the Drug Enforcement Administration, the Secret Service, and other federal agencies.

Except in the case of federal drug offenses, relatively few offenders break federal criminal laws, compared with the large numbers who break state criminal laws. For example, only small numbers of people violate the federal laws against counterfeiting and espionage, whereas large numbers violate state laws against assault, larceny, and drunken driving.

Expansion of Federal Involvement

Since the 1960s the federal government has expanded its role in dealing with crime, a policy area that has traditionally been the responsibility of state and local governments. The report of the U.S. President's Commission on Law Enforcement and Administration of Justice (1967:613) emphasized the need for greater federal involvement in crime control at the local level and urged that federal grants be directed to the states to support criminal justice initiatives. Since then, Congress has allocated billions of dollars for crime control efforts and passed legislation, national in scope, to deal with street crime, the "war on drugs," violent crime, terrorism, and juvenile delinquency.

Because many crimes span state borders, we no longer think of some crimes as being committed at a single location within a single state. For example, crime syndicates and gangs deal with drugs, pornography, and gambling on a national level. Thus, Congress expanded the powers of the FBI and other federal agencies to investigate criminal activities for which the states had formerly taken responsibility. As a national agency, the FBI can pursue criminal investigations across state borders better than any state agency can.

In addition, technology-based crimes, such as computer-fraud schemes and Internet-sourced child pornography, have also spurred new national laws from Congress because these illegal activities can cross both state and international borders. Moreover, federal officials have become increasingly active in pursuing arms dealers, narcotics traffickers, and terrorists who operate in other countries but whose harmful activities violate the laws of the United States. For example, Russian arms dealer Viktor Bout was arrested in Thailand and brought to the United States, as was reputed Jamaican drug kingpin Christopher Coke, who was brought to New York in 2010 to face trial (Weiser, 2011).

Disputes over jurisdiction may occur when an offense violates both state and federal laws. If the FBI and local agencies do not cooperate, they might each seek to

TABLE 1.1 Department of Homeland Security

Congress approved legislation to create a new federal agency dedicated to protecting the United States from terrorism. The legislation merges 22 agencies and nearly 170,000 government workers.

	Agencies Moved to the Department of Homeland Security	Previous Department or Agency
Border and Transportation Security	Immigration and Naturalization Service enforcement functions	Justice Department
	Transportation Security Administration	Transportation Department
	Customs Service	Treasury Department
	Federal Protective Services	General Services Administration
	Animal and Plant Health Inspection Service (parts)	Agriculture Department
Emergency Preparedness and Response	Federal Emergency Management Agency	(Independent Agency)
	Chemical, biological, radiological and nuclear response units	Health and Human Services Department
	Nuclear Incident Response Teams	Energy Department
	National Domestic Preparedness Office	FBI
	Office of Domestic Preparedness	Justice Department
	Domestic Emergency Support Teams	(From various departments and agencies)
Science and Technology	Civilian biodefense research program	Health and Human Services Department
	Plum Island Animal Disease Center	Agriculture Department
	Lawrence Livermore National Laboratory (parts)	Energy Department
Information Analysis and Infrastructure Protection	National Communications System	Defense Department
	National Infrastructure Protection Center	FBI
	Critical Infrastructure Assurance Office	Commerce Department
	National Infrastructure Simulation and Analysis Center	Energy Department
	Federal Computer Incident Response Center	General Services Administration
Secret Service	Secret Service including presidential protection units	Treasury Department
Coast Guard	Coast Guard	Transportation Department

Source: *New York Times*, November 20, 2002, p. A12.

catch the same criminals. This can have major implications if the agency that makes the arrest determines the court to which the case is brought. Usually, however, law enforcement officials at all levels of government seek to cooperate and to coordinate their efforts.

After the September 11, 2001, attacks on the World Trade Center and the Pentagon, the FBI and other federal law enforcement agencies focused their resources and efforts on investigating and preventing terrorist threats against the United States. As a result, the role of the FBI as a law enforcement agency has changed. One month after the attacks, 4,000 of the agency's 11,500 agents were dedicating their efforts to the aftermath of September 11. The FBI has continued to increase its attention to terrorism and cyber crimes in the subsequent years of the twenty-first century and thereby diminished its involvement in aspects of traditional law enforcement. In a 2011 speech, FBI Director Robert Mueller emphasized that "Terrorism, espionage, and cyber attacks are the FBI's top priorities" (Mueller, 2011a).

The reorientation of the FBI's priorities is just one of many changes made in federal criminal justice agencies to address the issues of national security and terrorism. The most significant expansion of the federal government occurred with the creation of a new Department of Homeland Security (DHS) through the consolidation of border security, intelligence, and emergency-response agencies from other departments of government (see Table 1.1). A new agency, the Transportation Security Administration (TSA), was created within DHS to assume responsibility for

Figure 1.1

Percentage (Rounded) of Criminal Justice Employees at Each Level of Government, 2006 The administration of criminal justice in the United States is very much a local affair, as these employment figures show. Only in corrections do states employ a greater percentage of workers than do cities and counties.

Source: Bureau of Justice Statistics, *Sourcebook of Criminal Justice Statistics, 2011* (Washington, DC: U.S. Government Printing Office, 2012), Table 1.21.2006.

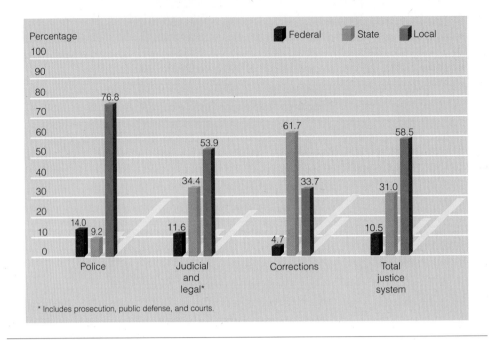

* Includes prosecution, public defense, and courts.

protecting travelers and interstate commerce by screening of passengers and their luggage at airports throughout the country.

Because both state and federal systems operate in the United States, criminal justice here is highly decentralized. As Figure 1.1 shows, almost two-thirds of all criminal justice employees work for local governments. The majority of workers in all of the subunits of the system—except corrections—are tied to local government. Likewise, the costs of criminal justice are distributed among federal, state, and local governments. The nation's economic problems since 2007 have reduced government budgets for criminal justice in many cities, counties, and states. Even the FBI faced the prospect of being unable to fill needed positions in 2012 as Congress sought to reduce federal government expenditures (R. Reilly, 2011). Thus, as we shall see throughout the chapters of this book, recent budget problems have forced criminal justice agencies at all levels of government to reduce law enforcement activities, release offenders early from prison, and take other measures to cope with a reduction in resources (Bluestein, 2011). These issues can have their greatest impact at the local level, especially when there are no longer enough police officers on duty to respond quickly to citizens' calls for assistance (LeDuff, 2011).

---

check point

4. What is the key feature of federalism?
A division of power between a central (national) government and regional (state) governments.

5. What powers does the national government have in the area of criminal justice?
Enforcement of federal criminal laws.

6. What factors have caused the expansion of federal laws and involvement in criminal justice?
The expansion of criminal activities across state borders; efforts to combat terrorism, cyber attacks, and international criminal activities.

stop & analyze

Is there a risk that the American system of criminal justice is too fragmented because authority is divided between three levels of government? List three problems that can arise because the United States lacks a single, specific authority to be in charge of running criminal justice agencies throughout the nation.

Criminal Justice as a Social System

To achieve the goals of criminal justice, many kinds of organizations—police, prosecution, courts, corrections—have been formed. Each has its own functions and personnel. We might assume that criminal justice is an orderly process in which a variety of professionals act on each case on behalf of society. To know how the system really works, however, we must look beyond its formal organizational structure. In doing so, we can use the concept of a **system**: a complex whole made up of interdependent parts whose actions are directed toward goals and influenced by the environment in which they function.

The system perspective emphasizes that criminal justice is made up of parts or subsystems, including police, courts, and corrections. Here, Judge Orlando Houston confers with prosecutors and defense attorneys during the Durham, North Carolina, trial of Michael Peterson, who was convicted of murdering his wife, Kathleen. Each participant brings his or her own perspective to the system.

The criminal justice system comprises several parts or subsystems. The subsystems—police, courts, corrections—have their own goals and needs but are also interdependent. When one unit changes its policies, practices, or resources, other units will be affected. An increase in the number of people arrested by the police, for example, will affect not only the judicial subsystem but also the probation and correctional subsystems. For criminal justice to achieve its goals, each part must make its own contribution; each must also have some contact with at least one other part of the system.

Criminal justice agencies and actors are depicted as functioning as a system, but this description should not be understood to imply that they cooperate fully, operate smoothly, or achieve efficiency in undertaking their responsibilities. It is a human system with flawed decisions, imperfect communication, and uneven distribution of resources. However, the various agencies and actors are connected to and dependent on each other in order to fulfill their assigned tasks.

Although understanding the nature of the entire criminal justice system and its subsystems is important, we must also see how individual actors play their roles. The criminal justice system is made up of a great many people doing specific jobs. Some, such as police officers and judges, are well known to the public. Others, such as bail bondsmen and probation officers, are less well known. A key concept here is **exchange**, meaning the mutual transfer of resources among individual actors, each of whom has goals that he or she cannot accomplish alone. Each needs to gain the cooperation and assistance of other individuals by helping them achieve their own goals. The concept of exchange allows interpersonal behavior to be seen as the result of individual decisions about the costs and benefits of different courses of action.

Many kinds of exchange relationships exist in the criminal justice system, some more visible than others. Probably the most obvious example is the **plea bargain**, in which the defense attorney and the prosecutor reach an agreement: The defendant agrees to plead guilty in exchange for a reduction of charges or for a lighter sentence. As a result of this exchange, the prosecutor gains a quick, sure conviction; the defendant achieves a shorter sentence, and the defense attorney can move on to the next case. Thus, the cooperation underlying the exchange promotes the goals of each participant. See "A Question of Ethics" at the end of the chapter, concerning the short jail sentence received by boxing champion Floyd Mayweather Jr.; then consider whether prosecutors' use of discretion in plea bargaining should be guided by a concern for equal treatment of all similarly situated offenders.

The concept of exchange serves as a reminder that decisions are the products of interactions among individuals and that the subsystems of the criminal justice system are tied together by the actions of individual decision makers. Figure 1.2 presents selected exchange relationships between a prosecutor and other individuals and agencies involved in the criminal justice process.

system A complex whole consisting of interdependent parts whose actions are directed toward goals and are influenced by the environment within which they function.

exchange A mutual transfer of resources: a balance of benefits and deficits that flow from behavior based on decisions about the values and costs of alternatives.

plea bargain A defendant's plea of guilty to a criminal charge with the reasonable expectation of receiving some consideration from the state for doing so, usually a reduction of the charge. The defendant's ultimate goal is a penalty lighter than the one formally warranted by the charged offense.

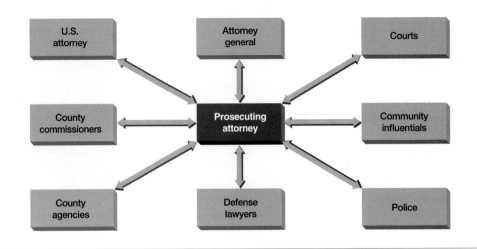

Figure 1.2

Exchange Relationships between Prosecutors and Others The prosecutor's decisions are influenced by relationships with other agencies and members of the community.

© Cengage Learning

check point

7. **What is a system?**
   A complex whole made up of interdependent parts whose actions are directed toward goals and influenced by the environment within which they function.

8. **What are the subsystems of the criminal justice system?**
   Police, courts, corrections.

9. **What is one example of an exchange relationship?**
   Plea bargaining.

stop & analyze

Is plea bargaining beneficial for society or does it inappropriately permit lawbreakers to escape appropriate punishment? Give two arguments favoring each side in this debate. Which side has the stronger arguments?

Characteristics of the Criminal Justice System

The workings of the criminal justice system have four major characteristics: (1) discretion, (2) resource dependence, (3) sequential tasks, and (4) filtering.

Discretion

discretion The authority to make decisions without reference to specific rules or facts, using instead one's own judgment; allows for individualization and informality in the administration of justice.

All levels of the justice process reflect a high degree of **discretion**. This term refers to officials' freedom to act according to their own judgment and conscience (see Table 1.2). For example, police officers decide how to handle a crime situation, prosecutors decide which charges to file, judges decide how long a sentence will be, and parole boards decide when an offender may be released from prison.

The extent of such discretion may seem odd, given that the United States is ruled by law and has created procedures to ensure that decisions are made in accordance with law. However, instead of a mechanical system in which decisions are dominated by law, criminal justice is a system in which actors may take many factors into account and exercise many options as they dispose of a case.

Two arguments are often made to justify discretion in the criminal justice system. First, discretion is needed because the system lacks the resources to treat every case the same way. If every violation of the law were pursued from

TABLE 1.2 Who Exercises Discretion?

Discretion is exercised by various actors throughout the criminal justice system.

These Criminal Justice Officials . . .	Must Often Decide Whether or How to . . .
Police	Enforce specific laws Investigate specific crimes Search people, vicinities, buildings Arrest or detain people
Prosecutors	File charges or petitions for adjudication Seek indictments Drop cases Reduce charges
Judges or Magistrates	Set bail or conditions for release Accept pleas Determine delinquency Dismiss charges Impose sentences Revoke probation
Correctional Officials	Assign to [which] type of correctional facility Award privileges Punish for infractions of rules Determine date and conditions of parole Revoke parole

Source: Bureau of Justice Statistics, *Report to the Nation on Crime and Justice*, 2nd ed. (Washington, DC: U.S. Government Printing Office, 1988), 59.

investigation through trial, the costs would be immense. Second, many officials believe that discretion permits them to achieve greater justice than rigid rules would produce.

Resource Dependence

Criminal justice agencies do not generate their own resources but depend on other agencies for funding. Therefore, actors in the system must cultivate and maintain good relations with those who allocate resources—that is, political decision makers, such as legislators, mayors, and city council members. Some police departments gain revenue through traffic fines and property forfeitures, but these sources cannot sustain their budgets.

Because budget decisions are made by elected officials who seek to please the public, criminal justice officials must also maintain a positive image and good relations with voters. If the police have strong public support, for example, the mayor will be reluctant to reduce the law enforcement budget. Criminal justice officials also seek positive coverage from the news media. Because the media often provide a crucial link between government agencies and the public, criminal justice officials may announce notable achievements while trying to limit publicity about controversial cases and decisions. In the second decade of the twenty-first century, resource issues have become especially difficult and important for criminal justice officials because of widespread and deep budget cuts in many cities, counties, and states (Bluestein, 2011).

Figure 1.3

Criminal Justice as a Filtering Process Decisions at each point in the system result in some cases being dropped while others are passed to the next point. Are you surprised by the small portion of cases that remain?

Sources: Estimates calculated from Thomas H. Cohen and Tracey Kyckelhahn, "Felony Defendants in Large Urban Counties, 2006," Bureau of Justice Statistics *Bulletin*, May 2010, Figure 1; FBI, *Crime in the United States, 2009* [Uniform Crime Reports], Tables 25 and 28; Jennifer L. Truman and Michael R. Rand, "Criminal Victimization, 2009," Bureau of Justice Statistics *Bulletin*, October 2010, Tables 1 and 11.

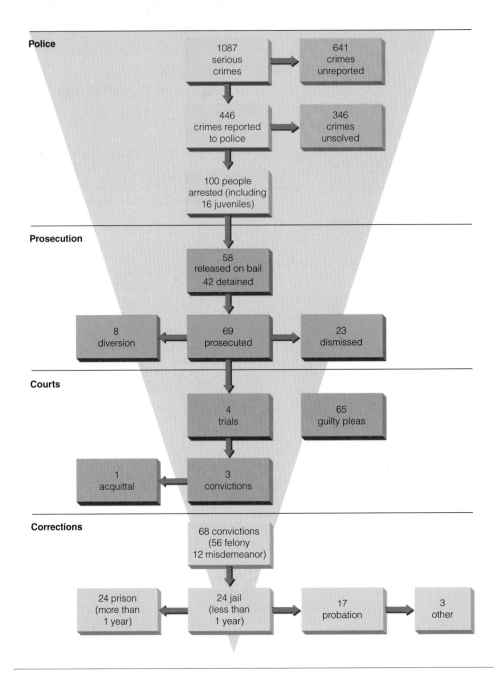

Police

1087 serious crimes	→	641 crimes unreported
446 crimes reported to police	→	346 crimes unsolved
100 people arrested (including 16 juveniles)		

Prosecution

58 released on bail 42 detained

8 diversion ← 69 prosecuted → 23 dismissed

Courts

4 trials   65 guilty pleas

1 acquittal ← 3 convictions

Corrections

68 convictions (56 felony 12 misdemeanor)

24 prison (more than 1 year) ← 24 jail (less than 1 year) → 17 probation → 3 other

Sequential Tasks

Decisions in the criminal justice system are made in a specific sequence. The police must arrest a person before the case is passed to the prosecutor to determine if charges should be brought. The prosecutor's decisions influence the nature of the court's workload. The accumulated decisions of police, prosecutors, and courts determine the number of offenders sent to corrections agencies. The sequential nature of the system is key to the exchange relationships among the justice system's decision makers, who depend on one another to achieve their goals. In other words, the system is highly interdependent partially because it is sequential.

Filtering

We can see the criminal justice system as a **filtering process**. At each stage some defendants are sent on to the next stage, while others are either released or processed under changed conditions. As shown in Figure 1.3, people who have

filtering process A screening operation; a process by which criminal justice officials screen out some cases while advancing others to the next level of decision making.

been arrested may be filtered out of the system at various points. Note that relatively few suspects are arrested in light of the number of crimes committed, and a portion of the arrestees will be released without being prosecuted or convicted. Some go free because the police decide that a crime has not been committed or that the evidence is not sound. The prosecutor may decide that justice would be better served by sending the suspect to a substance-abuse clinic. Many defendants will plead guilty and receive lesser punishments, judges may dismiss charges against others, and juries may acquit a few defendants. Most of the offenders who are actually prosecuted for serious charges will be convicted, however. Thus, the criminal justice system is often described as a funnel—only a portion of the cases that enter the system will result in conviction and punishment. Some people look at how few people end up in prison and conclude that the system is not tough enough on criminal offenders. Consider this idea as you read "Criminal Justice: Myth & Reality."

To summarize, the criminal justice system is composed of a set of interdependent parts (subsystems). This system has four key attributes: (1) discretion, (2) resource dependence, (3) sequential tasks, and (4) filtering. Using this framework, we look next at the operations of criminal justice agencies, and then examine the flow of cases through the system.

criminal justice myth & reality

Common Belief: The American criminal justice system is obviously not tough enough on criminal offenders, because so many of them go free and so few of them end up in prison.

- The filtering of people out of the justice system does not mean that the American system is not tough on offenders.
- In fact, the United States incarcerates more people and keeps them locked up for longer periods than do comparable democracies.
- The biggest challenge for police is gathering enough evidence to identify a suspect and justify making an arrest. This difficulty accounts for the largest gap between reported crimes and prosecutions.
- After a suspect is arrested, filtering occurs for a variety of reasons. Officials need proper evidence to prove guilt in order to move forward with cases. Sometimes the wrong person is arrested and further investigation leads to a release.
- The system also has limited resources. There are only so many police officers to investigate cases, prosecutors to prepare cases, courtrooms to process cases, and cells to hold detainees in jail and convicted offenders in prison.
- Thus, discretionary decisions must inevitably be made to use the system's limited resources to the greatest effect. Therefore, prosecutors focus their sustained attention on the most-serious cases and consider ways to speed the processing of lesser cases and first offenders through plea bargaining.
- When prosecutors have sufficient evidence and therefore move forward with a prosecution, they see very high conviction rates.

---

check point 10. **What are the major characteristics of the criminal justice system?**
Discretion, resource dependence, sequential tasks, filtering.

stop & analyze What is the most surprising aspect of Figure 1.3? Describe two aspects of the information presented in the figure that differ from your assumptions about the criminal justice system.

Operations of Criminal Justice Agencies

The criminal justice system has been formed to deal with people who are accused of violating the criminal law. Its subsystems consist of more than 60,000 public and private agencies with an annual budget of more than $214 billion and more than 2.4 million employees (Bureau of Justice Statistics, 2011b). Here we review the main parts of the criminal justice system and their functions.

Police

We usually think of the police as being on the "front line" in controlling crime. The term *police,* however, does not refer to a single agency or type of agency, but to many agencies at each level of government. The complexity of the criminal justice system can be seen in the large number of organizations engaged in law enforcement. There are only 50 federal law enforcement agencies in the United States, whereas 17,985 state and local law enforcement agencies operate (Reaves, 2011). Fifty

AP Images/The Day, Tim Cook

↑ As part of law enforcement responsibilities, the police must deal with a wide range of witnesses and victims in emotionally charged situations. What skills and personal qualities are required to respond to emergencies? What skills do officers need to deal one-to-one with traumatized victims and witnesses?

of these are state agencies. The remaining agencies are found in counties, cities, and towns, reflecting the fact that local governments dominate the police function. At the state and local levels, these agencies have more than one million full-time employees and a total annual budget that exceeds $80 billion (Reaves, 2011).

Police agencies have four major duties:

1. *Keeping the peace.* This broad and important mandate involves the protection of rights and persons in situations ranging from street-corner brawls to domestic quarrels.
2. *Apprehending violators and combatting crime.* This is the task that the public most often associates with police work, although it accounts for only a small portion of police time and resources.
3. *Preventing crime.* By educating the public about the threat of crime and by reducing the number of situations in which crimes are likely to be committed, the police can lower the rate of crime.
4. *Providing social services.* Police officers recover stolen property, direct traffic, give emergency medical aid, help people who have locked themselves out of their homes, and provide other social services.

Courts

The United States has a **dual court system** that consists of a separate judicial system for each state in addition to a national system. Each system has its own series of courts; the U.S. Supreme Court is responsible for correcting certain errors made in all other court systems. Although the Supreme Court can review cases from both the state and federal courts, it will hear only cases involving federal law or constitutional rights. State supreme courts are the final authority for cases that solely concern issues of state law.

With a dual court system, the law may be interpreted differently in various states. Although the wording of laws may be similar, state courts do not necessarily interpret the similarly worded laws the same way as the other courts do. To some extent, these variations reflect different social and political conditions. The dominant values of citizens and judges may differ from one region to another. Differences in interpretation may also be due to attempts by state courts to solve similar problems by different means. For example, before the Supreme Court ruled that evidence the police obtained in illegal ways should usually be excluded at trials, some states had already established rules barring the use of such evidence in their own courts.

dual court system A system consisting of a separate judicial system for each state in addition to a national system. Each case is tried in a court of the same jurisdiction as that of the law or laws broken.

adjudication The process of determining whether the defendant is guilty.

Courts are responsible for **adjudication**—determining whether or not a defendant is guilty. In so doing, they must use fair procedures that will produce just, reliable decisions. Courts must also impose sentences that are appropriate to the behavior being punished. Certain cases or offenders, such as drug cases or juvenile offenders, may be sent to specialized courts that focus on specific matters.

Corrections

On any given day, nearly seven million American adults (1 of every 33) are under the supervision of state and federal corrections systems (L. Glaze, 2011). There is no "typical" correctional agency or official. Instead, a variety of agencies and programs are provided by private and public organizations—including federal, state, and local governments—and carried out in many different community and closed settings.

Although the average citizen may equate corrections with prisons, less than 30 percent of convicted offenders are in prisons and jails; the rest are being supervised in the community. Probation and parole have long been important aspects of corrections, as have community-based halfway houses, work release programs, and supervised activities.

The federal government, all the states, most counties, and all but the smallest cities engage in corrections. Nonprofit private organizations such as the Young Men's Christian Association (YMCA) have also contracted with governments to perform correctional services. In recent years, for-profit businesses have also entered into contracts with governments to build and operate correctional institutions.

The police, courts, and corrections are the main agencies of criminal justice. Each is a part, or subsystem, of the criminal justice system. Each is linked to the other two subsystems, and the actions of each affect the others. These effects can be seen as we examine the flow of decision making within the criminal justice system.

Kevork Djansezian/Getty Images

⬆ Although prisons provide the most familiar image of corrections, in fact, two-thirds of offenders are in the community on probation, community-based sanctions, or parole. Do you ever notice the presence of convicted offenders serving their sentences in the community, or do they cause few problems that attract attention from the public?

check point

11. What are the four main duties of police?
Keeping the peace, apprehending violators and combatting crime, preventing crime, providing social services.

12. What is a dual court system?
A separate judicial system for each state in addition to a national system.

13. What are the major types of state and local correctional facilities and programs? What types of organizations operate them?
Prisons, jails, probation, parole, intermediate sanctions. Public, nonprofit, and for-profit agencies carry out these programs.

stop& analyze
What kinds of problems can arise from having state and federal law enforcement agencies and courts operating in the same city? Briefly describe two difficulties that citizens may face because two justice systems exist in one location; then consider the same scenario and describe two problems that may arise for either police or prosecutors.

The Flow of Decision Making in the Criminal Justice System

The processing of cases in the criminal justice system involves a series of decisions by police officers, prosecutors, judges, probation officers, wardens, and parole board members. At each stage in the process, they decide whether a case will move on to the next stage or be dropped from the system. Although the flowchart shown in Figure 1.4 appears streamlined, with cases entering at the top and moving swiftly toward the bottom, the actual route taken may be quite long and may involve many

Figure 1.4

The Flow of Decision Making in the Criminal Justice System Each agency is responsible for a part of the decision-making process. Thus, the police, prosecution, courts, and corrections are bound together through a series of exchange relationships.

© Cengage Learning

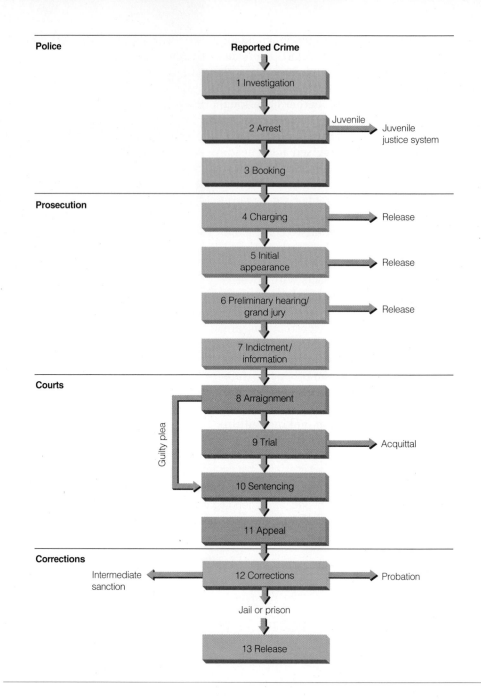

detours. At each step, officials have the discretion to decide what happens next. Many cases are filtered out of the system, others are sent to the next decision maker, and still others are dealt with informally.

Moreover, the flowchart does not show the influences of social relations or the political environment. In 2006, a retired FBI agent was charged with providing inside information to organized-crime figures so that informants could be murdered. It was then discovered that 30 years earlier this agent had been caught illegally selling unlicensed handguns to undercover agents of the U.S. Bureau of Alcohol, Tobacco, and Firearms. If this FBI agent had been prosecuted for the handgun sales, his career in the FBI would have been over and he would never have achieved the high-level position that later allegedly allowed him to assist mobsters. However, according to one former federal prosecutor involved in the handgun case in 1976, a high official in the U.S. Justice Department used his discretion to drop the gun charges. According to the former prosecutor, the high official "expressed no other reason not to prosecute the guy except the guy was a cop—and he didn't want to embarrass the [FBI]" (Feuer, 2006). The flowchart does not take into account that someone in authority might exercise discretion unfairly in favor of certain people, such as those with wealth or political connections.

Social relations and official discretion can create specific situations that make potential prosecutions more difficult. For example, in 2004, Colorado prosecutors dropped rape charges against basketball star Kobe Bryant after the alleged victim changed her mind about her willingness to testify against him (T. R. Reid, 2004). Instead, the alleged victim reportedly accepted an undisclosed sum of money from Bryant to settle a lawsuit that she had filed against him (Sarche, 2005). The prosecutors chose not to pursue this case without the victim's cooperation.

On the other hand, prosecutors and judges sometimes pressure witnesses to testify, even jailing some reluctant witnesses for contempt of court. In 2005, for example, a federal judge sent a news reporter to jail for initially failing to disclose sources concerning an investigation to identify the government officials who revealed the identity of a CIA officer. Thus, it is important to recognize that political influence, personal relationships, and specific circumstances may affect how officials' decisions shape the paths and outcomes of individual cases. Might Kobe Bryant have been convicted of rape if prosecutors in Colorado had chosen to exert more pressure on the reluctant witness? Would the victim have been willing to testify if Bryant, a millionaire athlete, had not paid her the money she sought in her lawsuit against him? There is no way to know. Such factors may influence decisions in ways that are not reflected in a simple description of decision-making steps. In the next section, as we follow the 13 steps of the criminal justice process, bear in mind that the formal procedures do not hold in every case. Discretion, political pressure, and other factors can alter the outcome for different individuals.

Steps in the Decision-Making Process

The criminal justice system consists of 13 steps that cover the stages of law enforcement, adjudication, and corrections. The system looks like an assembly line where decisions are made about *defendants*—persons charged with crimes. As these steps are described, recall the concepts discussed earlier: system, exchange, discretion, sequential tasks, and filtering. Be aware that the terms used for different stages in the process may differ from state to state and that the sequence of the steps differs in some parts of the country. In general, however, the flow of decision making follows this pattern:

1. *Investigation.* The process begins when the police believe that a crime has been committed. At this point an investigation is begun. The police typically depend on a member of the community to report the offense. Except for traffic and public-order offenses, it is unusual for the police to observe illegal behavior themselves. Most crimes have already been committed and offenders have left the scene before the police arrive, placing the police at a disadvantage in quickly finding and arresting the offenders.

2. *Arrest.* If the police find enough evidence showing that a particular person has committed a crime, an arrest may be made. An **arrest** involves physically taking a person into custody pending a court proceeding. This action not only restricts the suspect's freedom but also is the first step toward prosecution.

   Under some conditions, arrests may be made on the basis of a **warrant**—a court order issued by a judge authorizing police officers to take certain actions, such as arresting suspects or searching premises. In practice, most arrests are made without warrants. In some states, police officers may issue a summons or citation that orders a person to appear in court on a certain date. This avoids the need to hold the suspect physically until decisions are made about the case.

3. *Booking.* After an arrest, the suspect is usually transported to a police station for booking, in which a record is made of the arrest. When booked, the suspect

arrest The physical taking of a person into custody on the grounds that there is reason to believe that he or she has committed a criminal offense. Police are limited to using only reasonable physical force in making an arrest. The purpose of the arrest is to hold the accused for a court proceeding.

warrant A court order authorizing police officers to take certain actions, for example, to arrest suspects or to search premises.

may be fingerprinted, photographed, questioned, and placed in a lineup to be identified by the victim or witnesses. Before being questioned, all suspects in custody must also be warned that they have the right to counsel, that they may remain silent, and that any statement they make may be used against them later. Bail may be set so that the suspect learns what amount of money must be paid or what other conditions must be met to gain release from custody until the case is processed.

4. *Charging.* Prosecuting attorneys are the key link between the police and the courts. They must consider the facts of the case and decide whether there is reasonable cause to believe that an offense was committed and that the suspect committed the offense. The decision to charge is crucial because it sets in motion the adjudication of the case.

5. *Initial appearance.* Within a reasonable time after arrest, the suspect must be brought before a judge. At this point, suspects are given formal notice of the charge(s) for which they are being held, advised of their rights, and, if approved by the judge, given a chance to post bail. At this stage, the judge decides whether there is enough evidence to hold the suspect for further criminal processing. If enough evidence has not been produced, the judge will dismiss the case.

The purpose of bail is to permit the accused to be released while awaiting trial and to ensure that he or she will show up in court at the appointed time. Bail requires the accused to provide or arrange a surety (or pledge), usually in the form of money or a bond. The amount of bail is based mainly on the judge's view of the seriousness of the crime and the defendant's prior criminal record. Suspects may also be released on their own recognizance (also known as ROR)—a promise to appear in court at a later date without the posting of bail. In a few cases, bail may be denied and the accused held because he or she is viewed as a threat to the community.

6. *Preliminary hearing/grand jury.* After suspects have been arrested, booked, and brought to court to be informed of the charges against them and advised of their rights, a decision must be made as to whether there is enough evidence to proceed. The preliminary hearing, used in about half the states, allows a judge to decide whether there is probable cause to believe that a crime has been committed and that the accused person committed it. If the judge does not find probable cause, the case is dismissed. If there is enough evidence, the accused is bound over for arraignment on an **information**—a document charging a person with a specific crime.

In the federal system and in some states, the prosecutor appears before a grand jury, which decides whether there is enough evidence to file an **indictment** or "true bill" charging the suspect with a specific crime. The preliminary hearing and grand jury are designed to prevent hasty and malicious prosecutions, to protect people from mistakenly being humiliated in public, and to decide whether there are grounds for prosecution.

7. *Indictment/information.* If the preliminary hearing leads to an information or the grand jury vote leads to an indictment, the prosecutor prepares the formal charging document and presents it to the court.

8. *Arraignment.* The accused person appears in court to hear the indictment or information read by a judge and to enter a plea. Accused persons may plead guilty or not guilty, or in some states, stand mute. If the accused pleads guilty, the judge must decide whether the plea is made voluntarily and whether the person has full knowledge of the consequences. When a guilty plea is accepted as "knowing" and voluntary, there is no need for a trial and the judge imposes a sentence.

Plea bargaining may take place at any time in the criminal justice process, but it is likely to be completed just before or soon after arraignment. Very few criminal cases proceed to trial. Most move from the entry of the guilty plea to the sentencing phase.

information A document charging an individual with a specific crime. It is prepared by a prosecuting attorney and presented to a court at a preliminary hearing.

indictment A document returned by a grand jury as a "true bill" charging an individual with a specific crime on the basis of a determination of probable cause as presented by a prosecuting attorney.

9. *Trial.* For the small percentage of defendants who plead not guilty, the right to a trial by an impartial jury is guaranteed by the Sixth Amendment if the charges are serious enough to warrant incarceration for more than six months. In many jurisdictions, lesser charges do not entail the right to a jury trial. Most trials are summary or bench trials; that is, they are conducted without a jury. Because the defendant pleads guilty in most criminal cases, only about 10 to 15 percent of cases go to trial and only about 5 percent are heard by juries. Whether a criminal trial is held before a judge alone or before a judge and jury, the procedures are similar and are set out by state law and U.S. Supreme Court rulings. A defendant shall be found guilty only if the evidence proves beyond a reasonable doubt that he or she committed the offense.

10. *Sentencing.* Judges are responsible for imposing sentences. The intent is to make the sentence suitable to the offender and the offense within the limits set by the law. Although criminal codes place limits on sentences, the judge still typically has leeway. Among the judge's options are a suspended sentence, probation, imprisonment, or other sanctions such as fines and community service.

11. *Appeal.* Defendants who are found guilty may appeal convictions to a higher court. An appeal may be based on the claim that the trial court failed to follow the proper procedures or that constitutional rights were violated by the actions of police, prosecutors, defense attorneys, or judges. The number of appeals is small compared with the total number of convictions; further, in about 80 percent of appeals, trial judges and other officials are ruled to have acted properly. Even defendants who win appeals do not go free right away. Normally, the defendant is given a second trial, which may result in an acquittal, a second conviction, or a plea bargain to lesser charges.

12. *Corrections.* The court's sentence is carried out by the correctional subsystem. Probation, intermediate sanctions such as fines and community service, and incarceration are the sanctions most often imposed. Probation allows offenders to serve their sentences in the community under supervision. Youthful offenders, first offenders, and those convicted of minor violations are most likely to be sentenced to probation rather than incarceration. The conditions of probation may require offenders to observe certain rules—to be employed, maintain an orderly life, or attend school—and to report to their supervising officer from time to time. If these requirements are not met, the judge may revoke the probation and impose a prison sentence.

    Many new types of sanctions have been used in recent years. These intermediate sanctions are more restrictive than probation but less restrictive than incarceration. They include fines, intensive supervision probation, boot camp, home confinement, and community service.

    Whatever the reasons used to justify them, prisons exist mainly to separate criminals from the rest of society. Those convicted of misdemeanors usually serve their time in city or county jails, whereas felons serve time in state prisons. Isolation from the community is one of the most painful aspects of incarceration. Not only are letters and visits restricted, but supervision and censorship are ever present. In order to maintain security, prison officials make unannounced searches of inmates and subject them to strict discipline.

13. *Release.* Release may occur when the offender has served the full sentence imposed by the court, but most offenders are returned to the community under the supervision of a parole officer. Parole continues for the duration of the sentence or for a period specified by law. Parole may be revoked and the offender returned to prison if the conditions of parole are not met or if the parolee commits another crime.

To see the criminal justice process in action, read "The Criminal Justice Process," the story of Christopher Jones, who was arrested, charged, and convicted of serious crimes arising from the police investigation of a series of robberies. The story immediately follows this chapter.

Figure 1.5

The Criminal Justice Wedding Cake This figure shows that different cases are treated in different ways. Only a very few cases are played out as "high drama"; most are handled through plea bargaining and dismissals.

Source: Drawn from Samuel Walker, *Sense and Nonsense about Crime and Drugs*, 4th ed. (Belmont, CA: Wadsworth, 1998), 30–37.

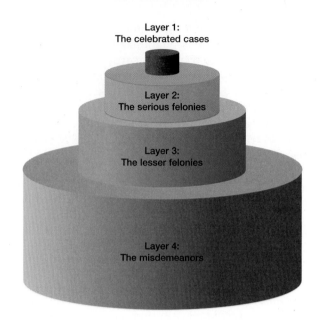

Layer 1:
The celebrated cases

Layer 2:
The serious felonies

Layer 3:
The lesser felonies

Layer 4:
The misdemeanors

The Criminal Justice Wedding Cake

Although the flowchart shown in Figure 1.4 is helpful, recall that not all cases are treated equally. The process applied to a given case, as well as its outcome, is shaped by many factors, including the importance of the case to decision makers, the seriousness of the charge, and the defendant's resources.

Some cases are highly visible, either because of the notoriety of the defendant or victim or because of the shocking nature of the crime. At the other extreme are "run-of-the-mill cases" involving minor charges and no media attention.

As shown in Figure 1.5, the criminal justice process can be compared to a wedding cake. This model shows clearly how different cases receive different kinds of treatment in the justice process.

Layer 1 of the "cake" consists of "celebrated" cases that are highly unusual, receive much public attention, result in a jury trial, and often drag on through many appeals. These cases embody the ideal of an adversarial system of justice in which each side actively fights against the other, either because the defendant faces a stiff sentence or because the defendant has the financial resources to pay for a strong defense. The highly publicized 2011 trial and conviction of Dr. Conrad Murray, the physician who prescribed medications that caused the death of singer Michael Jackson, serves as an example. Not all cases in Layer 1 receive national attention, however. From time to time, local crimes, especially cases of murder and rape, are treated in this way.

These cases serve as morality plays. The carefully crafted arguments of the prosecution and defense are seen as expressing key issues in our society or tragic flaws in individuals. Too often, however, the public concludes that all criminal cases follow this model.

felonies Serious crimes usually carrying a penalty of death or of incarceration for more than one year.

Layer 2 consists of **felonies** that are considered serious by officials. Here we see violent crimes committed by persons with long criminal records against victims unknown to them. Police and prosecutors speak of serious felonies as "heavy" cases that should result in "tough" sentences. In such cases the defendant has little reason to plead guilty and the defense attorney must prepare for trial.

Layer 3 also consists of felonies, but the crimes and the offenders are seen as less important than those in Layer 2. The offenses may be the same as in Layer 2, but the offender may have no record, and the victim may have had a prior relationship with the accused, for example. The main goal of criminal justice officials is to dispose of such cases quickly. For this reason, many are filtered out of the system, often through plea bargaining.

Layer 4 is made up of **misdemeanors**. About 90 percent of all cases fall into this category. They concern such offenses as public drunkenness, shoplifting, prostitution, disturbing the peace, and traffic violations. Looked on as the "garbage" of the system, these cases are handled by the lower courts, where speed is essential. Prosecutors use their discretion to reduce charges or recommend probation as a way to encourage defendants to plead guilty quickly. Trials are rare, processes are informal, and fines, probation, or short jail sentences result.

The wedding cake model is a useful way of viewing the criminal justice system. Cases are not treated equally; some are seen as very important, others as merely part of a large caseload that must be processed. When one knows the nature of a case, one can predict fairly well how it will be handled and what its outcome will be.

AP Images/Chuck Burton

⬆ In 2012, former presidential candidate John Edwards faced trial for violating campaign finance laws, including improperly using campaign contributions to support his mistress. The case had all of the earmarks of a Layer 1 case as the millionaire former U.S. senator claimed to be innocent and demanded a trial. Such cases embody the ideal of the due process model, with attorneys for each battling in front of the jury in a lengthy trial. Should society devote enough resources to the justice system so that all defendants—rich or poor—can have Layer 1, adversarial trials?

Crime Control versus Due Process

Models are simplified representations that illustrate important aspects of a system. As we saw in discussing the wedding cake model, they permit generalized statements and comparisons even though no one model necessarily portrays precisely the complex reality of specific situations. We now look at two more models to expand our picture of how the criminal justice system really operates.

In one of the most important contributions to systematic thought about the administration of justice, Herbert Packer (1968) described two competing models of the administration of criminal justice: the **crime control model** and the **due process model**. These are opposing ways of looking at the goals and procedures of the criminal justice system. The crime control model is much like an assembly line, whereas the due process model is like an obstacle course.

In reality, no one official or agency functions according to one model or the other. Elements of both models are found throughout the system. However, the two models reveal key tensions within the criminal justice process, as well as the gap between how the system is described and the way most cases are actually processed. Table 1.3 presents the major elements of each model.

Crime Control: Order as a Value The crime control model assumes that every effort must be made to repress crime. It emphasizes efficiency and the capacity to catch, try, convict, and punish a high proportion of offenders; it also stresses speed and finality. This model places the goal of controlling crime uppermost, putting less emphasis on protecting individuals' rights. As Packer points out, in order to achieve liberty for all citizens, the crime control model calls for efficiency

misdemeanors Offenses less serious than felonies and usually punishable by incarceration of no more than one year in jail, probation, or intermediate sanctions.

crime control model A model of the criminal justice system that assumes freedom is so important that every effort must be made to repress crime; it emphasizes efficiency, speed, finality, and the capacity to apprehend, try, convict, and dispose of a high proportion of offenders.

due process model A model of the criminal justice system that assumes freedom is so important that every effort must be made to ensure that criminal justice decisions are based on reliable information; it emphasizes the adversarial process, the rights of defendants, and formal decision-making procedures.

TABLE 1.3 Due Process and Crime Control Models Compared

What other comparisons can be made between the two models?

	Goal	Value	Process	Major Decision Point	Basis of Decision Making
Due Process Model	Preserve individual liberties	Reliability	Adversarial	Courtroom	Law
Crime Control Model	Repress crime	Efficiency	Administrative	Police/pretrial processes	Discretion

© Cengage Learning

in screening suspects, determining guilt, and applying sanctions to the convicted. Because of high rates of crime and the limited resources of law enforcement, speed and finality are necessary. All these elements depend on informality, uniformity, and few challenges by defense attorneys or defendants.

In this model, police and prosecutors decide early on how likely it is that the suspect will be found guilty. If a case is unlikely to end in conviction, the prosecutor may drop the charges. At each stage, from arrest to preliminary hearing, arraignment, and trial, established procedures are used to determine whether the accused should be passed on to the next stage. Instead of stressing the combative aspects of the courtroom, this model promotes bargaining between the state and the accused. Nearly all cases are disposed of through such bargaining, and they typically end with the defendant pleading guilty. Packer's description of this model as an assembly-line process conveys the idea of quick, efficient decisions by actors at fixed stations that turn out the intended product—guilty pleas and closed cases.

Due Process: Law as a Value If the crime control model looks like an assembly line, the due process model looks more like an obstacle course. This model assumes that freedom is so important that every effort must be made to ensure that criminal justice decisions are based on reliable information. It stresses the adversarial process, the rights of defendants, and formal decision-making procedures. For example, because people are poor observers of disturbing events, police and prosecutors may be wrong in presuming a defendant to be guilty. Thus, people should be labeled as criminals only on the basis of conclusive evidence. To reduce error, the government must be forced to prove beyond a reasonable doubt that the defendant is guilty of the crime. Therefore, the process must give the defense every opportunity to show that the evidence is not conclusive, and the outcome must be decided by an impartial judge and jury. According to Packer, the assumption that the defendant is innocent until proved guilty has a far-reaching impact on the criminal justice system.

In the due process model, the state must prove that the person is guilty of the crime as charged. Prosecutors must prove their cases while obeying rules dealing with such matters as the admissibility of evidence and respect for defendants' constitutional rights. Forcing the state to prove its case in a trial protects citizens from wrongful convictions. Thus, the due process model emphasizes particular aspects of the goal of doing justice. It protects the rights of individuals and reserves punishment for those who unquestionably deserve it. These values are stressed even though some guilty defendants may go free because the evidence against them is not conclusive enough. By contrast, the crime control model values efficient case processing and punishment over the possibility that innocent people might be swept up in the process.

check point 14. **What are the steps of the criminal justice process?**

(1) Investigation, (2) arrest, (3) booking, (4) charging, (5) initial appearance, (6) preliminary hearing/grand jury, (7) indictment/information, (8) arraignment, (9) trial, (10) sentencing, (11) appeal, (12) corrections, (13) release.

15. **What is the purpose of the wedding cake model?**

To show that not all cases are treated equally or processed in an identical fashion.

16. **What are the main features of the crime control model and the due process model?**

Crime control: Every effort must be made to repress crime through efficiency, speed, and finality. Due process: Every effort must be made to ensure that criminal justice decisions are based on reliable information; it stresses the adversarial process, the rights of defendants, and formal decision-making procedures.

stop& analyze Where in the wedding cake model is there a risk of incorrect or unjust outcomes? At the top—if effective defense lawyers persuade a judge or jury to acquit a guilty person? At the bottom—where quick, administrative processing lacks the opportunity for defense attorneys to challenge the nature and quality of evidence? Make an argument for which layer of the wedding cake—and its related processes—carries the greatest risk of error.

Crime and Justice in a Multicultural Society

One important aspect of American values is the principle of equal treatment. This value is prominently displayed in important national documents such as the Declaration of Independence and the Fourteenth Amendment to the Constitution, which guarantees the right to "equal protection." Critics of the criminal justice system argue that discretionary decisions and other factors produce racial discrimination. Discrimination calls into question the country's success in fulfilling the values that it claims to regard as supremely important. As such, it is instructive to look closely at whether or not discrimination exists in various criminal justice settings.

Disparity and Discrimination

African Americans, Hispanics, and other minorities are subjected to the criminal justice system at much higher rates than are the white majority (A. Baker, 2010; T. Cohen and Kyckelhahn, 2010; L. Glaze, 2011; Poston, 2011; Rainville and Smith, 2003; B. Reaves, 2006; Spohn, 2011; Ulmer, Light, and Kramer, 2011). For example:

- African American men are sent to jails and prisons at a rate 6 times greater than that of whites. The incarceration rate for Hispanic men is nearly 3 times greater than that for whites. For women, the rates are 2.5 times greater (African Americans) and 1.5 times greater (Hispanics).
- In sentencing for federal crimes, African American male offenders on average received sentences more than 20 percent longer than those imposed on comparable white male offenders and sentences for Hispanic men were nearly 7 percent longer.

Question: "I am going to read you a list of institutions in American society. Please tell me how much confidence you, yourself, have in each one."

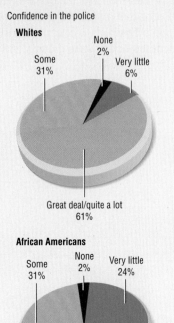

Confidence in the police

Whites

Some
31%

None
2%

Very little
6%

Great deal/quite a lot
61%

African Americans

Some
31%

None
2%

Very little
24%

Great deal/quite a lot
43%

Robert Nickelsberg/Getty Images

↑ Young African American and Hispanic men contend that they are always being hassled by the police. Is this perception the result of racism or effective police work?

- Studies of traffic stops regularly find that police stop and search African American and Hispanic drivers more frequently than white drivers, even though they are no more likely than whites to be found with weapons or drugs. In 2011 in Milwaukee, for example, African American drivers were 7 times more likely to be stopped and Hispanic drivers were 5 times more likely to be stopped. African American drivers were twice as likely to be searched.

- Forty-five percent of felony defendants in the 75 largest, most-populous counties were African American, although African Americans comprised only 14 percent of the population in those counties. Hispanics constituted 24 percent of felony defendants while only comprising 19 percent of the population.

- In the country's 40 most-populous counties, more than 60 percent of juvenile felony defendants were African Americans.

- A 2010 study in New York City concluded that African American and Hispanic pedestrians were 9 times more likely than whites to be stopped and searched by police, although they were less frequently found to be carrying illegal weapons and were no more likely than whites to be arrested.

The experiences of minority group members with the criminal justice system may contribute to differences in their views about the system's fulfillment of the goal of equal treatment (Lundman and Kaufman, 2003). Many young men, in particular, can describe multiple incidents when they were followed by officers, temporarily taken into custody, forced by police to hand over money and property, or subjected to physical force for no reason other than walking down the street (Peart, 2011; Brunson, 2007). See "What Americans Think" for more on this, and think about the impact on the criminal justice system, not just in respect to fairness, but also in relation to public cooperation with the police. As an African American college student in New York City wrote after the fifth time he was searched for no reason and, in the last search, actually handcuffed while the officers took his keys and illegally entered his apartment, "The police should consider the consequences for a generation of young people who want nothing to do with them—distrust, alienation and more crime" (Peart, 2011).

A central question is whether racial and ethnic disparities like those just listed are the result of discrimination (S. Walker, Spohn, and DeLone, 2011). A **disparity** is simply a difference between groups. Such differences can often be explained by legitimate factors. For example, the fact that 18- to 24-year-old men are arrested out of proportion to their numbers in the general population is a disparity explained by the fact that this age group produces more crime. It is not thought to be the result of public policy of singling out young men for arrest. **Discrimination** occurs when groups are differentially treated without regard to their behavior or qualifications, for example, if people of color are routinely sentenced to prison regardless of their criminal history. Thus, a disparity could result from either fair or unfair practices.

Explaining Disparities

Racial disparities in criminal justice are often explained in one of three ways: (1) people of color commit more crimes, (2) the criminal justice system is racially biased, with the result that people of color are treated more harshly, or (3) the criminal justice system expresses the racial bias found in society as a whole. We consider each of these views in turn.

Explanation 1: People of Color Commit More Crimes

Nobody denies that the proportion of minorities arrested and placed under correctional supervision (probation, jail, prison, parole) is greater than their proportion to the general population. However, people disagree over whether racial bias is responsible for the disparity.

Disparities in arrests and sentences might be due to legitimate factors. For example, prosecutors and judges are supposed to take into account differences between serious and petty offenses, and between repeat and first-time offenders. It follows that more people of color will end up in the courts and prisons if they are more likely to commit a greater number of serious crimes and have more-serious prior records than do whites (S. Walker, Spohn, and DeLone, 2011).

But why would minorities commit more crimes? The most extreme argument is that they are more predisposed to criminality. This assumes that people of color are a "criminal class." Research-based evidence does not support this view. Behavior that violates criminal laws is prevalent throughout all segments of society. For example, police made nearly 7.1 million arrests of *whites* in 2010, including more than 200,000 arrests for aggravated assault, 38,000 arrests for robbery, and more than 4,000 arrests for murder and manslaughter (FBI, 2011a). There are similar rates of illegal drug and marijuana use for whites, African Americans, and Hispanics (U.S. Department of Health and Human Services, 2007). Indeed, self-report studies show that nearly every adult American has committed an act for which he or she could be jailed. However, most are never caught for such common acts as using drugs, falsifying business-expense reports, drunken driving, cheating on taxes, or inflicting violence on an intimate partner.

Many of these kinds of crimes are difficult to detect or are low priorities for law enforcement agencies. In other instances, affluent perpetrators are better positioned to gain dismissals because of their status within the community, social networks, or access to high-quality legal representation.

In evaluating theories about possible links between race and crime, we must be aware that many commentators may be focusing only on crimes that resulted in prosecutions. Such limitations can distort an accurate understanding of this

Confidence in the criminal justice system

Whites

- Some 44%
- None 3%
- Very little 24%
- Great deal/quite a lot 28%

African Americans

- Some 36%
- Very little 37%
- Great deal/quite a lot 27%

Critical Thinking: Does it matter if different groups within society have different levels of confidence in the police and the criminal justice system? Make a list of three undesirable consequences that could emerge from these differences in opinions.

Source: Bureau of Justice Statistics, *Sourcebook of Criminal Justice Statistics, 2011*, Tables 2.11.2011 and 2.12.2011 (www.albany.edu/sourcebook).

disparity A difference between groups that may either be explained by legitimate factors or indicate discrimination.

discrimination Differential treatment of individuals or groups based on race, ethnicity, gender, sexual orientation, or economic status, instead of on their behavior or qualifications.

important issue. Race itself is not a cause of criminal behavior. Instead, any apparent associations between crime and race relate only to subcategories of people within racial and ethnic groups, such as poor, young men, as well as certain categories of crimes that are commonly investigated and prosecuted. Research links crime to social contexts, not to race (Bruce, 2003).

Crime problems evolve and change over time. Identity theft and computer crime, for example, cause economic losses in the billions of dollars, yet no one has claimed a link between these crimes and race. Even if we look at developments affecting "street crimes," we can see that factors other than race appear to create the contexts for criminal behavior. For example, one of the most significant crime problems to hit the United States at the dawn of the twenty-first century is the "meth crisis": the spread of highly addictive methamphetamine that can be "cooked" in homemade labs using over-the-counter medicines and readily available chemicals. Americans use this inexpensive, dangerous drug more often than crack cocaine or heroin. Yet this drug's use has been most prevalent among poor whites in rural areas and has contributed to burglaries and robberies by white addicts seeking to support their drug habits (Harkin, 2005). Similarly, many parts of the country have seen soaring rates for abuse and addiction of prescription painkillers, such as Vicodin and OxyContin, leading to burglaries and robberies with whites as the predominant perpetrators (Goodnough, 2011; Tavernise, 2011).

The link between crime and economic disadvantage is significant (Steffensmeier and Feldmeyer et al., 2011; McNulty and Bellair, 2003). The meth crisis has spread among poor whites in rural areas and small towns. Other kinds of crime prevail among the poor in urban areas. Further, minority groups suffer greatly from poverty and unemployment. If poor people seek to steal, it is likely to be through available means, whether burglaries at farmhouses or carjacking and shoplifting in urban areas. These sorts of crimes receive more attention from police than do crimes such as tax cheating, employee theft, and illegal stock transactions, which are associated with economic advantage. In light of the associations between race and poverty and between economic status and criminal opportunities, it is not surprising to find Native Americans, Hispanics, and African Americans to be overrepresented among perpetrators of certain categories of crimes, especially those that are the focus of police attention (Beckett, Nyrop, and Pfingst, 2006).

Explanation 2: The Criminal Justice System Is Racially Biased   Racial disparities may result if people who commit similar offenses are treated differently by decision makers in the criminal justice system because of their race or ethnicity. In this view, the fact that people of color are arrested more often than whites does not mean that they are more crime prone. Critics point to *racial profiling,* as described in the Close Up box, as an example of what many people believe is a racially biased activity by police (K. Johnson, 2010). Evidence of its existence has led to new laws and policies that require police to keep records about their traffic–law enforcement patterns (Engel, Calnon, and Bernard, 2002).

Despite efforts to monitor and prevent such activities, evidence that some police officers use race as the basis for stopping, searching, and arresting individuals persists (Alpert, 2007). Obviously, racial profiling activities—or the lack thereof—can vary from officer to officer and from police department to police department (P. Warren et al., 2006). The recent studies showing that African American drivers are 7 times more likely than white drivers to be stopped in Milwaukee, and African American pedestrians are 9 times more likely to be stopped and searched in New York City, echo prior research that provides evidence of racial bias (Poston, 2011; A. Baker, 2010). For example, a 2005 study of Texas law enforcement agencies reported that the Houston Police Department searched 12 percent of African American drivers and 9 percent of Hispanic drivers stopped by its officers, but searched only 3.7 percent of white drivers who were pulled over (Steward and Totman, 2005). A national study

Racial Profiling

Most people of all races and ethnic groups are never convicted of a crime, but stereotypes can work to brand all members of some groups with suspicion. These stereotypes are bad enough in the culture at large, but they also work their way into law enforcement through the use of criminal profiles, putting an undue burden on innocent members of these groups. Moreover, such actions produce stark collisions with important American values that we claim to hold dear, especially the values of equal treatment and fairness.

Many people of color, including well-known actors, prominent scholars, and successful doctors, can provide examples of being stopped and searched without justification. The evidence of profiling is not merely based on descriptions of specific incidents, however. Research has documented evidence of differential treatment. One study in Maryland found that African American motorists constituted 17 percent of the motorists and 17.5 percent of the speeders. But African American motorists were subjected to 77 percent of the automobile searches made by the police looking for contraband. Evidence of racial profiling in the criminal justice system is not limited to traffic enforcement. A study by the U.S. Government Accountability Office, the research agency that provides reports to Congress, discovered that African American women returning from abroad were 9 times as likely as white women to be subjected to X-ray searches at airports, even though white women were found to be carrying illegal contraband twice as often as African American women were.

Racial profiling need not be limited to African Americans. Hispanics in many locations claim that they are targeted by police who assume that they are illegal immigrants or drug traffickers. Since the tragic hijackings on September 11, many Muslims, including people of Middle Eastern and Asian ancestry, claim that they are subjected to groundless suspicion and questioning by the police and airport security officials as part of the war on terrorism.

Determining when and how the police should use race to assess suspects and situations involves a complicated balancing of public safety and civil liberties. Law enforcement experts insist that effective police work depends on quick analysis and that skin color is one factor among many—like dress and demeanor—that officers must consider. But minority leaders say that racial profiling is based on the presumption that African Americans and Hispanics are linked to crime or that Arab Americans might be linked to terrorism. This has led to the humiliation and physical abuse of innocent citizens. As a result, some police agencies have attempted to develop specific policies to steer their officers away from improper use of race and ethnicity as factors in their decisions to make stops and conduct searches.

 Researching the Internet

See one public-interest legal group's reports on racial profiling throughout the United States at the ACLU website, visit the Criminal Justice CourseMate at cengagebrain.com, then access the web links for this chapter.

For Critical Analysis

As you can see from this discussion, racial stereotypes held by law enforcement officers can contribute to stops and searches of specific people based on skin color or perceived ancestry. Is there any effective way to prevent criminal justice officials from using any degree of racial profiling? What impact does racial profiling have on people who believe that they have been subjected to it? Write a memo describing three steps you would take as a police chief to limit or stop racial profiling by your officers.

Sources: Drawn from Noah Kupferberg, "Transparency: A New Role for Police Consent Decrees," *Columbia Journal of Law and Social Problems* 42 (2008): 129–64; Ben Poston, "Racial Gap Found in Traffic Stops in Milwaukee," *Milwaukee Journal Sentinel*, December 3, 2011 (www.jsonline.com); Frederick Schauer, *Profiles, Probabilities, and Stereotypes* (Cambridge, MA: Harvard University Press, 2003); Christopher Stone, "Race, Crime, and the Administration of Justice," *National Institute of Justice Journal* (April 1999): 24–32; U.S. General Accounting Office, *U.S. Customs Service: Better Targeting of Airline Passengers for Personal Searches Could Produce Better Results* (Washington, DC: U.S. Government Printing Office, March 2000).

of traffic stops found that the odds of being searched were 50 percent higher for African American drivers and 42 percent higher for Hispanic drivers than for white drivers (Durose, Schmitt, and Langan, 2005; Engel and Calnon, 2004).

Is the criminal justice system racially biased? White Americans are less likely than African Americans to attribute the overrepresentation of minorities to biased decision making. A study published in 2008 found that 71 percent of African Americans believe that police bias is a "big reason" why minorities are disproportionately convicted of crimes and imprisoned, but only 37 percent of whites share this view (Unnever, 2008). Yet, the arrest rate of minority citizens is greater than their offense rates justify. According to data from the Bureau of Justice Statistics, victims of aggravated assaults identified their assailants as African Americans in 21 percent of cases, yet African Americans made up 34 percent of suspects arrested for aggravated assault. For rape cases, African Americans were 33 percent of the arrested suspects, but only 16 percent of the reported suspects (BJS, 2010).

With respect to sentencing, research indicates that African American and Hispanic men are less likely than white men to receive the benefit of prosecutors' discretionary recommendations for charge reductions for federal weapons crimes and for lesser sentences in cocaine prosecutions (Shermer and Johnson, 2010; Hartley, Maddan, and Spohn, 2007). A similar finding of racial disparities emerged in a study of who benefits from Florida judges' discretionary authority to "withhold adjudication" for people sentenced to probation so that they can avoid having a felony record if they successfully complete the terms of their probation (Bontrager, Bales, and Chiricos, 2005). African Americans and Hispanics, especially young men, were less likely than whites to benefit from discretionary decisions and other factors so that, in the findings of a recent study, "young black and Hispanic males bear the disproportionate brunt of sentencing in the federal courts" (Doerner and Demuth, 2010:23).

Research findings indicating the existence of bias do not mean that every minority defendant is treated disadvantageously when compared with police treatment of white defendants. Instead, the existence, nature, and extent of discrimination can vary from community to community (Britt, 2000). Thus, racial discrimination may be limited to specific types of cases, circumstances, and defendants (S. Walker, Spohn, and DeLeone, 2011).

Explanation 3: America Is a Racially Biased Society   Some people claim that the criminal justice system is racially biased because it is embedded in a racially biased society. In fact, some accuse the system of being a tool of a racially biased society.

Evidence of racial bias exists in the way society asks the criminal justice system to operate. For example, even after Congress reduced the amount of crack cocaine needed for a specific mandatory sentence in 2010, federal sentencing guidelines still punish users of crack cocaine more harshly than they do users of powder cocaine, even though the drugs are virtually identical in their chemical composition and effect on users (Eckholm, 2010). The key difference is that whites tend to use powder, whereas people of color in the inner cities tend to use crack. Thus the imposition of significantly harsher punishments for one form of the drug produces racial disparities in imprisonment rates. State and federal legislators emphasized lengthy prison sentences during the perceived "crack crisis" of the late twentieth century.

By contrast, government responses to the meth crisis of the early twenty-first century placed greater emphasis on prevention, such as limiting sales of over-the-counter medications used to manufacture meth, as well as treatment. For example, the state of Iowa's 2006 annual report entitled *Iowa's Drug Control Strategy* says, "More treatment and related resources need to be targeted to meth-addicted offenders . . . It is only by reducing the demand for meth and other drugs that we can hope to break the cycle of addiction" (Governor's Office on Drug Control Policy, 2006:8). Some observers suspect that the less-punitive orientation toward meth offenders, who are predominantly white, may reflect race-based attitudes that perceive crack cocaine offenders, many of whom have been African American, as more dangerous and less worthy of rehabilitation (A. Alexander, 2011).

Other evidence of racial bias in American society shows up in the stereotyping of offenders. For example, African American and Hispanic professionals have been falsely arrested when the police were looking for a person of color and these individuals happened to be "out of place." Judge Claude Coleman was handcuffed and dragged through crowds of shoppers in Short Hills, New Jersey, while protesting his innocence; Princeton University philosopher Cornel West was stopped on false cocaine charges while driving across Massachusetts; and law student Brian Roberts was pulled over by the police as he drove in an affluent St. Louis neighborhood on his way to interview a judge for a class project (Tonry, 1995).

If people of color are overrepresented in the justice system because of racial bias in society, the solution may seem a bit daunting. Nobody knows how to quickly rid a society of biased policies, practices, and attitudes.

check point >

17. What is meant by racial or ethnic disparities in criminal justice?
That racial and ethnic minorities are subjected to the criminal justice system at much higher rates than are the white majority.

18. What explanation put forward to account for such disparities is most clearly *not* supported by evidence?
Available evidence fails to support the claim that racial disparities exist because minorities commit more crime; instead, evidence of unequal treatment raises questions about the existence of racial bias.

stop & analyze
If race is influential throughout the criminal justice system, what are three steps that might be taken to attempt to reduce disparities and biased decision making?

a question of ethics

Think, Discuss, Write

In December 2011, boxing champion Floyd Mayweather Jr., was sentenced to 90 days in jail in Las Vegas after pleading guilty to domestic violence charges. The charges had been reduced from more-serious felony charges that could have produced a five-year prison sentence. By contrast, two weeks later in Huntsville, Alabama, Toriano Nicolas Porter was sentenced to 20 years in prison after being convicted of domestic violence charges. The significant disparity in sentences may reflect the influence of several factors, including the system of federalism that permits states to impose their own punishments for crimes that would be treated more lightly elsewhere. A particularly powerful factor is the prosecutor's use of discretion in deciding what charges to file and whether or not to engage in plea bargaining. Porter's long sentence resulted from the Alabama prosecutor labeling him as a "habitual offender" due to two prior felony convictions. However, Mayweather also had several prior convictions for assault, yet Nevada and Michigan prosecutors permitted him to plead to lesser charges in each case. Is this justice? Were prosecutors influenced in their decisions by Mayweather's wealth and fame? Did Mayweather benefit from hiring expensive, prominent attorneys to defend him?

Discussion/Writing Assignment
Do prosecutors have an ethical obligation to treat people the same if they are facing similar charges, no matter who they are? Imagine that you are a newly elected county prosecutor. How would you instruct your assistant prosecutors to handle cases? Could you avoid being influenced by the desire to gain quick convictions through pleas in order to preserve the limited resources of your office—scarce resources that would be stretched through an increase in time-consuming trials? Write a memo providing instructions for the assistant prosecutors. Be sure to address any ethical issues that influence your position. In a second brief memo, describe how the criminal justice system and the processing of cases in your county will be affected by your instructions.

Sources: ESPN.com, "Floyd Mayweather Released from Jail," September 10, 2010 (www.espn.go.com); Brian Lawson, "Huntsville Man Sentenced to 20 Years Following Domestic Violence Conviction," *Huntsville Times*, January 6, 2012 (http://blog.al.com); Lance Pugmire, "Mayweather Gets 90-Day Jail Sentence," *Los Angeles Times*, December 22, 2011 (www.latimes.com).

Understand the goals of the criminal justice system

→ Criminal laws define punishable acts that are wrongs in themselves (*mala in se*) or acts that legislators believe deserve punishment (*mala prohibita*).

→ The three goals of the criminal justice system are doing justice, controlling crime, and preventing crime.

→ Doing justice forms the basis for the rules, procedures, and institutions of the criminal justice system.

→ Controlling crime involves arresting, prosecuting, and punishing those who commit offenses.

→ Preventing crime requires the efforts of citizens as well as justice system officials.

Recognize the different responsibilities of federal and state criminal justice operations

→ Both the national and state systems of criminal justice enforce laws, try cases, and punish offenders.

→ Federal officials enforce laws defined by Congress.

→ Federal agencies have shifted greater attention to antiterrorist efforts since 9/11.

→ Most criminal law and criminal cases are under the authority of state criminal justice systems.

Analyze criminal justice from a systems perspective

→ Criminal justice is composed of many organizations that are interdependent and interact as they seek to achieve their goals.

→ The primary subsystems of criminal justice are police, courts, and corrections.

→ The key characteristics of the criminal justice system are discretion, resource dependence, sequential tasks, and filtering.

Identify the authority and relationships of the main criminal justice agencies, and understand the steps in the decision-making process for criminal cases

→ The processing of cases in the criminal justice system involves a series of decisions by police officers, prosecutors, judges, probation officers, wardens, and parole board members.

→ The criminal justice system consists of 13 steps that cover the stages of law enforcement, adjudication, and corrections.

Understand the criminal justice "wedding cake" concept as well as the due process and crime control models

→ The four-layered criminal justice wedding cake model shows that not all cases are treated equally.

→ The small top of the wedding cake represents the relatively small number of very serious cases that are processed through trials.

→ The lower, larger portions of the wedding cake represent the increasing frequency of plea bargaining for larger numbers of cases as one moves down toward less serious offenses.

→ The crime control model and the due process model are two ways of looking at the goals and procedures of the criminal justice system.

→ The due process model focuses on careful, reliable decisions and the protection of rights while the crime control model emphasizes efficient processing of cases in order to repress crime.

Recognize the possible causes of racial disparities in criminal justice

→ Analysts explain the disproportionate impact of the criminal justice system on minorities by examining the criminal behavior of different groups' members as well as how racial bias affects American society and the criminal justice system.

→ Research does not support any theories about race causing criminal behavior.

→ Evidence exists concerning differential treatment of members of various racial groups by criminal justice officials in some contexts.

Questions for Review

1. What are the goals of the criminal justice system?
2. What is a system? How is the administration of criminal justice a system?
3. Why is the criminal justice wedding cake more realistic than a linear model depicting the criminal justice system?
4. What are the major elements of Packer's crime control model and due process model?
5. What evidence exists concerning the impact of the criminal justice system on members of racial minority groups?

Key Terms and Cases

adjudication (p. 16)

arrest (p. 19)

crime control model (p. 23)

crimes (p. 5)

discretion (p. 12)

discrimination (p. 27)

disparity (p. 26)

dual court system (p. 16)

due process model (p. 23)

exchange (p. 11)

federalism (p. 7)

felonies (p. 22)

filtering process (p. 14)

indictment (p. 20)

information (p. 20)

mala in se (p. 5)

mala prohibita (p. 5)

misdemeanors (p. 23)

plea bargain (p. 11)

system (p. 11)

warrant (p. 19)

The State of Michigan versus Christopher Jones

In October 1998, police in Battle Creek, Michigan, investigated a string of six robberies that occurred in a ten-day period. People were assaulted during some of the robberies. One victim was beaten so badly with a power tool that he required extensive reconstructive surgery for his face and skull. The police received an anonymous tip on their Silent Observer hotline, which led them to put together a photo lineup—an array of photographs of local men who had criminal records. Based on the tip and photographs identified by the victims, the police began to search for two men who were well known to them, Christopher Jones and his cousin Fred Brown.

Arrest
Jones was a 31-year-old African American. A dozen years of struggle with cocaine addiction had cost him his marriage and several jobs. He had a criminal record stretching back several years, including attempted larceny and attempts at breaking and entering. Thus, he had a record of stealing to support his drug habit. He had spent time on probation and done a short stretch in a minimum-security prison and a boot camp. But he had never been caught with drugs or been accused of an act of violence.

Fearing that Jones would be injured or killed by the police if he tried to run or resist arrest, his parents called the police and told them he was holed up in the bedroom of their home. As officers surrounded the house, the family opened the door and showed the officers the way to the bedroom. Jones surrendered peacefully and was led to the waiting police car in handcuffs.

At the police station, a detective with whom Jones was acquainted read him his *Miranda* rights and then informed him that he was looking at the possibility of a life sentence in

prison unless he helped the police by providing information about Brown. Jones said he did not want to talk to the police, and he asked for an attorney. The police thus ceased questioning Jones, and he was taken to the jail.

Booking
At the jail, Jones was strip-searched, given a bright orange jumpsuit to wear, and photographed and fingerprinted. He was told that he would be arraigned the next morning. That night he slept on the floor of the overcrowded *holding cell*—a large cell where people are placed immediately upon arrest.

Arraignment
The next morning, Jones was taken to a room for video arraignment. A two-way camera system permitted Jones to see the district courtroom in the neighboring courthouse. At the same time, the judge and others could view him on a television screen. The judge informed Jones that he was being charged with breaking and entering, armed robbery, and assault with intent to commit murder. The final charge alone could draw a life sentence. Under Michigan law, these charges can be

filed directly by the prosecutor without being presented to a grand jury for indictment, as is required in federal courts and some other states. The judge set bail at $200,000.

At a second video arraignment several days later, Jones was informed that he faced seven additional counts of assault with intent to commit murder, armed robbery, unarmed robbery, and home invasion for four other robberies. Bond was set at $200,000 for each alleged robbery. Thus, he faced ten felony charges for the five robberies, and his total bail was $1 million.

Unable to make bail, Jones was held in the Calhoun County Jail to await his day in court. Eventually he would spend nine months in the jail before all of the charges against him were processed.

Defense Attorney
Under state court procedures, Jones was supposed to have a preliminary hearing within two weeks of his arraignment. At the preliminary hearing the district judge would determine whether enough evidence had been gathered to justify sending Jones's case up to the Calhoun County Circuit Court, which handled felony trials.

Jones received a letter informing him of the name of the private attorney appointed by the court to represent him, but he did not meet the attorney until he was taken to court for his preliminary hearing. Minutes before the hearing, the attorney, David Gilbert, introduced himself to Jones. Jones wanted to delay any preliminary hearing until a lineup could be held to test the victims' identifications of him as a robber. According to Jones, Gilbert said they must proceed with the preliminary hearing for the armed robbery case in which the victim was beaten with the power tool, because a witness had traveled from another state to testify. The testimony led the district judge to conclude that sufficient evidence existed to move that case to the circuit court on an armed robbery charge.

Lineup

Jones waited for weeks for the lineup to be scheduled. When he was taken to his rescheduled preliminary hearing, his attorney complained to the judge that the lineup had never been conducted. The judge ordered that the lineup be held as soon as possible.

At the lineup Jones and five other men stood in front of a one-way mirror. One by one, the victims of each of the six robberies looked at the men and attempted to determine if any were their assailant. At the end of each identification, one of the men was asked to step forward. Because he was asked to step forward only twice, Jones guessed that he was picked out by two of the victims.

Jones's defense attorney was unable to attend the lineup. Another attorney arrived and informed Jones that he would take Gilbert's place. Although Jones protested that the other men in the lineup were much shorter and older, he was disappointed that the substitute attorney was not more active in objecting that the other men looked too different from Jones to adequately test the victims' ability to make an accurate identification.

Preliminary Hearing

At the next preliminary hearing, the victims of the four additional robberies testified. Because they focused mainly on Brown as the perpetrator of the assaults and robberies, the defense attorney argued that many of the charges against Jones should be dropped. However, the judge determined that the victims' testimony provided enough evidence to send most of the charges against Jones to the circuit court.

Plea Bargaining

Jones waited for weeks in jail without hearing much from his attorney. Although he did not know it, the prosecutor was formulating a plea agreement and communicating to the defense attorney the terms under which some charges would be dropped in exchange for a guilty plea from Jones. A few minutes before a hearing on the proposed plea agreement, Gilbert told Jones that the prosecutor had offered

to drop all of the other charges if Jones would plead guilty to one count of unarmed robbery for the incident in which the victim was seriously injured by the power tool wielded by Brown, and one count of home invasion for another robbery. Jones did not want to accept the deal, because he claimed he was not even present at the robbery for which he was being asked to plead guilty to home invasion. According to Jones, the attorney insisted that this was an excellent deal compared with all of the other charges that the prosecutor could pursue. Jones still resisted.

In the courtroom, Judge James Kingsley read aloud the offer, but Jones refused to enter a guilty plea. Like the defense attorney, the judge told Jones that this was a favorable offer compared with the other more serious charges that the prosecutor could still pursue. Jones again declined.

As he sat in the holding area outside of the courtroom, Jones worried that he was making a mistake by turning down the plea offer. He wondered if he could end up with a life sentence if one of the victims identified him by mistake as having done a crime that was committed by Brown. When his attorney came to see him, he told Gilbert that he had changed his mind. They went right back into the courtroom and told the judge that he was ready to enter a guilty plea. As they prepared to plead guilty, the prosecutor said that as part of the agreement Jones would be expected to provide information about the other robberies and to testify against Brown. The defense attorney protested that this was not part of the plea agreement. Jones told the judge that he could not provide information about the home invasion to which he was about to plead guilty because he was not present at that robbery and had no knowledge of what occurred. Judge Kingsley declared that he would not accept a guilty plea when the defendant claimed to have no knowledge of the crime.

After the hearing, discussions about a plea agreement were renewed. Jones agreed to take a polygraph test so that the prosecutor could find out which robberies he knew about. Jones hoped to show prosecutors that his

involvement with Brown was limited, but no test was ever administered.

Scheduled Trial and Plea Agreement

Jones waited in jail for several more weeks. When Gilbert came to visit him, Jones was informed that the armed robbery trial was scheduled for the following day. In addition, the prosecutor's plea offer had changed. Brown had pleaded guilty to armed robbery and assault with intent less than murder and was facing a sentence of 25 to 50 years in prison. Because of Brown's guilty plea, the prosecutor no longer needed Jones as a witness against Brown. Thus, the prosecutor no longer offered robbery and home invasion pleas. He now wanted Jones to plead to the same charges as Brown in exchange for dropping the other pending charges. According to Jones, Gilbert claimed that the prosecutor would be very angry if he did not take the plea, and the attorney encouraged Jones to accept the plea by arguing that the prosecutor would otherwise pursue all of the other charges, which could bring a life sentence if Jones refused to plead guilty.

The next day, Jones was given his personal clothes to wear instead of the orange jail jumpsuit, because he was going to court for trial rather than a hearing. Prior to entering court the next day, Jones says Gilbert again encouraged him to accept the plea agreement in order to avoid a possible life sentence after trial. According to Jones, his attorney said that the guilty plea could be withdrawn if the probation office's sentencing recommendation was too high. Because he did not want to risk a life sentence, and believed he could later withdraw the plea, Jones decided to accept the offer.

With his attorney's advice, he entered a plea of "no contest" to the two charges. A "no contest" plea is treated the same way as a guilty plea for punishment purposes.

Before taking the plea, Judge Kingsley informed Jones that by entering the plea he would be waiving his right to a trial, including his right to question witnesses and to have the prosecutor prove his guilt beyond a reasonable doubt. Judge Kingsley then

continued

The State of Michigan versus Christopher Jones

read the charges of armed robbery and assault with intent to do great bodily harm and asked, "What do you plead?" Jones replied, "No contest." Then the judge asked a series of questions.

Judge Kingsley: "Mr. Jones, has anyone promised you anything other than the plea bargain to get you to enter this plea?"

Jones: "No."

Judge Kingsley: "Has anyone threatened you or forced you or compelled you to enter the plea?"

Jones: "No."

Judge Kingsley: "Are you entering this plea of your own free will?"

Jones: "Yes."

The judge reminded Jones that there had been no final agreement on what the ultimate sentence would be and gave Jones one last opportunity to change his mind about pleading "no contest." Jones repeated his desire to enter the plea, so the plea was accepted.

Immediately after the hearing Jones had second thoughts. According to Jones, "I was feeling uneasy about being pressured [by my attorney] to take the plea offer . . . [so I decided] to write to the judge and tell him about the pressures my attorney put upon me as well as [the attorney] telling me I had a right to withdraw my plea. So I wrote the judge that night." Jones knew he was guilty of stealing things in one robbery, but he had been unarmed.

When Gilbert learned that Jones had written the letter, he asked the judge to permit him to withdraw as Jones's attorney. Judge Kingsley initially refused. However, when Jones spoke in open court at his sentencing hearing about his criticisms of Gilbert, as well as his complaints about the prosecutor's handling of the lineup and the failure to administer the polygraph test, the judge decided to appoint a new defense attorney, Virginia Cairns,

to handle sentencing at a rescheduled hearing.

Presentence Investigation

Probation officers are responsible for conducting presentence investigations, in which they review offenders' records and interview the offenders about their education, work history, drug use, and family background before making recommendations to the judge about an appropriate punishment. The presentence report prepared by the probation office ultimately recommended 5 to 25 years for armed robbery and 4 to 7 years for assault.

Sentencing

Although arrested in October 1998, Jones was not sentenced until July 1999. At the hearing Judge Kingsley asked Jones if he would like to make a statement. Jones faced the judge as he spoke, glancing at his family and at the victim when he referred to them.

First and foremost, I would like to say what happened to the victim was a tragedy. I showed great remorse for that. He is in my prayers along with his family. Even though, your Honor, I'm not making any excuses for what I'm saying here today, the injuries the victim sustained were not at the hands of myself nor did I actually rob this victim. I was present, your Honor, as I told you once before, yes, I was. And it's a wrong. Again I'm not making any kind of excuse whatsoever. . . .

Your Honor, I would just like to say that drugs has clouded my memory, and my choices in the past. I really made some wrong decisions. Only times I've gotten into trouble were because of my drug use. . . . One of the worst decisions I really made was my involvement of being around the codefendant Fred Brown. That bothers me to this day because actually we didn't even get along. Because of my drug use again I chose to be around him.

Jones also talked about his positive record as a high school student and athlete, his work with the jail

minister, and his desire to talk to young people about his experiences to steer them away from drugs.

Attorney Cairns spoke next. She called the court's attention to several errors in the presentence report that recommended Jones serve 5–25 years for armed robbery and 4–7 years for assault. She emphasized letters of support from Jones's family, which she had encouraged them to write to the judge, describing his positive qualities and prospects for successful rehabilitation.

Next, the victim spoke about his injuries and how his $40,000 worth of medical bills had driven him to bankruptcy.

I went from having perfect vision to not being able to read out of my left eye. I got steel plates in my head. . . . They left me to die that morning. He took the keys to my car. . . . So today it's true, I don't think Mr. Jones should be sentenced same as Brown. That's who I want—I want to see him sentenced to the maximum. He's the one that crushed my skull with a drill. But Jones did hit me several times while Mr. Brown held me there to begin with. It's true that I did hit him with a hammer to get them off me. But he still was there. He still had the chance of not leaving me without keys to my car so I could get to a hospital. He still had the choice to stop at least and phone on the way and say there's someone that could possibly be dead, but he didn't. . . . You don't treat a human being like that. And if you do you serve time and pretty much to the maximum. I don't ask the Court for twenty-five years. That's a pretty long time to serve. And I do ask the Court to look at fifteen to twenty. I'd be happy. Thank you.

Gary Brand, the assistant prosecutor, rose and recommended a 20-year sentence and noted that Jones should be responsible for $35,000 in restitution to the victim and to the state for medical expenses and lost income.

Judge Kingsley then addressed Jones. He acknowledged that Jones's drug problem had led to his criminal activity. He also noted that Jones's family support was much stronger than that of most defendants. He chastised Jones for falling into drugs when life was tougher after enjoying a successful high school career. Judge Kingsley then proceeded to announce his sentencing decision.

You are not in my view as culpable as Mr. Brown. I agree with [the victim] that you were there. When I read your letter, Mr. Jones, I was a bit disturbed by your unwillingness to confront the reality of where you found yourself with Mr. Brown. You were not a passive observer to everything that went on in my view. You were not as active a participant as Mr. Brown. . . . What I'm going to do, Mr. Jones, is as follows: Taking everything into consideration as it relates to the armed robbery count, it is the sentence of the Court that you spend a term of not less than twelve years nor more than twenty-five years with the Michigan Department of Corrections. I will give you credit for the [261 days] you have already served.

The judge also ordered payment of $35,000 in restitution as a condition of parole. He concluded the hearing by informing Jones of his right to file an application for a leave to appeal.

Prison

After spending a few more weeks in jail awaiting transfer, Christopher Jones was sent to the state correctional classification center at Jackson for evaluation to determine to which of Michigan's 40 prisons he would be sent.

Prison security classifications range from level I for minimum to level VI for "supermaximum," high security. Jones was initially assigned to a level IV prison. Because Jones was a high school graduate who had previously attended a community college, he was one of the most highly educated prisoners in his institution. After working as the head clerk of the prison library in one prison, he was transferred to another prison, where he earned a certificate in substance abuse counseling. He taught classes on substance abuse and addiction for other prisoners before he was transferred to several different lower-security institutions where he took classes, worked when prison jobs were available, and waited until he was eligible for parole.

Parole

After being incarcerated for more than nine and a half years, Jones came up for consideration for parole. He was interviewed by a parole board member through a closed-circuit television connection. The parole member had a favorable view of the record of Jones's behavior and self-improvement activities in prison. He warned Jones about the consequences if he were to resume taking drugs or commit any crimes after being released. Because Jones had suffered two heart attacks in prison, perhaps as the result of damage to his arteries from drug use, smoking, and other unhealthy habits prior to being incarcerated, Jones assured the parole board member: "Don't worry. I know that if I ever touch drugs again, it will kill me. And I don't want to die." Several months later, Jones received word that his parole had been granted and he was released from prison after serving 10 years and 3 months of his 12-to-25-year sentence. He returned to his hometown facing the difficulties of finding a job in a depressed economy and attempting to reestablish relationships with his daughter and other family members.

A few months after his release, Jones was arrested and briefly placed in the county jail for violating his parole conditions by missing several appointments and drug tests with his parole officer. He was shaken by the thought of returning prison. He became very conscientious about fulfilling his parole conditions. He volunteered to speak to churches and youth groups about the dangers of drugs and even police officials began to invite him to speak to troubled youths. After working as a volunteer in a youth program, he was hired to work in a program for high school dropouts to help them earn their diploma and gain work skills.

Researching the Internet

The Jones case illustrates the important role of the defense attorney. Read the U.S. Supreme Court's decision about the attorney's responsibilities for presenting a strong defense. Go to the link for Supreme Court cases to find the case of *Wiggins v. Smith* (2003). To link to this website, visit the Criminal Justice CourseMate at cengagebrain.com, then access the web links for this chapter.

For Critical Analysis

Were any aspects of the processes and decisions in the Jones case unfair or improper? Did the outcome of the case achieve "justice"?

Sources: Calhoun County Circuit Court transcripts for plea hearing, May 20, 1999, and sentencing hearing, July 16, 1999; T. Christenson, "Two Charged in Violent Robberies," *Battle Creek Inquirer*, October 30, 1998, p. 1A; interview with Christopher Jones, St. Louis Correctional Facility, St. Louis, Michigan, October 19, 1999; letters to Christopher Smith from Christopher Jones, October and November 1999.

Crime and Crime Causation

Learning Objectives

⊙ Categorize crimes by their type

⊙ Recognize the different methods of measuring crime

⊙ Understand why some people are at higher risk of victimization than others

⊙ Recognize the negative consequences of victimization

⊙ Understand the theories put forward to explain criminal behavior

⊙ Analyze crime causation theories and women offenders

O n a sunny Saturday morning in January 2011, Tucson residents gathered outside a shopping center for a meet-and-greet with Representative Gabrielle Giffords. Congresswoman Giffords had recently been sworn in for her third term in the U.S. House of Representatives and she planned to talk with citizens about their concerns (K. Murphy and Riccardi, 2011). A young man approached Giffords and, without warning, fired a gun at her head at short range. Giffords collapsed, and the gunman continued to fire his weapon into the crowd (D. D. Nakamura, Hedgpeth, and Horwitz, 2011). Nineteen people were shot, with six of those mortally wounded. The victims ranged in age from 9 to 73. The shooter, Jared Loughner, a man with apparent mental problems, was tackled by a woman on the scene and then was restrained by three men in the crowd (Lacey, 2011). Giffords miraculously survived the shooting but spent months recuperating and regaining her ability to walk and speak.

As authorities studied the case, it became clear that Jared Loughner's behavior had been growing increasingly erratic in the months leading up to the shooting. In addition to posting materials on the Internet about such topics as mind control, Loughner had been suspended from Pima Community College after repeatedly disrupting classes and students studying in the library (Lacey, 2011). Did mental problems lead to his actions, was he motivated by political opposition to Giffords, or were there other reasons for his actions?

The event was highly publicized because of the number killed and wounded, and for the fact that the intended victim was a public figure. It was the type of crime that arouses the public's worst fears about being victims of random violence. The incident also raised significant questions about why anyone would commit such a terrible act. Yet as we consider the possible causes leading up to this crime, we also recognize that this shooting is not the typical crime. Obviously, thefts, minor assaults, and credit card fraud are much more common than murders are. Do the underlying motivations for all crimes have a common core? Or are there distinctly different causes of crime, depending on which crimes we examine? These and other questions serve to illuminate the issues of victimization and crime causation, the topics of this chapter.

The shooting of Giffords provides a context in which we can examine a number of important questions. For example, who are the crime victims in this case? Obviously, the innocent bystanders who were killed and wounded are victims. But what about their families? Are they also victims because they suffered psychological and emotional harm? What about the city of Tucson? Has its reputation as a safe place to live been destroyed? Will fewer people decide to move to Tucson, or to Arizona in general? What financial losses might the shopping center experience if it is known as the location of a terrible crime? What about members of the victims' hometown communities throughout Arizona? They lost relatives, friends, and neighbors; houses of worship lost parishioners—and society lost six citizens who might have made significant contributions to the well-being of their communities, the nation, or the world. Would it be proper to say that all people in society are also victims of the crime?

Loughner's actions cost the public thousands of dollars; law enforcement officers spent extra hours investigating the high-profile case. Additional time and money were spent reviewing and refining established safety procedures to ensure that law enforcement emergency-response planning and training could appropriately address such future situations. Moreover, members of the public may now feel less safe as a result of hearing about this shocking crime, which could have happened to anyone, anywhere. Does that make each of us—individually—a victim? We might feel as if we have lost a bit of our security and liberty if this event enhances our fears, nervousness, and discomfort when we wonder if any strangers around us—at the movies, at the ballpark, or in the mall—might have similar murderous plans.

These are important questions to consider, because how we answer them will define the scope of the subject of criminal victimization. In other words, when we talk about the victimizing consequences of crime, should we only talk about the individuals most directly harmed by a crime, or should we also consider people who suffer less-direct, but equally real, consequences? These questions actually have practical consequences under circumstances in which we speak of *victims' rights*, such as crime victims being entitled to compensation. We need to define what we mean by "victim" before we can implement any such policy.

An additional important question looms in this and every other criminal case: Why did the perpetrator do what he or she did? Criminal behavior is the main cause of criminal victimization. Scholars, policy makers, and the public have long pondered questions such as "What causes crime?" and "Why do criminal offenders cause harm to other human beings?" These questions have significant implications for the subject of criminal victimization. Theories about crime causation often influence government policies for controlling and punishing violations of criminal laws.

In order to understand the criminal justice system, we must understand the nature of crime and recognize the range of people affected by it. Chapter 1 introduced you to decision makers in the system, such as police and prosecutors, as well as to the processes for handling criminal cases. Here you will consider other key individuals: criminal offenders and their victims. You will also examine the nature and extent of crime—the key elements that tell us how many offenders and victims will likely cause or be affected by crime in a given year.

Types of Crime

Crimes can be classified in various ways, as you recall from the description in Chapter 1 of *mala in se* and *mala prohibita* crimes. They can also be classified as either felonies or misdemeanors, depending on whether the prescribed punishment is more than one year, or less than one year, in prison. A third scheme classifies crimes by the nature of the act. This approach has traditionally yielded six types of crime: visible crime, occupational crime, organized crime, victimless crime, political crime, and cyber crime. Each type has its own level of risk and reward, each arouses varying degrees of public disapproval, and each is committed by a certain kind of offender. New types of crime emerge as society changes. Cyber crimes committed through the use of computers and the Internet are becoming a major global problem.

Visible Crime

Visible crime, often called "street crime" or "ordinary crime," ranges from shoplifting to homicide. For offenders, such crimes are the least profitable and, because they are visible, the hardest to hide. These are the acts that the public regards as "criminal." The majority of law enforcement resources are employed to deal with them. We can divide visible crimes into three categories: violent crimes, property crimes, and public-order crimes.

visible crime An offense against persons or property, committed primarily by members of the lower class. Often referred to as "street crime" or "ordinary crime," this type of offense is the one most upsetting to the public.

Violent Crimes   Acts against people in which death or physical injury results are *violent crimes.* These include criminal homicide, assault, rape, and robbery. The criminal justice system treats them as the most serious offenses and punishes them accordingly. Although the public is most fearful of violence by strangers, many of these offenses are committed by people who know their victim.

Property Crimes   *Property crimes* are acts that threaten property held by individuals or by the state. Many types of crimes fall under this category, including theft, larceny, shoplifting, embezzlement, and burglary. Some property offenders are amateurs who occasionally commit these crimes because of situational factors such as financial need or peer pressure. In contrast, professional criminals make a significant portion of their livelihood from committing property offenses.

Public-Order Crimes   Acts that threaten the general well-being of society and challenge accepted moral principles are defined as *public-order crimes.* They include public drunkenness, aggressive panhandling, vandalism, and disorderly conduct. Although the police tend to treat these behaviors as minor offenses, some scholars argue that this type of disorderly behavior instills fear in citizens, leads to more-serious crimes, and hastens urban decay (Kelling and Coles, 1996). The definition and enforcement of such behaviors as crimes highlight the tensions between different interpretations of American values. Many people see such behavior as simply representing the liberty that adults enjoy in a free society to engage in offensive and self-destructive behavior that causes no concrete harm to other people. By contrast, other people see their own liberty limited by the need to be wary and fearful of actions by people who are drunk or out of control.

Those charged with visible crimes tend to be young men. Further, in many communities, members of minority groups tend to be overrepresented among those arrested and prosecuted for such offenses. Some argue that this is due to the class bias of a society that has singled out visible crimes for priority enforcement. They note that we do not focus as much police and prosecutorial attention on white-collar crimes, such as fraud and other acts committed by office workers and business owners, as we do on street crimes.

 In December 2011, former governor of Illinois, Rod Blagojevich, was sentenced to 16 years in prison for corruption. He was convicted of trying to sell the open Illinois senate seat, vacated upon former Senator Barack Obama's election to the presidency. In addition, he was found guilty of lying to federal investigators and of forcing people to contribute funds to his own campaign. Is such a long prison sentence appropriate for an individual who committed nonviolent financial crimes?

occupational crimes
Criminal offenses committed through opportunities created in a legal business or occupation.

organized crime A framework for the perpetuation of criminal acts—usually in fields such as gambling, drugs, and prostitution—providing illegal services that are in great demand.

money laundering Moving the proceeds of criminal activities through a maze of businesses, banks, and brokerage accounts so as to disguise their origin.

Occupational Crime

Occupational crimes are committed in the context of a legal business or profession. Often viewed as shrewd business practices rather than illegal acts, they are crimes that, if "done right," are never discovered. Such crimes are often committed by respectable, well-to-do people taking advantage of opportunities arising from business dealings. Such crimes impose huge costs on society. Although there are no precise figures on the cost of occupational crime to American society, some researchers estimate that losses due to occupational crime may be significantly higher than losses attributable to street crime. Some estimates indicate that for every $1 lost in street crime, about $60 is lost as a result of occupational crime (Friedrichs, 2010).

Organized Crime

Rather than referring to criminal acts per se, the term **organized crime** refers to the framework within which such acts are committed. A crime syndicate has an organizational structure, rules, a division of labor, and the capacity for ruthless violence and for corrupting law enforcement, labor and business leaders, and politicians (Jacobs and Panarella, 1998:160). Those active in organized crime provide goods and services to millions of people. They engage in any activity that provides a minimum of risk and a maximum of profit. Thus, organized crime involves a network of activities, usually cutting across state and national borders, which range from legitimate businesses to shady deals with labor unions to providing "goods"—such as drugs, sex, and pornography—that cannot be obtained legally. In recent years, organized crime has been involved in new services such as commercial arson, illegal disposal of toxic wastes, and **money laundering**. Some crime syndicates have also acquired significant funds through illegal recycling operations (K. Coleman, 2011). Few members of organized crime are arrested and prosecuted.

Although the public often associates organized crime with Italian Americans—indeed, the federal government indicted 73 members of the Genovese New York crime "family" in 2001 (Worth, 2001)—other ethnic groups have dominated at various times. Thirty-five years ago, one scholar noted the strangeness of America's "ladder of social mobility," in which each new immigrant group uses organized crime as one of the first rungs of the climb (Bell, 1967:150). However, debate about this notion continues, because not all immigrant groups have engaged in organized crime (Kenney and Finckenauer, 1995:38), and some nonimmigrants have also become involved in these crime syndicates (Mallory, 2012).

Over the last few decades, law enforcement efforts have greatly weakened the Italian American Mafia. An aging leadership, lack of interest by younger family members, and pressures from new immigrant groups have also contributed to the fall of the Mafia. Today African Americans, Hispanics, Russians, and Asians have formed organized-crime groups. Drug dealing has brought Colombian and Mexican crime groups to U.S. shores, and groups led by Vietnamese, Chinese, and Japanese have formed in California. Because these new groups do not fit the Mafia pattern, law enforcement agencies have had to find new ways to deal with them (Kleinknecht, 1996).

Just as multinational corporations have emerged during the past 20 years, organized crime has also developed global networks. Increasingly transnational criminal groups "live and operate in a borderless world" (Zagaris, 1998:1402). In the aftermath of the events of September 11, American law enforcement and intelligence officials increased their efforts to monitor and thwart international organizations that seek to attack the United States and its citizens. Many of these organizations use criminal activities, such as drug smuggling and stolen credit card numbers, to fund their efforts. Others steal under the pretext of "terrorism," while not embracing the ideals of terrorist groups; rather, they are mostly interested in making money (Rosenthal, 2008).

Douglas Engle/The New York Times/Redux

⬆ Sex workers such as this prostitute provide a service that is in demand but illegal. Are these willing and private exchanges truly "victimless"? Should this be a criminal activity?

Victimless Crimes

Victimless crimes involve a willing and private exchange of goods or services that are in strong demand but illegal—in other words, offenses against morality. Examples include prostitution, gambling, and drug sales and use. These crimes are called "victimless" because those involved do not feel that they are being harmed. Prosecution for these offenses is justified on the ground that society as a whole is harmed because the moral fabric of the community is threatened. However, using the law to enforce moral standards is costly. The system is swamped by these cases, which often require the use of police informers and thus open the door for payoffs and other kinds of corruption.

The "war on drugs" is the most obvious example of policies against one type of victimless crime. Possession and sale of drugs—marijuana, heroin, cocaine, opium, amphetamines—have been illegal in the United States for over a hundred years. Especially during the past 40 years, all levels of government have applied extensive resources to enforce these laws and punish offenders.

The crime-fighting duties of police patrol officers typically focus on visible crimes and victimless crimes. As we shall see in later chapters, police officers also fulfill other functions, such as order maintenance and public service.

victimless crimes Offenses involving a willing and private exchange of illegal goods or services that are in strong demand. Participants do not feel they are being harmed, but these crimes are prosecuted on the ground that society as a whole is being injured.

Political Crime

Political crime refers to criminal acts either by the government or against the government that are carried out for ideological purposes (F. E. Hagan, 1997:2). Political criminals believe they are following a morality that is above the law. Examples include James Kopp—arrested for murdering Dr. Barnett Slepian near Buffalo, New York, and for the murder of other doctors who performed abortions; and Eric Rudolph, who was convicted for the bombing of abortion clinics in Atlanta and Birmingham, and for the pipe-bomb explosion at the Atlanta Olympics. Similarly, shocking acts of violence that are labeled as terrorism, such as the 1995 bombing of the federal building in Oklahoma City by Timothy McVeigh and the 2001 attacks on the World Trade Center and Pentagon, often spring from political motivations.

In some authoritarian states, merely criticizing the government is a crime that can lead to prosecution and imprisonment. In Western democracies today, there are few political crimes other than treason, which is rare. For example, in 2009 a retired employee of the U.S. State Department and his wife were charged with being spies for Cuba. They reportedly stole government documents because of their ideological admiration for the Cuban government and hostile feelings toward the U.S. government—not because they were seeking financial payments from Cuba (G. Thompson, 2009). Many illegal acts, such as the World Trade Center and Oklahoma

political crime An act, usually done for ideological purposes, that constitutes a threat against the state (such as treason, sedition, or espionage); also describes a criminal act by the state.

City bombings, can be traced to political motives, but they are prosecuted as visible crimes under laws against bombing, arson, and murder rather than as political crimes per se.

Cyber Crime

Cyber crimes involve the use of computers and the Internet to commit acts against people, property, public order, or morality. Thus, cyber criminals have learned "new ways to do old tricks." Some use computers to steal information, resources, or funds. In 2010, the federal government's Internet Crime Complaint Center (IC3) received nearly 303,809 complaints about cyber crime, with most offenses related to nondelivery of purchased items (21.1 percent), identity theft (16.6 percent), and auction fraud (10.1 percent) (Internet Crime Complaint Center, 2011). Other criminals use the Internet to disseminate child pornography, to advertise sexual services, or to stalk the unsuspecting. The more sophisticated "hackers" create and distribute viruses designed to destroy computer programs or to gain control of computers from unsuspecting individuals. For example, a man in Minnesota hacked into his neighbors' Wi-Fi network to frame them for cyber crime—sending threatening emails to politicians and downloading child pornography (Kravets, 2011). You will read more about cyber crime in the discussion of criminal justice and technology in Chapter 14.

Which of these main types of crime is of greatest concern to you? If you are like most people, it is visible crime. Thus, as a nation, we devote most of our criminal justice resources to dealing with such crimes. To develop policies to address these crimes, however, we need to know more about the amount of crime and all the types of crimes that occur in the United States. One of the most disturbing crimes, which has gained much attention lately, is hate crime; see the Close Up box for more.

cyber crimes Offenses that involve the use of one or more computers.

Cyber crime is a growing problem that costs American businesses and individuals millions of dollars each year. Law enforcement officials work diligently to keep up with the criminals' computer expertise, technology, and methods of deception. How can American police effectively combat the evolving and spreading threat of cyber crime, especially when so many cyber criminals are located in other countries?

AP Images/Daniel Hulshizer

check point

1. **What are the six main types of crime?**
   Visible crime, occupational crime, organized crime, victimless crimes, political crime, cyber crime.

2. **What is the function of organized crime?**
   Organized crime usually provides goods and services that are in high demand but are illegal.

3. **What is meant by the term "victimless crimes"?**
   These are crimes against morality in which the people involved do not believe that anyone has been victimized.

stop & analyze

In 2011, several states legalized the use of medical marijuana; however, marijuana is classified as a "Schedule I" narcotic. According to the U.S. Drug Enforcement Administration's (DEA) definition this means, "Substances in this schedule have a high potential for abuse, have no currently accepted medical use in treatment in the United States, and there is a lack of accepted safety for use of the drug or other substance under medical supervision." Given this classification, does it make sense for states to be allowed to make marijuana use legal for medicinal purposes? Alternatively, should marijuana be removed from the list of Schedule I drugs? Provide a brief argument for the option you think that policy makers should adopt as this issue develops.

Hate Crimes: A New Category of Personal Violence

A New York City mosque is firebombed; Amish men and women are attacked in forcible hair-cutting incidents; a man beats two brothers, killing one, assuming they are a gay couple; a Chinese American soldier commits suicide after constant bullying by fellow soldiers due to his racial and cultural background. These are just a few of the more than 7,600 hate crimes reported to the police each year. Threats, assaults, and acts of vandalism against Arab Americans and individuals of Muslim American ancestry increased in the months following the events of September 11, 2001, but since that time has been decreasing (Disha, Cavendish, and King, 2011). Since 2006, however, hate crimes against victims based on sexual orientation have accounted for a higher percentage of total hate crimes reported—from 15.5 percent in 2006 to 19.3 percent in 2010 (FBI, 2007, 2011b).

Hate crimes focused on race, religion, or ethnicity can be found in the penal codes of 45 states and the District of Columbia. Some states also include crimes based on gender discrimination. In 2009, President Obama signed the Matthew Shepard and James Byrd Jr. Hate Crimes Prevention Act, which expanded federal law to cover hate crimes based on gender, sexual orientation, gender identity, or disability. Although the Ku Klux Klan, the World Church of the Creator, and Nazi-style "skinhead" groups represent the most visible perpetrators, most hate crimes are committed by individuals acting alone.

For example, analysts believe that an individual acting on his own sent threatening letters to African American actor Taye Diggs and his wife, white Broadway actress Idina Menzel, in 2004. In 2008, an Ohio man was arrested by the FBI for sending threatening letters to Supreme Court Justice Clarence Thomas and other African American men who are married to white women.

Hate crime laws have been challenged on the ground that they violate the right of free speech. Some argue that racial and religious slurs must be allowed on this basis. In response, supporters of hate crime laws say that limits must be placed on freedom of speech and that some words are so hateful that they fall outside the free-speech protection of the First Amendment.

In *Wisconsin v. Mitchell* (1993), the Supreme Court upheld a law providing for a severer sentence in cases in which the offender "intentionally selects the person against whom the crime [is committed] because of the race, religion, color, disability, sexual orientation, national origin or ancestry of that person." In a later case on a related issue, the Court decided that states can make it a crime to burn a cross with an intent to intimidate people (*Virginia v. Black,* 2003).

In an increasingly diverse society, hate crimes arguably hurt not only their victims but the social fabric itself. Democracy depends on people sharing common ideals and working together. Under this view, when groups are pitted against one another, the entire community suffers.

Researching the Internet
To see the American Psychological Association's analysis of hate crimes, visit the Criminal Justice CourseMate at cengagebrain.com, then access the web links for this chapter.

For Critical Analysis
Is criminal law an appropriate way to attack the problem of expressions of racial hatred? How can the criminal justice system help to define the line between free speech and hate speech?

Sources: Drawn from Anti-Defamation League, 2011, "Anti-Defamation League State Hate Crime Statutory Provisions" (http://www.adl.org/99hatecrime/state _hate_crime_laws.pdf); Ilir Disha, James C. Cavendish, and Ryan D. King, "Historical Events and Spaces of Hate: Hate Crimes against Arabs and Muslims in America, *Social Problems* 58(1): 21–46; Federal Bureau of Investigation, *Hate Crime Statistics, 2010* (Washington, DC: U.S. Department of Justice, 2011); Fox News, "Obama Signs Defense Policy Bill That Includes 'Hate Crime' Legislation," October 28, 2009 (http://www.foxnews.com); E. Harris, "Four Attacks in Queens with Homemade Firebombs," *New York Times,* January 2, 2012, p. A19; N. Jabail-Nash, "Hate Crime Murder: Attacker Thought Beating Victim Was Gay," CBS News, June 30, 2010; M. R. Kropko, "Ohio Writer of Racial Hate Letters Pleads Guilty," *USA Today,* May 15, 2008 (http://www.usatoday.com); E. Londoño and C. Davenport, "8 U.S. Soldiers Charged in Death of Comrade in Afghanistan," *Washington Post,* December 21, 2011 (http://www.washingtonpost.com); K. Palmer, "FBI Arrests Seven over Amish Beard Cutting Attacks," Reuters, November 23, 2011 (http://www.reuters .com); R. Parascandola and D. S. Morris, "Hate Crimes Investigation: Letters Threaten Actors," *New York Newsday,* December 5, 2004, p. A8.

How Much Crime Is There?

Many Americans believe that the crime rate is rising, even though it has generally declined since the 1980s (see "What Americans Think"). For example, the rate of violent crime decreased from 758.2 violent crimes per 100,000 people in 1991 to 403.6 violent crimes per 100,000 by 2010, including a 15.8 percent drop from 2006 to 2010 (FBI, 2011a: Table 1). According to the Bureau of Justice Statistics, "Rates of violent and property crime [measured by our survey] in 2009 were at the lowest overall levels recorded since 1973, the first year for which victimization estimates from the survey were produced" (Rand, 2010:1).

Question: "Is there more crime in the U.S. than there was a year ago, or less?"

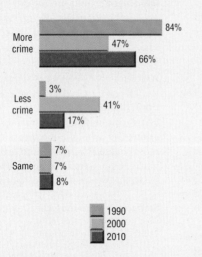

More crime — 84% (1990), 47% (2000), 66% (2010)

Less crime — 3% (1990), 41% (2000), 17% (2010)

Same — 7% (1990), 7% (2000), 8% (2010)

■ 1990
■ 2000
■ 2010

Critical Thinking: How might citizens' behavior—as well as the creation of law and policy—be affected when people have inaccurate perceptions about crime-rate trends?

Source: Gallup Poll, national survey of adults, reported December 21, 2010, as adapted by Bureau of Justice Statistics, *Sourcebook of Criminal Justice Statistics, 2010* (Washington, DC: U.S. Government Printing Office, 2010), Table 2.33.2010.

In December 2011 the FBI released preliminary crime statistics for the first half of 2011. The initial analysis showed a 6.4 percent decrease in violent crime. From January 2011 to June 2011, all types of violent crime decreased, with murder and aggravated assault down by about 6 percent (FBI, 2011c: Table 1). The largest decrease in violent crime occurred in the Midwest (9.7 percent), while the Northeast demonstrated the greatest decrease in homicide rates (12.1 percent) (FBI, 2011c: Table 2). Some scholars and law enforcement professionals were concerned when crime rates increased modestly in 2005 and 2006; however, the increase was small and crime rates still remain low compared with the rates from two decades ago.

Much of the discussion in this section concerns national crime data and trends that affect the United States as a whole. Individual cities and their police departments, however, need to be keenly aware of patterns of crime within their own neighborhoods. By monitoring crime rates and trends, they can decide how to deploy their officers and what strategies to employ. Many cities employ their own crime analysts to help identify and track crime problems. As you read "Careers in Criminal Justice," consider whether you would like to develop the knowledge and skills necessary to become a crime analyst.

One of the frustrations in studying criminal justice is the lack of accurate means of knowing the amount of crime. Surveys reveal that much more crime occurs than is reported to the police. This is referred to as the **dark figure of crime**.

dark figure of crime A metaphor that emphasizes the dangerous dimension of crimes that are never reported to the police.

Most homicides and auto thefts are reported to the police. In the case of a homicide, a body must be accounted for, and insurance companies require a police report before they will pay for a stolen car. But about 50 percent of rape victims do not report the attack. Figure 2.1 shows the percentage of victimizations reported to the police.

Until 1972, the only crimes counted by government were those that were known to the police and that made their way into the Federal Bureau of Investigation's Uniform Crime Reports (UCR). Since then, the Department of Justice has sponsored the National Crime Victimization Surveys (NCVS), which survey the public to find out how much victimization has occurred. One might hope that the data from these two sources would give us a clear picture of the amount of crime, crime trends, and the characteristics of offenders. However, the picture is blurred, perhaps even distorted, because of differences in the way crime is measured by the UCR and the NCVS.

The Uniform Crime Reports

Uniform Crime Reports (UCR) An annually published statistical summary of crimes reported to the police, based on voluntary reports to the FBI by local, state, and federal law enforcement agencies.

Issued each year by the FBI, the **Uniform Crime Reports (UCR)** are a statistical summary of crimes reported to the police. At the urging of the International Association of Chiefs of Police, Congress authorized this system in 1930 for compiling crime data (Rosen, 1995). The UCR data come from a voluntary national network of local, state, and federal law enforcement agencies, policing 94.6 percent of the U.S. population (FBI, 2012b).

With the sharp drop in crime in recent years, new pressures have been placed on police executives to show that their cities are following the national trend. Some officials have even falsified their crime statistics as promotions, pay raises, and departmental budgets have become increasingly dependent on positive data. For

Crime Analyst

Mark Bridge, Crime Analyst
City of Frederick, Maryland

Photo provided by Mark Bridge. © Cengage Learning

The primary responsibilities of the crime analyst's job include the following: conducting preliminary and advanced statistical analysis; compiling crime, arrest, and calls-for-service data; identifying trends and patterns in the data and generating maps, graphs, charts, and tables; briefing members of the command staff on crime patterns and intelligence matters; writing crime and intelligence analysis bulletins related to ongoing trends; making substantial contributions to the development and implementation of new analytical methods; and developing ways to collaborate with federal, state, and local agencies. Data used in crime analysis are derived from many resources, including record management systems (reports, incidents, arrests, and so forth), calls for service, field interviews, and probation and parole data.

A crime analyst must keep the police chief and shift commanders informed about trends in crime rates in various locations within a community. This allows those investing in law enforcement to see what they are getting for their dollar. It also allows for the budgeting and planning of future resources, such as the number of officers needed, which can be based on population growth, calls for service, crime rates, and other factors. Tactical analysis enables patrol and special details to focus on areas where their efforts are most needed. By analyzing data, crime analysts provide the peak days, times, and locations for crime problems within a community. Given a series of incidents that may involve the same suspect or suspects, the analyst can use forecasting techniques based on data from previous crimes to project the most likely dates, times, and places of the next crime.

Mark Bridge earned an undergraduate degree and a master's degree in criminal justice. He studied statistics, research methods, theories of crime, policing, and the operations of the criminal justice system. Prior to becoming a crime analyst, he worked in state government analyzing operations of the court system.

The biggest challenge of being a crime analyst is turning raw data into timely and useful information. There are a lot of sources to obtain information from, and you, as the analyst, must decide what to use and how to use it.

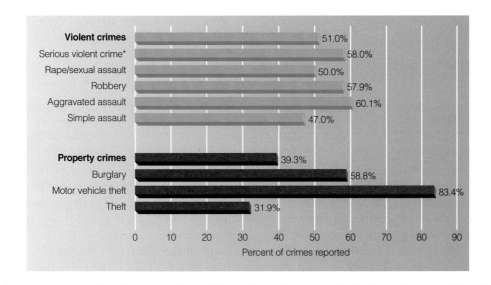

Figure 2.1
Violent and Property Victimizations Reported to the Police, 2010 Why are some crimes less likely to be reported to the police than others? What can be done to increase the likelihood that victims will report crimes to the police?

*Includes rape or sexual assault, robbery, and aggravated assault.

Source: Jennifer L. Truman, *Criminal Victimization, 2010* (Washington, DC: U.S. Department of Justice, 2011, Table 7).

example, an audit of police incident reports in Memphis in 2012 raised questions about whether the city's claims about reducing serious crimes were assisted by underreporting crimes in official crime reports (Maki, 2012). In 2005, leaders of police unions in New York City alleged that officers were pressured to report felonies as misdemeanors in order to help the city show favorable results (Moses, 2005).

TABLE 2.1 Uniform Crime Report Offenses

The UCR present data on 8 index offenses and 21 other crimes for which there is less information. A limitation of the UCR is that they tabulate only crimes that are reported to the police.

Part I (Index Offenses)	Part II (Other Offenses)
1. Criminal homicide	9. Other assaults
2. Forcible rape	10. Forgery and counterfeiting
3. Robbery	11. Fraud
4. Aggravated assault	12. Embezzlement
5. Burglary	13. Stolen property: Buying, receiving, possessing
6. Larceny/theft	14. Vandalism
7. Auto theft	15. Weapons (carrying, possessing, etc.)
8. Arson	16. Prostitution and commercialized vice
	17. Sex offenses
	18. Drug abuse violations
	19. Gambling
	20. Offenses against the family and children
	21. Driving under the influence
	22. Liquor laws
	23. Drunkenness
	24. Disorderly conduct
	25. Vagrancy
	26. All other offenses
	27. Suspicion
	28. Curfew and loitering laws (juvenile)
	29. Runaways (juvenile)

Source: Federal Bureau of Investigation, 2004, *Uniform Crime Reporting Handbook* (Washington, DC: U.S. Government Printing Office).

The Detroit Police Department was accused of misclassifying and undercounting homicides. Newspaper reporters conducted their own count and alleged that the police undercount helped the city avoid acknowledging that it had the nation's worst homicide rate (LeDuff and Esparza, 2009). Because the FBI relies on reports from local police departments, the UCR are inaccurate when agencies underreport crime.

The UCR use standard definitions to ensure uniform data on the 29 types of crimes listed in Table 2.1. For 8 major crimes—Part I (Index Offenses)—the data show factors such as age, race, and number of reported crimes solved. For the other 21 crimes—Part II (Other Offenses)—the data are less complete.

The UCR provide a useful but incomplete picture of crime levels. Because they cover only reported crimes, these reports do not include data on crimes for which people failed to call the police. Also, the UCR do not measure occupational crimes and other offenses that are not included in the 29 types covered. And because reporting is voluntary, police departments may not take the time to make complete and careful reports.

In response to criticisms of the UCR, the FBI has made some changes in the program that are now being implemented nationwide. Some offenses have been redefined, and police agencies are being asked to report more details about crime events. Using the **National Incident-Based Reporting System (NIBRS)**, police agencies are to report all crimes committed during an incident, not just the most serious one, as well as data on offenders, victims, and the places where they interact. While the UCR now count incidents and arrests for the 8 index offenses and count arrests for other crimes, the NIBRS provides detailed incident data on 46 offenses in 22 crime categories. The NIBRS distinguishes between attempted and completed crimes as well.

How is the NIBRS different from the UCR? In addition to including more types of crime than the UCR, NIBRS data are *disaggregated*—that is, rather than police departments reporting counts of crime to the FBI (as in the UCR), many jurisdictions now report information on individual crimes. Thanks to advances in technology and data transfer, police departments can now transfer data more easily than was possible when the UCR began collecting data from police departments in 1929. However, the reporting process is more difficult for NIBRS, and all agencies must adopt the same format for reporting data. These difficulties mean that not all states currently participate in the NIBRS system. As of December 2008, only nine states reported NIBRS data for every one of their jurisdictions (Delaware, Idaho, Michigan, Rhode Island, South Carolina, Tennessee, Vermont, Virginia, and West Virginia). Another four provide data for at least 90 percent of crimes committed in their states (Iowa, Montana, North Dakota, South Dakota). The remaining states report at least some crime through NIBRS or are in training to do so in the near future (JRSA, 2008).

National Incident-Based Reporting System (NIBRS) A reporting system in which the police describe each offense in a crime incident, together with data describing the offender, victim, and property.

The National Crime Victimization Surveys

As mentioned earlier, police agencies are aware that many crimes are not reported to them. In order to gain a better idea of the "dark figure of crime," the Census Bureau developed the **National Crime Victimization Surveys (NCVS)**. The NCVS is considered a "self-reported" measure of criminal behavior, because it uses survey research to ask people whether they've been victims of crime. Data have been gathered since 1972 on unreported as well as reported crimes. Interviews are conducted twice each year with a national probability sample of approximately 74,000 people in 41,000 households. The same people are interviewed twice a year for three years and asked if they have been victimized in the last six months (BJS, 2008).

National Crime Victimization Surveys (NCVS) Interviews of samples of the U.S. population conducted by the Bureau of Justice Statistics to determine the number and types of criminal victimizations and thus the extent of unreported as well as reported crime.

Each person is asked a set of "screening" questions (for example, "Did anyone beat you up, attack you, or hit you with something such as a rock or a bottle?") to determine whether he or she has been victimized. The person is then asked questions designed to elicit specific facts about the event, the offender, and any financial losses or physical injuries caused by the crime.

Besides the household interviews, surveys are carried out in the nation's 26 largest cities; separate studies are done to find out about the victimization of businesses. These data allow us to estimate how many crimes have occurred, learn more about the offenders, and note demographic patterns. The results show that for the crimes measured (rape, robbery, assault, burglary, theft) there were 18.7 million victimizations in 2010, which was down from 20.1 million in 2009 and 24.2 million in 2001 (Truman, 2011). This number is much higher than the number of crimes actually reported to the police.

Although the NCVS provide a more complete picture of the nature and extent of crime than do the UCR, they too have flaws (J. P. Lynch and Addington, 2007). Because government employees administer the surveys, the people interviewed are unlikely to report crimes in which they or members of their family took part. They also may not want to admit that a family member engages in crime, or they may be too embarrassed to admit that they have allowed themselves to be victimized more than once. In addition, the survey covers a limited range of crimes, and the relatively small sample of interviewees may lead to erroneous conclusions about crime trends for an entire country of over 300 million people (Mosher, Miethe, and Phillips, 2002).

TABLE 2.2 The UCR and the NCVS

Compare the data sources. Remember that the UCR tabulate only crimes reported to the police, whereas the NCVS are based on interviews with victims.

	Uniform Crime Reports	National Crime Victimization Survey
Offenses Measured	Homicide Rape Robbery (personal and commercial) Assault (aggravated) Burglary (commercial and household) Larceny (commercial and household) Motor vehicle theft Arson	Rape Robbery (personal) Assault (aggravated and simple) Household burglary Larceny (personal and household) Motor vehicle theft
Scope	Crimes reported to the police in most jurisdictions; considerable flexibility in developing small-area data	Crimes both reported and not reported to police; all data are for the nation as a whole; some data are available for a few large geographic areas
Collection Method	Police department reports to Federal Bureau of Investigation	Survey interviews: periodically measures the total number of crimes committed by asking a national sample of 43,000 households representing 76,000 people over the age of 12 about their experiences as victims of crime during a specific period
Kinds of Information	In addition to offense counts, provides information on crime clearances, persons arrested, persons charged, law enforcement officers killed and assaulted, and characteristics of homicide victims	Provides details about victims (such as age, race, sex, education, income, and whether the victim and offender were related) and about crimes (such as time and place of occurrence, whether or not reported to police, use of weapons, occurrence of injury, and economic consequences)
Sponsor	Department of Justice's Federal Bureau of Investigation	Department of Justice's Bureau of Justice Statistics

© Cengage Learning

The NCVS data are also imperfect because they depend on the victim's *perception* of an event. The theft of a child's lunch money by a bully may be reported as a crime by one person but not mentioned by another. People may say that their property was stolen when in fact they lost it. Moreover, people's memories of dates may fade, and they may misreport the year in which a crime occurred even though they remember the event itself clearly. In 1993 the Bureau of Justice Statistics made some changes in the NCVS to improve their accuracy and detail.

The next time you hear or read about crime rates, take into account the source of the data and its possible limitations. Table 2.2 compares the Uniform Crime Reports and the National Crime Victimization Surveys.

Trends in Crime

Experts agree that, contrary to public opinion and the claims of politicians, crime rates have not been steadily rising. The NCVS show that the victimization rate has been dropping steadily over the past decade. The greatest declines in victimizations between 2001 and 2010 were in aggravated assaults (decreased 40.7 percent) and motor vehicle theft (decreased 39.8 percent). Overall, victimizations decreased in every category during this time period, with a total 22.7 percent decrease in total crimes reported (Truman, 2011). The UCR data show similar results, with steady decreases in both violent and property crime reported to the police since 2001 (FBI, 2011a: Table 1).

Figure 2.2 displays four measures of violent crime, adjusted for changes made in the NCVS in 1992. The top two measures are based on the victimization survey; crimes recorded by the police and arrests are from the UCR and are presented

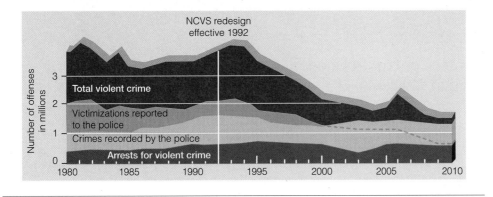

Figure 2.2

Four Measures of Serious Violent Crime Questions about homicides are not included in NCVS, so the data here include the assumption that the 12,996 homicides in 2010 were reported to the police.

Sources: Jennifer L. Truman, *Criminal Victimization, 2010* (Washington, DC: U.S. Department of Justice, 2011); FBI, *Crime in the United States, 2010* [Uniform Crime Reports] (http://www.fbi.gov).

© Cengage Learning

below these. Remember that the differences in the trends indicated by the NCVS and the UCR are explained in part by the different data sources and different populations on which their tabulations are based.

What explains the drop in both violent and property crime well below the 1973 levels? Among the reasons given by analysts are the aging of the baby boom population, the increased use of security systems, aggressive police efforts to keep handguns off the streets, and the dramatic decline in the use of crack cocaine. Other factors may include the booming economy of the 1990s and the quadrupling of the number of people incarcerated since 1970. Let us look more closely at how age distribution in the United States can be used to assess future crime levels.

Age Changes in the age makeup of the population are a key factor in the analysis of crime trends. It has long been known that men aged 16 to 24 are the most crime-prone group. The rise in crime in the 1970s has been blamed on the post–World War II baby boom. By the 1970s the "boomers" had entered the high-risk crime group of 16- to 24-year-olds. They composed a much larger portion of the U.S. population than ever before, so between 40 and 50 percent of the total arrests during that decade could have been attributed to the growth in the total population and in the size of the crime-prone age group. Likewise, the decline in most crime rates that began during the 1980s has been attributed to the maturing of the post–World War II generation. During the 1990s the 16- to 24-year age cohort was smaller than it had been at any time since the early 1960s, and many people believe that this contributed to the decline in crime.

In 1994 a small but influential group of criminologists predicted that by the year 2000 the number of young men in the 14- to 24-year-old cohort would greatly increase. It was argued that the decline in crime experienced in the 1990s was merely the "lull before the storm" (Steinberg, 1999:4WK). However, the predicted rise in violent crime has not occurred. In fact, after the homicide rate for young people peaked in 1993, it dropped to a new low in 2000 and has remained relatively stable (Puzzanchera and Kang, 2011).

There are many potential explanations for the continuing reductions in crime since the mid-1990s. Review "The Policy Debate" to learn about the pros and cons of tough crime policy and whether they can take credit for reductions in crime.

check point ▷ 4. **What are the two main sources of crime data?**
Uniform Crime Reports; National Crime Victimization Surveys.

5. **What are key factors in crime trends?**
Age cohorts and social conditions.

stop & analyze The state of Florida has experienced a 33 percent drop in crime since 1999, and many in the private and public sectors are looking for an explanation (K. Stanley, 2011). Some criminologists are examining the relationship between economics and crime. While many believe that worsening economic conditions will lead to more crime (people stealing food, for example), the trends show that the opposite seems to happen. Why would worsening economic conditions actually *decrease* the crime rate?

Have Tough Crime-Control Policies Caused a Decline in Crime?

There's good news and there's bad news. The good news is that the amount of crime in the United States has been decreasing in recent years. Significant reductions have been seen in every type of violent and property crime, and virtually every demographic group has experienced drops in violent victimization.

Any reduction in crime is welcome, but the bad news is that experts do not agree on the causes for the decline in crime. Have the tough crime-control policies of the past 20 years really reduced crime? Or have crime rates lessened because of factors unrelated to anything police, prosecution, courts, and corrections have done?

Some experts point out that there are more police officers on the streets, sentences are longer, and the probability upon conviction of going to prison is greater. They say the police have been more aggressive in dealing with public-order offenses, the waiting period for handgun purchases has been effective, and more than a million Americans are already in prison and off the streets. In other words, the police and other agencies of criminal justice have made the difference.

Other experts question the impact of tough policies. They point out that the number of men in the crime-prone age group is relatively low compared with that age group's percentage of the national population from the 1960s to the 1980s. Many also say that the tough crime policies, instead of reducing crime, have devastated minority communities and diverted resources from dealing with the poverty that underlies crime. They urge policies that "put justice back in criminal justice."

Although crime rates have been falling, fear of crime is rising. Some opinion surveys find that Americans rank crime among the nation's most prominent problems after the economy, wars, and terrorism. Arguably, crime should rank much lower, given the decrease in victimizations. Because views of crime are shaped more by television news than by statistics, Americans have an unrealistic picture of the crime problem. Grisly coverage of a murder scene on the evening news sticks in the mind in a way that the results of crime studies can never do.

Drugs and crime are perennially popular issues in U.S. politics.

Legislators respond easily to pressures to "do something about crime." Who can argue with that? They usually act by coming up with new laws mandating stiffer sentences and allocating more money for police and corrections. But is this the best direction for public policy?

For Tough Crime Control
Supporters of tough crime-control policies say that crime, especially violent crime, is a serious problem. Even though rates have declined, they argue, violence is still many times higher here than in other developed democracies. We must continue to pursue criminals through strict law enforcement, aggressive prosecutions, and the sentencing of career criminals to long prison terms. They claim that taking the pressure off now will pave the way for problems in the future.

Here is a summary of the arguments for tough crime-control policies:

- The United States has a serious crime problem. Its laws must ensure that offenders receive strict and certain penalties.
- Crime is not caused by poverty, unemployment, and other socioeconomic factors. Instead, crime causes poverty.

Crime Victimization

victimology A field of criminology that examines the role the victim plays in precipitating a criminal incident and also examines the impact of crimes on victims.

Until the past few decades, researchers paid little attention to crime victims. The field of **victimology**, which emerged in the 1950s, focuses attention on four questions: (1) Who is victimized? (2) What is the impact of crime? (3) What happens to victims in the criminal justice system? (4) What role do victims play in causing the crimes they suffer?

Who Is Victimized?

Not everyone has an equal chance of being a crime victim. Moreover, people who are victimized by crime in one year are also more likely to be victimized by crime in a subsequent year (Menard, 2000). Research also shows that members of certain demographic groups are more likely to be victimized than others.

- The expansion of the prison population has taken hardened criminals out of the community, thus contributing to the drop in crime.
- The police must have the resources and legal backing to pursue criminals.

Against Tough Crime Control

Opponents of the get-tough approach believe that better ways are available to deal with crime. They argue that crime is no more effectively controlled today than it was in the early 1970s and that in many respects the problem has worsened, especially in the poorest neighborhoods. Neither the war on crime nor the war on drugs has stopped the downward spiral of livability in these neighborhoods. Another price of the tough crime-control policies has been an erosion of civil rights and liberties—especially for racial and ethnic minorities. What is needed is an infusion of justice into the system.

Here is a summary of the arguments against tough crime-control policies:

- The get-tough policies have not significantly reduced crime.
- Resources should be diverted from the criminal justice system to get to the underlying causes of criminal behavior—poor housing, unemployment, and racial injustice.

- Tough incarceration policies have devastated poor communities. With large numbers of young men in prison, families live in poverty, and children grow up without guidance from their fathers and older brothers.
- Crime policies emphasizing community policing, alternatives to incarceration, and community assistance programs will do more to promote justice than will the failed get-tough policies of the past.

What Should U.S. Policy Be?

The justice system costs about $200 billion a year. Advocates of tough crime-control policies say that the high cost is worth the price, and that the aggressive and punitive policies of the past two decades have worked and reduced crime. Opponents of these policies respond that the police, courts, and corrections have had little impact on crime. Other factors, such as the booming economy of the 1990s and the smaller number of men in the crime-prone age cohort, have been responsible for the reduction. The recession that began in 2008 has caused many government agencies to rethink their spending. Some have found new ways to increase efficiency,

others are considering combining police and fire services into one, large agency.

Even though they are told that crime has gone down, Americans remain fearful. Their opinions translate into support for politicians who advocate the tough approach. No candidate for public office wants to be labeled "soft on crime." What would be the costs—economic and human—of continuing the get-tough policies? Would that same fearful public be affected?

Researching the Internet

To see a 2009 public-opinion study about alternatives to imprisonment as a policy for addressing crime, visit the Criminal Justice CourseMate at cengagebrain.com, then access the web links for this chapter.

For Critical Analysis

How can we determine which factors have caused the declines in crime rates? Are there ways to experiment with our public policies that might tell us which factors are most influential in affecting contemporary crime rates? Should the lowering crime rates cause us to create any new policies, shift our allocation of resources, or give less attention to crime as a policy issue?

Puzzling over this fact, victimologists have come up with several answers (Karmen, 2001:87). One explanation is that demographic factors (age, gender, income) affect lifestyle—people's routine activities, such as work, home life, and recreation. Lifestyles, in turn, affect people's exposure to dangerous places, times, and people (Varano et al., 2004). Consider, for example, that the homeless are at extremely high risk for physical and sexual victimization (Tyler and Beal, 2010). Thus, differences in lifestyles lead to varying degrees of exposure to risks (R. F. Meier and Miethe, 1993:466). Considering their theoretical perspective, think of people whose lifestyle includes going to nightclubs in a "shady" part of town. Such people run the risk of being robbed if they walk alone through a dark high-crime area at two in the morning to their luxury car. By contrast, older individuals who watch television at night in their small-town home have a very low chance of being robbed. But these cases do not tell the entire story. What other factors make victims more vulnerable than nonvictims?

Figure 2.3

Victimization Rates for Violent Crime Teenagers and young people have the highest victimization rate for violent crimes. Why are they more likely than other age groups to be victims of violent crime?

Source: Bureau of Justice Statistics, 2010, *Criminal Victimization in the United States, 2008 Statistical Tables* (Washington, DC: U.S. Department of Justice), Table 10, "Number of Victimizations and Victimization Rates for Persons 12 or Older by Race, Sex, and Age of Victims and Type of Crime."

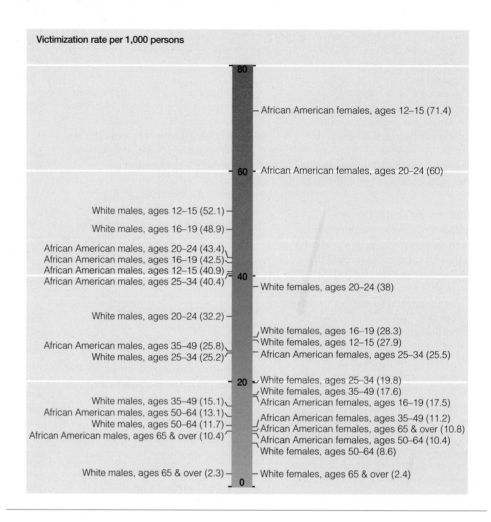

Women, Youths, Nonwhites

The lifestyle-exposure model and survey data shed light on the links between personal characteristics and the chance that one will become a victim. Figure 2.3 shows the influence of gender, age, and race on the risk of being victimized by a violent crime, such as rape, robbery, or assault. If we apply these findings to the lifestyle-exposure model, we might suggest that African American teenagers are most likely to be victimized because of where they live (urban, high-crime areas), how they may spend their leisure time (outside late at night), and the people with whom they may associate (violence-prone youths). Not surprisingly, juveniles who engage in a delinquent lifestyle are more likely to be victimized than those who do not (Melde, 2009). Lifestyle factors may also explain why elderly white men and women are least likely to be victimized by a violent crime. Perhaps it is because they do not go out at night, do not associate with people who are prone to crime, carry few valuables, and take precautions such as locking their doors. Thus, lifestyle choices directly affect the chances of victimization.

Race is a key factor in exposure to crime. African Americans and other minorities are more likely than whites to be raped, robbed, and assaulted. The rate of violent crime victimization for whites is 18.6 per 1,000 people, compared with 26.6 per 1,000 for African Americans (BJS, 2010: Table 5). For Hispanics, the rate is 17.1 per 1,000 (BJS, 2010: Table 7). White Americans are fearful of being victimized by African American strangers (Skogan, 1995:59). However, most violent crime is intraracial: Two-thirds of victims are of the same race as the attacker (BJS, 2010:

Table 42). These numbers simply reflect that African Americans and whites often live in separate neighborhoods. Most of their daily contacts are with people who share their demographic characteristics. And, most importantly, African American neighborhoods are much more likely to experience what scholars call "high levels of socioeconomic disadvantage" with respect to unemployment, quality of schools, quality of housing, and other factors associated with income and wealth (Lauritsen and White, 2001). These factors are often associated with higher levels of street crime, although, obviously, other kinds of crime, such as occupational crime and computer crime, occur more frequently in other settings.

Low-Income City Dwellers Income is also closely linked to exposure to crime. Americans with incomes below $7,500 annually experienced a victimization rate of 44 violent crimes per 1,000 people. By contrast, those with incomes in excess of $75,000 experienced only 12.9 violent crimes per 1,000 people (BJS, 2010: Table 14). Economic factors largely determine where people live, work, and seek recreation. For low-income people, these choices are limited. Some have to live in crime-prone areas, lack security devices to protect their homes, cannot avoid contact with people who are prone to crime, or cannot spend their leisure time in safe areas. Poor people and minorities have a greater risk of being victimized, because they are likely to live in inner-city zones with high rates of street crime. People with higher incomes have more lifestyle-exposure choices open to them and can avoid risky situations (R. F. Meier and Miethe, 1993:468). Living in a city is, in fact, a key factor in victimization. For example, motor vehicle theft is much more common in urban areas (10.0 victimizations per 1,000 population) compared to rural areas, with 2.2 victimizations per 1,000 people (BJS, 2010: Table 18).

In the inner cities, where drug dealing and drug use pose significant and visible problems, murder rates are higher than elsewhere. Like their killers, most of the victims tend to be young African Americans. The national homicide-victimization rate among African American men aged 18 to 24 is 91 for every 100,000 of the same group, about 8 times that for white men in the same age bracket (A. Cooper and Smith, 2011). But this does not tell the whole story, because homicide rates differ by city and state. In some cities and states, the gap between rates for African Americans and whites is even greater. Further, we cannot conclude that crime rates will be high in all poor urban areas. There is more crime in some poor areas than in others. Many factors besides poverty—such as the physical condition of the neighborhood, the residents' attitudes toward society and the law, the extent of opportunities for crime, and social control by families and government—can affect the crime rate of a given area.

© Michael Ventura/Alamy

According to the lifestyle-exposure model, demographic factors (age, gender, income) and exposure to dangerous places, times, and people influence the probability of being victimized. Based on this model, how would you assess your own risk of victimization?

Acquaintances and Strangers

The frightening image of crime in the minds of many Americans is the familiar scene played out in many movies and television shows in which a dangerous stranger grabs a victim on a dark street or breaks into a home at night. It is true

myth & reality | criminal justice

Common Belief: Women are more likely to be raped by a stranger than by someone they know.

- Most women take protective measures to avoid being attacked by strangers. They avoid walking alone at night, park their cars in well-lighted areas, or even carry weapons such as pepper spray.
- The "stranger-in-the-bushes" stereotype of rape certainly does occur, but women are significantly more likely to be raped by a friend or acquaintance than by a stranger.
- Approximately three-quarters of sexual assaults are perpetrated by someone the victim knows, whether an acquaintance, friend, or intimate partner (Truman, 2011).
- This misperception about the risk of sexual assault can lead women to take the wrong kinds of action to protect themselves from rape.
- For example, a college student drinking at a bar might fear walking alone at night and ask a male acquaintance she knows from one of her classes to walk her home. While this action has reduced her risk of being raped by a stranger, it may actually increase her risk of victimization by placing her alone in the company of someone she does not know very well.

© James Wiedel Photolibrary/Alamy

⬆ Although Americans often fear violent victimization at the hands of strangers, most violence against women is perpetrated by those with whom they are intimate—husbands, boyfriends, and former lovers. What policies could address this problem?

that many crimes are committed by strangers against people they have never seen before. However, most Americans do not realize the extent to which violent crimes occur among acquaintances, friends, and even relatives. In 2009, for example, female victims of violent crimes were victimized by strangers in only 31 percent of those crimes; acquaintances, spouses, boyfriends, or relatives committed 68 percent of the violent crimes against female victims. Although only 45 percent of male victims suffered violent crimes at the hands of acquaintances and relatives, that figure still constitutes a significant percentage of violent crimes (Truman and Rand, 2010: Table 7). As you read "Criminal Justice: Myth & Reality," consider how you evaluate your risk of victimization in different situations.

The kind of crime a victim suffers tends to depend on whether strangers or nonstrangers are the perpetrators. Most robberies are committed by strangers, but sexual assault victims are more likely to be victimized by someone they know (Truman and Rand, 2010: Table 7). These differences reflect, in part, the contexts in which these crimes occur. In robberies, valuables are taken from an individual by force and then the robber typically runs away. Thus, the scenario fits situations in which the robber hopes to escape without being caught or identified. This result is much more difficult for a robber who is known to the victim. By contrast, sexual assaults often take place in isolated or private locations. People are most likely to place themselves in isolated or private locations, such as inside a house or apartment, with someone they know.

People may be reluctant to report crimes committed by relatives, such as the theft of their own valuables by a relative with a substance-abuse problem. They may be upset about losing their valuables, but they do not want to see their son, daughter, or cousin arrested and sent to prison. If the perpetrators of such crimes know that their relatives will not report them, they may feel encouraged to victimize these people further in order to support a drug habit. Thus, the prior relationships among people may facilitate some crimes and keep victims from seeking police assistance.

The lifestyle-exposure model helps us understand some of the factors that increase or decrease the risk of being victimized, but what is the impact of crime on the nation and on individuals? We turn to this question in the next section.

The Impact of Crime

Crime affects not only the victim but all members of society. We all pay for crime through higher taxes, higher prices, and fear. These factors impinge on key American values such as individual liberty and protection of private property and personal wealth.

Costs of Crime Crime has many kinds of costs: (1) the economic costs—lost property, lower productivity, and medical expenses; (2) the psychological and emotional costs—pain, trauma, and diminished quality of life; and (3) the costs of operating the criminal justice system.

The cost of economic losses from crime in 2008 were estimated at $17.4 billion (BJS, 2010: Table 82); however, this value only includes the property lost through events such as theft or vandalism. Costs associated with damaged or lost property, lost work time, and medical expenses increase that value significantly. In addition, the intangible costs (pain, trauma, lost quality of life) to victims are difficult to estimate accurately. Adding the costs of operating the criminal justice system each year increases the total economic loss of criminal victimization. In the United States in 2007, approximately $228 billion was paid for police, courts, and corrections (Kyckelhahn, 2011). One study estimates the total cost of *each* homicide to be about $8.9 million, after adding the costs to victims and the government (McCollister, French, and Fang, 2010).

Government costs also increased in the aftermath of the September 11 tragedy as more money was spent on airport security, border patrols, and counterterrorist activities. These figures do not include the costs to consumers stemming from occupational and organized crime. For complaints filed with the Internet Crime Complaint Center, total reported losses increased from $264 million in 2008 to $560 million in 2009 (Internet Crime Complaint Center, 2010). It is difficult to estimate precise figures for economic losses, but clearly such losses are significant and appear to increase annually for crime such as Internet fraud and identity theft.

Question: "Is there any area near where you live—that is, within a mile—where you would be afraid to walk alone at night?"

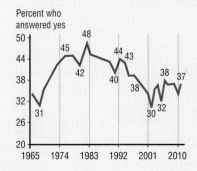

Critical Thinking: Should the government be more active in making the public aware about reduced crime rates and lessened risks of victimization? Alternatively, can increasing awareness about crime cause citizens to overreact to crime problems? In other words, might more information about crime lead to exaggerated fears rather than realistic ones?

Source: Copyright © 2010 Gallup, Inc. All rights reserved. The content is used with permission; however, Gallup retains all rights of republication (http://www.gallup.com/poll/144272 /Nearly-Americans-Fear-Walking-Alone-Night.aspx).

The costs of fighting crime came under increased scrutiny following the recession that began in late 2007. State agencies have begun to search for ways to save money, which frequently involve combining or sharing services with other agencies. In the state of Michigan, for example, several small police departments have been disbanded and local law enforcement is increasingly provided by larger neighboring police agencies. Such consolidation can increase response times, especially in rural areas. In other areas, 911 services are being shared by several agencies in an attempt to reduce operating budgets. Some areas are even taking the more drastic step of combining police and fire services into a single agency. Only time (and research) will determine if these cost-cutting measures also result in significant reductions in crime.

Fear of Crime   One impact of crime is fear. Fear limits freedom. Because they are fearful, many people limit their activities to "safe" areas at "safe" times. Fear also creates anxieties that affect physiological and psychological well-being. Ironically, the very people who have the least chance of being victimized, such as women and the elderly, are often the most fearful (Miethe, 1995). Not all Americans experience the same fears, but some people adjust their daily activities to prevent being victimized.

Since 1965, public-opinion polls have asked Americans whether they "feel more uneasy" or "fear to walk the streets at night." When people are afraid to walk near their homes, their freedom is limited. From 1972 to 1993, more than 40 percent of respondents indicated that fear of crime affected their nighttime activities in their neighborhoods. Coinciding with the declining crimes rates during the 1990s, the percentage of respondents who were fearful of walking near their homes dropped to 30 percent in 2001. However, as indicated in "What Americans Think," the percentage has remained around 37 percent since 2005—barely less than the percentages in some years with much higher national crime rates. Thus, a significant segment of the American public remains fearful despite the significant drop in crime rates over the past 20 years (Saad, 2010).

Although crime rates are down, Americans' fears seem to exceed actual victimization risks. As we have seen, people do not have a clear picture of the true risk of crime in their lives. They gain perceptions about crime from conversations at their workplace and from politicians' statements and campaign promises. Their views about crime also seem to be shaped more by what they see on television than by reality (Chiricos, Padgett, and Gertz, 2000). Although fewer than 8 percent of victimizations involve violent crime, such crimes are the ones most frequently reported by the media.

The Experience of Victims in the Criminal Justice System

After a crime has occurred, the victim is often forgotten. Victims may have suffered physical, psychological, and economic losses, yet the criminal justice system focuses on finding and prosecuting the offender.

Too often the system is not sensitive to the needs of victims. For example, defense attorneys may ask them hostile questions and attempt to paint them, rather than the defendant, as having caused the crime to occur. Similarly, whereas victims are a key source of evidence, the police and prosecutors may question them closely—and in a hostile fashion—to find out if they are telling the truth. Often the victim never hears the outcome of a case. Sometimes a victim comes face-to-face with the assailant who is out on bail or on probation. This can be quite a shock, especially if the victim assumed that the offender was in prison.

Victims may be forced to miss work and lose pay in order to appear at judicial proceedings. They may be summoned to court again and again, only to learn that the arraignment or trial has been postponed. Any recovered property may be held by the court for months as the case winds its way through the system. In short, after cases have been completed, victims may feel that they have been victimized twice, once by the offender and once by the criminal justice system.

During the past three decades, justice agencies have become more sensitive to the interests of crime victims. This has happened partly because victims often are the only witnesses to the crime and their help is needed. Many victims are not willing to provide such help if it involves economic and emotional costs. Some research indicates that victims are more likely to cooperate with the prosecutor if victim-assistance workers meet with them to provide comfort as well as information about how the court system operates (Dawson and Dinovitzer, 2001).

Various laws adopted in recent years provide funds to counsel victims and give financial compensation for injuries, although victims often do not receive enough timely information to take advantage of these programs (Sims, Yost, and Abbott, 2005). In addition, victims' rights statutes in many states permit crime victims to speak at sentencing and parole hearings and to receive information about any impending release of the offender who victimized them. The Justice for All Act passed by Congress in 2004 mandates such rights for victims in those criminal cases processed in the federal courts.

Victims' assistance laws raise questions about which individuals or family members can receive benefits as "victims" (Trulson, 2005). Questions about fairness may arise if some individuals receive different benefits than do other people. Read "A Question of Ethics" at the end of the chapter to consider whether the families of crime victims in general are treated fairly, compared with the families of 9/11 victims.

The Role of Victims in Crime

Victimologists study the role victims play in some crimes. Researchers have found that many victims behave in ways that facilitate the acts committed against them. This does not mean that it is the victim's fault that the crime occurred. It means instead that the victim's behavior may have led to the crime through consent, provocation, enticement, risk taking, or carelessness with property.

What do studies tell us about these situations? First, some people do not take proper precautions to protect themselves. For example, they leave keys in their cars or fail to lock their doors and windows at night. They seem to lack the "common sense" of understanding the price of living safely in modern society. Second, some victims provoke or entice another person to commit a crime. Arguing with a stranger at a bar can lead to criminal assaults. Third, some victims of nonstrangers are not willing to help with the investigation and prosecution. These behaviors do not excuse criminal acts, but they do force us to think about other aspects of the crime situation.

check point

6. **What are the main elements of the lifestyle-exposure model?**
   Demographic characteristics, adaptations, lifestyle, associations, exposure.

7. **What are some of the impacts of crime?**
   Fear, financial costs, emotional costs, lifestyle restrictions.

8. **Why do some crime victims feel mistreated by the criminal justice system?**
   The system focuses on finding and punishing the offender; police and lawyers often question victims closely, in an unsympathetic manner; victims do not always receive assistance that covers their medical expenses and other losses.

stop & analyze

Fear of crime among Americans has remained relatively stable since the mid-1990s; however, during this period the crime rate has decreased significantly. List two reasons that might explain this apparent "disconnect" between the perception of crime and the reality of crime. Why would the typical American fear crime at the same level, when the United States has become safer over the last 20 years?

Causes of Crime

Whenever news of a crime hits the headlines, whether the crime is a grisly murder or a complex bank fraud, the first question is "Why did he (or she) do it?" Do people commit crimes because they are poor, greedy, mentally ill, or just plain stupid? Do any of these explanations apply to the man who shot Gabrielle Giffords, who we read about in the chapter opening?

Various theories about the root causes of criminal behavior have been developed, and scholarly research regularly tests these theories. Using the scientific method, criminologists generate hypotheses, collect data, and derive findings about which theories best explain criminal behavior. When substantiated, these theories can provide the basis for new public policies aimed at preventing crime.

Criminology is concerned mainly with learning about criminal behavior, the nature of offenders, and how crime can be prevented. Research focuses mainly on the offender. Fewer questions are asked about how factors such as the economy, government policy, family, and education affect crime (Messner and Rosenfeld,

1994:45–47). In this section we look at the two major schools of criminological thought—classical and positivist. We will review biological, psychological, sociological, life course, and integrated theories of the causes of criminal behavior. We then take a look at women's criminal behavior and conclude with an overall assessment of the theories discussed in this section.

Classical and Positivist Theories

Two major schools of criminological thought are the classical and positivist schools. Each was pioneered by scholars who were influenced by the dominant intellectual ideas of their times.

The Classical School Until the eighteenth century, most Europeans explained criminal behavior in supernatural terms. Those who did wrong were "possessed" by the devil. Some Christians believed that all humanity had fallen with Adam and had remained in a state of total depravity ever since. Indictments often began, "[John Doe], not having the fear of God before his eyes but being moved and seduced by the instigation of the devil, did commit [a certain crime]." Before the eighteenth century, defendants had few rights. The accused had little chance to put forth a defense, confessions were obtained through torture, and the penalty for most offenses was physical punishment or death.

In 1764 Cesare Beccaria published *An Essay on Crimes and Punishment.* This was the first attempt to explain crime in secular, or worldly, terms, as opposed to religious terms. The book also pointed to injustices in the administration of criminal laws. Beccaria's ideas prompted reformers to try to make criminal law and procedures more rational and consistent. From this movement came **classical criminology**, whose main principles are as follows:

> **classical criminology** A school of criminology that views behavior as stemming from free will, demands responsibility and accountability of all perpetrators, and stresses the need for punishments severe enough to deter others.

1. Criminal behavior is rational, and most people have the potential to engage in such behavior.
2. People may choose to commit a crime after weighing the costs and benefits of their actions.
3. Fear of punishment is what keeps most people in check. Therefore, the severity, certainty, and speed of punishment affects the level of crime.
4. The punishment should fit the crime rather than the person who committed it.
5. The criminal justice system must be predictable, with laws and punishments known to the public.

Classical ideas declined in the nineteenth century, partly because of the rise of science and partly because its principles did not take into account differences among individuals or the way the crime was committed.

Neoclassical Criminology After remaining dormant for almost a hundred years, classical ideas took on new life in the 1980s, when America became more conservative. Some scholars argue that crimes may result from the rational choice of people who have weighed the benefits to be gained from the crime against the costs of being caught and punished. But they also recognize that criminal law must take into account the differences among individuals. To a large extent, sentencing reform, criticisms of rehabilitation, and greater use of incarceration stem from a renewed interest in classical ideas. However, the positivist school of thought is what has dominated American criminology since the start of the twentieth century.

> **positivist criminology** A school of criminology that views behavior as stemming from social, biological, and psychological factors. It argues that punishment should be tailored to the individual needs of the offender.

Positivist Criminology By the middle of the nineteenth century, as the scientific method began to take hold, the ideas of the classical school seemed old-fashioned. Instead, **positivist criminology** used science to study the body, mind, and environment of the offender. Science could help reveal why offenders committed crimes and how they could be rehabilitated. Here are the key features of this approach:

1. Human behavior is controlled by physical, mental, and social factors, not by free will.
2. Criminals are different from noncriminals.
3. Science can be used to discover the causes of crime and to treat deviants.

Understanding the main theories of crime causation is important because they affect how laws are enforced, guilt is determined, and crimes are punished. As we describe each of the theories, consider its implications for crime policies. For example, if biological theories are viewed as sound, then the authorities might try to identify potential offenders through genetic analysis and then segregate or supervise them. On the other hand, the acceptance of sociological theories might lead to efforts to end poverty, improve education, and provide job training.

Biological Explanations

The medical training of Cesare Lombroso (1836–1909) led him to suppose that physical traits distinguish criminals from law-abiding citizens. He believed that some people are at a more primitive state of evolution and hence are born criminal. These "throwbacks" have trouble adjusting to modern society. Lombroso's ideas can be summarized as follows (Lombroso, 1912/1968):

1. Certain people are **criminogenic**, that is, they are born criminals.
2. They have primitive physical traits such as strong canine teeth, huge jaws, and high cheekbones.
3. These traits are acquired through heredity or through alcoholism, epilepsy, or syphilis.

criminogenic Having factors thought to bring about criminal behavior in an individual.

Early biological studies traced the generations of specific families to count how many people in each violated criminal laws. These early studies may no longer seem credible to us, but they were taken seriously in their time and affected criminal justice for decades. For example, many states passed laws that required repeat offenders to be sterilized. It was assumed that crime could be controlled if criminal traits were not passed from parents to children. Not until 1942 did the U.S. Supreme Court declare required sterilization unconstitutional (*Skinner v. Oklahoma*).

Although **biological explanations** of crime were ignored or condemned as racist after World War II, they have attracted renewed interest. *Crime and Human Nature,* by James Q. Wilson and Richard Herrnstein (1985), reviews the research on this subject. Unlike the early positivists, the authors do not claim that any one factor explains criminality. Instead, they argue that biological factors predispose some individuals to commit crimes. Genetic makeup, body type, and IQ may outweigh social factors as predictors of criminality. The findings of research on nutrition, neurology, genetics, and endocrinology give some support to the view that these factors may contribute to violent behavior in some people (Brennan, Mednick, and Volavka, 1995:65). Other researchers have identified physiological factors associated with antisocial behavior, an association they see as a step toward considering a possible link between biology and offending (Cauffman, Steinberg, and Piquero, 2005).

biological explanations Explanations of crime that emphasize physiological and neurological factors that may predispose a person to commit crimes.

These new findings have given biological explanations a renewed influence and have reduced the dominance of sociological and psychological explanations. Scientists are doing further research to see if they can identify biological factors that make some people prone to violence and criminality (Fishbein, 1990:27). For example, a single gene can help predict which abused children are more likely to become violent or antisocial adults—abused children with this gene were twice as likely as other abused children to commit acts of violence (Hathaway, 2002). Other studies examine the role of nutrition, such as consumption of fish rich in omega-3 being associated with lower levels of hostility in young adults (Iribarren et al., 2004). Definitive research has revealed the impact of environmental lead, such as lead-based paint, on brain development and behavior (University of Pittsburgh Medical Center, 2005). Behavior may also be affected by head injuries, tumors in specific locations on the brain, and natural chemical imbalances within the body. These findings behind biology and behavior do not necessarily purport to seek a single explanation for crime. They merely demonstrate an increased recognition that biological factors influence certain kinds of behavior in some offenders.

Psychological Explanations

People have often viewed criminal behavior as being caused by a mental condition, a personality disturbance, or limited intellect. **Psychological explanations** of crime center on these ideas.

Sigmund Freud (1856–1939), now seen as one of the foremost thinkers of the twentieth century, proposed a psychoanalytic theory that crime is caused by unconscious forces and drives. Freud also claimed that early childhood experiences greatly affect personality development. Freud's followers expanded his theory, saying that the personality is made up of three parts: the id, ego, and superego. The id controls drives that are primarily sexual, the ego relates desires to behavior, and the superego (often referred to as the conscience) judges actions as either right or wrong. Psychoanalytic theory explains criminal behavior as resulting from either an undeveloped or an overdeveloped superego. For example, a person who commits a violent sex crime is thought to have an undeveloped superego, because the urges cannot be controlled. Alternatively, a person with an overdeveloped superego may suffer from guilt and anxiety. To reduce the guilt, the person may commit a crime, knowing that punishment will follow. To ensure punishment, the offender will unconsciously leave clues at the crime scene. Psychoanalysts say this occurred in the famous Loeb and Leopold murder of Bobby Franks in 1924 (Regoli and Hewitt, 1994).

In 2011, Anthony Sowell was sentenced to death after the decomposing bodies of 11 women were found at his Cleveland home. The victims had all been strangled to death. At his sentencing hearing, Sowell said, "This is not typical of me. I don't know what happened. I can't explain it." Does criminological theory help us understand what motivated Sowell to commit these acts?

AP Images/The Plain Dealer, Marvin Fong, Pool, File

psychological explanations
Explanations of crime that emphasize mental processes and behavior.

Psychiatrists have linked criminal behavior to such concepts as innate impulses, psychic conflict, and repression of personality. Such explanations propose that crime is a behavior that stems from abnormal urges and desires. Although the psychological approach takes many different forms, all are based on the idea that early personality development is a key factor in later behavior. The terms *psychopath, sociopath,* and *antisocial personality* refer to a person who is unable to control impulses, cannot learn from experience, and does not feel emotions, such as love. This kind of person is viewed as psychologically abnormal and may become a crazed killer or sex fiend.

Psychological theories have been widely criticized. Some critics point to the fact that it is hard to measure emotional factors and to identify people thought to be prone to crime. Others note the wide range of sometimes contradictory theories that take a psychological approach to crime.

Sociological Explanations

In contrast to psychological approaches, **sociological explanations** focus on the way that belonging to social groups shapes people's behavior. Sociologists believe that criminality is not inborn but caused by external factors. Thus, sociological theories of crime assume that contact with the social world, as well as such factors as race, age, gender, and income, mold the offender's personality and actions.

In the 1920s a group of researchers at the University of Chicago looked closely at aspects of urban life that seemed to be linked to crime: poverty, bad housing, broken families, and the problems faced by new immigrants. They found high levels of crime in those neighborhoods that had many opportunities for delinquent behavior and offered few legitimate means of earning a living.

From a sociological perspective, criminals are made, not born. Among the many theories stressing the influence of societal forces on criminal behavior, three types deserve special mention: social structure theories, social process theories, and critical theories.

Social Structure Theories
Social structure theories suggest that criminal behavior is related to social class. People in various social classes have quite different amounts of wealth, status, and power. Those in the lower class suffer from poverty, poor education, bad housing, and lack of political power. Therefore, members of the lower class, especially the younger members, are the most likely to engage in crime. Crime thus is created by the structure of society.

In 1938, the sociologist Robert Merton drew from theories about the role of social change and urbanization on crime. He stressed that social change often leads to a state of **anomie**, in which the rules or norms that guide behavior have weakened or disappeared. People may become anomic when the rules are unclear or they cannot achieve their goals. Under such conditions, antisocial or deviant behavior may result.

It is said, for example, that U.S. society highly values success but makes it impossible for some of its members to succeed. It follows that those who are caught in this trap may use crime as a way out. Theorists believe that this type of situation has led some ethnic groups into organized crime. Others argue that social disorganization brings about conditions in which, among other things, family structure breaks down, alcohol or drug abuse becomes more common, and criminal behavior increases. They assert that poverty must be ended and the social structure reformed if crime is to be reduced (R. J. Sampson and Wilson, 1995).

Contemporary theorists have drawn from social structure concepts and Merton's anomie theory to develop certain theories of crime causation. Prominent among modern approaches is the general theory of strain. According to this approach, negative relationships can lead to negative emotions. These emotions, particularly anger, are expressed through crime and delinquency. Strain is produced by the failure to achieve valued goals, which may particularly affect poor people in a society that values financial success. Strain is also produced by negative experiences, including unemployment, child abuse, criminal victimization, and family problems, which also tend to prevail in poor communities. Under this theory, those who cannot cope with negative experiences may be predisposed to criminal behavior (Liska and Messner, 1999:36–37).

As these ideas have become more refined, they have also been used to explain white-collar crime. To achieve even higher levels of success in a structure that values ever-increasing wealth, individuals may break rules and violate laws in order to enhance their personal success. As with "street" crime, white-collar criminals may commit crimes due to economic strain; but they may also be influenced by a perceived inability to reach a particular social status or work-related strain. These

sociological explanations
Explanations of crime that emphasize as causes of criminal behavior the social conditions that bear on the individual.

social structure theories
Theories that blame crime on the existence of a powerless lower class that lives with poverty and deprivation and often turns to crime in response.

anomie A breakdown or disappearance of the rules of social behavior.

strains, combined with other factors, can increase the likelihood that they will engage in white-collar crime (Agnew, Piquero, and Cullen, 2009).

Social Process Theories

social process theories
Theories that see criminality as normal behavior. Everyone has the potential to become a criminal, depending on (1) the influences that impel one toward or away from crime and (2) how one is regarded by others.

learning theories Theories that see criminal behavior as learned, just as legal behavior is learned.

theory of differential association The theory that people become criminals because they encounter more influences that view criminal behavior as normal and acceptable than they do influences that are hostile to criminal behavior.

control theories Theories holding that criminal behavior occurs when the bonds that tie an individual to society are broken or weakened.

labeling theories Theories emphasizing that the causes of criminal behavior are not found in the individual but in the social process that labels certain acts as deviant or criminal.

critical criminology Theories that assume criminal law and the criminal justice system are primarily a means of controlling the lower classes, women, and minorities.

Social Process Theories Despite such arguments, many criminologists believe that the social structure approach does not adequately explain criminality by middle-class and affluent people. More importantly, they fear that a focus on social structure erroneously emphasizes crime as primarily a problem of the poor. **Social process theories**, which date from the 1930s but did not gain recognition until the 1960s and 1970s, assume that any person, regardless of education, class, or upbringing, has the potential to become a criminal. However, some people are likely to commit criminal acts because of the circumstances of their lives. Thus, these theories try to explain the processes by which certain people become criminals.

There are three main types of social process theories: learning theories, control theories, and labeling theories.

Learning theories hold that criminal activity is learned behavior. Through social relations, some people learn how to be a criminal and acquire the values associated with that way of life. This view assumes that people imitate and learn from one another. Thus, family members and peers are viewed as major influences on a person's development.

In 1939, Edwin Sutherland proposed a type of learning theory called the **theory of differential association**, which states that behavior is learned through interactions with others, especially family members (Sutherland, 1947). Criminal behavior occurs when a person encounters others who are more favorable to crime than opposed to it. If a boy grows up in a family in which, say, an older brother is involved in crime, he is likely to learn criminal behavior. If people in the family, neighborhood, and gang believe that illegal activity is nothing to be ashamed of, this belief increases the chance that the young person will engage in crime.

Control theories hold that social links keep people in line with accepted norms (Gottfredson and Hirschi, 1990; Hirschi, 1969). In other words, all members of society have the potential to commit crime, but most are restrained by their ties to family, church, school, and peer groups. Thus, sensitivity to the opinion of others, commitment to a conventional lifestyle, and belief in the standards or values shared by friends all influence a person to abide by the law. A person who lacks one or more of these influences may engage in crime.

Finally, **labeling theories** stress the social process through which certain acts and people are labeled as deviant. As Howard Becker noted, society creates deviance—and, hence, criminality—"by making the rules whose infraction constitutes deviance, and by applying those rules to particular people and labeling them outsiders" (Becker, 1963, p. 9). Decisions that result in the imposition of labels do not necessarily affect all individuals in the same way. Thus, researchers are exploring the association between labels and specific categories of people labeled as offenders (Chiricos et al., 2007).

According to labeling theories, social control agencies, such as the police, courts, and corrections, are created to label certain people as outside the normal, law-abiding community. When they have been labeled, those people come to believe that the label is true. They take on a deviant identity and start acting in deviant ways. Labeling theory suggests the justice system creates criminals by labeling people in order to serve its own bureaucratic and political ends. Those who support this view call for decriminalization of drug use, gambling, and prostitution.

Critical Theories In the mid-1960s, the reigning biological, psychological, and sociological explanations of criminal behavior were challenged by scholars who developed theories known as **critical criminology**. These theories assume that criminal law and the justice system are designed by those in power, whose purpose is to oppress those who are not in power (particularly, the poor, women, and minorities). The powerful commit as many crimes as do the less powerful, it is argued, but unempowered individuals are more likely to be caught and punished. Those in power use the law to impose their version of morality on society in order to protect their property and safety. They also use their power to change the definitions of crime to cover acts they view as threatening.

Several different theories can be said to fall under the umbrella of critical criminology. **Social conflict theories** posit that crime is the result of conflict within societies. One type of social conflict theory has been proposed by critical, radical, or Marxist criminologists. It holds that the class structure causes certain groups to be labeled as deviant. In this view, "deviance is a status imputed to groups who share certain structural characteristics (e.g., powerlessness)" (Spitzer, 1975:639). Thus, the criminal law is aimed at the behavior of specific groups or classes. One result is that the poor are deeply hostile toward the social order, and this hostility is one factor in criminal behavior. Moreover, when the status quo is threatened, legal definitions of crime are changed in order to trap those who challenge the system. For example, vagrancy laws have been used to arrest labor union organizers, civil rights workers, and peace activists when those in power believed that their interests were threatened by these groups.

Feminist theories of crime are based on the idea that traditional theory centers on male criminality and ignores female offending. While this idea is adopted by all feminist theorists, some adopt less critical perspectives that integrate recognition of women's experiences into social process theories, psychological theories, and other existing approaches. Others, such as radical, Marxist, and socialist feminists, take a more critical view toward traditional, mainstream theories of crime. Recent feminist theorists underscore the need to integrate race and class issues with gender for a full understanding of crime (Chesney-Lind, 2006).

Like other theories about the causes of criminal behavior, sociological theories have been criticized. Critics argue that these theories are imprecise, unsupported by evidence, and based on ideology. Even so, sociological theories have served as the basis for many attempts to prevent crime and rehabilitate offenders.

Life Course Theories

Life course theories seek to identify factors that shape criminal careers, in order to explain when and why offenders begin to commit crimes and to see what factors lead individuals to stop their participation in crimes. Studies in this area often try to follow individuals from childhood through adulthood in order to identify the factors associated with beginning, avoiding, continuing, or ceasing criminal behavior. Criminal careers often begin at an early age; people who eventually become involved with crime often exhibit disruptive behavior, lack family support, and experiment with drinking and drugs as youths. Some theorists discuss *pathways* into crime, which may begin with minor habits of lying and stealing that lead to more-serious offenses. However, pathways into crime are not identical for all kinds of offenders (S. R. Maxwell and Maxwell, 2000). For example, those youths who engage in bullying and fighting may begin a pathway toward different kinds of crimes than do those who start out using drugs.

As identified by life course theorists, the factors that can impact criminal careers overlap with factors discussed in psychological, social structure, and social process theories, such as unemployment, failure in school, impulsiveness, and unstable families. In other words, life course theorists' ideas about factors associated with criminal behavior are consistent with factors identified in other theories. However, these theorists study criminal behavior from a broader perspective.

The research of Robert Sampson and John Laub is among the most influential in examining the life course and criminal careers (Laub and Sampson, 2003;

social conflict theories Theories that view crime as the result of conflict in society, such as conflict between economic classes caused by elites using law as a means to maintain power.

feminist theories Theories that criticize existing theories for ignoring or undervaluing women's experiences as offenders, victims, and people subjected to decision making by criminal justice officials. These theories seek to incorporate an understanding of differences between the experiences and treatment of men and women while also integrating consideration of other factors, such as race and social class.

life course theories Theories that identify factors affecting the start, duration, nature, and end of criminal behavior over the life of an offender.

Sampson and Laub, 1993). They reanalyzed and built on the famous studies of Sheldon and Eleanor Glueck that had followed the lives of 1,000 Boston-area boys from 1940 through the 1960s (Glueck and Glueck, 1950). Sampson and Laub gathered data on the same men in the 1990s, by which time the surviving "boys" from the original study were senior citizens.

Using their research, Sampson and Laub discuss informal and formal social controls over the life course. Unlike some researchers, who see youthful criminality as setting behavior patterns that continue into adulthood, Sampson and Laub emphasize *turning points* in life that move individuals away from criminal careers. For example, their study showed that military service, employment, and marriage served as particularly important factors leading away from criminal careers. By contrast, incarceration and alcohol abuse were associated with continued lawbreaking. Researchers have also sought to test other factors, such as the development of religiosity, but further studies are needed to see if such factors generate turning points away from crime (Giordano et al., 2008).

Life course explanations do not seek to identify a single or primary factor as the cause of criminal behavior. Instead, they try to identify and evaluate the timing, interaction, and results of complex factors that affect people's lives.

Integrated Theories

integrated theories Theories that combine differing theoretical perspectives into a larger model.

As the number of theoretical perspectives has grown, researchers have called for the development of **integrated theories** drawn from different disciplines— that is, theories that merge several perspectives on crime. In 1979, a group of researchers created a new theory from components of strain, social control, and social learning theories (D. S. Elliott, Ageton, and Cantor, 1979). From their data, they concluded that some juveniles enter delinquency through a combination of weak commitment to conventional norms (control theory) and vulnerability to delinquent peers (social learning theory). Others were more likely to become delinquent after forming strong commitments to conventional society (control theory), which are later weakened by their inability to achieve goals (strain theory). These weakened bonds lead to relationships with delinquent peers (social learning theory).

While the integration of theories makes sense, given the large array of factors that affect human behavior, there has been much debate about whether multiple theories can be integrated at all. For example, some theorists, such as Lombroso, believe that humans are inherently criminal and that positive social forces are needed to keep people from offending, while other theorists believe that people are generally not prone to criminal behavior but that negative forces can lure them into committing crime (Henry and Lanier, 2006). These issues are currently being debated by modern criminologists in an attempt to construct valid, integrated theories of crime.

Women and Crime

As mentioned earlier in this section, theories about causes of crime are almost all based on observations of men. That women commit crime less often than do men (and that most criminologists have historically been male) helps explain this fact (D. Klein, 1973). Traditionally, many people assumed that most women, because of their nurturing and dependent nature, could not commit serious crimes. Those who did commit crimes were labeled as "bad" or "fallen" women. Unlike male criminals, then, female criminals were viewed as moral offenders.

Most traditional theories of crime cannot explain two important facts about gender and offending. First, a theory must explain why women are less likely to commit crime than are men (the "gender gap"). Women accounted for approximately 25 percent of all arrests in 2010, with men responsible for the remaining 75 percent

(FBI, 2011a: Table 33). Second, a theory must explain why women commit different kinds of crime than do men—women are less likely to be arrested for violent crimes than are men, and women are more likely to be arrested for crimes such as embezzlement and prostitution (FBI, 2011a: Table 33).

Female suspects are less likely than male suspects to be arrested for any type of offense. In 2010, for example, 89 percent of arrested murder suspects and 87 percent of arrested robbery suspects were men. In addition, women are mostly likely to be arrested for larceny/theft than any other offense although they constituted only 44 percent of all arrestees for this offense (FBI, 2011a: Table 33).

Two books published in 1975 attempted to explain these facts about female offending. Rita Simon's *Women and Crime* and Freda Adler's *Sisters in Crime* both hypothesized that women's liberation would result in increases in female offending. While Adler and Simon disagreed about how the *types* of crime committed by women would be affected by women's liberation, both predicted the gender gap would be reduced significantly. Although there are still significant differences in patterns of criminal behavior by men and women, these books helped alert scholars to societal changes that affect women's status, self-image, behavior, and opportunities to commit crimes.

A Miami police officer arrests Josephine Martinez in 2008 as part of a crackdown on mortgage-fraud scams. How has women's participation in crime changed in recent decades?

Beginning in the 1990s, theorists recognized the importance of *social structure* in explaining female criminality. These theorists posit three things: that our society is structured in such a way as to create different opportunities for men and women in the workforce, that power differentials exist between men and women, and that important differences in sexuality shape the behavior of men and women (Messerschmidt, 1993).

Recent developments related to women and crime include life course theories, which focus on the paths taken by individuals through life and identify important turning points in people's lives. Recall that these "transitions" can affect individual behavior and lead people either to or away from criminal activity (Sampson and Laub, 1990). To explain gender and crime, feminist pathways researchers focus on the impact of critical life events, such as victimization, to determine why some women engage in criminal behavior. Research shows, for example, that many women working as prostitutes were sexually abused as children (Widom, 1995).

In recent years, scholars have pointed out the need to incorporate race and class into theories explaining female criminality. Known as "multiracial feminism," this perspective advocates not only the inclusion of race and class, but also an awareness that opportunities and transitions are shaped by our race, class, gender, sexuality, and many other relevant factors (Burgess-Proctor, 2006). Other research indicates that while the gender gap is growing smaller, this is primarily due to a decrease in male offending rather than an increase in female offending (Lauritsen, Heimer, and Lynch, 2009).

Assessing Theories of Criminality

Scholars have presented evidence to support aspects of each theory of crime (see Table 2.3). This does not mean, however, that the strength of supporting evidence is the same for each theory. In addition, some research may provide evidence for more than one theory. For example, research about the impact of neighborhoods may have implications for both social structure and social process theories (Kubrin and

TABLE 2.3 Major Theories of Criminality and Their Policy Implications

Scholars and the public support various types of policies. We know little about the real causes of crime, but note how many people think they have the answers!

Theory	Major Premise	Policy Implications	Policy Implementation
Biological	Genetic, biochemical, or neurological defects cause some people to commit crime.	Identification and treatment or control of persons with crime-producing biological factors. Selective incapacitation, intensive supervision.	1 Use of drugs to inhibit biological urges of sex offenders. 2 Use of controlled diet to reduce levels of antisocial behavior caused by biochemical imbalances. 3 Identification of neurological defects through CAT scans. Use of drugs to suppress violent impulses. 4 Special education for those with learning disabilities.
Psychological	Personality and learning factors cause some people to commit crime.	Treatment of those with personality disorders to achieve mental health. Those whose illegal behavior stems from learning should have their behavior punished so they will realize that crime is not rewarded.	1 Psychotherapy and counseling to treat personality disorders. 2 Behavior modification strategies, such as electric shock and other negative impulses, to change learned behavior. 3 Counseling to enhance moral development. 4 Intensive individual and group therapies.
Social Structure	Crime is the result of underlying social conditions such as poverty, inequality, and unemployment.	Actions taken to reform social conditions that breed crime.	1 Education and job-training programs. 2 Urban redevelopment to improve housing, education, and health care. 3 Community development to provide economic opportunities.
Social Process	Crime is normal learned behavior and is subject to either social control or labeling effects.	Individuals to be treated in groups, with emphasis on building conventional bonds and avoiding stigmatization.	1 Youth programs that emphasize positive role models. 2 Community organizing to establish neighborhood institutions and bonds that emphasize following society's norms. 3 Programs designed to promote family stability.
Critical	Criminal definitions and punishments are used by some groups to control other groups.	Fundamental changes in the political and social systems to reduce class conflict.	1 Development of programs to remove injustice in society. 2 Provision of resources to assist women, minorities, and the poor in dealing with the criminal justice system and other government agencies. 3 Modification of criminal justice to deal similarly with crimes committed by upper-class members and crimes committed by lower-class members.
Life Course	Offenders have criminal careers that often begin with pathways into youth crime but can change and end through turning points in life.	Foster positive turning points such as marriage and stable employment.	1 Policies to reduce entry pathways associated with youth incarceration and substance abuse. 2 Policies to promote educational success, full employment, successful marriages, and stable families.

© Cengage Learning

Stewart, 2006). When criminologists theorize that a recent rise in murders among young people in Boston is attributable, in part, to a "street culture" in which lethal violence is used to preserve reputations and respect (Llana, 2006), does that reflect social structure, social process, or some other theory? As yet, no theory is accurate enough to predict criminality or establish a specific cause for each offender's behavior.

The theories are limited in other ways as well. They tend to focus on visible crimes and the poor. They have less to say about upper-class or organized crime. Most of the theories also focus on male behavior. What is missing, and truly needed, is a theory that merges these disparate ideas about the causes of crime. Once we have a complete and testable account of what causes crime, we can develop better policies to deal with it.

a question of ethics

Think, Discuss, Write

Imagine the following scenarios: Two women—one in New York City and one in Chicago—arise early one morning to prepare to leave for their jobs at different insurance companies. As single parents, they both bear the responsibility of providing financial support as well as parental guidance to their children. After the Chicago woman parks in the underground garage next to her office building, an unfamiliar man sneaks up behind her, places a handgun against her face, and demands her purse and the keys to her car. Because she is startled and frightened, she drops her keys and reflexively bends to retrieve them. When she moves, the gun goes off and she is killed. In New York City, the woman is sitting at her desk in her office tower when suddenly her entire office suite bursts into flames in an explosion. She is killed instantly. The date is September 11, 2001. One woman has been killed in a parking garage in Chicago and the other has died in the hijackers' attack on the World Trade Center in New York City.

In the aftermath of the September 11 tragedy, Congress enacted legislation to compensate victims with financial awards that exceed those of standard victim compensation programs and instead match the kinds of significant awards that someone might win in a wrongful death lawsuit. Thus, the family of the woman killed at the World Trade Center would be eligible for significant financial support from the federal government to replace the income that she would have provided for her family. According to information available in 2011, the average award to a family of someone killed at the World Trade Center was $2 million. By contrast, the family of the woman killed in the Chicago parking garage would be eligible for a maximum of only $27,000 under the Illinois Crime Victims Compensation Act. Both women were killed during sudden attacks by strangers. Both women left behind children who had relied on them for financial support as well as emotional support and parental guidance.

Discussion/Writing Assignment
Is it ethical for the federal government to provide financial support for one victim's family but not for the other? Are there any persuasive reasons to treat the two families differently? Imagine that you are the advisor to a commission that must propose a policy concerning compensation for future crime victims as well as future victims of terrorist attacks. Write a memo explaining how you would treat these two groups for purposes of government compensation. Be sure to explain the reasons for your recommendation.

Sources: Illinois Attorney General's Office, "Crime Victim Compensation: Frequently Asked Questions by Relatives of Deceased Victims" (http://www.illinoisattorneygeneral.gov /victims/CV_FAQ_RelativesDeceased_0809.pdf); Ray Salazar, "How Does a Chicago Public Schools Student Survive a Sibling's Violent Death—Twice?," *The White Rhino: A Chicago Latino English Teacher* (blog) *Chicago Now*, August 23, 2011 (www.chicagonow.com); Aaron Smith, "The 9/11 Fund: Putting a Price on Life," CNN Money, September 7, 2011 (http://money.cnn.com).

Categorize crimes by their type

→ There are six broad categories of crime: visible crime, occupational crime, organized crime, victimless crime, political crime, and cyber crime.
→ Each type of crime has its own level of risk and profitability, each arouses varying degrees of public disapproval, and each has its own group of offenders with their own characteristics.

Recognize the different methods of measuring crime

→ The amount of crime is difficult to measure. The National Incident-Based Reporting System (NIBRS), Uniform Crime Reports (UCR), and National Crime Victimization Surveys (NCVS) are the best sources of crime data.
→ The complexity of crime statistics makes monitoring trends in crime a challenge.
→ Crime rates are affected by changes in social conditions, including demographic trends and unemployment rates.

Understand why some people are at higher risk of victimization than others

→ Young male residents of lower-income communities are among those most likely to be victimized by crime.
→ Because of the connection between race and social status in the United States, African Americans are more frequently victimized by crime than are whites.
→ A significant percentage of crimes, especially those against women, are committed by acquaintances and relatives of victims.

Recognize the negative consequences of victimization

→ Crime significantly affects all of society through financial and other costs.
→ Financial costs from white-collar crime, employee theft, and fraud lead to huge financial losses for businesses.
→ Medical costs, psychological effects, and insensitive treatment by justice system officials are among the burdens on individual crime victims.
→ Fear of crime may make everyone in society feel less free to go certain places or live their daily lives comfortably.

Understand the theories put forward to explain criminal behavior

→ The classical school of criminology emphasized reform—of criminal law, procedures, and punishments.
→ The rise of science led to the positivist school, which viewed behavior as stemming from social, biological, and psychological factors.
→ Positivist criminology has dominated the study of criminal behavior since the beginning of the twentieth century.
→ Biological theories of crime claim that physiological and neurological factors may predispose a person to commit crimes.
→ Psychological theories of crime propose that mental processes and behavior hold the key to understanding the causes of crime.
→ Sociological theories of crime emphasize as causes of criminal behavior the social conditions that bear on the individual. Three types of sociological theory are social structure theories, social process theories, and critical theories, including social conflict theories.
→ Feminist theories call attention to scholars' neglect of women's criminal behavior. Such theories often take a conflict perspective, but some feminist theorists may draw from other theoretical approaches in examining women and crime.
→ Life course theories consider pathways into crime and turning points, such as marriage, employment, and military service, that move individuals away from criminal careers.
→ Integrated theories combine components of theories from different disciplines. They attempt to provide a better explanation for crime than one single discipline can.

Analyze crime causation theories and women offenders

→ The criminality of women has only recently been studied. Some argue that, as society increasingly treats women and men as equals, the number of crimes committed by women will increase.
→ Theories of criminality are criticized for focusing too exclusively on lower-class and male perpetrators.

Questions for Review

1. What are the six types of crimes?
2. What are the positive and negative attributes of the two major sources of crime data?
3. Who is most likely to be victimized by crime?
4. What are the costs of crime?
5. How does the criminal justice system treat victims?
6. What are the major theories of criminality?
7. What have scholars learned about the criminal behavior of women?

Key Terms and Cases

anomie (p. 63)

biological explanations (p. 61)

classical criminology (p. 60)

control theories (p. 64)

criminogenic (p. 61)

critical criminology (p. 64)

cyber crimes (p. 44)

dark figure of crime (p. 46)

feminist theories (p. 65)

integrated theories (p. 66)

labeling theories (p. 64)

learning theories (p. 64)

life course theories (p. 65)

money laundering (p. 42)

National Crime Victimization Surveys (NCVS) (p. 49)

National Incident-Based Reporting System (NIBRS) (p. 49)

occupational crimes (p. 42)

organized crime (p. 42)

political crime (p. 43)

positivist criminology (p. 60)

psychological explanations (p. 62)

social conflict theories (p. 65)

social process theories (p. 64)

social structure theories (p. 63)

sociological explanations (p. 63)

theory of differential association (p. 64)

Uniform Crime Reports (UCR) (p. 46)

victimless crimes (p. 43)

victimology (p. 52)

visible crime (p. 41)

Criminal Justice and the Rule of Law

Learning Objectives

- Recognize the bases and sources of American criminal law

- Understand how substantive criminal law defines a crime and the legal responsibility of the accused

- Understand how procedural criminal law defines the rights of the accused and the processes for dealing with a case

- Recognize the U.S. Supreme Court's role in interpreting the criminal justice amendments to the Constitution

On a highway outside Pritchard, Alabama, in March 2005, the lead van carrying members of the Liberty University's men's lacrosse team slowed suddenly as a car in front of the van made a turn into a parking lot. The lacrosse team's second van did not slow down in time and plowed into the back of the first van, pushing it across the centerline and into the path of an oncoming truck. Amid screeching tires and sound of breaking glass, the truck crashed into the van. Many of the students were not wearing seat belts and were ejected from the vehicle. Three of students were hospitalized with very serious injuries (H. Brown, 2005). One of them, Chad Gurney, was listed in critical condition, ultimately leading to 20 surgeries for his head injuries and other medical issues resulting from the collision. Eventually, insurance companies paid Gurney a financial settlement for his injuries and he moved back home to Portland, Maine, to use the settlement money to begin his life again (Sharp, 2011).

Years later, the collision on the Alabama highway became the focus of debate in a criminal case. In May 2009, 27-year-old Gurney learned that the woman he had been dating for the past six weeks, 18-year-old Zoe Sarnacki, had been intimate with another man while Gurney was out of town. One night as she slept at his apartment, Gurney began to choke Zoe, ultimately strangling her to death. After abusing and decapitating her body, he arranged religious artifacts around the bed and then soaked the body and bed with gasoline, before striking a match to set everything on fire (Hench, 2011). When he was arrested, he expressed remorse and quickly settled a lawsuit filed by the victim's family.

The community of Portland was shocked by the horrific crime. How could anyone commit such terrible acts? Gurney entered a plea of not guilty by reason of insanity. His attorney, Sarah Churchill, argued that the defendant was legally insane at the time of the murder and therefore could not be punished for the crime. Dr. Harold Bursztajn, a psychiatrist from Harvard Medical School, testified that Gurney's mental illness was primarily the result of the brain injury from the highway collision as well as from his decision to stop taking narcotic pain medicines. Churchill argued that proof of Gurney's delusional thinking was evidenced in his interactions with friends, journal entries, emails, and text messages (T. Maxwell, 2011). Gurney had waived his right to a jury trial, and so Judge Roland Cole faced the prospect of deciding whether the defendant could be held legally responsible for the crime.

A criminal defendant's claim of insanity raises difficult questions for the justice system. Critics question whether such a defense should be available to permit people to avoid **legal responsibility** and punishment for their criminal acts. Should someone avoid imprisonment after committing the horrible acts for which Gurney was responsible? The defense attorney presented evidence that Gurney's behavior was the result of his mental disease and this evidence was backed by a respected psychiatrist from Harvard. In opposition, prosecutor Lisa Marchese presented the conclusions from two psychologists and a psychiatrist who examined Gurney and concluded that his personality

disorder did not prevent him from understanding the wrongfulness of his actions (T. Maxwell, 2011). Without having any professional training in psychology or medicine, how does a judge, or in other cases, a jury, decide whether a defendant is legally insane? Yet this is what our justice system asks these decision makers to determine. As in other cases raising this issue, Judge Cole heard evidence and expert testimony supporting both sides of the issue.

Ultimately, Judge Cole rejected the insanity defense (Sharp, 2011). He made a legal decision based on his assessment of whether the evidence demonstrated the existence of the defendant's insanity under the state's definition. He concluded that Gurney was not legally insane at the time of the murder and therefore he would be sentenced to prison for the crime. Had he been found legally insane, he would have been committed to a mental institution until doctors determined that he had recovered enough to be released. Instead, in March 2011 Judge Cole imposed a 60-year prison sentence on Gurney for the murder of Zoe Sarnacki. This was a 50-year sentence for the murder and an additional 10 years for arson. Gurney will need to serve at least 50 years before he might become eligible for early release (Hench, 2011).

In this chapter, we shall examine the primary components of criminal law. Substantive criminal law is developed through statutes enacted by the American people's elected representatives in state legislatures and Congress. It addresses the specific acts for which people will be punished as well as the circumstances in which people may not be held fully responsible for their actions. We shall also introduce procedural criminal law, which defines the procedures used in legal processes and the rights possessed by criminal suspects and defendants. Even though Gurney acknowledged that he committed the gruesome killing, he was still entitled to a trial and representation by an attorney as he attempted to show why he should not be held fully responsible for his actions. The right to counsel and the right to a fair trial are two of the elements provided by procedural criminal law. The precise nature of individuals' rights under procedural criminal law is determined by judges' interpretations of the U.S. Constitution, state constitutions, and relevant statutes enacted by Congress and state legislatures.

Foundations of Criminal Law

Like most Americans, you are probably aware that law and legal procedures are key elements of the criminal justice system. Americans are fond of saying that "we have a government of laws, not of men (and women)." According to our American values, we do not have a system based on the decisions of a king or dictator. In the United States, even our most powerful leaders have to make decisions within limits imposed by law. The government can seek to punish only people who violate defined laws, and their guilt has to be determined through procedures established by law.

Laws tell citizens what they can and cannot do. Laws also tell government officials when they can seek to punish citizens for violations and how they must go about it. Government officials, including the president of the United States, who take actions according to their own preferences run the risk that judges will order them to take different actions that comply with the law. In 2004, for example, the U.S. Supreme Court ordered then-President George W. Bush's administration to permit a U.S. citizen being held as a suspected terrorist to meet with an attorney and have opportunities to make arguments in court (*Hamdi v. Rumsfeld*). Government officials are expected to follow and enforce the law. Thus, in a democracy, laws are major tools for preventing government officials from seizing too much power or using power improperly.

Criminal law is only one category of law. Peoples' lives and actions are also affected by **civil law**, which governs business deals, contracts, real estate, and the like. For example, if you damage other people's property or harm them in an accident, they may sue you to pay for the damage or harm. By contrast, the key feature of criminal law is the government's power to punish people for damage they have done to society.

Among the two categories of criminal law, **substantive criminal law** defines actions that the government can punish. It also defines the punishments for such offenses. Often called the "penal code," substantive law answers the question "What is illegal?" Elected officials in Congress, state legislatures, and city councils write the substantive criminal laws. These legislators decide which kinds of behaviors are so harmful that they deserve to be punished. They also decide whether each violation should be punished by imprisonment, a fine, probation, or another kind of punishment. When questions arise about the meaning of substantive criminal laws, judges interpret the laws by seeking to fulfill the legislators' intentions.

By contrast, **procedural criminal law** defines the rules that govern how the laws will be enforced. It protects the constitutional rights of defendants and provides the rules that officials must follow in all areas of the criminal justice system. Many aspects of procedural criminal law are defined by legislatures, such as how bail will be set and which kind of preliminary hearing will take place before a trial. However, the U.S. Supreme Court and state supreme courts also play a key role in defining procedural criminal law. These courts define the meaning of constitutional rights in the U.S. Constitution and in state constitutions. Their interpretations of constitutional provisions create rules on issues such as when and how police officers can question suspects and when defendants can receive advice from their attorneys.

legal responsibility The accountability of an individual for a crime because of the perpetrator's characteristics and the circumstances of the illegal act.

civil law Law regulating the relationships between or among individuals, usually involving property, contracts, or business disputes.

substantive criminal law Law that defines acts that are subject to punishment and specifies the punishments for such offenses.

procedural criminal law Law defining the procedures that criminal justice officials must follow in enforcement, adjudication, and corrections.

---

check point

1. What is contained in a state's penal code?
Penal codes contain substantive criminal law that defines crimes and also punishments for those crimes.

2. What is the purpose of procedural criminal law?
Procedural criminal law specifies the defendant's rights and tells justice system officials how they can investigate and process cases.

stop & analyze

In 2011, the mayor of Baltimore proposed that the Maryland legislature enact a new law requiring a minimum 18-month prison sentence for anyone caught with an illegal, loaded firearm. Are legislators capable of predicting all of the consequences of such a law? List three of your own predictions about the consequences of such a law. In light of your predictions, is the proposed law a good idea?

State legislatures create criminal laws for their states and Congress creates national criminal laws. These laws define acts that are illegal and specify punishments for each offense. Are there additional criminal laws that contemporary legislators should create for your state?

© David Frazier/The Image Works

Substantive Criminal Law

Substantive criminal law defines acts that are subject to punishment and specifies the punishments. It is based on the doctrine that no one may be convicted of or punished for an offense unless the offense has been defined by the law. In short, people must know in advance what is required of them. Thus, no act can be regarded as illegal until it has been defined as punishable under the criminal law. While this sounds like a simple notion, the language of law is often confusing and ambiguous. As a result, judges must become involved in interpreting the law so that the meaning intended by the legislature can be understood.

Definitions and Classifications of Criminal Laws

In defining the behaviors deserving of punishment, legislatures also make decisions about the potential severity of punishments for various offenses. Typically, offenses are placed into specific categories according to the consequences that will follow. Crimes defined as **felonies** are those that can lead to incarceration for a year or more in state or federal prison as well as those subject to the death penalty. **Misdemeanors** are crimes for which the punishment may be a year or less in a county jail, but these are often punished with probation, fines, or community service instead. Some legislatures subdivide felonies and misdemeanors according to degrees of seriousness. For example, those crimes classified as third-degree felonies would lead to shorter sentences than the most serious crimes that are classified as first-degree felonies. Legislatures may also define a category of offenses as petty offenses, which are typically behaviors for which the punishment is only a small fine. Similarly, legislatures may define the most minor offenses as **civil infractions** that are punishable only by fines, do not make the violator subject to arrest, and do not produce any criminal record for the individual. For example, such actions as crossing a street against a traffic light ("jaywalking") or even possessing a small amount of marijuana for personal consumption can be defined as civil infractions if a legislature so chooses. Bear in mind that offenses within these classifications vary by state and that the terms used to define these classifications, such as petty offenses, may also vary in their meaning in each jurisdiction.

felonies Serious crimes usually carrying a penalty of death or of incarceration for more than one year in prison.

misdemeanors Offenses less serious than felonies and usually punishable by incarceration of no more than one year in jail, probation, or intermediate sanctions.

civil infractions Minor offenses that are typically punishable by small fines and that produce no criminal record for the offender.

Legislatures do not necessarily define categories of crimes solely according to idealistic assessments of the seriousness of each offense. Due to budget crises affecting various states, in 2009 several legislatures began to redefine specific nonviolent felonies as misdemeanors in an effort to reduce the number of people sent to prison and thus lower the associated costs to the state. For example, Montana raised the threshold dollar amount for a charge of felony theft from $1,000 to $1,500 (K. Johnson, 2011).

Legislatures do not act in isolation when developing definitions of crimes. Since the 1960s, they have been significantly influenced by the *Model Penal Code*. The American Law Institute, an organization of lawyers, judges, and law professors, set out to develop model definitions of crimes, which might help states to organize and standardize their many individual criminal statutes that had developed over the course of the nation's first two centuries of existence. With guidance from legal scholars' commentaries explaining the reasons for the individual provisions within the *Model Penal Code*, as well as observation of actions and experiences in other states, many states revised their criminal statutes in the 1960s and 1970s (Robinson and Dubber, 2007).

Federal and state penal codes often define criminal acts somewhat differently. To find out how a state defines an offense, one must read its penal code; this will give a general idea of which acts are illegal. To understand the court's interpretations of the code, one must analyze the judicial opinions that have sought to clarify the law.

The classification of criminal acts becomes complicated when statutes divide related acts, such as taking a person's life, into different offenses. For example, the definition of *criminal homicide* has been subdivided into degrees of murder and voluntary and involuntary manslaughter. In addition, some states have created new categories, such as reckless homicide, negligent homicide, and vehicular homicide. Each of these definitions involves slight variations in the action taken and the intention underlying the action. Did the individual plan in advance to kill someone, or was the death caused by a careless act by the offender? Table 3.1 shows the definition of offenses used in the Uniform Crime Reports, the measures described in Chapter 2 as one means to track crime rates each year that are available on the FBI's website. Beginning with the UCR issued in 2013, the FBI will use a new, gender-neutral definition of forcible rape that focuses solely on sexual penetration, without regard to whether the victim is female or male (U.S. Department of Justice, 2012). Under criminal homicide, there are important differences between intentional ("willful") homicides, which are labeled as murder and manslaughter deserving of severe punishment, and careless acts ("negligence") that lead to someone's death. These definitions are merely generic examples. Each state's actual statutes can have much more detailed wording to include various specific situations.

Criminal laws must be drafted carefully to define the specific actions and intentions that are regarded as deserving of punishment. Yet judgments must still be made by prosecutors, judges, and juries about whether specific actions occurred and what state of mind or intentions motivated the action. In October 2011, for example, two 12-year-olds pushed a shopping cart off the fourth floor of a parking garage in New York City and it struck a pedestrian on the sidewalk below, leaving her unconscious and suffering with a life-threatening head injury (Robbins, 2011). If the victim had died, would this be a willful killing that should be classified as murder or manslaughter, or was this a careless act that should be classified as negligent homicide?

A close examination of statutes from different states helps to illuminate similarities and differences in statutes and to indicate legislatures' efforts to be precise in their definitions. Compare the statutes defining murder in Idaho and Delaware that follow. You will see that they both emphasize intentional killing as a fundamental characteristic of murder, and that Idaho still uses the traditional phrase "malice aforethought" to mean specific intention. Look closely, however, and take note of the differences in the definitions and what the legislatures chose to emphasize in defining this crime for their states.

TABLE 3.1 Definitions of Offenses in the Uniform Crime Reports (Part I)

The exact descriptions of offenses differ from one state to another, but these UCR definitions provide a national standard that helps us distinguish among criminal acts.

1 Criminal homicide:

    a. Murder and nonnegligent manslaughter: the willful (nonnegligent) killing of one human being by another. Deaths caused by negligence, attempts to kill, assaults to kill, suicides, accidental deaths and justifiable homicides are excluded. Justifiable homicides are limited to (1) the killing of a felon by a law enforcement officer in the line of duty and (2) the killing of a felon by a private citizen.

    b. Manslaughter by negligence: the killing of another person through gross negligence. Excludes traffic fatalities. While manslaughter by negligence is a Part I crime, it is not included in the crime index.

2 Forcible rape*:

The carnal knowledge of a female forcibly and against her will. Included are rapes by force and attempts or assaults to rape. Statutory offenses (no force used—victim under age of consent) are excluded.

3 Robbery:

The taking or attempting to take anything of value from the care, custody, or control of a person or persons by force or threat of force of violence and/or by putting the victim in fear.

4 Aggravated assault:

An unlawful attack by one person upon another for the purpose of inflicting severe or aggravated bodily injury. This type of assault usually is accompanied by the use of a weapon or by means likely to produce death or great bodily harm. Simple assaults are excluded.

5 Burglary—breaking or entering:

The unlawful entry of a structure to commit a felony or a theft. Attempted forcible entry is included.

6 Larceny/theft (except motor vehicle theft):

The unlawful taking, carrying, leading, or riding away of property from the possession or constructive possession of another. Examples are thefts of bicycles or automobile accessories, shoplifting, pocket picking, or the stealing of any property or article that is not taken by force and violence or by fraud. Attempted larcenies are included. Embezzlement, "con" games, forgery, worthless checks, and so on, are excluded.

7 Motor vehicle theft:

The theft or attempted theft of a motor vehicle. A motor vehicle is self-propelled and runs on the surface and not on rails. Specifically excluded from this category are motorboats, construction equipment, airplanes, and farming equipment.

8 Arson:

Any willful or malicious burning or attempt to burn, with or without intent to defraud, a dwelling house, a public building, a motor vehicle or an aircraft, the personal property of another, and so on.

*Note: Beginning with the data collected in 2012 and reported in 2013, the new definition of forcible rape will be: "The penetration, no matter how slight, of the vagina or anus with any body part or object, or oral penetration by a sex organ of another person, without the consent of the victim."

Sources: Federal Bureau of Investigation, *Crime in the United States, 2001* (Washington, DC: U.S. Government Printing Office, 2007); U.S. Department of Justice, "Attorney General Eric Holder Announces Revisions to the Uniform Crime Report's Definition of Rape," Press Release, January 6, 2012 (http://www.fbi.gov).

Idaho Statutes, Title 18, Chapter 40, 18–4001. Murder Defined.

Murder is the unlawful killing of a human being including, but not limited to, a human embryo or fetus, with malice aforethought or the intentional application of torture to a human being, which results in the death of a human being. Torture is the intentional infliction of extreme and prolonged pain with the intent to cause suffering. The death of a human being caused by such torture is murder irrespective of proof of specific intent to kill; torture causing death shall be deemed the equivalent of intent to kill.

As you examine the definition produced by the Idaho legislature, do you see any particular values or policy priorities reflected in the choice of language? Is it possible that highly publicized homicides that occurred in a certain manner may have influenced the legislature's emphasis and choice of words? Now examine the Delaware statute defining murder and ask yourself those same questions.

Delaware Statutes, Title 11, Chapter 5, section 636. Murder in the first degree; class A felony.

A person is guilty of murder in the first degree when:

(1) The person intentionally causes the death of another person; (2) While engaged in the commission of, or attempt to commit, or flight after committing or attempting to

commit any felony, the person recklessly causes the death of another person; (3) The person intentionally causes another person to commit suicide by force or duress; (4) The person recklessly causes the death of a law-enforcement officer, corrections employee, fire fighter, paramedic, emergency medical technician, fire marshal or fire police officer while such officer is in the lawful performance of duties; (5) The person causes the death of another person by use of or detonation of any bomb or similar destructive device; (6) The person causes the death of another person in order to avoid or prevent the lawful arrest of any person, or in the course of and in furtherance of the commission or attempted commission of . . . escape after conviction.

Note that Delaware's legislature identified specific situations in which recklessly causing death would be punished as severely as intentionally causing the death of another person.

Police officers must carefully gather evidence at crime scenes in order to identify the proper suspect and then prove that the suspect actually committed the crime. They seek evidence relevant to each element in the definition of the specific law that was broken. For which crimes do you believe it is most difficult to obtain sufficient evidence to prove a suspect's guilt?

Are there any homicide situations that would clearly be murder in one of these states but would be manslaughter or other lesser degree of homicide in the other state? The examples demonstrate the authority of legislatures in each state to develop the specific definitions of crimes for their own states, including emphases on policy priorities that may not be evident in the statutes of other states.

Elements of a Crime

Legislatures define certain acts as crimes when they fulfill the seven principles under specific "attendant circumstances" while the offender has a certain state of mind. These three factors—the act, the attendant circumstances, and the state of mind or intent—are together called the *elements* of a crime. They can be seen in the following section from a state penal code:

> Section 3502. Burglary 1 Offense defined: A person is guilty of burglary if he enters a building or occupied structure, or separately secured or occupied portion thereof, with intent to commit a crime therein, unless the premises are at the time open to the public or the actor is licensed or privileged to enter.

The elements of burglary are, therefore, entering a building or occupied structure (the act) with the intent to commit a crime therein (state of mind) at a time when the premises are not open to the public and the actor is not invited or otherwise entitled to enter (attendant circumstances). For an act to be a burglary, all three elements must be present.

Although most definitions of crimes focus on specific acts that produce harms to persons or property, some crimes involve specific intentions and plans, even if those plans are never carried out. Obviously, planning is a form of action, but the action itself may never produce a specific harm. Yet that can be the basis for a criminal conviction and punishment. The criminal law includes conspiracies and attempts, even when the lawbreaker does not complete the intended crime (Cahill, 2007a). These are called **inchoate** or **incomplete offenses**. For example, people can be prosecuted for planning to murder someone or hiring a "hit man" to kill someone. The potential for grave harm from such acts justifies the application of the government's power to punish.

inchoate or **incomplete offenses** Conduct that is criminal even though the harm that the law seeks to prevent has not been done but merely planned or attempted.

Figure 3.1

The Seven Principles of Criminal Law These principles of Western law provide the basis for defining acts as criminal and the conditions required for successful prosecution.

© Cengage Learning

A crime is	
1 legally proscribed	(legality)
2 human conduct	(*actus reus*)
3 causative	(causation)
4 of a given harm	(harm)
5 which conduct coincides	(concurrence)
6 with a blameworthy frame of mind	(*mens rea*)
7 and is subject to punishment	(punishment)

Seven Principles of Criminal Law

In analyzing the definitions of crimes and the elements necessary to lead to conviction and punishment, legal scholar Jerome Hall (1947) summarized the major principles of Western criminal law that must be present. To convict a defendant of a crime, prosecutors must prove that all seven principles have been fulfilled (see Figure 3.1).

1. *Legality.* There must be a law that defines the specific action as a crime. Offensive and harmful behavior is not illegal unless it has been prohibited by law before it was committed. The U.S. Constitution forbids *ex post facto laws,* or laws written and applied after the fact. Thus, when the legislature defines a new crime, people can be prosecuted only for violations that occur after the new law has been passed.

2. *Actus reus.* Criminal laws are aimed at human acts, including acts that a person failed to undertake. The U.S. Supreme Court has ruled that people may not be convicted of a crime simply because of their status. Under this *actus reus* requirement, for a crime to occur there must be an act of either commission or omission by the accused. In *Robinson v. California* (1962), for example, the Supreme Court struck down a California law that made being addicted to drugs a crime. States can prosecute people for using, possessing, selling, or transporting drugs when they catch them performing these acts, but states cannot prosecute them for the mere status of being addicted to drugs.

3. *Causation.* For a crime to have been committed, there must be a causal relationship between an act and the harm suffered. In Ohio, for example, a prosecutor tried to convict a burglary suspect on a manslaughter charge when a victim, asleep in his house, was killed by a stray bullet as officers fired at the unarmed, fleeing suspect. The burglar was acquitted on the homicide charge because his actions in committing the burglary and running away from the police were not the direct cause of the victim's death (Bandy, 1991).

4. *Harm.* To be a crime, an act must cause harm to some legally protected value. The harm can be to a person, property, or some other object that a legislature deems valuable enough to deserve protection through the government's power to punish. This principle is often questioned by those who feel that they are not committing a crime, because they may be causing harm only to themselves. Laws that require motorcyclists to wear helmets have been challenged on this ground. Such laws, however, have been written because legislatures see enough forms of harm to require protective laws. These forms of harm include injuries to helmetless riders, tragedy and loss for families of injured cyclists, and the medical costs imposed on society for head injuries that could have been prevented.

5. *Concurrence.* For an act to be considered a crime, the intent and the act must be present at the same time (J. Hall, 1947). Let us imagine that Joe is planning to murder his archenemy, Bill. He spends days planning how he will abduct Bill and carry out the murder. While driving home from work one day, Joe accidentally hits and kills a jogger who suddenly—and foolishly—runs across the busy street without looking. The jogger turns out to be Bill. Although Joe

had planned to kill Bill, he is not guilty of murder, because the accidental killing was not connected to Joe's intent to carry out a killing.

6. *Mens rea.* The commission of an act is not a crime unless it is accompanied by a guilty state of mind. This concept is related to intent. It seeks to distinguish between harm-causing accidents, which generally are not subject to criminal punishment, and harm-causing crimes, in which some level of intent is present. As discussed previously, certain crimes require a specific level of intent; examples include first-degree murder, which is normally a planned, intentional killing, and larceny, which involves the intent to deprive an owner of his or her property permanently and unlawfully. Later in this chapter we examine several defenses, such as necessity and insanity, that can be used to assert that a person did not have **mens rea**—"guilty mind" or blameworthy state of mind— and hence should not be held responsible for a criminal offense. The element of *mens rea* becomes problematic when there are questions about an offender's capacity to understand or plan harmful activities, as when the perpetrator is mentally ill or a child. The defense attorneys in Chad Gurney's murder case, described at the beginning of the chapter, sought to attack the *mens rea* element by claiming he was legally insane at the time that the crime was committed.

mens rea "Guilty mind" or blameworthy state of mind, necessary for legal responsibility for a criminal offense; criminal intent, as distinguished from innocent intent.

Exceptions to the concept of *mens rea* are strict liability offenses involving health and safety, in which it is not necessary to show intent. Legislatures have criminalized certain kinds of offenses in order to protect the public. For example, a business owner may be held responsible for violations of a toxic-waste law whether or not the owner actually knew that his employees were dumping pollutants into a river. Other laws may apply strict liability to the sale of alcoholic beverages to minors. The purpose of such laws is to put pressure on business owners to make sure that their employees obey regulations designed to protect the health and safety of the public. Courts often limit the application of such laws to situations in which recklessness or indifference is present.

7. *Punishment.* There must be a provision in the law calling for punishment of those found guilty of violating the law. The punishment is enforced by the government and may carry with it social stigma, a criminal record, loss of freedom, and loss of rights.

The seven principles of substantive criminal law allow authorities to define certain acts as being against the law and provide the accused with a basis for mounting a defense against the charges. During a criminal trial, defense attorneys will often try to show that one of the seven elements either is unproved or can be explained in a way that is acceptable under the law. Read the Careers in Criminal Justice box about Denver criminal defense attorney Abraham Hutt and consider the important role played by such attorneys in seeking to make sure that only truly guilty defendants are convicted and punished.

Defenses against Criminal Charges

Defendants' attorneys can use several defenses to seek to avoid criminal convictions in cases for which defendants actually committed the acts proscribed by criminal law. These defenses are traditionally divided into justifications and excuses (Samaha, 2011). Justifications focus on the act and whether the act was socially acceptable under the circumstances. Justifications are actions based on self-defense or necessity in which the individual reasonably felt obligated to cause harm, but the actions were those that are recognized and accepted by society as essential to the individual's self-preservation. Excuses focus on the actor and whether the actor fulfilled the elements required for being held responsible under a criminal statute. Excuses are defenses that under specific circumstances either eliminate (e.g., insanity) or diminish (e.g., intoxication) criminal responsibility because the individual did not possess the knowledge, state of mind, or intent required for a criminal conviction (Milhizer, 2004).

As indicated by these general descriptions of justifications and excuses, of the seven principles of criminal law, *mens rea* is crucial in establishing responsibility

Criminal Defense Attorney

Abraham V. Hutt, Criminal Defense Attorney,
Private Practice, Denver, Colorado

Photo provided by Abraham V. Hutt. © Cengage Learning

Defense attorneys must interview their clients and relevant witnesses when hired by a defendant or appointed by a court to handle criminal cases. These interviews may occur under difficult circumstances in jails or on street corners in tough neighborhoods. Defense attorneys must find all relevant evidence and evaluate that evidence in anticipation of how the prosecution will present its version of the case. They spend a significant amount of time in offices doing legal research, preparing legal documents, and reviewing legal papers. They also must appear in court to represent their clients at hearings where bail is set and judges consider whether there is sufficient evidence for a case to move forward. Defense attorneys discuss possible plea agreements with prosecutors. Occasionally, one of their cases will move through the entire justice process and become the subject of a trial. In the courtroom, defense attorneys present arguments and evidence to show the weaknesses in the prosecution's case.

When a guilty verdict is issued, they may continue to represent their clients in the appeals process.

To become a lawyer in the United States, people must earn a four-year college degree in any subject before going to law school for three years of postgraduate study. Gaining admission to law school is a competitive process, so people interested in legal careers must work hard during college, earn good grades, and gain good scores on the Law School Admissions Test (LSAT). After graduating from law school, prospective lawyers must pass a state's bar exam in order to receive a license to practice law. Each state has its own bar exam, which typically lasts two days. A separate ethics exam may also be required. In most states, one day is devoted to a six-hour multiple-choice test on six subjects that are common to all states (contract, criminal, tort, evidence, property, and constitutional law). The other day involves six hours of essays on 12 or more subjects focused on state law, including business associations, taxation, and family law.

During college, Abraham Hutt spent two summers as an intern with the Colorado State Public Defender's Office, where he worked as an investigator interviewing witnesses and helping lawyers prepare to represent defendants who were too poor to hire their own attorneys. For one year after college, he worked as an investigator for a former public defender who became a private-practice attorney, representing criminal defendants who could afford to pay for legal representation. Hutt then went to law school for three years, passed the Colorado bar exam, and worked in a small law firm that specialized in criminal defense. Eventually, he started his own law firm that focused on criminal cases.

In preparing for a trial, a defense attorney is obligated to question the prosecutor's version of events and the truthfulness of any witness whose testimony is disputed by the accused. . . . Members of the public often erroneously believe that the defense attorney's goal is to prevent guilty people from receiving the punishment that they deserve. In fact, our adversarial justice system relies on defense attorneys to make sure that all mitigating information about the accused and his or her circumstances are made known to the prosecutor and the court and to require that prosecutors are actually able to prove that defendants are guilty beyond a reasonable doubt with lawfully obtained evidence. Our system is based on the principle that any person the government accuses of a crime is entitled to the assistance of a legal counselor and advocate who will stand up in that person's defense, no matter how harsh the accusations or how troubled the person's background. Without defense attorneys, the fundamental human dignity of many accused people would regularly be trampled by the system. . . . Similarly, without defense attorneys there would be no check or balance to the power of prosecutors and judges and no one to ensure that prosecutors follow the law and courts respect the constitutional rights of people drawn into the criminal justice process.

for the act. To obtain a conviction, the prosecution must show that the offender not only committed the illegal act but also did so in a state of mind that makes it appropriate to hold him or her responsible for the act. In 2011, two Indiana boys pleaded guilty in the shooting death of the older boy's stepfather. The 15-year-old received a 30-year prison sentence and his 12-year-old accomplice was sentenced to 25 years (R. Green, 2011). Were these young boys old enough to plan their crimes and understand the consequences of their actions? Is a child capable of forming the same intent to commit a crime that an adult can form? The analysis of *mens rea* is

Criminal Intent and the Appropriateness of Punishment

In 2009, an 18-year-old in Ohio was accused of beating his mother so badly that she died a few days later from internal injuries. Is this a clear-cut case of criminal responsibility? The suspect is an adult whose intentional violent actions caused a death. In this case, however, the suspect has autism. He has a limited ability to communicate, using specific words and phrases that only his mother understood. In his jail cell, the deputies positioned a television set just outside the bars and played recordings of *The Price Is Right* over and over again because watching his favorite show kept him calm. Friends and relatives were permitted to bring barbecue potato chips, McDonald's Happy Meals, and items from his bedroom at home as jail officials, lawyers, and judges tried to determine how best to detain him safely as judicial processes moved forward to decide whether he was competent to stand trial.

In Arizona in 2008, an eight-year-old boy shot his father and another man at point-blank range with a hunting rifle that his father had given him for his birthday. He stopped and reloaded as he shot each victim at least four times. He was charged with premeditated murder. Some news reports indicated that the boy was tired of being spanked by his father. Was this an intentional act of homicide? Apparently, yes. But should a child so young be held criminally responsible in the same manner as an adult?

In South Carolina, a 12-year-old boy walked into his grandparents' bedroom one night and killed them with two blasts of a shotgun as they slept. He was a troubled boy who lived with his grandparents because he had been abandoned by his mother and had serious conflicts with his father. At the time, he was taking an antidepressant medication prescribed by doctors—but one that cannot be prescribed for teenagers in some countries because it is known to affect thinking and behavior, and carries a risk of suicide. Could the medication have affected his thinking so that he actually did not have the requisite intent to commit the crime? Did he really know what he was doing that night?

All three of these examples raise serious questions about how we evaluate *mens rea* and determine whether someone is capable of forming criminal intent. Advances in modern science affect such situations. For example, the development and use of new medications may lead to unintended consequences for people's clarity of thought and control over their own actions. In addition, greater understanding of mental conditions and neuroscience—the science of the brain and thinking—may help us analyze the capabilities of people with specific medical conditions. Yet there will always be difficult decisions to be made.

In Ohio, a judge ordered the autistic homicide suspect be moved from the jail to a state residential facility for developmentally disabled people while the court system decided whether he should stand trial. The boy in Arizona was eventually permitted to plead guilty to one count of negligent homicide instead of facing trial on two counts of first-degree murder. He was ordered to remain under the custody and supervision of the state until age 18, with further determinations to be made about whether he should live in a juvenile detention facility, be sent to a treatment facility, be placed with foster parents, or be permitted to live with his mother. If he stayed out of trouble until age 18, his record would be expunged.

By contrast, the South Carolina boy, Christopher Pittman, was unsuccessful in challenging the *mens rea* element of the crime by pointing to the effects of his medication. He was sentenced to 30 years in prison for murder. The U.S. Supreme Court declined to hear his appeal.

Researching the Internet
To read about other cases that raise issues concerning *mens rea*, including cases that use the insanity defense, visit the Criminal Justice CourseMate at cengagebrain.com, then access the web links for this chapter.

For Critical Analysis
What rule could we formulate that would guide us in determining which individuals were capable of forming criminal intent and are deserving of punishment? Alternatively, how could we use a case-by-case approach effectively to analyze the capability of each defendant? Would we advance the goal of justice by thinking about appropriate treatment instead of punishment when such questions arise about a defendant? What would you decide about each of the three defendants profiled here? Write a memo detailing how each of the three defendants should have been punished and/or given treatment.

Sources: *Akron Beacon Journal*, "Son of Late KSU Professor Sent to State Facility," March 27, 2009 (http://www.ohio.com); Associated Press, "Autistic Murder Defendant Poses Challenges," March 19, 2009 (http://www.msnbc.com); articles from the *New York Times* (http://www.nytimes.com): S. Dewan and B. Meier, "Boy Who Took Antidepressants Is Convicted in Killings," February 15, 2005; J. Dougherty and A. O'Connor, "Prosecutors Say Boy Methodically Shot His Father," November 11, 2008; S. Moore, "Boy, 9, Enters a Guilty Plea in 2 Killings in Arizona," February 20, 2009.

difficult because the court must inquire into the defendant's mental state at the time the offense was committed. It is not easy to know what someone was thinking when he or she performed an act. Moreover, as discussed in the Close Up box, factors such as age, the effects of medications, and specific medical conditions can complicate the task of deciding whether someone acted with the intent necessary to deserve criminal punishment.

Although many defendants admit that they committed the harmful act, they may still plead not guilty. They may do so not only because they know that the state must prove them guilty but also because they—or their attorneys—believe that *mens rea* was not present. Accidents are the clearest examples of such situations: The defendant argues that it was an accident that the pedestrian suddenly crossed into the path of the car.

The absence of *mens rea,* as we have seen, does not guarantee a verdict of not guilty in every case. In most cases, however, it relieves defendants of responsibility for acts that would be labeled criminal if they had been intentional. Besides the defense of accidents, there are eight defenses based on lack of criminal intent: self-defense, necessity, duress (coercion), entrapment, infancy, mistake of fact, intoxication, and insanity. These defenses are often divided into two categories, justifications and excuses.

Justification Defenses

Justification defenses focus on whether the individual's action was socially acceptable under the circumstances despite causing a harm that the criminal law would otherwise seek to prevent.

Self-Defense   A person who feels that he or she is in immediate danger of being harmed by another person may ward off the attack in *self-defense.* The laws of most states also recognize the right to defend others from attack, to protect property, and to prevent a crime. For example, in August 2002, T. J. Duckett, an African American football player for the NFL's Seattle Seahawks, was attacked by three white men who also yelled racial slurs at him as he walked toward his car after a concert. After Duckett lost a tooth and suffered a cut that required four stitches when he was struck with a bottle in the surprise attack, the 250-pound running back defended himself. He knocked one attacker unconscious and caused a second attacker to be hospitalized with injuries. The third attacker ran away. The attackers received the most serious injuries, yet they faced criminal charges because Duckett was entitled to defend himself with reasonable force against an unprovoked criminal assault (Winkeljohn, 2002).

The level of force used in self-defense cannot exceed the person's reasonable perception of the threat (K. W. Simons, 2008). Thus, a person may be justified in shooting a robber who is holding a gun to her head and threatening to kill her, but homeowners generally are not justified in shooting an unarmed burglar who has left the house and is running across the lawn.

Necessity   Unlike self-defense, in which a defendant feels that he or she must harm an aggressor to ward off an attack, the *necessity* defense is used when people break the law in order to save themselves or prevent some greater harm. A person who speeds through a red light to get an injured child to the hospital or breaks into a building to seek refuge from a hurricane could claim to be violating the law out of necessity.

In 2011, for example, a man in San Francisco was acquitted on charges of illegally carrying a concealed weapon when the jury heard that he borrowed the handgun in order to retrieve his niece's baby food from a car while visiting a housing project in a high-crime neighborhood where he had previously been robbed ("Man Acquitted," 2011). The jury accepted the necessity of his conduct, which under other circumstances, would have provided the basis for a criminal conviction.

Excuse Defenses

Excuse defenses focus on the actor and whether he or she possessed the knowledge or intent needed for a criminal conviction.

Duress (Coercion)   The defense of *duress* arises when someone commits a crime because he or she is coerced by another person. During a bank robbery, for instance, if an armed robber forces one of the bank's customers at gunpoint to drive the getaway car, the customer would be able to claim duress. However, courts generally are not willing to accept this defense if people do not try to escape from the situation.

Entrapment Entrapment is a defense that can be used to show lack of intent. The law excuses a defendant when it is shown that government agents have induced the person to commit the offense. That does not mean the police may not use undercover agents to set a trap for criminals, nor does it mean the police may not provide ordinary opportunities for the commission of a crime. But the entrapment defense may be used when the police have acted so as to induce the criminal act.

Entrapment raises tough questions for judges, who must decide whether the police went too far toward making a crime occur that otherwise would not have happened (Carlon, 2007). The key question is the predisposition of the defendant. In 1992 the Supreme Court stressed that the prosecutor must show beyond a reasonable doubt that a defendant was predisposed to break the law before he or she was approached by government agents. The Court's decision invalidated the conviction of a Nebraska farmer who purchased child pornography after receiving multiple solicitation letters from law enforcement officials pretending to be pen pals and bookstore operators (*United States v. Jacobson*).

AP Images/Fred Beckham, pool

In 2011, a three-judge panel in Connecticut found Stephen Morgan to be "not guilty by reason of insanity" for first-degree murder charges after he stalked and shot a female student in the Wesleyan University bookstore. The judges ordered that he be committed to a secure psychiatric facility. Should people with severe mental problems who kill others receive psychiatric treatment rather than the full punishment of a prison sentence?

entrapment The defense that the individual was induced by the police to commit the criminal act.

Infancy Anglo American law excuses criminal acts by children under age seven on the grounds of their *infancy* and lack of responsibility for their actions—*mens rea* is not present. Also called *immaturity*, this excuse is based on the recognition that young children do not yet have the capacity to think about and understand appropriate behavior and the consequences of their actions. Common law has presumed that children aged 7–14 are not liable for their criminal acts; however, prosecutors have been able to present evidence of a child's mental capacity to form *mens rea*. Juries can assume the presence of a guilty mind if it can be shown, for example, that the child hid evidence or tried to bribe a witness. As a child grows older, the assumption of immaturity weakens. Since the development of juvenile courts in the 1890s, children generally have been tried using rules that are different from those applied to adults. In some situations, however, children may be tried as adults—if, for example, they are repeat offenders or are charged with a particularly heinous crime. Because of the public's concerns about violent crimes by young people, in the 1990s it became increasingly common to see prosecutors seek to hold children responsible for serious crimes in the same manner that adults are held responsible. As mentioned in the "Close Up" on page 83, in 2008 the U.S. Supreme Court declined to hear an appeal from Christopher Pittman, who, as a 12-year-old, killed his grandparents, was tried as an adult, and was sentenced to 30 years.

Mistake of Fact The courts have generally upheld the view that ignorance of the law is no excuse for committing an illegal act. But what if there is a *mistake of fact*? If an accused person has made a mistake on some crucial fact, that may serve as a defense (Christopher, 1994). For example, suppose some teenagers ask your permission to grow sunflowers in a vacant lot behind your home. You help them weed the garden and water the plants. Then it turns out that they are growing marijuana. You were not aware of this because you have no idea what a marijuana plant looks like. Should you be convicted for growing an illegal drug on your property? The answer depends on the specific degree of knowledge and intent that the prosecution must prove for that offense. The success of such a defense may also depend on the extent to which jurors understand and sympathize with your mistake.

For example, in 2008 a college professor attending a professional baseball game bought his seven-year-old son a bottle of "lemonade." Because he and his family seldom watch television, however, he had no idea that "hard lemonade" even existed. Thus, he made a mistake of fact by purchasing an alcoholic beverage for his underage son. When police officers spotted the child drinking the beverage, the boy was taken from the custody of his parents for a few days until officials decided that it was an unintentional mistake. If prosecutors had pursued criminal charges against the professor, his fate would have depended on whether the jury believed his claim of making an ignorant mistake of fact in purchasing the alcoholic "lemonade" for a child (Dickerson, 2008).

Intoxication   The law does not relieve an individual of responsibility for acts performed while voluntarily intoxicated. There are, however, cases in which *intoxication* can be used as a defense, as when a person has been tricked into consuming a substance without knowing that it may cause intoxication. Christopher Pittman's attorney attempted unsuccessfully to use this defense by arguing that the boy's prescribed antidepressant drugs caused his violent behavior. Other complex cases arise in which the defendant must be shown to have had a specific, rather than a general, intent to commit a crime. For example, people may claim that they were too drunk to realize that they had left a restaurant without paying the bill. Drunkenness can also be used as a mitigating factor to reduce the seriousness of a charge.

In 1996, the U.S. Supreme Court narrowly approved a Montana law that barred the use of evidence of intoxication, even for defendants who claimed that their condition prevented them from forming the specific intent necessary to be guilty of a crime (*Montana v. Egelhoff*). Thus, states may enact laws that prevent the use of an intoxication defense.

Insanity   The defense of *insanity* has been a subject of heated debate. It is available in all but four states (Idaho, Montana, Nevada, and Utah). The public believes that many criminals "escape" punishment through the skillful use of psychiatric testimony. Yet, less than 1 percent of incarcerated offenders are held in mental hospitals because they were found "not guilty by reason of insanity." The insanity defense is rare and is generally used only in serious cases or where there is no other valid defense.

Over time, U.S. courts have used five tests of criminal responsibility involving insanity: the *M'Naghten* Rule, the Irresistible Impulse Test, the *Durham* Rule, the *Model Penal Code*'s Substantial Capacity Test, and the test defined in the federal Comprehensive Crime Control Act of 1984. These tests are summarized in Table 3.2. One important feature of the insanity defense is the opportunity for state and federal laws to impose on defendants the burden of demonstrating their mental capacity. The prosecution bears the burden of proving the defendant's guilt beyond a reasonable doubt, but the Supreme Court has said laws "may place the burden of persuasion on a defendant to prove insanity as the applicable law defines it, whether by a preponderance of the evidence or to some more convincing degree" (*Clark v. Arizona*, 2006). Thus, if the defendant raises an insanity defense in a case, the law of that jurisdiction will dictate whether the defendant must present evidence to persuade the judge or jury about his or her insanity, or whether the prosecutor must prove that the defendant did not fit the legal definition of insanity at the time of the crime.

***M'Naghten* Rule**   More than a dozen states use the *M'Naghten* Rule, which was developed in England in 1843. In that year Daniel M'Naghten was acquitted of killing Edward Drummond, a man he had thought was Sir Robert Peel, the prime minister of Great Britain. M'Naghten claimed that he had been delusional at the time of the killing. The British court developed a standard for determining criminal responsibility known as the "right-from-wrong test." It asks whether "at the time of the committing of the act, the party accused was laboring under such a defect of reason, from disease of the mind, as not to know the nature and quality of the act he was doing, or if he did know it that he did not know he was doing what was wrong" (*M'Naghten's Case*, 1843).

TABLE 3.2 Insanity Defense Standards

The standards for the insanity defense have evolved over time.

Test	Legal Standard Because of Mental Illness
M'Naghten (1843)	"Didn't know what he was doing or didn't know it was wrong."
Irresistible Impulse (1897)	"Could not control his conduct."
Durham (1954)	"The criminal act was caused by his mental illness."
Model Penal Code (1972)	"Lacks substantial capacity to appreciate the wrongfulness of his conduct or to control it."
Comprehensive Crime Control Act	"Lacks capacity to appreciate the wrongfulness of his conduct."

Source: National Institute of Justice, *Crime File*, "Insanity Defense," a film prepared by Norval Morris (Washington, DC: U.S. Government Printing Office, n.d.).

Irresistible Impulse Test Four states supplemented the *M'Naghten* Rule with the Irresistible Impulse Test. Because psychiatrists argued that some people can feel compelled by their mental illness to commit criminal actions even though they recognize the wrongfulness of their conduct, the Irresistible Impulse Test was designed to bring the *M'Naghten* Rule in line with modern psychiatry. This test excuses defendants when a mental disease was controlling their behavior even though they knew that what they were doing was wrong.

Durham Rule The *Durham* Rule, originally developed in New Hampshire in 1871, was adopted by the Circuit Court of Appeals for the District of Columbia in 1954 in the case of *Durham v. United States.* Under this rule, the accused is not criminally responsible "if an unlawful act is the product of mental disease or mental defect."

Model Penal Code's Substantial Capacity Test It was argued that the *Durham* Rule offered no useful definition of "mental disease or defect." By 1972 (*United States v. Brawner*), the federal courts had overturned the *Durham* Rule in favor of a modified version of a test proposed in the *Model Penal Code* (a penal code developed by the American Bar Association as a model of what "should" be). By 1982, all federal courts and about half of the state courts had adopted the *Model Penal Code's* Substantial Capacity Test, which states that a person is not responsible for criminal conduct "if at the time of such conduct as a result of mental disease or defect he lacks substantial capacity either to appreciate the criminality [wrongfulness] of his conduct or to conform his conduct to the requirements of law." The Substantial Capacity Test broadens and modifies the *M'Naghten* and Irresistible Impulse rules. By stressing "substantial capacity," the test does not require that a defendant be unable to distinguish right from wrong.

In Chad Gurney's case, discussed in the opening of the chapter, Maine law required Gurney to persuade the judge that, in accordance with the Substantial Capacity test, "Gurney was psychotic at the time of the killing, was severely delusional and he lacked the capacity to understand the consequences of his actions" (T. Maxwell, 2011). The judge was not persuaded by Gurney's attorney to rule in favor of this argument.

Comprehensive Crime Control Act The Comprehensive Crime Control Act of 1984 changed the federal rules on the insanity defense by limiting it to those who are unable, as a result of severe mental disease or defect, to understand the nature or wrongfulness of their acts. This change means that the Irresistible Impulse Test cannot be used in the federal courts. It also shifts the burden of proof from the prosecutor to the defendant, who has to prove his or her insanity. Further, the act creates a new procedure whereby a person who is found not guilty only by reason of insanity must be committed to a mental hospital until he or she no longer poses a danger to society. These rules apply only in federal courts, but they are spreading to the states.

All of the insanity tests are difficult to apply. Moreover, deciding what to do with someone who has been found not guilty by reason of insanity poses significant difficulties. Finally, jurors' fears about seeing the offender turned loose might affect their decisions about whether the person was legally insane at the time of the crime.

John Hinckley's attempt to assassinate President Ronald Reagan in 1981 reopened the debate on the insanity defense. Television news footage showed that Hinckley had shot the president. Yet, with the help of psychiatrists, Hinckley's lawyers counteracted the prosecution's efforts to persuade the jury that Hinckley was sane. When Hinckley was acquitted, the public was outraged, and several states acted to limit or abolish the insanity defense. Twelve states introduced the defense of "guilty but mentally ill" (Klofas and Yandrasits, 1989:424). This defense allows a jury to find the accused guilty but requires that he or she be given psychiatric treatment while in prison (L. A. Callahan et al., 1992).

check point

3. **What are the seven principles of criminal law?**
   Legality, *actus reus,* causation, harm, concurrence, *mens rea,* and punishment.

4. **What are the defenses in substantive criminal law?**
   Self-defense, necessity, duress (coercion), entrapment, infancy, mistake of fact, intoxication, insanity.

5. **What are the tests of criminal responsibility used for the insanity defense?**
   M'Naghten Rule (right-from-wrong test), Irresistible Impulse Test, *Durham* Rule, *Model Penal Code,* Comprehensive Crime Control Act.

stop & analyze

Look through the list of justification and excuse defenses and choose one that is the *least* important or necessary. Make three arguments for abolishing that defense. What would be the risks and consequences of abolishing the defense? What is the strongest argument in favor of keeping it?

Procedural Criminal Law

Procedural law defines how the state must process cases. According to procedural due process, accused persons must be tried in accordance with legal procedures. The procedures include providing the rights granted by the Constitution to criminal defendants. As we saw in Chapter 1, the due process model is based on the premise that freedom is so valuable that efforts must be made to prevent erroneous decisions that would deprive an innocent person of his or her freedom. Rights are not only intended to prevent the innocent from being wrongly convicted. They also seek to prevent unfair police and prosecution practices aimed at guilty people, such as conducting improper searches, using violence to pressure people to confess, and denying defendants a fair trial.

The importance of procedural law has been evident throughout history. U.S. history contains many examples of police officers and prosecutors harassing and victimizing those who lack political power, including poor people, racial and ethnic minorities, and unpopular religious groups. The development of procedural safeguards through the decisions of the U.S. Supreme Court has helped protect citizens from such actions. In these decisions, the Supreme Court may favor guilty people by ordering new trials or may even release them from custody because of the weight it places on protecting procedural rights and preventing police misconduct.

Individual rights and the protection against improper deprivations of liberty represent central elements of American values. Americans expect that their rights will be protected. At the same time, however, the protection of rights for the criminally accused can clash with competing American values that emphasize the control of crime as an important component of protecting all citizens' freedom of movement and sense of security. Because the rules of procedural criminal law can sometimes lead to the release of guilty people, some observers regard them as weighted too heavily in favor of American values emphasizing individual rights rather than equally valid American values that emphasize the protection of the community.

Public opinion does not always support the decisions by the Supreme Court and other courts that uphold the rights of criminal defendants and convicted offenders. Many Americans would prefer if other goals for society, such as stopping crime and ensuring that guilty people are punished, took a higher priority over the protection of rights. Such opinions raise questions about Americans' commitment to the rights described in the Bill of Rights. Public-opinion data indicate that most first-year college students believe that courts have placed too much emphasis on the rights of criminal defendants. This view, while reduced since 1998, remains stronger than in 1971. Although male and female students' support for rights differed in 1971, there is less difference between the two groups in later years (see "What Americans Think"). Do you agree that there are too many rights?

Unlike substantive criminal law, which is defined by legislatures through statutes, procedural criminal law is defined by courts through judicial rulings. Judges interpret the provisions of the U.S. Constitution and state constitutions, and those interpretations

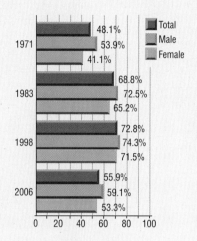

Percentage of first-year college students who agree with the statement "There is too much concern in the courts for the rights of criminals."

Critical Thinking: Can you identify specific rights that give too much protection to criminal defendants? Would there be any risks from reducing the rights available in the criminal justice process?

Source: Bureau of Justice Statistics, *Sourcebook of Criminal Justice Statistics Online* (http://www.albany.edu/sourcebook/), Table 2.92.2006.

establish the procedures that government officials must follow. Because it has the authority to review cases from state supreme courts as well as from federal courts, the U.S. Supreme Court has played a major role in defining procedural criminal law. The Supreme Court's influence stems from its power to define the meaning of the U.S. Constitution, especially the Bill of Rights—the first ten amendments to the Constitution, which list legal protections against actions of the government. Although public opinion may clash with Supreme Court rulings, the Supreme Court can make independent decisions because its appointed members cannot be removed from office by the voters but only through impeachment for misconduct.

The Bill of Rights and the Fourteenth Amendment

The U.S. Constitution contained few references to criminal justice when it was ratified in 1788 and 1789. Because many people were concerned that the document did not set forth the rights of individuals in enough detail, ten amendments were added in 1791. These first ten amendments are known as the **Bill of Rights**. American students typically gain exposure to the provisions of the Bill of Rights through required high school classes on civics and American government. Thus many Americans know that rights concerning free speech and religion are contained in the First Amendment. Because of public debates about its meaning, many Americans also know that the Second Amendment contains the phrase "the right of the people to keep and bear arms, shall not be infringed." The details of the other numbered amendments are often not as familiar because they tend to receive less attention in politicians' speeches and news media articles. As described in The Policy Debate feature, the Second Amendment is one of several amendments in the Bill of Rights that has implications for criminal

Bill of Rights The first ten amendments added to the U.S. Constitution to provide specific rights for individuals, including criminal justice rights concerning searches, trials, and punishments.

The first Congress debated and approved the Bill of Rights, the first ten amendments to the U.S. Constitution. These amendments provided protections for suspects and defendants in the federal criminal justice process. Decisions by the U.S. Supreme Court later applied these protections to state court criminal cases, too. What might the American criminal justice system look like if it lacked the procedural rights provided by the Bill of Rights?

JOHN ADAMS. MORRIS. HAMILTON. JEFFERSON.
LEADERS OF THE CONTINENTAL CONGRESS.

justice. However, the Second Amendment is not one of the four amendments that directly concern procedural criminal law. Instead, it is at the heart of debates about criminal justice policies that are shaped by judges' interpretations of the Constitution, scholars' studies of crime and violence, interest groups' beliefs about constitutional rights, and legislators' decisions about needed laws.

Procedural criminal law is shaped by four specific amendments in the Bill of Rights, as well as by the Fourteenth Amendment, which was created in 1868 after the Civil War. The Fourth Amendment bars unreasonable searches and seizures. The Fifth Amendment outlines basic due process rights in criminal cases. For example, consistent with the assumption that the state must prove the defendant's guilt, protection against **self-incrimination** means that persons cannot be forced to respond to questions whose answers may reveal that they have committed a crime. The protection against **double jeopardy** means that a person may be subjected to only one prosecution or punishment for a single offense within the same jurisdiction. The Sixth Amendment provides for the right to a speedy, fair, and public trial by an impartial jury, as well as the right to counsel. The Eighth Amendment bars excessive bail, excessive fines, and cruel and unusual punishments.

The texts of these four procedural criminal law amendments in the Bill of Rights are included here. Refer back to these as you read the sections that follow. The first ten amendments were ratified on December 15, 1791. The Fourteenth Amendment, which was ratified on July 28, 1868, also impacts procedural criminal law by providing rights to due process and equal protection of the laws. Unlike these four amendments that are primarily concerned with criminal justice, the Fourteenth Amendment also applies to a variety of other contexts, such as prohibiting racial discrimination in public schools and other government facilities and programs.

Fourth Amendment: The right of the people to be secure in their persons, houses, papers, and effects, against unreasonable searches and seizures, shall not be violated, and no Warrants shall issue, but upon probable cause, supported by Oath or affirmation, and particularly describing the place to be searched, and the persons or things to be seized.

Fifth Amendment: No person shall be held to answer for a capital or otherwise infamous crime, unless on a presentment or indictment of a Grand Jury, except in cases arising in

self-incrimination The act of exposing oneself to prosecution by being forced to respond to questions when the answers may reveal that one has committed a crime. The Fifth Amendment protects defendants against compelled self-incrimination.

double jeopardy The subjecting of a person to prosecution more than once in the same jurisdiction for the same offense; prohibited by the Fifth Amendment.

Should Ex-Felons' Gun Ownership Rights Be Restored?

In 2009, more than 729,000 people were released from American prisons and returned to their home communities. The number of ex-felons gaining release is increasing as states seek ways to reduce the expense of imprisonment. It is much less expensive to have offenders under parole supervision in the community than it is to incarcerate them. These releases coincide with two developments. First, because of attention to voting rights for ex-offenders, there has been a political push to restore all constitutional rights for ex-offenders after they successfully complete their prison sentences and parole supervision within the community. Second, the U.S. Supreme Court issued decisions declaring that the Second Amendment grants to individuals the right to own handguns in their homes for personal protection (*District of Columbia v. Heller,* 2008) and that this Second Amendment right should limit gun regulations imposed by cities and states as well as the federal government (*McDonald v. Chicago,* 2010). As a result, debates have emerged about whether gun-ownership rights should be restored for ex-felons. Proponents argue that ex-felons should have their gun rights restored, especially those who face daily dangers from living in high-crime neighborhoods and therefore need the necessary means to protect themselves and their families.

For Restoring Gun-Ownership Rights for Ex-Felons

Supporters of the restoration of gun-ownership rights focus on the fact that ex-offenders who have completed their punishment should be reintegrated into the community, recognized as equal citizens, and permitted to rebuild their lives with full citizenship rights.

The arguments for restoring gun-ownership rights are these:

- Ex-offenders have completed their punishment and need to be regarded as full and equal citizens in order to be reintegrated into the society.
- Many ex-offenders live in high-crime neighborhoods and they need to be able to protect their homes and families.
- Gun ownership is a basic right guaranteed for all Americans by the Second Amendment.
- States that have enacted laws to expand opportunities for citizens to possess and carry guns have not experienced increases in crime rates as a result.

Against Restoring Gun-Ownership Rights for Ex-Felons

Opponents of restoration of gun-ownership rights raise concerns about permitting the possession of firearms for people whose past behavior demonstrated that they lacked self-control, acted in a violent manner, or otherwise failed to obey society's rules. As a result, there would be grave risks of additional shootings and homicides that might have been prevented by barring ex-felons from owning guns or approving gun ownership on an individual case-by-case basis.

The arguments against permitting ex-felons to own guns are these:

- The Second Amendment does not guarantee gun rights for all Americans; the Supreme Court's decision specifically said: "nothing in our opinion should be taken to cast doubt on longstanding prohibitions on the possession of firearms by felons and the mentally ill."
- Congress and state legislatures can enact reasonable restrictions on gun ownership by specific categories of people as long as they do not prohibit handguns kept in the homes of people with established records of being law-abiding citizens.
- In states that require restoration of gun-ownership rights, there have been highly publicized shootings committed by mentally ill and otherwise troubled ex-felons.
- In addition to risks of shootings and homicides, gun ownership by ex-felons whose lives lack evidence of self-control, organizational skills, and concern for safety will also increase risks of gun accidents involving children, suicides, and the theft of unsecured firearms in burglaries and robberies.

What Should U.S. Policy Be?

What impact will the restoration of gun-ownership rights for ex-felons have on American society? Is it an essential element of reintegrating ex-offenders that all citizenship rights be restored? Will the availability of legal guns for ex-felons increase shootings, homicides, and other crimes, and thereby harm society?

Researching the Internet

To read the Supreme Court's opinions on the nature of Second Amendment rights as well as examples of concerns raised by ex-felons' possession of guns, visit the Criminal Justice CourseMate at cengagebrain.com, then access the web links for this chapter.

For Critical Analysis

Are gun-ownership rights essential to ex-felons' successful reintegration into American society, to the restoration of their status as equal citizens, and to the protection of their families? Alternatively, is society subject to increased danger and harm when ex-felons can readily own guns? What policy do you see as best for the United States? Give three reasons for your conclusion about this issue.

---

the land or naval forces, or in the Militia, when in actual service in time of War or public danger; nor shall any person be subject for the same offence to be twice put in jeopardy of life or limb; nor shall be compelled in any criminal case to be a witness against himself, nor be deprived of life, liberty, or property, without due process of law; nor shall private property be taken for public use, without just compensation.

Sixth Amendment: In all criminal prosecutions, the accused shall enjoy the right to a speedy and public trial, by an impartial jury of the State and district wherein the crime shall have been committed, which district shall have been previously ascertained by law, and to be informed of the nature and cause of the accusation; to be confronted with the witnesses against him; to have compulsory process for obtaining witnesses in his favor, and to have the Assistance of Counsel for his defense.

Eighth Amendment: Excessive bail shall not be required, nor excessive fines imposed, nor cruel and unusual punishments inflicted.

For most of American history, the Bill of Rights did not apply to most criminal cases, because it was designed to protect people from abusive actions by the federal government. It did not seek to protect people from state and local officials, who handled nearly all criminal cases. This view was upheld by the U.S. Supreme Court in the 1833 case of ***Barron v. Baltimore***. However, as we shall see shortly, this view gradually changed in the late nineteenth and early twentieth centuries.

The Fourteenth Amendment and Due Process

After the Civil War, three amendments were added to the Constitution. These amendments were designed to protect individuals' rights against infringement by state and local government officials. The Thirteenth Amendment abolished slavery and the Fifteenth Amendment attempted to prohibit racial discrimination in voting; these had little impact on criminal justice. However, the Fourteenth Amendment profoundly affected it by barring states from violating people's right to due process of law. Its key language says that "no State shall . . . deprive any person of life, liberty, or property, without due process of law; nor deny to any person within its jurisdiction the equal protection of the laws." These rights to due process and equal protection served as a basis for protecting individuals from abusive actions by local government officials. However, the terms *due process* and *equal protection* are so vague that it was left to the U.S. Supreme Court to decide if and how these new rights applied to the criminal justice process.

For example, in ***Powell v. Alabama* (1932)**, the Supreme Court ruled that the due process clause required states to provide attorneys for poor defendants facing the death penalty. This decision stemmed from a notorious case in Alabama in which nine African American men, known as the "Scottsboro boys," were quickly convicted and condemned to death for allegedly raping two white women, even though one of the alleged victims later admitted that she had lied about the rape (Goodman, 1994).

In these early cases, the justices had not developed clear rules for deciding which specific rights applied to state and local officials as components of the due process clause of the Fourteenth Amendment. They implied that procedures must meet a standard of **fundamental fairness**. In essence, the justices simply reacted against brutal situations that shocked their consciences. In doing so, they showed the importance of procedural criminal law in protecting individuals from abusive and unjust actions by government officials.

The Due Process Revolution

From the 1930s to the 1960s, the fundamental fairness doctrine was supported by a majority of the Supreme Court justices. It was applied on a case-by-case basis, not always consistently. After Earl Warren became chief justice in 1953, he led the Supreme Court in a revolution that changed the meaning and scope of constitutional rights. Instead of requiring state and local officials merely to uphold fundamental fairness, the Court began to require them to abide by the specific provisions of the Bill of Rights (Marceau, 2008). Through the process of **incorporation**, the Supreme Court during the Warren Court era declared that elements of the Fourth, Fifth, Sixth, Eighth, and other amendments were part of the due process clause of the Fourteenth Amendment. Previously, states could design their own procedures so long as those procedures passed the fairness test. Under Warren's leadership, however, the Supreme

---

***Barron v. Baltimore* (1833)** The protections of the Bill of Rights apply only to actions of the federal government.

***Powell v. Alabama* (1932)** An attorney must be provided to a poor defendant facing the death penalty.

fundamental fairness A legal doctrine supporting the idea that so long as a state's conduct maintains basic standards of fairness, the Constitution has not been violated.

incorporation The extension of the due process clause of the Fourteenth Amendment to make binding on state governments the rights guaranteed in the first ten amendments to the U.S. Constitution (the Bill of Rights).

Court's new approach imposed detailed procedural standards on the police and courts.

As it applied more and more constitutional rights against the states, the Court made decisions that favored the interests of many criminal defendants. These defendants had their convictions overturned and received new trials because the Court believed that it was more important to protect the values underlying criminal procedure than single-mindedly to seek convictions of criminal offenders. In the eyes of many legal scholars, the Warren Court's decisions made criminal justice processes consistent with the American values of liberty, rights, and limited government authority.

To critics, however, these decisions made the community more vulnerable to crime and thereby harmed American values by diminishing the overall sense of liberty and security in society. Warren and the other justices were strongly criticized by politicians, police chiefs, and members of the public. These critics believed that the Warren Court was rewriting constitutional law in a manner that gave too many legal protections to criminals who harm society. In addition, Warren and his colleagues were criticized for ignoring established precedents that defined rights in a limited fashion.

From 1962 to 1972, the Supreme Court, under Chief Justices Earl Warren (1953–1969) and Warren Burger (1969–1986), applied most criminal justice rights in the U.S. Constitution against the states. By the end of this period, the process of incorporation was nearly complete. Criminal justice officials at all levels—federal, state, and local—were obligated to respect the constitutional rights of suspects and defendants.

AP Images/Evan Vucci

⬆ Police need to conduct searches and examine people's property as part of criminal investigations. They also need to search in order to prevent crimes by people who might conceal weapons, drugs, or other illegal items at airports, borders, nightclubs, and stadiums. All searches must either be done with warrants or be "reasonable" under judges' interpretations of the Fourth Amendment. Have you had your clothes or property examined by police or security guards? Is every examination of property a "search" under the Fourth Amendment? Is this dog "searching" the luggage?

The Fourth Amendment: Protection against Unreasonable Searches and Seizures

The Fourth Amendment limits the ability of law enforcement officers to search a person or property in order to obtain evidence of criminal activity. It also limits the ability of the police to detain a person without proper justification (Taslitz, 2010). When police take an individual into custody or prevent an individual from leaving a location, such detentions are considered to be "seizures" under the Fourth Amendment. As we shall examine in greater detail in Chapter 6, the Fourth Amendment does not prevent the police from conducting searches or making arrests; it merely protects people's privacy by barring "unreasonable" searches and arrests. It is up to the Supreme Court to define the situations in which a search or seizure is reasonable or unreasonable.

The justices also face challenges in defining such words as *searches* and *seizures*. For example, in 2005 the Supreme Court ruled that no issues concerning Fourth Amendment rights arose when a K-9 officer had a trained police dog sniff the exterior of a vehicle that was stopped for a traffic violation (Lunney, 2009). The dog indicated to the officer that the car's trunk contained marijuana, and that discovery led to a criminal conviction. However, unlike a *search,* for which officers must have proper justifications, the use of the dog did not require any justification, because the dog's scent-based examination of the vehicle's exterior did not invade the driver's right to privacy (*Illinois v. Caballes,* 2005). Read "A Question of Ethics" at the end of the chapter to consider police officers' use of an electronic device to monitor the movements of a suspect's car and the Supreme Court's consideration of whether this action constituted a "search" that affected the suspect's privacy.

Because different Supreme Court justices do not always agree on the Constitution's meaning, the definitions of these words and the rules for police searches can change as the makeup of the Court changes.

The wording of the Fourth Amendment makes clear that the authors of the Bill of Rights did not believe that law enforcement officials should have the power to pursue criminals at all costs. The Fourth Amendment's protections apply both to suspects and to law-abiding citizens. Police officers are supposed to follow the rules for obtaining search warrants, and they are not permitted to conduct unreasonable searches even when trying to catch dangerous criminals. As we shall see in Chapter 6, improper searches that lead to the discovery of criminal evidence can lead judges to bar police and prosecutors from using that evidence to prove the suspect's guilt. Thus, police officers need to be knowledgeable about the rules for searches and seizures and to follow those rules carefully when conducting criminal investigations.

Police face challenges in attempting to respect Fourth Amendment rights while also actively seeking to prevent crimes and catch offenders. Officers may be tempted to go too far in investigating crimes without an adequate basis for suspicion and thereby violate Fourth Amendment rights. The discussion of racial profiling in Chapter 1 illustrates one aspect of the risk that officers will, by conducting stops and searches without an appropriate basis, use their authority in ways that collide with the Fourth Amendment (Antonovics and Knight, 2009).

The Fifth Amendment: Protection against Self-Incrimination and Double Jeopardy

The Fifth Amendment clearly states some key rights related to the investigation and prosecution of criminal suspects. For example, the protection against compelled self-incrimination seeks to prevent authorities from pressuring people into acting as witnesses against themselves. Presumably, this right also helps protect against torture or other rough treatment when police officers question criminal suspects. In Chapter 6, we shall discuss the Fifth Amendment rules that guide officers in questioning criminal suspects. Improper questioning can affect whether evidence obtained through that questioning can be used in court.

Because of the right that protects against double jeopardy imposed by the Fifth Amendment, a person charged with a criminal act may be subjected to only one prosecution or punishment for that offense in the same jurisdiction. The purpose of the right is to prevent the government from trying someone over and over again until a conviction is obtained (Coffin, 2010). Generally, a person acquitted of a crime at trial cannot be tried again for that same crime. As interpreted by the Supreme Court, however, the right against double jeopardy does not prevent a person from facing two trials or receiving two sanctions from the government for the same criminal acts (L. Griffin, 2010). Because a single criminal act may violate both state and federal laws, for example, a person may be tried in both courts. Thus, when Los Angeles police officers were acquitted of assault charges in a state court after they had been videotaped beating motorist Rodney King, they were convicted in a federal court for violating King's civil rights. In yet another case, the Supreme Court permitted Alabama to pursue kidnapping and murder charges against a man who had already been convicted for the same murder in Georgia, because the victim was kidnapped in one state and killed in the other (*Heath v. Alabama,* 1985). Thus, the protection against double jeopardy does not prevent two different trials based on the same criminal acts as long as the trials are in different jurisdictions and based on different charges, a violation of the Georgia murder law being a different charge than a violation of the Alabama murder law even when both charges concern the same killing.

grand jury Body of citizens drawn from the community to hear evidence presented by the prosecutor in order to decide whether enough evidence exists to file charges against a defendant.

One of the rights in the Fifth Amendment, the entitlement to indictment by a grand jury before being prosecuted for a serious crime, applies only in federal courts. This is one of the few rights in the Bill of Rights that the Supreme Court never applied to the states. A **grand jury** is a body of citizens drawn from the community to hear evidence from the prosecutor in order to determine whether there is a sufficient basis to move forward with a criminal prosecution (Washburn, 2008). Some states use grand juries by their own choice; they are not required to do so by the Fifth Amendment. Other states simply permit prosecutors to file charges directly against criminal suspects.

The Sixth Amendment: The Right to Counsel and a Fair Trial

The Sixth Amendment includes several provisions dealing with fairness in a criminal prosecution. These include the rights to counsel, to a speedy and public trial, and to an impartial jury.

The Right to Counsel Although the right to counsel in a criminal case had prevailed in federal courts since 1938, not until the Supreme Court's landmark decision in **Gideon v. Wainwright (1963)** was this requirement made binding on the states. Many states already provided attorneys, but in this ruling the Court forced all of the states to meet Sixth Amendment standards. In previous cases, the Court, applying the doctrine of fundamental fairness, had ruled that states must provide poor people with counsel only when this was required by the special circumstances of the case. A defense attorney had to be provided when conviction could lead to the death penalty, when the issues were complex, or when a poor defendant was either very young or mentally handicapped.

Although the *Gideon* ruling directly affected only states that did not provide poor defendants with attorneys, it set in motion a series of cases that affected all the states by deciding how the right to counsel would be applied in various situations. Beginning in 1963, the Court extended the right to counsel to preliminary hearings, initial appeals, postindictment identification lineups, and children in juvenile court proceedings. Later, however, the Burger Court declared that attorneys need not be provided for discretionary appeals or for trials in which the only punishment is a fine (*Ross v. Moffitt,* 1974; *Scott v. Illinois,* 1979). Even in recent years, the Supreme Court has continued to clarify the extent of the right to counsel (M. A. McCall, McCall, and Smith, 2008). In 2008, for example, the Court determined that counsel must be provided to indigent defendants at an early stage in the process during the initial appearance before a judge at a preliminary hearing (*Rothgery v. Gillespie*). The Court also declared that trial judges can require that mentally ill defendants be represented by defense attorneys, even when those defendants wish to represent themselves in court (*Indiana v. Edwards*, 2008).

Because defense attorneys are an important component of a legal process that uses an adversarial system to pursue the truth and protect rights, defendants' conversations and communications with attorneys are secret. Prosecutors are not entitled to know what defendants tell their attorneys, even if they admit their guilt. As part of the effort to combat terrorism, however, in the aftermath of 9/11 the federal government proposed that it should gain the authority to monitor conversations between jailed defendants and their attorneys. Others believe that defense attorneys should have an obligation to reveal information that might help to solve any crime. Do you think such proposals improperly weaken Sixth Amendment rights? See "What Americans Think" to compare your view with those of people surveyed in North

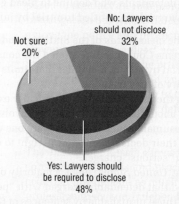

Question: "Should lawyers be required to disclose what their clients told them in private when that information will help to solve crimes?"

Not sure: 20%

No: Lawyers should not disclose 32%

Yes: Lawyers should be required to disclose 48%

Critical Thinking: How would our system be different if lawyers could not maintain the confidentiality of their clients' statements? What would be the costs and benefits of following the views of the largest group of respondents to this survey?

Note: Statewide poll of 600 North Carolina voters conducted in October 2005 by Research 2000.

Source: Matthew Eisley, "Nearly Half Favor Disclosure," *Raleigh News and Observer*, October 24, 2005 (http://www.newsobserver.com).

Gideon v. Wainwright (1963) Indigent defendants have a right to counsel when charged with serious crimes for which they could face six or more months of incarceration.

The Eighth Amendment protects offenders serving prison sentences. Under judges' interpretations of the Eighth Amendment, prisoners are entitled to food, shelter, sanitation facilities, and limited medical care. Is the maintenance of humane living conditions in prison an appropriate application of the protection against "cruel and unusual punishments"?

AP Images/LM Otero

Release on Bail   The purpose of bail is to allow for the release of the accused while he or she is awaiting trial. The Eighth Amendment does not require that all defendants be released on bail, only that the amount of bail not be excessive. Many states do not allow bail for those charged with some offenses, such as murder, and there seem to be few limits on the amounts that can be required. In 1987 the Supreme Court, in *United States v. Salerno and Cafero,* upheld provisions of the Bail Reform Act of 1984 that allow federal judges to detain without bail suspects who are considered dangerous to the public.

Excessive Fines   The Supreme Court ruled in 1993 that the forfeiture of property related to a criminal case can be analyzed for possible violation of the excessive fines clause (*Austin v. United States*). In 1998 the Court declared for the first time that forfeiture constituted an impermissible excessive fine. In that case, a man failed to comply with the federal law requiring that travelers report if they are taking $10,000 or more in cash outside the country (C. E. Smith, 1999). There is no law against transporting any amount of cash. The law only concerns filing a report to the government concerning the transport of money. When one traveler at a Los Angeles airport failed to report the money detected in his suitcase by a cash-sniffing dog trained to identify people who might be transporting money for drug dealers, he was forced to forfeit all $357,000 that he carried in his luggage. Because there was no evidence that the money was obtained illegally and because the usual punishment for the offense would only be a fine of $5,000, a slim five-member majority on the Supreme Court ruled that the forfeiture of all the traveler's money constituted an excessive fine (*United States v. Bajakajian,* 1998). It remains to be seen whether the Court's recent interest in violations of the excessive fines clause will limit law enforcement agencies' practices in forcing criminal defendants to forfeit cash and property.

Cruel and Unusual Punishments   The nation's founders were concerned about the barbaric punishments that had been inflicted in seventeenth- and eighteenth-century Europe, where offenders were sometimes burned alive or stoned to death—hence the ban on "cruel and unusual punishment." The Warren Court set the standard for judging issues of cruel and unusual punishments in a case dealing with a former soldier who was deprived of U.S. citizenship for deserting his post during World War II (*Trop v. Dulles,* 1958). Chief Justice Earl Warren declared that judges must use

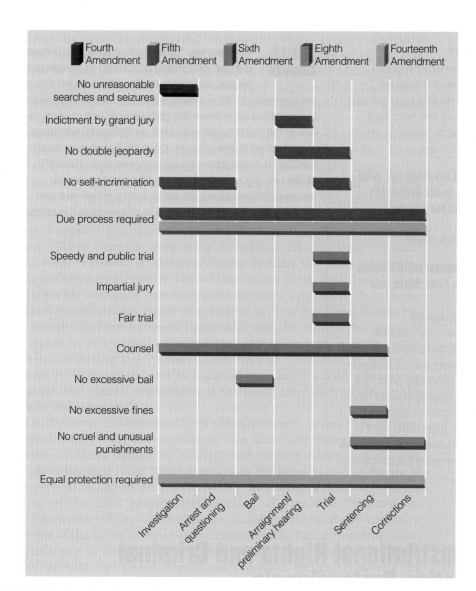

Figure 3.2
Protections of Constitutional Rights The Bill of Rights and the Fourteenth Amendment protect defendants during various phases of the criminal justice process.
© Cengage Learning

the values of contemporary society to determine whether a specific punishment is cruel and unusual.

Through the use of this test, punishments may be declared unconstitutional for being either disproportionate to the offense or comparable to a form of torture through the infliction of physical or psychological pain. In recent years, the Supreme Court has seldom regarded punishments other than the death penalty as disproportionate to any crime for which a legislature chooses to mandate it. The Court reinforced this view in 2003 by endorsing California's sentences of 25 years to life for offenders convicted of three felonies, even in a case when the third offense was merely shoplifting some children's videos from K-Mart (*Lockyer v. Andrade,* 2003). With respect to juvenile offenders, however, a majority of justices declared that life sentences without possibility of parole were unconstitutionally disproportionate for nonhomicide offenses (*Graham v. Florida,* 2010).

The Court's test has been used in death penalty cases, but the justices have strongly disagreed over the values of American society on this issue. The Supreme Court's decisions in death penalty cases are extensively discussed in Chapter 9.

Since the 1950s, the rights of defendants in state criminal trials have greatly expanded. The Supreme Court has incorporated most portions of the Fourth, Fifth, Sixth, and Eighth Amendments. Figure 3.2 shows the amendments that protect defendants at various stages of the criminal justice process.

Francom, a 30-year-old father of two young daughters, was hit six times and subsequently died from his wounds. Five other officers were hospitalized with gunshot wounds after the incident and Stewart was taken into custody and hospitalized with non-life-threatening injuries (Muskal, 2012).

The Utah police officers who were shot that day did not predict the lethal danger that they would face in carrying out a routine drug search. They had no information suggesting that an armed man with military training inside the house would shoot at them. Of course, as veteran police officers, they were constantly aware of the possibility that their jobs might someday place them in extreme danger. Indeed, they may have known about the highly publicized news stories one week earlier reporting a national increase in police officers shot to death while on duty: 68 in 2011 as compared to only 40 in 2008 (Cratty, 2011). Despite such knowledge, officers place themselves in potential danger every day. After the shooting started, many of their fellow officers bravely risked their lives, including one officer who was not part of the task force but was seriously injured after he rushed to the scene to provide help when calls about gunfire came over his police radio (Carlisle, 2012).

Who would choose a career that might entail life-threatening danger? What attracts people to a public-service career that brings them into situations of conflict? Further, how do the police, on an individual as well as an organizational level, carry out their duties in the face of such risks?

In this chapter, we examine several aspects of policing. A brief history of the police precedes discussion of the types of law enforcement agencies in the United States. We also examine the recruitment and training of contemporary police officers, the police subculture, and the functions, organization, and policies of policing.

The Development of Police in the United States

Law and order is not a new concept; it has been a subject of debate since the first police force was formed in London in 1829. Looking back even further, we find that the Magna Carta of 1215 placed limits on constables and bailiffs. Reading between the lines of that historic document reveals that the modern problems of police abuse, maintenance of order, and the rule of law also existed in thirteenth-century England. Further, current remedies—recruiting better-qualified people to serve as police, stiffening the penalties for official misconduct, creating a civilian board of control—were suggested even then to ensure that order was kept in accordance with the rule of law.

The English Roots of the American Police

The roots of American policing lie in the English legal tradition. Three major aspects of American policing evolved from that tradition: (1) limited authority, (2) local control, and (3) fragmented organization. Like the British police, but unlike police in continental Europe, the police in the United States have limited authority; their powers and duties are specifically defined by law. England, like the United States, has no national police force; instead, 43 regional authorities are headed by elected commissioners who appoint the chief constable. Above these local authorities is the home secretary of the national government, which provides funding and can intervene in cases of police corruption, mismanagement, and discipline. In the United States, policing is fragmented: There are many types of agencies—constable, county sheriff, city police, FBI—each with its own special jurisdiction and responsibilities.

frankpledge A system in old English law in which members of a tithing (a group of ten families) pledged to be responsible for keeping order and bringing violators of the law to court.

Systems for protecting citizens and property existed before the thirteenth century. The **frankpledge** system required that groups of ten families, called *tithings*, agree to uphold the law, keep order, and bring violators to a court. By custom, every male person above the age of 12 was part of the system. When a man became aware that a crime had occurred, he was obliged to raise a "hue and cry" and to join others in his tithing to track down the offender. The tithing was fined if members did not perform their duties.

Over time, England developed a system in which individuals were chosen within each community to take charge of catching criminals. The Statute of Winchester, enacted in 1285, set up a parish constable system. Members of the community were still required to pursue criminals, just as they had been under the frankpledge system, but now a constable supervised those efforts. The constable was a man chosen from the parish to serve without pay as its law enforcement officer for one year. The constable had the power to call the entire community into action if a serious disturbance arose. Watchmen, who were appointed to help the constable, spent most of their time patrolling the town at night to ensure that "all's well" and to enforce the criminal law. They were also responsible for lighting street lamps and putting out fires.

Not until the eighteenth century did an organized police force evolve in England. With the growth of commerce and industry, cities expanded while farming declined as the main source of employment and the focus of community life. In the larger cities, these changes produced social disorder.

In the mid-eighteenth century, novelist Henry Fielding and his brother, Sir John Fielding, led efforts to improve law enforcement in London. They wrote newspaper articles to inform the public about crime, and they published flyers describing known offenders. After Henry Fielding became a magistrate in 1748, he organized a small group of "thief-takers" to pursue and arrest lawbreakers. The government was so impressed with Fielding's Bow Street Amateur Volunteer Force (known as the Bow Street Runners) that it paid the participants and attempted to form similar groups in other parts of London.

After Henry Fielding's death in 1754, these efforts declined. As time went by, however, many saw that the government needed to assert itself in enforcing laws and maintaining order. London, with its unruly mobs, had become an especially dangerous place. In the early 1800s, several attempts were made to create a centralized police force for London. While people saw the need for social order, some feared that a police force would threaten the freedom of citizens and lead to tyranny. Finally, in 1829 Sir Robert Peel, home secretary in the British Cabinet, pushed Parliament to pass the Metropolitan Police Act, which created the London police force.

This agency was organized like a military unit, with a thousand-man force commanded by two magistrates, later called "commissioners." The officers were called "bobbies" after Sir Robert Peel. In the British system, cabinet members who oversee government departments are chosen from the elected members of Parliament. Thus, because Peel supervised it, the first police force was under the control of democratically elected officials.

Under Peel's direction, the police had a four-part mandate:

1. To prevent crime without using repressive force and to avoid having to call on the military to control riots and other disturbances
2. To maintain public order by nonviolent means, using force only as a last resort to obtain compliance
3. To reduce conflict between the police and the public
4. To show efficiency through the absence of crime and disorder rather than through visible police actions (P. K. Manning, 1977:82)

In effect, this meant keeping a low profile while maintaining order. Because of fears that a national force would threaten civil liberties, political leaders made every effort to focus police activities at the local level. These concerns were transported to the United States.

Policing in the United States

As with other institutions and areas of public policy, the development of formal police organizations reflected the social conditions, politics, and problems of different eras of American history. The United States drew from England's experience but implemented policing in its own way.

The Colonial Era and the Early Republic

As settlers arrived in North America from Europe and eventually moved westward from the East Coast, they relied on each other for assistance and protection in all matters, from weather disasters to conflicts with Native Americans. They also needed to protect themselves and their neighbors from those who might cause harm through theft or other crimes.

Along the East Coast, the colonists drew from their experiences in England by adopting the English offices of constable, sheriff, and night watchman as the first positions with law enforcement responsibilities. Boston's **watch system** began before 1640. Such systems served to warn of dangers ranging from fires to crime. Each male citizen was required to be a member of the watch, but paid watchmen could be hired as replacements. Although the watch system originally operated at night, cities eventually began to have daytime watches, too. Over time, cities began to hire paid, uniformed watchmen to deal with public danger and crime (S. Walker, 1999).

In the South, **slave patrols** developed as organized forces to prevent slave revolts and to catch runaway slaves. These patrols had full power to break into the homes of slaves who were suspected of keeping arms, to physically punish those who did not obey their orders, and to arrest runaways and return them to their masters. Under the watch system in northern cities, watchmen reacted to calls for help. By contrast, the mobility of slave patrols positioned them to operate in a proactive manner by looking for African Americans whom whites feared would disrupt society, especially the economic system of slavery. Samuel Walker (1999) describes the slave patrols as a distinctly American form of law enforcement and the first modern police force in the United States.

Beginning in the 1830s and continuing periodically for several decades, many American cities experienced violent riots. Ethnic conflicts, election controversies, hostility toward nonslave blacks and abolitionists, mob actions against banks during economic declines, and violence in settling questions of morality, such as the use of alcohol—all these factors contributed to fears that a stable democracy would not survive. The militia was called in to quell large-scale conflicts, because constables and watchmen proved ineffective in restoring order (Uchida, 2005). These disorders, along with perceptions of increased problems with serious crimes, helped push city governments to consider the creation of professional police forces.

American policing is often described in terms of three historical periods: the political era (1840–1920), the professional model era (1920–1970), and the community policing era (1970–present) (Kelling and Moore, 1988). This description has been criticized because it applies only to the urban areas of the Northeast and does not take into account the very different development of the police in rural areas of the South and West. Still, it remains a useful framework for exploring the organization of the police, the focus of police work, and the strategies employed by police (H. Williams and Murphy, 1990).

The Political Era: 1840–1920

The period from 1840 to 1920 is called the political era because of the close ties that were formed between the police and local political leaders at that time. In many cities, the police seemed to work for the mayor's political party rather than for the citizens. This relationship served both groups in that the political "machines" recruited and maintained the police while the police helped the machine leaders get out the vote for favored candidates. Ranks in the police force were often for sale to the highest bidder, and many officers took payoffs for not enforcing laws on drinking, gambling, and prostitution (S. Walker, 1999).

---

watch system Practice of assigning individuals to night observation duty to warn the public of fires and crime that was first introduced to the American colonies in Boston and that later evolved into a system of paid, uniformed police.

slave patrols Distinctively American form of law enforcement in southern states that sought to catch and control slaves through patrol groups that stopped and questioned African Americans on the roads and elsewhere in public places.

In the United States, as in England, the growth of cities led to pressures to modernize law enforcement. Around 1840 the large cities began to create police forces. In 1845 New York City established the first full-time, paid police force. Boston and Philadelphia were the first to add a daytime police force to supplement the night watchmen; other cities—Chicago, Cincinnati, New Orleans—quickly followed.

By 1850, most major cities had created police departments organized on the English model. A chief, appointed by the mayor and city council, headed each department. The city was divided into precincts, with full-time, paid patrolmen assigned to each. Early police forces sought to prevent crimes and keep order through the use of foot patrols. The officer on the beat dealt with crime, disorder, and other problems as they arose.

In addition to foot patrols, the police performed service functions, such as caring for derelicts, operating soup kitchens, regulating public health, and handling medical and social emergencies. In cities across the country, the police provided beds and food for homeless people. In station houses, overnight "lodgers" might sleep on the floor or sometimes in clean bunkrooms (Monkkonen, 1981:127). The police became general public servants as well as crime control officers.

Police developed differently in the South because of the existence of slavery and the agrarian nature of that region. As noted previously, the first organized police agencies with full-time officers developed in cities with large numbers of slaves (Charleston, New Orleans, Richmond, and Savannah), where white owners feared slave uprisings (Rousey, 1984:41).

Culver Pictures

During the political era, the officer on a neighborhood beat dealt with crime and disorder as it arose. Police also performed various social services, such as providing beds and food for the homeless. Should today's police officers devote more time to providing social services for the public?

Westward expansion in the United States produced conditions quite different from those in either the urban East or the agricultural South. The frontier was settled before order could be established. Thus, those who wanted to maintain law and order often had to take matters into their own hands by forming vigilante groups.

One of the first official positions created in rural areas was that of sheriff. Although the sheriff had duties similar to those of the "shire reeves" of seventeenth-century England, the American sheriff was elected and had broad powers to enforce the law. As elected officers, sheriffs had close ties to local politics. They also depended on the men of the community for assistance. This is how the *posse comitatus* (Latin for "power of the county"), borrowed from fifteenth-century Europe, came into being. Local men above age 15 were required to respond to the sheriff's call for assistance, forming a body known as a posse.

After the Civil War, the federal government appointed U.S. marshals to help enforce the law in the western territories. Some of the best-known folk heroes of American policing were U.S. Marshals Wyatt Earp, Bat Masterson, and Wild Bill Hickok, who tried to bring law and order to the "Wild West" (Calhoun, 1990). While some marshals did extensive law enforcement work, most had mainly judicial duties, such as keeping order in the courtroom and holding prisoners for trial.

During the early twentieth century, much of the United States became more urban. This change blurred some of the regional differences that had helped define policing in the past. In addition, growing criticism of the influence of politics on the police led to efforts to reform the nature and organization of the police. Specifically, reformers sought to make police more professional and to reduce their ties to local politics.

sheriff Top law enforcement official in county government who was an exceptionally important police official during the country's westward expansion and continues to bear primary responsibility for many local jails.

U.S. marshals Federal law enforcement officials appointed to handle duties in western territories and today bear responsibility for federal court security and apprehending fugitives.

During the professional model era, the police saw themselves as crime fighters. Yet many inner-city residents saw them as a well-armed, occupying force that did not support efforts to advance civil rights and racial equality. If you looked out your window and saw these heavily armed Oklahoma City SWAT team members in your neighborhood, would you have any concerns about how your neighbors might perceive the dress, demeanor, and actions of these officers? Might you have a different reaction if you lived in your city's poorest neighborhood?

AP Images/The Oklahoman, Michael Dounes

The Professional Model Era: 1920–1970

American policing was greatly influenced by the Progressive movement. The Progressives were mainly upper-middle-class, educated Americans with two goals: more-efficient government and more government services to assist the less fortunate. A related goal was to reduce the influence of party politics and patronage (favoritism in handing out jobs) in government. The Progressives saw a need for professional law enforcement officials who would use modern technology to benefit the whole of society, not just local politicians.

The key to the Progressives' concept of professional law enforcement is found in their slogan, "The police have to get out of politics, and politics has to get out of the police." August Vollmer, the chief of police of Berkeley, California, from 1909 to 1932, was a leading advocate of professional policing. He initiated the use of motorcycle units, handwriting analysis, and fingerprinting. With other police reformers, such as Leonhard Fuld, Raymond Fosdick, Bruce Smith, and O. W. Wilson, he urged that the police be made into a professional force, a nonpartisan agency of government committed to public service. This model of professional policing has six elements:

1. The force should stay out of politics.
2. Members should be well trained, well disciplined, and tightly organized.
3. Laws should be enforced equally.
4. The force should use new technology.
5. Personnel procedures should be based on merit.
6. The main task of the police should be fighting crime.

Refocusing attention on crime control and away from maintaining order probably did more than anything else to change the nature of American policing. The narrow focus on crime fighting broke many of the ties that the police had formed with the communities they served. By the end of World War I, police departments had greatly reduced their involvement in social services. Instead, for the most part, cops became crime fighters.

O. W. Wilson, a student of Vollmer, was another leading advocate of professionalism. He earned a degree in criminology at the University of California in 1924 and became the chief of police of Wichita, Kansas, in 1928. By reorganizing the department and fighting police corruption, he came to national attention. He promoted the use of motorized patrols, efficient radio communication, and rapid response. He believed that one-officer patrols were the best way to use personnel and that the two-way radio, which allowed for supervision by commanders, made officers more efficient (Reiss, 1992:51). He rotated assignments so that officers on patrol would not become too familiar with people in the community (and thus prone to corruption). In 1960, Wilson became the superintendent of the Chicago Police Department with a mandate to end corruption there.

The new emphasis on professionalism had also spurred the formation of the International Association of Chiefs of Police (IACP) in 1902 and the Fraternal Order of Police (FOP) in 1915. Both organizations promoted training standards, the use of new technologies, and a code of ethics.

By the 1930s the police were using new technologies and methods to combat serious crimes. Officers became more effective against crimes such as murder, rape, and robbery—an important factor in gaining citizen support.

In the 1960s, the civil rights and antiwar movements, urban riots, and rising crime rates challenged many of the assumptions of the professional model. In their attempts to maintain order during public demonstrations, police officers found themselves enforcing laws that tended to discriminate against African Americans and the poor. The number of low-income racial minorities living in the inner cities was growing, and the professional style kept the police isolated from the communities they served. In the eyes of many inner-city residents, the police were an occupying army keeping them at the bottom of society, not public servants helping all citizens.

Although the police continued to portray themselves as crime fighters, as crime rates rose, citizens became aware that the police often were not effective in this role.

The Community Policing Era: 1970–Present Beginning in the 1970s, calls were heard for a move away from the crime-fighting focus and toward greater emphasis on keeping order and providing services to the community. Research studies revealed the complex nature of police work and the extent to which day-to-day practices deviated from the professional ideal. The research also questioned the effectiveness of the police in catching and deterring criminals.

Three findings of this research are especially noteworthy:

1. Increasing the number of patrol officers in a neighborhood had little effect on the crime rate.
2. Rapid response to calls for service did not greatly increase the arrest rate.
3. Improving the percentage of crimes solved is difficult.

Such findings undermined acceptance of the professional crime-fighter model. Critics argued that the professional style isolated the police from the community and reduced their knowledge about the neighborhoods they served, especially when police patrolled in cars. Instead, it was argued, police should get out of their cars and spend more time meeting and helping residents. Reformers hoped that closer contact with citizens would not only permit the police to help them in new ways but would also make citizens feel safer, knowing that the police were available and interested in their problems.

In a provocative article titled "Broken Windows: The Police and Neighborhood Safety," James Q. Wilson and George L. Kelling argued that policing should work more on "little problems" such as maintaining order, providing services to those in need, and adopting strategies to reduce the fear of crime (1982:29). They based their approach on three assumptions:

1. Neighborhood disorder creates fear. Areas with street people, youth gangs, prostitution, and drunks are high-crime areas.
2. Just as broken windows are a signal that nobody cares and can lead to worse vandalism, untended disorderly behavior is a signal that the community does not care. This also leads to worse disorder and crime.

 Community policing encourages personal contact between officers and citizens, especially interactions that facilitate citizens' cooperation with and support for the police. Is your own interest in criminal justice affected by your view of police officers and interactions with them?

3. If the police are to deal with disorder and thus reduce fear and crime, they must rely on citizens for assistance.

Advocates of the **community policing** approach urge greater use of foot and bicycle patrols so that officers will become known to citizens, who in turn will cooperate with the police. They believe that through attention to little problems, the police may not only reduce disorder and fear but also improve public attitudes toward policing (Kelling, 1985).

Closely related to the community policing concept is **problem-oriented policing**. Herman Goldstein, the originator of this approach, argued that instead of focusing on crime and disorder, the police should identify the underlying causes of problems such as noisy teenagers, battered spouses, and abandoned buildings used as drug houses. In doing so they could reduce disorder and fear of crime (Goldstein, 1979). Closer contacts between the police and the community might then reduce the hostility that has developed between officers and residents in many urban neighborhoods (Sparrow, Moore, and Kennedy, 1990).

community policing
Approach to policing that emphasizes close personal contact between police and citizens and the inclusion of citizens in efforts to solve problems, including vandalism, disorder, youth misbehavior, and crime.

problem-oriented policing
Community policing strategy that emphasizes solving problems of disorder in a neighborhood that may contribute to fear of crime and crime itself.

In *Fixing Broken Windows*, written in response to the Wilson and Kelling article, George L. Kelling and Catherine Coles (1996) call for strategies to restore order and reduce crime in public spaces in U.S. communities. Many cities instructed police to pay greater attention to "quality-of-life crimes" by arresting subway fare-beaters, rousting loiterers and panhandlers from parks, and aggressively dealing with those who are obstructing sidewalks, harassing others, and soliciting. By handling these "little crimes," the police not only help restore order but also often prevent worse crimes. In New York, for example, searching fare-beaters often yielded weapons, questioning a street vendor selling hot merchandise led to a fence specializing in stolen weapons, and arresting a person for urinating in a park resulted in the discovery of a cache of weapons. This shift of emphasis still retains police officers' crime-fighter role.

The federal government created the Office of Community Oriented Policing Services, more commonly known as the "COPS Office," which provides grants for hiring new officers and developing community policing programs. Between 1995 and 2003, the COPS Office supplied nearly $7 billion to 13,000 state and local agencies to hire 118,000 new officers and implement training and other programs (Uchida, 2005). In 2009, the Obama administration provided $1 billion additional dollars to the COPS Office to fund the hiring of police officers around the nation as part of the stimulus program to revive the national economy (N. A. Lewis, 2009).

In the 1980s, critics questioned whether the professional model really ever isolated police from community residents (S. Walker, 1984). Others wondered whether the opportunity to receive federal money and hire new officers led departments to use the language of community policing in portraying their activities even though they never fully adopted the new methods.

The Next Era: Homeland Security? Scarce Resources?

Although many local police departments continue to emphasize community policy, after 9/11 homeland security and antiterrorist efforts became two of the highest priorities for the federal government. As we shall see in Chapter 5, this event shifted the federal government's funding priorities for law enforcement and led to a reorganization of federal agencies. This shift also affected state and local police. According to Craig Uchida, "Priorities for training, equipment, strategies, and funding have transformed policing once again—this time focusing on homeland security" (2005:38). Federal money for state and local police agencies moved toward supplying emergency preparedness training, hazardous-materials gear, equipment for detecting bombs and other weapons of mass destruction, and the collection of intelligence data. In public comments, a few police officials have referred to "terrorist-oriented policing," but how such a concept or emphasis would be defined at the local level is not clear (Kerlikowske, 2004). Some observers believe that a shift toward homeland security may appeal to traditionalists in law enforcement who prefer to see themselves as heroically catching "bad guys."

In the aftermath of the nation's economic crisis of 2008 and its continuing effects, all levels of government cut their budgets as tax revenues diminished. Federal funding to support local policing became more uncertain and local governments faced their own budget shortfalls. A direct effect for many communities was a reduction in the number of police officers and a corresponding loss of police services. For the most seriously affected cities and counties, this development can overwhelm any sustained focus on homeland security or even efforts to maintain community policing. In Michigan, for example, the city of Flint (population 100,000), reduced its police force by two-thirds, leading one officer to comment, "Sometimes, we don't [respond] to a [citizen's] call for two days" (LeDuff, 2011). Local cuts also affect other agencies' resources as county sheriffs must send officers to handle duties previously covered by a village's officers, and state police must similarly share their personnel. For example, New Jersey state police had to handle many criminal investigations and patrols in the city of Camden after 168 city police officers lost their jobs because of a budget cut (C. Baxter, 2011).

Community policing will not disappear. Many police executives remain committed to its purposes and principles. However, budget issues may limit their ability to fulfill their ideal vision of policing. In addition, federal funding for local policing is more limited and reflects an emphasis on emergency preparedness and homeland security.

---

check point

1. **What three main features of American policing were inherited from England?**
   Limited authority, local control, organizational fragmentation.

2. **What are the historical periods of American policing?**
   Colonial era and early republic; political era, professional model era, community policing era.

3. **What were the major recommendations of the Progressive reformers?**
   The police should be removed from politics, police should be well trained, the law should be enforced equally, technology should be used, merit should be the basis of personnel procedures, the crime-fighting role should be prominent.

stop & analyze

If you were a police chief in a city plagued by difficult crime problems, how might your distribution and use of police officers differ if you emphasized the crime-fighter role instead of community policing? Would you do anything differently if you were equally committed to both goals?

5

Policing: Contemporary Issues and Challenges

Learning Objectives

- ➔ Understand the everyday actions of police
- ➔ Recognize the ways police can abuse their power and the challenges of controlling this abuse
- ➔ Identify the methods that can be used to make police more accountable to citizens
- ➔ Understand the delivery of police services
- ➔ Analyze patrol strategies that departments employ
- ➔ Recognize the importance of connections between the police and the community
- ➔ Identify issues and problems that emerge from law enforcement agencies' increased attention to homeland security
- ➔ Understand the policing and related activities undertaken by private sector security management

I n New York City's Times Square, one of the busiest areas for tourists walking to restaurants, stores, and Broadway theaters, a sidewalk vendor who sells T-shirts noticed smoke coming out of an SUV that was parked awkwardly with its engine running and hazard lights flashing. He called out to a nearby police officer on horseback who approached the suspicious vehicle and smelled gunpowder (A. Baker and Rashbaum, 2010). The officer immediately radioed for assistance and, on this warm May evening in 2010, the New York City Police Department sprang into action,

141

simultaneously carrying out several of the important functions that police provide for society.

The attack on the World Trade Center on 9/11 heightened New York City officers' awareness to the risks of bombs and other threats to public safety. Moreover, through training and experience, the force was particularly well prepared to respond to a suspicious situation. Officers immediately worked to evacuate a ten-block area around Times Square, which entailed notifying thousands of people that they must move away from the scene, and then blocking off the area to prevent access.

The bomb squad arrived, donned their protective gear, and sent a robotic device to examine the vehicle. They discovered propane canisters, gasoline, and fireworks connected to battery-operated clocks. It was a crude bomb that apparently malfunctioned in the process of detonating. Despite its rudimentary construction, the bomb had the potential to kill many people, given that it was planted in a crowded pedestrian area (A. Baker and Rashbaum, 2010).

As the bomb-squad officers dismantled the device, police investigators had already discovered that the vehicle's license plate was not registered to the SUV, but instead to a pickup truck that recently had been taken to a Connecticut junkyard. Although the vehicle identification number (VIN) for the SUV had been removed from the dashboard and the door, a detective located a hidden VIN number underneath the vehicle—one that the bomber had not removed. Using the recovered VIN number and license-plate registration, the NYPD officers, joined by FBI agents and other federal law enforcement officials from the Joint Terrorism Task Force, interviewed both the pickup-truck owner and the prior owner of the SUV. Using this information they were able to identify a suspect—Faisal Shahzad—a naturalized U.S. citizen who had been born in Pakistan and whose American business career had faltered (Rashbaum, Mazzetti, and Baker, 2010).

FBI agents went to the suspect's apartment and interviewed the landlord. They then placed the apartment under surveillance and Shahzad soon arrived there. When he left the apartment again, they followed him and, despite losing him briefly on the highway, they eventually caught up with him at the airport and arrested him as he boarded a plane for Dubai. In just 53 hours from the moment the smoking bomb had been noticed in Times Square, the police used their investigative skills to identify and arrest the suspect (Rashbaum and Baker, 2010). Eventually, Shahzad pleaded

guilty to the attempted bombing and was sentenced to spend the rest of his life in federal prison (M. Wilson, 2010).

This case illustrates the range of responsibilities and challenges facing police officers. It demonstrates the diverse missions that the police must simultaneously carry out—duties ranging from emergency response to crowd control to criminal investigation.

The 9/11 terrorist attack on the World Trade Center drew worldwide attention to courageous actions taken by hundreds of police officers and firefighters on that day. Many of these law enforcement officers and emergency responders lost their lives in the collapse of the twin towers and its aftermath. Until that day, few Americans had cause or reason to recognize the importance of law enforcement agencies at the various levels of government or to appreciate the numerous ways these officers serve society. Now there is much wider recognition that police officers are not merely crime fighters. They are essential civil servants who can act quickly and professionally to coordinate responsive efforts in the face of threats to public safety—whether the dangers be human caused or the result of natural disasters.

In this chapter, we examine several aspects of the continuing challenges faced by American police in protecting lives and property. We focus on the actual work of the police as they pursue suspects, prevent crimes, and otherwise serve the public. The police must be organized so that patrol efforts are coordinated, investigations carried out, arrests made, evidence gathered, and violators prosecuted. Moreover, police responsibilities must be performed effectively in a variety of contexts, with an increasingly diverse society. As shown by the Times Square example, law enforcement officials must routinely tackle issues that might not be considered in the realm of traditional crime prevention, such as public-safety emergencies and natural disasters. Because each of these responsibilities must be executed while maintaining the highest principles and professional standards, we will examine the issues of police ethics, misconduct, and accountability. This chapter also looks at the emerging challenges stemming from homeland security and antiterrorist efforts. We will conclude by discussing the role of private security officials in advancing society's interests in public safety and crime prevention. All of the topics explored in this chapter demonstrate the wide range of issues and problems handled by public police and private security officials in the twenty-first century, as they work toward advancing society's goals of order, safety, and security.

Everyday Action of Police

We saw in Chapter 4 how the police are organized and which three functions of policing—law enforcement, order maintenance, and service—compose their mandate. We have also recognized that police officers must be guided by policies developed by their superiors as to how policing is to be implemented. Police officers' actions and effectiveness also depend on the resources available to them, as illustrated by the example of computers in patrol cars that will be discussed in greater detail in Chapter 14. In this section, we look at the everyday actions of the police as they deal with citizens in often highly discretionary ways. We then discuss domestic violence, to show how the police respond to serious problems.

Question: "I am going to read you a list of institutions in American society. Please tell me how much confidence you, yourself, have in each one—a great deal, quite a lot, some, or very little: the police?"

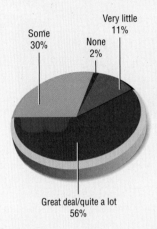

Some 30%

Very little 11%

None 2%

Great deal/quite a lot 56%

Critical Thinking: Nearly half of Americans asked indicate that they lack complete confidence in the police. Why might these skeptical viewpoints exist? What impact might these viewpoints have on the interactions between police and people in the community?

Source: Bureau of Justice Statistics, *Sourcebook of Criminal Justice Statistics, 2011*, Table 2.12.2011 (http://www.albany.edu /sourcebook/).

Encounters between Police and Citizens

To carry out their mission, the police must have the public's confidence, because they depend on the public to help them identify crime and carry out investigations (see "What Americans Think"). Each year 1 in 5 Americans has face-to-face contact with law enforcement officers. A third of these contacts involve people seeking help or offering assistance. Another third involve witnessing or reporting a crime. A little less than a third say that the police initiated the contact.

Although most people are willing to help the police, factors such as fear and self-interest keep some from cooperating. Many people who avoid calling the police do so because they think it is not worth the effort and cost. They do not want to spend time filling out forms at the station, appearing as a witness, or confronting a neighbor or relative in court. In some low-income neighborhoods, citizens are reluctant to assist the police, because their past experience has shown that contact with law enforcement "only brings trouble." Without information about a crime, the police may decide not to pursue an investigation. Clearly, citizens have influence over the work of the police through their decisions to call or not to call them. As a result, officers learn that developing and maintaining effective communication with people is essential to doing their job.

Citizens expect the police to act both effectively and fairly—in ways consistent with American values. Yet police departments have little direct control over the actions of individual officers. Departments have policies about when to conduct searches and other matters concerning officers' interactions with members of the public. However, officers possess the discretion to decide for themselves when to stop a driver, when to frisk a pedestrian, and when to make an arrest. Sometimes these individual decisions will violate policy or even ignore the legal rights of citizens. Thus police officers' decisions about how to use their discretion have significant impact on how people are treated and how they feel about the criminal justice system.

Police Discretion

Police officers have the power to deprive people of their liberty, to arrest them, to take them into custody, and to use force to control them. In carrying out their professional responsibilities, officers are expected to exercise *discretion*—to make

© Michael Newman/PhotoEdit, Inc.

Police officers use their discretion to make many decisions. Who should be stopped and questioned? When should an arrest be made? Who needs an encouraging word and who needs a stern warning? In making decisions, officers can significantly impact the lives of people who come into contact with the criminal justice system. Are there ways that supervisors could better monitor officers' use of discretion?

choices in often ambiguous situations as to how and when to apply the law. Discretion can involve ignoring minor violations of the law or holding some violators to rule-book standards. It can mean arresting a disorderly person or just taking that person safely home. In the final analysis, the officer on the scene must define the situation, decide how to handle it, and determine whether and how the law should be applied. Five factors are especially important:

1. *The nature of the crime.* The less serious a crime is to the public, the more freedom officers have to ignore it.
2. *The relationship between the alleged criminal and the victim.* The closer the personal relationship, the more variable the use of discretion. Family squabbles may not be as grave as they appear, and police are wary of making arrests, because a spouse may later decide not to press charges.
3. *The relationship between the police and the criminal or victim.* A polite complainant will be taken more seriously than a hostile one. Similarly, a suspect who shows respect to an officer is less likely to be arrested than one who does not.
4. *Race/ethnicity, age, gender, class.* Research studies show that some officers are more likely to investigate behavior (e.g., make stops and searches) and strictly enforce the law against young, minority, poor men while being more lenient to the elderly, to whites, and to affluent women.
5. *Departmental policy.* The policies of the police chief and city officials promote more or less discretion.

domestic violence The term commonly used to refer to intimate partner violence or violent victimizations between spouses, boyfriends, and girlfriends, or those formerly in intimate relationships. Such actions account for a significant percentage of the violent victimizations experienced by women.

Violence between spouses or intimate partners, typically called **domestic violence**, provides a good example of the role of police discretion. Twenty-six percent of violent victimizations experienced by women are at the hands of spouses or boyfriends (Truman and Rand, 2010). Until the 1970s and 1980s, many male officers treated such events as private matters for couples to handle themselves, rather than as crimes, even when there was clear evidence of violence and injuries. In light of lawsuits and lobbying on behalf of injured women, nearly half of the states and the District of Columbia eventually developed policies to require the arrest of suspects in violent incidents, without a warrant, even if the officer did not witness the crime (Hoctor, 1997). In addition, most large departments and police academies have programs to educate officers about domestic violence and the victimization of women. Yet, even though we can point to policy changes imposed to deal with domestic violence, the fact remains that the officer in the field is the one who must handle these situations. Each context may differ, both in terms of the officer's perceptions about what occurred and with respect to the victim's desire to see the abuser arrested and punished (Hirschel and Hutchinson, 2003). As with most law enforcement situations, laws, guidelines, and training can help; however, as is often true in police work, in the end the discretion of the officer inevitably determines what actions will be taken (R. C. Davis et al., 2008).

Police officers possess significant discretion because so much of their work is conducted independently, beyond the observation and supervision of superior officers. Officers' independence and discretion also raises risks of improper police behavior and corruption, the topics we will examine in the next section. For police to fulfill their responsibilities properly, we count on them to be ethical and professional in all of their decisions and actions. These issues affect all aspects of police functions and performance.

check point

1. **Why do patrol officers have so much discretion?**
   They deal with citizens, often in private, and are charged with maintaining order and enforcing laws. Many of these laws are ambiguous and deal with situations in which the participants' conduct is in dispute.

2. **Why have police in the past failed to make arrests in domestic violence situations?**
   Officers assumed family conflicts are private matters and were often insensitive to the victimization of women.

stop& analyze

Discretion is a necessary element of police officers' tools to handle situations that they encounter. Yet discretion may be used inappropriately. List two actions you would take, if you were a police chief, to improve the discretionary decision making of your officers.

Police Abuse of Power

Police officers can break the law and disobey departmental policies through corruption, favoritism, discrimination, and the failure to carry out their duties properly. Periodically, police corruption and abuse of power become major issues on the public agenda (Skolnick and Fyfe, 1993). In particular, the illegal use of violence by law enforcement officers and the criminal activities associated with police corruption can gain news media attention and anger the public. Although most officers do not engage in misconduct, these problems deserve study because they raise questions about how much the public can control and trust the police.

Use of Force

Although most people cooperate with the police, officers must at times use force to make arrests, control disturbances, and deal with the drunken or mentally ill. Thus, police may use *legitimate* force to do their job. It is when they use *excessive* force that they violate the law. But which situations and actions constitute **excessive use of force**? Both officers and experts debate this question.

Citizens use the term *police brutality* to describe a wide range of practices, from the use of profane or abusive language to physical force and violence. As shown in "What Americans Think," the percentage of Americans who believe that police brutality exists where they live has increased over the past four decades.

Stories of police brutality are not new. However, unlike the untrained officers of the early 1900s, today's officers are supposed to be professionals who know the rules and understand the need for proper conduct. Yet, a 2011 report by the Los Angeles Sheriff's Department identified instances of improper conduct, such as a deputy who shot at a driver who bumped into his vehicle in a fast-food restaurant parking lot, and another who sought to cover up the fact that she had fired her gun at a burglary suspect (Faturechi, 2011). Concerns are heightened by the fact that the public cannot know how often police engage in abusive behavior, even when it comes to light, because most violence remains hidden from public view (Weitzer, 2002). In 2008,

excessive use of force Applications of force against individuals by police officers that violate either departmental policies or constitutional rights by exceeding the level of force permissible and necessary in a given situation.

Question: "In some places in the nation there have been charges of police brutality. Do you think there is any police brutality in your area, or not?"

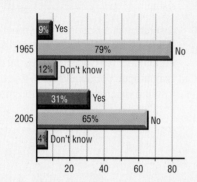

Critical Thinking: What do you believe has caused the public's increased perception of improper police behavior? Is it because more police behave unprofessionally? More news media coverage of such incidents? Less public acceptance of police use of force generally? If you were a police chief, what are three steps that you would take to try to counteract this rise in negative public views about police behavior?

Source: Gallup Poll, January 3, 2006, reprinted from Bureau of Justice Statistics, *Sourcebook of Criminal Justice Statistics, 2011*, Table 2.0001.2005 (http://www.albany.edu/sourcebook/).

a news helicopter filmed a dozen Philadelphia police officers beating and kicking a criminal suspect who had just been pulled from a car (Hurdle, 2008). If not for the video, how would the public know that the incident had happened? Without direct proof, will the public believe criminal suspects who claim to have been beaten by police? How can we prevent such incidents, especially when they occur without witnesses?

The concept "use of force" takes many forms in practice. We can arrange the various types of force on a continuum ranging from most severe (civilians shot and killed) to least severe ("come-alongs," or being grasped by an officer) (Terrill, 2005). How often must force be used? Most research has shown that in police contacts with suspects, force is used infrequently and the type of force used is usually at the low end of the continuum—toward the less severe. Resistance by a suspect can contribute to the officers' decision to use force (R. Johnson, 2011; J. H. Garner, Maxwell, and Heraux, 2002). A report by the National Institute of Justice summarized general conclusions from research about use of force (K. Adams, 1999):

1. Police use force infrequently.
2. Police use of force typically occurs in the lower end of the force spectrum and involves grabbing, pushing, or shoving.
3. Use of force typically occurs when police are trying to make an arrest and the suspect is resisting.

Although more studies are needed, other research indicates that use of force is not necessarily linked to an officer's personal characteristics such as age, gender, and ethnicity (Klahm and Tillyer, 2010). However, a small percentage of officers may be disproportionately involved in use-of-force situations. In addition, use of force occurs more frequently when police are dealing with people affected by drugs, alcohol, or mental illness (Lord and Sloop, 2010). By law, the police have the authority to use force if necessary to make an arrest, keep the peace, or maintain public order. But the questions of just how much force is necessary and under what conditions force may be used are complex and open to debate.

When police kill a suspect or bystander while trying to make an arrest, their actions may produce public outrage and hostility. Fears about the possibility of similar public disorders arose in 2005 when a police officer fired ten shots that killed a 13-year-old boy who was driving a stolen car. The officer fired in the aftermath of a chase when the boy skidded across a sidewalk and then struck a police car while backing up (Chavez, 2005). The incident led Los Angeles police officials to revise their policies about firing at moving vehicles.

An analysis of New York City's detailed records on police shootings in 2010 showed drops in the use of firearms that coincided with the drop in crime rate over the preceding decade. Police opened fire at people fewer than 40 times in 2010, compared with 147 times in 1996 (Harris, 2011; A. Baker, 2008). One troubling question that lingers is whether the New York City police are more inclined to use firearms against members of minority groups (Gill and Pasquale-Styles, 2009). In cities throughout the country, the use of deadly force in apprehending suspects has become a deeply emotional issue with a direct connection to race relations. Nearly 90 percent of those shot by the New York City police in the late 1990s were African American or Hispanic. Similarly, in 2010, reports show that 53 percent of those shot were African American, 26 percent were Hispanic, 15 percent were white, and 6 percent were Asian American

(Harris, 2011). Data from other U.S. cities also raises questions about the use of force against minorities.

The risk of lawsuits by victims of improper police shootings and other injury-producing uses of force looms over police departments and creates an incentive for administrators to impose standards for the proper use of force (H. Lee and Vaughn, 2010). In addition to the use of firearms, police officers have caused deaths and injuries with choke holds and by striking people in the head with flashlights or batons (Klingler, 2012). Injuries can also result from seemingly routine procedures such as placing a suspect in handcuffs that are too tight.

As long as officers carry weapons, some improper uses of force, including shootings, will occur. Officers who are angry or otherwise guided by improper motives may use unnecessary force in situations beyond public view. See "A Question of Ethics" at the end of the chapter for an example of excessive force caught on video. Police administrators have limited tools available to restrain unethical officers. Training, internal review of incidents, and the disciplining or firing of quick-trigger officers may help reduce the use of unnecessary force.

As a result of lawsuits by people injured at the hands of the police, departments have sought new means of applying force in ways that will not produce injuries. Some of the new methods center on specific holds and pressure points that officers can use to incapacitate people temporarily without causing permanent harm; officers can learn these techniques through training. In addition, police departments seek new weapons that use less-than-lethal force. In Chapter 14, when we discuss the impact of technology on police practices, we shall examine new weapons that use electric shocks, projectiles, and chemical sprays. These new weapons also pose serious risks, including the possibility that officers will resort too quickly to such weapons when situations could be solved through patience and persuasion (Adang and Mensink, 2004).

Police grab a protester off his bike after he taunted them at a protest against free-trade policies during a meeting of international leaders in Miami, Florida. Does this appear to be an appropriate use of force? Do police officers sometimes use force out of anger rather than out of necessity?

Corruption

Police corruption has a long history in America. Early in the twentieth century, city officials organized liquor and gambling businesses for their personal gain. In many cities, ties between politicians and police officials assured that favored clients would be protected and competitors harassed. Much of the Progressive movement's efforts to reform the police aimed at combating such corrupt arrangements.

police corruption Police officers' violations of law and departmental policy for personal gain or to help their family and friends.

Although such political ties have diminished in most cities, corruption still exists. In 2011, for example, 30 Baltimore police officers were charged in an extortion scheme in which they received thousands of dollars in exchange for steering accident victims to a towing service that was not authorized to do business with the city (Fenton, 2011). Sometimes corruption is defined so broadly that it ranges from accepting a free cup of coffee to robbing businesses or beating suspects. Obviously, corruption is not easily defined, and people disagree about what it includes. As a useful starting point, we can focus on the distinction between corrupt officers who are "grass eaters" and those who are "meat eaters."

"Grass eaters" are officers who accept payoffs that the routines of police work bring their way. These officers may accept gifts from businesses or take a $20 bribe instead of writing a traffic ticket. "Meat eaters" are officers who actively use their power for personal gain. For example, several Chicago police officers were convicted in 2011 of robbing drug dealers and conducting illegal searches in order to steal money and drugs (Meisner, 2011). Although meat eaters are few, their actions make headlines when discovered. By contrast, because grass eaters are numerous, they make corruption seem acceptable and promote a code of secrecy that brands any officer who exposes corruption as a traitor.

Officers are often placed in situations where they can be tempted to enrich themselves by stealing money, property, or drugs, or by accepting favors, gifts, and bribes. If you were a police chief, how would you reduce the risks of police corruption?

If police administrators judge success merely by the maintenance of order on the streets and a steady flow of arrests and traffic citations, they may not have any idea what their officers actually do while on patrol. Officers therefore may learn that they can engage in improper conduct without worrying about investigations by supervisors as long as there is order on the streets and they keep their activities out of the public spotlight.

Over time, illegal activity may become accepted as normal. Ellwyn Stoddard, who studied "blue-coat crime," has said that it can become part of an "identifiable informal 'code'" (Stoddard, 1968:205). He suggests that officers are socialized to the code early in their careers. Those who "snitch" on other officers may be ostracized. Recent research shows that officers risk retaliation from peers if they break the code (Cancino and Enriquez, 2004). When corruption comes to official attention, officers protect the code by distancing themselves from the known offender rather than stopping their own improper conduct (C. Cooper, 2009; Stoddard, 1968).

New police officers must be instilled with a sense of ethics and professionalism in both their formal and informal training. Because of the significant discretion enjoyed by police and their independence in undertaking daily tasks, it is not possible for administrators to detect or prevent all misconduct. The public depends on officers to take seriously the responsibilities that come with the uniform and badge. When investigations reveal improper conduct by police, we must always wonder what impact that misconduct will have on the public trust in and cooperation with law enforcement officers.

check point

3. **What kinds of problems arise with police use of force?**
Risks that force will be used in ways that exceed what is needed for a specific situation; risks that force is applied disproportionately to minority group members.

4. **What is the difference between grass eaters and meat eaters?**
Grass eaters are officers who accept payoffs that police work brings their way. Meat eaters are officers who aggressively misuse their power for personal gain.

stop & analyze If you were a police chief, what three actions might you take to better prepare your officers to make discretionary decisions that include respect for ethical standards and adherence to proper professional standards for conduct?

Civic Accountablility

Making the police responsive to citizen complaints without burdening them with a flood of such grievances is difficult. The main challenge to improving police accountability is to use enough citizen input to force police to follow the law and departmental guidelines without restricting their ability to carry out their primary functions. At present, four less-than-perfect techniques are used in efforts to control the police: (1) internal affairs units, (2) civilian review boards, (3) standards and accreditation, and (4) civil liability lawsuits. We now look at each of these in turn.

Internal Affairs Units

The community must be confident that the department has procedures to ensure that officers will protect the rights of citizens. Yet, department complaint procedures often seem designed to discourage citizen input. People with complaints cannot always be certain that the police department will take any meaningful action.

Depending on the size of the department, a single officer or an entire section can serve as an **internal affairs unit** that receives and investigates complaints against officers. An officer charged with misconduct can face criminal prosecution or disciplinary action leading to resignation, dismissal, or suspension. Officers assigned to the internal affairs unit have duties similar to those of the inspector general's staff in the military. They must investigate complaints against other officers. Hollywood films and television series depict dramatic investigations of drug dealing and murder, but investigations of sexual harassment, alcohol or drug problems, misuse of force, and violations of departmental policies are more common.

The internal affairs unit must receive enough resources to fulfill its mission. It must also have direct access to the chief. Internal affairs investigators find the work stressful because their status prevents them from maintaining close relationships with other officers. They may face a wall of silence from fellow officers as they investigate complaints of misconduct within a department.

internal affairs unit A branch of a police department that receives and investigates complaints alleging violation of rules and policies on the part of officers.

Civilian Review Boards

If a police department cannot show that it effectively combats corruption among officers, the public will likely demand that the department be investigated by a **civilian review board**. The Bay Area Regional Transit (BART) system in California created such a citizens' board in the aftermath of a BART police officer's fatal shooting of an unarmed African American man under controversial circumstances (Melendez, 2011). Such a board allows complaints to be channeled through a committee of people who are not sworn police officers. The organization and powers of civilian review boards vary, but all oversee and review how police departments handle citizen complaints. The boards may also recommend remedial action. They do not have the power to investigate or discipline individual officers, however (S. Walker and Wright, 1995).

The main argument made by the police against civilian review boards is that people outside law enforcement do not understand the problems of policing. The police contend that civilian oversight lowers morale and hinders performance, claiming that officers will be less effective if they must worry about possible disciplinary actions. In reality, however, the boards have not been harsh.

The effectiveness of civilian review boards has not been tested, but their presence may improve police–citizen relations.

civilian review board Citizens' committee formed to investigate complaints against the police.

Standards and Accreditation

One way to increase police accountability is to require that police actions meet nationally recognized standards. The movement to accredit departments that meet these standards has gained momentum during the past decade. It has the support of the **Commission on Accreditation for Law Enforcement Agencies (CALEA)**, a private nonprofit corporation formed by four professional associations: the International Association of Chiefs of Police (IACP), the National Organization of Black Law Enforcement Executives (NOBLE), the National Sheriffs' Association (NSA), and the Police Executive Research Forum (PERF).

Police accreditation is voluntary. Departments contact CALEA, which helps them in their efforts to meet the standards. This process involves self-evaluation by departmental executives, the development of policies that meet the standards, and the training of officers. The CALEA representative acts like a military inspector general, visiting the department, examining its policies, and seeing if the standards are met in its daily operations. Departments that meet the standards receive certification. Administrators

Commission on Accreditation for Law Enforcement Agencies (CALEA) Nonprofit organization formed by major law enforcement executives' associations to develop standards for police policies and practice; on request, will review police agencies and award accreditation upon meeting those standards.

can use the standards as a management tool, training officers to know the standards and to be accountable for their actions. Obviously, the standards do not guarantee that police officers in an accredited department will not engage in misconduct. However, the guidelines serve as a major step toward providing clear guidance to officers about proper behavior. Accreditation can also show the public a department's commitment to making sure officers carry out their duties in an ethical, professional manner.

Civil Liability Lawsuits

Civil lawsuits against departments for police misconduct can increase police accountability. In 1961, the U.S. Supreme Court ruled that Section 1983 of the Civil Rights Act of 1871 allows citizens to sue public officials for violations of their civil rights. The high court extended this opportunity for **Section 1983 lawsuits** in 1978 when it ruled that individual officials and local agencies may be sued when a person's civil rights are violated by an agency's "customs and usages." If an individual can show that harm was caused by employees whose wrongful acts were the result of these "customs, practices, and policies, including poor training and supervision," then he or she can sue a local agency (*Monell v. Department of Social Services of the City of New York*, 1978).

> **Section 1983 lawsuits** Civil lawsuits authorized by a federal statute against state and local officials and local agencies when citizens have evidence that these officials or agencies have violated their federal constitutional rights.

Lawsuits charging police officers with brutality, improper use of weapons, dangerous driving, and false arrest are brought in both state and federal courts. Often, these lawsuits provide the basis for punishing officers who violate constitutional rights. Rights that are often subject to lawsuits are the Fourth Amendment right against unreasonable seizures, when police use excessive force or make improper arrests, and the Fourth Amendment right against unreasonable searches, when police wrongly search a house without a warrant.

In many states, people have received damage awards in the millions of dollars, and police departments have settled some suits out of court. In 2011, for example, the city of Philadelphia agreed to pay $1.2 million to the family of an unarmed man who was shot in the head by a police officer on New Year's Eve (Gorenstein, 2011). In 2009, Philadelphia paid amounts ranging from $690 to $750,000 to resolve 22 lawsuits and complaints about police (Gorenstein, 2011). Civil liability rulings by the courts tend to be simple and severe: Officials and municipalities are ordered to pay a sum of money, and the courts can enforce that judgment. The threat of significant financial awards gives police departments a strong incentive to improve the training and supervision of officers (Vaughn, 2001).

---

check point >

5. **What are the four methods used to increase the civic accountability of the police?**
Internal affairs units, civilian review boards, standards and accreditation, civil liability suits.

6. **What is an internal affairs unit?**
A unit, within a police department, designated to receive and investigate complaints alleging violation of rules and policies on the part of officers.

7. **Why are civilian review boards criticized by police officers?**
Police officers often fear that citizens do not understand the nature of law enforcement work and therefore will make inaccurate decisions about what constitutes improper behavior by officers.

stop & analyze
What are two arguments in favor of using only professionals in investigating and deciding whether police acted improperly? What are two arguments in favor of treating citizens as essential participants in these processes? Which set of arguments is more persuasive?

Delivery of Police Services

Law enforcement agencies attempt to structure their organization and processes to provide effective service to the public amid the reality of limited resources. In a contemporary era of significant budget cuts and reductions in personnel affecting agencies in various parts of the country, police departments must make difficult decisions about how to set priorities (Rudolph, 2012). These decisions include such matters as how to distribute officers on patrol and how to prioritize requests for assistance from the public.

Increasingly, police administrators look to **evidence-based policing** as a tool for making decisions about deployment of personnel and officers' duties on patrol (Gross-Shader, 2011). Evidence-based policing involves the examination of social science research on crime and policing, and the translation of that research into practical strategies for police departments to employ when addressing crime and other problems. With respect to crime prevention, for example, evidence-based policing draws from research studies that guide police to proactively employ specific strategies aimed at targeted locations within a city or town (Lum, Koper, and Telep, 2011). Otherwise, officers deployed on general patrols throughout an entire city would be less effective in preventing crime than when they are engaged in specific activities at targeted trouble spots. The effective use of evidence-based policing can be enhanced through cooperation and communication between law enforcement officials and criminal justice researchers.

> **evidence-based policing** The deployment of police personnel and development of police strategies based on the utilization of results from social science studies on the nature of crime and other social problems and the effectiveness of past efforts to address these problems.

Police Response

In a free society, people do not want police to stand on every street corner and ask them what they are doing. Thus, the police are mainly **reactive** (responding to citizen calls for service) rather than **proactive** (initiating actions in the absence of citizen requests). Studies of police work show that 81 percent of actions result from citizen telephone calls, 5 percent are initiated by citizens who approach an officer, and only 14 percent are initiated in the field by an officer. These facts affect the way departments are organized and the way the police respond to incidents.

> **reactive** Occurring in response, such as police activity in response to notification that a crime has been committed.

Because they are mainly reactive, the police usually arrive at the scene only after the crime has been committed and the perpetrator has fled. This means that the police are hampered by the time lapse and sometimes by inaccurate information given by witnesses. For example, a mugging may happen so quickly that victims and witnesses cannot accurately describe what occurred. In about a third of cases in which police are called, no one is present when the police arrive on the scene.

> **proactive** Acting in anticipation, such as an active search for potential offenders that is initiated by the police without waiting for a crime to be reported. Arrests for victimless crimes are usually proactive.

Citizens have come to expect that the police will respond quickly to every call, whether it requires immediate attention or can be handled in a more routine manner. This expectation has produced **incident-driven policing**, in which calls for service are the primary instigators of action. Studies have shown, though, that less than 30 percent of calls to the police involve criminal law enforcement—most calls concern order maintenance and service (S. Walker, 1999:80). To a large extent, then, reports by victims and observers define the boundaries of policing.

> **incident-driven policing** Policing in which calls for service are the primary instigators of action.

Most residents in urban and suburban areas can call 911 to report a crime or obtain help or information. The 911 system has brought a flood of calls to police departments—many not directly related to police responsibilities. In Baltimore a "311 system" has been implemented to help reduce the number of nonemergency calls, estimated as 40 percent of the total calls. Residents have been urged to call 311 when they need assistance that does not require the immediate dispatch of an officer. Studies found that this innovation reduced calls to 911 and resulted in extremely high public support (Mazerolle et al., 2003).

To improve efficiency, police departments use a **differential response** system that assigns priorities to calls for service. This system assumes that it is not always necessary to rush a patrol car to the scene when a call is received. The appropriate response depends on several factors—such as whether the incident is in progress,

> **differential response** A patrol strategy that assigns priorities to calls for service and chooses the appropriate response.

Common Belief: If more police officers actively patrolled the streets, instead of having so many at headquarters sitting in offices, crime rates in a city would certainly decline.

- Crime rates are shaped by a complex variety of factors that seem unrelated to the number of officers in a city's police department.
- Some cities with the highest number of officers per capita on the streets also have the highest crime rates.
- In addition, patrols do not necessarily reduce crime. Officers cannot be everywhere at once.
- Cities that have attempted to flood neighborhoods with officers often simply see criminals move their activities to a different location.
- Research raises questions about whether more-numerous patrols will necessarily impact crime rates.

CompStat Approach to crime prevention and police productivity measurement pioneered in New York City and then adopted in other cities that involves frequent meetings among police supervisors to examine detailed crime statistics for each precinct and develop immediate approaches and goals for problem solving and crime prevention.

clearance rate The percentage of crimes known to the police that they believe they have solved through an arrest; a statistic used to measure a police department's productivity.

has just occurred, or occurred some time ago, as well as whether anyone is or could be hurt.

The police do use proactive strategies such as surveillance and undercover work to combat some crimes. When addressing victimless crimes, for example, they must rely on informers, stakeouts, wiretapping, stings, and raids. Because of the current focus on drug offenses, police resources in many cities have been assigned to proactive efforts to apprehend people who use or sell illegal drugs. As you read "Criminal Justice: Myth & Reality," consider whether the use of proactive strategies will reduce crime.

Productivity

Following the lead of New York City's **CompStat** program, police departments in Baltimore, New Orleans, Indianapolis, and some smaller cities emphasized precinct-level accountability for crime reduction (Bass, 2012; Rosenfeld, Fornango, and Baumer, 2005). Through twice-weekly briefings before their peers and senior executives, precinct commanders must explain the results of their efforts to reduce crime. In the CompStat approach, they are held responsible for the success of crime control efforts in their precincts as indicated by crime statistics (Weisburd, Mastrofski, et al., 2003). Essential to this management strategy is timely, accurate information. Computer systems have been developed to put up-to-date crime data into the hands of managers at all levels (Willis, Mastrofski, and Weisburd, 2004). This allows discussion of department-wide strategies and puts pressure on low producers (Sherman, 1998:430; Silverman, 1999). The CompStat approach has raised questions as to how police work should be measured. It has also raised questions about how to integrate this centralized approach for measuring performance with community policing, a decentralized strategy for crime prevention, order maintenance, and fear reduction (Willis, Mastrofski, and Kochel, 2010).

Quantifying police work is difficult in part because of the wide range of duties and day-to-day tasks of officers. In the past, the crime rate and the clearance rate

→ The use of crime statistics for CompStat discussions with precinct commanders is a way to measure productivity and a method of using evidence as the basis for police strategy. Should knowledge of statistics and research methods be required for officers who attain supervisory positions that involve decisions about personnel deployment and crime-prevention strategies?

© Peter Casolino/New Haven Register

have been used as measures of "good" policing. A lower crime rate might be cited as evidence of an effective department, but critics note that factors other than policing affect this measure. Like other public agencies, the police departments and the citizens in a community have trouble gauging the quantity and quality of police officers' work (see "What Americans Think").

The **clearance rate**—the percentage of crimes known to police that they believe they have solved through an arrest—is a basic measure of police performance. The clearance rate varies by type of offense. In reactive situations this rate can be low. For example, the police may learn about a burglary hours or even days after it has occurred; the clearance rate for such crimes is only about 13 percent. Police have much more success in handling violent crimes, in which victims often know their assailants; the clearance rate for such cases is 46 percent.

These measures of police productivity are sometimes supplemented by other data, such as the number of traffic citations issued, illegally parked cars ticketed, and suspects stopped for questioning, as well as the value of stolen goods recovered. These additional ways of counting work done reflect the fact that an officer may work hard for many hours but have no arrests to show for his or her efforts. Yet, society may benefit even more when officers spend their time in activities that are hard to measure, such as calming disputes, becoming acquainted with people in the neighborhood, and providing services to those in need. Some research indicates that officers who engage in activities that produce higher levels of measurable productivity, such as issuing citations or making arrests, also receive higher numbers of citizen complaints about alleged misconduct (Lersch, 2002).

Question: "How would you rate the police in your community on the following?"

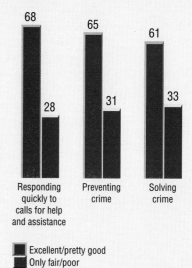

Responding quickly to calls for help and assistance: 68, 28

Preventing crime: 65, 31

Solving crime: 61, 33

■ Excellent/pretty good
■ Only fair/poor

Critical Thinking: Do you have actual knowledge about police performance or do you merely have perceptions? What may shape your perceptions—news coverage, experiences of friends and relatives, other influences? If some people's opinions are based on perceptions rather than on personal experience, what steps could a police chief take to improve the department's image?

Note: Percentages do not add to 100, because some respondents declined to answer specific questions.

Source: Bureau of Justice Statistics, *Sourcebook of Criminal Justice Statistics, 2003*, Table 2.22 (http://www.albany.edu/sourcebook/pdf/t222.pdf).

8. What is evidence-based policing?
Police strategies and deployment of resources developed through examination of research on crime, social problems, and previously used strategies.

9. What is differential response?
Policy that gives priority to calls according to whether an immediate or delayed response is warranted.

10. What are examples of measures of police productivity?
Crime statistics (CompStat), clearance rate, traffic citations.

If you were a police chief, how would you measure your officers' productivity? Suggest two possible measures and list the advantages and disadvantages of each.

Patrol Functions

Patrol is often called the backbone of police operations. The word *patrol* is derived from a French word, *patrouiller*, which once meant "to tramp about in the mud." This is an apt description of a function that one expert has described as "arduous, tiring, difficult, and performed in conditions other than ideal" (Chapman, 1970:ix). For most Americans, "policing" is the familiar sight of a uniformed and armed patrol officer, on call 24 hours a day.

Every local police department has a patrol unit. Even in large departments, patrol officers account for up to two-thirds of all **sworn officers**—those who have taken an oath and received the powers to make arrests and to use necessary force in accordance with their duties. In small communities, police operations are not specialized, and the patrol force is the department. As we have seen, the patrol officer must be prepared for any imaginable situation and must perform many duties.

Television portrays patrol officers as always on the go—rushing from one incident to another and making several arrests in a single shift. A patrol officer may indeed be called to deal with a robbery in progress or to help rescue people from a burning building. However, the patrol officer's life is not always so exciting, and often involves routine and even boring tasks such as directing traffic at accident scenes and road construction sites.

Most officers, on most shifts, do not make even one arrest. To better understand patrol work, examine Figure 5.1 and note how the police of Wilmington, Delaware, allocate time to various activities.

The patrol function has three parts: answering calls for help, maintaining a police presence, and probing suspicious circumstances. Patrol officers are well suited to answering calls, because they usually are near the scene and can move quickly to provide help or catch a suspect. At other times they engage in **preventive patrol**—that is, making the police visible and their presence known in an effort to deter crime and to make officers available to respond quickly to calls. Whether walking the streets or cruising in a car, the patrol officer is on the lookout for suspicious people and behavior. With experience, officers come to trust their own ability to spot signs of suspicious activity that merit stopping people on the street for questioning.

Patrol officers' duties sound fairly straightforward, yet these officers often find themselves in complex situations requiring sound judgments and careful actions. As the first to arrive at a crime scene, the officer must comfort and give aid to victims, identify and question witnesses, control crowds, and gather evidence. These roles call for creativity and good communication skills.

sworn officers Police employees who have taken an oath and been given powers by the state to make arrests and to use necessary force, in accordance with their duties.

preventive patrol Making the police presence known, to deter crime and to make officers available to respond quickly to calls.

Figure 5.1
Time Allocated to Patrol Activities by the Police of Wilmington, Delaware The time spent on each activity was calculated from records for each police car unit. Note the range of activities and the time spent on each.
Source: Jack R. Greene and Carl B. Klockars, "What Police Do," in *Thinking about Police*, 2nd ed., ed. Carl B. Klockars and Stephen D. Mastrofski (New York: McGraw-Hill, 1991), 279.

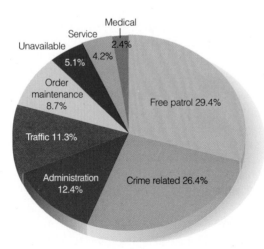

Free patrol: park and walk

Crime related: officer in trouble, suspicious person/vehicle, crime in progress, alarm, investigate crime not in progress, serve warrant/subpoena, assist other police

Administration: meal break, report writing, firearms training, police vehicle maintenance, at headquarters, court related

Traffic: accident investigation, parking problems, motor vehicle driving problems, traffic control, fire emergency

Order maintenance: order maintenance in progress, animal complaint, noise complaint

Service: service related

Medical: medical emergency, at local hospital

Because the patrol officers have the most direct contact with the public, their actions, in large part, determine the image of the police and their relations with the community. Moreover, successful investigations and prosecutions often depend on patrol officers' actions in questioning witnesses and gathering evidence after a crime.

Investigation

All cities with a population of more than 250,000, and 90 percent of smaller cities, have officers called **detectives**, who are assigned to investigative duties. Detectives make up 15 percent of police personnel. Compared with patrol officers, they enjoy a higher status in the department: Their pay is higher, their hours are more flexible, and they are supervised less closely. Detectives do not wear uniforms and their work is considered more interesting than that of patrol officers. In addition, they engage solely in law enforcement rather than in order maintenance or service work; hence, their activities conform more closely to the image of the police as crime fighters.

A police officer in Santa Ana, California, dusts the door of a stolen car to look for fingerprints. Police departments use various forensic techniques to discover evidence. Some techniques are used at crime scenes, while others involve tests in scientific laboratories. Which techniques are likely to be the most effective?

detectives Police officers, typically working in plainclothes, who investigate crimes that have occurred by questioning witnesses and gathering evidence.

Within federal law enforcement agencies, the work of special agents is similar to that of detectives. In agencies such as the FBI, DEA, and Secret Service, special agents are plainclothes officers who focus on investigations. One key difference between federal special agents and detectives in local departments is that federal agents are more likely to be proactive in initiating investigations to prevent terrorism, drug trafficking, and other crimes. Local detectives are typically reactive, responding to crimes already discovered.

Detectives typically become involved after a crime has been reported and a patrol officer has done a preliminary investigation. The job of detectives is mainly to talk to people—victims, suspects, witnesses—to find out what happened. On the basis of this information, detectives develop theories about who committed the crime; they then set out to gather the evidence that will lead to arrest and prosecution.

In performing an investigation, detectives depend not only on their own experience but also on technical experts. Much of the information they need comes from criminal files, lab technicians, and forensic scientists. Many small departments turn to the state crime laboratory or the FBI for such information. Often depicted as working alone, detectives, in fact, operate as part of a team.

Apprehension   The discovery that a crime has been committed sets off a chain of events leading to the capture of a suspect and the gathering of the evidence needed to convict that person. It may also lead to several dead ends, such as a lack of clues pointing to a suspect or a lack of evidence to link the suspect to the crime.

The process of catching a suspect has three stages: detection of a crime, preliminary investigation, and follow-up investigation. Depending on the outcome of the investigation, these three steps may be followed by a fourth: clearance and arrest. As shown in Figure 5.2, these actions are designed to use criminal justice resources to arrest a suspect and assemble enough evidence to support a charge.

American police have long relied on science in gathering, identifying, and analyzing evidence. The public has become increasingly aware of the wide range of scientific testing techniques used for law enforcement purposes, through the television drama *CSI: Crime Scene Investigation* and its spin-offs (S. Stephens, 2007). As we will examine in greater detail in Chapter 14, scientific analysis of fingerprints, blood, semen, hair, textiles, soil, weapons, and other materials has helped the police identify criminals.

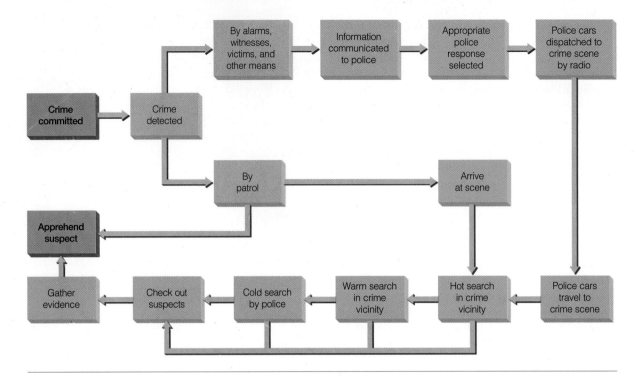

Figure 5.2

The Apprehension Process Apprehension of a felony suspect results from a sequence of actions by patrol officers and detectives. Coordination of these efforts is key to solving major crimes.

© Cengage Learning

Special Operations

Patrol and investigation are the two largest and most important units in a police department. In metropolitan areas, however, special units are set up to deal with specific types of problems. The most common of such units concern traffic, vice, juveniles, and SWAT (strategic weapons and tactics) teams. Some cities also have units to deal with organized crime and drugs. Even with such special units in place, however, regular patrol officers and investigators continue to deal individually in their daily work with the drugs, juvenile delinquency, and other problems that are targeted by special units.

It is increasingly common for police agencies to cooperate with each other in multiagency task forces to better address specialized problems that are not confined to a specific spot in one city. Such task-force participation is especially prevalent for the largest cities. For example, more than 80 percent of cities larger than 250,000 participate in antiterrorism task forces, and more than a third of such cities participate in human-trafficking task forces (Reaves, 2010).

As we examine the special units used by many departments, bear in mind that individual officers may receive special assignments, too. A good example is the development of **school resource officers (SROs)**, police officers assigned to high schools under contractual arrangements between public schools and local police departments. More than 85 percent of police departments in cities ranging in size from 25,000 to 500,000 have officers assigned to SRO duty (Reaves, 2010). School resource officers provide a visible presence that may deter misconduct and they have full authority to enforce laws as well as school rules. They are expected to develop relationships with students, which will permit them to provide advice and guidance. These officers are positioned to help develop positive relationships between young people and police. In addition, they frequently give formal talks in classrooms to educate students about law and the criminal justice system (Finn et al., 2005). The use of SROs represents a particularly important form of individualized special assignment because it shows in one specific setting how police officers' functions and duties extend well beyond the crime-fighting image that is commonly associated with law enforcement.

school resource officers (SROs) Police officers assigned for duty in schools to assist in order maintenance while also developing positive relationships with students that may assist in delinquency prevention.

Traffic Traffic regulation is a major job of the police. The police regulate the flow of vehicles, investigate accidents, and enforce traffic laws. This work may not seem to have much to do with crime fighting or order maintenance, but in fact it does. Besides helping to maintain order, enforcement of traffic laws educates the public by promoting safe driving habits and provides a visible service to the community.

Traffic work is mostly proactive and permits officers to use broad discretion about whom to stop and whether to issue a citation. Traffic duty can also help the police catch criminals. In enforcing traffic laws, patrol officers can stop cars and question drivers. Stolen property and suspects linked to other criminal acts are often found this way. Most departments can now automatically check license numbers against lists of wanted vehicles and suspects.

Vice Enforcement of vice laws depends on proactive police work, which often involves the use of undercover agents and informers. Most big-city police departments have a vice unit. Strict enforcement of these laws requires that officers receive wide discretion. They often must engage in degrading and dangerous activities, such as posing as prostitutes or drug dealers, in order to catch lawbreakers. The special nature of vice work requires members of the unit to be well trained in the legal procedures required for arrests to lead to convictions.

The potential for corruption in this type of police work presents some administrative problems. Undercover officers are in a position to blackmail gamblers and drug dealers, and they may also be offered bribes. In addition, officers working undercover must be transferred when their identities become known.

Drug Law Enforcement Many large cities have a bureau to enforce drug laws. These agencies may include task forces that deal with organized crime or with gangs involved in drug dealing. Some groups may use sting operations to arrest drug sellers on the street; still others may provide drug education in the community.

Drug enforcement sometimes reflects the goal of *aggressive patrol*, or assigning resources so as to get the largest number of arrests and to stop street dealing. Police executives believe that they must show dealers and the community that drug laws are actively enforced. Streets on which drugs are dealt openly can be flooded with officers who engage in proactive stops and questionings. There are risks, however, that drug dealers will simply move their operations to new locations.

Many public officials argue that drugs should be viewed as a public-health problem rather than as a crime problem. Critics of current policies believe that society would benefit more from drug-treatment programs, which can help some people to stop using drugs, than from police actions that fill prisons without doing much to reduce drug use.

---

check point

11. What are the three parts of the patrol function?
Answering calls for assistance, maintaining a police presence, probing suspicious circumstances.

12. What are the four steps in the apprehension process?
(1) Detection of crime, (2) preliminary investigation, (3) follow-up investigation, (4) clearance and arrest.

13. What are three kinds of special operations units that police departments often employ?
Traffic, vice, narcotics.

stop & analyze

Think about the city or town where you live. Is there a need for a special operations unit in your police department? Why or why not? Give two reasons for your answer.

Issues in Patrolling

In the last 30 years, much research has been done on police methods of assigning tasks to patrol officers, deploying them, and communicating with them. Although the conclusions have been mixed, these studies have caused experts to rethink some aspects of patrolling. However, even when researchers agree on which patrol practices are the most effective, those practices often run counter to the desires of departmental personnel. For example, foot patrol may be a key component of community-policing strategies, but many officers would rather remain in squad cars than walk the pavement. Police administrators, therefore, must deal with many issues to successfully develop and implement effective patrol strategies.

Assignment of Patrol Personnel

In the past it has been assumed that patrol officers should be assigned where and when they will be most effective in preventing crime, keeping order, and serving the public. For the police administrator, the question has been "Where should the officers be sent, when, and in what numbers?" There are no guidelines to answer this question, and most assignments seem to be based on the notion that patrols should be concentrated in "problem" neighborhoods or in areas where crime rates and calls for service are high. Thus, the assignment of officers is based on factors such as crime statistics, 911 calls, degree of urbanization, pressures from business and community groups, ethnic composition, and socioeconomic conditions. Experimentation with different strategies in various cities has led to numerous choices for police leaders. In addition, research on these strategies sheds light on the strengths and weaknesses of various options. We shall examine several options in greater detail: (1) preventive patrol, (2) hot spots, (3) foot versus motorized patrol, (4) aggressive patrol, and (5) community policing.

Preventive Patrol   Preventive patrol has long been thought to help deter crime. Many have argued that a patrol officer's moving through an area will keep criminals from carrying out illegal acts. In 1974, this assumption was tested in Kansas City, Missouri. The surprising results shook the theoretical foundations of American policing (Sherman and Weisburd, 1995).

In the Kansas City Preventive Patrol Experiment, a 15-beat area was divided into three sections, each with similar crime rates, population characteristics, income levels, and numbers of calls to the police. In one area, labeled "reactive," all preventive patrol was withdrawn, and the police entered only in response to citizens' calls for service. In another section, labeled "proactive," preventive patrol was raised to as much as 4 times the normal level; all other services were provided at the same levels as before. The third section was used as a control, with the usual level of services, including preventive patrol, maintained. After observing events in the three sections for a year, the researchers concluded that the changes in patrol strategies had had no major effects on the amount of crime reported, the amount of crime as measured by citizen surveys, or citizens' fear of crime (Kelling, Pate, et al., 1974). Neither a decrease nor an increase in patrol activity had any apparent effect on crime.

Despite contradictory findings of other studies using similar research methods, the Kansas City finding "remains the most influential test of the general deterrent effects of patrol on crime" (Sherman and Weisburd, 1995:626). Because of this study, many departments have shifted their focus from law enforcement to maintaining order and serving the public. Some have argued that if the police cannot prevent crime by changing their patrol tactics, they may serve society better by focusing patrol activities on other functions while fighting crime as best they can.

Hot Spots   In the past, patrols were organized by "beats." It was assumed that crime can happen anywhere, and the entire beat must be patrolled at all times. Research shows, however, that crime is not spread evenly over all times and places. Instead, direct-contact predatory crimes, such as muggings and robberies, occur when three elements converge: motivated offenders, suitable targets, and the absence of anyone who could prevent the violation. This means that resources should be focused on *hot spots*, places where crimes are likely to occur. The deployment of personnel in this manner can prevent crimes from occurring.

Advocates of evidence-based policing argue that "place-based policing," such as focusing on hot spots, can prevent crime and also reduce arrests and costs of processing cases (Aden and Koper, 2011). According to David Weisburd, "If place-based policing were to become the central focus of police crime prevention, rather than arrest and apprehension of offenders, we would likely see at the same time a reduction in prison populations and an increase in crime prevention effectiveness of the police" (2011:16).

Administrators can assign officers to **directed patrol**—a proactive strategy designed to direct resources to known high-crime areas. Research indicates that directed-patrol activities focused on suspicious activities and locations can reduce violent gun crime (McGarrell et al., 2001). Observers fear that the extra police pressure may simply cause lawbreakers to move to another area (Goldkamp and Vilcica, 2008).

directed patrol A proactive form of patrolling that directs resources to known high-crime areas.

Foot versus Motorized Patrol One of the most frequent citizen requests is for officers to be put back on the beat. This was the main form of police patrol until the 1930s, when motorized patrol came to be viewed as more effective. Foot patrol and bicycle patrol are used in the majority of cities larger than 10,000 residents, including approximately 90 percent of cities with 50,000 or more inhabitants (Hickman and Reaves, 2006). However, departments typically use these strategies only in selected neighborhoods or districts with a high business or population density. Most patrolling is still conducted in cars. Cars increase the amount of territory that officers can patrol. With advances in communications technologies and onboard computers, patrol officers have direct links to headquarters and to criminal information databases. Now the police can be quickly sent where needed, with crucial information in their possession.

In contrast to police in vehicles, officers on foot stay close to the daily life of the neighborhood. They detect criminal activity and apprehend lawbreakers more easily than do car patrols. In addition, recent research indicates that foot patrols can be effective in reducing criminal activities at crime hot spots in neighborhoods (Ratcliffe et al., 2011).

Aggressive Patrol **Aggressive patrol** is a proactive strategy designed to maximize police activity in the community. It takes many forms, such as "sting" operations, firearms confiscation, raids on crack houses, programs that encourage citizens to list their valuables, and the tracking of high-risk parolees. Some have argued that the effect of the police on crime depends less on how many officers are deployed in an area than on what they do while they are there.

aggressive patrol A patrol strategy designed to maximize the number of police interventions and observations in the community.

The zero-tolerance policing of the 1990s in New York City is an example of aggressive patrol linked to the "broken windows" theory. As you will recall, this theory asserts "that if not firmly suppressed, disorderly behavior in public will frighten citizens and attract predatory criminals, thus leading to more serious crime problems" (Greene, 1999:172). Thus, the police should focus on minor, public-order crimes such as aggressive panhandling, graffiti, prostitution, and urinating in public. By putting more police on the streets, decentralizing authority to the precinct level, and instituting officer accountability, the zero-tolerance policy was judged to be a factor in reducing New York City's crime rate (Messner, Galea, et al., 2007; Rosenfeld, Fornango, and Rengifo, 2007).

Aggressive policing has also been applied as part of the war on drugs, with police officers stopping many vehicles and frisking pedestrians on certain streets. In Detroit, aggressive, zero-tolerance police practices reduced gang-related crime in targeted precincts (Bynum and Varano, 2002). Police departments also use aggressive patrol strategies to track high-risk parolees and apprehend them if they commit new offenses.

Many police chiefs credit aggressive take-back-the-streets tactics with reducing urban crime rates in the past two decades. In some cities, however, there are questions about whether such tactics have harmed police–community relations through searches and arrests that neighborhood residents view as unjustified. If you were a police chief, what patrol strategy would you choose and what specific goals would you seek to advance?

Research now raises questions about whether the "broken windows" approach actually reduces crime. Several studies present new analyses of data that challenge claims that aggressive policing is what caused crime reduction during the 1990s (Harcourt and Ludwig, 2006). Moreover, the "broken windows" approach might actually lead to citizen hostility. In some urban neighborhoods, there are rumblings that aggressive patrol has gone too far and is straining police relations with young African Americans and Hispanics.

Community Policing To a great extent, community policing has been seen as the solution to problems with the crime-fighter stance that prevailed during the professional model era (P. V. Murphy, 1992). Community policing consists of attempts by the police to involve residents in making their own neighborhoods safer. Based on the belief that citizens are often concerned about local disorder as well as crime in general, this strategy emphasizes cooperation between the police and citizens in identifying community needs and determining the best ways to meet them (Reisig, 2010; M. Moore, 1992).

Community policing has four components (Skolnick and Bayley, 1986):

1. Community-based crime prevention
2. Changing the focus of patrol activities to nonemergency services
3. Making the police more accountable to the public
4. Decentralizing decision making to include residents

As indicated by these four components, community policing requires a major shift in the philosophy of policing. In particular, police officials must view citizens both as customers to be served and as partners in the pursuit of social goals, rather than as a population to be watched, controlled, and served reactively (Morash, Ford, White, et al., 2002). Although crime control may remain a priority in community policing, the change in emphasis can strengthen police effectiveness for order maintenance and service (Zhao, He, et al., 2003).

Departments that view themselves as emphasizing community policing do not necessarily share identical patrol strategies and initiatives (Thurman, Zhao, and Giacomazzi, 2001). Some departments emphasize identifying and solving problems related to disorder and crime. Other departments work mainly on strengthening local neighborhoods. A department's emphasis can affect which activities become the focus of officers' working hours. The common element in community-policing programs is a high level of interaction between officers and citizens and the involvement of citizens in identifying problems and solving them.

problem-oriented policing
An approach to policing in which officers routinely seek to identify, analyze, and respond to the circumstances underlying the incidents that prompt citizens to call the police.

A central feature of community policing for many departments is **problem-oriented policing**, a strategy that seeks to find out what is causing citizens to call for help (Weisburd, Telep, et al., 2010; Goldstein, 1990). The police seek to identify, analyze, and respond to the conditions underlying the events that prompt people to call the police (Maguire, Uchida, and Hassell, 2012; Cordner and Biebel, 2005; DeJong, Mastrofski, and Parks, 2001). Knowing those conditions, officers can enlist community agencies and residents to help resolve them. Recent research indicates that problem-solving approaches can impact various crimes, including drug sales and homicides (Corsaro, Brunson, and McGarrell, 2012; Chermak and McGarrell, 2004). Police using this approach do not just fight crime (M. D. White et al., 2003); they address a broad array of other problems that affect the quality of life in the community.

The Future of Patrol

Preventive patrol and reactive response to calls for help have been the hallmarks of policing in the United States for the past half century. However, research done in the past 30 years has raised many questions about which patrol strategies police should employ. The rise of community policing has shifted law enforcement toward problems that affect residents' quality of life. The continuing development of evidence-based policing is producing greater attention to place-based strategies, such as hot spots. Police forces need to use patrol tactics that fit the needs of the neighborhood. Neighborhoods with crime hot spots may require different strategies than do neighborhoods where residents are concerned mainly with order maintenance. Many researchers believe that traditional patrol efforts have focused too narrowly on crime control, neglecting the order maintenance and service activities for which police departments were originally formed. Critics have urged the police to become more community oriented.

The current era of budget cuts and reductions in police-force personnel will constrict many police chiefs' flexibility in their use of officers. It remains to be seen how financial problems will reduce various forms of patrol or if they push departments, by necessity, toward either a purely reactive or hot-spot emphasis. Some cities already face the worst-case scenario of having every patrol shift reduced to so few officers that they are unable to respond to all calls about felonies (LeDuff, 2011).

How the national effort to combat terrorism will affect local police-patrol operations remains uncertain. Since the attacks of September 11, state and local police have assumed greater responsibility for investigating bank robberies and other federal crimes as the FBI and other federal agencies devote significant attention to catching people connected with terrorist organizations. In addition, even local police officers must be ready to spot suspicious activities that might relate to terrorist activity. They are the first responders in a bombing or other form of attack. Obviously, federal law enforcement officials must work closely with local police in order to be effective. The new concerns will not alter traditional police responsibilities for crime fighting, order maintenance, and service, but they will provide an additional consideration as police administrators plan how to train and deploy their personnel.

check point

14. **What are the advantages of foot patrol? Of motorized patrol?**
   Officers on foot patrol have greater contact with residents of a neighborhood, thus gaining their confidence and assistance. Officers on motorized patrol have a greater range of activity and can respond speedily to calls.

15. **What is aggressive patrol?**
   A proactive strategy designed to maximize the number of police interventions and observations in a community.

16. **What are the major elements of community policing?**
   Community policing emphasizes order maintenance and service. It attempts to involve members of the community in making their neighborhoods safe. Foot patrol and decentralization of command are usually part of community-policing efforts.

stop & analyze

If you were a police chief, what approaches to patrol would you choose to implement? Give three reasons for your answer.

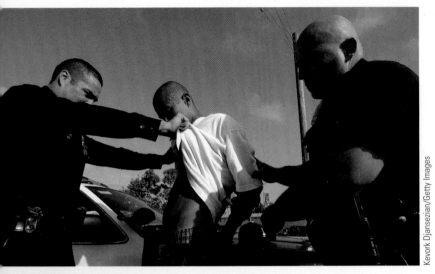

In multicultural America, police must be sensitive to the perspectives and customs of many different groups. They must enforce the law while treating people equally and upholding civil liberties. These responsibilities can be difficult when people are angry or uncooperative. Have you heard about situations in which police officers' emotions, such as anger or frustration, affected their decisions or behavior?

Kevork Djansezian/Getty Images

Police and the Community

The work of a police officer in a U.S. city can be very difficult, involving hours of boring, routine work interrupted by short spurts of dangerous crime fighting. Although police work has always been frustrating and dangerous, officers today must deal with situations ranging from helping the homeless to dealing with domestic violence to confronting shoot-outs at drug deals gone sour. Yet, police actions are sometimes mishandled by officers or misinterpreted by the public, making some people critical of the police.

Special Populations

Urban police forces must deal with a complex population. City streets contain growing numbers of people suffering from mental illness, homelessness, alcoholism, drug addiction, or serious medical conditions such as acquired immune deficiency syndrome (AIDS) (Reuland, 2010; Hails and Borum, 2003). In addition, they may find youthful runaways and children victimized by their parents' neglect. Several factors have contributed to increasing numbers of "problem" people on the streets. These factors include overcrowded jails, cutbacks in public assistance, and the closing of many psychiatric institutions, which must then release mental health patients. Most of these individuals do not commit crimes, but their presence disturbs many of their fellow citizens and thus they may contribute to fear of crime and disorder (T. Coleman and Cotton, 2010).

Patrol officers cooperate with social-service agencies in helping individuals and responding to requests for order maintenance. Police departments have developed various techniques for dealing with special populations, such as the use of Crisis Intervention Teams (CIT) in conjunction with social-service agencies (Franz and Borum, 2011). In some cities, mobile units are equipped with restraining devices and medical equipment to handle disturbed people.

Clearly, dealing with special populations is a major problem for police in most cities. Each community must develop policies so that officers will know when and how they are to intervene when a person may not have broken the law but is upsetting residents. Inevitably, police officers will make mistakes in some situations. For instance, their interactions with troubled people sometimes lead to tragic consequences, such as using lethal force against deaf or mentally ill people whose actions are misperceived as threatening. In 2003, a controversy erupted in Denver after police shot a legally blind, mentally handicapped teenager who was holding a knife (Felch, 2003).

Policing in a Multicultural Society

In the last half century, the racial and ethnic composition of the United States has changed. During the mid-twentieth century, many African Americans moved from rural areas of the South to northern cities. In recent years, immigrants from Central and South America have become the fastest-growing minority group in many cities. Latinos are now the largest minority population in the nation. Immigrants from Eastern Europe, Russia, the Middle East, and Asia have entered the country in greater numbers than before.

Policing requires trust, understanding, and cooperation between officers and the public. People must be willing to call for help and provide information about wrongdoing. But in a multicultural society, relations between the police and minorities are complicated by stereotypes, cultural variations, and language differences. Most of these immigrants come from countries with cultural traditions and laws that differ from those in the United States. These traditions may be unfamiliar to American police officers. Further, some immigrants cannot communicate easily in English. Lack of familiarity, difficulties in communicating, and excessive suspicion can increase the risk that officers will violate the American principle of equal treatment of all people (C. E. Smith, McCall, and Perez McCluskey, 2005).

Like other Americans who have limited personal experience or familiarity with people from different backgrounds, officers may attribute undesirable traits to members of minority groups. Treating people according to stereotypes, rather than as individuals, creates tensions that harden negative attitudes. As you read the "Close Up," consider how officers' decisions to intrude upon people's liberty by stopping and searching them on the streets may affect attitudes toward the police.

Public opinion surveys have shown that race and ethnicity play a key role in determining people's attitudes toward the police. As seen in "What Americans Think," questions of fair treatment by the police differ among racial groups (Stewart et al., 2009; Gabbidon and Higgins, 2009). Young, low-income, racial-minority men carry the most negative attitudes toward the police (Gabbidon, Higgins, and Potter, 2011; S. Walker, Spohn, and DeLeone, 2007). Inner-city neighborhoods—the areas that need and want effective policing—often significantly distrust the police; citizens may therefore fail to report crimes and refuse to cooperate with the police (Carr, Napolitano, and Keating, 2007). Encounters between officers and members of these communities are often hostile and sometimes lead to large-scale disorders. In January 2008, hundreds of protestors marched in Lima, Ohio, to express their outrage that police officers, when entering a home to look for a male drug suspect, had shot and killed a young African American woman and wounded her toddler. Twenty-seven percent of Lima's 38,000 residents are African American, yet only two of the city's 77 police officers are African American (Maag, 2008). All aspects of officers' responsibilities, including service, order maintenance, and crime control, can suffer when police officers and the communities they serve lack cooperation and trust.

What Americans Think

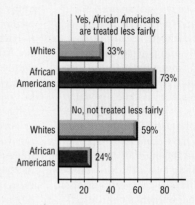

Question: "Just your impression, are African Americans in your community treated less fairly than whites in the following situations? How about in dealing with the police, such as traffic incidents?"

Yes, African Americans are treated less fairly

Whites — 33%
African Americans — 73%

No, not treated less fairly

Whites — 59%
African Americans — 24%

Critical Thinking: Can individual police officers take actions that will improve the perceptions and relationship between police and residents in a community? If so, what can officers do?

Source: Gallup Poll, June 2–24, 2007 (http://www.gallup.com).

Community Crime Prevention

There is a growing awareness that the police cannot control crime and disorder on their own. Social control requires involvement by all members of the community. **Community crime prevention** can be enhanced if government agencies

community crime prevention Programs through which criminal justice officials cultivate relationships with and rely on assistance from citizens in preventing crime and apprehending offenders within neighborhoods.

Living under Suspicion

One of the most invasive discretionary decisions made by police officers is the determination of when to do a warrantless search. As we will see in Chapter 6, there are specific situations in which police officers are authorized to search people and places without seeking approval from a judge in the form of a search warrant. One key situation that interferes with people's privacy and liberty is a stop-and-frisk search. This does not mean that officers are supposed to have complete discretion to simply feel the outer clothing of anyone walking down the street to see if the individual is carrying a weapon, drugs, or other evidence of criminal activity. Indeed, the original Supreme Court decisions in *Terry v. Ohio* (1968) was quite specific about the circumstances in which such searches could be done on the spot and to avoid giving police officers complete freedom to do searches based on hunches or other unjustified grounds. According to the *Terry* decision, "where a police officer observes unusual conduct which leads him to reasonably conclude in light of his experience that criminal activity may be afoot and that the persons with whom he is dealing may be armed and presently dangerous," the officer may stop the individual and conduct a limited search of the outer clothing. Unfortunately, studies in a number of cities indicate that some officers may be more inclined to conclude "criminal activity may be afoot" when they see African Americans or Latinos, and less likely to reach that conclusion when they see whites who may be engaged in the same questionable behaviors.

A review of New York City police records showed that its officers conducted 575,000 stop-and-frisk searches in 2009. Whites constitute the largest racial group in the city, more than 40 percent of the city's population in the first decade of the twenty-first century, yet the number of African Americans and Latinos subjected to stop-and-frisk searches was many times more than the number of whites subjected to such searches. During 2009, there were nearly 490,000 stop-and-frisk searches of African Americans and Latinos and only 53,000 stop-and-frisk searches of whites. Yet whites were more likely to be found illegally carrying weapons, 1.7 percent of whites versus only 1.1 percent of African Americans. Such findings raise concerns that officers are more likely to look for actual indications of potential criminal behavior before searching whites but more freely search African Americans and Latinos without the proper basis articulated in the original *Terry v. Ohio* decision. A sophisticated statistical analysis of New York City stop-and-frisk searches from the late 1990s concluded that "police were more willing to stop minority group members with less reason" (Gelman et al., 2007: 821).

Indicators of racial differences in the rate of discretionary stops and searches by police officers are not limited to large cities. For example, a 2011 study of the Lansing, Michigan, police department found that, although Latinos make up only 10 percent of the city's population, they were subjected to 33 percent of the discretionary searches conducted by officers in conjunction with traffic stops.

What do these racial disparities mean for Americans who are members of racial and ethnic minority groups? Can minority citizens avoid feeling as if they are constantly under suspicion if they see, through their own experiences or the experiences of friends and relatives, that they are much more likely than white Americans to be stopped and searched by the police?

and neighborhood organizations cooperate. Across the country, community programs to help the police have proliferated (Wehrman and DeAngelis, 2011; Arthur et al., 2010; Zhao, Gibson, et al., 2002). The federal government has funded and facilitated intergovernmental cooperation and citizen involvement through a variety of programs, including Project Safe Neighborhoods, an anticrime program with a significant focus on antigang efforts and the reduction in illegal firearms.

More than six million Americans belong to citizen crime-watch groups, which often have direct ties to police departments. Many communities also use the Crime Stoppers Program to enlist public help in solving crimes. Television and radio stations present the "unsolved crime of the week," sometimes with cash rewards given for information that leads to the conviction of the offender. Although these programs help solve some crimes, the number solved remains small compared with the total number of crimes committed.

In 2007, the number of stop-and-frisk searches of African Americans in New York City was equal to more than 21 percent of the African American population of the city. By contrast, the number of such searches directed at whites was equal to less than 3 percent of the white population. How might such figures—and the thousands of experiences that they represent—affect people's views about the police? Are there risks that discretionary decisions that lead to racial disparities will ultimately harm policing by making people distrustful and unwilling to help the police?

While these disparities in the application of police discretion are cause for concern, there is also visible progress toward fair and appropriate treatment. Like many other departments, the Lansing Police Department pays outside researchers to study their traffic stops and searches each year because the department wants to be educated about its officers' actions and to use the findings to develop additional training and to improve supervision, if necessary. In 2010, the Arizona state legislature sought to require officers to ask people about their immigration status. The law raised fears that it would push officers to engage in racial profiling, especially with respect to Latinos. Although the

law was put on hold by a court order, police departments moved forward with additional training for their officers about the proper bases for searches and how to avoid accusations of racial profiling. Some observers believe that the additional training is helping to reduce bias and errors in officers' decisions about when a stop is legally justified.

For Critical Analysis

Are racial and ethnic disparities in the number of stop-and-frisk searches a cause for concern, or is there no real reason to be bothered because the rate of arrests for whites from such searches is actually higher than that for African Americans and Latinos—at least in New York City? Should we worry about a brief frisk of the external clothing when such actions may help to reduce crime by deterring criminals from carrying guns and increase law enforcement's ability to catch terrorists and other dangerous individuals? List two arguments supporting the position that this is a small intrusion that helps to make society safer. List two opposing arguments that portrays these disparities as a matter of serious concern. Where do you stand?

Researching the Internet

Read Bryonn Bain's provocative article, "Walking While Black: The Bill of Rights for Black Men." As you read, you will understand his angry tone and use of offensive language. Bain, an African American man and former class president at Columbia University, was a second-year student at Harvard Law when he was arrested and jailed as he walked down the sidewalk in New York City. He had been carelessly misidentified as responsible for a minor crime. To link to the website, visit the Criminal Justice CourseMate at cengagebrain .com, then access the web links for this chapter.

Sources: Al Baker, "Minorities Frisked More but Arrested at Same Rate," *New York Times*, May 12, 2010 (www.nytimes .com); Andrew Gelman, Jeffrey Fagan, and Alex Kiss, "An Analysis of the New York City Police Department's 'Stop-and-Frisk' Policy in the Context of Claims of Racial Bias," *Journal of the American Statistical Association*, 102:813–23 (2007); Kevin Grasha, "Reporter Finds LPD Searched Minorities' Cars More Than Whites," *Lansing State Journal*, May 5, 2011 (www.lsj.com); J. J. Hensley, "Arizona Immigration Law: Police Profiling Training Paid Off, Some Say," *Arizona Republic*, April 23, 2011 (www .azcentral.com).

---

check point

17. What "special populations" pose challenges for policing?
Runaways and neglected children; people who suffer from homelessness, drug addiction, mental illness, or alcoholism.

18. What factors make policing in a multicultural society difficult?
Stereotyping, cultural differences, language differences.

19. How are citizen watch groups and similar programs helpful to the police?
They assist the police by reporting incidents and providing information.

stop & analyze

What innovative approaches to training police officers might help them be more effective in serving and working with people in contemporary American neighborhoods? Provide three ideas for training experiences that might help officers become more effective.

Homeland Security

The aftermath of 9/11 has brought expansion, redirection, and reorganization among law enforcement agencies, especially those at the federal level. For instance, the emphasis on counterterrorism has led to an increase in intelligence analysts in the FBI, from 1,023 holding that position in September 2001 to more than 3,118 in September 2011. Over that same time period, the number of FBI special agents assigned to national security duties increased from 2,514 to 4,815 (Mueller, 2011b). The creation of the Department of Homeland Security, the reordering of crime control policies away from street crime and drugs to international and domestic terrorism, and the great increase in federal money directed against the war against terrorism are greatly affecting law enforcement at all levels of government.

This new thrust in policy has shifted the focus of the FBI from the investigation of local street crimes to cases of international and domestic terrorism. FBI Director Robert Mueller has acknowledged that, following 9/11, many criminal investigations had to be set aside as many agents directed their attention toward al-Qaeda and related threats. Further, the bureau has come to rely on state and local law enforcement to fill the gaps that the FBI could not respond to, such as bank robberies, which are crimes under both federal and state laws.

To meet the challenges of terrorist threats and the increasingly international nature of criminal organizations, U.S. agencies have dramatically boosted the number of officers stationed in foreign countries. The FBI has 70 overseas offices known as Legal Attaches or Legats. These offices focus on coordination with law enforcement personnel in other countries. Their activities are limited by the formal agreements negotiated between the United States and each host country. In many other countries, American agents are authorized only to gather information and facilitate communications between countries. American agencies are especially active in working with other countries on counterterrorism, drug trafficking, and cyber crime (Mueller, 2011b).

Another vehicle for international antiterrorist and anticrime efforts is **Interpol**—the International Criminal Police Organization—created in 1946 to foster cooperation among the world's police forces. Based today in Lyon, France, Interpol maintains an intelligence database and serves as a clearinghouse for information gathered by agencies of its 186 member nations, including the United States. Interpol's six priority crime areas are (1) drugs and criminal organizations, (2) public safety and terrorism, (3) financial and high-tech crime, (4) trafficking in human beings, (5) fugitive apprehension, and (6) corruption (http://www.interpol.int).

Interpol The International Criminal Police Organization formed in 1946 and based in France with the mission of facilitating international cooperation in investigating transnational criminal activities and security threats.

Preparing for Threats

The events of September 11 altered the priorities of government agencies and pushed law enforcement agencies at the federal, state, and local levels to make plans for the possibility of future significant threats to homeland security. The FBI and DHS make concerted efforts to identify and combat risks in order to reduce the threat of additional attacks. The FBI switched a significant portion of its personnel away from traditional crime control activities in order to gather intelligence on people within the United States who may pose a threat to the nation. At the same time, the creation of the DHS reflected a desire to have better coordination between agencies that were previously scattered through the federal government. The DHS also instituted new security procedures at airports and borders as a means of identifying individuals and contraband that pose threats. Many critics believe that the federal government has not done enough to protect ports and critical infrastructure, including nuclear power plants, information systems, subway systems, and other elements essential for the functioning of U.S. society. Attacks with devastating consequences could range from computer hackers disabling key military information systems or computerized controls at energy companies to a suicide airline hijacker hitting a nuclear power or chemical plant. If an attack should target and disable any of these entities, it would fall to local police to maintain order and rescue victims.

Security at borders is an important component of homeland security. **U.S. Border Patrol** agents do not merely look for illegal immigrants and drug traffickers; they must also be aware that terrorists might try to sneak across the border, bringing with them weapons, explosives, and other dangerous materials.

Police agencies have traditionally gathered **law enforcement intelligence** about criminal activities and organizations, especially in their efforts to monitor motorcycle gangs, hate groups, drug traffickers, and organized crime. The new emphasis on homeland security broadens the scope of information that agencies need to gather (Kris, 2011). According to Jonathan White (2004), police must be trained to look for and gather information about such things as

U.S. Border Patrol agents and other officials who work for U.S. Customs and Border Protection have been trained to give extra attention to the threat of terrorism. They still retain traditional responsibilities for laws related to immigration, drug trafficking, and smuggling, but all of these issues are now recognized as important components of homeland security. Should the United States impose greater restrictions on entry into our country? What would be the economic and political impact of such restrictions?

- Emergence of radical groups, including religious groups
- Suspicious subjects observing infrastructure facilities
- Growth of phony charities that may steer money to terrorists
- Groups with links to foreign countries
- Unexpected terrorist information found during criminal searches
- Discovery of bomb-making operations

Local police agencies need training that focuses on what to look for and whom to contact if any suspicious activities or materials are discovered. One effort to share information emerged in the form of **fusion centers** (Perrine, Speirs, and Horwitz, 2010). These are state and local intelligence operations that use law enforcement analysts and sophisticated computer systems to compile and analyze clues and then pass along refined information to various agencies (O'Harrow, 2008). The federal government has provided nearly $250 million for the development and operation of these centers. Read about the job of an Intelligence Analyst in "Careers in Criminal Justice," the growing occupational category that describes the professionals who are central to the operation of fusion centers.

The emphasis on information analysis and coordination among agencies at all levels of U.S. government, as well as coordination with foreign governments, also impacts law enforcement operations concerning other major problems, such as drug trafficking, money laundering, gun smuggling, and border security. For example, homeland security efforts overlap with initiatives to combat transnational street gangs. For instance, the MS-13 gang from Central America has spread from Los Angeles to such places as Washington, D.C., and Charlotte, North Carolina, bringing with it various criminal activities, including a series of gang-related homicides (Lineberger, 2011).

Within local police departments, the emphasis on homeland security has led to changes in training, equipment, and operations to prepare first responders to deal with the possibility of weapons of mass destruction and terrorist attacks (Magda, Canton, and Gershon, 2010). The police must also develop regional coordination with neighboring communities and state governments, because large-scale emergencies require the resources and assistance of multiple agencies. Communities need plans for conducting evacuations of buildings and neighborhoods. Police officials must work more closely with firefighters, public-health officials, and emergency medical services to prepare for anything from a

U.S. Border Patrol Federal law enforcement agency with responsibility for border security by patrolling national land borders and coastal waters to prevent smuggling, drug trafficking, and illegal entry, including entry by potential terrorists.

law enforcement intelligence Information, collected and analyzed by law enforcement officials, concerning criminal activities and organizations, such as gangs, drug traffickers, and organized crime.

fusion centers Centers run by states and large cities that analyze and facilitate sharing of information to assist law enforcement and homeland security agencies in preventing and responding to crime and terrorism threats.

Intelligence Analyst

Erin Goff, Intelligence Analyst,
Ohio Department of Public Safety, Division of Homeland Security

Photo provided by Erin Goff. © Cengage Learning

Assigned duties for intelligence analysts vary according to the specific mission of the federal or state agency in which they work. Intelligence analysts collect and analyze information about financial transactions, communication patterns, informants' tips, individuals' and organizations' actions, and other activities that might reveal threats to public safety. By continuously sifting through available information, they produce intelligence products, such as reports, statistical analyses, and suspicious-activities notices concerning potential criminal events and threats to homeland security. They also conduct specific research projects, present briefings to law enforcement and other officials, and write reports and other materials that can be used to warn, inform, and train officials.

Qualifications for the position vary according to an agency's specific needs. In general, candidates need experience and skill in research and writing. Critical-thinking skills are especially important, as is the ability to communicate effectively, both orally and in writing. Intelligence analysts must also have an understanding of the criminal justice system and the functions and relationships of various agencies in all levels of governments. Because training and experience in such areas as research, computers, intelligence software programs, and statistics can be important, intelligence analysts typically are college graduates who have studied criminal justice and other relevant subjects.

In preparing for her career as an intelligence analyst, Erin Goff earned both undergraduate and graduate degrees in criminal justice. In addition, she gained experience in the field as a graduate student by working on federally funded projects through which university professors and other experts provided training for police departments concerning homeland security issues.

The biggest challenge I face on a daily basis is the constantly changing picture of terrorism. There are always new threat streams using tactics we've never seen and we are forced to adapt our information analysis. As with other areas of criminal justice, it is essential to stay one step ahead, so I regularly seek additional education to enhance my formal knowledge. In addition, I continuously discuss emerging information and issues with other intelligence analysts.

bomb to a bioterrorist attack using anthrax, smallpox, or other harmful agents. Some of these threats require the acquisition of new equipment, such as protective suits for suspected biological or chemical hazards, or communications equipment that can be used to contact multiple agencies. Many police departments are giving renewed attention to training specialized teams, such as bomb squads and SWAT teams, that will intervene in emergency situations. In addition, they must give all officers additional training on coordination with outside agencies, evacuation procedures for malls and hospitals, and containment of hazardous materials (Perin, 2009).

check point > **20. What have law enforcement officials done to enhance the protection of homeland security?**
Planning and coordinating with other agencies, intelligence gathering, new equipment, and training.

stop& analyze In light of the budget cuts affecting state and local government, imagine that you are a governor who must recommend choices about how to allocate shrinking resources. If faced with the following choices—reduce money for homeland security and law enforcement intelligence, reduce money for state police patrols and criminal investigation, or raise taxes—which would you choose and why? Give three reasons for your answer.

New Laws and Controversies

The hijackers' devastating attacks on September 11, 2001, spurred a variety of government actions intended to protect homeland security and combat terrorism. The Bush administration asserted new presidential powers to arrest and detain indefinitely without trial Americans whom it accused of terrorist activities. In 2004, however, the U.S. Supreme Court ruled that the president does not possess unlimited authority and that American detainees are entitled to challenge their confinement through court procedures (*Hamdi v. Rumsfeld*, 2004). The Supreme Court's decision illustrates one aspect of the challenge facing the United States: how to provide government with sufficient power to fight terrorism while also protecting individuals' constitutional rights.

In 2011, the National Defense Authorization Act, which provides annual funding for the military, included provisions permitting terrorism suspects to be arrested and detained indefinitely and permitting the military to detain and question terrorism suspects on American soil. These provisions generated harsh criticism from civil libertarians who feared the expansion of governmental powers and the potential for Americans to be denied their rights. However, members of Congress claimed that the wording was carefully designed to balance individuals' rights with national security. President Obama expressed misgivings about the language but signed the bill into law in December 2011 (Klain, 2012; Nakamura, 2011).

Other controversies arose concerning new state and federal statutes created after September 11. Both Congress and state legislatures enacted new laws aimed at addressing various aspects of homeland security. More than 30 states added new terrorism-related laws. These laws ranged from narrow to broad—from statutes addressing specific problems to authorizations of new powers for law enforcement officials and the definition of new crimes. At the narrow end of the spectrum, for example, Virginia passed a law to make it more difficult for foreign nationals to obtain a driver's license without possession of specific legal documents. This was in direct response to the discovery that several of the September 11 hijackers had obtained Virginia driver's licenses.

Because new laws provide tools for justice system officials, controversies can arise when those officials apparently stretch their authority beyond the intentions of the relevant statutes. For example, prosecutors in several cases have used new terrorism laws as a means to prosecute people for criminal acts that are not commonly understood to be related to terrorism. In New York, for example, one of the first prosecutions under the state's antiterrorism laws enacted after September 11 arose when the Bronx district attorney charged street gang members for various crimes. There was no allegation that the gang members had connections to any foreign terrorist networks. Instead, the prosecutor used the state's antiterrorism law to charge gang members with shootings committed with the intent to intimidate or coerce a civilian population (Garcia, 2005). In another example, a North Carolina prosecutor charged the operator of a small meth lab under a terrorism statute for manufacturing a nuclear or chemical weapon ("Charging Common Criminals," 2003). These cases generated criticism in newspaper editorials and raised concerns that government officials would exploit terrorism laws for improper purposes.

The most controversial legislation came from Congress in the form of the Uniting and Strengthening America by Providing Appropriate Tools Required to Intercept and Obstruct Terrorism Act. It is best known by its shorthand name, the **USA PATRIOT Act**. The PATRIOT Act moved quickly through Congress after the September 11 attacks and covered a wide range of topics, including the expansion of government authority for searches and surveillance and the expansion of definitions and penalties for crimes related to terrorism. Critics have raised concerns about many provisions because of fears that the government's assertions of excessive power will violate individuals' rights (Ahmadi, 2011; Lichtblau, 2008; Dority, 2005). The PATRIOT Act makes it easier for law enforcement officials

USA PATRIOT Act A federal statute passed in the aftermath of the terrorist attacks of September 11, 2001, that broadens government authority to conduct searches and wiretaps and that expands the definitions of crimes involving terrorism.

to monitor email and obtain "sneak-and-peek" warrants, in which they secretly conduct searches and do not inform the home or business owner that the premises have been searched until much later (K. M. Sullivan, 2003). The PATRIOT Act also authorizes warrantless searches of third-party records, such as those at libraries, financial institutions, phone companies, and medical facilities. This provision has sparked an outcry from librarians and booksellers and was cited by many of the 150 communities across the country that passed resolutions protesting the excessive authority granted to government by the Act (J. Gordon, 2005). Despite the outcry, Congress approved an extension of the PATRIOT Act's key provisions in 2011 (Mascaro, 2011).

The PATRIOT Act defines domestic terrorism as criminal acts dangerous to human life that appear intended to intimidate civilians or influence public policy by intimidation. It also makes it a crime to provide material support for terrorism. Conservatives fear the law could be used against antiabortion protestors who block entrances at abortion clinics as well as their financial supporters. Liberals fear that it could be used against environmental activists and their financial supporters (Zerwas, 2011; Lithwick and Turner, 2003).

The debates about new laws enacted as part of homeland security and counterterrorist efforts illustrate the struggle to maintain American values of personal liberty, privacy, and individual rights while simultaneously ensuring that law enforcement personnel have sufficient power to protect the nation from catastrophic harm.

Now that we have considered the government's role in homeland security, we turn our attention to the private sector. Corporations and other entities must safeguard their assets, personnel, and facilities. They, too, have heightened concerns about terrorism and other homeland security issues. For example, nuclear power plants, chemical factories, energy companies, and other private facilities make up part of the nation's critical infrastructure. Because terrorists might target such facilities, private sector officials must address these concerns, just as they have long needed to address other security issues such as employee theft, fires, and trade secrets.

---

check point > **21. What are the criticisms directed at the USA PATRIOT Act?**
Permits too much government authority for searches and wiretaps; defines domestic terrorism in ways that might include legitimate protest groups.

stop& analyze Are you willing to give up any of your rights and liberties in order to grant the government more power to take actions to strengthen homeland security? If so, which rights and liberties? If not, why not?

Security Management and Private Policing

Only a few years ago, the term *private security* called to mind the image of security guards, people with marginal qualifications for other occupations who ended up accepting minimal wages to stand guard outside factories and businesses. This image reflected a long history of private employment of individuals who served limited police-patrol functions. In recent years, by contrast, private sector activities related to policing functions have become more complex and important.

Many threats have spurred an expansion in security management and private policing; these include (1) an increase in crime in the workplace; (2) an increase in fear (real or perceived) of crime; (3) the fiscal crises of the states, which have limited public-police protection; and (4) increased public and business awareness and use of more cost-effective private security services (Steden and Sarre, 2007; Cunningham, Strauchs, and Van Meter, 1990). Today, if one speaks of people employed in private security, it would be more accurate to envision a variety of occupations ranging from traditional security guards to computer security experts to high-ranking corporate vice presidents responsible for planning and overseeing safety and security at a company's industrial plants and office complexes around the world.

Retail and industrial firms spend nearly as much for private protection as all localities spend for police protection. Many government entities hire private companies to provide security at specific office buildings or other facilities. In addition, private groups, such as residents of wealthy suburbs, have hired private police to patrol their neighborhoods. There are now more officers hired by private security companies than there are public police (Strom et al., 2010).

AP Images/Damian Dovarganes

⬆ Contemporary security managers are well-educated professionals with administrative experience and backgrounds in management and law. Here, Hemanshu Nigam, a former federal prosecutor, poses at the offices of Fox Interactive Media, where he is the chief security officer. Nigam is responsible for online safety and security. Are there any businesses or industries that do not need the services of security personnel in today's fast-changing world?

Functions of Security Management and Private Policing

Top-level security managers have a range of responsibilities that require them to fulfill multiple roles that separate individuals would handle in the public sector. For their corporations, they simultaneously function as police chiefs, fire chiefs, emergency-management administrators, and computer-security experts. They hire, train, and supervise expert personnel to protect corporate computer systems that may contain credit card numbers, trade secrets, confidential corporate financial information, and other data sought by hackers intent on causing destruction or stealing money. Frequently they combat cyber criminals who are attacking their computer resources from overseas and are therefore beyond the reach of U.S. law enforcement officials. They also plan security systems and emergency-response plans for fires and other disasters. Such plans include provisions for evacuating large buildings and coordinating their efforts with local police and fire departments in a variety of locales. In addition, they develop security systems to prevent employee theft that may involve sophisticated schemes to use company computer systems to transfer financial assets for illegal purposes. Because so many American companies own manufacturing plants and office buildings overseas, security companies must often implement their services in diverse countries around the globe.

At lower levels, specific occupations in private security compare more closely with those of police officers. Many security personnel are the equivalent of private sector detectives. They must investigate attacks on company computer systems or activities that threaten company assets. Thus, for example, credit card companies have large security departments that use computers to monitor unusual activity on individual customers' credit cards, which may signal that a thief is using the card. Private sector detectives must also investigate employee theft. Because this criminal activity extends beyond simple crimes such as stealing money from a store's cash register, investigations might examine whether people are making false reports on expense accounts, using company computers to run private businesses, or misspending company money.

Other activities compare more directly to those of police patrol officers, especially those of security officers who must guard specific buildings, apartments, or stores. The activities of these private security personnel vary greatly: Some act merely as guards and call the police at the first sign of trouble, others have the power to carry out patrol and investigative duties similar to those of police officers, and still others rely on their own presence and the ability to make a citizen's arrest to deter lawbreakers.

Private Police and Homeland Security

Private sector corporations control security for vital facilities in the United States, including nuclear power plants, oil refineries, military manufacturing facilities, and other important sites (Nalla, 2002). Fires, tornadoes, or earthquakes at such sites could release toxic materials into the air and water. Thus, emergency planning is essential for public safety (Simonoff et al., 2011). Moreover, because these sites are now recognized as potential targets of terrorist attacks, the role and effectiveness of security managers matter more than ever to society. They must work closely with law enforcement executives and other government officials to institute procedures that reduce known risks and to participate in emergency preparedness planning.

Private Employment of Public Police

The officials responsible for asset protection, safety, and security at the top levels of major corporations are often retired police administrators or former military personnel. For example, New York Police Commissioner Raymond Kelly served as Senior Managing Director of Global Corporate Security for a Wall Street financial firm after he left his position as Director of the U.S. Customs Service and before he was appointed to serve as police commissioner. The reliance on people with public sector experience for important positions in private security management reflects the fact that asset protection and security management have only recently become emphasized as topics in college and university programs. Thus, relatively few professionals have yet gained specific educational credentials in this important area. As a result, the placement of retired law enforcement officials in high-level positions has often created opportunities for strategic communication and coordination between top-level security managers and public sector police administrators.

At operational levels of security management, private security and local police often make frequent contact. Private firms are usually eager to hire public-police officers on a part-time basis. Although police departments may forbid moonlighting by their officers, some departments simultaneously facilitate and control the hiring of their officers by creating specific rules and procedures for off-duty employment. For example, the New York City Police Department coordinates a program called the Paid Detail Unit. Event planners, corporations, and organizations can hire uniformed, off-duty officers for $33 per hour. The police department must approve all events at which the officers will work, and the department imposes an additional 10 percent administrative fee for the hiring of its officers. Thus, the department can safeguard against officers working for organizations and events that will cause legal, public relations, or other problems for the police department. The department can also monitor and control how many hours its officers work so that private, part-time employment does not lead them to be exhausted and ineffective during their regular shifts.

Several models have been designed to manage off-duty employment of officers. Some approaches can lead to controversy, as in New Orleans in 2011 when several high-ranking police officials were revealed to be earning six-figure incomes beyond their police salaries by imposing "coordination fees" as part of their authority over choosing which officers would perform security work at movie sets, football games, and other private settings (McCarthy, 2012).

The *department contract model* permits close control of off-duty work, because firms must apply to the department to have officers assigned to them. New York

City's system fits this model. Officers chosen for off-duty work are paid by the police department, which is reimbursed by the private firm, along with an overhead fee. Departments usually screen employers to make sure that the proposed use of officers will not conflict with the department's needs.

The *officer contract model* allows each officer to find off-duty employment and to enter into a direct relationship with the private firm. Officers must apply to the department for permission, which is granted if the employment standards listed earlier are met. Problems can arise when an officer acts as an employment agent for other officers. This can lead to charges of favoritism and nepotism, with serious effects on discipline and morale.

In the *union brokerage model*, the police union or association finds off-duty employment for its members. The union sets the standards for the work and bargains with the department over the pay, status, and conditions of the off-duty employment.

The Public–Private Interface

The relationship between public and private law enforcement is a concern for police officials. Because private agents work for the people who employ them, their goals might not always serve the public interest. Questions have arisen about the power of private security agents to make arrests, conduct searches, and take part in undercover investigations. A key issue is the boundary between the work of the police and that of private agencies.

One such area is criminal activity within a company. Many security managers in private firms tend to treat crimes by employees as internal matters that do not concern the police. They report UCR index crimes to the police, but employee theft, insurance fraud, industrial espionage, commercial bribery, and computer crime tend not to be reported to public authorities. In such cases, the chief concern of private firms is to prevent losses and protect assets. Most of these incidents are resolved through internal procedures (private justice). When such crimes are discovered, the offender may be convicted and punished within the firm by forced restitution, loss of the job, and the spreading of information about the incident throughout the industry. Private firms often bypass the criminal justice system so they do not have to deal with prosecution policies, administrative delays, rules that would open the firms' internal affairs to public scrutiny, and bad publicity. Thus, the question arises: To what extent does a parallel system of private justice exist with regard to some offenders and some crimes (M. Davis, Lundman, and Martinez, 1991)?

Recruitment and Training

Higher-level security managers are increasingly drawn from college graduates with degrees in criminal justice who have taken additional coursework in such subjects as business management and computer science. These graduates are attracted to the growing private sector employment market for security-related occupations, because the jobs often involve varied, complex tasks in a white-collar work environment. In addition, they often gain corporate benefits such as quick promotion, stock options, and other perks unavailable in public sector policing.

By contrast, the recruitment and training of lower-level private security personnel present a major concern to law enforcement officials and civil libertarians (Enion, 2009; Strickland, 2011). These personnel carry the important responsibility of guarding factories, stores, apartments, and other buildings. Often on the scene when criminal activity occurs, they are the private security personnel most likely to interact with the public in emergency situations. Moreover, any

Today's security personnel must be aware of numerous potential threats and have the necessary training and equipment to communicate with law enforcement officials. If security guards are minimum-wage employees, are they likely to have the qualifications and commitment to provide adequate security at important private enterprises such as chemical factories and nuclear-power plants?

failure to perform their duties could lead to a significant and damaging event, such as a robbery or a fire. Lack of coordination and communication between public and private agencies has led to botched investigations, destruction of evidence, and overzealousness.

Growing awareness of this problem has led to efforts to have private security agents work more closely with the police. Current efforts to enhance coordination involve emergency planning, building security, and general crime prevention. However, effective coordination may be hampered if private firms lack standards for hiring and conduct little training for their employees.

In spite of these important responsibilities, which parallel those of police patrol officers, studies have shown that such personnel often have little education and training. A national study in 2008 found that 46 percent of private security officers had a high school diploma or even less education and only 12 percent had bachelor's degrees. In addition, the median annual pay for private security officers is less than half that of police officers. Many private security officers are paid only minimum wage (Strom et al., 2010). Because the pay is low, the work often attracts people who cannot find other jobs or who seek temporary work. For example, private security firms in San Francisco reported annual staff turnover rates as high as 300 percent because their low pay and benefits led employees continually to seek higher-paying jobs, especially when better-paid public sector security work opened up, such as jobs as airport screeners (Lynem, 2002).

The growth of private policing has brought calls for the screening and licensing of its personnel. However, there has been no systematic national effort to standardize training and licensing for private security personnel. As indicated in Figure 5.3, only eight states require all private security officers to be licensed. Other states require licensing only for contractual security officers or those carrying firearms. Remarkably, sixteen states require no licensing at all (Strom et al., 2010).

The regulations that do exist tend to focus on contractual, as opposed to proprietary, private policing. Contractual security services are provided for a fee by locksmiths, alarm specialists, polygraph examiners, and firms such as Brink's, Burns, and Wackenhut, which provide guards and detectives. States and cities often require contract personnel to be licensed and bonded. Similar services are sometimes provided by proprietary security personnel, who are employed directly

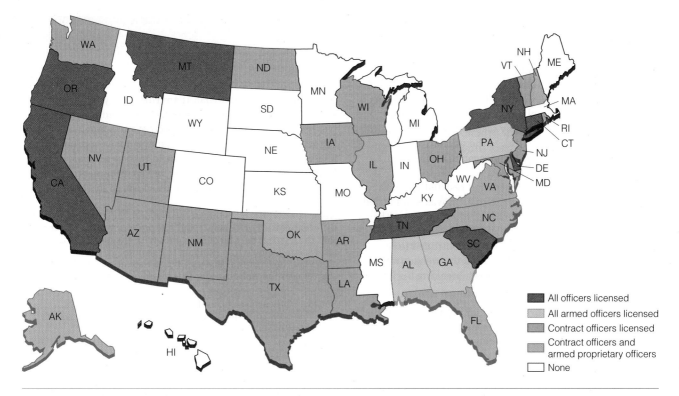

Figure 5.3
Licensing Requirements for Security Officers by State, 2009

Source: K. Strom, M. Berzofsky, B. Shook-Sa, K. Barrick, C. Daye, N. Horstmann, and S. Kinsey. *The Private Security Industry: A Review of the Definitions, Available Data Sources, and Paths Moving Forward*. Report prepared for Bureau of Justice Statistics, December 2010 (https://www.ncjrs.gov/pdffiles1/bjs/grants/232781.pdf).

Legend:
- All officers licensed
- All armed officers licensed
- Contract officers licensed
- Contract officers and armed proprietary officers
- None

by the organizations they protect—retail stores, industrial plants, hospitals, and so forth. Except for those who carry weapons, proprietary security personnel are not usually regulated by the state or city. Certainly, the importance of private security and its relation to public policing demands further exploration of these and related issues in the years to come.

check point

22. What has caused the growth of security management and private policing?
Companies' recognition of the need to protect assets and to plan for emergencies, as well as problems with employee theft, computer crime, and other issues that require active prevention and investigation.

23. What are the three models for private employment of police officers?
Department contract model, officer contract model, and union brokerage model.

stop & analyze

To what extent can private security replace public police when police personnel and services are reduced due to state and city budget cuts? Give two examples of situations or places where private security can fill the gap and two situations where private security cannot effectively provide replacement services.

6

Police and Law

Learning Objectives

→ Know the extent of police officers' authority to stop people and to conduct searches of people, their vehicles, and other property

→ Recognize how police officers seek warrants in order to conduct searches and make arrests

→ Identify situations in which police officers can examine property and conduct searches without obtaining a warrant

→ Analyze the purpose of the privilege against compelled self-incrimination

→ Understand the exclusionary rule and situations in which it applies

Tucson, Arizona, police officers received an anonymous tip about possible drug activity at a house. When they arrived at the residence, Rodney Gant answered the door, provided the requested identification, and told the officers that the home's owner would return later. After the officers left the scene, a records check indicated that Gant was subject to arrest under an outstanding warrant. The warrant had been issued when he failed to appear for a court hearing after being caught driving with a suspended license. When the officers returned to the house, they saw Gant driving a car up the street and then parking it at the end of the home's driveway. They arrested Gant, handcuffed him, placed him in the backseat of a patrol car, and then locked the patrol car's doors. Two officers their authority to halt that individual's movement, then a seizure has occurred and the Fourth Amendment requires that the seizure be reasonable.

One form of seizure is an arrest. This involves taking a suspect into custody. Property can also be subject to seizure, especially if it is evidence in a criminal case.

A **stop** is a brief interference with a person's freedom of movement for a duration that can be measured in minutes, usually under an hour. An interference with freedom of movement that lasts several hours risks being viewed as exceeding the proper duration of a stop and requires greater justification. When police require a driver to pull over in order to receive a traffic citation, that is a stop. Such stops can affect the rights of both drivers and passengers, especially if the stop leads to a search of the individuals or the vehicle (*Brendlin v. California*, 2007; V. Amar, 2008). In order to be permissible under the Fourth Amendment, stops must be justified by **reasonable suspicion**—a situation in which specific articulable facts lead officers to conclude that the person may be engaging in criminal activity. Officers cannot legally make stops based on hunches; they must be able to describe specific aspects of the person's appearance, behavior, and circumstances that led them to conclude that the person should be stopped in order to investigate the occurrence of a crime. As we shall see, however, the courts permit police officers to make many kinds of stops without reasonable suspicion. Such stops can occur, for example, at border crossing points where preventing illegal activities, such as smuggling and drug trafficking, is especially important. Thus, everyone can be stopped in certain situations even if there is no specific basis to suspect them of wrongdoing.

Use of Force and the Fourth Amendment

In Chapter 5 we examined problems stemming from excessive use of force by police officers. Such actions reflect on the application of discretion, ethics, professionalism, and training of officers. When people sue police officers for violating constitutional rights through the excessive use of force, they claim their Fourth Amendment right against "unreasonable seizures" has been violated. Although many people assume that an improper shooting or beating inflicted by a police officer might violate the Eighth Amendment prohibition on cruel and unusual punishments, the Supreme Court has interpreted this Eighth Amendment right to protect only individuals who are being "punished" by the justice system, namely people who have been convicted of crimes. For people who have not been convicted of a crime, such as those encountered by the police in free society, the use of excessive force by government officials falls under the coverage of the Fourth Amendment. According to the Supreme Court, when police officers victimize individuals through the use of excessive force, those individuals have suffered an "unreasonable seizure."

Until the 1980s, the police had broad authority to use deadly force in pursuing suspected felons. Police in about half the states were guided by the common-law principle that allowed the use of whatever force was necessary to arrest a fleeing felon. In 1985, the Supreme Court set a new standard in *Tennessee v. Garner*, ruling that the police may not use deadly force in apprehending fleeing felons "unless it is necessary to prevent the escape and the officer has probable cause to believe that the suspect poses a significant threat of death or serious physical injury to the officer or others."

The standard set by *Tennessee v. Garner* presents problems, because it can be difficult to judge how dangerous a suspect may be. Because officers must make quick decisions in stressful situations, the Supreme Court and other courts cannot create clear rules that will guide police in every context that arises. However, to clarify the rules for police, the Supreme Court justices also established the standard of "objective reasonableness," saying that the officer's use of deadly force should be judged in terms of its reasonableness for the specific situation that confronts the

stop Government officials' interference with an individual's freedom of movement for a duration that typically lasts less than one hour and only rarely extends for as long as several hours.

reasonable suspicion A police officer's belief based on articulable facts that would be recognized by others in a similar situation as indicating that criminal activity is afoot and necessitates further investigation that will intrude on an individual's reasonable expectation of privacy.

Tennessee v. Garner **(1985)** Deadly force may not be used against an unarmed and fleeing suspect unless necessary to prevent the escape and unless the officer has probable cause to believe that the suspect poses a significant threat of death or serious injury to the officers or others.

officer and requires the officer to make a quick decision about appropriate actions to take (*Graham v. Connor*, 1989). This means that the use of the deadly force—or any form of force—should be judged from the point of view of the officer on the scene. The Court's decision recognized that "officers are often forced to make split-second judgments— in circumstances that are tense, uncertain, and rapidly evolving—about the amount of force that is necessary in a particular situation" (Georgiady, 2008).

Arrest is the physical taking of a person into custody. What legal requirements must be met to make this a valid arrest? What limits are placed on the officers?

The Concept of Arrest

An arrest is a significant deprivation of liberty, because a person is taken into police custody, transported to the police station or jail, and processed into the criminal justice system. Because arrests involve a more significant intrusion on liberty, they require a higher level of justification. Unlike stops, which require only reasonable suspicion, all arrests must be supported by **probable cause**. Probable cause exists when sufficient evidence is available to support the reasonable conclusion that a person has committed a crime. To obtain an arrest warrant, the police must provide a judicial officer with sufficient evidence to support a finding of probable cause. Alternatively, police officers' on-the-street determinations of probable cause can produce discretionary warrantless arrests. A judge subsequently examines such arrests for probable cause, in a hearing that must occur shortly after the arrest, typically within 48 hours. If the judge determines that the police officer was wrong in concluding that probable cause existed to justify the arrest, the suspect is released from custody.

probable cause An amount of reliable information indicating that it is more likely than not that evidence will be found in a specific location or that a specific person is guilty of a crime.

Warrants and Probable Cause

Imagine that you are a judge. Two police officers come to your chambers to ask you to authorize a search warrant. They swear that they observed frequent foot traffic of suspicious people going in and out of a house. Moreover, they swear that a reliable informant told them that he was inside the house two days earlier and saw crack cocaine being sold. Does this information rise to the level of probable cause, justifying issuance of a search warrant? Can you grant a warrant based purely on the word of police officers, or do you need more-concrete evidence?

These questions are important not only for judges but for prosecutors as well. Police and prosecutors must work closely together. If the police have made errors in seeking warrants or conducting searches, evidence could be excluded from use at trial and, as a result, prosecutors could lose their cases through no fault of their own.

The Fourth Amendment requires that "no Warrants shall issue, but upon probable cause, supported by Oath or affirmation, and particularly describing the place to be searched, and the persons or things to be seized." These particular elements of the Amendment must be fulfilled in order to issue a warrant. If they are not, then a defendant may later challenge the validity of the warrant. The important elements are, first, the existence of probable cause. Second, evidence must be presented to the judicial officer and be supported by "oath or affirmation," which typically means that police officers must say "yes" when the judicial officer asks them if they swear or affirm that all information presented is true to the best of their knowledge. This requirement may be fulfilled by presenting an **affidavit** from the police officers, which is a written statement confirmed by oath or affirmation. Third, the warrant must describe the specific place to be

affidavit Written statement of fact, supported by oath or affirmation, submitted to judicial officers to fulfill the requirements of probable cause for obtaining a warrant.

check point

1. **What is a search?**
   A government intrusion into an individual's reasonable expectation of privacy.

2. **What is the plain view doctrine?**
   The plain view doctrine permits officers to observe and seize illegal items that are visible to them when they are in a location in which they are legally permitted to be.

3. **What is the difference between an arrest and a stop?**
   An arrest requires probable cause and involves taking someone into custody for prosecution, whereas a stop is a brief deprivation of freedom of movement based on reasonable suspicion.

4. **What do police officers need to demonstrate in order to obtain a warrant?**
   The existence of probable cause by the totality of circumstances in the case.

stop& analyze

What are two examples of situations that you believe should be considered "unreasonable searches" in violation of the Fourth Amendment? What is it about those searches that makes them "unreasonable"?

Warrantless Searches

In day-to-day police work, the majority of searches take place without a warrant. It is in this area that the courts have been most active in defining the term *unreasonable*. Six kinds of searches may be legally conducted without a warrant and still uphold the Fourth Amendment: (1) special needs beyond the normal purposes of law enforcement, (2) stop and frisk on the streets, (3) search incident to a lawful arrest, (4) exigent circumstances, (5) consent, and (6) automobile searches. We examine these forms of warrantless searches in this section.

Special Needs beyond the Normal Purposes of Law Enforcement

In certain specific contexts, law enforcement officials have a justified need to conduct warrantless searches of every individual passing through. The use of metal detectors to examine airline passengers, for example, occurs in a specific context in which the need to prevent hijacking justifies a limited search of every passenger. Here, the Supreme Court does not require officers to have any suspicions, reasonable or otherwise, about the illegal activities of any individual (Loewy, 2011).

Similarly, warrantless searches take place at the entry points into the United States—border crossings, ports, and airports (Chacon, 2010). The government's interests in guarding against the entry of people and items (weapons, drugs, toxic chemicals, and so forth) that are harmful to national interests outweigh the individuals' expectations of privacy. Typically, these border stops involve only a few moments as customs officers check any required documents such as passports and visas, ask where the person traveled, and ask what the person is bringing into the United States. The customs officers may have a trained dog sniff around people and their luggage, checking for drugs or large amounts of cash. At the Mexican and Canadian borders and at international airports, people may be chosen at random to have their cars and luggage searched. They may also be chosen for such searches because their behavior or their answers to questions arouse the suspicions of customs officers.

The Supreme Court has expanded the checkpoint concept by approving systematic stops to look for drunken drivers along highways. Michigan's state police implemented a sobriety checkpoint program. They set up a checkpoint at which they stopped every vehicle and briefly questioned each driver (*Michigan Department of State Police v. Sitz*, 1990). A group of citizens filed lawsuits alleging that checkpoints violated drivers' rights. However, the Court said that police can systematically stop drivers in order to seek information. The Court more recently approved checkpoints to ask drivers whether they had witnessed an accident (*Illinois v. Lidster*, 2004).

The U.S. Supreme Court has not given blanket approval for every kind of checkpoint or traffic stop that police might wish to use. The Court forbids random stops of vehicles by officers on patrol (*Delaware v. Prouse*, 1979). Officers must have a basis for a vehicle stop, such as an observed violation of traffic laws. The Court also ruled that a city cannot set up a checkpoint in order to check drivers and passengers for possible involvement in drugs or other crimes. The Court declared that a general search for criminal evidence does not justify the use of a checkpoint. Again, such stops must be narrowly focused on a specific objective, such as checking for drunken drivers (*City of Indianapolis v. Edmond*, 2000).

⬆ The U.S. Supreme Court has declared that police may set up sobriety checkpoints in which they establish roadblocks and stop all cars in an effort to detect drunk drivers. Do you think such road-blocks interfere with the rights of drivers who have done nothing to raise suspicions about improper behavior?

As you reflect on the importance and challenges of conducting warrantless stops and searches in the protection of national borders (MacCormack, 2011), consider whether you would be interested in a career with the U.S. Border Patrol, as described in "Careers in Criminal Justice."

Stop and Frisk on the Streets

Police officers possess the authority to make stops and limited searches of individuals on the streets when specific circumstances justify such actions. In the landmark case of **Terry v. Ohio (1968)**, the Court upheld the stop-and-frisk procedure when a police officer had good reasons to conclude that a person endangered the public by being involved in criminal activity. In the *Terry* case, a plainclothes detective in downtown Cleveland observed men walking back and forth to look in the window of a store and then conferring with each other. He suspected that they might be preparing to rob the store. He approached the men, identified himself as a police officer, patted down their clothing, and found unlicensed handguns on two individuals. Those individuals challenged the legality of the search.

Although the justices supported the detective's authority to conduct the pat-down search based on his observations of the men's suspicious behavior, they struck a careful balance between police authority and individuals' rights by specifying the circumstances in which such a pat-down search—more commonly known as a **stop-and-frisk search**—can occur. In the *Terry* decision, the Court specifies the following criteria, all of which must be present, to define a legal stop and frisk:

> We merely hold today that
>
> [1] where a police officer observes unusual conduct
> [2] which leads him reasonably to conclude in light of his experience
> [3] that criminal activity may be afoot and
> [4] that the persons with whom he is dealing may be armed and presently dangerous,
> [5] where in the course of investigating this behavior
> [6] he identifies himself as a policeman and makes reasonable inquiries,
> [7] and where nothing in the initial stages of the encounter serves to dispel his reasonable fear for his own or others' safety,

Terry v. Ohio (1968)
Supreme Court decision endorsing police officers' authority to stop and frisk suspects on the streets when there is reasonable suspicion that they are armed and involved in criminal activity.

stop-and-frisk search
Limited search approved by the Supreme Court in *Terry v. Ohio* that permits police officers to pat down the clothing of people on the street if there is reasonable suspicion of dangerous criminal activity.

Border Patrol Agent

Karl Huether, U.S. Border Patrol Agent,
U.S. Border Patrol, Arizona

Photo provided by Karl Huether. © Cengage Learning

The United States Border Patrol is the mobile, uniformed law enforcement arm of the U.S. Customs and Border Protection (CBP) within the Department of Homeland Security. Since the terrorist attacks of September 11, 2001, the focus of the Border Patrol has shifted to include emphasis on the detection, apprehension and/or deterrence of terrorists and terrorist weapons. Its overall mission remains unchanged: to detect and prevent the illegal entry of undocumented immigrants and contraband into the United States. Together with other law enforcement officers, the Border Patrol helps maintain borders that work—facilitating the flow of legal immigration and goods while preventing the illegal trafficking of people and contraband.

The Border Patrol is specifically responsible for patrolling the 6,000 miles of Mexican and Canadian international land borders and 2,000 miles of coastal waters surrounding Florida and Puerto Rico. Agents work around the clock on assignments, in all types of terrain and weather conditions. Agents also work in many isolated communities throughout the United States.

To become a United States Border Patrol Agent, one must meet a few basic qualifications. A candidate must be a U.S. citizen, possess a valid automobile driver's license, and pass the CBP Border Patrol entrance exam. Candidates must also have substantial work experience. A four-year college degree may substitute for the required work experience, or candidates may qualify through a combination of education and work experience.

Karl Huether earned an undergraduate degree in criminal justice, as well as a certificate in homeland security studies. In addition, he gained experience in the field of criminal justice through participation in internships with state police and state probation offices.

As a Border Patrol Agent, I face different challenges every day when I go out into the field. Line watch is one of the most crucial activities that a Border Patrol Agent will conduct. While conducting line watch, agents detect, prevent, and apprehend terrorists, undocumented aliens, and smugglers of aliens at or near the land border. To make line watch successful, agents must keep up with daily intelligence reports, training, and the laws which are enforced by the U.S. Border Patrol.

[8] he is entitled for the protection of himself and others in the area to conduct a carefully limited search of the outer clothing of such persons in an attempt to discover weapons which might be used to assault him.

These factors impose an obligation on police officers to make observations, draw reasonable conclusions, identify themselves, and make inquiries before conducting the stop-and-frisk search. In addition, the reasonableness of the search must be justified by a reasonable conclusion that a person is armed, thereby requiring the officer to act in order to protect him- or herself and the public.

As we discuss later with respect to the "exclusionary rule," a suspect who, during a frisk search, is found to be carrying drugs or a weapon can seek to have the evidence excluded from use in court if the stop-and-frisk was not justified by proper observations and reasonable suspicion. Typically, a judge will believe the police officer's version of events rather than accept the claims of a person found to be carrying illegal items. Sometimes, however, the officer's version of events may not be persuasive. When an officer claims to have seen a lump under a suspect's jacket while the officer was standing 20 yards away on a busy street, judges may doubt whether an officer can reasonably draw such conclusions from such a distance. In New York City, for example, concerns arose in 2008 that police officers were regularly searching anyone they saw on the streets, even though the officers did not have the proper justifications established in *Terry v. Ohio* and later cases. In response, federal judges closely examined officers' versions of events. In nearly two dozen cases, the judges concluded that the police officers either were not being truthful or were not carefully following the *Terry* rules (Weiser, 2008).

Court decisions have given officers significant discretion to decide when factors that justify a stop-and-frisk search exist. For example, if officers see someone running at the sight of police in a high-crime neighborhood, their observation can be one consideration in determining whether a stop-and-frisk search is justified (*Illinois v. Wardlow*, 2000). Thus, officers need not actually see evidence of a weapon or interact with the suspect prior to making the stop.

The Supreme Court also expanded police authority by permitting officers to rely on reports from reliable witnesses as the basis for conducting the stop and frisk (*Adams v. Williams*, 1972). However, an unverified anonymous tip does not serve as an adequate reason for a stop-and-frisk search (*Florida v. J. L.*, 2000).

⬆ The stopping and frisking of an individual must be carried out according to the law. What does the law require in this situation?

Search Incident to a Lawful Arrest

The authority to undertake a warrantless search incident to a lawful arrest is not limited by the crime for which the arrestee has been taken into custody. Even someone arrested for a traffic offense can be searched. Although there is no reason to suspect the person has a weapon or to believe that evidence related to the offense will be found in the person's pockets (*United States v. Robinson*, 1973), the arrestee is subject to the same arrest-scene search as someone taken into custody for murder.

The justification for searches of arrestees emerged in the Supreme Court's decision in **Chimel v. California (1969)**. The officers must be sure that the arrestee does not have a weapon that could endanger the officers or others in the vicinity. The officers must also look for evidence that might be destroyed or damaged by the arrestee before or during the process of transporting the individual to jail. Officers are permitted to search the arrestee and the immediate area around the arrestee.

Officers can also make a protective sweep through other rooms where the suspect may recently have been. However, the arrest would not justify opening drawers and conducting a thorough search of an entire house. If, after the arrest, officers have probable cause to conduct a more thorough search, they must obtain a warrant that specifies the items that they seek and the places where they will search.

In a traffic stop, because officers possess the authority to make arrests for minor offenses, including acts that would normally only be subject to traffic citations, officers have opportunities to use arrests of drivers as a basis for conducting warrantless searches of automobiles (*Virginia v. Moore*, 2008). However, the search of the passenger compartment must be limited to areas within reach of the arrestee. Remember that in *Arizona v. Gant* (2009), the case that opened this chapter, a majority of justices barred the search of an automobile after an arrest when the handcuffed driver posed no danger to the officers and could not reach into the car to destroy evidence.

Chimel v. California (1969) Supreme Court decision that endorsed warrantless searches for weapons and evidence in the immediate vicinity of people who are lawfully arrested.

Exigent Circumstances

Officers can make an arrest without a warrant when there are **exigent circumstances**. This means that officers are in the middle of an urgent situation in which they must act swiftly and do not have time to go to court to seek a warrant. With respect to arrests, for example, when officers are in hot pursuit of a fleeing suspected felon, they need not stop to seek a warrant and thereby risk permitting the suspect to get away (*Warden v. Hayden*, 1967). Similarly, exigent circumstances can justify the warrantless entry into a home or other building and an accompanying search that flows from the

exigent circumstances When there is an immediate threat to public safety or the risk that evidence will be destroyed, officers may search, arrest, or question suspects without obtaining a warrant or following other usual rules of criminal procedure.

officers' response to the urgent situation. For example, the Supreme Court approved police officers' warrantless entry into a home when, on being called to the scene of a loud party, they observed through the home's window a violent altercation between a teenager and an adult (*Brigham City, Utah v. Stuart*, 2006). The unanimous decision by Chief Justice John Roberts said that "law enforcement officers may enter a home without a warrant to render emergency assistance to an injured occupant or to protect an occupant from imminent injury." After the officers make the warrantless entry, the plain view doctrine permits them to examine and seize any criminal evidence that they can see in the course of actions taken to address the exigent circumstances.

In *Cupp v. Murphy* (1973), a man voluntarily complied with police officers' request that he come to the police station to answer questions concerning his wife's murder. At the station, officers noticed a substance on the man's fingernails that they thought might be dried blood. Over his objections, they took a sample of scrapings from his fingernails and ultimately used that tissue as evidence against him when he was convicted of murdering his wife. The Supreme Court said the search was properly undertaken under exigent circumstances. If officers had taken the time to seek a warrant, the suspect could have washed his hands and the evidence would have been lost.

Police officers can use the exigent circumstances justification for warrantless searches for the purpose of seeking evidence. To justify such searches, they do not need to show that there was a potential threat to public safety. As a practical matter, police officers make quick judgments about undertaking certain searches. If incriminating evidence is discovered, courts may be asked after the fact to determine whether the urgency of the situation justified a warrantless search and whether the nature and purpose of the search were reasonable. Judges are usually reluctant to second-guess a police officer's on-the-spot decision that the urgency of a situation required an immediate warrantless search. For example, in 2011, the Supreme Court decided a case concerning police officers who followed a drug suspect into an apartment building and then smelled marijuana outside one apartment while hearing sounds that they believed could be the destruction of evidence. The Court ruled that the officers could legally kick in the door and enter the apartment, based on exigent circumstances, even though it turned out that it was not the apartment that their drug suspect had entered (*Kentucky v. King*).

Consent

If people consent to a search, officers do not need probable cause or even any level of suspicion to justify the search. Consent effectively absolves law enforcement officers of any risk that evidence will be excluded from use at trial or that they will be found liable in a civil lawsuit alleging a violation of Fourth Amendment rights.

A **consent search** provides a valuable investigatory tool for officers who wish to conduct warrantless searches. Officers in many police departments are trained to ask people if they will consent to a search. Thus, some officers ask every motorist during a traffic stop, "May I search your car?" Or, if called to the scene of a domestic dispute or a citizen complaint about noise, the officers may say, "Do you mind if I look around the downstairs area of your house?" Criminal evidence is often uncovered in such consent searches—a fact that may indicate that many citizens do not know that they have the option to say "no" when officers ask for permission to search. Moreover, some citizens may fear that they will look more suspicious to the officer if they say "no," so they agree to searches in order to act as if they have nothing to hide. In addition, in **United States v. Drayton** (2002), the Supreme Court said that police officers do not have to inform people of their right to say "no" when asked if they wish to consent to a search.

In deciding if a permissible consent search has occurred, one must address two key issues. First, the consent must voluntary. Police officers may not use coercion or threats to obtain consent. Even subtler tricks, such as dishonestly telling someone that there is a search warrant and thereby implying that the person has no choice but to consent, will result in the search being declared improper (*Bumper v. North Carolina*, 1968). Second, the consent must be given by someone who possesses authority to give consent and thereby waive the right. Someone cannot, for example, consent to have

consent search A permissible warrantless search of a person, vehicle, home, or other location based on a person with proper authority or the reasonable appearance of proper authority voluntarily granting permission for the search to take place.

United States v. Drayton (2002) Judicial decision declaring that police officers are not required to inform people of their right to decline to be searched when police ask for consent to search.

his or her neighbor's house searched. The resident in a dwelling can consent to a search of that dwelling. A controversial Supreme Court decision said that the police may not search when one resident of a dwelling is present and objects, even if another resident consents to the search of the house (*Georgia v. Randolph*, 2006). In some circumstances, a permissible search may occur if the officers reasonably believe that they have been given permission to search by someone who possesses such authority even if, for example, it later turns out that the person is a former rather than a current resident of the apartment searched (*Illinois v. Rodriguez,* 1990).

Automobile Searches

The U.S. Supreme Court first addressed automobile searches in *Carroll v. United States* (1925), a case in which federal agents searched a car for illegal alcohol. The *Carroll* case, in which the warrantless search was approved, provided an underlying justification for permitting such searches of automobiles. In essence, because cars are mobile, they differ greatly from houses and other buildings. Automobiles can be driven away and disappear in the time that it would take for police to ask a judicial officer for a search warrant.

Police officers have significant authority to search automobiles and to issue commands to people riding in vehicles. For example, during a traffic stop, officers can order passengers as well as the driver to exit the vehicle, even if there is no basis for suspicion that the passengers engaged in any wrongdoing (*Maryland v. Wilson*, 1997).

Two key questions arise in automobile searches: (1) When can officers stop a car? and (2) How extensively can they search the vehicle? Many automobile searches arise as a result of traffic stops. A stop can occur when an officer observes a traffic violation, including defective safety equipment, or when there is a basis for reasonable suspicion concerning the involvement of the car, its driver, or its passengers in a crime. Police officers are free to make a visible inspection of a car's interior by shining a flashlight inside and looking through the window. They can also look at the vehicle identification number on the dashboard and inside the door of a validly stopped vehicle (*New York v. Class*, 1986).

All sworn officers can make traffic stops, even if they are in unmarked vehicles and serving in special vice or detective bureaus that do not normally handle traffic offenses (*Whren v. United States*, 1996). A traffic violation by itself, however, does not provide an officer with the authority to search an entire vehicle (*Knowles v. Iowa*, 1998). Only specific factors creating reasonable suspicion or probable cause will justify officers' doing anything more than looking inside the vehicle.

For example, the arrest of a driver justifies the search of a passenger's property or other locations in the vehicle if there is reason to believe that those locations could contain criminal evidence or weapons (*Wyoming v. Houghton*, 1999). In addition, the Court has expanded officers' authority to search automobiles even when no formal arrest has yet occurred. In *Michigan v. Long* (1983), the Court approved a search of the car's interior around the driver's seat after officers found the car in a ditch and the apparently intoxicated driver standing outside the car. The Supreme Court justified the search as an expansion of the *Terry* doctrine. In effect, the officers were permitted to "frisk" the car in order to protect themselves and others by making sure no weapon was available to the not-yet-arrested driver. Such a search requires that the officers have reasonable suspicion that the person stopped may be armed and may pose a threat to the officers. As described in "Criminal Justice: Myth & Reality," there are also opportunities for officers to search closed containers within a vehicle.

Common Belief: Under the Fourth Amendment's requirements for searches, only judges make determinations of "probable cause," and they do so in order to decide whether to issue a search warrant.

- In *California v. Acevedo* (1991), the Supreme Court said that officers could search anywhere in the car for which they have probable cause to search. This includes a search of closed containers within the car.
- The officers themselves, rather than a judge, determine whether probable cause exists before conducting the warrantless search of the vehicle.
- If the defense attorney seeks to have evidence from such a search excluded as improperly obtained, it may be difficult for a judge to second-guess an officer's decisions.
- The judge must make an after-the-fact evaluation based on the officer's description of the facts and circumstances, and thus the officer's determination of probable cause is likely to stand as the basis for an automobile search.
- If officers are suspicious of a driver who has been stopped for a traffic violation and they are eager to search the vehicle, is there a risk that they will be less careful than a judge in deciding whether probable cause exists to justify a complete search?

TABLE 6.1 Warrantless Searches

The Supreme Court has ruled that there are circumstances when a warrant is not required.

Case	Decision
Special needs	
Michigan Department of State Police v. Sitz (1990)	Stopping motorists systematically at roadblocks designed for specific purposes, such as detecting drunken drivers, is permissible.
City of Indianapolis v. Edmond (2000)	Police traffic checkpoints cannot be justified as a generalized search for criminal evidence, they must be narrowly focused on a specific objective.
Stop and frisk	
Terry v. Ohio (1968)	Officers may stop and frisk suspects on the street when there is reasonable suspicion that they are armed and involved in criminal activity.
Adams v. Williams (1972)	Officers may rely on reports from reliable witnesses as the basis for conducting a stop and frisk.
Illinois v. Wardlow (2000)	When a person runs at the sight of police in a high-crime area, officers are justified in using the person's flight as a basis for forming reasonable suspicion to justify a stop and frisk.
Incident to an arrest	
Chimel v. California (1969)	To preserve evidence and protect the safety of the officer and the public after a lawful arrest, the arrestee and the immediate area around the arrestee may be searched for weapons and criminal evidence.
United States v. Robinson (1973)	A warrantless search incident to an arrest is not limited by the seriousness of the crime for which the arrestee has been taken into custody.
Exigent circumstances	
Warden v. Hayden (1967)	When officers are in hot pursuit of a fleeing suspect, they need not stop to seek a warrant and thereby risk permitting the suspect to get away.
Cupp v. Murphy (1973)	Officers may seize evidence to protect it if taking time to seek a warrant creates a risk of its destruction.
Consent	
Bumper v. North Carolina (1968)	Officers may not tell falsehoods as a means of getting a suspect to consent to a search.
United States v. Drayton (2002)	An officer does not have to inform people of their right to refuse when he or she asks if they wish to consent to a search.
Automobiles	
Carroll v. United States (1925)	Because by their nature automobiles can be easily moved, warrantless searches are permissible when reasonable suspicion of illegal activity exists.
New York v. Class (1986)	An officer may enter a vehicle to see the vehicle identification number when a car has been validly stopped pursuant to a traffic violation or other permissible justification.
California v. Acevedo (1991)	Officers may search throughout a vehicle when they believe they have probable cause to do so.
Maryland v. Wilson (1997)	During traffic stops, officers may order passengers as well as the driver to exit the vehicle, even if there is no basis for suspicion that the passengers engaged in any wrongdoing.
Knowles v. Iowa (1998)	A traffic violation by itself does not provide an officer with the authority to search an entire vehicle. There must be reasonable suspicion or probable cause before officers can extend their search beyond merely looking inside the vehicle's passenger compartment.

© Cengage Learning

inventory search
Permissible warrantless search of a vehicle that has been "impounded"—meaning that it is in police custody—so that police can make a record of the items contained in the vehicle.

The Court permits thorough searches of vehicles, without regard to probable cause, when police officers inventory the contents of impounded vehicles (*South Dakota v. Opperman*, 1976). This means that containers found within the course of the **inventory search** may also be opened and searched when the examination of such containers is consistent with a police department's inventory policies.

Table 6.1 reviews selected Supreme Court cases concerning those circumstances in which the police do not need a warrant to conduct a search or to seize evidence.

5. In what situations do law enforcement's special needs justify stopping an automobile without reasonable suspicion?
Warrantless stops of automobiles are permitted at international borders and sobriety checkpoints (unless barred within a specific state by its own supreme court) or when there is reasonable suspicion of a traffic violation or other wrongdoing.

6. What is an exigent circumstance?
An urgent situation in which evidence might be destroyed, a suspect might escape, or the public would be endangered if police took the time to seek a warrant for a search or an arrest.

7. What two elements must be present for a valid consent to permit a warrantless search?
Voluntary consent by a person with proper authority to consent.

Imagine that you were stopped for speeding while driving down a highway. If the officer gives you a warning rather than a ticket, how would you answer if the police officer then said to you, "Do you mind if I look in the trunk of your car?" What reasons would motivate your decision about how to answer? What concerns might someone have about what the officer could do upon hearing the answer "no"?

Questioning Suspects

The Fifth Amendment contains various rights, including the one most relevant to police officers' actions in questioning suspects. The relevant words of the amendment are "No person shall . . . be compelled in any criminal case to be a witness against himself." The privilege against compelled self-incrimination should not be viewed as simply a legal protection that seeks to assist individuals who may be guilty of crimes. By protecting individuals in this way, the Fifth Amendment discourages police officers from using violent or otherwise coercive means to push suspects to confess.

In addition to discouraging the physical abuse of suspects, the privilege against compelled self-incrimination can also diminish the risk of erroneous convictions. When police officers use coercive pressure to seek confessions, they create a significant risk that innocent people will confess to crimes they did not commit. The worst-case scenario took place in the film *In the Name of the Father* (1993), based on a true story in England, in which police officers gain a confession from a bombing suspect, whom they know to be innocent, by placing a gun in the suspect's mouth and threatening to pull the trigger. This example from England took place at a time when people there were afraid of terrorist acts by militants who sought to use violence to force Great Britain to remove its soldiers and governing institutions from Northern Ireland. Since 9/11, many Americans feel similar fears about their own country's vulnerability to terrorists. See "What Americans Think" to assess how the threat of terrorism may have influenced the public's views on coercive questioning of terrorism suspects.

Miranda Rules

The decision by the Supreme Court in ***Miranda v. Arizona*** (1966) said that as soon as the investigation of a crime begins to focus on a particular suspect and he or she is taken into custody, the so-called *Miranda* warnings must be read aloud before

Miranda v. Arizona (1966)
U.S. Supreme Court decision declaring that suspects in custody must be informed of their rights to remain silent and be represented during questioning.

Question: "How do you feel about the use of torture against suspected terrorists to obtain information about terrorism activities? Can that often be justified, sometimes be justified, rarely be justified, or never be justified?"

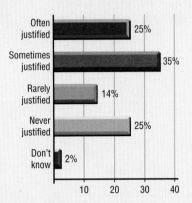

Often justified — 25%
Sometimes justified — 35%
Rarely justified — 14%
Never justified — 25%
Don't know — 2%

Critical Thinking: Those respondents to the poll who believe that torture is justified in certain circumstances presumably also believe that torture is an effective way to obtain desired information. Alternatively, it is possible that the infliction of severe fear, pain, and discomfort will lead a tortured suspect to provide a false confession or inaccurate information out of sheer desperation—especially if the person really does not possess any pertinent information. How would you write a law that specifies when torture or coercive methods are allowed but that also ensures protection from excessive abuse or the infliction of pain? Is it possible to draft such a law in a workable manner?

Source: AP-GfK Poll conducted by GfK Roper Public Affairs and Corporate Communications, May 5–9, 2011 (www.pollingreport.com/terror.htm).

questioning can begin. Suspects must be told four things:

1. They have the right to remain silent.
2. If they decide to make a statement, it can and will be used against them in court.
3. They have the right to have an attorney present during interrogation or to have an opportunity to consult with an attorney.
4. If they cannot afford an attorney, the state will provide one.

Prior to the *Miranda* decision, police officers in some places solved crimes by picking up a poor person or an African American and torturing him or her until a confession was produced. In *Brown v. Mississippi* (1936), the Supreme Court ruled that statements produced after police beat suspects were inadmissible, but it did not insist that counsel be available at the early stages of the criminal process.

Two rulings in 1964 laid the foundation for the *Miranda* decision. In *Escobedo v. Illinois*, the Court made the link between the Fifth Amendment right against self-incrimination and the Sixth Amendment right to counsel. Danny Escobedo was questioned at the police station for 14 hours without counsel, even though he asked to see his attorney. He finally made incriminating statements that the police said were voluntary. The Court's ruling specified that defendants have a right to counsel

> when the investigation is no longer a general inquiry into an unsolved crime, but has begun to focus on a particular suspect, the suspect has been taken into police custody, [and] the police carry out a process of interrogations that lends itself to eliciting incriminating statements.

The Court effectively expanded the right to counsel to apply at an early point in the criminal justice process as a means to guard against law enforcement officers' actions that might violate the Fifth Amendment privilege against compelled self-incrimination. In *Massiah v. United States* (1964), the Supreme Court declared that the questioning of the defendant by a police agent outside of the presence of defense counsel violated the defendant's rights.

The *Miranda* warnings only apply to what are called custodial interrogations. If police officers walk up to someone on the streets and begin asking questions, there is no need to inform the person of his rights. The justices say that people know they can walk away when an officer asks them questions in a public place. When police have taken someone into custody, however, the Supreme Court sees risks of excessive pressure. The loss of liberty and isolation experienced by detained suspects can make them vulnerable to abusive interrogation techniques, especially when interrogations take place out of view of anyone other than police officers. When a suspect is alone in a room with the police, will anyone believe the suspect if he or she claims to have been beaten? If the police say that the suspect confessed, will anyone believe the suspect if he or she denies this? The *Miranda* warnings and presence of counsel during questioning are supposed to prevent such abuses (C. E. Smith, 2010b).

The Court has permitted police officers to forgo *Miranda* warnings when a threat to public safety would result from police taking the time to provide the warnings. This exception is similar to the exigent circumstance justification for warrantless searches. The underlying premise is that some urgent, socially significant situation outweighs the necessity of respecting individuals' rights. In the case that created this **"public safety" exception**, police officers chased an armed man into a supermarket after a reported assault. When they found him with an empty shoulder holster, they asked, "Where's the gun?" after he was handcuffed but before he had been informed of his *Miranda* rights (*New York v. Quarles*, 1984). His statement in response to the question could be used against him in court, because the public's safety might have been threatened if the police had taken the time to read him his rights before asking any questions.

Police interrogations often occur when suspects have just been arrested and are feeling disoriented, confused, and afraid. Under such circumstances, are you confident that suspects will truly understand the nature of their rights before consenting to be questioned without an attorney present?

The Supreme Court continues to refine and clarify the requirements of *Miranda* warnings (Kinports, 2011; Dery, 2011). Most recently, in *Berghuis v. Thompkins* (2010), the Court concluded that a suspect being questioned cannot assert his right to remain silent by remaining silent in the face of continued questioning by an officer. Instead, he must actually tell the officer that he is asserting his right to remain silent in order to seek an end to the officer's questioning (Weisselberg, 2011). The Court permitted police to vary the precise words used to provide the warnings in *Florida v. Powell* (2010). The Court approved the officers' delivery of the warnings even though they failed to make clear that the suspect has a right to consult with an attorney throughout the entire questioning process and not just, as they stated it to the suspect, "before answering questions." And in *J. D. B. v. North Carolina* (2011), a case concerning police officers' questioning of a seventh-grader at school, the Court declared that juveniles may be entitled to *Miranda* warnings even in some situations in which an adult could freely walk away from the police and thus not be considered a detained suspect entitled to warnings.

"public safety" exception
Exception to *Miranda* requirements that permits police to immediately question a suspect in custody without providing any warnings, when public safety would be jeopardized by their taking the time to supply the warnings.

Although some legal commentators and police officials have criticized the *Miranda* warnings and urged the Court to eliminate the rule, the Supreme Court strongly repeated its endorsement of the *Miranda* requirement in 2000 (*Dickerson v. United States*). In declaring that *Miranda* warnings are required by the Constitution, Chief Justice William Rehnquist's majority opinion stated that "*Miranda* has become embedded in routine police practice to the point where the warnings have become part of our national culture." Rehnquist's conclusion was reinforced by a national survey of police chiefs, in which more than three-quarters of respondents supported the Supreme Court's decision to keep the *Miranda* rule in place (Zalman and Smith, 2007).

The Consequences of *Miranda*

Miranda rights must be provided before questions are asked during custodial interrogations. However, police officers have adapted their techniques in various ways that enable them to question suspects without any impediment from the warnings. For example, officers may ask questions while standing on the suspect's doorstep before making an arrest. Even after arrest, the courts do not require that police inform suspects of their rights immediately. Thus, after taking a suspect into custody, some officers may delay providing *Miranda* warnings in case the suspect talks on his or her own. The suspect may be kept in the backseat of a car as officers drive around town, or the suspect may be left alone in a room at the police station. Some suspects will take the initiative to talk to officers because of feelings of guilt. Other suspects may start conversations with officers because they are so eager to convince the officers that they have an alibi or that they want to cooperate. This may lead the suspect to provide contradictory statements that will help build the case.

Officers are also trained in interrogation techniques that are intended to encourage suspects to talk despite *Miranda* warnings (Weisselberg, 2008). The words of the warnings are so familiar from their use in television police shows that many suspects never stop to think about the message being conveyed. In addition, officers may pretend to sympathize with the suspect (Leo, 1996). For example, they may say such things as, "We know that you had a good reason to go after that guy with a knife. Tell us how it happened." Police officers are not required to be truthful in speaking to suspects. They are permitted to use deception to induce suspects to talk. It is not uncommon for officers to say, untruthfully, "We have five witnesses that saw you do it. If you tell us everything right now, we may be able to get you a good deal." In reality, there were no witnesses and there will be no deal. Do such statements constitute improper pressure in violation of *Miranda*? Probably not—as long as the officers do not threaten suspects in ways that make them fear for their physical safety or the safety of their loved ones. Read "A Question of Ethics" at the end of the chapter and consider whether the Houston police officer's techniques for questioning suspects are consistent with the letter and intent of the *Miranda* rule.

Many suspects talk to the police despite being informed of their right to remain silent and their right to have an attorney present during questioning. Some suspects do not fully understand their rights (Rogers et al., 2011). They may believe that they will look guilty by remaining silent or asking for an attorney. They therefore feel that they must talk to officers if they are to have any hope of claiming innocence. More importantly, many suspects believe (often accurately) that they will gain a more favorable charge or plea bargain if they cooperate with officers as fully and as early as possible.

In 2004, the Supreme Court warned police officers not to try to get around *Miranda* warnings by questioning unwarned suspects and obtaining incriminating statements and then giving the warnings and asking the suspects to repeat their statements again. In *Missouri v. Seibert* (2004), Justice Souter's majority opinion concluded,

> upon hearing warnings only in the aftermath of interrogation and just after making a confession, a suspect would hardly think he had a genuine right to remain silent, let alone persist in so believing once the police began to lead him over the same ground again. . . . Thus, when *Miranda* warnings are inserted in the midst of coordinated and continuing interrogation, they are likely to mislead and "depriv[e] a defendant of knowledge essential to his ability to understand the nature of his rights and the consequences of abandoning them."

Some commentators have argued that officers' efforts to get around the *Miranda* requirement could be prevented by requiring that all police interrogations be video recorded, to provide proof that suspects' statements are voluntary. Several states have introduced video-recording requirements, but they are often limited to certain categories of cases, such as murders or serious felonies (L. Lewis, 2007). It remains to be seen whether such requirements will become more universal.

8. What are *Miranda* rights?

Officers must inform suspects, *before* custodial interrogation, of their right to remain silent, the prosecution's authority to use any of the suspect's statements, the right to the presence of an attorney during questioning, and the right to have an attorney appointed if the suspect is too poor to hire one.

9. What is the "public safety" exception?

Officers can ask questions of suspects in custody without first providing *Miranda* warnings when public safety would be threatened by their taking the time to supply the warnings.

10. How have police officers adapted their practices in light of *Miranda*?

Officers ask questions before suspects are in custody, use techniques to pretend to befriend or empathize with suspects being questioned, and misinform suspects about the existence of evidence demonstrating their guilt.

stop & analyze

Should police officers be permitted to lie to suspects during questioning, such as falsely claiming that they have eyewitnesses or other evidence of a suspect's guilt? Do such strategies create any risks, such as innocent people feeling hopelessly doomed and admitting guilt in order to seek a plea to a lesser charge? Write an argument in favor of giving police flexibility to use such strategies as well as an argument against permitting dishonest statements. Which argument do you support? Why?

The Exclusionary Rule

What happens when police commit rights violations? One primary remedy is the exclusion of evidence from court. In 1914, the U.S. Supreme Court declared in *Weeks v. United States* that federal courts must exclude any evidence that was obtained through an improper search by federal law enforcement agents. In *Weeks*, U.S. marshals searched a home without a warrant and found incriminating evidence. According to the Court,

> if letters and private documents can thus be seized and held and used in evidence against a citizen accused of an offense, the protection of the Fourth Amendment, declaring his right to be secure against such searches and seizures, is of no value, and, so far as those thus placed are concerned, might as well be stricken from the Constitution.

Thus, the Court required that the improperly obtained evidence be excluded from use in court, even if it meant that a guilty person might go free because of a lack of enough evidence to gain a conviction. As a result of this **exclusionary rule** created by the Court, it was assumed that law enforcement officers would obey the Fourth Amendment to avoid the loss of incriminating evidence. Later, the exclusionary rule was also applied to Fifth Amendment violations caused by improper questioning, such as a failure to inform arrested individuals of their *Miranda* rights. Read the "Comparative Perspective" to consider whether the United States should draw from practices in other countries to refine the exclusionary rule and its impact on criminal cases.

The exclusionary rule does not necessarily require that cases against defendants be dismissed when constitutional rights have been violated. The prosecution can continue, but improperly obtained evidence may not be used. In some cases, other

exclusionary rule The principle that illegally obtained evidence must be excluded from trial.

Police officers must take care to follow the rules for conducting proper searches that obey court rulings defining the Fourth Amendment protection against "unreasonable searches and seizures." Evidence will be excluded when the Fourth Amendment is violated, unless the police officers' actions fall within a specific exception to the exclusionary rule.

valid evidence of guilt may exist in the form of witness testimony or confessions. As described by one scholar with experience as a prosecutor,

> during my seven years as a federal prosecutor, . . . I could see that the rule's mandatory nature forced police and federal agents to think about the rules before they acted. It caused both federal and local law-enforcement authorities to train their agents in the constitutional rules in order to [avoid] evidentiary exclusion. . . . Nor was it my impression that any significant number of cases were lost as a result of the rule, especially prosecutions of violent felonies (Bradley, 2010:212).

The Application of the Exclusionary Rule to the States

In *Wolf v. Colorado* **(1949)**, the Supreme Court incorporated the Fourth Amendment. However, the justices declined to apply the exclusionary rule to the states, because they believed states could develop their own remedies to handle improper searches by police. The situation changed during the Supreme Court tenure of Chief Justice Earl Warren (1953–1969), when the Court incorporated most of the criminal justice–related rights in a way that required state law enforcement officials to adhere to the same rules federal law enforcement officials had to follow. Not until *Mapp v. Ohio* **(1961)** did the Court apply the exclusionary rule to the states.

Why did the Supreme Court see the exclusionary rule as necessary? Several reasons emerge in *Weeks v. United States* **(1914)** and *Mapp*. First, *Weeks* declared that the exclusionary rule is essential to make the Fourth Amendment meaningful. In essence, the justices believed that constitutional rights are nullified if government officials are permitted to benefit by violating those rights. Second, *Mapp* indicated that the exclusionary rule is required by the Constitution. Third, the majority opinion in *Mapp* concluded that alternatives to the exclusionary rule do not work. The opinion noted that many states had found that nothing short of exclusion of evidence would work to correct constitutional rights violations and limit the number of violations that occur. Fourth, the *Mapp* opinion argued that the use of improperly obtained evidence by officials who are responsible for upholding the law only serves to diminish respect for the law. Fifth, the *Mapp* decision indicates that the absence of an exclusionary rule would diminish the protection of all rights because it would permit all constitutional rights "to be revocable at the whim of any police officer who, in the name of law enforcement itself, chooses to suspend . . . [the] enjoyment [of rights]." Sixth, the exclusionary rule is justified in *Mapp* as an effective means of deterring police and prosecutors from violating constitutional rights.

The existence of the exclusionary rule demonstrates the Supreme Court's conclusion that it is sometimes necessary to risk setting a guilty criminal free to ensure that constitutional rights are protected.

Exceptions to the Exclusionary Rule

The exclusionary rule has many critics who claim that the Court's decision hampers police investigations and allows guilty criminals to go free. However, research has not clearly supported claims about the negative consequences of the exclusionary rule. Studies of the impact of the exclusionary rule have produced two consistent findings. First, only a small minority of defendants file

© Mitch Wojnarowicz/Amsterdam Recorder/The Image Works

Wolf v. Colorado **(1949)**
Supreme Court decision in which the Fourth Amendment was applied against searches by state and local police officers, but the exclusionary rule was not imposed as the remedy for violations of the Fourth Amendment by these officials.

Mapp v. Ohio **(1961)**
Supreme Court decision that applied the exclusionary rule as the remedy for improper searches by state and local officials.

Weeks v. United States **(1914)**
Supreme Court decision applying the exclusionary rule as the remedy for improper searches by federal law enforcement officials.

The Exclusionary Rule in Canada and Europe

The exclusionary rule in the United States is mandatory when evidence is obtained in violation of the Fourth and Fifth Amendments, unless the circumstances fit certain exceptions, such as the "good faith" and "inevitable discovery" situations discussed in this section of the chapter. By contrast, other countries' legal systems often consider the issue of exclusion on a case-by-case basis for searches, whereas exclusion is more consistently enforced when improper questioning of suspects occurs.

In the Canadian case of *R. v. Grant* (2009), a pedestrian was stopped and surrounded by police officers without any reasonable suspicion of wrongdoing. When asked, the pedestrian admitted that he was illegally carrying a gun. After he was convicted of the crime, the Canadian Supreme Court examined whether the gun should have been excluded from evidence since it was obtained through an improper stop. The Court applied a three-part test to consider whether the evidence should have been excluded. It considered,

1. the seriousness of the violation of the Canadian Charter of Rights by the police officers' conduct;
2. the impact of the violation on the rights of the accused; and

3. society's interests in having the evidence examined at trial as part of the merits of the case.

In applying these factors to the case, the Court held that the gun was properly admitted into evidence. Presumably, if the evidence had been obtained through an involuntary search, a forceful home invasion, or other more flagrant invasion of rights, the Court's test would have weighed more heavily in favor of the accused. In cases where the exclusionary rule has been applied in Canada, the emphasis has been on maintaining the image of the judicial system for upholding rights and laws rather than an emphasis on deterring improper behavior by the police.

In Germany, there is also a case-by-case consideration of circumstances when improper searches are challenged and defendants seek to have evidence excluded. In each case, the judge must balance the protection of the suspect's rights against the interests of society in having useful evidence fully examined and lawbreakers punished for their crimes. German courts frequently admit evidence from improper searches, although exclusion is more likely to occur for flagrant violations of citizens' privacy, such as improperly gaining access to medical records or improper electronic surveillance.

With respect to improper questioning of suspects in custody, however, Canada, Germany, England, and France all impose exclusion more consistently. Scholars believe that the stronger application of the exclusionary rule for questioning reflects serious concerns about the risk of false confessions if people feel trapped, pressured, and denied their rights during questioning. By contrast, controversies about searches arise in a wider of variety of circumstances, many of which involve relatively modest intrusions on rights and, moreover, which produce reliable evidence of guilt (e.g., weapons, drugs, stolen goods, etc).

For Critical Analysis

Should the United States consider a two-track approach to the exclusionary rule with greater emphasis on exclusion for violations of *Miranda* rights but more case-by-case decisions for improper searches? Give three reasons to support your answer to this question. What will be the impact and effect of the approach that you advocate?

Sources: Craig M. Bradley, "Interrogation and Silence: A Comparative Study," *Wisconsin International Law Journal* 27:271–97 (2009); Craig M. Bradley, "Reconceiving the Fourth Amendment and the Exclusionary Rule," *Law and Contemporary Problems* 73:211–38 (2010); Tracey Tyler, "Should Evidence be Allowed if Police Break the Law?," *Toronto Star,* August 8, 2009 (www.thestar.com).

---

a "motion to suppress," which is used to ask a judge to exclude evidence that has allegedly been obtained in violation of the defendant's rights. Second, only a very small fraction of motions to suppress evidence are granted (Uchida and Bynum, 1991; S. Walker, 2001). Despite continuing debates about the rule's impact and effectiveness (Dripps, 2010), the Supreme Court began creating exceptions to the exclusionary rule after Warren Burger became chief justice in 1969.

"Good Faith" Exception The Supreme Court created a **"good faith" exception** to the exclusionary rule when officers use search warrants **(United States v. Leon, 1984)**. *Good faith* means that the officers acted with the honest belief that they were following the proper rules, but the judge issued the warrant improperly. In addition, the reliance and honest belief must be reasonable. If officers knew that a judge issued a warrant based on no evidence whatsoever, the officers could not claim that they reasonably and honestly relied on the warrant. But when officers present evidence of probable cause to the judge and the judge issues a warrant based

"good faith" exception
Exception to the exclusionary rule that permits the use of improperly obtained evidence when police officers acted in honest reliance on a defective statute, a warrant improperly issued by a magistrate, or a consent to search by someone who lacked authority to give such permission.

United States v. Leon (1984)
Supreme Court decision announcing the "good faith" exception to the exclusionary rule.

TABLE 6.2 Exclusionary Rule

The Supreme Court has created the exclusionary rule as a means of ensuring that Fourth and Fifth Amendment rights are protected. It has also provided exceptions to this rule.

Case	Decision
Exclusionary rule *Mapp v. Ohio* (1961)	Because the Fourth Amendment protects people from unreasonable searches and seizures by all law enforcement officials, evidence found through improper searches or seizures must be excluded from use at state and federal trials.
"Good faith" exception *United States v. Leon* (1984)	When officers act in good faith reliance on a warrant, the evidence will not be excluded even if the warrant was issued improperly.
"Inevitable discovery" exception *Nix v. Williams* (1984)	Improperly obtained evidence can be used when it would later have inevitably been discovered without improper actions by the police.

© Cengage Learning

on information that actually falls below the standard of probable cause, the officers may use evidence found in the resulting search, because it was the judge who made the error, not the police (Cammack, 2010). However, evidence can still be excluded if officers undertake a warrantless search based on their own discretionary decision, even if they honestly (but wrongly) believe that such a search is permitted in such circumstances.

"Inevitable Discovery" Rule   Another important exception to the exclusionary rule is the **"inevitable discovery" rule** (Grubman, 2011). This rule arose from a case involving the tragic abduction and murder of a young girl. The police sought an escapee from a psychiatric hospital who was seen carrying a large bundle. The man being sought contacted an attorney and arranged to surrender to police in a town 160 miles away from the scene of the abduction. The Supreme Court subsequently found that the police improperly questioned the suspect outside of the presence of his attorney while driving him back to the city where the abduction occurred (*Brewer v. Williams*, 1977). The Court declared that the girl's body and the suspect's statements had to be excluded from evidence because they were obtained in violation of his rights. Thus, his murder conviction was overturned and he was given a new trial. At the second trial, he was convicted again. However, at the second trial, the prosecution used the body in evidence against him based on the claim that search parties would have found the body eventually even without his confession. There was a search team within two and one-half miles of the body at the time that it was found. In ***Nix v. Williams* (1984)**, the Supreme Court agreed that the improperly obtained evidence can be used when it would later have been inevitably discovered, without improper actions by the police. Table 6.2 summarizes selected Supreme Court decisions regarding the exclusionary rule as it applies to the Fourth and Fifth Amendments.

When the Court issued its decisions in *Weeks* and *Mapp*, it appeared that the exclusion of evidence would be guided by a trial judge's answer to the question,

"inevitable discovery" rule
Supreme Court ruling that improperly obtained evidence can be used when it would later have been inevitably discovered by the police.

***Nix v. Williams* (1984)**
Legal decision in which the Supreme Court created the "inevitable discovery" exception to the exclusionary rule.

"Did police violate the suspect's rights?" By contrast, through the development of exceptions to the rule, the Court shifted its focus to the question, "Did the police make an error that was so serious that the exclusion of evidence is required?" For example, the "good faith" exception established in *United States v. Leon* (1984) emphasizes the fact that officers did what they thought they were supposed to do. The decision did not rest on the fact that the suspect's Fourth Amendment rights were violated by a search conducted with an improper warrant. Thus, the Supreme Court's creation of exceptions to the exclusionary rule has given police officers the flexibility to make specific kinds of errors in an increasing variety of situations without jeopardizing the admissibility of evidence that may help establish a defendant's guilt (Nolasco, del Carmen, and Vaughn, 2011).

In 2009, some commentators speculated that the Supreme Court was deeply divided on the issue of whether to eliminate the exclusionary rule (Liptak, 2009). Five justices declined to apply the exclusionary rule to the case of an improper search, when a man was wrongly arrested because of sloppy record keeping in a police database that erroneously informed the officers that there was an arrest warrant (*Herring v. United States*, 2009). As you read the excerpt from the Supreme Court's *Herring* opinion in the "Close Up," note how the five justices in the majority have a narrow view of the exclusionary rule's purposes for deterring police misconduct. By contrast, the four dissenters claim that the exclusionary rule is needed to protect the public in a broader fashion against preventable mistakes by law enforcement agencies.

Critics of the exclusionary rule hope that this decision moved the Court one step closer to abolishing the rule. In reality, the fate of the rule will be determined by new justices, who could go either way (C. E. Smith, McCall, and McCall, 2009). In the immediate future, it seems unlikely that President Barack Obama would appoint new justices who would favor the elimination of the exclusionary rule, but presidents cannot always predict accurately how their nominees will decide specific issues.

---

check point

11. Why was the exclusionary rule created and eventually applied to the states?

The exclusionary rule was created to deter officers from violating people's rights, and the Supreme Court considers it an essential component of the Fourth and Fifth Amendments.

12. What are the criticisms of the exclusionary rule?

The rule is criticized for hampering police investigations and permitting some guilty people to go free.

13. What are the main exceptions to the exclusionary rule?

A "good faith" exception in warrant situations; cases in which evidence would have been discovered by the police inevitably anyway ("inevitable discovery" rule).

stop & analyze

When you add up the pros and cons, does the exclusionary rule provide a needed benefit for our society and justice system? Describe three situations in which the exclusionary rule should definitely apply—*or* list three reasons why the exclusionary rule should be abolished. Give two reasons why you would either treat *Miranda* cases differently than search cases, or why you would treat them in the same manner with respect to the issue of excluding improperly obtained evidence.

Herring v. United States, 555 U.S. 135 (2009)

Chief Justice John Roberts delivered the opinion of the Court [on behalf of Justices Antonin Scalia, Anthony Kennedy, Clarence Thomas, and Samuel Alito].

Facts: Police officers asked the court clerk in a neighboring county whether there were any warrants outstanding for Bennie Herring. Computer records indicated that there was a warrant for Herring's arrest based on his failure to appear in court on a felony charge. Relying on that information, the officers arrested Herring and searched both him and his vehicle. They found methamphetamine in his pocket. They also found a pistol in his vehicle and, as a convicted felon, his possession of that pistol constituted as crime. Subsequently, it turned out that there was no outstanding warrant for Herring. The warrant in question had been withdrawn five months earlier but the information had not been corrected in the computer database. Because the search incident to arrest was conducted in reliance on an invalid arrest, Herring sought to have the exclusionary rule applied to prohibit the prosecution's use of the drugs and pistol as bases for the criminal charges against him.

The Fourth Amendment forbids "unreasonable searches and seizures," and this usually requires the police to have probable cause or a warrant before making an arrest. What if an officer reasonably believes there is an outstanding arrest warrant, but that belief turns out to be wrong because of a negligent bookkeeping error by another police employee? The parties here agree that the ensuing arrest is still a violation of the Fourth Amendment, but dispute whether contraband found during a search incident to that arrest must be excluded in a later prosecution.

Our cases establish that such suppression is not an automatic consequence of a Fourth Amendment violation. Instead, the question turns on the culpability of the police and the potential of exclusion to deter wrongful police conduct. Here the error was the result of isolated negligence attenuated from the arrest. We hold that in these circumstances the jury should not be barred from considering all the evidence.

***

For purposes of deciding this case, . . . we accept the parties' assumption that there was a Fourth Amendment violation. The issue is whether the exclusionary rule should be applied.

***

First, the exclusionary rule is not an individual right and applies only where it "'result[s] in appreciable deterrence.'" . . . We have repeatedly rejected the argument that exclusion is a necessary consequence of a Fourth Amendment violation. . . . Instead we have focused on the efficacy of the rule in deterring Fourth Amendment violations in the future. . . .

In addition, the benefits of deterrence must outweigh the costs. . . .

***

The extent to which the exclusionary rule is justified by these deterrence principles varies with the culpability of the law enforcement conduct. As we said in *Leon*, "an assessment of the flagrancy of the police misconduct constitutes an important step in the calculus" of applying the exclusionary rule. . . .

***

An error that arises from nonrecurring and attenuated negligence is thus far removed from the core concerns that led us to adopt the rule in the first place. And in fact since *Leon*, we have never applied the rule to exclude evidence obtained in violation of the Fourth Amendment, where the police conduct was no more intentional or culpable than this.

To trigger the exclusionary rule, police conduct must be sufficiently deliberate that exclusion can meaningfully deter it, and sufficiently culpable that such deterrence is worth the price paid by the justice system. As laid out in our cases, the exclusionary rule serves to deter deliberate, reckless, or grossly negligent conduct, or in some circumstances recurring or systemic negligence. The error in this case does not rise to that level.

***

If the police have been shown to be reckless in maintaining a warrant system, or to have knowingly made false entries to lay the groundwork for future false arrests, exclusion would certainly be justified under our cases should such misconduct cause a Fourth Amendment violation. . . .

***

In light of our repeated holdings that the deterrent effect of suppression must be substantial and outweigh any harm to the justice system, *e.g., Leon*, 468 U.S., at 909–910, we conclude that when police mistakes are the result of negligence such as that described here, rather than systemic error or reckless disregard of constitutional requirements, any marginal deterrence does not "pay its way." *Id.,* at 907–908, n. 6 [internal quotation marks omitted]. In such a case, the criminal should not "go free because the constable has blundered." . . .

Justice Ruth Bader Ginsburg, with whom Justice John Paul Stevens, Justice David Souter, and Justice Stephen Breyer join, dissenting.

***

The exclusionary rule is "a remedy necessary to ensure that" the Fourth Amendment's prohibitions "are observed in fact." . . .

***

Beyond doubt, a main objective of the rule "is to deter—to compel respect for the constitutional guaranty in the only effectively available way—by removing the incentive to disregard it." . . . But the rule also serves other important purposes: It "enabl[es] the judiciary to avoid the taint of partnership in official lawlessness," and it "assur[es] the people—all potential victims of unlawful government conduct—that the government would not profit from its lawless behavior, thus minimizing the risk of seriously undermining popular trust in government."

* * *

The exclusionary rule, it bears emphasis, is often the only remedy effective to redress a Fourth Amendment violation. . . . Civil liability will not lie for "the vast majority of [F]ourth [A]mendment violations—the frequent infringements motivated by commendable zeal, not condemnable malice." . . . Criminal prosecutions or administrative sanctions against the offending officers and injunctive relief against widespread violations are an even farther cry.

* * *

The record reflects no routine practice of checking the database for accuracy, and the failure to remove the entry for Herring's warrant was not discovered until Investigator Anderson sought to pursue Herring five months later. Is it not altogether obvious that the Department could take further precautions to ensure the integrity of its database? The Sheriff's Department "is in a position to remedy the situation and might well do so if the exclusionary rule is there to remove the incentive to do otherwise." . . .

Is the potential deterrence here worth the costs it imposes? . . . In light of the paramount importance of accurate recordkeeping in law enforcement, I would answer yes, . . .

Electronic databases form the nervous system of contemporary criminal justice operations. In recent years, their breadth and influence have dramatically expanded. Police today can access databases that include not only the updated National Crime Information Center (NCIC), but also terrorist watchlists, the Federal Government's employee eligibility system, and various commercial databases. . . . Moreover, States are actively expanding information sharing between jurisdictions. . . . As a result, law enforcement has an increasing supply of information within its easy electronic reach. . . .

The risk of error stemming from these databases is not slim. . . . [L]aw enforcement databases are insufficiently monitored and often out of date. . . . Government reports describe, for example, flaws in NCIC databases, terrorist watchlist databases, and databases associated with the Federal Government's employment eligibility verification system.

Inaccuracies in expansive, interconnected collections of electronic information raise grave concerns for individual liberty. "The offense to the dignity of the citizen who is arrested, handcuffed, and searched on a public street simply because some bureaucrat has failed to maintain an accurate computer database" is evocative of the use of general warrants that so outraged the authors of our Bill of Rights. . . .

* * *

First, by restricting suppression to bookkeeping errors that are deliberate or reckless, the majority leaves Herring, and others like him, with no remedy for violations of their constitutional rights. . . . [T]he police department itself is not liable for the negligent acts of its employees, ... Moreover, identifying the department employee who committed the error may be impossible.

Second, I doubt that police forces already possess sufficient incentives to maintain up-to-date records.

* * *

Third, even when deliberate or reckless conduct is afoot, the Court's assurance will often be an empty promise: How is a poor defendant to make the required showing? If the answer is that a defendant is entitled to discovery (and if necessary, an audit of police databases), . . . then the Court has imposed a considerable administrative burden on courts and law enforcement.

Negligent recordkeeping errors by law enforcement threaten individual liberty, are susceptible to deterrence by the exclusionary rule, and cannot be remedied effectively through other means. Such errors present no occasion to further erode the exclusionary rule. The rule "is needed to make the Fourth Amendment something real; a guarantee that does not carry with it the exclusion of evidence obtained by its violation is a chimera." . . . In keeping with the rule's "core concerns," . . . suppression should have attended the unconstitutional search in this case.

Researching the Internet
The U.S. Department of Homeland Security posts online the transcripts of their training sessions at the Federal Law Enforcement Training Center concerning the exclusionary rule and searches. To link to the website, visit the Criminal Justice CourseMate at cengagebrain.com, then access the web links for this chapter.

For Critical Analysis
As you read the two perspectives in the opinion concerning the purposes and benefits of the exclusionary rule, which viewpoint was more persuasive? Give three reasons why one opinion was more convincing than the other.

own counsel. Clark's guilty plea was the culmination of an 18-month process, starting from the discovery of the victim's body and ending with the defendant's official admission of guilt (A. Griffin, 2011a). The plea represented months of police investigation in addition to negotiations that took place between the prosecutor, David Strollo, and Clark's defense attorneys. At the time of the actual hearing to enter the plea, Judge Fasano's primary role was to ensure that Clark understood that he would be voluntarily giving up many rights, including the right to a trial by jury.

The last image of Annie Le alive came from security camera footage that showed her entering the science laboratory building where she conducted cancer research and where Clark worked as a lab-animal caretaker. Le disappeared on September 8, 2009, and the case shocked and frightened the Yale University community. Her body was found days later, battered and hidden behind a wall in the science building. Clark was eventually arrested and made his first appearance in court in October 2009; he stood silently as the judge set bail at $3 million—an amount that the lab technician could not possibly pay. Unable to make bail, he was locked up to await the processing of his case (A. Griffin, 2011b).

At a later pretrial proceeding, Clark entered a "not guilty" plea, following his attorneys' advice to waive his right to a preliminary hearing at which the prosecutors would present evidence to justify the charges against him. In anticipation of a possible jury trial, the defense attorneys' advice may have reflected an attempt to limit the amount of incriminating evidence revealed in court and relayed in the news media in advance of the trial. Over the months that followed, the police collected and analyzed additional evidence from the crime scene, the prosecutors awaited DNA test results, and the defense attorneys engaged in discussions with Prosecutor Strollo about a possible plea agreement. Ultimately, Clark, age 26, agreed to plead guilty in exchange for a 44-year prison sentence from which he would not be eligible for release until he was 70 years old (A. Griffin, 2011a).

Because of the high stakes and uncertainty that surround criminal trials, most defendants plead guilty as they get closer to the prospect of being judged by a random group of citizens drawn from the community.

Court organization and processes serve to structure the interactions of attorneys and judges who ultimately produce the outcomes in criminal cases. Prosecutors create incentives for guilty pleas by offering reductions in charges and sentences in exchange for admissions of guilt. Defense attorneys advise their clients by predicting the likelihood that a jury might issue a guilty verdict, weighing it against the advantages of taking a plea deal. Even if specific incentives are not offered, defendants may plead guilty if only to demonstrate to the judge that they are taking responsibility for their actions. They may hope that such honesty will lead the judge to soften the sentence. Meanwhile, judges oversee court processes, bear responsibility for ensuring that rules are followed and defendants' rights are protected, and make decisions about punishments.

Raymond Clark's case demonstrates the power and importance of prosecutors and defense attorneys. Defense attorneys must advise their clients and make strategic decisions about whether to plead guilty and, if a case goes to trial, what tactics to use during proceedings. Prosecutors determine who will be charged with a crime and which charges they will face. Prosecutors communicate with victims' families and may seek their approval for plea-negotiation offers. In the Raymond Clark case, the prosecutor accommodated the request of Annie Le's family that the plea bargain include a sexual-assault charge in addition to the murder charge (A. Griffin, 2011a).

The American criminal justice system places great power and responsibility in the hands of attorneys for each side in a criminal case. The prosecutor and defense attorney are the most influential figures in determining the outcomes of criminal cases. Their discretionary decisions and negotiations determine people's fates. As we shall see in this chapter, the justice system's ability to handle cases and produce fair results depends on the dedication, skill, and enthusiasm of these lawyers. In addition, the lawyers who become judges assume important duties for overseeing court proceedings that decide whether accused defendants will be found guilty and punished. When you read the job requirements and overview of what it takes to be a prosecutor in "Careers in Criminal Justice" later in the chapter, imagine the impact of your decisions on people's lives if you pursued such a career.

The Functions and Structure of American Courts

The United States has a dual court system. Separate federal and state court systems handle matters throughout the nation. Other countries have a single national court system, but American rules and traditions permit states to create their own court systems to handle most legal matters, including most crimes.

In the United States, both state and federal courts use the **adversarial process** to protect the rights of defendants and examine evidence to determine whether a defendant is guilty. In the adversarial process, a professional attorney, trained in the rules of evidence and the strategies of advocacy, represents each side—the prosecution (government) and defense (defendant). These attorneys challenge each other's evidence and arguments while trying to persuade the judge or jury about the defendant's guilt or lack thereof. Even when the attorneys negotiate a guilty plea without going to trial, they are supposed to adopt an adversarial stance that represents the interests of their side. Although they may hold friendly and cooperative discussions, the content of these discussions often reflects probing, bluffing, compromising, and disagreeing. In the adversarial context of American courts, judges often act like referees at a sporting event. They oversee the interactions and enforce the rules without imposing their will on the presentation of evidence by attorneys. The adversarial process is derived from British law and can be found in the United States and other former British colonies. By contrast, other countries typically use an **inquisitorial process,** in which the judge takes an active role in questioning witnesses and asserts herself into the investigation of the case and the examination of evidence.

adversarial process Court process, employed in the United States and other former British colonies, in which lawyers for each side represent their clients' best interests in presenting evidence and formulating arguments as a means to discover the truth and protect the rights of defendants.

The federal courts oversee a limited range of criminal cases. For example, they deal with people accused of violating the criminal laws of the national government. Federal crimes include counterfeiting, kidnapping, smuggling, and drug trafficking, among others. But such cases account for only a small portion of the criminal cases that pass through U.S. courts each year. For every offender sentenced to incarceration by federal courts, more than ten offenders are sent to prisons and jails by state courts, because most crimes are defined by state laws (BJS, 2011b). This disparity may grow wider as federal law enforcement agencies increasingly emphasize antiterrorism activities rather than traditional crime control investigations. The gap is even greater for misdemeanors, because state courts bear the primary responsibility for processing the lesser offenses, such as disorderly conduct, that arise on a daily basis.

inquisitorial process Court process, employed in most countries of the world, in which the judge takes an active role in investigating the case and examining evidence by, for example, questioning witnesses.

State supreme courts monitor the decisions of lower courts within their own states by interpreting state constitutions and statutes. Although most are named, the "Supreme Court" of the state, in a few states they have different names. In New York, in particular, the top court is called the New York Court of Appeals, and "supreme courts" in that state are trial courts. The U.S. Supreme Court oversees both court systems by interpreting the U.S. Constitution, which protects the rights of defendants in federal and state criminal cases (Smith, DeJong and McCall, 2011).

A third court system operates in several states; this adds to the issues of complexity and coordination that the country's decentralized courts face. Native Americans have tribal courts, whose authority is endorsed by congressional statutes and Supreme Court decisions, with **jurisdiction** over their own people on tribal land. The existence of tribal courts permits Native American judges to apply their people's cultural values in resolving civil lawsuits and processing certain criminal offenses (Goldberg, 2010).

jurisdiction The geographic territory or legal boundaries within which control may be exercised; the range of a court's authority.

The Functions of Courts

Courts serve many important functions for society. We often picture courts as the settings for criminal trials, much like those portrayed on television shows such as *Law and Order.* When courts focus on criminal matters, through bail hearings, preliminary hearings, plea bargaining, and trials, they are serving a *norm enforcement* function for society. A *norm* is a value, standard, or expectation concerning people's behavior. In other words, courts play a central role in enforcing society's rules and standards for behavior—a function that contributes to peace and stability in society. In addition, courts handle a wide variety of matters beyond criminal justice, matters that benefit society in ways that extend beyond merely determining the guilt of and punishments for criminal defendants.

Courts also handle *dispute processing* for society. When people disagree about contracts, money, property, and personal injuries in ways that they cannot resolve on their own, they file lawsuits seeking government intervention on their behalf. Presumably the availability of courts for dispute processing helps avoid the possibility that people will resort to violence when they become angry about disagreements with business partners, neighbors, and others. In criminal justice, the dispute-processing function plays a significant role when people file lawsuits against police officers or correctional officials for violating constitutional rights. As a result of such lawsuits, judges may order prisons to change their procedures or order police officers or their departments to pay thousands of dollars to compensate a citizen for an erroneous arrest, excessive use of force, or the improper search of a home.

Courts also engage in *policy making*, especially the highest courts, such as state supreme courts and the U.S. Supreme Court. When judges interpret the U.S. Constitution or other forms of law and thereby define the rights of individuals, they are simultaneously telling police officers, correctional officers, and other officials what they can and cannot do. Such judicial decisions determine how searches will be conducted, how suspects will be questioned, and how prisons will be managed. This function makes courts in the United States especially important and powerful, because judges in other countries usually do not have the authority to tell officials throughout all levels of government how to carry out their jobs.

The Structure of Courts

Both the federal and state court systems have trial and appellate courts. There are three levels of courts: trial courts of limited jurisdiction, trial courts of general jurisdiction, and appellate courts.

Cases begin in a trial court, which handles determinations of guilt and sentencing. **Trial courts of limited jurisdiction** handle only misdemeanors, lawsuits for small amounts of money, and other specific kinds of cases. The full range of felony cases and all other civil lawsuits are heard in **trial courts of general jurisdiction**. Trial courts are the arenas in which evidence is presented, witnesses give testimony and are questioned by attorneys, and lawyers make arguments about the guilt (or lack thereof) of criminal defendants. These are the courts in which jury trials take place and judges impose prison sentences. The federal system has no limited jurisdiction trial courts. All federal cases begin in the general jurisdiction trial courts, the U.S. district courts.

Cases move to intermediate **appellate courts** if defendants claim that errors by police or the trial court contributed to their convictions. Further appeals may be filed with a state supreme court or the U.S. Supreme Court, depending on which court system the case is in and what kind of legal argument is being made. Unlike trial courts, appellate courts do not have juries, nor do lawyers present evidence. Instead, lawyers for each side make arguments about specific alleged errors of law or procedure that the trial judge failed to correct during the proceeding that determined the defendant's guilt. Thus, the written and oral arguments presented in an entire appellate case may focus on a single question, such as, "Should the trial judge have excluded the defendant's confession because the police did not adequately inform

trial courts of limited jurisdiction Criminal courts with trial jurisdiction over misdemeanor cases and preliminary matters in felony cases. Sometimes these courts hold felony trials that may result in penalties below a specific limit.

trial courts of general jurisdiction Criminal courts with jurisdiction over all offenses, including felonies. In some states, these courts also hear appeals.

appellate courts Courts that do not try criminal cases but hear appeals of decisions of lower courts.

The Supreme Court of the United States has the final word on questions concerning interpretations of the U.S. Constitution. Should a small group of appointed judges possess such power in a democracy?

The justices of the U.S. Supreme Court in 2012 (and year of appointment): *front row* (*left to right*) Clarence Thomas (1991); Antonin Scalia (1986); John Roberts (Chief Justice—2005); Anthony Kennedy (1988); Ruth Bader Ginsburg (1993); *back row*: Sonia Sotomayor (2009); Stephen Breyer (1994); Samuel Alito (2006); Elena Kagan (2010).

her about *Miranda* rights?" Appellate judges often decide cases by issuing elaborate written opinions to explain why they answered the question at issue in a certain way (C. Jacobs and Smith, 2011).

All states have courts of last resort (usually called state supreme courts), and all but a few have an intermediate-level appellate court (usually called courts of appeals). In the federal system, the U.S. Supreme Court is the court of last resort, and the U.S. circuit courts of appeals are the intermediate appellate courts. The U.S. Supreme Court, with its nine justices, controls its own caseload by choosing 75 to 85 cases to hear from among the 7,000 cases submitted annually. It takes the votes of four justices for the Supreme Court to decide to grant a request to hear a case. After the justices consider the written and oral arguments in the cases selected for hearing, a majority vote will determine the outcome and the rule of law to be expressed in the Court's majority opinion. Many decisions are unanimous, but other cases are decided by a narrow 5-to-4 vote when the justices are deeply divided. For example, when the Court decided in 2010 that the Second Amendment's "right to bear arms" that gives law-abiding adults the constitutional right to own and keep handguns in their homes applies against city and state laws as well as federal law, the justices split 5-to-4 in reaching the decision (*McDonald v. City of Chicago*, 2010; Miller, 2011). Close decisions can be overturned in later years if the new justices appointed to replace retiring justices bring viewpoints to the Court that differ from those of their predecessors.

Although the basic, three-tiered structure is found throughout the United States, the number of courts, their names, and their specific functions vary widely. For example, in state systems, 13,000 trial courts of limited jurisdiction typically handle traffic cases, small claims, misdemeanors, and other less serious matters. These courts handle 90 percent of all criminal matters. Some limited jurisdiction courts bear responsibility for a specific category of cases, sometimes including serious offenses. These courts were developed as part of a movement to create **problem-solving courts** that would directly address recurring problems or troubled individuals that appeared in court repeatedly. Drug courts, for example, attempt to combine rehabilitation, close supervision, and the threat of punishment to push drug offenders to shake free from substance-abuse problems (Rempel et al., 2012; Rockwell, 2008). Mental health courts, which are expanding across the country, seek to handle cases of nonviolent offenders with mental disorders and to develop appropriate treatment, supervision, and assistance instead of incarceration (Heaphy, 2011;

problem-solving courts Lower-level local courts dedicated to addressing particular social problems or troubled populations. Examples of such courts include drug courts, domestic violence courts, and mental health courts.

Figure 7.1

The Dual Court System of the United States and Routes of Appeal Whether a case enters through the federal or state court system depends on which law has been broken. The right of appeal to a higher court exists in either system.

© Cengage Learning

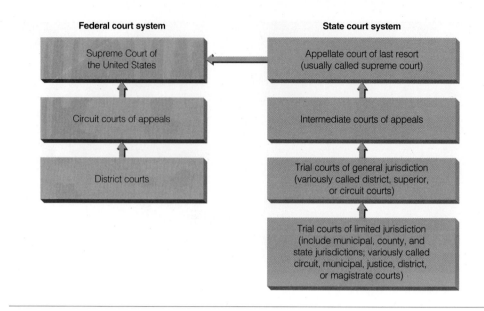

Kimber, 2008). Some cities have developed domestic violence courts to give focused attention to recurring problems of violence within families and among those with intimate relationships (Boyd, 2011; Gover, MacDonald, and Alpert, 2003). Other cities have dedicated judges' time to addressing problems of veterans or the homeless (S. Burns, 2010).

The federal system begins with the U.S. district courts, its trial courts of general jurisdiction. In the states, these courts have a variety of names (circuit, district, superior, and others) and are reserved for felony cases or substantial lawsuits. These are the courts in which trials take place, judges rule on evidence, and juries issue verdicts. Figure 7.1 shows the basic structure of the dual court system.

American trial courts are highly decentralized. Local political influences and community values affect the courts: Local officials determine their budgets, residents make up the staff, and operations are managed so as to fit community needs. Only a few small states have a court system organized on a statewide basis, with a central administration and state funding. In most of the country, the criminal courts operate under the state penal code but are staffed, managed, and financed by county or city governments. Many of these courts have been significantly burdened by budget cuts since the onset of the nation's economic crisis in 2008. State courts in 42 states experienced budget cuts in 2011, and the New York state courts alone experienced a budget reduction of $170 million (Favate, 2012). These cutbacks often shrink the number of court support personnel and lead to case backlogs. Often, less money is available to fund defense attorneys for the poor—such as the public defenders who represented Raymond Clark in the chapter opening. The federal courts, by contrast, have central administration and funding, although judges in each district help shape their own courts' practices and procedures.

Lower courts, especially at the state level, do not always display the dignity and formal procedures of general jurisdiction trial courts and appellate courts. Instead, they may function informally. Decisions and processes in one judge's courtroom may differ from those in another courtroom. In most urban areas, local courts process seemingly endless numbers of people through the crime control model (see Chapter 1), and each defendant's "day in court" usually lasts only a few minutes. People expect their local courts to adhere to the standards that reflect American values of justice. Many are critical when the courts do not meet these ideals (Dyer, 2012).

1. **What is the dual court system?**
Separate federal and state court systems handling cases in the United States.

2. **What different categories of courts exist within each court system?**
The federal system is made up of the Supreme Court of the United States, circuit courts of appeals, and district courts. State court systems are made up of an appellate court of last resort, intermediate appellate courts (in most states), trial courts of general jurisdiction, and trial courts of limited jurisdiction.

3. **What does it mean for courts to be decentralized?**
Operated, controlled, and funded by local communities, not a statewide administration. Most state and county courts are decentralized.

 Will contemporary budget crises lead to greater centralization in state court systems? What actors might resist moves toward centralization?

To Be a Judge

People tend to see judges as the most powerful actors in the criminal justice process. Their rulings and sentencing decisions influence the actions of police, defense attorneys, and prosecutors. For example, if judges treat certain crimes lightly, police and prosecutors may be less inclined to arrest and prosecute people who commit those offenses. Although judges are thought of primarily in connection with trials, some of their work—signing warrants, setting bail, arraigning defendants, accepting guilty pleas, and scheduling cases—takes place outside the formal trial process.

More than any other person in the system, the judge is expected to embody justice, ensuring that the right to due process is upheld and that the defendant receives fair treatment. The prosecutor and the defense attorney each represent a "side" in a criminal case. By contrast, the judge's black robe and gavel symbolize impartiality. Both within and outside the courthouse, the judge is supposed to act according to a well-defined role. Judges are expected to make careful, consistent decisions that uphold the ideal of equal justice for all citizens (McKee, 2007; Dyer, 2012). At the end of the chapter, read "A Question of Ethics" about a federal judge who sent a highly offensive email joke, that he admitted was "racist," concerning President Obama. Can such a judge truly embody justice and ensure that every defendant receives a fair trial?

Who Becomes a Judge?

In U.S. society, the position of judge, even at the lowest level of the judicial hierarchy, brings high status. Public service, political power, and prestige in the community may matter more than a high-paying job to those who aspire to the judiciary. Many judges take a significant cut in pay to assume a position on the bench (Tillman, 2012). Unlike private practice attorneys, who often work over 50 hours per week preparing cases and counseling clients, judges can typically control their own working hours and schedules better. Although judges carry heavy caseloads, they frequently decide for themselves when to go home at the end of the workday. The ability to control one's own work schedule is therefore an additional attraction for lawyers interested in becoming judges.

Judges bear important responsibilities for ensuring that both prosecutors and defense attorneys follow proper law and procedure. They must be certain that the rights of defendants are protected during court proceedings. Here, Judge Roosevelt Robinson instructs the jury during a trial in Portland, Oregon. What qualifications do you think someone should have to become a judge?

Historically, the vast majority of judges have been white men with strong political connections. Women and members of minority groups had few opportunities to enter the legal profession prior to the 1960s and thus were seldom considered for judgeships. In 2010, women comprised 26 percent of state judiciaries, including 31 percent of judges on state appellate courts, 24 percent on general jurisdiction trial courts, and 30 percent on limited jurisdiction courts (National Association of Women Judges, 2011). Contemporary political factors in many cities dictate that a portion of judges be drawn from specific demographic groups as political party leaders seek to gain the support of various segments of the voting public. Thus, overall 7 percent of state trial judges are African American, 4 percent are Latino, 2 percent are Asian or Pacific Islander in ancestry, and less than one-half of one percent are Native American (American Bar Association, 2010). These figures reflect great progress in advancing equal opportunity since the 1960s, but this still demonstrates significant underrepresentation of every demographic group except white males. A majority of Americans are female, but women hold only one quarter of judgeships. In addition, 2010 U.S. Census figures show the country's population to be 12.6 percent African American, 16.3 percent Latino, 5.7 percent Asian or Pacific Islander, and 1 percent Native American (Humes, Jones, and Ramirez, 2011). The percentages for diversity among judges are markedly lower.

Comparing the racial and ethnic makeup of the judiciary with that of the defendants in courts raises important questions (Nava, 2008). If middle-aged white men hold nearly all the power to make judgments about people from other segments of society, will people believe that decisions about guilt and punishment are being made in an unfair manner? Will people think that punishment is being imposed on behalf of a privileged segment of society rather than on behalf of the entire, diverse U.S. society? Moreover, the political connections necessary to gain judgeships continue to disadvantage women and members of racial minority groups in many communities. Because judges both symbolize the law and make important decisions about law, the lack of diversity in the judiciary provides a visible contrast with American values related to equal opportunity.

Functions of the Judge

Although people usually think that a judge's job is to preside at trials, in reality the work of most judges extends to all aspects of the judicial process. Defendants see a judge whenever decisions about their future are being made: when bail is set, pretrial motions are made, guilty pleas are accepted, a trial is conducted, a sentence is pronounced, and appeals are filed (see Figure 7.2). However, judges' duties are not limited to making such decisions about criminal defendants within the courtroom; judges also perform administrative tasks outside of it. Judges have three major roles: adjudicator, negotiator, and administrator.

Adjudicator   Judges must assume a neutral stance in overseeing the contest between the prosecution and the defense. They must apply the law in ways that uphold the rights of the accused in decisions about detention, plea, trial, and sentence. Judges receive a certain amount of discretion in performing these tasks—for example, in setting bail—but they must do so according to the law. They must avoid any conduct that could appear biased (Geyh, 2012).

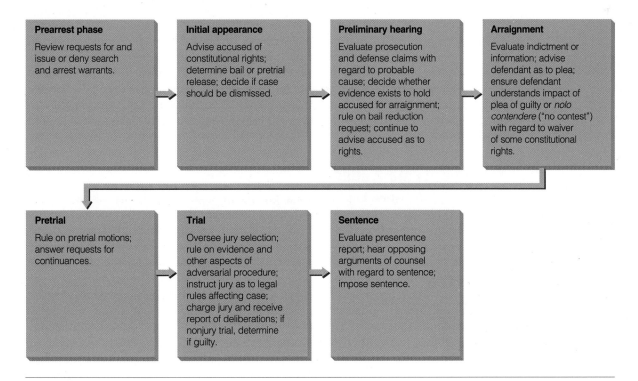

Prearrest phase	Initial appearance	Preliminary hearing	Arraignment
Review requests for and issue or deny search and arrest warrants.	Advise accused of constitutional rights; determine bail or pretrial release; decide if case should be dismissed.	Evaluate prosecution and defense claims with regard to probable cause; decide whether evidence exists to hold accused for arraignment; rule on bail reduction request; continue to advise accused as to rights.	Evaluate indictment or information; advise defendant as to plea; ensure defendant understands impact of plea of guilty or *nolo contendere* ("no contest") with regard to waiver of some constitutional rights.

Pretrial	Trial	Sentence
Rule on pretrial motions; answer requests for continuances.	Oversee jury selection; rule on evidence and other aspects of adversarial procedure; instruct jury as to legal rules affecting case; charge jury and receive report of deliberations; if nonjury trial, determine if guilty.	Evaluate presentence report; hear opposing arguments of counsel with regard to sentence; impose sentence.

Figure 7.2

Actions of a Trial Court Judge in Processing a Felony Case Throughout pretrial and trial processes, the judge ensures that legal standards are upheld; he or she maintains courtroom decorum, protects the rights of the accused, meets the requirement of a speedy trial, and makes certain that case records are maintained properly.

© Cengage Learning

Negotiator Many decisions that determine the fates of defendants take place outside of public view, in the judge's private chambers. These decisions come about through negotiations between prosecutors and defense attorneys about plea bargains, sentencing, and bail conditions. Judges spend much of their time in their chambers talking with prosecutors and defense attorneys. They often encourage the parties to work out a guilty plea or agree to proceed in a certain way. The judge may act as a referee, keeping both sides on track in accordance with the law. Sometimes the judge takes a more active part in the negotiations, suggesting terms for an agreement or even pressuring one side to accept an agreement (Carodine, 2010).

Administrator A seldom-recognized function of most judges is managing the courthouse. In urban areas, a professional court administrator may direct the people who keep records, schedule cases, and do the many other jobs that keep a system functioning. But even in cities, judges are in charge of their own courtroom and staff. In rural areas, which do not usually employ professional court administrators, the judges' administrative tasks may expand to include managing labor relations, budgeting, as well as maintenance of the courthouse building. As administrator, the judge must deal with political actors such as county commissioners, legislators, and members of the state executive bureaucracy. Chief judges in large courts may also use their administrative powers to push other judges to cooperate in advancing the court's goals of processing cases in a timely manner (Jacob, 1973). For judges whose training as lawyers focused on learning law and courtroom advocacy skills, managing a complex organization with a sizeable budget and many employees can pose a major challenge (Levy, 2011; C. E. Smith and Feldman, 2001).

Many observers argue that a fourth role of judges is emerging in some court systems. They see judges acting as "problem solvers" in newly developed problem-solving courts discussed earlier in this chapter that seek to address the problems related to drugs, mental health, struggling veterans, and domestic violence (S. Burns, 2010). These innovative courts steer people to treatment programs rather than jail. Because judges typically have no training in psychology or social work, critics worry that the development of the problem-solver role will lead judges to make decisions about matters in which they lack expertise.

How to Become a Judge

The quality of justice depends to a great extent on the quality of those who make decisions about guilt and punishment. Because judges have the power to deprive a citizen of his or her liberty through a prison sentence, judges should be thoughtful, fair, and impartial. When a judge is rude or hasty or allows the courtroom to become noisy and crowded, the public may lose confidence in the fairness and effectiveness of the criminal justice process.

Five methods are used to select state trial-court judges: **partisan election**, **nonpartisan election**, gubernatorial appointment, legislative selection, and merit selection. Some states use a combination of methods from among these approaches. Table 7.1 shows the method used in each of the states. All the methods bring up persistent concerns about the desired qualities of judges. By contrast, federal judges are nominated by the president and confirmed by a majority vote of the U.S. Senate. Federal judgeships also involve politics and questions about nominees' qualifications because presidents typically choose judges who are members of their own political party (Geyh, 2012). In addition, a judgeship can be a reward for loyal service to a political party's campaigns and fundraising efforts.

Selection by public voting occurs in more than half the states and has long been part of this nation's tradition. This method of judicial selection embodies the underlying American value of democracy because it permits the citizens to control the choice of individuals who will receive the power to make decisions in civil and criminal cases. The fulfillment of this American value also helps ensure that judges will remain connected to the community and demonstrate sensitivity to the community's priorities and concerns (Griffen, 2011). The American value of democracy may, however, have detrimental consequences if it pressures judges to follow a community's prejudices rather than make independent decisions using their best judgment in each case (Pratt, 2011; Saphire and Moke, 2008). Retired U.S. Supreme Court Justice Sandra Day O'Connor has mounted a public campaign against selecting judges through elections because of her concerns about the impact on the appearance of justice, especially as judicial candidates must solicit campaign contributions and subsequently may make decisions affecting their contributors (Geyh, 2012).

When lawyers are first elected to serve as judges, they obviously have no prior experience in deciding cases or supervising courthouse operations. As a result, judges must learn on the job. This clashes with the belief that judges are trained to "find the law" and to apply neutral judgments. In Europe, by contrast, prospective judges are given special training in law school to become professional judges. These trained judges must serve as assistant judges and lower-court judges before they can become judges in general trial and appellate courts (Provine, 1996).

Election campaigns for lower-court judgeships tend to be low-key contests marked by little controversy. Usually, only a small portion of the voters participate, judgeships are not prominent on the ballot, and candidates do not discuss controversial issues because of ethical considerations. Most candidates run on the same two claims that reveal relatively little to the voters about how they will make specific decisions as judges: "I have the best prior experience" and "I'll be tough on

partisan election An election in which candidates openly endorsed by political parties are presented to voters for selection.

nonpartisan election An election in which candidates' party affiliations are not listed on the ballot.

TABLE 7.1 Methods Used by States to Select Judges

States use different methods to select judges. Note that many judges are initially appointed to fill a vacancy, giving them an advantage if they must run for election at a later date.

Partisan Election	Nonpartisan Election	Gubernatorial Appointment	Legislative Selection	Merit Selection
Alabama	Arizona (some trial courts)	California (appellate)	South Carolina	Alaska
Illinois	Arkansas	Maine	Virginia	Arizona (appellate)
Indiana (trial)	California (trial)	Massachusetts (court of last resort)		Colorado
Louisiana	Florida (trial)			Connecticut
New Mexico	Georgia	New Jersey		Delaware
New York (trial)	Idaho			Florida (appellate)
Pennsylvania (initial)	Kentucky			Hawaii
Tennessee (trial)	Michigan			Indiana (appellate)
Texas	Minnesota			Iowa
West Virginia	Mississippi			Kansas
	Montana			Maryland
	Nevada			Massachusetts (trial, intermediate appellate)
	North Carolina			Missouri
	North Dakota			Nebraska
	Ohio			New Hampshire
	Oklahoma (trial)			New York (appellate)
	Oregon			Oklahoma (appellate)
	Pennsylvania (retention)			Rhode Island
	South Dakota (trial)			South Dakota (appellate)
	Washington			Tennessee (appellate)
	Wisconsin			Utah
				Vermont
				Wyoming

Source: American Judicature Society, 2012, "Judicial Selection in the States" (http://www.ajs.org).

crime." Recent research reveals, however, that even lower-level judicial races are becoming more competitive as candidates raise money and seek connections with interest groups (Abbe and Herrnson, 2002). Political parties typically want local judgeships to be elected posts, because they can use courthouse staff positions to reward party loyalists. When a party member wins a judgeship, courthouse jobs may become available for campaign workers, because the judge often chooses clerks, bailiffs, and secretaries.

In contrast, elections for seats on state supreme courts frequently receive statewide media attention. Because of the importance of state supreme courts as policy-making institutions, political parties and interest groups may devote substantial energy to organizing and funding the election campaigns of their preferred candidates. When organized interests contribute tens of thousands of

Question: "Please tell me how you would rate the honesty and ethical standards of judges—very high, high, average, low, or very low."

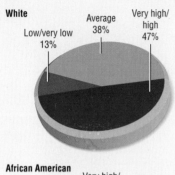

White

Average 38%

Low/very low 13%

Very high/high 47%

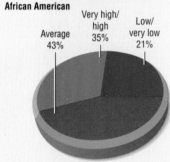

African American

Very high/high 35%

Average 43%

Low/very low 21%

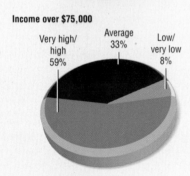

Income over $75,000

Average 33%

Very high/high 59%

Low/very low 8%

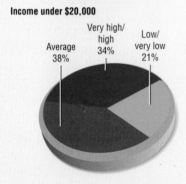

Income under $20,000

Very high/high 34%

Average 38%

Low/very low 21%

Critical Thinking: What might explain the divergent perceptions by race and income? Should these differing perceptions cause concern for judges who are worried about the image of the judicial branch of government?

Source: Bureau of Justice Statistics, *Sourcebook of Criminal Justice Statistics, 2011* (http://bjs.ojp.usdoj.gov/), Table 2.0017.2010.

dollars to judicial campaigns, questions sometimes arise about whether the successful candidates who received those contributions will favor the interests of their donors when they begin to decide court cases (Geyh, 2012).

Some states have tried to reduce the influence of political parties in the selection of judges while still allowing voters to select judges. These states hold nonpartisan elections in which only the names of candidates, not their party affiliations, appear on the ballot. However, political parties are often strongly involved in such elections. In Ohio, for example, the Republican and Democratic political parties hold their own primary elections to choose the judicial candidates whose names will go on the nonpartisan ballot for the general election. In other states, party organizations raise and spend money on behalf of candidates in nonpartisan elections.

Public opinion data show that Americans express concern about the influence of politics on judges, especially with respect to elected judges. If so many Americans are concerned about judges' involvement in political campaigns, why do so many states still rely on elections to select judges?

Merit selection, which combines appointment and election, was first used in Missouri in 1940 and has since spread to other states. When a judgeship becomes vacant, a nominating commission made up of citizens and attorneys evaluates potential appointees and sends the governor the names of three candidates, from which the replacement is chosen. After one year, a referendum is held to decide whether the judge will stay on the bench. The ballot asks, "Shall Judge X remain in office?" The judge who wins a majority vote serves out the term and can then be listed on the ballot at the next election (Cady and Phelps, 2008).

Public opinion polls indicate that Americans are divided in their views about judges' honesty and ethics, and these divisions are based, in part, on race and income. It is unclear whether judges' image would improve if merit selection were more widespread (see "What Americans Think" for specific data).

Merit selection is designed to remove politics from the selection of judges and supposedly allows the voters to unseat judges. However, interest groups sometimes mount publicity campaigns during retention elections in order to turn out judges with whom they disagree on a single issue or to open an important court seat so that a like-minded governor can appoint a sympathetic replacement. It may be difficult for judges to counteract a barrage of one-sided inflammatory television commercials focusing on a single issue such as capital punishment (T. V. Reid, 2000). If merit-selected judges feel intimidated by interest groups that might threaten their jobs at the next retention election, the independence of the judiciary will diminish (Breslin, 2010).

4. What are judges' main functions?
Adjudicator, negotiator, administrator.

5. Why do political parties often prefer that judges be elected?
To ensure that courthouse positions are allocated to party workers.

6. What are the steps in the merit-selection process?
When a vacancy occurs, a nominating commission is appointed that sends the governor the names of approved candidates. The governor must fill the vacancy from the list. After a year's term, a referendum is held to ask the voters whether the judge should be retained.

What is the best way to select judges? List three arguments for the method that you favor. List three arguments against a method that you do not prefer.

The Prosecutorial System

Prosecuting attorneys make discretionary decisions about whether to pursue criminal charges, which charges to make, and what sentence to recommend. They represent the government in pursuing criminal charges against the accused. Except in a few states, no higher authority second-guesses or changes these decisions. Thus, prosecutors are more independent than most other public officials. As with other aspects of American government, prosecution is mainly a task of state and local governments because most crimes violate state laws. The vast majority of state criminal cases are handled in the 2,341 county-level offices of the prosecuting attorney—known in various states as the district attorney, state's attorney, commonwealth attorney, or county attorney—who pursues cases that violate state law. Prosecutors have the power to make independent decisions about which cases to pursue and what charges to file. They can also drop charges and negotiate arrangements for guilty pleas. Since 2008, budget cuts have forced many prosecutors' offices to cut staff and, as a result, reduce defendants' charges and offer attractive plea deals more frequently in order to process cases efficiently (CBS Chicago, 2011; Singer, 2008).

Federal cases are prosecuted by **United States attorneys**. One U.S. attorney and a staff of assistant U.S. attorneys prosecute cases in each of the 94 U.S. district courts. Each state has an elected **state attorney general**, who usually has the power to bring prosecutions in certain cases. A state attorney general may, for example, handle a statewide consumer fraud case if a chain of auto repair shops is suspected of overcharging customers. In Alaska, Delaware, and Rhode Island, the state attorney general also directs all local prosecutions.

Read "Careers in Criminal Justice" to see the responsibilities and career path of an elected prosecutor in a major county.

Politics and Prosecution

Except in a few states, such as Alaska, Connecticut, and New Jersey, prosecutors are elected, usually for a four-year term; local politics thus heavily influence the office. By seeking to please voters, many prosecutors have tried to use their local office as a springboard to a higher office—such as state legislator, governor, or member of Congress.

Prosecutors may choose certain cases for prosecution in order to gain the favor of voters, or investigate charges against political opponents and public officials to

merit selection A reform plan by which judges are nominated by a commission and appointed by the governor for a given period. When the term expires, the voters approve or disapprove the judge for a succeeding term. If the judge is disapproved, the committee nominates a successor for the governor's appointment.

prosecuting attorney A legal representative of the state with sole responsibility for bringing criminal charges. In some states, this person is referred to as the district attorney, state's attorney, commonwealth attorney, or county attorney.

United States attorneys Officials responsible for the prosecution of crimes that violate the laws of the United States. Appointed by the president and assigned to a U.S. district court jurisdiction.

state attorney general Chief legal officer of a state, responsible for both civil and criminal matters.

Prosecuting Attorney

Kym Worthy, Prosecuting Attorney,
Wayne County, Michigan

AP Images/Carlos Osorio

A county's elected prosecutor oversees a staff of assistant prosecutors and support personnel in directing the investigation and prosecution of cases within the county. Wayne County, Michigan, which includes the city of Detroit, is one of the ten largest counties in the United States. The Wayne County prosecutor's office handles tens of thousands of cases each year. The prosecutor's office works with law enforcement agencies to investigate crimes, apply for search and arrest warrants, and gather evidence concerning criminal suspects. The prosecutor and her assistant prosecutors make decisions about which suspects to charge with crimes and what charges to pursue against each suspect. Prosecutors decide whether to offer opportunities for defendants to plead guilty in exchange for dropping specific charges for suspects accused of multiple crimes, reducing the severity of charges, or recommending specific sentences. They must discuss and negotiate with defense attorneys in defining these plea agreements. Prosecutors also present evidence in trials when defendants decline to plead guilty. They try to present enough evidence to prove a defendant's guilt "beyond a reasonable doubt." Prosecutors in many states may also be involved in appeals if they must fight against defense attorneys' claims that convictions should be thrown out because of errors by the trial judge. In some states, the state attorney general's office may have primary responsibility for representing the prosecution in appeals.

Kym Worthy completed her undergraduate degree at the University of Michigan and earned her law degree at the University of Notre Dame Law School. She spent ten years as an assistant prosecuting attorney in Wayne County before being elected to a trial court judgeship. After nearly a decade as a trial court judge, she resigned from the bench in order to seek the position of Wayne County Prosecuting Attorney when the previous elected prosecutor resigned. With her significant experience as both an assistant prosecutor and a trial judge, she was elected as prosecutor in 2004 and overwhelmingly reelected in 2008.

When you let the facts and evidence guide you, then you just do the right thing. And the minute I feel that I'm letting any outside pressures dictate what I do, that's the day I no longer should have this position. Any prosecutors that let outside forces dictate how they handle a case or how they dispose of a case other than the facts and the law really shouldn't be doing the job.

Source: Sven Gustafson, "Wayne County Prosecutor Kym Worthy: No One Is above the Law," *Michigan Business Review*, March 4, 2009 (http://www.mlive.com /businessreview).

→ The U.S. Attorney in Illinois, Patrick Fitzgerald, is known for his determination and evenhandedness in prosecuting officials from both political parties, including Republican I. Lewis Libby, who was the chief advisor to former Vice President Dick Cheney, and Democrat Rod Blagojevich, the former governor of Illinois. What kinds of political pressures can confront prosecutors?

Chuck Berman/MCT/Landov

get the public's attention. Political factors may also cause prosecutors to apply their powers unevenly within a community. Prosecutors' discretionary power can create the impression that some groups or individuals receive harsh treatment while others receive protection (Podgor, 2010).

Discretion in decision making also creates the risk of discrimination. For example, some scholars see prosecutors' decisions as reflecting biases based on race, social class, and gender (Frohmann, 1997), but other researchers believe that studies have not yet documented the full extent of discrimination by prosecutors (S. Walker, Spohn, and DeLeone, 2011). Several studies raise questions about discrimination in specific situations, such as prosecutors' decisions to seek the death penalty (Unah, 2010; Sorensen and Wallace, 1999). For the criminal justice system to fulfill American values concerning equality and fairness, prosecutors must use their decision-making authority carefully to avoid inequality and injustice (Butler, 2010; Kotch and Mosteller, 2010).

The Prosecutor's Influence

Most decision makers in the criminal justice system are involved in only one part of the process. However, prosecutors are involved at multiple stages and can therefore exert great influence through the use of their broad discretion in decision making (Krischke, 2010). From arrest to final disposition of a case, prosecutors can make choices that largely determine the defendant's fate. The prosecutor decides which cases to prosecute, selects the charges to be brought, recommends the bail amount, approves agreements with the defendant, and urges the judge to impose a particular sentence (Kenny, 2009).

Throughout the justice process, prosecutors' links with the other actors in the system—police, defense attorneys, judges—shape the prosecutors' decisions. Prosecutors may, for example, recommend bail amounts and sentences that match the preferences of particular judges. They may make "tough" recommendations in front of "tough" judges but tone down their arguments before judges who favor leniency or rehabilitation. Similarly, the other actors in the system may adjust their decisions and actions to match the preferences of the prosecutor. For example, police officers' investigation and arrest practices tend to reflect the prosecutor's priorities. Thus, prosecutors influence the decisions of others while also shaping their own actions in ways that reinforce their relationships with police, defense attorneys, and judges.

Prosecutors gain additional power from the fact that their decisions and actions take place away from public view. For example, a prosecutor and a defense attorney may strike a bargain whereby the prosecutor reduces a charge in exchange for a guilty plea or drops a charge if the defendant agrees to seek psychiatric help. In such instances, they reach a decision on a case in a way that is nearly invisible to the public.

The Prosecutor's Roles

As "lawyers for the state," prosecutors face conflicting pressures to press charges vigorously against lawbreakers while also upholding justice and the rights of the accused (O'Brien, 2009). These pressures are often called "the prosecutor's dilemma." In the adversarial system, prosecutors must do everything they can to win a conviction, but as members of the legal profession they must see that justice is done even if it means that the accused is not convicted. Even so, they always face the risk of "prosecutor's bias," sometimes called a "prosecution complex." Although they are supposed to represent all the people, including the accused, prosecutors may view themselves as instruments of law enforcement. Thus, as advocates on behalf of the state, their strong desire to close each case with a conviction may keep them from recognizing unfair procedures or evidence of innocence. As discussed in the "Close Up," it can be very difficult to hold prosecutors accountable if they ignore the interests of justice in their single-minded pursuit of a criminal conviction.

The Accountability of Prosecutors

How can prosecutors be held accountable if they violate their responsibilities and the principles of justice? In theory, if the public hears about prosecutorial misconduct, the democratic selection process will enable voters to elect a new prosecutor in most states. As mentioned earlier, because so many of prosecutors' discretionary decisions are not visible to the news media and public, voters may lack the information necessary to provide the accountability mechanism for improper conduct.

People can file lawsuits against police officers and corrections officers to hold them accountable for violating citizens' rights or improperly causing injuries and property damage. By contrast, the American legal system generally shields prosecutors and judges from the risk of lawsuits by granting them immunity, in much the same manner that the president and governors enjoy immunity in most circumstances. These are the officials who need to use their best judgment in making tough decisions and the law is designed to protect them from being guided by fear of liability in making those decisions. However, this immunity from lawsuits effectively removes an important and effective accountability mechanism that might otherwise deter misconduct and provide remedies for citizens who are victimized by such misconduct.

In 2011, the U.S. Supreme Court decided the case of *Connick v. Thompson*, concerning a man who spent 18 years in prison and came within one month of being executed for a murder that he did not commit. Only a stroke of luck resulting from a private detective's discovery of a crime lab report in the

New Orleans Police Crime Lab files saved Thompson from execution.

Prosecutors have a legal obligation to provide defense attorneys with all evidence that might indicate a defendant's innocence. In *Brady v. Maryland* (1963) the Supreme Court declared that in their efforts to get a conviction, prosecutors cannot hide evidence that is helpful to the defense. To do so, prosecutors would greatly increase the likelihood of innocent people being erroneously found guilty. In the *Thompson* case, New Orleans prosecutors hid evidence from the defendant's counsel. One prosecutor went so far as to remove a blood-stained piece of cloth from the evidence room, which, if tested by the defense and compared to the defendant's blood type could have proved the defendant's innocence to one of the crimes for which he was convicted. Indeed, the prosecutor possessed a lab report indicating that the blood did not match Thompson's blood type, but that information did not become available to Thompson's attorneys until the investigator discovered it in the crime lab files 18 years later. When the prosecutor in question was dying of cancer, he confessed to another prosecutor that he had intentionally hidden evidence that would have been helpful to the defendant. In addition, there were other issues raised concerning the failure of the prosecutors to accurately reveal the nature of witness statements taken during the investigation of the crime.

After he was found to be innocent and released from prison, Thompson sued the prosecutor's office for violating his rights by failing to train assistant prosecutors of their obligation

to share relevant evidence. A jury awarded him $14 million dollars in the lawsuit. Despite evidence that the assistant prosecutors—as well as the chief prosecutor—were not fully aware of the legal requirements of the *Brady* rule, a narrow five-member majority on the Supreme Court threw out the jury award and found that Thompson had not proved his case. Indeed, their ruling made clear that prosecutors seldom, if ever, should be subject to lawsuits, even when prosecutors acknowledge the intentional violation of a suspect's rights and a wrongly convicted man spent many years on death row as a result.

Researching the Internet

Read the Supreme Court's opinion in the *Thompson* case, including the strong objections voiced by the four dissenting justices who concluded that Thompson was entitled to the money that he was awarded by the jury in his lawsuit. To link to the website, visit the Criminal Justice CourseMate at cengagebrain.com, then access the web links for this chapter.

For Critical Analysis

Should citizens have the opportunity to sue prosecutors for violations of legal rights? If such lawsuits are not permitted, how will society otherwise make sure that prosecutors do their jobs properly? What would be the consequences if prosecutors could be sued for rights violations or wrongful convictions? Would that pressure prosecutors to act properly? Would it open the floodgates to lawsuits by vengeful criminal defendants whose rights were not actually violated? Are there alternative mechanisms that could more effectively keep prosecutors accountable?.

Although all prosecutors must uphold the law and pursue charges against lawbreakers, they may perform these tasks in different ways. Their personal values and professional goals, along with the political climate of their city or county, may cause them to define the prosecutor's role differently than do prosecutors in other places. For example, a prosecutor who believes that young offenders can be rehabilitated may take different actions than one who believes that young offenders should receive the same punishments as adults. One might send juveniles to counseling programs, whereas the other would seek to process them though the adult system of courts and corrections. A prosecutor with no assistants and few resources for conducting jury trials may be forced to embrace effective plea bargaining, whereas a prosecutor in a wealthier county may have more options when deciding whether to take cases to trial.

When prosecutors are asked about their roles in the criminal justice process, the following four functions are often mentioned:

1. *Trial counsel for the police.* Prosecutors who see their main function in this light believe that they should reflect the views of law enforcement in the courtroom and take a crime-fighter stance in public.
2. *House counsel for the police.* These prosecutors believe that their main function is to give legal advice so that arrests will stand up in court.
3. *Representative of the court.* Such prosecutors believe that their main function is to enforce the rules of due process to ensure that the police act according to the law and uphold the rights of defendants.
4. *Elected official.* These prosecutors may be most responsive to public opinion. The political impact of their decisions is one of their main concerns.

Each of these roles involves a different view of the prosecutor's "clients" as well as his or her own responsibilities. In the first two roles, prosecutors appear to believe that the police are the clients of their legal practice. Take a moment to think about who might be the clients of prosecutors who view themselves as representatives of the court or as elected officials.

Discretion of the Prosecutor

Because they have such broad discretion, prosecutors can shape their decisions to fit different interests (K. Griffin, 2009). They might base their decisions on a desire to impress voters through tough "throw-the-book-at-them" charges in a highly publicized case (Maschke, 1995). Decisions may also be driven by changing events in society. For example, when American opinion held that the greed of business people had helped to create the economic crisis of 2008, certain prosecutors placed new emphasis on pursuing criminal charges for fraudulent business transactions and mortgage loans (Segal, 2009). Decisions by prosecutors might also stem from their personal values, such as an emphasis on leniency and rehabilitation for young offenders (Ferguson, 2009). They may also shape their decisions to please local judges by, for example, accepting plea agreements that will keep the judges from being burdened by too many time-consuming trials. Prosecutors who have doubts about whether available evidence actually proves the defendant's guilt may just shrug their shoulders and say, "I'll just let the jury decide" rather than face public criticism for dropping charges. Any or all of these motives may shape prosecutors' decisions, because there is generally no higher authority to tell prosecutors how they must do their jobs. From the time the police turn a case over to the prosecutor, the prosecutor has almost complete control over decisions about charges and plea agreements (M. Stephens, 2008).

Research has also shown that the staffing levels of individual prosecutor's offices may affect decisions to pursue felony charges. If offices lack sufficient resources to pursue all possible cases, prosecutors may establish priorities and then reduce or dismiss charges in cases deemed less important. This has increasingly affected decisions in many prosecutors' offices in light of budget cuts in state and local government (Stensland, 2011).

If you were a prosecutor, what would you consider to be the most important factors in deciding whether to pursue a case? Would you have any concerns about the possibility of prosecuting an innocent person? If a prosecutor pursues a case against someone who the prosecutor does not really believe is guilty of a crime, does this pose an ethical problem?

After deciding that a case should be prosecuted, the prosecutor has great freedom in deciding what charges to file. Criminal incidents may involve several laws, so the prosecutor can often bring a single charge or more than one. Suppose that Smith, who is armed, breaks into a grocery store, assaults the proprietor, and robs the cash drawer. What charges can the prosecutor file? By virtue of having committed the robbery, the accused can be charged with at least four crimes: breaking and entering, assault, armed robbery, and carrying a dangerous weapon. Other charges or **counts** may be added, depending on the nature of the incident. A forger, for instance, may be charged with one count for each act of forgery committed. By filing as many charges as possible, the prosecutor strengthens his or her position in plea negotiations. In effect, the prosecutor can use discretion in deciding the number of charges and thus increase the prosecution's supply of "bargaining chips" (M. Simons, 2010).

The discretionary power to set charges does not give the prosecutor complete control over plea bargaining, however. Defense attorneys strengthen their position in the **discovery** process, in which information from the prosecutor's case file must be made available to the defense. For example, the defense has the right to see any statements made by the accused during interrogation by the police, as well as the results of any physical or psychological tests. This information tells the defense attorney about the strengths and weaknesses of the prosecution's case. The defense attorney may use it to decide whether a case is hopeless or whether engaging in tough negotiations is worthwhile.

The prosecutor's discretion does not end with the decision to file a certain charge. After the charge has been made, the prosecutor may reduce it in exchange for a guilty plea or enter a notation of *nolle prosequi* (*nol. pros.*). The latter is a freely made decision to drop the charge, either as a whole or as to one or more counts (Bowers, 2010). When a prosecutor decides to drop charges, no higher authorities can force him or her to reinstate them. When guilty pleas are entered, the prosecutor uses discretion in recommending a sentence.

Key Relationships of the Prosecutor

Prosecutors do not base their decisions solely on formal policies and role conceptions (Fridell, 1990). Relationships with other actors in the justice system also influence their choices. Despite their independent authority, prosecutors must consider how police, judges, and others will react. They depend on these other officials in order to prosecute cases successfully. In turn, the success of police, judges, and correctional officials depends on prosecutors' effectiveness in identifying and convicting lawbreakers. Thus, these officials build exchange relationships in which they cooperate with each other.

Police Prosecutors depend on the police to provide both the suspects and the evidence needed to convict lawbreakers. Because they cannot investigate crimes on their own, prosecutors are not in command of the types of cases brought to them. Thus, the police control the initiation of the criminal justice process by investigating crimes and arresting suspects. These actions may be influenced by various factors, such as pressure on police to establish an impressive crime-clearance record. As a result, police actions may create problems for prosecutors if, for example, the police make many arrests without gathering enough evidence to ensure conviction.

Victims and Witnesses Prosecutors depend on the cooperation of victims and witnesses (Rhodes et al., 2011). Although prosecutors can pursue a case whether or not a victim wishes to press charges, many prosecutors will not do so when the key testimony and other necessary evidence must come from a victim who is unwilling to cooperate (Dawson and Dinovitzer, 2001). In some cases, the decision to prosecute may be influenced by the victim's assertiveness in persuading the prosecutor to file charges (Stickels, Michelsen, and Del Carmen, 2007).

The decision to prosecute is often based on an assessment of the victim's role in his or her own victimization and the victim's credibility as a witness. If a victim has a criminal record, the prosecutor may choose not to pursue the case in the belief that

count Each separate offense of which a person is accused in an indictment or an information.

discovery A prosecutor's pretrial disclosure to the defense of facts and evidence to be introduced at trial.

nolle prosequi An entry, made by a prosecutor on the record of a case and announced in court, indicating that the charges specified will not be prosecuted. In effect, the charges are thereby dismissed.

a jury would not consider the victim a credible witness—despite the fact that the jury will never learn that the victim has a criminal record. If a victim is poorly dressed, uneducated, or somewhat inarticulate, the prosecutor may be inclined to dismiss charges out of fear that a jury would find the victim unpersuasive (Stanko, 1988). Research indicates that victim characteristics, such as moral character, behavior at the time of the incident, and age, influence decisions to prosecute sexual assault cases more than does the actual strength of the evidence against the suspect (Spears and Spohn, 1997). Studies have shown that prosecutions succeed most when aimed at defendants accused of committing crimes against strangers (Boland et al., 1983). When the victim is an acquaintance, a friend, or even a relative of the defendant, he or she may refuse to act as a witness, and prosecutors and juries may view the offense as less serious (Beichner and Spohn, 2012).

Judges and Courts The sentencing history of each judge gives prosecutors an idea of how a case may be treated in the courtroom. Prosecutors may decide to drop a case if they believe that the judge assigned to it will not impose a serious punishment. Because prosecutors' offices have limited resources, they cannot afford to waste time pursuing charges in front of a specific judge who shows a pattern of dismissing those types of charges. Interactions with defense attorneys also affect prosecutors' decisions, as in the case of plea bargains.

The Community Public opinion and the media can play a crucial role in creating an environment that either supports or scrutinizes the prosecutor. Like police chiefs and school superintendents, county prosecutors will not remain in office long if they fall out of step with community values. They will likely lose the next election to an opponent who has a better sense of the community's priorities.

Many cities are experimenting with innovations designed to enhance communication and understanding between prosecutors and the community. One innovation called *community prosecution* gives specific assistant prosecutors continuing responsibilities for particular neighborhoods. These prosecutors may become known to people in the neighborhood, attend community meetings and social functions, and learn about residents' specific concerns. In so doing, they can build relationships that will help them gather information and identify witnesses when crimes occur (Porter, 2011).

Prosecutors' relationships and interactions with police, victims, defense attorneys, judges, and the community form the core of the exchange relations that shape decision making in criminal cases. Other relationships, such as those with news media, federal and state officials, legislators, and political-party officials, also influence prosecutors' decisions. This long list of actors illustrates that prosecutors do not base their decisions solely on whether a law has been broken. The occurrence of a crime is only the first step in a decision-making process that may vary from one case to the next. Sometimes charges are dropped or reduced. Sometimes plea bargains are negotiated quickly. Sometimes cases move through the system to a complete jury trial. In every instance, relationships and interactions with a variety of actors both within and outside the justice system shape prosecutors' discretionary decisions.

Decision-Making Policies

Despite the many factors that potentially affect prosecutors' decisions, we can draw some general conclusions about how prosecutors approach their office. Prosecutors develop their own policies on how cases will be handled. These policies shape the decisions made by the assistant prosecutors and thus greatly affect the administration of justice (Holleran, Beichner and Spohn, 2010). Within the same state, prosecutors may pursue different goals in forming policies on which cases to pursue, which ones to drop, and which ones to plea bargain. For example, prosecutors who wish to maintain a high conviction rate will drop cases with weak evidence. Others, concerned about using limited resources effectively, will focus most of their time and energy on the most serious cases.

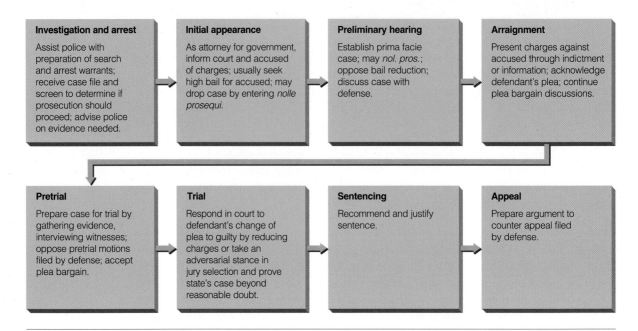

Figure 7.3

Typical Actions of a Prosecuting Attorney in Processing a Felony Case The prosecutor has certain responsibilities at various points in the process. At each point, the prosecutor is an advocate for the state's case against the accused.

© Cengage Learning

Some prosecutors' offices make extensive use of screening and tend not to press charges. Guilty pleas are typically the main method of processing cases. Because pleas of not guilty strain the prosecutors' and courts' trial resources, there are strong reasons to offer incentives to defendants to plead guilty. Some offices process cases soon after the police bring them to the prosecutor's attention, sometimes diverting or referring them to other agencies; others have disposition occurring as late as the first day of trial. The period from the receipt of the police report to the start of the trial is thus a time of review in which the prosecutor uses discretion to decide what actions should be taken.

The **accusatory process** is the series of activities that take place from the moment a suspect is arrested and booked by the police to the moment the formal charge—in the form of an indictment or information—is filed with the court. In an indictment, evidence is presented to a grand jury composed of citizens who determine whether to issue a formal charge. Grand juries are used in the federal system and in states where legislatures have mandated their use for serious charges. In jurisdictions that do not use grand juries, the prosecutor has full control of the charging decision when the filing of an information initiates prosecution. In other words, when an information is used to present formal charges, no body of citizens can protect a suspect from wrongful prosecution until the case goes to trial and a trial jury hears the case. However, earlier in the process judges may decide at preliminary hearings that there is insufficient evidence to support the pursuit of the charges; in such circumstances, a judge can order that the charges be dismissed.

Clearly, the prosecutor's established policies and decisions play a key role in determining whether charges will be filed against a defendant. Keep in mind, though, that the prosecutor's decision-making power is not limited to decisions about charges. As shown in Figure 7.3, the prosecutor makes important decisions at each stage, both before and after a defendant's guilt is determined. Because the prosecutor's involvement and influence span the justice process, from seeking search warrants during early investigations to arguing against postconviction appeals, the prosecutor is a highly influential actor in criminal cases. No other participant in the system is involved in so many different stages of the criminal process.

accusatory process The series of events from the arrest of a suspect to the filing of a formal charge (through an indictment or information) with the court.

check point

7. What are the roles of the prosecutor?
Trial counsel for the police, house counsel for the police, representative of the court, elected official.

8. How does the prosecutor use discretion to decide how to treat each defendant?
The prosecutor can determine the type and number of charges, reduce the charges in exchange for a guilty plea, or enter a *nolle prosequi* (thereby dropping some or all of the charges).

9. What are the prosecutor's key exchange relationships?
Police, victims and witnesses, defense attorneys, judges, the community.

stop & analyze

Do prosecutors' exchange relationships contribute to or distract from the goal of achieving justice in each case? List two arguments for recognizing benefits from exchange relationships and two arguments about negative consequences from such relationships.

The Defense Attorney: Image and Reality

In an adversarial process, the **defense attorney** is the lawyer who represents accused and convicted persons in their dealings with the criminal justice system. Most Americans have seen defense attorneys in action on television dramas such as *Boston Legal* and *Law and Order*. In these dramas, defense attorneys vigorously battle the prosecution, and the jury often finds their clients innocent. These images gain strength from news stories about prominent defense attorneys, such as Chicago's Ed Genson, who represented Illinois governor Rod Blagojevich during initial impeachment proceedings, and who won an acquittal from child pornography charges for singer R. Kelly in 2008 (St. Clair, 2008). Although these images are drawn from reality, they do not give a true picture of the typical defense attorney, focusing as they do on the few highly publicized cases that result in jury trials. By contrast, most cases find resolution through plea bargaining, discretionary dismissals, and similar decisions by actors in the justice system. In these cases, the defense attorney may seem less like the prosecutor's adversary and more like a partner in the effort to dispose of cases as quickly and efficiently as possible through negotiation (Edkins, 2011).

All the key courtroom actors discussed in this chapter—judges, prosecutors, and defense attorneys—are lawyers who met the same educational requirements. After becoming lawyers, however, they made different decisions about what career to pursue. Some people cannot understand why anyone would want to be a defense attorney and work on behalf of criminals. However, defense attorneys work for people who are *accused* of crimes. Under the American system of criminal justice, defendants are supposedly presumed to be innocent. Indeed, many of them will have charges reduced or dismissed. Others will be found not guilty. Thus, characterizing defense attorneys as representing only criminals is simply not accurate. Moreover, many lawyers who choose to work as defense attorneys see themselves as defending the Bill of Rights by ensuring that prosecutors actually respect the Constitution and provide proof beyond a reasonable doubt before defendants are convicted and punished.

defense attorney The lawyer who represents accused offenders and convicted offenders in their dealings with criminal justice.

Billy Martin, a prominent defense attorney who has represented such clients as NFL star Michael Vick and U.S. Senator Larry Craig, gives closing arguments in the manslaughter trial of former NBA basketball star Jayson Williams. An effective defense requires respect, openness, and trust between attorney and client. Do defense attorneys need special skills and personal qualities?

The Role of the Defense Attorney

To be effective, defense attorneys must have knowledge of law and procedure, skill in investigation, experience in advocacy, and, in many cases, relationships with prosecutors and judges that will help a defendant obtain the best possible outcome.

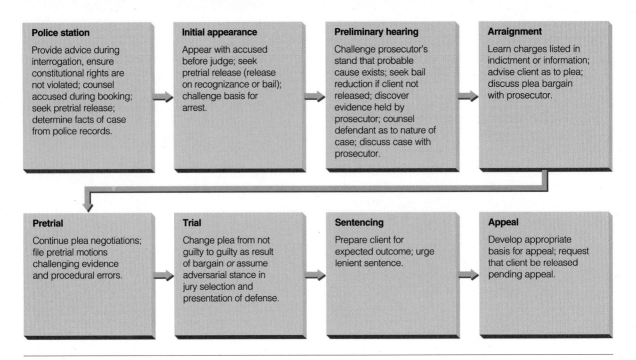

Police station

Provide advice during interrogation, ensure constitutional rights are not violated; counsel accused during booking; seek pretrial release; determine facts of case from police records.

Initial appearance

Appear with accused before judge; seek pretrial release (release on recognizance or bail); challenge basis for arrest.

Preliminary hearing

Challenge prosecutor's stand that probable cause exists; seek bail reduction if client not released; discover evidence held by prosecutor; counsel defendant as to nature of case; discuss case with prosecutor.

Arraignment

Learn charges listed in indictment or information; advise client as to plea; discuss plea bargain with prosecutor.

Pretrial

Continue plea negotiations; file pretrial motions challenging evidence and procedural errors.

Trial

Change plea from not guilty to guilty as result of bargain *or* assume adversarial stance in jury selection and presentation of defense.

Sentencing

Prepare client for expected outcome; urge lenient sentence.

Appeal

Develop appropriate basis for appeal; request that client be released pending appeal.

Figure 7.4

Typical Actions of a Defense Attorney Processing a Felony Case Defense attorneys are advocates for the accused. They have an obligation to challenge points made by the prosecution and to advise clients of their constitutional rights.

© Cengage Learning

In the American legal system, the defense attorney performs the key function of ensuring that the prosecution proves its case in court or possesses substantial evidence of guilt before a guilty plea leads to conviction and punishment.

As shown in Figure 7.4, the defense attorney advises the defendant and protects his or her constitutional rights at each stage of the criminal justice process. The defense attorney advises the defendant during questioning by the police, represents him or her at each arraignment and hearing, and serves as advocate for the defendant during the appeal process. Without understanding the technical details of law and court procedures, defendants have little ability to effectively represent themselves in court. The defense attorney therefore ensures that prosecutors and judges understand and respect the defendant's rights.

While filling their roles in the criminal justice system, defense attorneys also psychologically support defendants and their families. Relatives are often bewildered, frightened, and confused. The defense attorney is the only legal actor available to answer the question "What will happen next?" In short, the attorney's relationship with the client matters a great deal. An effective defense requires respect, openness, and trust between attorney and client. If the defendant refuses to follow the attorney's advice, the lawyer may feel obliged to withdraw from the case in order to protect his or her own professional reputation.

Realities of the Defense Attorney's Job

How well do defense attorneys represent their clients? Attorneys who are inexperienced, uncaring, or overburdened have trouble representing their clients effectively. The attorney may quickly agree to a plea bargain and then work to persuade the defendant to accept the agreement. The attorney's self-interest in disposing of cases quickly, receiving payment, and moving on to other cases may cause the attorney to, in effect, work with the prosecutor to pressure the defendant to plead guilty. Skilled defense attorneys also consider plea bargaining in the earliest stages of a case; however, unlike their unskilled counterparts, these lawyers would be guided by their role as advocate for the defendant, not by outside pressures. In many cases, a negotiated plea with a predictable sentence serves the defendant better than does a trial spent fending off more-serious charges. An effective defense attorney does not try to take every case all the way to trial.

The defense attorney's job is all the more difficult because neither the public nor defendants fully understand the attorney's duties and goals. The public often views defense attorneys as protectors of criminals. When in fact, the attorney's basic duty is not to save criminals from punishment but to protect constitutional rights, keep the prosecution honest in preparing and presenting cases, and prevent innocent people from being convicted (Flowers, 2010). Surveys indicate that lawyers place much greater emphasis on the importance of right to counsel than does the public. Look at the issues presented in "What Americans Think." Do you think that the public may underestimate the necessity of representation by an attorney? Do you agree with the majority of defense attorneys in the survey, or are they too protective of rights for people who might threaten American society?

Three groups of private practice lawyers can be called specialists in criminal defense because they handle criminal cases on a regular basis. The first group is composed of nationally known attorneys who charge large fees in highly publicized cases. The second group, found in each large city, is composed of the lawyers of choice for defendants who can afford to pay high fees. These attorneys make handsome incomes by representing white-collar criminals, drug dealers, and affluent people charged with crimes. The third and largest group of attorneys in full-time criminal practice is composed of courthouse regulars who accept many cases for small fees and who participate daily in the criminal justice system as either retained or assigned counsel. These attorneys handle a large volume of cases quickly. They negotiate guilty pleas and try to convince their clients that these agreements are beneficial. They depend on the cooperation of prosecutors, judges, and other courtroom actors, with whom they form exchange relationships in order to reach plea bargains quickly.

In addition to these defense specialists, many private attorneys sometimes take criminal cases. These attorneys often have little trial experience and lack well-developed relationships with other actors in the criminal justice system. In fact, their clients might be better served by a courthouse regular who has little interest in each case but whose relationships with prosecutors and judges will produce better plea bargains.

As mentioned earlier in the chapter, government-salaried attorneys called *public defenders* handle criminal cases for defendants who are too poor to hire their own attorneys. These attorneys focus exclusively on criminal cases and usually develop significant expertise. They cannot always devote as much time as they want to each case, because they often have heavy caseloads.

what americans think

Question: The American Bar Association, the largest national association of lawyers, surveyed a small sample of defense attorneys about their views on issues related to the government's response to terrorism.*

The terrorism laws passed by Congress have made the U.S. safer.

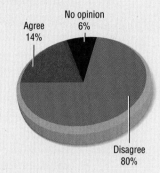

No opinion 6%
Agree 14%
Disagree 80%

Privacy rights have been unduly compromised as a result of antiterror efforts.

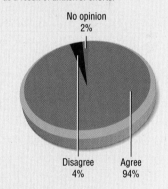

No opinion 2%
Disagree 4%
Agree 94%

Would you be willing to represent Osama Bin Laden in federal court?

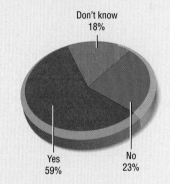

Don't know 18%
Yes 59%
No 23%

*Poll taken prior to the death of Osama bin Laden in 2011.

Source: Mark Hansen and Stephanie Francis Ward, "The 50-Lawyer Poll," *ABA Journal*, September 2007 (http://www.abajournal.com).

The Environment of Criminal Practice

Defense attorneys have a difficult job. Much of their work involves preparing clients and their relatives for the likelihood of conviction and punishment. Even when they know that their clients are guilty, they may become emotionally involved because they are the only judicial actors who know the defendants as human beings and see them in the context of their family and social environment.

Most defense lawyers constantly interact with lower-income clients whose lives and problems are depressing. These attorneys might also visit the local jail at all hours of the day and night. Clearly, their work setting is far removed from the fancy offices and expensive restaurants of the world of corporate attorneys. As described by one defense attorney, "The days are long and stressful. I spend a good deal of time in jail, which reeks of stale food and body odor. My clients often think that because I'm court-appointed, I must be incompetent" (Lave, 1998:14).

Defense lawyers must also struggle with the fact that criminal practice does not pay well. Public defenders garner fairly low salaries, and attorneys appointed to represent poor defendants receive small sums. If private attorneys do not demand payment from their clients at the start of the case, they may find that they must persuade the defendants' relatives to pay—because many convicted offenders have no incentive to pay for legal services while sitting in a prison cell. To perform their jobs well and gain satisfaction from their careers, defense attorneys must focus on goals other than money, such as their key role in protecting people's constitutional rights. However, that they are usually on the losing side can make it hard for them to feel like professionals and enjoy the high self-esteem and satisfying work that is characteristic of the careers of other highly educated people. Because they work on behalf of criminal defendants, they may also face suspicion from the public.

Counsel for Indigents

Since the 1960s, the Supreme Court has interpreted the "right to counsel" in the Sixth Amendment to the Constitution as requiring that the government provide attorneys for indigent defendants who face the possibility of going to prison or jail. *Indigent defendants* are those who are too poor to afford their own lawyers. The Court has also required that attorneys be provided early in the criminal justice process, to protect suspects' rights during questioning and pretrial proceedings. See Table 7.2 for a summary of key rulings on the right to counsel.

Research on felony defendants indicates that 78 percent of those prosecuted in the 75 largest counties and 66 percent of those prosecuted in federal courts received publicly provided legal counsel (Harlow, 2000). The portion of defendants who are provided with counsel because they are indigent has increased greatly in the past three decades. For example, in the 22 states with public defender offices funded by state government rather than county or city governments, criminal caseloads increased by 20 percent from 1999 to 2007 (Langton and Farole, 2010). Government-salaried public defenders alone received 5.5 million cases of indigent criminal defendants in 2007, a figure that does not include thousands of indigents represented by private attorneys who are paid by government on a case-by-case basis (Farole and Langton, 2010).

The quality of counsel given to indigent defendants has spurred debate. Ideally, experienced lawyers would be appointed soon after arrest to represent the defendant in each stage of the criminal justice process. Ideal conditions do not always exist, however. As we have seen, inexperienced and uncaring attorneys may be appointed. Some attorneys have little time to prepare the case. Even conscientious attorneys may be unable to provide top-quality counsel if they have heavy caseloads or do not receive enough money to enable them to spend the time required to handle the case well. For example, in 15 of 22 states with state-funded public defender offices and three-quarters of the county-funded public defender offices in 27 other states, the defense attorneys had caseloads that exceeded the U.S. Department of Justice's recommended guidelines (Farole and Langton, 2010; Langton and Farole, 2010). If attorneys lack either the time

TABLE 7.2 The Right to Counsel: Major Supreme Court Rulings

Case	Year	Ruling
Powell v. Alabama	1932	Indigents facing the death penalty who are not capable of representing themselves must be given attorneys.
Johnson v. Zerbst	1938	Indigent defendants must be provided with attorneys when facing serious charges in federal court.
Gideon v. Wainwright	1963	Indigent defendants must be provided with attorneys when facing serious charges in state court.
Douglas v. California	1963	Indigent defendants must be provided with attorneys for their first appeal.
Miranda v. Arizona	1966	Criminal suspects must be informed about their right to counsel before being questioned in custody.
United States v. Wade	1967	Defendants are entitled to counsel at "critical stages" in the process, including postindictment lineups.
Argersinger v. Hamlin	1972	Indigent defendants must be provided with attorneys when facing misdemeanor and petty charges that may result in incarceration.
Ross v. Moffitt	1974	Indigent defendants are not entitled to attorneys for discretionary appeals after their first appeal is unsuccessful.
Strickland v. Washington	1984	To show ineffective assistance of counsel violated the right to counsel, defendants must prove that the attorney committed specific errors that affected the outcome of the case.
Murray v. Giarratano	1989	Death row inmates do not have a right to counsel for habeas corpus proceedings asserting rights violations in their cases.

© Cengage Learning

or the desire to interview the client and prepare the case, they may simply persuade defendants to plead guilty right there in the courtroom during their first and only conversation. Of course, not all publicly financed lawyers who represent poor defendants ignore their clients' best interests. Even so, the quality of counsel received by the poor

A public defender represents indigent clients and carries a heavy caseload under difficult conditions. The quality of representation for poor defendants may vary from courthouse to courthouse, depending on the knowledge and efforts of the attorneys, caseloads, and administrative pressures to resolve cases quickly. How can we improve the quality of defense in criminal cases?

© Paul Sakuma/AP/Corbis

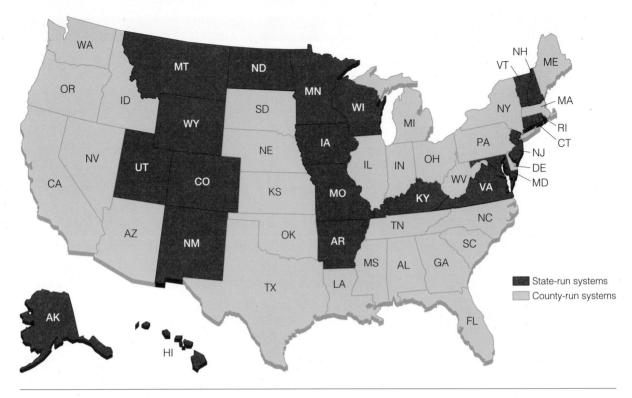

Figure 7.5

State-Run Public Defender Offices and County-Run Indigent Defense Systems Note that county-run systems, in particular, may use different representation models (appointed, contract, or public defender) in counties within a given state, or use more than one method within a county.

Source: Lynn Langton and Donald Farole Jr., "State Public Defender Programs, 2007," *Bureau of Justice Statistics Special Report*, September 2010, NCJ 228229.

may vary from courthouse to courthouse, depending on the quality of the attorneys, conditions of defense practice, and administrative pressure to reduce the caseload.

Ways of Providing Indigents with Counsel

There are three main ways of providing counsel to indigent defendants: (1) the **assigned counsel** system, in which a court appoints a private attorney to represent the accused; (2) the **contract counsel** system, in which an attorney, a nonprofit organization, or a private law firm contracts with a local government to provide legal services to indigent defendants for a specified dollar amount; and (3) **public defender** programs, which are public or private nonprofit organizations with full-time or part-time salaried staff. Figure 7.5 shows the states that have statewide, centrally administered public defender systems and the other states that have county-based systems for indigent defense that may include the use of public defenders, appointed counsel, or contract counsel.

The methods for providing defense attorneys and the quality of defense services may depend on the money available to pay attorneys. In the states where counties must fund their own defense services, resources—and the quality of indigent defense—may vary from county to county within a single state. As the chief state public defender in Ohio said with respect to the 88 counties in his state's county-run system, "When you have the state of Ohio law being enforced and defended in 88 different ways . . . you end up with huge disparities in cost, quality and efficiency," (A. Manning, 2012).

Issues of resources and quality are complicated by budget cuts in the current era of economic recovery. For example, in 2010, Gwinnett County, Georgia, cut the compensation for court-appointed defense attorneys from $75 to $65 per hour for serious felony cases, with even lower pay rates for misdemeanors and out-of-court activities (Simmons and Rankin, 2010). In Oklahoma, the indigent defense system

assigned counsel An attorney in private practice assigned by a court to represent an indigent. The attorney's fee is paid by the government with jurisdiction over the case.

contract counsel An attorney in private practice who contracts with the government to represent all indigent defendants in a county during a set period of time and for a specified dollar amount.

public defender An attorney employed on a full-time, salaried basis by a public or private nonprofit organization to represent indigents.

TABLE 7.3 Fees Paid to Assigned Counsel in Noncapital Felony Cases

State	Out-of-Court Hourly Rate	In-Court Hourly Rate	Per-Case Maximum
Alaska	$50	$60	$4,000 trial; $2,000 plea
Georgia	$40	$60	None
Hawaii	$90	$90	$6,000
Maryland	$50	$50	$3,000
New York	$75	$75	$4,400
North Carolina	$65	$65	None
North Dakota	$65	$65	$2,000
Federal	$100	$100	$7,000

Sources: Darryl K. Brown, "The Next Steps in Reform: Epiphenomenal Indigent Defense," *Missouri Law Review* 30 (2010): 913; "Economics of CJA Representations Costly to Attorneys," *The Third Branch* 40 (4), April 2008 (http://www.uscourts.gov/News/TheThirdBranch.aspx); Spangenberg Group, "Rates of Compensation Paid to Court-Appointed Counsel in Non-Capital Felony Cases at Trial: A State-by-State Overview," American Bar Association Information Program, June 2007.

suffered a $1.5 million budget cut resulting in its attorneys being assigned 400 to 500 cases per year (Bisbee, 2010).

Assigned Counsel   In the assigned counsel system, the court appoints a lawyer in private practice to represent an indigent defendant. This system is widely used in small cities and in rural areas, but even some city public defender systems assign counsel in some cases, such as a case with multiple defendants, where a conflict of interest might result if a public lawyer represented all of them.

Assigned counsel systems are organized on either an ad hoc or a coordinated basis. In ad hoc assignment systems, private attorneys tell the judge that they are willing to take the cases of indigent defendants. When an indigent requires counsel, the judge either assigns lawyers in rotation from a prepared list or chooses one of the attorneys who are known and present in the courtroom. In coordinated assignment systems, a court administrator oversees the appointment of counsel.

Use of the ad hoc system raises questions about the loyalties of the assigned counsel. Are they trying to vigorously defend their clients or are they trying to please the judges to ensure future appointments? In states where judges run for election, there are concerns about lawyers donating to judges' political campaigns. Judges could return the favor by supplying their contributors with criminal defense assignments.

The fees paid to assigned defenders are often low compared with what a lawyer might otherwise charge. As described by one attorney, "The level of compensation impacts the level of representation. . . . If an attorney takes [an appointed criminal case], it means they lose the opportunity to take other cases at higher rates" (*Third Branch*, 2008a). Whereas a private practice attorney might charge clients at rates that exceed $200 per hour, hourly rates for appointed counsel in Cook County (Chicago), Illinois, are merely $40 per hour for in-court tasks and $30 per hour for out-of-court tasks. These same rates have been in place for more than 30 years. Defense attorneys receive the low rate of $40 per hour for out-of-court work in Oklahoma, Oregon, Alabama, South Carolina, and Tennessee. Many other states pay only $50 to $75 per hour (Spangenberg Group, 2007). The average hourly overhead cost for attorneys—the amount they must make just to pay their secretaries, office rent, and telephone bills— is $64 ("Economics of CJA Representations," 2008). If their hourly fees fall short of their overhead costs, then attorneys actually lose money when spending time on these cases. Look at Table 7.3 to see examples of fees paid to assigned defense counsel.

8

Pretrial Procedures, Plea Bargaining, and the Criminal Trial

Learning Objectives

➔ Understand the pretrial process in criminal cases

➔ Recognize how the bail system operates

➔ Understand the context of pretrial detention

➔ Analyze how and why plea bargaining occurs

➔ Know why cases go to trial and how juries are chosen

➔ Identify the stages of a criminal trial

➔ Understand the basis for an appeal of a conviction

Shelley Malil swung the knife wildly through empty air, as if slashing at an imaginary attacker. The actor, best known for his role as one of Steve Carrell's fellow electronics store employees in the popular movie, *The Forty-Year-Old Virgin*, demonstrated to the hushed jury and other onlookers in the California courtroom how he had defended himself against an attack. The knife employed by Malil in the 2010 trial was made of rubber, unlike the actual kitchen knife in his hand when he stabbed his girlfriend, Kendra Beebe, 24 times at her home in 2008. Malil was on trial for attempted murder, assault with a deadly weapon, and burglary. He faced the possibility of receiving a sentence of 21 years to life in prison if convicted (S. Gordon, 2010b).

Guided through the retelling of events by the questions of his defense attorney, Matthew Roberts, Malil consistently claimed that he thought David Maldonado, the man he saw sipping wine with Beebe outside her home, was sneaking up to attack him from behind. Malil claimed he was defending himself as he swung the knife wildly and was shocked to later discover that he had stabbed Beebe numerous times, fortunately without killing her.

When Beebe testified under questioning from deputy district attorney Keith Watanabe, she described Malil walking into her yard with a knife and stabbing her three times in her side. According to Watanabe, the couple had quarreled the previous day and Malil had stolen various items from Beebe. On cross-examination, defense attorney Roberts got Beebe to admit that she had previously lied under oath during a separate child-custody hearing that did not involve Malil. Roberts claimed to the jurors that Beebe's previous lies in a court proceeding meant that they should not believe her version of events in this case (S. Gordon, 2010a).

The American system regards the trial as the best method for determining a defendant's guilt. This is especially true when the defendant can afford to pay for an attorney to mount a vigorous defense. However, a trial is not a scientific process. Instead of calm, consistent evaluations of evidence, trials involve unpredictable human perceptions and reactions. Attorneys know that a mix of citizens drawn from society may react in a variety of ways and reach different conclusions in response to the attorneys' presentations of evidence and the testimony of witnesses. Ultimately, the San Diego County jurors demonstrated that they did not believe Malil's testimony. They deliberated

for less than four hours before finding Malil guilty of attempted murder and assault with a deadly weapon. Three months later at the sentencing hearing, Superior Court Judge Harry Elias sentenced Malil to life in prison with the possibility of parole. Under California's system, it is possible that good behavior could lead to Malil's release on parole in as few as nine years (Spagat, 2010).

Because of the high stakes and uncertainty that surround criminal trials, most defendants plead guilty as they get closer to the prospect of being judged by a random group of citizens drawn from the community. Even the cases of prominent defendants, who can afford to pay top-notch attorneys, are often determined by plea bargaining. For example, multimillionaire movie star Mel Gibson entered a plea in March 2011 to misdemeanor battery charges after he allegedly punched his girlfriend in 2010 (Cieply, 2011). In his plea deal, Gibson agreed to a sentence of 36 months of probation and 52 weeks of domestic violence counseling (McCartney, 2011). Gibson gained a specific sentence and spared his children from the embarrassment of a lengthy proceeding covered by newspapers and television. The prosecutor gained a quick conviction without expending time and other resources.

In this chapter, we examine the steps in the criminal justice process from arrest to dismissal or conviction. We give particular attention to bail, plea bargaining, and trials—the processes and decisions that most influence whether people will lose their liberty or otherwise receive punishment. As we shall see, interactions and decisions involving judges, prosecutors, and defense attorneys guide the outcomes from these important processes.

From Arrest to Trial or Plea

At each stage of the pretrial process, key decisions are made that move some defendants to the next stage of the process and filter others out of the system. An innocent person could be arrested on the basis of mistaken identification or misinterpreted evidence (Streib, 2010; Huff, 2002). However, pretrial processes ideally force prosecutors and judges to review the available evidence and dismiss unnecessary charges against people who should not face trial and punishment. These processes stem from the American value of due process. Americans believe that people should be entitled to a series of hearings and other procedural steps in which their guilt is proved, before they should be subjected to punishments such as the loss of liberty through incarceration.

After arrest, the accused is booked at the police station. This process includes taking photographs and fingerprints, which form the basis of the case record. Within 48 hours of a warrantless arrest, the defendant is usually taken to court for the initial appearance to hear which charges are being pursued, to be advised of his or her rights, and to receive the opportunity to post bail. At the initial appearance, the judge also must confirm that evidence exists to establish probable cause that the accused committed a crime and thereby is eligible to be prosecuted. If the police used an arrest warrant to take the suspect into custody, evidence has already been presented to a judge who believed that it was strong enough to support a finding of probable cause to proceed against the defendant.

Often, the first formal meeting between the prosecutor and the defendant's attorney is the **arraignment**: the formal court appearance in which the charges against the defendant are read and the defendant, advised by his or her lawyer, enters a plea of either guilty or not guilty. Most defendants will initially plead not guilty, even if they are likely to plead guilty at a later point. This is because, thus far, the prosecutor and defense attorney usually have had little chance to discuss a potential plea bargain. The more serious the charges, the more likely the prosecutor and defense attorney will need time to assess the strength of the other side's case. Only then can plea bargaining begin.

AP Images/Todd Davis, Pool

⬆ Criminal defendants typically make several court appearances as the judge reaches decisions about evidence and the protection of each defendant's due process rights. Does the American system reduce the risk of error by using a multistep process to examine evidence, protect rights, and determine guilt?

At the time of arraignment, prosecutors begin to evaluate the evidence. This screening process greatly affects the lives of accused persons, whose fate rests largely on the prosecutor's discretion (Covey, 2011). If the prosecutor believes the case against the defendant is weak, the charges may be dropped. Prosecutors do not wish to waste their limited time and resources on cases that will not stand up in court. A prosecutor may also drop charges if the alleged crime is minor, if the defendant is a first offender, or if the prosecutor believes that the few days spent in jail before arraignment have provided enough punishment for the alleged offense. Jail overcrowding or the need to work on more-serious cases may also influence the decision to drop charges. In making these decisions, prosecutors at times may discriminate against the accused because of race, wealth, or some other factor, or they may discriminate against certain victims, such as women who have been sexually assaulted by an intimate partner or other acquaintance (A. Davis, 2008; Spohn and Holleran, 2001).

Defense attorneys use pretrial proceedings to challenge the prosecution's evidence. They make **motions** to the court requesting that an order be issued to bring about a specific action. For example, the defense may seek an order for the prosecution to share certain evidence, or for the exclusion of evidence that was allegedly obtained through improper questioning of the suspect or an improper search.

As Figure 8.1 shows, prosecutors use their decision-making power to filter many cases out of the system. The 100 cases illustrated are typical felony cases. The percentage of cases varies from city to city, depending on such factors as the effectiveness of police investigations and prosecutors' policies about which cases to pursue. In the figure, nearly half of those arrested did not ultimately face felony prosecutions. A small number of defendants were steered toward diversion programs (Alarid and Montemayor, 2010). A larger number had their cases dismissed for various reasons, including lack of evidence, the minor nature of the charges, or first-time offender status. Some of the 17 sentenced to probation may actually be imprisoned if the offenders commit a crime after release into the community. In these cases, the prosecutor simply chooses to pursue revocation of probation or

arraignment The court appearance of an accused person in which the charges are read and the accused, advised by a lawyer, pleads guilty or not guilty.

motion An application to a court requesting that an order be issued to bring about a specific action.

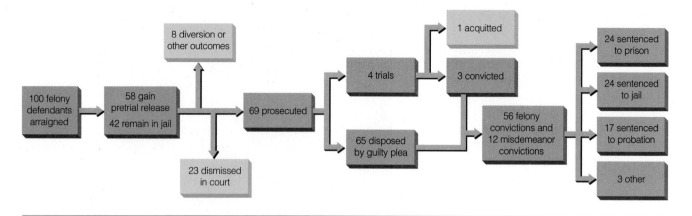

Figure 8.1

Typical Outcomes of 100 Urban Felony Cases Prosecutors and judges make crucial decisions during the period before trial or plea. Once cases are bound over for disposition, guilty pleas are many, trials are few, and acquittals are rare.

Source: Thomas H. Cohen and Tracy Kyckelhahn, "Felony Defendants in Large Urban Counties, 2006," Bureau of Justice Statistics *Bulletin*, May 2010, NCJ 228944.

parole, typically an easier and quicker process than proving guilt for a new crime (Weisberg, 2010; Kingsnorth, MacIntosh, and Sutherland, 2002).

During the pretrial process, defendants are exposed to the informal, "assembly-line" atmosphere of the lower criminal courts. Often, decisions are quickly made about bail, arraignment, pleas, and the disposition of cases. Moving cases through court quickly seems to be the main goal of many judges and attorneys during the pretrial process. Courts throughout the nation face pressure to limit the number of cases going to trial. This pressure may affect the decisions of both judges and prosecutors, as well as the defense attorneys who seek to maintain good relationships with them. American courts often have too little funding, too few staff members, and too little time to give detailed attention to each case, let alone to the time and resources needed for a full trial. Resource scarcity is a growing problem due to the budget cuts experienced by many state and local court systems (Bluestein, 2011).

check point

1. **What are the purposes of the initial appearance, arraignment, and motions?**
   The initial appearance determines if there is probable cause to support the arrest. Arraignments involve the formal reading of charges and the entry of a plea. Motions seek information and the vindication of defendants' rights.

2. **Why and how are cases filtered out of the system?**
   Cases are filtered out through the discretionary decisions of prosecutors and judges when they believe that there is inadequate evidence to proceed, or when prosecutors believe that their scarce resources are best directed at other cases.

stop & analyze

Do prosecutors hold too much power in the pretrial process in light of their discretionary decisions about charging and plea bargaining? List two risks and two benefits from giving prosecutors significant authority over pretrial decisions.

Bail: Pretrial Release

It is often stated that defendants are presumed innocent until proved guilty or until they enter a guilty plea. However, people who are arrested are taken to jail. They are deprived of their freedom and, in many cases, subjected to miserable living conditions while they await the processing of their cases. The idea that people who are presumed innocent can lose their freedom—sometimes for many months—as their cases work their way toward trial, clashes with the American values of freedom and liberty. It is not clear how committed Americans are to preserving the ideal of freedom for people who have not yet been convicted of crimes. Such concerns may have further diminished in the aftermath of September 11, as the federal government began to hold persons suspected of terrorism, labeled "enemy combatants," without providing any bail hearing, evidence of guilt, or access to defense attorneys. The outcry against such deprivations of liberty has come from civil rights groups and attorneys rather than from the general public (Tashima, 2008).

A conflict is bound to occur between the American value of individual liberty and the need to keep some criminal suspects in jail in order to protect society from violent people or from those who may try to escape prosecution. However, not every person charged with a criminal offense need be detained. Thus, bail and other release methods are used on the condition that the defendants will appear in court as required.

Bail is a sum of money or property, specified by the judge, that defendants present to the court as a condition of pretrial release. They forfeit the bail if they do not appear in court as scheduled. Although people are generally entitled to a bail hearing as part of their right to due process, there is no constitutional right to release on bail, nor even a right to have the court set an amount as the condition of release. The Eighth Amendment to the U.S. Constitution forbids excessive bail, and state bail laws are usually designed to prevent discrimination in setting bail. They do not guarantee, however, that all defendants will have a realistic chance of being released before trial. A study in New York City found that among 19,137 cases for which bail was set at $1,000 or less, 87 percent of those defendants could not post bail and they remained in jail for an average of 16 days while their cases were processed (Secret, 2010). Such statistics about the risk of pretrial detention for large numbers of poor people raise the possibility that such defendants may feel pressured to plead guilty, whether or not they are in fact guilty, simply to obtain a sentence of probation for minor offenses and thereby more quickly gain their freedom from custody.

Because the accused is presumed to be innocent, bail should not be used as punishment. The amount of bail should therefore be high enough to ensure that the defendant appears in court for trial—but no higher. As we have seen, however, this is not the only purpose of bail. The community must be protected from the crimes that some defendants would likely commit while out on bail (Karnow, 2008). Congress and some of the states have passed laws that permit *preventive detention* of defendants when the judge concludes that they pose a threat to the community while awaiting trial (Wiseman, 2009).

bail An amount of money, specified by a judge, to be paid as a condition of pretrial release to ensure that the accused will appear in court as required.

The Reality of the Bail System

The reality of the bail system is far from the ideal. The question of bail may arise at the police station, at the initial court appearance in a misdemeanor case, or at the arraignment in most felony cases. For minor offenses, police officers may have a standard list of bail amounts. For serious offenses, a judge will set bail in court. In both cases, those setting bail may have discretion to set differing bail amounts for various suspects, depending on the circumstances of each case. The speed of decision making and lack of information available at the moment of setting bail can enhance differential treatment. As described by the prosecutor in Staten Island, one of the

→ Each year, 20 percent of felony defendants out on bail fail to appear for scheduled court hearings. Some forget court dates or misunderstand instructions. Others intentionally skip town. Nearly all of them are eventually found, frequently by bail agents and their employees. Should such profit-seeking, private businesses be so deeply involved in the criminal justice process?

© Spencer Grant/Alamy

law enforcement personnel. In the federal system, U.S. marshals are the main law enforcement officials in the court system and are responsible for court security, prisoner transport, and tracking down fugitives.

Setting Bail

When the police set bail at the station house for minor offenses, they usually apply a standard amount for a particular charge. By contrast, when a judge sets bail, the amount of bail and conditions of release result from interactions among the judge, prosecutor, and defense attorney. These actors discuss the defendant's personal qualities and prior record. The prosecutor may stress the seriousness of the crime, the defendant's record, and negative personal characteristics. The defense attorney, if one has been hired or appointed at this point in the process, may stress the defendant's good job, family responsibilities, and place in the community. Like other aspects of bail, these factors may favor affluent defendants over the poor, the unemployed, and people with unstable families. Yet, many of these factors provide no clear information about how dangerous a defendant is or whether he or she will appear in court. The amount of bail may also reflect the defendant's social class or even racial or ethnic discrimination by criminal justice officials (M. Johnson and Johnson, 2012).

Reforming the Bail System

Studies of pretrial detention in such cities as Philadelphia and New York have raised questions about the need to hold defendants in jail. Criticisms of the bail system focus on judges' discretion in setting bail amounts, the fact that the poor are deprived of their freedom while the affluent can afford bail, the negative aspects of bail agents, and jail conditions for those detained while awaiting trial.

In response to such criticisms, efforts to reform the bail system have arisen. Such efforts often focus on reducing the number of defendants held in jail. As such, the percentage of defendants released on bail has increased in recent decades, in part because of the use of certain pretrial release methods, which we now discuss.

Citation   A **citation**, or summons, to appear in court—a "ticket"—is often issued to a person accused of committing a traffic offense or some other minor violation. By issuing the citation, the officer avoids taking the accused person to the station house

citation A written order or summons, issued by a law enforcement officer, directing an alleged offender to appear in court at a specific time to answer a criminal charge.

for booking and to court for arraignment and setting of bail. Citations are now being used for more-serious offenses, in part because the police want to reduce the amount of time they spend booking minor offenders and waiting in arraignment court for their cases to come up.

Release on Recognizance

Pioneered in the 1960s by the Vera Institute of Justice in New York City, the **release on recognizance (ROR)** approach is based on the assumption that judges will grant releases if the defendant is reliable and has roots in the community. Soon after the arrest, court personnel talk to defendants about their job, family, prior record, and associations (Kim and Denver, 2011). They then decide whether to recommend release. In the first three years of the New York project, more than ten thousand defendants were interviewed and about 3,500 were released. Only 1.5 percent failed to appear in court at the scheduled time, a rate almost 3 times better than the rate for those released on bail (Goldfarb, 1965). Programs in other cities have had similar results, although Sheila Royo Maxwell's research (1999) raises questions about whether women and property-crime defendants on ROR are less likely than other defendants to appear in court.

release on recognizance (ROR) Pretrial release granted, on the defendant's promise to appear in court, because the judge believes that the defendant's ties to the community guarantee that he or she will appear.

Ten Percent Cash Bail

Although ROR is a useful alternative to money bail, judges are unwilling to release some defendants on their own recognizance. Illinois, Kentucky, Nebraska, Oregon, and Pennsylvania have **percentage bail** programs in which the defendants deposit with the court an amount of cash equal to 10 percent of their bail. When they appear in court as required, this amount is returned minus a 1 percent fee for administrative costs. Begun in Illinois in 1964, this plan is designed to release as many defendants as possible without using bail agents.

percentage bail Defendants may deposit a percentage (usually 10 percent) of the full bail with the court. The full amount of the bail is required if the defendant fails to appear. The percentage of bail is returned after disposition of the case, although the court often retains 1 percent for administrative costs.

Bail Fund

An innovative program developed in New York City in 2009 is called the Bronx Freedom Fund. Poor people who are represented by the Bronx Defenders, a nonprofit organization that handles defense for indigent defendants, can receive loans from the fund in order to post bail and gain pretrial release (Clisura, 2010). The fund was created to prevent poor defendants from languishing in jail merely because they cannot pay a relatively small amount of money. Those freed on bail are monitored and assisted through the relationship between the fund and the defense attorneys. The organization's website claims that 93 percent of defendants assisted by the fund returned for their court appearances. In other locations, churches and other organizations have sometimes engaged in parallel activities by loaning money for bail. However, such programs are probably most effective when the loans are tied to contact, assistance, and supervision with people, such as counselors or defense attorneys, who remind defendants about court dates and otherwise help them to avoid violating conditions of bail.

Bail Guidelines

To deal with the problem of unequal treatment, reformers have written guidelines for setting bail. The guidelines specify the standards judges should use in setting bail and also list appropriate bail amounts. Judges are expected to follow the guidelines but may deviate from them in special situations. The guidelines take into account the seriousness of the offense and the defendant's prior record in an effort to protect the community and ensure that released suspects will likely return for court appearances.

Preventive Detention

Reforms have been suggested by those concerned with unfairness in the bail system as well as by those concerned with stopping crime. Critics of the bail system point to a link between release on bail and the commission of crimes, arguing that the accused can commit other crimes while awaiting trial. A study of the nation's most populous counties found that 21 percent of felony defendants released on bail were rearrested for another crime (Kyckelhahn and Cohen, 2008). To address this problem, legislatures have passed laws permitting detention of defendants without bail.

preventive detention
Holding a defendant for trial, based on a judge's finding that if the defendant were released on bail, he or she would endanger the safety of any other person and the community or would flee.

For federal criminal cases, Congress enacted the Bail Reform Act of 1984, which authorizes **preventive detention**. Under the act, if prosecutors recommend that defendants be kept in jail, a federal judge holds a hearing to determine (1) if there is a serious risk that the person will flee; (2) if the person will obstruct justice or threaten, injure, or intimidate a prospective witness or juror; or (3) if the offense is one of violence or one punishable by life imprisonment or death. On finding that any of these factors makes setting bail impossible without endangering the community, the judge can order the defendant be held in jail until the case is completed (C. E. Smith, 1990).

Critics of preventive detention argue that it violates the Constitution's due process clause because the accused is held in custody until a verdict is rendered (Wiseman, 2009). However, the Supreme Court has ruled that it is constitutional. The preventive detention provisions of the Bail Reform Act of 1984 were upheld in ***United States v. Salerno and Cafero* (1987)**. The justices said that preventive detention was a legitimate use of government power because it was not designed to punish the accused. Instead, it deals with the problem of people who commit crimes while on bail. By upholding the federal law, the Court also upheld state laws dealing with preventive detention (M. Johnson and Johnson, 2012).

Supporters of preventive detention claim that it ensures that drug dealers, who often treat bail as a business expense, cannot flee before trial. Research has shown that the nature and seriousness of the charge, a history of prior arrests, and drug use all have a strong bearing on the likelihood that a defendant will commit a crime while on bail.

***United States v. Salerno and Cafero* (1987)**
Preventive detention provisions of the Bail Reform Act of 1984 are upheld as a legitimate use of government power designed to prevent people from committing crimes while on bail.

---

check point

3. What factors affect whether bail is set and how much money or property a defendant must provide to gain pretrial release?
Bail decisions are based primarily on the judge's evaluation of the seriousness of the offense and the defendant's prior record. The decisions are influenced by the prosecutor's recommendations and the defense attorney's counterarguments about the defendant's personal qualities and ties to the community.

4. What methods are used to facilitate pretrial release for certain defendants?
Police citations, release on own recognizance (ROR), 10 percent cash bail, and bail fund.

stop & analyze

If you were the governor of a state that had never introduced reforms to reduce pretrial detention, which approach would you propose—10 percent cash bail, bail fund, release on own recognizance, bail guidelines, or citation? Make two arguments in favor of the approach that you would choose.

Pretrial Detention

People who are not released before trial must remain in jail. Often called the ultimate ghetto, American jails hold almost 600,000 people on any one day. Most of the people in jail are poor, half are in pretrial detention, and the rest are serving sentences (normally of less than one year) or are waiting to be moved to state prison or to another jurisdiction (Clear, Cole, and Reisig, 2009).

Urban jails also contain troubled people, many with mental health and drug abuse problems, whom police have swept off the streets. Michael Welch calls this process, in which the police remove socially offensive people from certain areas, "social sanitation" (Welch, 1994:262). Conditions in jails are often much harsher

For t
know
or co
crim
inste
inter
deter
court
plea
quick
same
cases

C
guilty
the S
New
descr
that
made
"'Plea
admi
it is
crimi
comm

Ir
heart
in *Bl*
benefi
are ac
attorn
cases
punis
of a j
less th
Prosec
gain a
been g
and re
bargai
to pre
case. S
Judges
what s
recom
provic
given

Be
approp
Tenne
aimed
charge
on plea
becaus
their ii

than those in prisons. People awaiting trial are often held in barracks-like cells along with sentenced offenders. Thus, a "presumed innocent" pretrial detainee might spend weeks in the same confined space with troubled people or sentenced felons (Beck, Karberg, and Harrison, 2002). The problems of pretrial detention may be even worse in other countries where suspects languish in jail during the slow-moving processing of criminal cases. Read the "Comparative Perspective" on pretrial detention in the Philippines for a different perspective on the experience of pretrial detainees. What factors help keep detainees in American jails from experiencing the hardships endured by those in jails in the Philippines?

The period just after arrest is the most frightening and difficult time for suspects. Imagine freely walking the streets one minute and being locked in a small space with a large number of troubled and potentially dangerous cell mates the next. Suddenly, you have no privacy and must share an open toilet with hostile strangers. You have been fingerprinted, photographed, searched, and questioned—treated like the "criminal" that the police and the criminal justice system consider you to be (Schlanger, 2008). You are alone with people whose behavior you cannot predict and left to worry about what might happen. If you are female, you may be placed in a cell by yourself. Given the stressful nature of arrest and jailing, it is little wonder that most jail suicides and psychotic episodes occur during the first hours of detention.

Other factors can make the shock of arrest and detention even worse. Many people are arrested for offenses they committed while under the influence of drugs or alcohol. They may be less able than others to cope with their new situation. Young arrestees who face the risk of being victimized by older, stronger cell mates may sink into depression. Detainees also worry about losing their jobs while in jail, because they do not know if or when they will be released.

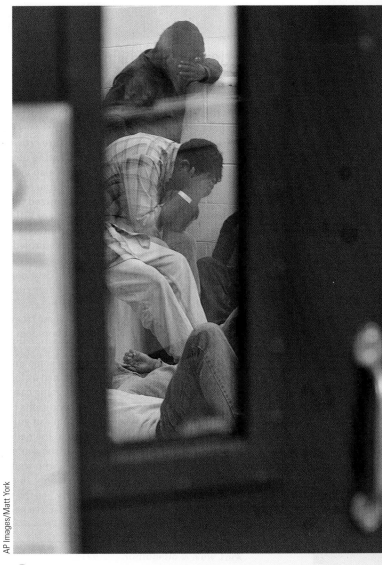

AP Images/Matt York

Jails holding pretrial detainees may be crowded and lack education and counseling programs. Spending time in detention can be frightening and difficult as people worry about what will happen to them. Why do you think the suicide rate in jails is higher than that in prisons?

Although most Americans arrested for felonies have their cases adjudicated within six months, other felony defendants can wait more than a year (Kyckelhahn and Cohen, 2008). Imagine the hardships for the 38 percent of arrestees who cannot gain pretrial release if they are among those who must wait six months to a year before the courts complete the processing of their cases. The psychological and economic hardships faced by pretrial detainees and their families can be significant and prolonged.

Pretrial detention not only imposes stresses and hardships that may reach a crisis level; it can also affect the outcomes of cases (McCoy, 2007). People in jail can give little help to their attorneys. They cannot help find witnesses and perform other useful tasks on their own behalf. In addition, they may feel pressured to plead guilty in order to end their indefinite stay in jail. Even if they believe that they should not be convicted of the crime charged, they may prefer to start serving a prison or jail sentence with a definite end point. Some may even gain quicker release on probation or in a community corrections program by pleading guilty, whereas they might stay in jail for a longer period by insisting on their innocence and awaiting a trial.

Pre

Rayn

Despi
cused
trial,
pines
unde:
trial.
and u
deten
sente:
tuber
disea:
where
wron;
ees ty

Jai
a lack
jail ne
Jail w
is use
with i
a roor
enoug
The m
is the
detair
clothi
even f
must i

chec
poir

→ In 2009, two Pennsylvania judges, Michael Conahan (back left) and Mark Ciavarella (center), pleaded guilty to wire fraud and income tax fraud charges. They had taken more than $2.6 million in kickback payments from private companies that managed juvenile detention facilities, in exchange for sentencing juvenile offenders to serve time in those facilities. Should officials who violate the public's trust be permitted to gain reduced sentences through plea bargains?

AP Images/Times Tribune, Pamela Suchy

Exchange Relationships in Plea Bargaining

As we have seen, plea bargaining is a set of exchange relationships in which the prosecutor, the defense attorney, the defendant, and sometimes the judge participate. All have specific goals, all try to use the situation to their own advantage, and all are likely to see the exchange as a success.

Plea bargaining does not always occur in a single meeting between the prosecutor and defense attorney. One study showed that plea bargaining is a process in which prosecutors and defense attorneys interact again and again as they move further along in the judicial process. As time passes, the discovery of more evidence or new information about the defendant's background may strengthen the prosecutor's hand (Emmelman, 1996). Often, the prosecution rather than the defense is in the best position to obtain new evidence (Cooney, 1994). However, the defense attorney's position may gain strength if the prosecutor does not wish to spend time preparing for a trial.

Tactics of Prosecutor and Defense

Plea bargaining between defense counsel and prosecutor is a serious game in which friendliness and joking can mask efforts to advance each side's cause. Both sides use various strategies and tactics (D. M. Brown, 2009). Each tries to impress the other with its confidence in its own case while pointing out weaknesses in the other side's case. An unspoken rule of openness and candor usually keeps the relationship on good terms. Little effort is made to conceal information that could later be useful to the other side in the courtroom. Studies show that the outcomes of plea bargaining may depend on the relationships between prosecutors and individual attorneys, as well as the defense counsel's willingness to fight for the client (Champion, 1989).

A tactic that many prosecutors bring to plea bargaining sessions is the multiple-offense indictment. Multiple-offense charges are especially important to prosecutors in handling difficult cases—for instance, those in which the victim is reluctant to provide information, the value of the stolen item is unclear, or the evidence may not be reliable. Prosecutors often file charges of selling a drug when they know they can probably convict only for possession. Because the accused persons know that the penalty for selling is much greater, they are tempted to plead guilty to the lesser charge rather than risk a longer sentence, even if the probability of conviction on the more serious charge is uncertain. Such tactics can be especially powerful when the potential punishment upon conviction at trial would be severe (Erhard, 2008).

Defense attorneys may threaten to ask for a jury trial if concessions are not made (D. M. Bowen, 2009). To strengthen their hand further, they may also file pretrial motions that require a formal response by the prosecutor. Another tactic is to seek to reschedule pretrial activities in the hope that, with delay, witnesses will become unavailable, media attention will die down, and memories of the crime will grow weaker by the time of the trial. Rather than resort to such legal tactics, however, some attorneys prefer to bargain on the basis of friendship.

Pleas without Bargaining

Studies have shown that in many courts give-and-take plea bargaining does not occur for certain types of cases, yet they have as many guilty pleas as do other courts (Eisenstein, Flemming, and Nardulli, 1988). The term *bargaining* may be misleading in that it implies haggling. Many scholars argue that guilty pleas emerge after the prosecutor, the defense attorney, and sometimes the judge have reached an agreement to "settle the facts" (Utz, 1978). In this view, the parties first study the facts of a case. What were the circumstances of the event? Was it really an assault or was it more of a shoving match? Did the victim antagonize the accused? Each side may hope to persuade the other that its view of the defendant's actions is backed up by provable facts. The prosecution wants the defense to believe that strong evidence proves its version of the event. The defense attorney wants to convince the prosecution that the evidence is not solid and that there is a risk of acquittal if the case is heard by a jury.

In some cases, the evidence is strong and the defense attorney has little hope of persuading the prosecutor otherwise. Through their discussions, the prosecutor and defense attorney seek to reach a shared view of the provable facts in the case. Once they agree on the facts, they will both know the appropriate charge, and they can agree on a sentence according to the locally defined going rate. At that point, a guilty plea can be entered without any formal bargaining, because both sides agree on what the case is worth in terms of the seriousness of the charge and the usual punishment. This process may be thought of as *implicit plea bargaining*, because shared understandings create the expectation that a guilty plea will lead to a less-than-maximum sentence, even without any exchange or bargaining.

As we saw in Chapter 7, the going rates for sentences for particular crimes and offenders depend on local values and sentencing patterns. Often, both the prosecutor and the defense attorney belong to a particular local legal culture and thus share an understanding about how cases should be handled. Thus, they may both know right away what the sentence will be for a first-time burglar or second-time robber. The sentence may differ in another courthouse, because the local legal culture and going rates vary.

Legal Issues in Plea Bargaining

In *Boykin v. Alabama* (1969), the U.S. Supreme Court ruled that, before a judge may accept a plea of guilty, defendants must state that the plea was made voluntarily. Judges have created standard forms with questions for the defendant to affirm in open court before the plea is accepted. Trial judges also must learn whether the defendant understands the consequences of pleading guilty and ensure that the plea is not obtained through pressure.

In 2012, the Supreme Court issued a pair of potentially far-reaching decisions confirming that defendants are entitled to effective assistance of counsel during the plea bargaining process. In *Missouri v. Frye* (2012), a lawyer failed to inform his client about a favorable plea bargain offer from the prosecutor. In *Lafler v. Cooper* (2012), the defense attorney gave the defendant bad advice about a potential plea agreement by being mistaken about the actual seriousness of the offense for which

Boykin v. Alabama (1969) Before a judge may accept a plea of guilty, defendants must state that they are making the plea voluntarily.

Missouri v. Frye (2012) Criminal defendants' Sixth Amendment right to counsel includes protection against ineffective assistance of counsel in the plea bargaining process, such as defense attorneys' failures to inform their clients about plea bargain offers.

the defendant could be charged and convicted at trial (Liptak, 2012). It remains to be seen how these decisions will impact plea bargaining, but many observers predict that more plea offers will be placed in writing and that trial judges will provide closer supervision over the plea bargaining process to guard against attorney mistakes that disadvantage defendants (Goode, 2012).

Can a trial court accept a guilty plea if the defendant claims to be innocent? In *North Carolina v. Alford* (1970), the Court allowed a defendant to enter a guilty plea for the purpose of gaining a lesser sentence, even though he maintained that he was innocent. However, the Supreme Court also stated that trial judges should not accept such a plea unless a factual basis exists for believing that the defendant is in fact guilty.

Another issue is whether the plea agreement will be fulfilled. If the prosecutor has promised to recommend a lenient sentence, the promise must be kept (*Santobello v. New York*, 1971). As ruled in *Ricketts v. Adamson* (1987), defendants must also keep their side of the bargain, such as testifying against a codefendant. However, in *Bordenkircher v. Hayes* (1978), the justices ruled that prosecutors may threaten to seek more-serious charges, as long as such charges are supported by evidence, if defendants refuse to plead guilty. Some scholars criticize this decision as imposing pressures on a defendant that are not permitted elsewhere in the justice process (O'Hear, 2006).

Criticisms of Plea Bargaining

Among the many concerns about plea bargaining, two primary criticisms stand out. The first argues that plea bargaining is unfair because defendants give up some of their constitutional rights, especially the right to trial by jury (O'Keefe, 2010). The second stresses sentencing policy and points out that plea bargaining reduces society's interest in appropriate punishments for crimes. In urban areas with high caseloads, harried judges and prosecutors are said to make concessions based on administrative needs, resulting in lighter sentences than those required by the penal code.

Plea bargaining also comes under fire because it is hidden from judicial scrutiny. Because the agreement is most often made at an early stage, the judge has little information about the crime or the defendant and thus cannot adequately evaluate the case.

Other critics believe that overuse of plea bargaining breeds disrespect and even contempt for the law. They say criminals look at the judicial process as a game or a sham, much like other "deals" made in life.

Critics also contend that it is unjust to penalize people who assert their right to a trial, by giving them stiffer sentences than they would have received if they had pleaded guilty. The evidence here is debated (D. Abrams, 2011), although it is widely believed that an extra penalty is imposed on defendants who take up the court's time by asserting their right to a trial (Ulmer, Eisenstein, and Johnson, 2010).

Finally, another concern about plea bargaining is that innocent people will plead guilty to acts that they did not commit. Although it is hard to know how often this happens, some defendants have entered guilty pleas when they have not committed the offense (J. Bowen, 2008). It may be hard for middle-class people to understand how anyone could possibly plead guilty when innocent. However, people with little education and low social status may lack the confidence to say "no" to an attorney who strongly encourages them to plead guilty.

People may also lack confidence in court processes. What if you feared that a jury might convict you and send you to prison for 20 years based on circumstantial evidence (such as being in the vicinity of the crime and wearing the same color shirt as the robber that day)? Might you plead guilty and take a five-year sentence, even if you knew that you were innocent? How much confidence do you have that juries and judges will always reach the correct result? Poor people, in particular, may feel helpless in the stressful climate of the courthouse and jail. If they lack faith in the system's ability to protect their rights and find them not guilty, they may accept a lighter punishment rather than risk being convicted for a serious offense.

North Carolina v. Alford (1970) A plea of guilty by a defendant who maintains his or her innocence may be accepted for the purpose of a lesser sentence.

Ricketts v. Adamson (1987) Defendants must uphold the plea agreement or suffer the consequences.

Bordenkircher v. Hayes (1978) A defendant's rights were not violated by a prosecutor who warned that refusing to enter a guilty plea would result in a harsher sentence.

7. Why does plea bargaining occur?

It serves the self-interest of all relevant actors: defendants gain certain, less-than-maximum sentences; prosecutors gain swift, sure convictions; defense attorneys get prompt resolution of cases; judges preside over fewer time-consuming trials.

8. What are the criticisms of plea bargaining?

Defendants might be pressured to surrender their rights; society's mandated criminal punishments are improperly reduced.

stop& analyze

The U.S. Supreme Court's decision in *North Carolina v. Alford* (1970) says that a judge can accept a guilty plea from someone who claims to be actually innocent. Does the acceptance of such pleas diminish the justice system's goal of punishing only those who are guilty of crimes? If you were a judge, would you accept such pleas? Write a brief statement explaining your position.

Trial: The Exceptional Case

If cases are not dismissed or terminated through plea bargaining, they move forward for trial. The seriousness of the charge is probably the most important factor influencing the decision to go to trial. Murder, felonious assault, or rape—all charges that bring long prison terms—may require judge and jury, unless the defendant fears a certain conviction and therefore seeks a negotiated plea deal. When the penalty is harsh, however, many defendants seem willing to risk the possibility of conviction at trial. Table 8.1 shows the differences in the percentages of defendants going to trial for offenses of varying severity. Notice that homicide offenses, which carry the most significant punishments, produce a higher percentage of trials than do other crimes.

Trials determine the fates of very few defendants. Although the right to trial by jury is ingrained in American ideology—it is mentioned in the Declaration of Independence, the U.S. Constitution and three of its amendments, and myriad opinions of the U.S. Supreme Court—year in and year out fewer than 9 percent of felony cases go to trial. Of these, only about half are jury trials; the rest are **bench trials**, presided over by a judge without a **jury**. In 2006, trials produced only 5 percent of felony convictions in the nation's 75 most populous counties (Cohen and Kyckelhahn, 2010). Defendants may choose a bench trial if they believe a judge will be more capable of making an objective decision, especially if the charges or evidence are likely to arouse emotional reactions in jurors.

bench trials Trials conducted by a judge who acts as fact finder and determines issues of law. No jury participates.

jury A panel of citizens selected according to law and sworn to determine matters of fact in a criminal case and to deliver a verdict of guilty or not guilty.

TABLE 8.1 Percentage of Indicted Cases That Went to Trial, by Offense

The percentages of cases that went to trial differ both by offense and by jurisdiction. Typically, it seems that the stiffer the possible penalty, the greater the likelihood of a trial. However, a prosecutor may be able to gain guilty pleas even in the most serious cases.

Jurisdiction	Homicide	Rape/Sexual Assault	Robbery	Assault	Drug Offenses
State courts, 75 largest counties	44%	7%	6%	6%	2%
Federal courts	16	—	4	8	4
Mercer County, NJ (Trenton)	12	0	3	<1	<1

Sources: Adapted from Thomas H. Cohen and Tracy Kyckelhahn, *Felony Defendants in Large Urban Counties, 2006*, Washington, DC: Bureau of Justice Statistics (2010); "Mercer County Prosecutor's Annual Report 2009" (2010); *Sourcebook of Criminal Justice Statistics 2009*, Table 5.24.2009.

Sitting between his attorneys, defendant Dr. Conrad Murray listens to the presentation of evidence against him in a California courtroom in 2011. The jury convicted him of manslaughter in the death of singer Michael Jackson. He was accused of improperly supplying and administering prescription drugs that caused Jackson's death. What other kinds of cases are likely to be processed through jury trials?

The rates of trials also vary from city to city. This difference stems, in part, from the local legal culture. Think about how prosecutors' policies or sentencing practices in different cities may increase or decrease the incentives for a defendant to plead guilty. In addition, defense attorneys and prosecutors in different courthouses may have their own understandings about which cases should produce a plea bargain because of agreements (or disagreements) about the provable facts and the going rate of sentences for an offense.

Trials take considerable time and resources. Attorneys frequently spend weeks or months preparing—gathering evidence, responding to their opponents' motions, planning trial strategy, and setting aside a day to several weeks to present the case in court. From the perspective of judges, prosecutors, and defense attorneys, plea bargaining presents an attractive alternative for purposes of completing cases quickly.

Jury Trial

Trials are based on the idea that the prosecution and defense will compete as adversaries before a judge and jury so that the truth will emerge. As such, the rules of criminal law, procedure, and evidence govern the conduct of the trial. Above the battle, the judge ensures that the rules are followed and that the jury impartially evaluates the evidence and reflects the community's interests. In a jury trial, the jury alone evaluates the facts in a case. The adversarial process and inclusion of jurors in decision making often make trial outcomes difficult to predict. The verdict hinges not only on the nature of the evidence but also on the effectiveness of the prosecution and defense and on the jurors' attitudes. Does this adversarial and citizen-based process provide the best mechanism for finding the truth and doing justice in our most serious criminal cases?

However one assesses their effectiveness, juries perform six vital functions in the criminal justice system:

1. Prevent government oppression by safeguarding citizens against arbitrary law enforcement
2. Determine whether the accused is guilty on the basis of the evidence presented
3. Represent diverse community interests so that no one set of values or biases dominates decision making
4. Serve as a buffer between the accused and the accuser
5. Promote knowledge about the criminal justice system by learning about it through the jury-duty process
6. Symbolize the rule of law and the community foundation that supports the criminal justice system

As a symbol of law, juries demonstrate to the public, as well as to defendants, that decisions about depriving individuals of their liberty will be made carefully by a group of citizens who represent the community's values. In addition, juries provide the primary element of direct democracy in the judicial branch of government. Citizens have the opportunity to participate directly in decision making within the judicial branch of government. However, as indicated in "What Americans Think," Americans have divided views on the fairness of the jury process.

Williams v. Florida
(1970) Juries of fewer than 12 members are constitutional.

In the United States, a jury in a criminal trial traditionally comprises 12 citizens, but some states now allow as few as 6 citizens to make up a jury. This reform was recommended to modernize court procedures and reduce expenses. It costs less for the court to contact, process, and pay a smaller number of jurors. The use of small juries was upheld by the Supreme Court in **Williams v. Florida (1970)**. Six states use juries with fewer than 12 members in noncapital felony cases, and a larger number of states use small juries for misdemeanors. In *Burch v. Louisiana* (1979), the Supreme Court ruled that 6-member juries must vote unanimously to convict a defendant, but unanimity is not required for larger juries. Some states permit juries to convict defendants by votes of 10–2 or 9–3. The change to 6-person juries has its critics, who charge that the smaller group is less representative of the conflicting views in the community and too quick to bring in a verdict (Diamond et al., 2009; A. R. Amar, 1997).

The Trial Process

The trial process generally follows eight steps: (1) selection of the jury, (2) opening statements by prosecution and defense, (3) presentation of the prosecution's evidence and witnesses, (4) presentation of the defense's evidence and witnesses, (5) presentation of rebuttal witnesses, (6) closing arguments by each side, (7) instruction of the jury by the judge, and (8) decision by the jury. The details of each step may vary according to each state's rules. Although the proportion of trials may be small, understanding each step in the process and considering the broader impact of this institution are both important.

Jury Selection   The selection of the jury, outlined in Figure 8.3, is a crucial first step in the trial process. Because people always apply their experiences, values, and biases in their decision making, prosecutors and defense attorneys actively seek to identify potential jurors who may be automatically sympathetic or hostile to their side. When they believe they have identified such potential jurors, they try to find ways to exclude those who may sympathize with the other side, while striving to keep those who may favor their side. Lawyers do not necessarily achieve these goals, because the selection of jurors involves the decisions and interactions of prosecutors, defense attorneys, and judges, each of whom has different objectives in the selection process.

Jurors are selected from among the citizens whose names have been placed in the jury pool. The composition of the jury pool tremendously affects the ultimate composition of the trial jury. In most states, the jury pool is drawn from lists of registered voters, but research has shown that nonwhites, the poor,

Question: "How often do most people who are on trial have a jury that is fair and impartial?"

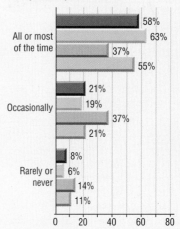

Perceptions of juries' fairness

All or most of the time	58% / 63% / 37% / 55%
Occasionally	21% / 19% / 37% / 21%
Rarely or never	8% / 6% / 14% / 11%

Question: "Who would you trust more to give a fair verdict?"

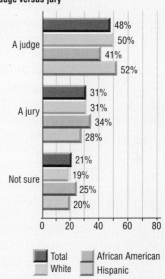

Judge versus jury

A judge	48% / 50% / 41% / 52%
A jury	31% / 31% / 34% / 28%
Not sure	21% / 19% / 25% / 20%

Total
White
African American
Hispanic

Critical Thinking: What might lead people to lack faith in the fairness of juries? Does it matter if this reflects an overall lack of faith in the justice system rather than specific experience with jury trials? Are there reasons for officials in the justice system to worry about the reduced levels of confidence expressed by specific demographic groups?

Source: The Harris Poll, "Just under Three in Five Americans Believe Juries Can Be Fair and Impartial All or Most of the Time," Harris Interactive, January 21, 2008 (www.harrisinteractive.com).

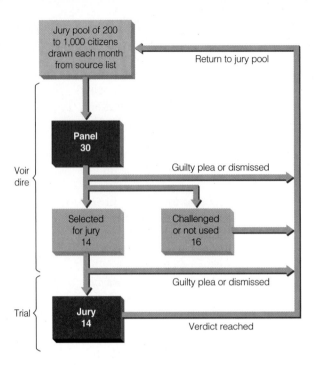

Figure 8.3

Jury Selection Process for a 12-Member Jury Potential jurors are drawn at random from a source list. From this pool, a panel is selected and presented for duty. The voir dire examination may remove some, whereas others will be seated. The 14 jurors selected include two alternates.

© Cengage Learning

and young people register to vote at much lower rates than does the rest of the population. As a result, members of these groups are underrepresented on juries (Sommers, 2009).

In many cases, the presence or absence of these groups may make no difference in the ultimate verdict. In some situations, however, members of these groups may assert themselves in discussion and interpret evidence differently than do their older, white, middle-class counterparts who dominate the composition of juries (Cornwell and Hans, 2011). For example, the poor, nonwhites, and young people may be more likely to have had unpleasant experiences with police officers and therefore be less willing to believe automatically that police officers always tell the truth. Today, courts may supplement the lists of registered voters with other lists, such as those for driver's licenses, hunting licenses, and utility bills, in an effort to diversify the jury pool (Hannaford-Agor, 2011).

Several states are also considering increases in jurors' daily pay; Texas, for example, has gone from $6 per day to $40 per day in trials lasting more than one day. It is hoped that such efforts will make jury service more attractive for poor people who might otherwise avoid participating because they cannot afford to lose pay by missing work (Axtman, 2005). In addition, judges have increasing concerns about small-business owners as well as people worried about losing their jobs who seek to avoid jury duty for financial reasons (Weiss, 2009b; C. J. Williams, 2010). Unfortunately, the current era of budget cuts has hampered efforts to increase financial incentives for participation. Many jurisdictions, including Cleveland, Ohio, and Topeka, Kansas, reduced jurors' pay to save money (Dubail, 2009; KTKA News, 2011).

Retired people and homemakers with grown children tend to be overrepresented on juries, because they are less inconvenienced by serving and are often less likely to ask to be excused because of job responsibilities or child care problems. To make jury duty less onerous, many states have moved to a system called "one-day-one-trial," in which jurors serve for either one day or for the duration of one trial.

The courtroom process of **voir dire** (which means "to speak the truth") is used to question prospective jurors in order to screen out those who might be biased or otherwise incapable of making a fair decision (C. Harrison, 2011). Attorneys for each side, as well as the judge, may question jurors about their background, knowledge of the case, and acquaintance with any participants in the case. Jurors will also be

voir dire A questioning of prospective jurors to screen out people the attorneys think might be biased or otherwise incapable of delivering a fair verdict.

asked whether they or their immediate family members have been crime victims or otherwise involved in a criminal case in a manner that may prevent them from making open-minded decisions about the evidence and the defendant. If a juror's responses indicate that he or she will not be able to make fair decisions, the juror may be **challenged for cause**. The judge must rule on the challenge, but if the judge agrees with the attorney, then the juror is excused from that specific case (Arterton, 2008). There is usually no limit on the number of jurors that the attorneys may challenge for cause.

Although challenges for cause ultimately fall under the judge's control, the prosecution and defense can exert their own control over the jury's composition through the use of **peremptory challenges**. With these, the prosecution and defense can exclude prospective jurors without giving specific reasons. Attorneys use peremptory challenges to exclude jurors who they think will be unsympathetic to their arguments (Hoffman, 1999). Attorneys usually use hunches about which jurors to challenge; little evidence suggests that they can accurately identify which jurors will sympathize with their side or not (M. S. White, 1995). Normally, the defense is allowed eight to ten peremptory challenges, and the prosecution six to eight.

The use of peremptory challenges has raised concerns that attorneys can use them to exclude, for example, African American jurors when an African American is on trial or Latino jurors when there is a Latino defendant (Bagnato, 2010; Price 2009; Enriquez and Clark, 2007). In a series of decisions in the late 1980s and early 1990s (such as *Batson v. Kentucky*, 1986), the Supreme Court prohibited using peremptory challenges to systematically exclude potential jurors because of their race or gender. In practice, however, the enforcement of this prohibition is up to the trial judge (C. E. Smith and Ochoa, 1996). If a trial judge is willing to accept flimsy excuses for race-based and gender-based exclusions, then the attorneys can ignore the ban on discrimination (Bray, 1992).

Some lawyers believe that trials are won or lost in jury selection. If a lawyer succeeds in seating a favorable jury, he or she may have a receptive audience that will readily support the lawyer's arguments and evidence.

Opening Statements   After the jury has been selected, the trial begins. The clerk reads the complaint (indictment or information) detailing the charges, and the prosecutor and the defense attorney may, if they desire, make opening statements to the jury to summarize the position that each side intends to take. The statements are not evidence. The jury is not supposed to regard the attorneys' statements as proving or disproving anything about the case.

Presentation of the Prosecution's Evidence   One of the basic protections of the American criminal justice system is the presumption that the defendant is innocent until proved guilty. The prosecution carries the burden of proving beyond a reasonable doubt, within the demands of the court procedures and rules of evidence, that the individual named in the indictment committed the crime. This does not mean that absolute certainty is required, only that the evidence sufficiently excludes all reasonable doubt.

In presenting evidence to the jury, the prosecution must establish a case showing that the defendant is guilty. Evidence is classified as real evidence, demonstrative evidence, testimony, direct evidence, and circumstantial evidence. **Real evidence** might include such objects as a weapon, business records, fingerprints, or stolen property. These are real objects involved in the crime. **Demonstrative evidence** is presented for jurors to see and understand without testimony. Real evidence is one form of demonstrative evidence; other forms include maps, X-rays, photographs, models, and diagrams. Most evidence in a criminal trial, however, consists of the **testimony** of witnesses. Witnesses at a trial must be legally competent. Thus, the judge may be required to determine whether the witness whose testimony is challenged has the intelligence to tell the truth and the ability to recall what was seen. Witnesses with inadequate intelligence or mental problems might not be regarded as qualified to

challenge for cause Removal of a prospective juror by showing that he or she has some bias or some other legal disability. The number of such challenges available to attorneys is unlimited.

peremptory challenge Removal of a prospective juror without giving any reason. Attorneys are allowed a limited number of such challenges.

real evidence Physical evidence—such as a weapon, records, fingerprints, and stolen property—involved in the crime.

demonstrative evidence Evidence that is not based on witness testimony but that demonstrates information relevant to the crime, such as maps, X-rays, and photographs; includes real evidence involved in the crime.

testimony Oral evidence provided by a legally competent witness.

→ Prosecutors and defense attorneys present various forms of evidence during trials, including physical objects ("real evidence") as well as witness testimony. Do you think that the communication skills and persuasiveness of some attorneys could distract the jurors' attention from the actual evidence presented in the case?

direct evidence Eyewitness accounts.

circumstantial evidence Evidence provided by a witness from which a jury must infer a fact.

present testimony. **Direct evidence** refers to eyewitness accounts such as "I saw John Smith fire the gun." **Circumstantial evidence** requires that the jury infer a fact from what the witness observed: "I saw John Smith walk behind his house with a gun. A few minutes later I heard a gun go off, and then Mr. Smith walked toward me holding a gun." The witness's observation that Smith had a gun and that the witness then heard a gun go off does not provide direct evidence that Smith fired his gun; however, the jury may link the described facts and infer that Smith fired his gun. After a witness has given testimony, counsel for the other side may cross-examine him or her.

Because many cases rely on scientific evidence, especially in the form of experts' testimony about DNA, blood spatters, bullet fragments and trajectories, and the nature of physical injuries, there are concerns that judges and juries do not fully understand the information presented (Cheng, 2005). Determinations of guilt may hinge on the effectiveness of the presentation of such evidence rather than the accuracy and verifiability of the scientific conclusions (McAuliff and Duckworth, 2010). Some prosecutors fear that the prevalence of definitive scientific evidence in television crime dramas may cause jurors to expect scientific evidence in each case, such as DNA, in order to issue a guilty verdict. As discussed in the "Close Up," there are debates about whether a "*CSI* effect" [*Crime Scene Investigation*] has affected jurors' expectations and made it more difficult for prosecutors to gain convictions in cases for which there is only witness testimony and no scientific evidence.

The attorney for each side challenges the other side's presentation of evidence. If evidence violates the rules, reflects untrustworthy hearsay, is a statement of opinion, or is not relevant to the issues in the case, an attorney will object to its presentation. In effect, the attorney is asking the judge to rule that the jury cannot consider the opponent's questionable evidence.

After the prosecution has presented all of the state's evidence against the defendant, the court is informed that the people's case rests. It is common for the defense then to ask the court to direct the jury to bring forth a verdict of not guilty. Such a motion is based on the defense argument that the state has not presented enough evidence to prove its case. If the motion is sustained by the judge (it rarely is), the trial ends; if it is overruled, the defense presents its evidence.

The "*CSI* Effect" and Jurors' Expectations about Scientific Evidence

The CBS television network enjoys great success with three popular crime dramas entitled *CSI: Crime Scene Investigation* set in Las Vegas, Miami, and New York. Other networks emulated the success of CBS by creating their own shows, including *Bones* (Fox network) and *Body of Proof* (ABC), based on the scientific techniques for the investigation of crimes and the development of criminal evidence. The public's fascination with the forensic science portrayed in these television shows has led some prosecutors to complain about an escalation in jurors' unrealistic expectations about the necessity of presenting DNA analysis or other scientific evidence in order to establish guilt in each criminal trial. In reality, many criminal investigations and prosecutions are not based on DNA, fingerprints, or other scientific evidence. Instead, prosecutors present witness testimony and circumstantial evidence about a suspect's presence in a certain location and relationship with the victim. However, some prosecutors came to fear that jurors will not render a guilty verdict without the presentation of scientific evidence. Even if the purported "*CSI* effect" is a myth, if prosecutors are fearful of jurors' expectations, this might make prosecutors more reluctant to take cases to trial and thereby pressure them to offer more favorable plea agreements to the defendant.

Research on the so-called "*CSI* effect" raises questions about whether jurors are actually less inclined to convict defendants in the absence of scientific evidence. Surveys indicate that jurors may expect to see specific kinds of scientific evidence, but this expectation may be related to a more general "tech effect" of Americans using technology in their daily lives rather than watching specific television shows. Moreover, the increased expectation for scientific evidence does not necessarily mean that jurors will not vote to convict a defendant without it.

While the existence of a "*CSI* effect" continues to be debated by lawyers, judges, and scholars, prosecutors face a very real issue of deciding how, if at all, they will address the issue, just in case it affects jurors in a specific trial. One problem may be a lack of resources to actually gather and evaluate all potential scientific evidence for every case. For example, many crime labs have delays of many months due to backlogs for DNA evidence and other materials requiring scientific analysis. While a prosecutor might wait for definitive DNA testing on evidence in a murder case, should the same resources and time be devoted to analyzing all evidence in a burglary case? Prosecutors' options include educating jurors very directly about scientific evidence and why it may not exist in certain cases.

 Researching the Internet

Read about the National Institute of Justice's website. To link to the website, visit the Criminal Justice CourseMate at cengagebrain.com, then access the web links for this chapter.

For Critical Analysis

Should society devote substantial additional resources to the collection, analysis, and storage of scientific evidence for all criminal cases? In times of budget cuts at all levels of government, what other departments and programs should be cut in order to devote more resources to criminal justice investigations? List two arguments about what ought to be done or, alternatively, whether attempting to educate jurors about these issues will adequately address the matter.

Sources: Simon Cole and Rachel Dioso-Villa, "Investigating the '*CSI* Effect': Media and Litigation Crisis in Criminal Law," *Stanford Law Review* 61:1335–73 (2009); Laura Huey, "'I've Seen This On CSI': Criminal Investigators' Perceptions about the Management of Public Expectations in the Field," *Crime, Media, Culture* 6 (1): 49–68 (April 2010); Donald E. Shelton, "The '*CSI* Effect': Does It Really Exist?," *National Institute of Justice Journal* 259: March 2008 (www.nij.gov).

Presentation of the Defense's Evidence The defense is not required to answer the case presented by the prosecution. As it is the state's responsibility to prove the case beyond a reasonable doubt, it is theoretically possible—and in fact sometimes happens—that the defense rests its case immediately, as we have seen. Usually, however, the accused's attorney employs one strategy or a combination of three strategies: (1) contrary evidence is introduced to rebut or cast doubt on the state's case, (2) an alibi is offered, or (3) an affirmative defense is presented. As discussed in Chapter 3, defenses include self-defense, insanity, duress, and necessity.

A key issue for the defense is whether the accused will take the stand. The Fifth Amendment protection against self-incrimination means that the defendant does not have to testify. The Supreme Court has ruled that the prosecutor may not comment on, nor can the jury draw inferences from, the defendant's decision not to appear in his or her own defense. The decision is not made lightly, because if the defendant does testify, the prosecution may cross-examine. *Cross-examination*, which is questioning by the opposing attorney, is broader than direct examination.

The prosecutor may question the defendant not only about the crime but also about his or her past, including past criminal convictions. On the other hand, if the defendant does not testify, jurors may make assumptions about the defendant's guilt, even though they have been instructed not to do so.

When singer R. Kelly was acquitted of child pornography charges by a Chicago jury in 2008, the defense attorneys used every argument that they could, including arguments that were not consistent with each other (Streitfeld, 2008). Their objective was to cast doubt on the prosecution's case. The case hinged on whether a VHS tape showed Kelly having sex with a specific underage girl. The defense suggested that the tape showed another man who looked like Kelly, that computer manipulation had made the tape look like Kelly, or that the tape was made with models and prostitutes who looked like Kelly and the alleged victim. The defense attorneys did not need to prove Kelly's innocence; they just needed to raise questions in the jurors' minds about the accuracy of the prosecution's claims. R. Kelly never testified in court and thereby avoided cross-examination about any aspects of his private life and past behavior (St. Clair and Ataiyero, 2008).

Presentation of Rebuttal Witnesses   When the defense's case is complete, the prosecution may present witnesses whose testimony is designed to discredit or counteract testimony presented on behalf of the defendant. If the prosecution brings rebuttal witnesses, the defense has the opportunity to question them and to present new witnesses in rebuttal.

Closing Arguments by Each Side   When each side has completed its presentation of the evidence, the prosecution and defense make closing arguments to the jury. The attorneys review the evidence of the case for the jury, presenting interpretations of the evidence that favor their own side. The prosecutor may use the summation to connect the individual pieces of evidence in a way that forms a basis for concluding that the defendant is guilty. The defense may set forth the applicable law and try to show that the prosecution has not proved its case beyond a reasonable doubt. Each side may remind the jury of its duty to evaluate the evidence impartially and not to be swayed by emotion. Yet, some attorneys may hope that the jurors react emotionally, especially if they think that those emotions will benefit their side.

Judge's Instructions to the Jury   The jury decides the facts of the case, but the judge determines the law. Before the jurors depart for the jury room to decide the defendant's fate, the judge instructs them on how the law should guide their decision. The judge may discuss basic legal principles such as proof beyond a reasonable doubt, the legal requirements necessary to show that all the elements have been proved by the prosecution, or the rights of the defendant. More-specific aspects of the law bearing on the decision—such as complicated court rulings on the nature of the insanity defense or the ways certain types of evidence have been gathered—may be included in the judge's instructions. In complicated trials, the judge may spend an entire day instructing the jury.

The concept of **reasonable doubt** forms the heart of the jury system. As we have seen, the prosecution is not required to prove the guilt of the defendant beyond all doubt. Instead, if a juror is

> satisfied to a moral certainty that this defendant...is guilty of any one of the crimes charged here, you may safely say that you have been convinced beyond a reasonable doubt. If your mind is wavering, or if you are uncertain...you have not been convinced beyond a reasonable doubt and must render a verdict of not guilty. (S. Phillips, 1977:214)

Listening to the judge may become an ordeal for the jurors, who must hear and understand perhaps two or three hours of instruction on the law and the evidence (Bradley, 1992). It is assumed that somehow jurors will fully absorb these details on first hearing them, so that they will thoroughly understand how they are supposed to decide the case in the jury room (Kramer and Koenig, 1990). In fact, the length,

reasonable doubt The standard used by a jury to decide if the prosecution has provided enough evidence for conviction.

complexity, and legalistic content of jury instructions make them difficult for many jurors to comprehend (Daftary-Kapur, Dumas, and Penrod, 2010). The jurors may be confused by the instructions and reach a decision through an inaccurate understanding of the law that applies to the case, such as the legal definitions of intent, premeditation, and other elements of the crime that must be proved in order to justify a conviction (Bornstein and Green, 2011; Armour, 2008).

Decision by the Jury After they have heard the case and received the judge's instructions, the jurors retire to a room where they have complete privacy. They elect a foreperson to run the meeting, and deliberations begin. Until now, the jurors have been passive observers of the trial, unable to question witnesses or to discuss the case among themselves; now they can discuss the facts that have been presented. The jury may request that the judge reread to them portions of the instructions, ask for additional instructions, or hear portions of the transcript detailing what was said by specific witnesses.

Throughout their deliberations the jurors may be *sequestered*—kept together day and night, away from the influences of newspapers and conversations with family and friends. If jurors are allowed to spend nights at home, they are ordered not to discuss the case with anyone. The proliferation of cell phones, personal computers, and social media presents new problems for judges seeking to focus the jury's attention solely on information presented in court. Read "A Question of Ethics" at the end of the chapter to see how new laws take aim at jurors' improper use of technology to either gather or announce information about a trial.

If the jury becomes deadlocked and cannot reach a verdict, the trial ends with a hung jury and the prosecutor must decide whether to try the case over again in front of a new jury. When a verdict is reached, the judge, prosecution, and defense reassemble in the courtroom to hear it. The prosecution or the defense may request that the jury be polled: Each member individually tells his or her vote in open court. This procedure presumably ensures that no juror has felt pressured to agree with the other jurors.

Evaluating the Jury System

Individual jurors differ in their processing of information and interactions with others (Gunnell and Ceci, 2010). A classic study at the University of Chicago Law School found that, consistent with theories of group behavior, participation and influence in the jury process are related to social status. Men were found to be more active participants than were women, whites more active than minority members, and the better educated more active than those less educated. Much of the discussion in the jury room was not directly concerned with the testimony but rather with trial procedures, opinions about the witnesses, and personal reminiscences (Strodtbeck, James, and Hawkins, 1957). Recent research has reinforced these results (Cornwell and Hans, 2011). Because of group pressure, only rarely did a single juror produce a hung jury (Sundby, 2010). Some jurors may doubt their own views or go along with the others if everyone else disagrees with them. Additional studies have upheld the importance of group pressure on decision making (Hastie, Penrod, and Pennington, 1983).

An examination of trials in the 75 largest counties found that 76 percent of jury trials ended in convictions, compared with 82 percent of bench trials (Kyckelhahn and Cohen, 2008). These numbers alone do not reveal whether judges and juries decide cases differently. However, research on trials provides clues about differences between these two decision makers.

Juries tend to take a more liberal view of such issues as self-defense than do judges and are likely to minimize the seriousness of an offense if they dislike some characteristic of the victim (S. J. Adler, 1994). For example, if the victim of an assault is a prostitute, the jury may minimize the assault. Perceived characteristics of the defendant may also influence jurors' assessments of guilt (Abwender and Hough, 2001). Judges have more experience with the justice process. They are more likely than juries to convict defendants based on evidence that researchers characterize as moderately strong (Eisenberg et al., 2005). As explained by the premier jury researchers Valerie Hans and Neil Vidmar (2008: 227):

> [T]he jury's distinctive approach of common sense justice, and the judges' greater willingness to convict based on the same evidence, best explain why juries and judges sometimes reach different conclusions. These juror values affect the verdicts primarily in trials in which the evidence is relatively evenly balanced and a verdict for either side could be justified.

In recent years, the American Bar Association and other groups have worked to introduce reforms that might improve the quality of juries' decision making (Post, 2004). For example, some courts now permit jurors to take notes during trials and submit questions that they would like to see asked of witnesses (Bornstein and Greene, 2011). Other courts permit jurors to submit questions to the judge during the trial (Mardar, 2010). There are also efforts to make judges' instructions to the jury more understandable through less reliance on legal terminology. It is hoped that jurors can make better decisions if they have more information and a better understanding of the law and the issues in a case.

---

check point

9. **What functions do juries serve in the criminal justice system?**
Safeguard citizens against arbitrary law enforcement, determine the guilt of the accused, represent diverse community interests and values, serve as buffer between accused and accuser, become educated about the justice system, and symbolize the law.

10. **What is voir dire?**
The jury selection process in which lawyers and/or judges ask questions of prospective jurors and make decisions about using peremptory challenges and challenges for cause to shape the jury's composition.

11. **What are the stages in the trial process?**
Jury selection, attorneys' opening statements, presentation of prosecution's evidence, presentation of defense's evidence, presentation of rebuttal witnesses, closing arguments by each side, judge's instructions to the jury, and jury's decision.

stop & analyze

If you were charged with tax evasion, would you prefer a trial in front of a judge or jury? Why? Would you make a different choice if you were charged with injuring a small child when texting while driving?

Appeals

Imposition of a sentence does not mean that the case is necessarily over; the defendant typically has the right to appeal the verdict to a higher court, and the right to counsel continues through the first appeal (Heise, 2009). Some states have limited the right to appeal when defendants plead guilty. An **appeal** is based on a claim that one or more errors of law or procedure were made during the investigation, arrest, or trial process (C. E. Smith, 2000b). Such claims usually assert that the trial judge made errors in courtroom rulings or by improperly admitting

appeal A request to a higher court that it review actions taken in a trial court.

evidence that the police gathered in violation of some constitutional right. A defendant might base an appeal, for example, on the claim that the judge did not instruct the jury correctly or that a guilty plea was not made voluntarily.

Appeals are based on questions of procedure, not on issues of the defendant's guilt or innocence. The appellate court will not normally second-guess a jury. Instead, it will check to make sure that the trial followed proper procedures (Shay, 2009). If there were significant errors in the trial, then the conviction is set aside. The defendant may be tried again if the prosecutor decides to pursue the case again. Thus a successful appeal may merely lead to reconviction on the charges in a second trial.

AP Images/Bob Child

In appellate courts, several judges sit as a group to hear and decide cases. The appeals process provides an opportunity to correct errors that occurred in trial court proceedings. What are the advantages and disadvantages of having a group of appeals court judges decide a case together?

Most criminal defendants must file an appeal shortly after trial to have an appellate court review the case. By contrast, many states provide for an automatic appeal in death penalty cases (Alarcon, 2007). The quality of defense representation is important, because the appeal must usually meet short deadlines and carefully identify appropriate issues (Wasserman, 1990).

A case originating in a state court is first appealed through that state's judicial system. When a state case involves a federal constitutional question, however, a later appeal can go to the U.S. Supreme Court. State courts decide almost four-fifths of all appeals.

Most appeals do not succeed in gaining either a new trial, a new sentence, or an outright acquittal. In almost 80 percent of the cases examined in one study (Chapper and Hanson, 1989), the decision of the trial courts was affirmed. Most of the other decisions produced new trials or resentencing; very few decisions (1.9 percent) produced acquittals on appeal.

Habeas Corpus

After people use their avenues of appeal, they may pursue a writ of habeas corpus if they claim that their federal constitutional rights were violated during the lower-court processes (King and Hoffmann, 2011). Known as "the great writ" from its traditional role in English law and its enshrinement in the U.S. Constitution, **habeas corpus** is a judicial order requesting that a judge examine whether an individual is being properly detained in a jail, prison, or mental hospital. If there is no legal basis for the person to be held, then the judge may grant the writ and order the person to be released. In the context of criminal justice, convicted offenders claim that their imprisonment is improper because one of their constitutional rights was violated during the investigation or adjudication of their case. Statutes permit offenders convicted in both state and federal courts to pursue habeas corpus actions in the federal courts. After first seeking favorable decisions by state appellate courts, convicted offenders can start their constitutional claims anew in the federal district courts and subsequently pursue their habeas cases in the federal circuit courts of appeal and the U.S. Supreme Court.

Overall, only about 1 percent of habeas petitions succeed (Flango, 1994). In one study, less than one-half of one percent of noncapital habeas petitioners gained a

habeas corpus A writ or judicial order requesting the release of a person being detained in a jail, prison, or mental hospital. If a judge finds the person is being held improperly, the writ may be granted and the person released.

favorable judicial decision but more than 12 percent of habeas petitioners in death penalty cases demonstrated a rights violation (King, Cheesman, and Ostrom, 2007). One reason may be that an individual has no right to be represented by counsel when pursuing a habeas corpus petition. Few offenders have sufficient knowledge of law and legal procedures to identify and present constitutional claims effectively in the federal courts (Hanson and Daley, 1995).

In 1996, the Antiterrorism and Effective Death Penalty Act placed additional restrictions on habeas corpus petitions. The statute was quickly approved by the U.S. Supreme Court. These reforms were based, in part, on a belief that prisoners' cases were clogging the federal courts (C. E. Smith, 1995). Ironically, habeas corpus petitions in the federal courts have increased by 50 percent since the passage of the restrictive legislation (Scalia, 2002). By imposing strict filing deadlines for petitions, the legislation may have inadvertently focused more prisoners' attention on the existence of habeas corpus and thereby encouraged them to move forward with petitions in order to meet the deadlines.

Evaluating the Appellate Process

The public seems to believe that many offenders are being "let off" through the appellate process. Some critics have argued that opportunities for appeal should be limited. They claim that too many offenders delay imposition of their sentences and that others completely evade punishment by filing appeals endlessly. This practice not only increases the workload of the courts but also jeopardizes the concept of the finality of the justice process. However, given that 90 percent of accused persons plead guilty, the number of cases that might be appealed is relatively small.

The appeals process performs the important function of righting wrongs. It also helps ensure consistency in the application of law by judges in different courts. Beyond that, its presence constantly influences the daily operations of the criminal justice system, as prosecutors and trial judges must consider how a higher court might later evaluate their decisions and actions.

check point >

12. How does the appellate court's job differ from that of the trial court?

Unlike trial courts, which have juries, hear evidence, and decide if the defendant is guilty or not guilty, appellate courts focus only on claimed errors of law or procedure in trial court proceedings. Victory for a defendant in a trial court means an acquittal and instant freedom. Victory in an appellate court may mean only a chance at a new trial—which often leads to a new conviction.

13. What is a habeas corpus petition?

The habeas corpus process may be started after all appeals have been filed and lost. Convicted offenders ask a federal court to review whether any constitutional rights were violated during the course of a case investigation and trial. If rights were violated, the person's continued detention in prison or jail may be improper.

stop& analyze

Do criminal offenders have too many opportunities to challenge convictions? List two benefits and two costs of having an appeals process and a habeas corpus process.

Think, Discuss, Write

The everyday usage of personal technology and social media has invaded the jury box and is affecting criminal trials. Judges around the country now warn jurors that they may not check their cell phones during trials or tweet updates about the trial. Moreover, jurors are not allowed to go online during breaks in order to carry out their own investigations about the case or to read commentary about it. There have been some instances where jurors looked online for information about the defendant's background or details of the crime that were not presented in evidence in court. The use of these outside sources violates the rules of evidence and court procedure. Jurors are supposed to remain open-minded and rely solely on the evidence presented by the attorneys for each side. If jurors gather outside information or post information about the trial on Facebook, judges may be forced to declare a mistrial, necessitating a new trial with a new jury. Such consequences are very costly in terms of time and money for the court. The California legislature became so concerned about the problems that it created a new law, effective in 2012, authorizing judges to send jurors to jail for contempt of court if they disobey court instructions concerning electronic devices in court, including not posting updates on social media and not looking online for information about the case.

Discussion/Writing Assignment

If you were a juror hearing testimony during a trial and you noticed a fellow juror slyly holding his smartphone under the bottom of his jacket, what would you do? Does it matter if you have no idea whether the other juror is just checking his text messages or merely checking the time? What if the testimony in the trial made it obvious to you that the defendant was clearly guilty of the crime? Would you feel any pressure to avoid triggering a mistrial by reporting the other juror? Write a description of the factors, if any, that would guide your decision about what to do. Also describe whether you would take action and, if so, what action.

Sources: Bob Egelko, "Jurors to Be Told Not to Tweet under New Law," *San Francisco Chronicle*, August 6, 2011 (www.sfgate.com); Stephanie Francis Ward, "Tweeting Jurors to Face Jail Time with New California Law," *American Bar Association Journal Daily News*, August 8, 2011 (www.abajournal.com).

summary

Understand the pretrial process in criminal cases

→ Pretrial processes determine the fates of nearly all defendants through case dismissals, decisions defining charges, and plea bargains, all of which affect more than 90 percent of cases.

→ Defense attorneys use motions to their advantage to gain information and delay proceedings to benefit their clients.

Recognize how the bail system operates

→ The bail process provides opportunities for many defendants to gain pretrial release, but poor defendants may be disadvantaged by their inability to come up with the money or property needed to secure release. Some preventive detention statutes permit judges to hold defendants considered dangerous or likely to flee.

→ Bail agents, also known as bail bondsmen, are private businesspeople who charge a fee to provide money for defendants' pretrial release. Their activities create risks of corruption and discrimination in the bail process, but bail agents may also help the system by reminding defendants about court dates.

→ Although judges bear the primary responsibility for setting bail, prosecutors are especially influential in recommending amounts and conditions for pretrial release.

→ Initiatives to reform the bail process include police-issued citations, release on own recognizance (ROR), percentage bail, bail guidelines, and preventive detention.

Understand the context of pretrial detention

→ Despite the presumption of innocence, pretrial detainees endure difficult conditions in jails that often contain mixed populations of convicted offenders, detainees, and troubled people. The shock of being jailed creates risks of suicide and depression.

Analyze how and why plea bargaining occurs

→ Most convictions are obtained through plea bargaining, a process that exists because it fulfills the self-interest of prosecutors, judges, defense attorneys, and defendants.

→ Plea bargaining is facilitated by exchange relations between prosecutors and defense attorneys. In many courthouses, there is little actual bargaining, as outcomes are determined through the implicit bargaining process of settling the facts and assessing the going rate of punishment according to the standards of the local legal culture.

→ Plea bargaining has been criticized for pressuring defendants to surrender their rights and for reducing the sentences imposed on offenders.

Know why cases go to trial and how juries are chosen

→ Americans tend to presume that, through the dramatic courtroom battle of prosecutors and defense attorneys, trials are the best way to discover the truth about a criminal case.

→ Only about 5 percent of cases go to trial, and half of those are typically bench trials in front of a judge, not jury trials.

→ Typically, cases go to trial because they involve defendants who are wealthy enough to pay attorneys to fight to the very end or because they involve charges that are too serious to create incentives for plea bargaining.

→ Juries serve vital functions for society by preventing arbitrary action by prosecutors and judges, educating citizens about the justice system, symbolizing the rule of law, and involving citizens from diverse segments of the community in judicial decision making.

→ The U.S. Supreme Court has ruled that juries need not be made up of 12 members, and 12-member juries can, if permitted by state law, convict defendants by a less-than-unanimous super-majority vote.

Identify the stages of a criminal trial

→ The trial process consists of a series of steps: jury selection, opening statements, presentation of prosecution's evidence, presentation of defense's evidence, presentation of rebuttal witnesses, closing arguments, judge's jury instructions, and jury's decision.

→ The jury selection process, especially in the formation of the jury pool and the exercise of peremptory challenges, often creates juries that do not fully represent all segments of a community.

→ Rules of evidence dictate what kinds of information may be presented in court for consideration by the jury. Types of evidence are real evidence, demonstrative evidence, testimony, direct evidence, and circumstantial evidence.

Understand the basis for an appeal of a conviction

→ Convicted offenders have the opportunity to appeal, although defendants who plead guilty, unlike those convicted through a trial, often have few grounds for an appeal.

→ Appeals focus on claimed errors of law or procedure in the investigation by police and prosecutors, or in the decisions by trial judges. Relatively few offenders win their appeals, and most who do simply gain an opportunity for a new trial, not release from jail or prison.

→ After convicted offenders have used all of their appeals, they may file a habeas corpus petition to seek federal judicial review of claimed constitutional rights violations in their cases. Very few of such petitions succeed.

Questions for Review

1. What is bail and how has it been reformed to limit its traditionally harsh impact on poor defendants?
2. Why are some defendants held in pretrial detention?
3. Why does plea bargaining exist?
4. Given that there are so few jury trials, what types of cases would you expect to find adjudicated in this manner? Why?
5. What is the purpose of the appeals process?

Key Terms and Cases

appeal (p. 268)

arraignment (p. 245)

bail (p. 247)

bench trials (p. 259)

challenge for cause (p. 263)

circumstantial evidence (p. 264)

citation (p. 250)

demonstrative evidence (p. 263)

direct evidence (p. 264)

habeas corpus (p. 269)

jury (p. 259)

motion (p. 245)

percentage bail (p. 251)

peremptory challenge (p. 263)

preventive detention (p. 252)

real evidence (p. 263)

reasonable doubt (p. 266)

release on recognizance
(ROR) (p. 251)

testimony (p. 263)

voir dire (p. 262)

Bordenkircher v. Hayes
(1978) (p. 258)

Boykin v. Alabama (1969) (p. 257)

Missouri v. Frye (2012) (p. 257)

North Carolina v. Alford
(1970) (p. 258)

Ricketts v. Adamson (1987) (p. 258)

Santobello v. New York
(1971) (p. 255)

*United States v. Salerno
and Cafero* (1987) (p. 252)

Williams v. Florida (1970) (p. 261)

THIS ENTRANC
FOR FEDERAL
EMPLOYEES
INCLUDING
HANDICAPPED
FEDERAL
EMPLOYEES

9

Punishment and Sentencing

Learning Objectives

→ Recognize the goals of punishment

→ Identify the types of sentences judges can impose

→ Understand what really happens in sentencing

→ Analyze whether the system treats wrongdoers equally

In the final weeks of 2011, several nationally publicized criminal cases reached their conclusions as judges in New York, Chicago, and Los Angeles imposed sentences on offenders convicted amid the glare of television lights and the constant commentary of talk-show hosts. Because the accused were public figures, their sentences help illuminate the purposes of punishment in the American criminal justice system; but they also raise difficult questions about the appropriateness and fairness of prison sentences imposed on people convicted of different offenses.

In New York City, U.S. District Judge Richard Holwell imposed a sentence of 11 years in federal prison, a $10 million fine, and the forfeiture of $53.8 million on Raj Rajaratnam, the head of an investment hedge fund who illegally used inside information from tipsters within corporations to reap profits from his investments. Observers regarded this as the longest prison sentence ever for using insider information to illegally make investments, although longer sentences had been imposed previously on investment executives who directly stole money from their clients (Lattman, 2011). In this case, Rajaratnam did not directly steal money from any specific individuals; however, he broke the law when he used unfair insider knowledge to

his own advantage when deciding which corporations' stock to purchase for investment. In imposing a sentence that was less than the 19- to 24-year sentence requested by prosecutors, Judge Holwell said he was taking into consideration Rajaratnam's "good works" in generously contributing financial assistance for victims of a tsunami in the country of Sri Lanka as well as for victims of the terrorist attacks on New York City on September 11, 2001 (Lattman, 2011).

Former Illinois Governor Rod Blagojevich was sentenced to 14 years in federal prison by U.S. District Judge James Zagel. Blagojevich was convicted of 18 corruption charges, including that of seeking to sell the U.S. senate seat vacated when former Illinois Senator Barack Obama was elected to the presidency in 2008. The jury listened to recordings from telephone wiretaps as well as other secret recordings in which then-Governor Blagojevich was heard illegally seeking campaign donations in exchange for the Senate appointment. Other recordings served as evidence of his efforts to affect state policies related to hospitals and a racetrack (M. Davey, 2011). Although Blagojevich had maintained his innocence through the trial, at his sentencing hearing he apologized for his action and said, "I have nobody to blame but myself for my stupidity and actions, words, things that I did, that I thought I could do" (M. Davey, 2011). In imposing the sentence, Judge Zagel alluded to a history of political corruption among Illinois politicians in saying: "The harm here is not measured in the value of property or money, . . . The harm is the erosion of public trust in government" (M. Davey, 2011).

In contrast to the long federal prison sentences imposed on Blagojevich and Rajaratnam, in Los Angeles, Dr. Conrad Murray received the maximum-allowable sentence of four years in state custody for involuntary manslaughter, with the recognition that he would serve only half of the sentence because new California laws addressing prison costs and overcrowding had reduced requirements for the actual time to be served by offenders. Murray was convicted for his role in the death of superstar singer Michael Jackson. The court heard that Murray had improperly administered a powerful sedative drug while caring for Jackson at the star's home. The drug Murray used was one that is typically administered only in hospitals under close supervision. The jury also heard evidence that Murray had failed to call 911 immediately when Jackson slipped into unconsciousness and died (Medina, 2011).

The outcomes of these criminal cases bring up many questions about the role of sentencing in the criminal justice system. Did these sentences achieve justice? Did they appropriately advance society's goals? Which goals? For example, should causing a person's death draw a markedly shorter sentence than crimes involving illegal campaign contributions or violations of laws about investing money? Were the sentences for Blagojevich and Rajaratnam largely intended to frighten other politicians and investment executives from engaging in illegal activities? Or were the sentences focused solely on punishing these two offenders for their specific crimes? As such questions indicate, criminal behavior may produce a wide range of punishments that depend on the goals being pursued by officials who make laws and determine sentences.

The criminal justice system aims to solve three basic issues: (1) What conduct is criminal? (2) What determines guilt? and (3) What should be done with the guilty? Earlier chapters emphasized the first two questions. The answers given by the legal system to the first question compose the basic rules of society: Do not murder, rob, sell drugs, commit treason, and so forth. The law also spells out the process for determining guilt or innocence; however, the administrative and interpersonal considerations of the actors in the criminal justice system greatly affect this process. In this chapter, we begin to examine the third problem: sanction and punishment. First, we consider the four goals of punishment: retribution, deterrence, incapacitation, and rehabilitation. We then explore the forms punishment takes to achieve its goals. These are incarceration, intermediate sanctions, probation, and death. Finally, we look at the sentencing process and how it affects punishment.

The Goals of Punishment

Criminal sanctions in the United States have four main goals: retribution (deserved punishment), deterrence, incapacitation, and rehabilitation. Ultimately, all criminal punishment aims at maintaining the social order, but the justifications for sentencing proceed from the American values of justice and fairness. There is no universal agreement, however, on how to make the severity of punishment just and fair. Further, the justice sought by crime victims often conflicts with fairness to offenders.

Punishments reflect the dominant values of a particular moment in history. By the end of the 1960s, for example, the number of Americans who were sentenced to imprisonment decreased because of a widespread commitment to rehabilitating offenders. By contrast, since the mid-1970s an emphasis on imposing strong punishments for the purposes of retribution, deterrence, and incapacitation has resulted in record numbers of offenders being sentenced to prison. At the beginning of the twenty-first century, voices are calling for the addition of *restorative justice* as a fifth goal of the criminal sanction.

Retribution—Deserved Punishment

Retribution is punishment inflicted on a person who has harmed other people and so deserves to be penalized (Cahill, 2007b). The biblical expression "An eye for an eye, a tooth for a tooth" illustrates the philosophy underlying this kind of punishment. Retribution means that those who commit a particular crime should be punished alike, in proportion to the gravity of the offense or to the suffering it has caused others. Retribution is deserved punishment; offenders must "pay their debts."

retribution Punishment inflicted on a person who has harmed others and so deserves to be penalized.

Some scholars claim that the desire for retribution is a basic human emotion. They maintain that if the state does not provide retributive sanctions to reflect community revulsion at offensive acts, citizens will take the law into their own hands to punish offenders. Under this view, the failure of government to satisfy the people's desire for retribution could produce social chaos.

This argument may not be valid for all crimes, however. If a rapist is inadequately punished, then the victim's family and other members of the community may be tempted to exact their own retribution. But what about a young adult smoking marijuana? If the government failed to impose retribution for this offense, would the community care? The same apathy may hold true for offenders who commit other nonviolent crimes that modestly impact society. Even in these seemingly trivial situations, however, retribution may serve as a necessary public reminder of the general rules of law and the important values they protect.

Since the late 1970s, retribution as a justification for the criminal sanction has aroused new interest, largely because of dissatisfaction with the philosophical basis and practical results of rehabilitation. Using the concept of "just deserts or deserved punishment" to define retribution, some theorists argue that one who infringes on the rights of others deserves to be punished. This approach rests on the philosophical view that punishment is a moral response to harm inflicted on society (Bronsteen, 2010). In effect, these theorists believe that basic morality demands that wrongdoers be punished (von Hirsch, 1976). According to this view, punishment should be applied only for the wrong inflicted and not primarily to achieve other goals such as deterrence, incapacitation, or rehabilitation.

Deterrence

Many people see criminal punishment as a basis for affecting the future choices and behavior of individuals. Politicians frequently talk about being "tough on crime" to send a message to would-be criminals. The roots of this approach, called *deterrence*, lie in eighteenth-century England among the followers of social philosopher Jeremy Bentham.

Bentham was struck by what seemed to be the pointlessness of retribution. His fellow reformers adopted Bentham's theory of utilitarianism, which holds that human behavior is governed by the individual's calculation of the benefits versus the costs of his or her acts. Before stealing money or property, for example, potential offenders would consider the punishment that others have received for similar acts and would thereby be deterred.

There are two types of deterrence. **General deterrence** presumes that members of the general public, on observing the punishments of others, will conclude that the costs of crime outweigh the benefits. For general deterrence to be effective, the public must receive constant reminders of the likelihood and severity of punishment for various acts. They must believe that they will be caught, prosecuted, and given a specific punishment if they commit a particular crime. Moreover, the punishment must be severe enough to instill fear of the consequences of committing crimes. For example, Jim Cramer, a close observer of Wall Street executives and the host of the CNBC show, *Mad Money*, commented on the reaction of corporate executives to the sentences imposed on Rod Blagojevich and Raj Rajaratnam. According to Cramer, "It took their collective breaths away. . . . They are still reeling from the Raj sentence. . . . Nothing scares these guys more than jail time" (J. Warren, 2011). Whether or not Cramer is correct, there are some judges who believe that there is a general-deterrence benefit from stiff sentences for high-profile offenders. Yet not all judges share that view, as one news reporter noted when he asked two judges about whether high-profile sentences can deter people seeking to advance their own greed for money and power. According to the reporter, both judges laughed and one said, "Deter greed, eh? . . . Good luck!" (J. Warren, 2011).

By contrast, **specific deterrence** targets the decisions and behavior of offenders who have already been convicted. Under this approach, the amount and kind of punishment are calculated to discourage that criminal from repeating the offense. The punishment must be severe enough to cause the criminal to say, "The consequences of my crime were too painful. I will not commit another crime, because I do not want to risk being punished again." As you can see in "What Americans Think," many people have doubts about specific deterrence and its potential impact on many lawbreakers.

The concept of deterrence presents obvious difficulties (Stafford and Warr, 1993). Deterrence assumes that all people think before they act. As such, deterrence does not account for the many people who commit crimes while under the influence of drugs or alcohol, or those whose harmful behavior stems from psychological problems or mental illness. Deterrence also does not account for people who act impulsively when stealing or damaging property. In other cases, the low probability

Tim Boyle/Bloomberg via Getty Images

⬆ The fourteen-year sentence imposed on former Illinois Governor Rod Blagojevich for corrupt activities while in office was considered by many observers to be a surprisingly long sentence. Some people believe that such stiff sentences will have a general deterrent effect and prevent misconduct by other elected officials. Other people believe that greed is such a powerful motive that many people violate the law despite the risks involved. Are there any particular types of crimes that are likely to be prevented when people hear about harsh sentences for those offenses?

general deterrence
Punishment of criminals that is intended to be an example to the general public and to discourage the commission of offenses.

specific deterrence
Punishment inflicted on criminals to discourage them from committing future crimes.

of being caught defeats both general and specific deterrence. To be generally deterrent, punishment must be perceived as relatively fast, certain, and severe. See "Criminal Justice: Myth & Reality" to explore the problems underlying fulfillment of the deterrence goal.

Knowledge of the effectiveness of deterrence is limited as well (Kleck et al., 2005). For example, social science cannot measure the effects of general deterrence, because only those who are not deterred come to the attention of researchers. A study of the deterrent effects of punishment would have to examine the impact of different forms of the criminal sanction on various potential lawbreakers. How can we truly determine how many people—or even if any people—stopped themselves from committing a crime for any reason, let alone because they were deterred by the prospect of prosecution and punishment? Therefore, although legislators often cite deterrence as a rationale for certain sanctions, no one really knows the extent to which sentencing policies based on deterrence achieve their objectives. Because contemporary U.S. society has shown little ability to reduce crime by imposing increasingly severe sanctions, the effectiveness of deterrence for many crimes and criminals should be questioned (Tonry, 2008).

Question: "Would you agree or disagree that serving time in prison or jail reduces the likelihood a person will commit more crime in the future?"

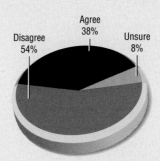

Agree 38%

Disagree 54%

Unsure 8%

Critical Thinking: If specific deterrence is ineffective, then what other goal or goals—general deterrence, retribution, incapacitation, or rehabilitation—should be emphasized in determining what punishments to impose on criminal offenders?

Source: Christopher Hartney and Susan Marchionna, "Attitudes of U.S. Voters toward Nonserious Offenders and Alternatives to Incarceration," *Focus: Views from the National Council on Crime and Delinquency*, Washington, DC: NCCD (June 2009), p. 4.

Incapacitation

Incapacitation assumes that society can use detention in prison or execution to keep offenders from committing further crimes. Many people express such sentiments, urging officials to "lock 'em up and throw away the key!" In primitive societies, banishment from the community was the usual method of incapacitation. In earlier periods of American history, offenders often agreed to move away or to join the army as an alternative to some other form of punishment. In the United States today, imprisonment serves as the usual method of incapacitation. Offenders can be confined within secure institutions and effectively prevented from committing additional harm against society for the duration of their sentence. Capital punishment is the ultimate method of incapacitation. Any sentence that physically restricts an offender may incapacitate the person, even when the underlying purpose of the sentence is retribution, deterrence, or rehabilitation.

Sentences based on incapacitation are future oriented. Whereas retribution requires focusing on the harmful act of the offender, incapacitation looks at the offender's potential actions. If the offender is likely to commit future crimes, then the judge may impose a severe sentence—even for a relatively minor crime.

For example, under the incapacitation theory, a woman who kills her abusive husband as an emotional reaction to his verbal insults and physical assaults could receive a light sentence. As a one-time impulse killer who felt driven to kill by unique circumstances, she is not likely to commit additional crimes. By contrast, a woman who shoplifts merchandise and has been convicted of the offense on ten previous occasions may receive a severe sentence. In a case like this, the criminal record and type of crime indicate that she will commit additional crimes if released. Thus, incapacitation focuses on characteristics of the offenders instead of aspects of their offenses.

incapacitation Depriving an offender of the ability to commit crimes against society, usually by detaining the offender in prison.

Common Belief: Long sentences will deter people from committing crimes, because they will stop themselves from causing harm to society out of fear of the severe punishments that await them.

- Effective deterrence requires two elements: (1) potential offenders must think rationally, weighing the costs and benefits of crimes before committing criminal acts, and (2) potential offenders must fear that they will be caught.
- In fact, many offenders do not think rationally. They act impulsively in deciding to rob someone or steal an item from a store. They may also be driven by substance-abuse problems that cloud their ability to think rationally and/or create an immediate need for money in order to obtain drugs and alcohol.
- In addition, many offenders do not believe that they will be caught. They erroneously believe that they are smarter than the police or that they are committing their crime in a manner that will let them escape without being apprehended.
- When offenders are overconfident about their ability to get away with crimes, then deterrence is unlikely to prevent them from committing illegal acts.
- Moreover, some offenders do not fear the prospect of prison. They regard stretches in prison as merely an inevitable part of their lives.
- All of the foregoing factors mean that legislators should not assume that severe sentences will have a deterrent effect, even if they themselves think, "I would never commit crimes if sentences were long and mandatory."

Does it offend your sense of justice that a person could receive a severer sentence for shoplifting than for manslaughter? This question embodies one of the criticisms of incapacitation. Questions also arise about how to determine the length of sentence. Presumably, offenders will not be released until the state is reasonably sure that they will no longer commit crimes. However, can we accurately predict any person's behavior? Moreover, on what grounds can we punish people for anticipated behavior that we cannot accurately predict? In addition, there are questions about whether incapacitative policies will lead to an overall reduction in crime rates if there are other social forces that continue to foster criminal behavior among people living in various contexts in American society (Stahlkopf, Males, and Macallair, 2010).

In recent years, greater attention has been paid to the concept of **selective incapacitation**, whereby offenders who repeat certain kinds of crimes receive long prison terms. Research has suggested that a relatively small number of offenders commit a large number of violent and property crimes (Clear, 1994). Burglars, for example, tend to commit many offenses before they are caught. Thus, these "career criminals" should be locked up for long periods (Auerhahn, 1999). Such policies could be costly, however. Not only would correctional facilities have to be expanded, but the number of expensive, time-consuming trials also might increase if severer sentences caused more repeat offenders to plead not guilty. Another difficulty with this policy is that we cannot accurately predict which offenders will commit more crimes upon release (Vitiello, 2008).

selective incapacitation Making the best use of expensive and limited prison space by targeting for incarceration those individuals whose incapacity will do the most to reduce crime in society.

rehabilitation The goal of restoring a convicted offender to a constructive place in society through some form of vocational or educational training or therapy.

Rehabilitation

Rehabilitation refers to the goal of restoring a convicted offender to a constructive place in society through some form of training or therapy. Americans want to believe that offenders can be treated and resocialized in ways that allow them to lead a crime-free, productive life upon release. Over the last hundred years, rehabilitation advocates have argued for techniques that they claim identify and treat the causes of criminal behavior. If the offender's criminal behavior is assumed to result from some social, psychological, or biological imperfection, the treatment of the disorder becomes the primary goal of corrections.

Rehabilitation focuses on the offender. Its objective does not imply any consistent relationship between the severity of the punishment and the gravity of the crime. People who commit lesser offenses can receive long prison sentences if experts believe effective rehabilitation requires it. By contrast, a murderer might win early release by showing signs that the psychological or emotional problems that led to the killing have been corrected.

According to the concept of rehabilitation, offenders are treated, not punished, and they will return to society when they are "cured." Consequently, if adhering to this philosophy, judges should not set fixed sentences but rather ones with maximum and minimum terms so that parole boards can release inmates when they have been rehabilitated.

From the 1940s until the 1970s, the goal of rehabilitation was so widely accepted that treatment and reform of the offender were generally regarded as the only issues worth serious attention. Crime was assumed to be caused by problems affecting individuals, and modern social sciences had the tools to address those problems. During the past 30 years, however, researchers and others have questioned the assumptions of the rehabilitation model. Studies of the results of rehabilitation programs have challenged the idea that criminal offenders can be cured (Martinson, 1974). Moreover, scholars no longer take for granted that crime is caused by identifiable, curable problems such as poverty, lack of job skills, low self-esteem, and hostility toward authority. Instead, some argue that we cannot identify the cause of criminal behavior for individual offenders.

During the first decade of the twenty-first century, rehabilitation reemerged as a goal of corrections. As we shall see in Chapter 13, it came to be discussed and applied through the concept of "reentry" rather than through a declaration that rehabilitation is a primary goal of the justice system (Butterfield, 2004a). States and the federal government endured significant financial costs through the expansion of prison systems and the growth of prison populations, caused by the imposition of severer prison sentences during the preceding two decades. Eventually, they confronted the reality that hundreds of thousands of prisoners were returning to society each year after serving long sentences. In addition, as governments at all levels experienced budget crises, officials sought ways to reduce prison populations. Thus, policies and programs emerged that were intended to prepare offenders for successful integration into society (Eckholm, 2008b). These programs are rehabilitative in nature, by providing education, counseling, skill training, and other services to help change offenders' behavior and prospects for success in society. Public opinion generally supports efforts to reform offenders through such rehabilitative efforts (Cullen, 2007).

Restorative justice seeks to repair the damage done to the victim and community by an offender's criminal act. Here, Susanna Kay Cooper sits next to David Lee Myers as she looks at the photo of his dead wife. Cooper pled guilty to vehicular homicide in the death of Elaine Myers, received a 34-month prison sentence, and agreed to enter into talks with the victim's family.

A New Approach to Punishment: Restorative Justice

In keeping with the focus on community justice for police, courts, and corrections, many people are calling for **restorative justice** to be added to the goals of the criminal sanction (Basemore and Umbreit, 1994; J. Braithwaite, 2007). The restorative justice perspective views crime as more than a violation of penal law. The criminal act practically and symbolically denies community. It breaks trust among citizens and requires community members to determine how "to contradict the moral message of the crime that the offender is above the law and the victim beneath its reach" (Clear and Karp, 1999:85). Crime victims suffer losses involving damage to property and self. The primary aim of criminal justice should be to repair these losses (Waldman, 2007). Crime also challenges the heart of community, to the extent that community life depends on a shared sense of trust, fairness, and interdependence.

Shifting the focus to restorative justice requires a three-way approach that involves the offender, the victim, and the community. This approach may include mediation in which the three actors devise a punishment that all agree is fair and just, by which the offender can try to repair the harm done to victims and community. Communities in Vermont have well-established restorative justice programs through which alternative punishments, public apologies, restitution, and interaction between offenders and victims seek to advance both accountability and restoration (Dzur, 2011). This new approach to criminal justice means that losses suffered by the crime victim are restored, the threat to local safety is removed, and the offender again becomes a fully participating member of the community. As yet, restorative justice represents a small minority of sanctions. To see how the four main punishment goals might be enacted in real life, consider again the sentencing of

restorative justice
Punishment designed to repair the damage done to the victim and community by an offender's criminal act.

TABLE 9.1 The Goals of Punishment

At sentencing, the judge usually gives reasons for the punishments imposed. Here are statements that Judge James Zagel might have given former Illinois Governor Rod Blagojevich, each promoting a different goal for the sanction.

Goal	Judge's Possible Statement
Retribution	I am imposing this sentence because you deserve to be punished for the harm to our democratic system of government caused by violating laws concerning political corruption. Your criminal behavior is the basis of the punishment. Justice requires that I impose a sanction at a level that illustrates the importance that the community places on government officials' compliance with anticorruption laws.
Deterrence	I am imposing this sentence so that your punishment for corruption will serve as an example and deter others who may contemplate similar actions. In addition, I hope that this sentence will deter you from ever again committing an illegal act.
Incapacitation	I am imposing this sentence so that you will be incapacitated and hence unable to engage in political corruption in the free community during the length of this term.
Rehabilitation	The trial testimony and information contained in the presentence report make me believe that there are aspects of your personality that led to the political corruption. I am therefore imposing this sentence so that you can receive treatment that will rectify your behavior so you will not commit another crime.

© Cengage Learning

former Governor Rod Blagojevich for political corruption. Table 9.1 shows various hypothetical sentencing statements that the judge might have given, depending on prevailing correctional goals.

As we next consider how such goals are expressed though the various forms of punishment, keep in mind the underlying goal—or mix of goals—that justifies each form of sanction.

check point

1. **What are the four primary goals of the criminal sanction?**
   Retribution, deterrence, incapacitation, rehabilitation.

2. **What are the difficulties in showing that a punishment acts as a deterrent?**
   It is impossible to show who has been deterred from committing crimes, punishment isn't always certain, people act impulsively rather than rationally, people commit crimes while on drugs.

stop & analyze

What do you think should be the primary goal of the criminal sanction? List two problems or challenges to the achievement of that goal.

Forms of the Criminal Sanction

Incarceration, intermediate sanctions, probation, and death are the basic ways that the criminal sanction, or punishment, is applied. The United States does not have a single, uniform set of sentencing laws. The criminal codes of each of the states and of the federal government specify the punishments. Each code differs to some extent in the severity of the punishment for specific crimes and in the amount of discretion given judges to tailor the sanction to the individual offender.

As we examine the various forms of criminal sanction, bear in mind that applying these legally authorized punishments gives rise to complex problems. Judges often receive wide discretion in determining the appropriate sentence within the parameters of the penal code.

Incarceration

Imprisonment is the most visible penalty imposed by U.S. courts. Although less than 30 percent of people under correctional supervision are in prisons and jails, incarceration remains the standard for punishing those who commit serious crimes. Imprisonment is thought to contribute significantly to deterring potential offenders. However, incarceration is expensive. It also creates the problem of reintegrating offenders into society upon release.

In penal codes, legislatures stipulate the types of sentences and the amount of prison time that can be imposed for each crime. Three basic sentencing structures are used: (1) indeterminate sentences (36 states), (2) determinate sentences (14 states), and (3) mandatory sentences (all states). Each type of sentence makes certain assumptions about the goals of the criminal sanction, and each provides judges with varying degrees of discretion.

AP Images/Charlie Litchfield

⬆ Of all correctional measures, incarceration represents the greatest restriction on freedom. These inmates are part of America's huge incarcerated population. Since 1980, the number of Americans held in prisons and jails has quadrupled. What are the costs to society from having such a large population of prisoners?

Indeterminate Sentences When the goal of rehabilitation dominated corrections, legislatures enacted **indeterminate sentences** (often called indefinite sentences) (Fisher, 2007). In keeping with the goal of treatment, indeterminate sentencing gives correctional officials and parole boards significant control over the amount of time a prisoner serves. Penal codes with indeterminate sentences stipulate a minimum and a maximum amount of time to be served in prison (for example, 1 to 5 years, 10 to 15 years, or 1 year to life). At the time of sentencing, the judge informs the offender about the range of the sentence. The offender also learns that he or she will probably be eligible for parole at some point after the minimum term has been served. The parole board determines the actual release date. Because it is based on the idea that the time necessary for treatment cannot be set, the indeterminate sentence is closely associated with rehabilitation.

indeterminate sentence A period, set by a judge, that specifies a minimum and a maximum time to be served in prison. Sometime after the minimum, the offender may be eligible for parole.

Determinate Sentences Dissatisfaction with the rehabilitation goal and support for the concept of deserved punishment led many legislatures in the 1970s to shift to **determinate sentences** (Dansky, 2008). With a determinate sentence, a convicted offender is imprisoned for a specific period (for example, 2 years, 5 years, 15 years). At the end of the term, minus credited *good time* (to be discussed shortly), the prisoner is automatically freed. The time of release depends neither on participation in treatment programs nor on a parole board's judgment concerning the offender's likelihood of returning to criminal activities.

Some determinate-sentencing states have adopted penal codes that stipulate a specific term for each crime category. Others allow the judge to choose a range of time to be served. Some states emphasize a determinate **presumptive sentence**: The legislature, or often a commission, specifies a term based on a time range (for example, 14 to 20 months) into which most cases should fall. Only in special circumstances should judges deviate from the presumptive sentence. Whichever variation is used, however, the offender theoretically knows at sentencing the amount of time to be served. One objective of determinate sentencing is that, by reducing the judge's discretion, legislatures can limit sentencing disparities and ensure that sentences correspond to those the elected lawmakers believe are appropriate (Engen, 2009).

determinate sentence A sentence that fixes the term of imprisonment at a specific period.

presumptive sentence A sentence for which the legislature or a commission sets a minimum and maximum range of months or years. Judges are to fix the length of the sentence within that range, allowing for special circumstances.

Mandatory Sentences As part of the public's fear and anger about crime, politicians and the public periodically complain that offenders are released before serving sufficiently long terms, and legislatures have responded (Zimring, 2007). All states and the federal government now have some form of **mandatory sentences** (often called mandatory minimum sentences), stipulating some minimum period of incarceration that people convicted of selected crimes must serve. The judge may

mandatory sentence A sentence determined by statutes and requiring that a certain penalty be imposed and carried out for convicted offenders who meet certain criteria.

(mandatory minimum)

consider neither the circumstances of the offense nor the background of the offender, and he or she may not impose nonincarcerative sentences. Mandatory prison terms are most often specified for violent crimes, drug violations, habitual offenders, or crimes in which a firearm was used.

The "three strikes and you're out" laws adopted by 26 states and the federal government provide an example of mandatory sentencing (Schultz, 2000). These laws require that judges sentence offenders with three felony convictions (in some states two or four convictions) to long prison terms, sometimes to life without parole. In some states, these laws have inadvertently clogged the courts, lowered the rates of plea bargaining, and caused desperate offenders to violently resist arrest. Mandatory minimum sentences resulted in a great increase in the number of drug offenders serving very long terms in America's prisons, mostly for nonviolent offenses (Gezari, 2008). Across the country, mandatory prison terms are applied more often to African American drug offenders than to their white counterparts (Crawford, 2000).

A study in California found a reduction in repeat offenders' participation in certain kinds of crimes, but a troubling increase in the violence of third-strike offenses (Iyengar, 2008). This raises the possibility that career criminals who are willing to risk the three-strikes ultimate punishment may commit more-serious crimes, such as robbery, since the penalty will be no greater than that for a lesser felony, such as larceny (Fisman, 2008). The study also raised the possibility that offenders with prior strikes may be inclined to migrate to other states, thus merely moving their criminal activities to a new location (Iyengar, 2008).

In recent years, state governments have been forced to cut their budgets as the nation's economic woes caused a decline in tax revenues; consequently, there has been increased attention to the high cost of long, mandatory sentences. Some states initiated changes in sentencing in an effort to alleviate prison overcrowding and reduce their corrections budgets (Riccardi, 2009). In addition, mandatory sentences faced reexamination because of concerns that certain sentences are unfair. For example, in 2010, Congress reformed mandatory cocaine sentencing laws which, due to differential treatment of crack cocaine and powder cocaine, had led to lengthier sentences for many African American offenders who had been the primary users and sellers of crack cocaine. The change in the law still does not treat crack cocaine offenses identically with powder cocaine offenses, for which white offenders were heavily represented, but it did reduce the number of crack offenders subjected to the mandatory five-year sentence that previously applied (P. Baker, 2010).

The Sentence versus Actual Time Served Regardless of how much discretion judges have to fine-tune the sentences they give, the prison sentences that are imposed may bear little resemblance to the actual amount of time served. In reality, parole boards in indeterminate-sentencing states have broad discretion in release decisions once the offender has served a minimum portion of the sentence. In addition, offenders can have their prison sentence reduced by earning **good time** for good behavior, at the discretion of the prison administrator.

good time A reduction of an inmate's prison sentence, at the discretion of the prison administrator, for good behavior or participation in vocational, educational, or treatment programs.

Most states have good-time policies. Days are subtracted from prisoners' minimum or maximum term for good behavior or for participating in various types of vocational, educational, or treatment programs. Correctional officials consider these policies necessary for maintaining institutional order and for reducing crowding. Good-time credit serves as an incentive for prisoners to follow institutional rules, because recently earned credits can be taken away for misbehavior (King and Sherry, 2008). Prosecutors and defense attorneys also take good time into consideration during plea bargaining. In other words, they think about the actual amount of time a particular offender will likely serve.

The amount of good time one can earn varies among the states, usually from 5 to 10 days a month. In some states, once 90 days of good time are earned, they are vested; that is, the credits cannot be taken away as a punishment for misbehavior. Prisoners who then violate the rules risk losing only days not vested.

Contemporary budget crises have led several states to increase good time credits as a means to reduce prison populations through quicker release from custody

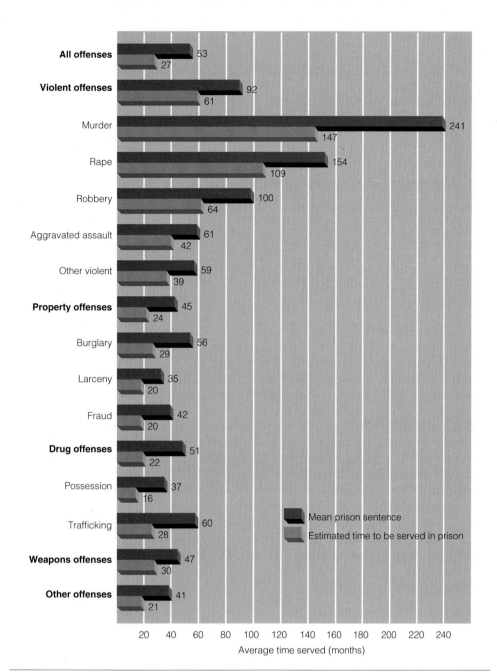

Figure 9.1
Estimated Time Served in State Prison Compared with Mean Length of Sentence
Most offenders serve a third or less of their mean sentences. Why is there such a difference between the sentence and actual time served?
Sources: Matthew R. Durose and Patrick A. Langan, "Felony Sentences in State Courts, 2004," Bureau of Justice Statistics *Bulletin*, July 2007; "State Court Sentencing of Convicted Felons, 2004—Statistical Tables," Table 1.5 (http://www.ojp.usdoj.gov /bjs/abstract/scscfst.htm).
© Cengage Learning

Chart data:

Offense	Mean prison sentence	Estimated time to be served in prison
All offenses	53	27
Violent offenses	92	61
Murder	241	147
Rape	154	109
Robbery	100	64
Aggravated assault	61	42
Other violent	59	39
Property offenses	45	24
Burglary	56	29
Larceny	35	20
Fraud	42	20
Drug offenses	51	22
Possession	37	16
Trafficking	60	28
Weapons offenses	47	30
Other offenses	41	21

Average time served (months)

(Homan, 2010). In 2010, for example, Louisiana made well-behaved prisoners eligible to receive a 35-day credit for every 30 days served. The change was expected to reduce the state's prison population by 2,386 prisoners in the first year and save the state $7 million in the first year alone (KATC, 2010).

More than 30 states also grant **earned time** that may be offered in addition to good time. Unlike good time, which is based on good behavior, earned time is awarded for participation in education, vocational, substance abuse, and other rehabilitation programs. Earned time may also be awarded for work assignments, such as when low-security prisoners work on disaster relief, conservation projects, or fighting wildfires (Lawrence, 2009). Several states have expanded the use of earned time as part of their budget-reduction strategies for shrinking expensive prison populations.

Judges in the United States often prescribe long periods of incarceration for serious crimes, but good time, earned time, and parole reduce the amount of time spent in prison. Figure 9.1 shows the estimated time actually served by offenders in state prisons, versus the average (mean) sentence.

earned time Reduction in a prisoner's sentence as a reward for participation in educational or other rehabilitation programs, and for work assignments, such as disaster relief and conservation projects.

TABLE 9.2 Estimated Cost Savings for Florida from Increased Use of Intermediate Sanctions (based on 2009 costs)

Sanction	First–Year Cost per Offender	Total First-Year Cost for 100 Offenders	Potential Savings per 100 Offenders
Prison	$20,272	$2,027,200	—
Supervision with GPS monitoring	$5,121	$806,954	$1,220,246
Probation and restitution centers	$9,492	$1,639,211	$387,989
Day reporting	$4,191	$917,823	$1,109,377
Residential drug treatment	$10,539	$1,419,529	$607,671

Source: Florida Office of Program Policy Analysis and Government Accountability, *Intermediate Sanctions for Non-Violent Offenders Could Produce Savings*, Report No. 10-27, March 2010, p. 3.

This type of national data often hides the impact of variations in sentencing and releasing laws in individual states. In many states, because of prison crowding and release policies, offenders serve less than 20 percent of their sentences. In other states, where three-strikes and truth-in-sentencing laws are employed, the average time served will be longer than the national average.

Truth in Sentencing *Truth in sentencing* refers to laws that require offenders to serve a substantial proportion (usually 85 percent for violent crimes) of their prison sentence before being released on parole (Mayrack, 2008). Truth in sentencing became such a politically attractive idea that the federal government allocated almost $10 billion for prison construction to those states adopting truth in sentencing (Donziger, 1996). Critics maintain, however, that truth in sentencing increases prison populations at a tremendous cost. The concept is less attractive today to many states beset by budget problems as they try to reduce their prison populations through greater flexibility in sentencing and early release (Riccardi, 2009).

Intermediate Sanctions

intermediate sanctions A variety of punishments that are more restrictive than traditional probation but less severe and less costly than incarceration.

Prison crowding and the low levels of probation supervision have spurred interest in the development of **intermediate sanctions**, punishments that are less severe and less costly than prison but more restrictive than traditional probation (R. Warren, 2007). Intermediate sanctions provide a variety of restrictions on freedom, such as fines, home confinement, intensive probation supervision, restitution to victims, community service, boot camp, and forfeiture of possessions or stolen property. In 2010, Florida's Office of Program Policy Analysis and Government Accountability noted that more than 24,000 of the state's prison inmates were convicted of nonviolent offenses and had no prior convictions for violent offenses (Florida Office of Program Policy, 2010). As indicated in Table 9.2, the agency estimated that the state could enjoy substantial financial savings through the increased use of intermediate sanctions rather than imprisonment.

In advocating intermediate punishments, Norval Morris and Michael Tonry (1990) stipulate that these sanctions should not be used in isolation, but rather in combination, to reflect the severity of the offense, the characteristics of the offender, and the needs of the community. In addition, intermediate punishments must be supported and enforced by mechanisms that take seriously any breach of the conditions of the sentence. If the law does not fulfill its promises, offenders may feel that they have "beaten" the system, which makes the punishment meaningless. Citizens who perceive any ineffectiveness in the system may develop the attitude that nothing but stiffer prison sentences will actually impose punishment.

Probation

The most frequently applied criminal sanction is **probation**, a sentence that an offender serves in the community under supervision. Nearly 60 percent of adults under correctional supervision are on probation. Ideally, under probation, offenders attempt to straighten out their lives. Probation is a judicial act granted by the grace of the state, not extended as a right. Conditions are imposed specifying how an offender will behave through the length of the sentence. Probationers may have to undergo regular drug tests, abide by curfews, enroll in educational programs or remain employed, stay away from certain people or parts of town, and meet regularly with probation officers. If probationers do not meet the required conditions, the supervising officer recommends to the court that the probation be revoked and that the remainder of the sentence be served in prison. Probation may also be revoked for commission of a new crime.

Although probationers serve their sentences in the community, the sanction is often tied to incarceration. In some jurisdictions, the court is authorized to modify an offender's prison sentence, after a portion is served, by changing it to probation. This is often referred to as **shock probation** (or *split probation*): An offender is released after a period of incarceration (the "shock") and resentenced to probation. An offender on probation may be required to spend intermittent periods, such as weekends or nights, in jail. Whatever its specific terms, a probationary sentence will emphasize and require guidance and supervision in the community.

Probation is generally advocated as a way of rehabilitating offenders whose crimes are not serious or whose past records are clean. It is viewed as less expensive yet more effective than imprisonment. For example, imprisonment may embitter youthful or first-time offenders and mix them with hardened criminals so that they learn more-sophisticated criminal techniques.

probation A sentence that the offender is allowed to serve under supervision in the community.

shock probation A sentence in which the offender is released after a short incarceration and resentenced to probation.

Death

Although other Western democracies abolished the death penalty years ago, the United States continues to use it (C. E. Smith, 2010a). Capital punishment was imposed and carried out regularly prior to the late 1960s. Amid debates about the constitutionality of the death penalty and with public opinion polls showing opposition to it, the U.S. Supreme Court suspended its use from 1968 to 1976. Eventually, the Court decided that capital punishment does not violate the Eighth Amendment's prohibition of cruel and unusual punishments. Executions resumed in 1977 as a majority of states began, once again, to sentence murderers to death.

During the 1980s, the number of people facing the death penalty increased steadily, with the number of people sentenced to death exceeding the number of actual executions, so that from the early 1990s onward there have been more than 3,000 offenders on death rows awaiting execution. As of May 2012, there were 3,195 people awaiting execution in 33 death penalty states, two states (New Mexico and Connecticut) that had offenders awaiting execution prior to their abolition of capital punishment in 2009 and 2012 respectively, federal prisons (60 offenders), and U.S. military prisons (6 offenders) (www.deathpenaltyinfo.org). Two-thirds of those on death row are in the South. The greatest number of death row inmates are in California, Texas, Florida, and Pennsylvania (see Figure 9.2).

One of the most striking contemporary developments affecting the death penalty is the decline in both offenders sentenced to death each year and the number of executions actually carried out. The imposition of death sentences peaked during the period from 1994 through 1996, when 312 to 315 offenders were sentenced to death during each of those years. By contrast, since 2006, fewer than 130 offenders have been sentenced to death annually, with the largest drop occurring most recently as 104 offenders were sentenced to death row in 2010. Moreover, in 2011 only 78 offenders had received death sentences as of December 15, 2011. Executions peaked at 98 in 1999 and declined so that there were only 37 in 2008, and not more than 52 in any year thereafter (Death Penalty Information Center, 2011). Many scholars attribute this trend to the heavy news media attention to the discovery and release of innocent people who had been

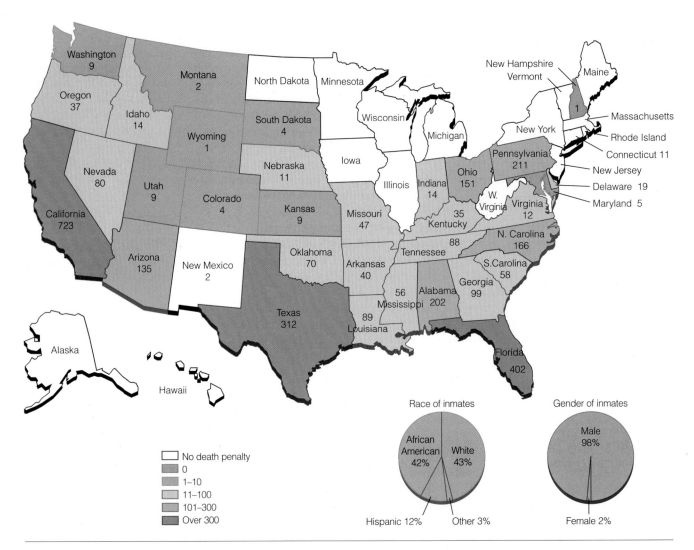

Figure 9.2

Death Row Census, 2012 Many of the inmates on death row are concentrated in certain states. African Americans make up about 13 percent of the U.S. population but 42 percent of the death row population. How might you explain this higher percentage of death sentences in proportion to population?

Note: The two offenders on death row in New Mexico remain under the sentence of death, although the state abolished the death penalty for crimes in 2009 and thereafter. The same is true for the 11 offenders on death row in Connecticut after the state abolished the death penalty in 2012.

Source: Death Penalty Information Center, *Facts about the Death Penalty*, May 2, 2012, p. 2.

sentenced to death (Baumgartner, Linn, and Boydstun, 2010). In March 2012, Edward Lee Elmore was released after spending more than 30 years on death row in South Carolina after courts determined that prosecutors had hidden evidence indicating that he was innocent of the murder for which he was convicted. Elmore was one of 141 wrongly convicted offenders released from death row since 1977 (Death Penalty Information Center, www.deathpenaltyinfo.org). Public-opinion polls indicate less support across American society for the death penalty in recent years. These statistics presumably include those Americans called for jury duty who are asked to decide whether to impose death sentences, as opposed to prison sentences, in murder cases. As you examine Figure 9.3 showing the decline in death sentences and executions since the Supreme Court's reactivation of capital punishment in 1977, bear in mind that there were more than 3,000 offenders on death row for most of this period since the early 1990s. The data merely show the trends in new sentences and executions.

Over this time period, 7,351 convicted murderers were sent to death row, but only 1,277 executions occurred nationally. This gap reflects both the lengthy appeals

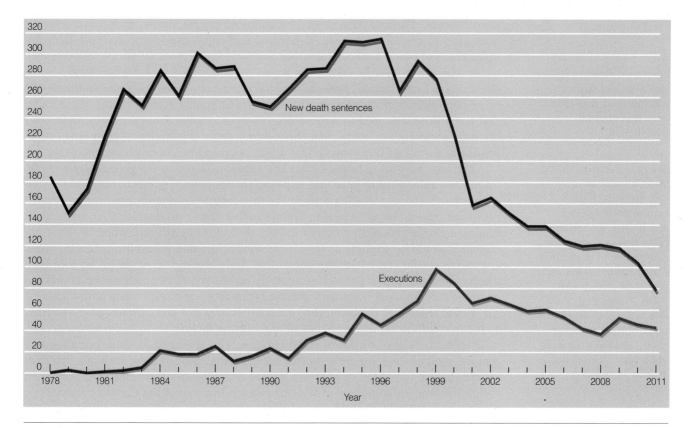

Figure 9.3

New Death Sentences and Executions, 1978–2011 The decline in death sentences and executions is attributed to shifts in public opinion affected by highly publicized cases of innocent people wrongly sent to death row. Does this trend indicate that the United States will eventually abolish the death penalty as the countries of Western Europe have done?

Sources: Bureau of Justice Statistics, *Sourcebook of Criminal Justice Statistics* (2011); Death Penalty Information Center, *The Death Penalty in 2011: Year End Report*, December 2011 (www.deathpenaltyinfo.org).

process that lasts many years for death penalty cases and individual states' varying commitments to actually carrying out executions. As indicated in Figure 9.2, for example, California leads the nation with 723 offenders sentenced to death, but the state has carried only 13 executions since the resumption of the death penalty in 1977 (www .deathpenaltyinfo.org). Thus the death penalty in California, as well as in a number of other states, is largely symbolic as these states' governors and prosecutors have not uniformly pushed forward to see executions occur. By contrast, the states that carry out most executions are few in number. Five states—Texas, Virginia, Oklahoma, Florida, and Missouri—together account for nearly two-thirds of the total executions carried out in the United States since 1977 (Death Penalty Information Center, 2011). Texas has carried out 480 executions in that time period, thereby demonstrating greater commitment by its public officials to put the punishment into practice. Indeed, in several cases, Texas has been accused of showing insufficient concern with careful reviews of cases and there are accusations that the state may have executed one or more innocent people by failing to be careful about guarding against errors and by being unwilling to admit the possibility of errors (Mann, 2011). Thus it appears that the political values and culture of a specific state affect not only whether the state's laws permit capital punishment, but also the practical decisions that determine how frequently executions are carried out.

The Death Penalty and the Constitution Death differs from other punishments in that it is final and irreversible. The Supreme Court has therefore examined the decision-making process in capital cases to ensure that it fulfills the Constitution's requirements regarding due process, equal protection, and cruel and unusual punishments. Because life is in the balance, capital cases must be conducted according to higher standards of fairness and more-careful procedures than are other kinds of cases. Several important Supreme Court cases illustrate this concern.

In **Furman v. Georgia** (1972), the Supreme Court ruled that the death penalty, as administered, constituted cruel and unusual punishment. The decision invalidated the death penalty laws of 39 states and the District of Columbia. A majority of justices found that the procedures used to impose death sentences were arbitrary and unfair. Over the next several years, more than three dozen states eventually enacted new capital punishment statutes that provided for different procedures in death penalty cases.

The new laws were tested before the Supreme Court in **Gregg v. Georgia** (1976). The Court upheld those laws that required the sentencing judge or jury to take into account specific aggravating and mitigating factors in deciding which convicted murderers should be sentenced to death. Further, the Court decided that, rather than having a single proceeding determine the defendant's guilt and whether the death sentence would be applied, states should use "bifurcated proceedings." In this two-part process, the defendant has a trial that finds him guilty or not guilty and then a separate hearing that focuses exclusively on the issues of punishment. It seeks to ensure a thorough deliberation before someone receives the ultimate punishment.

Under the *Gregg* decision, the prosecution uses the punishment phase hearing to focus attention on the existence of aggravating factors, such as excessive cruelty or a defendant's prior record of violent crimes. The defense may focus on mitigating factors, such as the offender's youthfulness, mental condition, or lack of a criminal record. Before the judge or jury can decide to impose a death sentence, they must weigh these aggravating and mitigating factors. Because of the Court's emphasis on fair procedures and individualized decisions, state appellate courts review trial court procedures in virtually every capital case.

After **McCleskey v. Kemp** (1987), opponents of the death penalty felt disappointed that the U.S. Supreme Court failed to accept strong statistical evidence showing racial discrimination in the administration of the death penalty. In this case, the Court rejected an equal protection clause challenge to Georgia's death penalty law. Warren McCleskey, an African American, was sentenced to death for killing a white police officer. Before the U.S. Supreme Court, McCleskey's attorney cited an elaborate research study that showed a disparity in the imposition of the death penalty in Georgia, based on the race of the victim and, to a lesser extent, the race of the defendant (Baldus, Woodworth, and Pulaski, 1994). In particular, when African American men were murdered, there was little likelihood that the death penalty would be pursued. When an African American man was convicted of killing a white person, the likelihood of the death penalty increased dramatically (M. R. Williams, Demuth, and Holcomb, 2007).

By a 5-to-4 vote, the justices rejected McCleskey's assertion that Georgia's capital-sentencing practices produced racial discrimination that violated the equal protection clause of the Constitution. The slim majority of justices declared that McCleskey would have to prove that the decision makers acted with a discriminatory purpose in deciding his particular case. The Court also concluded that statistical evidence showing discrimination throughout the Georgia courts did not provide adequate proof. McCleskey was executed in 1991. The decision made it very difficult to prove the existence of racial discrimination in capital cases because prosecutors and judges rarely make statements that openly indicate a discriminatory motive. Yet, when analyzed through the methods of social science, the patterns of decisions that determine which murderers receive the death penalty instead of imprisonment indicate that racial disparities are often present when looking at a state court system as whole. Thus there are continuing concerns that death penalty cases can be infected with racial bias (R. N. Walker, 2006).

In June 2002, the Supreme Court broke new ground in a way that heartened opponents of the death penalty. First, in **Atkins v. Virginia** (2002), it ruled that execution of developmentally disabled individuals was unconstitutional. In the case, the Court used the older term "mentally retarded" to describe these individuals. Daryl Atkins,

Furman v. Georgia (1972)
The death penalty, as administered, constitutes cruel and unusual punishment.

Gregg v. Georgia (1976)
Death penalty laws are constitutional if they require the judge and jury to consider certain mitigating and aggravating circumstances in deciding which convicted murderers should be sentenced to death. Proceedings must also be divided into a trial phase and a punishment phase, and there must be opportunities for appeal.

McCleskey v. Kemp (1987)
The Supreme Court rejects a challenge of Georgia's death penalty on grounds of racial discrimination.

Atkins v. Virginia (2002)
Execution of developmentally disabled offenders is unconstitutional.

who has an IQ of 59, was sentenced to death for killing Eric Nesbitt in a 7-Eleven store parking lot. As the majority opinion noted, the characteristics of developmentally disabled offenders, people with IQs of less than 70, "undermine the strength of the procedural protections." This point is in keeping with the argument of mental health experts who say their suggestibility and willingness to please leads developmentally disabled people to confess. At trial, they have problems remembering details, locating witnesses, and testifying credibly in their own behalf.

The Supreme Court further reduced the scope of capital punishment, in ***Roper v. Simmons (2005)***. A slim majority of justices decided that offenders cannot be sentenced to death for crimes that they committed before they reached the age of 18. Prior to that decision, the United States was among only a half-dozen countries in the entire world with laws that permitted death sentences for juveniles. The same five-member majority also ruled that the death penalty cannot be imposed as a punishment for the crime of child rape (*Kennedy v. Louisiana*, 2008).

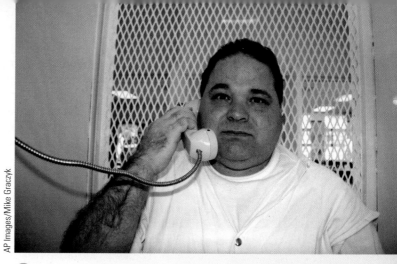

Prisoners sentenced to death typically must wait several years as their cases move through the appeals process. Michael Rodriguez was among a group of Texas prison escapees who killed a police officer during a robbery in 2000. Here he was interviewed on death row just two weeks prior to his execution by lethal injection in August 2008. Should appeals in death penalty cases be accelerated so as to speed up executions, or would speedy appeals increase the risk of executing an innocent person?

Because the Court was deeply divided on these issues, some observers wonder if further changes in the Court's composition may lead to a reversal of these decisions.

Roper v. Simmons (2005)
Execution of offenders for crimes committed while under the age of 18 is unconstitutional.

All states use lethal injection as the means to conduct executions, although a few states permit the condemned prisoners to choose the electric chair or another means that was in existence at the time of their conviction (Liptak, 2008a). Lethal injection remains controversial as a method of execution because of botched executions. In these cases, prolonged and painful deaths resulted from improperly inserted needles or malfunctioning tubes that carry the chemicals (Radelet, 2004). The constitutionality of lethal injection as a means of execution was examined by the U.S. Supreme Court in *Baze v. Rees* (2008). All of the justices concluded that the attorneys for the death row inmates had not proved that the use of lethal injection violates the Eighth Amendment. New issues will arise concerning lethal injection because the drugs used by most states for such executions are difficult to obtain and few companies manufacture them. In 2011, the federal Drug Enforcement Administration seized an execution drug purchased by the state of Georgia from a supplier in Great Britain because Georgia did not hold a proper license to import that drug (Sack, 2011). It remains to be seen if these shortages affect the number of executions or whether states will simply change the combination of drugs used for their executions in order to use those drugs that are more easily available.

The future of the death penalty's treatment by the Supreme Court will depend on such factors as who is elected president of the United States in 2012, and thereafter, and thereby appoints new justices to the nation's highest court. The newest justices appointed by President Obama, Justice Sonia Sotomayor (confirmed in 2009) and Justice Elena Kagan (confirmed in 2010) had not yet addressed the issue of capital punishment directly by mid-2012. Thus their impact on the issue, like that of future appointees, remains to be seen.

Continuing Legal Issues The case law since *Furman* indicates that capital punishment is legal so long as it is imposed fairly. However, opponents continue to raise several issues in litigation and in arguments presented to legislatures and the public (Acker, 2007). Just as developmentally disabled and juvenile offenders have been excluded from eligibility for the death penalty, some people argue that mentally ill offenders should also be excluded. Issues have arisen about the effectiveness of representation provided for capital defendants by defense attorneys. Many critics are concerned about the impact of using death-qualified juries from selection processes that exclude as jurors those citizens who are strongly opposed to capital punishment. Research raises questions about whether such juries are more inclined to find defendants guilty and impose capital punishment (Summers, Hayward, and Miller, 2010). Other cases continue to raise issues about methods of execution and the lengthy periods that condemned offenders spend on death row because of appeals. We now look at several contemporary issues.

Execution of the Mentally Ill
As we saw in Chapter 3, insanity is a recognized defense for commission of a crime. Moreover, the Supreme Court has said that people who become insane after entering prison cannot be executed (*Ford v. Wainwright*, 1986). But many people with mental illnesses do not meet the legal tests for insanity. They can be convicted of crimes and punished, and there is no guarantee that they will receive psychiatric treatment in prison. What happens if these people commit capital crimes? Is it appropriate to execute people whose mental illnesses may have affected their behavior? Opponents of the death penalty will undoubtedly seek to persuade the Supreme Court that mentally ill offenders should be excluded from capital punishment, following the rulings regarding developmentally disabled offenders and juveniles convicted of murder.

Effective Counsel
In *Strickland v. Washington* (1984), the Supreme Court ruled that defendants in capital cases had the right to representation that meets an "objective standard of reasonableness." As noted by Justice Sandra Day O'Connor, the appellant must show "that there is a reasonable probability that, but for the counsel's unprofessional errors, the result of the proceeding would be different." Although it is possible to identify errors made by an attorney, it can be difficult to persuade judges that anything less than truly major errors actually affected the outcome of the case.

In the past decade, the public has learned of cases placing the defense attorney's competency in doubt, such as the case of a defense attorney sleeping during a murder trial. In 1999, the *Chicago Tribune* conducted an extensive investigation of capital punishment in Illinois. Reporters found that 33 defendants sentenced to death since 1977 were represented by attorneys who had been, or were later, disbarred or suspended for conduct that was "incompetent, unethical or even criminal." These attorneys included David Landau, who was disbarred one year after representing a Will County defendant sentenced to death, and Robert McDonnell, a convicted felon and the only lawyer in Illinois to be disbarred twice. McDonnell represented four men who landed on death row (Armstrong and Mills, 1999).

These highly publicized cases may have caught the attention of the Supreme Court. In 2003, the Court issued a decision that seemed designed to remind lawyers and judges about the need for competent defense attorneys in capital cases. In *Wiggins v. Smith* (2003), the Court found that the Sixth Amendment right to counsel was violated when a defense attorney failed to present mitigating evidence concerning the severe physical and sexual abuse suffered by the defendant during childhood. Whether the justices create clearer or stricter standards for defense attorneys remains to be seen.

Death-Qualified Juries
Should people who are opposed to the death penalty be excluded from juries in capital cases? In **Witherspoon v. Illinois (1968)**, the Supreme Court held that potential jurors who have general objections to the death penalty or whose religious convictions oppose its use cannot be automatically excluded from jury service in capital cases. However, it upheld the practice of removing, during voir dire (preliminary examination), those people whose opposition is so strong as to "prevent or substantially impair the performance of their duties." Such jurors have become known as *"Witherspoon excludables."* The decision was later reaffirmed in *Lockhart v. McCree* (1986).

Because society is divided on capital punishment, opponents argue that death-qualified juries do not represent a cross section of the community (Summers, Hayward, and Miller, 2010). Researchers have also found that "juries are likely to be

Witherspoon v. Illinois **(1968)** Potential jurors who object to the death penalty cannot be automatically excluded from service; however, during voir dire, those who feel so strongly about capital punishment that they could not give an impartial verdict may be excluded.

nudged toward believing the defendant is guilty and toward an imposition of the death sentence by the very process of undergoing death qualification" (Luginbuhl and Burkhead, 1994:107).

Mark Costanzo (1997) points to research indicating that death qualification has several impacts. First, those who are selected for jury duty are more conviction prone and more receptive to aggravating factors presented during the penalty phase. A second, subtler impact is that jurors answering the questions about their willingness to vote for a death sentence often conclude that both defenders and prosecutors anticipate a conviction and a death sentence.

The Death Penalty: A Continuing Controversy

Various developments in the twenty-first century appear to indicate a weakening of support for capital punishment in the United States. In May 2000 the New Hampshire legislature became the first in more than two decades to vote to repeal the death penalty; however, the governor vetoed the bill. New York's capital punishment law was declared unconstitutional by its own state courts in 2004. The New Jersey state legislature and governor eliminated the death penalty in that state in 2007. Subsequently, the legislature of New Mexico (Urbina, 2009), as well as the House of Representatives in New Hampshire (Chiaramida, 2009), voted to abolish capital punishment. The governor of New Mexico signed the law, but New Hampshire's Senate and governor blocked enactment (as the governor in 2000 had done). The Maryland legislature declined to follow the governor's request to abolish the death penalty, but instead severely restricted the application of the punishment in that state by requiring DNA evidence and a videotaped confession in any murder case for which the prosecution seeks capital punishment (Wagner, 2009).

In March 2011, the governor of Illinois signed a law that eliminated capital punishment. He also commuted the sentences of the 15 offenders on death row so that they will now serve sentences of life without parole (Schwartz and Fitzsimmons, 2011). Illinois had not executed an offender since 2000, when it was discovered that a number of innocent people had been sentenced to death due to flaws in the justice system, including the use of dishonest jailhouse informants and incompetent defense attorneys. In 2012, Connecticut's legislature and governor abolished capital punishment for future crimes. Unlike Illinois, Connecticut took New Mexico's approach by leaving its 11 currently condemned murderers on death row to face eventual execution (Applebome, 2012)

Concerns about the conviction of innocent people may lead some other states to reconsider the use of capital punishment. Simultaneously, the extraordinary costs of capital trials and appeals are likely to deter many states from seeking to use the punishment widely in murder cases. Because the costs of trials are typically placed on county government, small counties frequently cannot afford to seek the death penalty in murder cases as these trials can last for weeks and require the services of expensive scientific testing and expert witnesses. On the other hand, a future terrorism attack on the United States may intensify public support for capital punishment and spur efforts to expand the penalty. Thus it remains to be seen whether the nation will continue to see diminishing use of the death penalty.

Although public-opinion polls still reflect significant support for the death penalty (see "What Americans Think"), the number of executions remains low.

what americans think

Question: "If you could choose between the following two approaches, which do you think is the better penalty for murder—the death penalty or life imprisonment with absolutely no possibility of parole?"

Death penalty 49%

Life imprisonment 46%

No opinion 6%

Critical Thinking: What reasons would people likely give for preferring life without parole as a sentence for murder instead of the death penalty?

Source: Frank Newport, "In U.S., 64% Support Death Penalty for Murder," Gallup Poll, November 8, 2010. Reprinted by permission of the Gallup Organization.

Should the Death Penalty Be Abolished?

The applicability of the death penalty has diminished in the twenty-first century. The execution moratorium imposed by Illinois Governor George Ryan in January 2000 reinvigorated debate on the death penalty. His announcement was soon followed by a national poll that found support for the penalty to be the lowest in 19 years, the release of a national study of appeals that found two-thirds of death penalty cases are flawed and overturned by higher courts, and research questioning the quality of counsel given to many defendants. Subsequently, the U.S. Supreme Court reduced the applicability of capital punishment by excluding the developmentally disabled and juveniles from executions. In 2011, the Illinois legislature and Governor Pat Quinn approved legislation to end capital punishment in that state, just as New Jersey had done in 2007 and New Mexico did in 2009. Connecticut did the same in 2012.

Opponents of capital punishment continue the fight to abolish it. They argue that poor people and minorities receive a disproportionate number of death sentences. They also believe that executing people who are teenage, insane, or developmentally disabled is barbaric.

Even the proponents of capital punishment remain dissatisfied with how it is applied. They point to the fact that although more than 3,200 convicted murderers wait on death row, the number of executions since 1976 has never exceeded 98 per year and has declined through the first years of the twenty-first century.

The appeals process is a major factor halting this pace, given that it can delay executions for years.

For the Death Penalty

Supporters argue that society should apply swift, severe punishments to killers to address the continuing problems of crime and violence. Execution should occur quite soon after conviction so that the greatest deterrent value will result. They say that justice requires that a person who murders another must be executed. To do less is to denigrate the value of human life.

The arguments for the death penalty include the following:

- The death penalty deters criminals from committing violent acts.
- The death penalty achieves justice by paying killers back for their horrible crimes.
- The death penalty prevents criminals from doing further harm while on parole.
- The death penalty is less expensive than holding murderers in prison for life.

Against the Death Penalty

Opponents believe that the death penalty lingers as a barbaric practice from a less civilized age. They point out that most other developed democracies in the world have ceased to execute criminals. Opponents challenge the death penalty's claims for effectiveness in reducing crime. They also raise concerns about whether the punishment can be applied without errors and discrimination.

The arguments against the death penalty include the following:

- No hard evidence proves that the death penalty is a deterrent.
- It is wrong for a government to participate in the intentional killing of citizens.
- The death penalty is applied in a discriminatory fashion.
- Innocent people have been sentenced to death.
- Some methods of execution are inhumane, causing painful, lingering deaths.

What Should U.S. Policy Be?

With more and more people now being sentenced to death row but fewer than sixty individuals executed each year, death penalty policy is at a significant crossroads. Will the United States increase the pace of executions, allow the number of capital offenders in prison to keep growing, or take a middle ground that satisfies neither side completely, such as life imprisonment without parole for convicted murderers?

Researcing the Internet

Compare the perspectives presented at the websites of Pro-Death Penalty and the Death Penalty Information Center. You can access them both by going to the Criminal Justice CourseMate at cengagebrain.com, and clicking on the web links for this chapter.

For Critical Analysis

Evaluate the pros and cons of the death penalty debate. What political factors might influence your state's legislators to abolish, modify, or retain the death penalty?

Recent surveys show that the public is split when asked to choose between life imprisonment (without parole) and death. Does this mean that Americans are ambivalent about carrying out the punishment? What might it say about capital punishment in the next decade? Debate on this important public-policy issue has gone on for more than two hundred years, yet there is still no consensus (see "The Policy Debate" for more).

TABLE 9.3 The Punishment of Offenders

The goals of the criminal sanction are carried out in a variety of ways, depending upon the provisions of the law, the characteristics of the offender, and the discretion of the judge. Judges may impose sentences that combine several forms to achieve punishment objectives.

Form of Sanction	Description	Purposes
Incarceration	Imprisonment	
Indeterminate sentence	Specifies a maximum and minimum length of time to be served	Incapacitation, deterrence, rehabilitation
Determinate sentence	Specifies a certain length of time to be served	Retribution, deterrence, incapacitation
Mandatory sentence	Specifies a minimum amount of time that must be served for given crimes	Incapacitation, deterrence
Good time	Subtracts days from an inmate's sentence because of good behavior or participation in prison programs	Rewards behavior, relieves prison crowding, helps maintain prison discipline
Intermediate sanctions	Punishment for those requiring sanctions more restrictive than probation but less restrictive than prison	Retribution, deterrence
Administered by the judiciary		
Fine	Money paid to state by offender	Retribution, deterrence
Restitution	Money paid to victim by offender	Retribution, deterrence
Forfeiture	Seizure by the state of property illegally obtained or acquired with resources illegally obtained	Retribution, deterrence
Administered in the community		
Community service	Requires offender to perform work for the community	Retribution, deterrence
Home confinement	Requires offender to stay in home during certain times	Retribution, deterrence, incapacitation
Intensive probation supervision	Requires strict and frequent reporting to probation officer	Retribution, deterrence, incapacitation
Administered institutionally		
Boot camp/shock incarceration	Short-term institutional sentence emphasizing physical development and discipline, followed by probation	Retribution, deterrence, rehabilitation
Probation	Allows offender to serve a sentence in the community under supervision	Retribution, incapacitation, rehabilitation
Death	Execution	Incapacitation, deterrence, retribution

The criminal sanction takes many forms, with offenders punished in various ways to serve various purposes. Table 9.3 summarizes how these sanctions operate and how they reflect the underlying philosophies of punishment.

3. What are the three types of sentences used in the United States?

Determinate, indeterminate, and mandatory sentences.

4. What are thought to be the advantages of intermediate sanctions?

Intermediate sanctions give judges a greater range of sentencing alternatives, reduce prison populations, cost less than prison, and increase community security.

5. What requirements specified in *Gregg v. Georgia* must exist before a death sentence can be imposed?

Judge and jury must be able to consider mitigating and aggravating circumstances, proceedings must be divided into a trial phase and a punishment phase, and there must be opportunities for appeal.

stop& analyze

Which goals of punishment are advanced by intermediate sanctions? Do intermediate sanctions adequately advance those goals? Imagine that you are a state legislator. For which crimes would you vote to authorize the use of intermediate sanctions? Which goals would you be seeking to advance with those punishments?

The Sentencing Process

Regardless of how and where guilt has been determined—misdemeanor court or felony court, plea bargain or adversarial context, bench or jury trial—judges hold the responsibility for imposing sentences. Often difficult, sentencing usually involves more than applying clear-cut principles to individual cases. In one case, a judge may decide to sentence a forger to prison as an example to others, even though the offender poses no threat to community safety and probably does not need rehabilitative treatment. In another case, the judge may impose a light sentence on a youthful offender who has committed a serious crime but may be a candidate for rehabilitation if moved quickly back into society.

Legislatures establish the penal codes that set forth the sentences judges can impose. These laws generally give judges discretion in sentencing. Judges may combine various forms of punishment in order to tailor the sanction to the offender. The judge may specify, for example, that the prison terms for two charges are to run either concurrently (at the same time) or consecutively (one after the other), or that all or part of the period of imprisonment may be suspended. In other situations, the offender may receive a combination of a suspended prison term, a fine, and probation. Judges may suspend a sentence as long as the offender stays out of trouble, makes restitution, or seeks medical treatment. They may also delay imposing any sentence but retain the power to set penalties at a later date if the offender misbehaves.

Within the discretion allowed by the code, various elements influence the decisions of judges (B. D. Johnson, 2006). Social scientists believe that several factors influence the sentencing process: (1) the administrative context of the courts, (2) the attitudes and values of judges, (3) the presentence report, and (4) sentencing guidelines.

The Administrative Context of the Courts

Judges are strongly influenced by the administrative context within which they impose sentences. As a result, differences are found, for example, between the assembly-line style of justice in misdemeanor courts and the more formal proceedings in felony courts.

Misdemeanor Courts: Assembly-Line Justice

Misdemeanor or lower courts have limited jurisdiction because typically they can impose only jail sentences of less than one year. These courts hear about 90 percent of criminal cases. Whereas felony cases are processed in lower courts only for arraignments and preliminary hearings, misdemeanor cases are processed completely in the lower courts. Only a minority of cases adjudicated in lower courts end in jail sentences. Most cases result in fines, probation, community service, restitution, or a combination of these.

Most lower courts are overloaded and allot minimal time to each case. Judicial decisions are mass produced because actors in the system share three assumptions. First, any person appearing before the court is guilty, because the police and prosecution have presumably filtered out doubtful cases. Second, the vast majority of defendants will plead guilty. Third, those charged with minor offenses will be processed in volume, with dozens of cases being decided in rapid succession within a single hour. The citation will be read by the clerk, a guilty plea entered, and the sentence pronounced by the judge for one defendant after another.

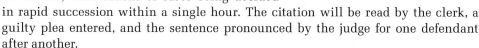

In misdemeanor cases, judges' sentencing decisions may be influenced by many factors, including the defendant's remorse, the availability of space for new offenders in the county jail, and the defendant's prior record. Here, Eric Feltner, a former government official in Missouri, is sentenced to probation and community service for public display of explicit sexual materials. Is it important for judges to impose comparable sentences on offenders who are convicted of similar crimes?

Defendants whose cases are processed through the lower court's assembly line may appear to receive little or no punishment. However, people who get caught in the criminal justice system experience other punishments, whether or not they are ultimately convicted. A person who is arrested but eventually released still incurs various tangible and intangible costs. Time spent in jail awaiting trial, the cost of a bail bond, and days of work lost create an immediate and concrete impact. Poor people may lose their jobs or be evicted from their homes if they fail to work and pay their bills for even a few days. For most people, simply being arrested is a devastating experience. It is impossible to measure the psychological and social price of being stigmatized, separated from family, and deprived of freedom.

Felony Courts Felony cases are processed and felony offenders are sentenced in courts of general jurisdiction. Because of the seriousness of the crimes, the atmosphere is more formal and generally lacks the chaotic, assembly-line environment of misdemeanor courts. Caseload burdens can affect how much time individual cases receive. Exchange relationships among courtroom actors can facilitate plea bargains and shape the content of prosecutors' sentencing recommendations. Sentencing decisions are ultimately shaped, in part, by the relationships, negotiations, and agreements among the prosecutor, defense attorney, and judge. Table 9.4 shows the types of felony sentences imposed for conviction on different charges.

Attitudes and Values of Judges

All lawyers recognize that judges differ from one another in their sentencing decisions. Administrative pressures, the conflicting goals of criminal justice, and the influence of community values partly explain these differences. Sentencing decisions also depend on judges' attitudes concerning the offender's blameworthiness, the protection of the community, and the practical implications of the sentence (Steffensmeier and Demuth, 2001).

TABLE 9.4 Types of Felony Sentences Imposed by State Courts

Although a felony conviction is often equated with a prison sentence, almost a third of felony offenders receive probation.

Most Serious Conviction Offense	Percentage of Felons Sentenced to		
	Prison	Jail	Probation
All offenses	41	28	27
Murder	93	2	3
Rape	72	15	10
Robbery	71	14	13
Burglary	49	24	24
Larceny	34	34	28
Drug possession	33	31	30
Drug trafficking	41	26	29
Weapons offenses	45	28	25

Note: For persons receiving a combination of sanctions, the sentence designation came from the most severe penalty imposed—prison being the most severe, followed by jail and then probation. Rows do not add up to 100% because a small percentage of offenders for each crime were sentenced to other nonincarceration sanctions.

Source: Sean Rosenmerkel, Matthew R. Durose, and Donald Farole Jr., "Felony Sentences in State Courts, 2006—Statistical Tables," *Bureau of Justice Statistics Statistical Tables*, December 2009, p. 4.

Blameworthiness concerns such factors as offense severity (such as violent crime or property crime), the offender's criminal history (such as recidivist or first timer), and role in commission of the crime (such as leader or follower). For example, a judge might impose a harsh sentence on a repeat offender who organized others to commit a serious crime.

Protection of the community hinges on similar factors, such as dangerousness, recidivism, and offense severity. However, it centers mostly on the need to incapacitate the offender or to deter would-be offenders.

Finally, the practical implications of a sentence can affect judges' decisions. For example, judges may take into account the offender's ability to "do time," as in the case of an elderly person. They may also consider the impact on the offender's family; a mother with children may receive a different sentence than a single woman would. Finally, costs to the corrections system may play a role in sentencing, as judges consider probation officers' caseloads or prison crowding (Steffensmeier, Kramer, and Streifel, 1993). The "Close Up" gives examples of judges' sentencing decisions in prominent cases.

Presentence Report

presentence report A report, prepared by a probation officer, that presents a convicted offender's background and is used by the judge in selecting an appropriate sentence.

Even though sentencing is the judge's responsibility, the **presentence report** has become an important ingredient in the judicial mix. Usually, a probation officer investigates the convicted person's background, criminal record, job status, and mental condition to suggest a sentence that is in the interests of both the offender and society. Although the presentence report serves primarily to help the judge select the sentence, it also assists in the classification of probationers, prisoners, and parolees for treatment planning and risk assessment. In the report, the probation officer makes judgments about what information to include and what conclusions to draw from that information. In some states, however, probation officers present only factual material to the judge and make no sentencing recommendation. Because

Judges and Sentencing

In March 2011, Andrew Stein, the former president of the New York City Council and a former candidate for Congress, stood before U.S. Magistrate Judge Ronald Ellis to hear his sentence for entering a guilty plea to one misdemeanor charge of failing to pay federal income taxes. Stein had created a phony company to hide money and avoid paying taxes on that money. He was originally charged with a felony for lying to federal investigators, but his attorney negotiated a plea agreement for him to accept responsibility for one misdemeanor for failing to pay taxes on $1 million of income in 2008. Stein also agreed to pay taxes for the years 2003 to 2008, although his plea permitted him to avoid criminal charges for failing to pay taxes in all but one year (2008) within that time period.

Stein delivered an emotional plea for leniency. In his five-minute statement, he choked up as he admitted to making a "terrible, terrible mistake." He suggested that his long career in public service should be considered as a factor in granting leniency.

Judge Ellis remarked that he had entered the courtroom expecting to sentence Stein to serve time behind bars, but he changed his mind as he listened to Stein and as he considered the 14 letters written on Stein's behalf by prominent lawyers, journalists, and entertainment figures. He ultimately sentenced Stein to three years' probation and 500 hours of community service.

In a different federal income tax case in 2008, movie star Wesley Snipes was charged with failing to pay taxes on $58 million in income over the course of a decade. Instead of negotiating a plea agreement, Snipes went to trial and a jury acquitted him of serious conspiracy and tax fraud charges. The jury apparently believed that he relied on misguided advice from an accountant who told him that he was not required to pay taxes. However, the jury convicted him of three separate misdemeanor counts of failing to file tax returns for the three years after he had been informed by the federal government that he was, indeed, required to file a return.

At his sentencing, Snipes apologized for making mistakes and offered checks totaling $5 million to begin payment on his back taxes. Snipes was not emotional and the federal prosecutor complained that Snipes never mentioned the word "taxes," never directly admitted that he should have paid his taxes, and did not show any remorse. U.S. District Judge William Terrell Hodge gave Snipes the maximum sentence of three years in prison, one year for each misdemeanor count.

Were these two sentences fair? Are they comparable? Snipes was convicted of failing to file his tax return, while Stein pled guilty to tax evasion—yet Snipes received the much more significant sentence. Did Snipes receive extra punishment for failing to fully apologize and accept responsibility? Did he receive extra punishment because the government accused him of owing additional money—even though the jury acquitted him of the charge of tax evasion? Did he receive extra punishment for refusing to plead guilty and for ultimately taking his case to a time-consuming, expensive jury trial? By contrast, did Stein receive leniency for having so many prominent friends willing to write letters to the judge?

Researching the Internet
Look at the website of the U.S. Sentencing Commission to see what percentage of convicted tax offenders are sentenced to probation and the average sentence for tax offenders sentenced to prison. To link to the website, visit the Criminal Justice CourseMate at cengagebrain.com, then access the web links for this chapter.

For Critical Analysis
Consider the precise charges for which Stein and Snipes were convicted. Which one was convicted of the more serious acts? Write down the sentence that you would have given to each of these defendants in order to achieve justice. What punishment goals are advanced by the sentences that you designed?

---

the probation officers do not necessarily follow evidentiary rules, they may include hearsay statements as well as firsthand information.

In the federal court system, the presentence report is supplemented by an additional report written by a pretrial services officer (PSO). This report focuses on the defendant's behavior and compliance with conditions while out on bail—prior to trial or plea or between the date of conviction and the date of sentencing.

The presentence report is one means by which judges ease the strain of decision making. The report lets judges shift partial responsibility to the probation department. Because a substantial number of sentencing alternatives are open to judges, they often rely on the report for guidance.

Sentencing Guidelines

Since the 1980s, **sentencing guidelines** have been established in the federal courts and in more than two dozen states. Such guidelines indicate to judges the expected sanction for particular types of offenses. They are intended to limit the sentencing

sentencing guidelines A mechanism to indicate to judges the expected sanction for certain offenses, in order to reduce disparities in sentencing.

TABLE 9.5 Minnesota Sentencing Guidelines Grid (presumptive sentence length in months)

The italicized numbers in the grid are the range within which a judge may sentence without the sentence being considered a departure. The criminal-history score is computed by adding one point for each prior felony conviction, one-half point for each prior gross-misdemeanor conviction, and one-quarter point for each prior misdemeanor conviction.

Severity of Offense (Illustrative Offenses)		Criminal-History Score						
		0	1	2	3	4	5	6 or more
Murder, second degree (intentional murder, drive-by shootings)	XI	306 *261–367*	326 *278–391*	346 *295–415*	366 *312–439*	386 *329–463*	406 *346–480*	426 *363–480*
Murder, third degree Murder, second degree (unintentional murder)	X	150 *128–180*	165 *141–198*	180 *153–216*	195 *166–234*	210 *179–252*	225 *192–270*	240 *204–288*
Assault, first degree Controlled substance crime, first degree	IX	86 *74–103*	98 *84–117*	110 *94–132*	122 *104–146*	134 *114–160*	146 *125–175*	158 *135–189*
Aggravated robbery, first degree Controlled substance crime, second degree	VIII	48 *41–57*	58 *50–69*	68 *58–81*	78 *67–93*	88 *75–105*	98 *84–117*	108 *92–129*
Felony DWI	VII	36	42	48	54 *46–64*	60 *51–72*	66 *57–79*	72 *62–84*
Controlled substance crime, third degree	VI	21	27	33	39 *34–46*	45 *39–54*	51 *44–61*	57 *49–68*
Residential burglary Simple robbery	V	18	23	28	33 *29–39*	38 *33–45*	43 *37–51*	48 *41–57*
Nonresidential burglary	IV	12	15	18	21	24 *21–28*	27 *23–32*	30 *26–36*
Theft crimes (over $5,000)	III	12	13	15	17	19 *17–22*	21 *18–25*	23 *20–27*
Theft crimes ($5,000 or less) Check forgery ($251–$2,500)	II	12	12	13	15	17	19	21 *18–25*
Sale of simulated controlled substance	I	12	12	12	13	15	17	19 *17–22*

⬜ At the discretion of the judge, up to a year in jail and/or other nonjail sanctions can be imposed instead of prison sentences as conditions of probation for most of these offenses. If prison is imposed, the presumptive sentence is the number of months shown.

⬜ Presumptive commitment to state prison for all offenses.

Note: First-degree murder has a mandatory life sentence and is excluded from the guidelines by law.

Source: Minnesota Sentencing Guidelines Commission, *Minnesota Sentencing Guidelines and Commentary*, revised August 1, 2010.

discretion of judges and to reduce disparity among sentences given for similar offenses. Although statutes provide a variety of sentencing options for particular crimes, guidelines attempt to direct the judge to more-specific actions that should be taken. The range of sentencing options provided for most offenses centers on the seriousness of the crime and on the criminal history of an offender.

Legislatures and, in some states and the federal government, commissions construct sentencing guidelines as a grid of two scores (Tonry, 1993). As shown in Table 9.5, the Minnesota Guidelines, one dimension relates to the seriousness of the offense, the other to the likelihood of offender recidivism. The offender score is obtained by totaling the points allocated to such factors as the number of juvenile offenses, adult misdemeanors, and adult felony convictions; the number of times incarcerated; the status of the accused at the time of the last offense, whether on probation or parole or escaped from confinement; and employment status or educational achievement. Judges look at the grid to see what sentence should be imposed on a particular offender who has committed a specific offense. Judges may go outside the guidelines if aggravating or mitigating circumstances exist; however, they must provide a written explanation of their reasons for doing so (Fischman and Schanzenbach, 2011).

Sentencing guidelines are to be reviewed and modified periodically so that recent decisions will be included. Given that guidelines are constructed on the basis of past sentences, some critics argue that because the guidelines reflect only what has happened, they do not reform sentencing. Others question the choice of characteristics included in the offender scale and charge that some are used to mask racial criteria. Paula Krautt (2002) found differences in drug-trafficking sentences among federal district and circuit courts. However, Lisa Stolzenberg and Stewart J. D'Alessio (1994) studied the Minnesota guidelines and found, compared with pre-guideline decisions, an 18 percent reduction in disparity for the prison/no-prison outcome and a 60 percent reduction in disparity of length of prison sentences.

Although guidelines make sentences more uniform, many judges object to having their discretion limited in this manner (Zimmerman, 2011). However, Peter Rossi and Richard Berk (1997) found a fair amount of agreement between the sentences prescribed in the federal guidelines and those desired by the general public.

The future of sentencing guidelines is uncertain. In 2004, the U.S. Supreme Court decided that aspects of Washington State sentencing guidelines violated the Sixth Amendment right to trial by jury, by giving judges too much authority to enhance sentences based on unproved factual determinations (*Blakely v. Washington*). One year later, the Supreme Court applied the *Blakely* precedent to the federal sentencing guidelines and found a similar violation of the Sixth Amendment when judges enhance sentences based on their own determinations (*United States v. Booker*, 2005). In effect, federal judges are expected to consult the guidelines, but they are not mandatory and federal judges can make reasonable deviations (Wu and Spohn, 2010). In 2008, however, the Supreme Court ruled that federal judges are not required to give advance notice to defendants prior to imposing a sentence that varies from the guidelines (*Irizarry v. United States*, 2008). Yet, most sentences in federal courts remain in conformity with the guidelines (U.S. Sentencing Commission, 2006). Observers anticipate that the U.S. Supreme Court will need to revisit this issue in order to provide guidance about how sentencing guidelines can be properly designed and applied. For example, in 2011 the Court determined that federal judges can consider evidence of an offender's rehabilitation in imposing a sentence that is below those specified in sentencing guidelines (*Pepper v. United States*, 2011).

Judges' decisions have profound impacts on the lives of people drawn into the criminal justice system. Would you want to make sentencing decisions that determine the fates of people convicted of crimes? Consider how you would perform as a judge when you read "Careers in Criminal Justice." In addition, bear these considerations in mind as you assume the role of a judge and design a sentence for a controversial 2012 case as described at the end of the chapter in "A Question of Ethics."

Who Gets the Harshest Punishment?

Harsh, unjust punishments can occur because of sentencing disparities and wrongful convictions. The prison population in most states contains a higher proportion of African American and Hispanic men than occurs in the general population. Are these disparities caused by racial prejudices and discrimination, or are other factors at work? Wrongful conviction takes place when people who are in fact innocent are nonetheless found guilty by plea or verdict. It also occurs in those cases in which the conviction of a truly guilty person is overturned on appeal because of due process errors.

Racial Disparities Studies of racial disparities in sentencing are inconclusive. Because some studies show disparities in specific states or cities, though, there are grave concerns about the possibility of racial discrimination. Studies of sentencing

District Associate Judge

Ottumwa, Iowa
Kirk Daily, District Associate Judge

Photo provided by Kirk Daily. © Cengage Learning

Under Iowa law, district associate judges have the authority to hear Class D felonies as well as serious and aggravated misdemeanors. Substance-abuse crimes can form a significant component of the court's docket. Such crimes include operating a motor vehicle while intoxicated and possession of controlled substances. The penalties for crimes handled by this limited-jurisdiction court can range from probation and other community-based sanctions to one year in county jail and up to

five years in state prison. Thus, these judges' decisions significantly impact the lives of people charged with such crimes.

Judges in such courts make determinations of probable cause and decide whether to issue search warrants. They also conduct preliminary hearings in criminal cases. District associate judges also have jurisdiction over civil suits when the amount in controversy is $10,000 or less. Finally, these judges handle appeals for both criminal and civil matters that have been decided in the limited-jurisdiction magistrate court

After graduating from college and law school, Kirk Daily entered private law practice as an attorney in his hometown of Ottumwa, Iowa. The career path to a judgeship, whether in a system of elected judges or appointed judges, typically depends on building a solid reputation for wisdom, intelligence, ethics, and industriousness. Daily gained significant knowledge and experience in many areas of law

through a broad, general law practice that ranged from representing criminal defendants for serious crimes, including murder, to civil cases such as medical malpractice and divorce. The breadth of his experience as a lawyer provided exceptionally good training for his later role as judge. As a judge, he must use his knowledge of law to make decisions concerning a wide variety of cases, both criminal and civil. Iowa uses a merit-selection process for choosing judges, and Daily's solid experience and impressive performance as an attorney led to his selection for a judgeship.

Substance abuse crimes, such as the use and manufacture of methamphetamine and drunk driving, take up a great deal of my time. There are high recidivism rates among substance abusers, and their cases require a high level of follow-up supervision to assist these individuals to deal with their addictions. In sentencing substance abusers, judges must often weigh public safety against treatment. Creating a sentence that aims to treat a person's addiction, rather than simply imposing prison, increases a judge's options.

in Pennsylvania, for example, found that there is a "high cost of being black, young (21–29 years), and male." Sentences given these offenders resulted in a higher proportion going to prison and incurring longer terms (Steffensmeier, Ulmer, and Kramer, 1998). While supporting the Pennsylvania results, research in Chicago, Kansas City, Missouri, and Miami found variation among the jurisdictions as to sentence length (Spohn and Holleran, 2000). Other research shows disproportionate effects on African American men being sent to prison through mandatory punishments and sentence enhancements (Schlesinger, 2011).

Do these disparities stem from the prejudicial attitudes of judges, police officers, and prosecutors? Are African Americans and Hispanics viewed as a "racial threat" when they commit crimes of violence and drug selling, which are thought to be spreading from the urban ghetto to the "previously safe places of the suburbs" (Crawford, Chiricos, and Kleck, 1998:484)? Are enforcement resources distributed so that certain groups are subject to closer scrutiny than are other groups?

Scholars have pointed out that the relationship between race and sentencing is complex and that judges consider many defendant and case characteristics. According to this view, judges assess not only the legally relevant factors of blameworthiness, dangerousness, and recidivism risk, but also race, gender, and age characteristics (Steen, Engen, and Gainey, 2005). The interconnectedness of these variables, not judges' negative attitudes, is what culminates in the disproportionately severe sentences given young black men.

Federal sentencing guidelines were adjusted in 2007 and 2008 to reduce the impact of a highly criticized source of racial disparities in prison sentences for offenders convicted of cocaine-related offenses. The federal sentencing guidelines for crack cocaine offenses—which disproportionately affected African American defendants—were adjusted to be more closely aligned with shorter sentences for possessing and selling similar amounts of powder cocaine, crimes more commonly associated with white offenders. The U.S. Sentencing Commission voted to apply these new guidelines retroactively, meaning that offenders currently serving long sentences for crack cocaine offenses were eligible to be resentenced to shorter terms in prison. In many cases, this adjustment led to the release in 2008 of offenders who had already served for longer periods than those required under the new sentencing guidelines (Gezari, 2008; *Third Branch*, 2008b). As mentioned earlier, President Obama signed into law a new federal statute that reduced, but did not eliminate, the disparities in mandatory sentences for crack and powder cocaine offenders (Eckholm, 2010).

AP Images/The Southern, Paul Newton

In recent years, the development of DNA evidence has contributed to the reinvestigation of cases and the release of people sent to prison for crimes that they did not commit. Here, James Harden gained release in 2011 after spending 20 years in prison. His innocence was discovered when DNA tests proved that he did not commit the rape and murder for which he was imprisoned. How could criminal justice processes be changed to reduce the risks of erroneous convictions?

Wrongful Convictions A serious dilemma for the criminal justice system concerns people who are wrongly convicted and sentenced. Whereas the public expresses much concern over those who "beat the system" and go free, they pay comparatively little attention to those who are innocent yet convicted. Many of these people are wrongly convicted because victims and witnesses make mistakes in identifying alleged criminals from photographs and lineups.

The development of DNA technology has increased the number of people exonerated after being convicted. However, many cases do not have DNA evidence available. C. Ronald Huff notes that "because the great majority of cases do not produce biological material to be tested, one can only speculate about the error rate in those cases" (2002:2). Even when there is DNA evidence available, the U.S. Supreme Court has ruled that convicted offenders do not have a constitutional right to have the stored evidence tested. According to a five-member majority on the Court, state legislatures and Congress should develop their own rules concerning opportunities to have old evidence tested (*District Attorney's Office v. Osborne*, 2009). Every year, national attention focuses on several cases in which innocent people have been erroneously convicted, yet there is no way to know how many more innocent people may be wrongly confined in prisons today.

Whether from racial discrimination or wrongful convictions, unjust punishments do not serve the ideals of justice. Such punishments raise fundamental questions about the criminal justice system and its links to the society it serves.

check point > **6. What are the four factors thought to influence the sentencing behavior of judges?** The administrative context of the courts, the attitudes and values of judges, the presentence report, and sentencing guidelines.

stop& analyze If your son were arrested for a crime and you believed his claim that he was innocent, are there any steps you could take to reduce the likelihood that he would be subject to an erroneous conviction? Make a list of what you might do to help your son.

Prosecution, Adjudication, and Sentencing

Written by Chuck Terry

Los Angeles County has the largest jail system in the country. On any given day it houses roughly 20,000 inmates. As I walked into the main jail I was so sick I could hardly stand. Once the chains were removed I was placed in a holding tank with other "new arrivals." Whereas getting booked at the city jail took less than an hour, here it took two days. Remember, I had yet to be formally charged and had not had contact with an attorney.

As time passed, more and more bodies were packed inside the tank. Before long we were standing shoulder to shoulder, butt to butt, like sardines in a can. My nightmare was at a high point. I felt like I wouldn't be able to do this much longer—like I might collapse or lose consciousness. Right then this guy looked at me and said, "Hey, brother, you're sick as hell aren't you?" When I said yes, he directed those around me to move over just enough so I could sit down. Never have I been so glad to sit.

We were eventually herded into a larger holding tank that had one seatless toilet and a sink for everyone. In this world privacy does not exist. Hours are spent in these concrete enclosures with others who are arrested for everything from public drunkenness to robbery. Most are addicts, skid-row winos, homeless people, or a mixture of all three. Many have mental problems. Within these rooms one hears a constant mixture of echoes from slamming cell doors, people yelling, wailing, vomiting, and laughing. Strange how, over time, I got used to it.

The next step of the journey involved being strip-searched. As our clothes were removed, the stench of body odor permeated the room. It took effort not to gag. After having every orifice of our naked bodies examined by deputies, we were steered to a shower area, given about thirty seconds to wash, and then sprayed with bug repellent. Next came jail clothing, a wool blanket, and a towel.

Before being assigned to a cell we were photographed, fingerprinted, and given receipts for our property. Finally, after nearly two days, I was led to a four-man cell—my next temporary home. There were already six men living there—two sleeping on the floor (these cells had enough space for two bunks, a toilet, a sink, and about thirty inches between the bunks). I, along with two of the others, slept on the concrete floor. Whereas they slept directly underneath each of the bunks, I took the space between them—and was glad to have it. No mattress. No pillow. But the blanket and the space sure were nice.

I welcomed the chance to rest. I still couldn't sleep, but it felt good to just lie there. Around 3:30 A.M. a guard came down the tier (the walkway in front of the rows of cells), waking up people whose names were on the daily court list. I was one of the fortunate few. Within a few minutes the cell door opened and I was guided to a holding tank where I waited with other court-bound men to be taken downstairs for breakfast. Once given food and seated, we had about three minutes to eat.

Our next stop was an area containing dozens of holding tanks—each acting as way stations for different courts. Deputies, reading names and court destinations from printouts, directed us to the appropriate tanks. I soon learned that I'd be going to the Torrance court.

Before long we could hear the rattling of chains—a signal that we would soon be departing. As our names were called, we walked forward and placed our wrists in cuffs. After we were chained, we were led out of the jail into a parking lot where a huge fleet of black-and-white buses sat, waiting to take us to courts all over the county.

A jail bus ride can be an eventful occasion. For a short time you are almost in the world. Through steel-meshed windows you see cars, buildings, parks, streetlights, and people who are free—including women. Many of the men yell and joke about whatever crosses their mind. Others stare idly through the steel grillwork—silent and serious looking. Five days after my arrest I was finally going before a judge.

After arriving at the Torrance courthouse, we were taken to a basement holding tank and unchained. Because I didn't have money for a lawyer I was assigned a public defender (PD), whom I met through the bars of a holding cell located next to the courtroom. His name was Robert Harrison. Like every other lawyer I ever had, he was white.

He carried a briefcase packed with papers, had a suit on, and looked like he was in his late twenties. Although clearly hurried, he treated me with respect. After introducing himself he informed me that this would be my initial appearance and that I'd be back in two weeks for a preliminary hearing. Our meeting took about three minutes.

During the initial appearance I was arraigned in municipal court (the lower, or misdemeanor, court), which meant being legally charged, given a set amount of bail, and given a date on which to return. The district attorney (DA) and public defender introduced themselves to the judge as participants in the case. The entire proceeding took less than a minute. Afterward, as bailiffs escorted me from the courtroom, my PD told me, "See you soon."

Two weeks later, still in jail and running on no sleep, I returned for my preliminary hearing—the phase of the process in which the district attorney tries to convince the court that a felony has been committed while the PD shoots for dismissal based on lack of evidence or an unlawful arrest. The woman who called the police testified that she had seen suspicious activity around my room—strangers coming and going. The police testified that I evaded arrest. The heroin, money, and other drugs taken from my pockets and room were used as evidence. My PD tried to get the case dismissed by arguing that the police searched me without probable cause. The DA said the search had been lawful. The court ruled against me, and I was bound over for arraignment in the superior court (felony court). After the hearing, my lawyer told me, "It doesn't look good." I asked him, "How much time do you think I'll have to do?" He said I'd "better plan on doing five" (that meant years and that meant prison).

Arraignment in the superior court came two weeks later. This time, as well as being told what I was charged with, I made a plea. In another brief meeting before the hearing, my lawyer told me, "When they ask you to plead, say 'Not guilty.' The judge will then set a trial date. Before that time arrives I hope to know more about what the DA wants from this case." I did as he suggested and a trial date was set. Within a few weeks my PD came to visit me in the county jail to tell me about a deal being offered by the district attorney. If I pled guilty to possession of a controlled substance (heroin), the rest of the charges would be dropped and I would be sent to the Southern California Regional Guidance Center at Chino—state prison, for a ninety-day evaluation, a process designed to assist the court at sentencing. He said, "Because of the evidence in this case I don't think we'd have a chance to win at trial. If you take the deal there is the possibility that a positive evaluation by the people at Chino might influence the judge to send you to a drug program. The worst-case scenario, though, is two to ten years for possession. On the other hand, if you go to trial and lose, you will most likely get five to fifteen years for possession with the intent to sell."

I knew my situation was bleak. The court already had a presentence investigation (PSI) report from my last case, in which I received jail time and probation. I didn't think I had a chance of being found not guilty for my current charges. Plus I had heard about guys getting breaks after going to Chino. So the deal sounded good and I went for it.

To formally accept the deal I had to plead guilty in court to the charge of possession of heroin. My PD told me I needed to understand that doing so must be a decision I willingly made and that the judge possibly would not accept the deal. Finally, there were no guarantees as to what type of sentence I'd get. He said he'd recommend a drug program, but the chances were good that I'd have to do prison time, regardless of what type of evaluation I received from Chino.

When the court date arrived I appeared in Judge Barrett's courtroom. The district attorney told the judge that in exchange for a guilty plea to possession of a controlled substance, the people would agree to drop the rest of the charges. My PD said that we agreed. Then the judge said, "Mr. Terry, before accepting this plea I must ensure that you are doing so voluntarily. Has anyone coerced you in any way to plead guilty to this charge?" I said, "No." "Has anyone promised that you will receive a specific sentence if you plead guilty?" "No." "Do you understand that you do not have to make this plea and that you have a right to a trial by a jury of your peers?" "Yes." "And understanding all this, do you waive that right at this time?" By now I was wondering if I was making a mistake. It seemed as if the judge was trying to talk me out of it. I looked at my PD for assurance. He nodded his head, indicating it was OK. I said, "Yes." After accepting my plea of guilty the judge sent me to Chino as expected and said that sentencing would take place upon my return to court.

The "evaluation" from the ninety-day observation came from a twenty-minute interview by a counselor who recommended a drug program and a fifteen-minute interview by a psychologist (nicknamed San Quentin Sally) who said I was a threat to society and belonged in prison. Within three months I was back in the county jail awaiting my final court date.

Finally, five days after I returned from Chino, I was again taken before Judge Barrett for sentencing. Inside the courtroom, before the actual hearing took place, my PD showed me a copy of the evaluation from Chino that clearly indicated the likelihood of a prison sentence. San Quentin Sally not only recommended prison but also said I was a chronic liar with a dismal future. Once I read that I lost all hope for a drug program. Right then I also felt alone, isolated, like it was me against the world and I was definitely losing. I had no friends or family in the courtroom, I was surrounded by strangers dressed in suits and fancy dresses, and the only person who seemed to care about my well-being was my PD.

When the hearing began, the DA used my criminal history and the evaluation from Chino as justification for a prison sentence. My PD suggested a drug program because I had an extensive history of addiction and no arrests for violent crimes. He pointed out that this was also the conclusion of the counselor at Chino. Before imposing the sentence, the judge asked me if I had anything to say. I said no. Then he said, "After considering all sides of this matter I feel little choice but to send you to the department of corrections for the term prescribed by law. I understand you have a problem with drugs, but you've had your chances in the past. It is my hope that when you get to prison you do something to better yourself so when you get out you can live a normal, decent life. With this said, I sentence you to do not less than two but no more than ten years in the California Department of Corrections for possession of narcotics."

I felt good that day when they chained me up to take me back to the county jail. It had been a while since I got arrested, and I was finally headed for the last leg of my journey. I figured that with the time I had already spent in custody, plus good time, I would be out within eighteen months to two years.

Jails contain both pretrial detainees, who are presumptively innocent until proved guilty, and convicted offenders awaiting transfer to prison or serving short sentences. Should as-yet-unconvicted detainees, some of whom may eventually be found not guilty, experience the same conditions and deprivations as convicted offenders inside jails? Or should pretrial detainees be kept in separate areas and given more-extensive privileges? What if the jail lacks the space and resources to treat the groups differently?

the jail inmates are sentenced offenders under correctional authority. Thus, many experts argue that jails have outgrown police administration.

Inmate Characteristics

The mixture of offenders of widely diverse ages and criminal histories in U.S. jails is an often-cited problem. Because criminal justice professionals view most inmates as temporary residents, they make little attempt to classify them for either security or treatment purposes. Horror stories of the mistreatment of young offenders by older, stronger, and more violent inmates occasionally come to public attention. The physical condition of most jails aggravates this situation, because most are old, overcrowded, and lacking in basic facilities. Many sentenced felons prefer to move on to state prison, where the conditions tend to be better.

Because inmate turnover is high and because local control provides an incentive to keep costs down, jails usually lack correctional services. They do not usually offer recreational facilities or treatment programs, and medical services are generally minimal. Such conditions add to the idleness and tensions of the inmates. Suicides and high levels of violence are hallmarks of many jails. In any one year, almost half the people who die while in jail have committed suicide.

Fiscal Problems

Jails help control crime but also drain local revenues. The tension between these two public interests often surfaces in debates over expenditures for jail construction and operation. Because revenues often fall short, many jails are overcrowded, lack programs, and do not have enough officers for effective supervision. In some areas, multicounty jails serve an entire region as a means of operating facilities in a cost-efficient way.

As criminal justice policy has become more punitive, jails, like prisons, have become crowded. Even with new construction and with alternatives such as release on recognizance programs, diversion, intensive probation supervision, and house arrest with electronic monitoring, the jail population continues to rise. The annual cost of operating jails heavily burdens local governments and this burden has become more difficult in an era of budget cuts and layoffs of sheriff's deputies and other jail officers. In New Jersey, for example, the Camden County Jail was forced to lay off 60 corrections officers in 2011—one-quarter of the workforce—due to severe budget difficulties, even though the facility handles a high volume of detainees in one of the most crime-plagued places in the state (Osborne, 2011).

4. What agencies of the U.S. government are responsible for prisons and probation?
The Federal Bureau of Prisons, which handles prisons, and the Administrative Office of the U.S. Courts, which handles probation.

5. What agencies of state government are responsible for prisons, probation, intermediate sanctions, and parole?
Prisons: department of corrections (executive branch). *Probation:* judiciary or executive department. *Intermediate sanctions:* judiciary, probation department, department of corrections. *Parole:* executive agency.

6. What are the functions of jails?
Holding of offenders before trial and incarceration of offenders sentenced to short terms.

stop& analyze Does a philosophical problem arise when convicted offenders are sent to privately run prisons and jails? In criminal law, the government imposes punishment on people for breaking the laws made by the government. Does this mean that only the government should administer the punishment? List two arguments either supporting or opposing the idea that all criminal punishment should be administered by government.

The Law of Corrections

Prior to the 1960s, most courts maintained a **hands-off policy** with respect to corrections. Only a few state courts had recognized rights for offenders. Most judges felt that prisoners and probationers did not have protected rights and that courts should not interfere with the operational agencies dealing with probation, prisons, and parole.

Since the 1960s, however, offenders have gained access to the courts to contest correctional officers' decisions and challenge aspects of their punishment that they believe violate basic rights. Judicial decisions have defined and recognized the constitutional rights of probationers, prisoners, and parolees, as well as the need for policies and procedures that respect those rights. As you read "Criminal Justice: Myth & Reality," consider your own views about the recognition of constitutional rights for convicted criminal offenders.

hands-off policy Judges should not interfere with the administration of correctional institutions.

Constitutional Rights of Prisoners

The U.S. Supreme Court decision in *Cooper v. Pate* (1964) signaled the end of the hands-off policy. The court said that through the Civil Rights Act of 1871 (referred to here as Section 1983), state prisoners were *persons* whose rights are protected by the Constitution. The act imposes *civil liability* on any official who violates someone's constitutional rights. It allows suits against state officials to be heard in the federal courts. Because of *Cooper v. Pate*, the federal courts now recognize that prisoners may sue state officials over such things as brutality by guards, inadequate nutrition and medical care, theft of personal property, and the denial of basic rights.

The first successful prisoners' rights cases involved the most excessive of prison abuses: brutality and inhumane physical conditions. Gradually, however, prison litigation has focused more directly on the daily activities of the institution, especially on the administrative rules that regulate inmates' conduct (C. E. Smith, 2007). This focus has resulted in a series of court decisions concerning the First, Fourth, Eighth, and Fourteenth Amendments to the Constitution. (See Chapter 3 for the full text of these amendments.)

Cooper v. Pate (1964) Prisoners are entitled to the protection of the Civil Rights Act of 1871 and may challenge in federal courts the conditions of their confinement.

11

Incarceration and Prison Society

Learning Objectives

- → Describe how contemporary institutions differ from the old-style "big-house" prisons
- → Understand the three models of incarceration that have predominated since the 1940s
- → Explain how a prison is organized
- → Know how a prison is governed
- → Understand the role of correctional officers in a prison
- → Explain the characteristics of the incarcerated population
- → Discuss what prison is like for men and for women
- → List some of the programs and services available to prisoners
- → Describe the nature of prison violence

We're crowded into the Department of Corrections' bus, 20 convicts en route to the state prison. I'm handcuffed to two other men, the chains gleaming dully at wrists and ankles. The man on my right lifts his hand to smoke, the red eye of his cigarette burning through the darkness of the van. When he exhales, the man at my left coughs, the sound in his lungs suggesting that he's old, maybe sick. I want to ask what he's in for. But I don't speak, restrained by my fear, a feeling that rises cold up the back of my spine. For a long time no one else speaks either, each man locked in his own thoughts. It's someone up front, a kid, his voice brittle with fear, who speaks first. "What's it like down there—in the joint? Is it as bad as they say?"

"Worse," someone answers. "Cell blocks are dirty. Overcrowded. Lousy chow. Harassment. Stabbings."

"How do you live there?"

"You don't exactly live. You go through the motions. Eat, sleep, mind your own business. Do drugs when you can get them. Forget the world you came from."

This description of the "way in" was written by an inmate who was incarcerated in the Arizona penal system for seven years. It conveys much of the anxiety not only of the new "fish" but also of the old con. What goes on inside U.S. prisons? What does incarceration mean to the inmates, the guards, the administrators, the public? Are the officers in charge or do the prisoners "rule the joint"? In the Close Up box on page 345, Michael Santos describes his anxiety as a 24-year-old first-time offender entering the U.S. Federal Penitentiary in Atlanta.

In this chapter, we focus on the goals of incarceration, the challenges of management, and the inmate's experience. Discussion also centers on violence in prison and the policies and programs intended to keep correctional institutions from boiling over.

The Modern Prison: Legacy of the Past

American correctional institutions have always been more varied than the way movies or novels portray them. Fictional depictions of prison life are typically set in a fortress, the "big house"—the maximum-security prisons where the inmates are tough and the guards are just as tough or tougher. Although big houses predominated in much of the country during the first half of the twentieth century, many prisons were based on other models. In the South, for instance, prisoners worked outside at farm labor, and the massive walled structures were not so common.

The typical big house of the 1940s and 1950s was a walled prison with large, tiered cell blocks, a yard, shops, and industrial workshops. About 2,500 prisoners served their time in each institution. They came from both urban and rural areas, were usually poor, and, outside the South, were predominantly white. The prison society was essentially isolated, with restricted access to visitors, mail, and other communication. Prisoners' days were strictly structured, with rules enforced by the guards. A basic division stood between inmates and staff; rank was observed and discipline maintained. In the big house, few treatment programs existed; custody stood as the primary goal.

During the 1960s and early 1970s, when the rehabilitation model prevailed, many states built new prisons and converted others into "correctional institutions." Treatment programs administered by counselors and teachers became a major part of prison life, although the institutions continued to give priority to the custody goals of security, discipline, and order.

During the past 30 years, as the population of the United States has changed, so has the prison population. The number of African American and Hispanic inmates has greatly increased. More inmates come from urban areas, and more have been convicted of drug-related and violent offenses. Former street gangs, often organized along racial lines, today regroup inside prisons; such gangs have raised the level of violence in many institutions.

Further, the focus of corrections has shifted to crime control, which emphasizes the importance of incarceration. Not only has the number of people in prison greatly increased, but many states have removed educational and recreational amenities from institutions.

One Man's Walk through Atlanta's Jungle

Michael G. Santos

I was not expecting to receive the southern hospitality for which Atlanta is famous when the bus turned into the penitentiary's large, circular drive, but neither did I expect to see a dozen uniformed prison guards—all carrying machine guns—surround the bus when it stopped. A month in transit already had passed by the time we made it to the U.S. Penitentiary (USP) in Atlanta, the institution that would hold me (along with over two thousand other felons) until we were transferred to other prisons, we were released, or we were dead.

I left the jail in Tacoma, Washington, on the first of August, but I didn't see the huge gray walls that surround USP Atlanta until the first of September. That month was spent in a bus operated by the U.S. Marshal Service as it moved across the country, picking up federal prisoners in local jails and dropping them off at various Bureau of Prison facilities.

As I crossed the country, I listened to tales from numerous prisoners who sat beside me on the bus. There wasn't much to discuss except what was to come. Each of us was chained at the hands and feet. There were neither magazines to read nor music playing. Mostly people spoke about a riot that had taken place behind USP Atlanta's walls a few months earlier. A lot of the men had been to prison before, and Atlanta would be nothing new. Those prisoners only talked about reuniting with old friends, explaining prison routine, or sat like stone-cold statues waiting for what was to come. I'd never been confined before, so it was hard to tune out the stories that others were telling. While I was listening, though, I remember telling myself that I would survive this sentence. No matter what it took, I would survive.

I was in my early 20s, younger than perhaps every other prisoner on the bus. Pimples spotted my face as I began my term, but I was certain my black hair would be white by the time I finished. I had been sentenced to forty-five years by a U.S. district court judge in Tacoma on charges related to cocaine trafficking. I was expected to serve close to thirty years before release. It was hard then—just as it is hard now—to believe the sentence was real. The best thing I could do, I reasoned, was to stay to myself. I'd heard the same rumors that every suburban kid hears about prison. I was anxious about what was to come, but I was determined to make it out alive and with my mind intact. Now it was all to begin!

After the bus stopped, the guards began calling us off by last name and prison number. It is not easy to walk with a twelve-inch chain connected to each ankle, and wrists bound to a chain that runs around the waist, but when my name was called, I managed to wobble through the bus's aisle, hop down the steps, and then begin the long march up the stairs leading to the fortress. As I was moving to the prison's doors, I remember glancing over my shoulder, knowing it would be the last time I'd see the world from the outside of prison walls for a long time.

Once inside the institution, the guards began unlocking my chains. About fifty other prisoners arrived with me that day, so the guards had plenty of chains to unlock, but their work didn't stop there. They also had to squeeze us through the dehumanizing admissions machine. The machine begins with photographs, fingerprints, and interrogations. Then comes the worst part, the strip search, where each prisoner stands before a prison official, naked, and responds to the scream: "Lift up your arms in the air! Let me see the back of your hands! Run your fingers through your hair! Open your mouth! Stick your tongue out! Lift your balls! Turn around! Bend over! Spread your ass! Wider! Lift the bottom of your feet! Move on!"

The strip search, I later learned, is a ritual Atlanta's officers inflict on prisoners every time they have contact with anyone from outside the walls, and sometimes randomly as prisoners walk down the corridor.

There was a lot of hatred behind those walls. Walking through the prison must be something like walking through a jungle, I imagined, not knowing whether others perceive you as predator or prey, knowing that you must remain always alert, watching every step, knowing that the wrong step may be the one that sucks you into the quicksand. The tension is ever present; I felt it wrapped all over, under and around me. I remember it bothering me that I didn't have enough hatred, because not hating in the jungle is a weakness. As the serpents slither, they spot that lack of hatred and salivate over a potential target.

Every prisoner despises confinement, but each must decide how he or she is going to do the time. Most of the men run in packs. They want the other prisoners either to run with them or run away from them. I wasn't interested in doing either. Instead of scheming on how I could become king of the jungle, I thought about ways that I could advance my release date. Earning academic credentials, keeping a clean record, and initiating projects that would benefit the communities both inside and outside of prison walls seemed the most promising goals for me to achieve. Yet working toward such goals was more dangerous than running with the pack; it didn't take me long to learn that prisoners running in herds will put forth more energy to cause others to lose than they will to win themselves. Prison is a twisted world, a menagerie.

I found that a highly structured schedule would not only move me closer to my goals, but also would limit potential conflicts inside the prison. There is a pecking order in every prison, and prisoners vying for attention don't want to see others who are cutting their own path. I saw that bullies generally look for

continued

One Man's Walk through Atlanta's Jungle

weaker targets, so I began an exercise routine that would keep me physically strong. If I were strong, I figured, others would be more reluctant to try me. Through discipline, I found, I could develop physical strength. Yet I've never figured out how to develop the look of a killer, or the hatred off which that look feeds.

I don't know whether the strategies I have developed for doing time are right for everyone. But they are working for me. Still, I know that I may spend many more years in prison. The only fear I have—and as I'm working on my eighth year, it's still here—is that someone will try me and drag me into an altercation that may jeopardize my spotless disciplinary record. I've been successful in avoiding the ever-present quicksand on my walk through the jungle so far, but I know that on any given day, something may throw me off balance, or I may take a wrong step. And one wrong step in this jungle can drown me in quicksand, sucking me into the abysmal world of prison forever. That wrong step also could mean the loss of life, mine or someone else's.

In prison, more than anywhere else I know, understanding that some things are beyond an individual's sphere of control is vital. No matter how much preparation is made, the steel and concrete jungle is a dangerous place in which to live.

Researching the Internet

Michael Santos is now incarcerated at the Federal Prison Camp in Taft, California. While in prison he has completed bachelor's and master's degrees. He is the author of *About Prison* (Belmont, CA: Wadsworth, 2004) and *Inside: Life behind Bars in America* (New York: St. Martin's Press, 2006), and four other books. You can contact Santos through his website by going to the Criminal Justice CourseMate at cengagebrain.com and accessing the links to this chapter.

Source: Written for this book by Michael G. Santos. In 1987, he was sentenced to 45 years in prison for drug trafficking. Because of his impeccable disciplinary record, he looks forward to release in 2013.

custodial model A model of incarceration that emphasizes security, discipline, and order.

rehabilitation model A model of incarceration that emphasizes treatment programs to help prisoners address the personal problems and issues that led them to commit crimes.

Today, prisoners are less isolated from the outside world than before. As we have seen, the Supreme Court has ruled on issues of communication and access to information for prisoners, weighing their constitutional rights against the need for order and safety within the prison walls. Another difference from the past is that correctional officers have used collective bargaining to improve their working conditions.

Although today's correctional administrators seek to provide humane incarceration, they must struggle with limited resources and shortages of cell space. Thus, the modern prison faces many of the difficult problems that confront other parts of the criminal justice system: racial conflicts, legal issues, limited resources, and growing populations. Despite these challenges, can prisons still achieve their objectives? The answer to this question depends, in part, on how we define the goals of incarceration.

check point

> 1. **How does today's prison differ from the big house of the past?**
>
> The characteristics of the inmate population have changed, more inmates are from urban areas and have been convicted for drug-related or violent offenses, the inmate population is fragmented along racial and ethnic lines, prisoners are less isolated from the outside world, and correctional officers have used collective bargaining to improve their working conditions.

stop & analyze

With access to television, telephones, and, in an increasing number of prison systems, email communications (F. Green, 2011), prisoners are not as isolated from the outside world as they once were. What are some possible negative and positive consequences of this increased contact? How might this affect life inside prisons?

Goals of Incarceration

Citing the nature of inmates and the need to protect staff and the community, most people consider security the dominant purpose of a prison. High walls, barbed-wire fences, searches, checkpoints, and regular counts of inmates serve the security function: Few inmates escape. More importantly, the features set the tone for the daily operations. Prisons stand as impersonal, quasi-military places where strict discipline, minimal amenities, and restrictions on freedom serve to punish criminals.

Three models of incarceration have predominated since the early 1940s: the custodial, rehabilitation, and reintegration models. Each is associated with one style of institutional organization.

1. The **custodial model** assumes that prisoners have been incarcerated for the purpose of incapacitation, deterrence, or retribution. It emphasizes security, discipline, and order in subordinating the prisoner to the authority of the warden. Discipline is strict, and most aspects of behavior are regulated. Having prevailed in corrections before World War II, this model dominates most maximum-security institutions today.

2. The **rehabilitation model**, developed during the 1950s, emphasizes treatment programs designed to reform the offender. According to this model, security and housekeeping activities are viewed primarily as preconditions for rehabilitative efforts. Because all aspects of the organization should center on rehabilitation, professional treatment specialists carry a higher status than do other employees. Since the rethinking of the rehabilitation goal in the 1970s, treatment programs still exist in most institutions, but few prisons conform to this model today.

3. The **reintegration model** is linked to the structures and goals of community corrections. Recognizing that prisoners will be returning to society, this model emphasizes maintaining the offenders' ties to family and community as a method of reform. Prisons following this model gradually give inmates greater freedom and responsibility during their confinement, moving them to halfway houses or work release programs before giving them community supervision.

Question: "State prison systems could offer the following four alternative prison policies for people who have committed nonviolent crime. What would you prefer the state implement?"

Policy 1: Treat prison as punishment and do not offer rehabilitation services to people either during their time in prison or after their release.

Policy 2: Make state-funded rehabilitation services available to incarcerated people while they are serving time in prison.

Policy 3: Make state-funded rehabilitation services available to incarcerated people only after they have been released from prison.

Policy 4: Make state-funded rehabilitation services available to incarcerated people both while they are in prison and after they have been released from prison.

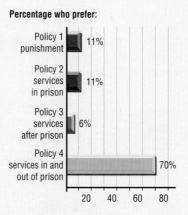

Percentage who prefer:

- Policy 1 punishment — 11%
- Policy 2 services in prison — 11%
- Policy 3 services after prison — 6%
- Policy 4 services in and out of prison — 70%

Critical Thinking: A study of public attitudes on punishment found that women tend to be more supportive of rehabilitation than men are. List two reasons why this gender difference in attitudes might exist.

Note: May not add to 100% due to rounding and missing responses.

Source: Barry Krisberg and Susan Marchionna. "Attitudes of U.S. Voters toward Prison Rehabilitation and Reentry Policies," *Focus: Views from the National Council on Crime and Delinquency* (April) (Oakland, CA: National Council on Crime and Delinquency, 2006).

Although one can find correctional institutions that conform to each of these models, most prisons are mainly custodial. Nevertheless, treatment programs do exist, and because almost all inmates return to society at some point, even the most custodial institutions must prepare them for their reintegration. See "What Americans Think" for a look at how the public views the goals of incarceration.

Much is asked of prisons. As Charles Logan notes, "We ask them to correct the incorrigible, rehabilitate the wretched, deter the determined, restrain the dangerous, and punish the wicked" (Logan, 1993:19). Because prisons are expected to pursue many different and often incompatible goals, they are almost doomed to

reintegration model A model of a correctional institution that emphasizes maintaining the offender's ties to family and community as a method of reform, recognizing that the offender will be returning to society.

fail as institutions. Logan believes that the mission of prisons is confinement. He argues that imprisonment serves primarily to punish offenders fairly and justly through lengths of confinement proportionate to the seriousness of their crimes. He summarizes the mission of prison as follows: "to keep prisoners—to keep them in, keep them safe, keep them in line, keep them healthy, and keep them busy—and to do it with fairness, without undue suffering, and as efficiently as possible" (Logan, 1993:21). If the purpose of prisons is punishment through confinement under fair and just conditions, what are the implications of this purpose for correctional managers?

check point > 2. **What three models of prison have predominated since the 1940s?**
The custodial, rehabilitation, and reintegration models.

stop & analyze Given the complex challenges facing today's prisons—including increased racial diversity within prisons, the greater likelihood of gang membership, and states' need to reduce corrections budgets—which model of prison administration seems best suited to addressing these challenges?

Prison Organization

The prison's physical features and function set it apart from almost every other institution and organization in modern society. It is a place where a group of employees manage a group of captives. Prisoners must live according to the rules of their keepers, and their movements remain sharply restricted. Unlike managers of other government agencies, prison managers

- Cannot select their clients
- Have little or no control over the release of their clients
- Must deal with clients who are there against their will
- Must rely on clients to do most of the work in the daily operation of the institution—work they are forced to do and for which they are not paid
- Must depend on the maintenance of satisfactory relationships between clients and staff

Given these unique characteristics, how should a prison be run? What rules should guide administrators? As the description just given indicates, wardens and other key personnel are asked to perform a difficult job, one that requires skilled and dedicated managers.

Most prisons are expected to fulfill goals related to keeping (custody), using (working), and serving (treating) inmates. Because individual staff members are not equipped to perform all functions, separate lines of command organize the groups of employees that carry out these different tasks. One group is charged with maintaining custody over the prisoners, another group supervises them in their work activities, and a third group attempts to treat them.

The custodial employees are the most numerous. They are typically organized along military lines, from warden to captain to officer, with accompanying pay differentials down the chain of command. The professional personnel associated with the using and serving functions, such as industry supervisors, clinicians, and teachers, are not part of the custodial structure and have little in common with its staff. All employees are responsible to the warden, but the treatment personnel and the civilian supervisors of the workshops have their own salary scales and titles. Figure 11.1 presents the formal organization of staff responsibilities in a typical prison.

The multiple goals and separate lines of command often cause ambiguity and conflict in the administration of prisons. For example, the goals imposed on

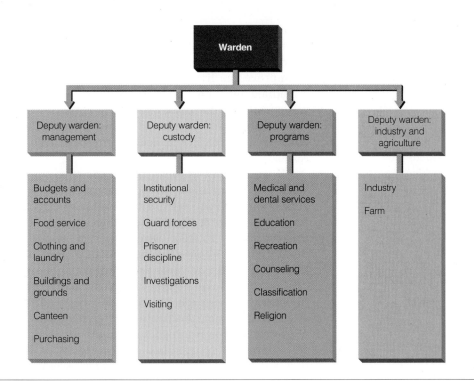

Figure 11.1
Formal Organization of a Prison for Adult Felons
Prison staff are divided into various sections consistent with the goals of the organization. Custodial employees are the most numerous.

© Cengage Learning

prisons are often contradictory and unclear. Conflict between different groups of staff (custodial versus treatment, for instance), as well as between staff and inmates, presents significant challenges for administrators.

How, then, do prisons function? How do prisoners and staff try to meet their own goals? Although the U.S. prison may not conform to the ideal goals of corrections and the formal organization may bear little resemblance to the ongoing reality of the informal relations, order *is* kept and a routine *is* followed.

---

check point > **3. How do prisons differ from other organizations in society?**
It is a place where a group of workers manages a group of captives.

stop & analyze How might the multiple goals of prisons collide with each other? Select two of the goals and describe how the pursuit of one goal may make the effective attainment of the other goal more difficult.

Governing a Society of Captives

Much of the public believes that prisons are operated in an authoritarian manner. In such a society, correctional officers give orders and inmates follow orders. Strictly enforced rules specify what the captives may and may not do. Staff members have the right to grant rewards and to inflict punishment. In theory, any inmate who does not follow the rules could be placed in solitary confinement. Because the officers have a monopoly on the legal means of enforcing rules and can call in the state police and the National Guard if necessary, many people believe that no question should arise as to how the prison is run. Read "Criminal Justice: Myth & Reality" to test your perceptions about the power of correctional officials.

What quality of life should be maintained in prison? According to John DiIulio, a good prison is one that "provides as much order, amenity, and service as possible given the human and financial resources" (1987:12). *Order* is here defined as the absence of individual or group misconduct that threatens the safety of others—for example, assault, rapes, and other forms of violence or threat. *Amenities* include

Common Belief: Because correctional officers have access to guns, clubs, tear gas, and other weapons, they can readily control the behavior of prisoners through the threat of force or, if necessary, the use of force, including lethal force.

- Although prison officials typically have firearms locked in an accessible area for emergencies, and the correctional officers in towers or walking outside the prison's perimeter carry guns, most correctional officers cannot carry weapons.
- These officers must supervise, question, and frisk prisoners close at hand and in a context in which they are heavily outnumbered by the prisoners. If they carried weapons, they might easily be overpowered and have their weapons taken by the prisoners.
- Thus, effective officers cannot rely on the threat of force to accomplish their daily tasks smoothly. Instead, they must encourage the cooperation and obedience of the prisoners by communicating effectively, establishing their own reputations for toughness and fairness, and showing some understanding and flexibility in the enforcement of minor rules.
- If a violent event or uprising occurs, prison staff members will use force to restore order. However, the use of force throughout the day is not an efficient way to keep the institution running smoothly.
- Moreover, there are now legal rules that limit when and how force may be used, and prisoners may file lawsuits for rights violations and personal injuries suffered through the improper use of force.

anything that enhances the comfort of the inmates, such as good food, clean cells, and recreational opportunities. *Service* includes programs designed to improve the lives of inmates: vocational training, remedial education, and work opportunities. Here, too, we expect inmates to be engaged in activities during incarceration that will make them better people and enhance their ability to lead crime-free lives upon release.

If we accept the premise that inmates, staff, and society need well-run prisons, what problems must correctional administrators address? The correctional literature points to four factors that make governing prisons different from administering other public institutions: (1) the defects of total power, (2) the limitation on the rewards and punishments officials can use, (3) the co-optation of correctional officers by inmates through exchange relationships, and (4) the strength of inmate leadership. After reviewing each of these research findings, we examine what kind of administrative systems and leadership styles ensure that prisons are safe and humane and serve inmates' needs.

The Defects of Total Power

Imagine a prison society in which officers could use force to rule hostile and uncooperative inmates. Prisoners could legally be isolated from one another, physically abused until they cooperate, and put under continuous surveillance. Although all of these things are possible, such practices would probably not be countenanced for long, because the public expects correctional institutions to be run humanely.

In reality, the power of officers is limited, because many prisoners have little to lose by misbehaving, and unarmed officers have only limited ability to force compliance with rules. Perhaps more important is the fact that forcing people to follow commands is an inefficient way to make them carry out complex tasks; efficiency further diminishes because of the ratio of inmates to officers (typically 40 to 1) and the intrinsic potential danger.

Rewards and Punishments

Correctional officers often rely on rewards and punishments to gain cooperation. To maintain security and order among a large population in a confined space, they impose extensive rules of conduct. Instead of using force to ensure obedience, however, they reward compliance by granting privileges and punish rule violators by denying these same privileges.

To promote control, officers may follow any of several policies. One is to offer cooperative prisoners rewards such as choice job assignments, residence in the honor unit, and favorable parole reports. Inmates who do not break rules receive good time. Informers may also be rewarded, and administrators may ignore conflict among inmates on the assumption that it keeps prisoners from uniting against authorities.

The system of rewards and punishments has some deficiencies. One is that the punishments for rule breaking do not represent a great departure from the prisoners' usual circumstances. Because inmates already lack many freedoms and valued goods—heterosexual relations, money, choice of clothing, and so on—not being allowed to attend, say, a recreational period does not carry much weight. Further, inmates receive authorized privileges at the start of the sentence and lose them if rules are broken, but officials authorize few rewards for progress or exceptional behavior. However, as an inmate approaches release, opportunities for furloughs, work release, or transfer to a halfway house can serve as incentives to obey rules.

Gaining Cooperation: Exchange Relationships

One way that correctional officers obtain inmate cooperation is by tolerating minor rule infractions in exchange for compliance with major aspects of the custodial regime. The correctional officer plays the key role in these exchange relationships. Officers and prisoners remain in close proximity both day and night—in the cell block, workshop, dining hall, recreation area, and so on. Although the formal rules require a social distance between officers and inmates, the physical closeness makes them aware that each relies on the other. The officers need the cooperation of the prisoners so that they will look good to their superiors, and the inmates count on the officers to relax the rules or occasionally look the other way. For example, officers in a Midwestern prison told researcher Stan Stojkovic that flexibility in rule enforcement especially mattered as it related to the ability of prisoners to cope with their environment. As one officer said, "Phone calls are really important to guys in this place. You cut off their calls and they get pissed. So what I do is give them a little extra and they are good to me." Yet the officers also told Stojkovic that prison personnel would be crazy to intervene to stop illicit sex or drug use (Stojkovic, 1990:214).

Correctional officers must take care not to pay too high a price for the cooperation of their charges. Under pressure to work effectively with prisoners, officers may be blackmailed into doing illegitimate favors in return for cooperation. Officers who establish *sub-rosa*, or secret, relationships can be manipulated by prisoners into smuggling contraband or committing other illegal acts. Corrections officers are caught each year smuggling drugs and cell phones to prisoners. In addition, bans on cigarettes inside some prisons have created a lucrative and tempting market for corrections officers to smuggle tobacco into institutions and receive payments from the prisoners' relatives. Because scarce tobacco can be worth hundreds of dollars per bag, unethical officers can significantly enhance their incomes through such smuggling—at the same time that they risk being arrested and sent to prison themselves for such illegal activity (Ingold, 2011). At the end of the chapter, "A Question of Ethics" presents a recent example of such risks of co-optation for corrections officers.

AP Images/Elaine Thompson

⬆ Officers face significant challenges in maintaining order and safety, especially when many prisons are understaffed and inmates far outnumber those in authority. What qualities and skills do correctional officers need in order to be effective?

Inmate Leadership

In the traditional prison of the big-house era, administrators enlisted the inmate leaders to help maintain order. Inmate leaders had been "tested" over time so that they were neither pushed around by other inmates nor distrusted as stool pigeons. Because the staff could rely on them, they served as the essential communications link between staff and inmates. Their ability to acquire inside information and gain access to higher officials brought inmate leaders the respect of other prisoners and special privileges from officials. In turn, they distributed these benefits to other prisoners, thus bolstering their own influence within the prison society.

Prisons seem to function more effectively now than they did in the recent past. Although prisons are more crowded, riots and reports of violence have declined. In many prisons, the inmate social system may have reorganized, so that correctional officers again can work through prisoners respected by fellow inmates. Yet, some observers contend that when wardens maintain order in this way, they enhance the positions of some prisoners at the expense of others. The leaders profit by receiving illicit privileges and favors, and they influence other prisoners by distributing benefits.

Further, descriptions of the contemporary maximum-security prison raise questions about administrators' ability to run these institutions using inmate leadership. In most of today's prisons, inmates are divided by race, ethnicity, age, and gang affiliation, so that no single leadership structure exists.

The Challenge of Governing Prisons

The factors of total power, rewards and punishments, exchange relationships, and inmate leadership exist in every prison and must be managed. How they are managed greatly influences the quality of prison life. John DiIulio's research (1987) challenged the common assumption of many correctional administrators that "the cons run the joint." Instead, successful wardens have made their prisons function well by applying management principles within the context of their own style of leadership. Prisons can be governed, violence minimized, and services provided to the inmates if correctional executives and wardens exhibit leadership. Although governing prisons poses an extraordinary challenge, it can be and has been effectively accomplished.

check point > 4. **What four factors make governing prisons different from administering other public institutions?**
The defects of total power, a limited system of rewards and punishments, exchange relations between correctional officers and inmates, and the strength of inmate leadership.

stop & analyze Think about the type of rewards that correctional officers can use to recognize and encourage good behavior among prisoners. What types of rewards would you expect to be most effective, and why?

Correctional Officers: The Linchpins of Management

A prison is simultaneously supposed to keep, use, and serve its inmates. The achievement of these goals depends heavily on the performance of its correctional officers. Their job is not easy. Not only do they work long and difficult hours with a hostile client population, but their superiors also expect them to do so with few resources or punishments at their disposal. Most of what they are expected to do must be accomplished by gaining and keeping the cooperation of the prisoners.

The Officer's Role

Over the past 30 years, the correctional officer's role has changed greatly. No longer responsible merely for "guarding," the correctional officer now stands as a crucial professional who has the closest contact with the prisoners and performs a variety of tasks. Officers are expected to counsel, supervise, protect, and process the inmates under their care. But the officer also works as a member of a complex bureaucratic organization and is expected to deal with clients impersonally and to follow formal procedures. Fulfilling these contradictory role expectations is difficult in itself, and the physical closeness of the officer and inmate over long periods exacerbates this difficulty.

Recruitment of Officers

Employment as a correctional officer is neither glamorous nor popular. The work is thought to be boring, the pay is low, and career advancement is minimal. Studies have shown that one of the primary incentives for becoming involved in correctional work is the financial security that civil service status provides (Schlosser, Safran, and Sbaratta, 2010). In addition, because most correctional facilities are located in rural areas, prison work often is better than other available employment. Because correctional officers are recruited locally, most of them are

Much of the work of correctional officers involves searches and counting. Officers have a saying: "We're all doing time together, except guards are doing it in eight-hour shifts." What are the professional rewards—if any—of working as a correctional officer?

rural and white (see Figure 11.2), in contrast to the majority of prisoners, who come from urban areas and are often either African American or Hispanic (see Figure 11.3 page 356). Yet, some correctional officers see their work as a way of helping people, often the people most in need in U.S. society.

Today, because they need well-qualified, effective correctional officers, states seek to recruit quality personnel. Salaries have been raised so that the average annual pay runs from about $25,000 per year in some southern and rural states to over $65,000 in states such as New Jersey and California (Bureau of Labor Statistics, 2009). In addition to their salaries, most officers can earn overtime pay, supplementing base pay by up to 30 percent. However, low salaries; the massive increase in the prison population; and a tougher, more violent class of prisoners have all probably contributed to a shortage of correctional officers in some states.

Correctional administrators have made special efforts to recruit women and minorities. Today, approximately 30 percent of correctional officers belong to minority groups, and 33 percent of officers are women (see Figure 11.2). Female officers are no longer restricted to working with female offenders. For example, in South Carolina, approximately 41 percent of correctional officers are women. In Arkansas, 51 percent of officers are women. In the Federal Bureau of Prisons, only 27 percent of staff were women in 2012 (Bureau of Prisons, 2012; C. G. Camp, 2003; Stephan, 2008).

States generally require cadets, or new recruits, to complete a preservice training program. The length of preservice training varies from state to state. For example, cadets in California and Michigan receive 640 hours of training (California Department of Corrections and Rehabilitation, 2010; Michigan Department of Corrections, 2012). In contrast, new recruits in Kentucky receive only 40 hours of classroom training, but follow this up with a second phase of training. These new recruits remain on probation while working for the first eight months of their tenure as corrections officers (Kleymeyer, 2010). In most states, new cadets receive at least a rudimentary knowledge of the job and correctional rules. Classroom work includes learning about report writing, communicable diseases, inmate classification, self-defense, and use of force. The classroom work, however, often bears little resemblance to problems confronted on the cell block or in the yard. On completing the course, the new officer is placed under the supervision of an experienced officer. On the job, the new officer experiences real-life situations and

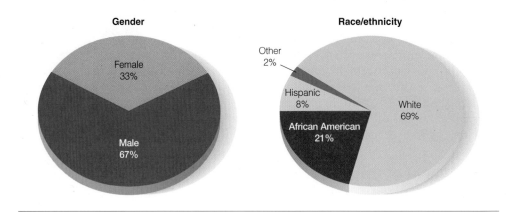

Figure 11.2

Characteristics of Correctional Officers Compare these pie charts to the data found in Figure 11.3. How do correctional officers differ from those incarcerated in terms of sex and race/ethnicity?

Source: J. J. Stephan and J. C. Karberg, *Census of State and Federal Correctional Facilities, 2000* (Washington, DC: U.S. Department of Justice, 2003).

learns the necessary techniques and procedures. Through encounters with inmates and officers, the recruit becomes socialized to life behind the walls and gradually becomes part of that subculture.

For most correctional workers, being a custodial officer is a dead-end job. Although officers who perform well may be promoted to higher ranks, such as correctional counselor, few ever move into administrative positions. However, in some states and in the Federal Bureau of Prisons, people with college degrees can move up the career ladder to management positions without having to rise through the ranks of the custodial force.

Use of Force

The use of force by correctional officers, as that by the police, generates much controversy. Although corporal punishment and the excessive use of force are not permitted, correctional officers use force in many situations. They often confront inmates who challenge their authority or are attacking other inmates. Though unarmed and outnumbered, officers must maintain order and uphold institutional rules. Under these conditions they feel justified in using force.

All correctional agencies now have policies regarding the legitimate use of force. Officers violating these policies may face an inmate lawsuit and dismissal. There are five situations in which the use of force is legally acceptable:

1. *Self-defense.* If officers are threatened with physical attack, they may use a level of force that is reasonable to protect themselves from harm.
2. *Defense of third persons.* As in self-defense, an officer may use force to protect an inmate or another officer. Again, only reasonably necessary force may be used.
3. *Upholding prison rules.* If prisoners refuse to obey prison rules, officers may need to use force to maintain safety and security. For example, if an inmate refuses to return to his or her cell, using handcuffs and forcefully transferring the prisoner may be necessary.
4. *Prevention of a crime.* Force may be used to stop a crime, such as theft or destruction of property, from being committed.
5. *Prevention of escapes.* Officers may use force to prevent escapes, because they threaten the well-being of society and order within correctional institutions. Some agencies limit the use of deadly force to prisoners thought to be dangerous, whereas others require warning shots.

Correctional officers face challenges to self-control and professional decision making. Inmates often "push" officers in subtle ways such as moving slowly, or they use verbal abuse to provoke officers. Correctional officers are expected to run a "tight ship" and maintain order, often in situations where they are outnumbered and dealing with troubled people. In confrontational situations, they must defuse hostility yet uphold the rules—a difficult task at best.

check point ▷ 5. **Name three of the five legally acceptable reasons for the use of force.**
Self-defense, defense of third persons, upholding prison rules, prevention of crime, prevention of escapes.

stop& analyze What should happen when a corrections officer uses force in an inappropriate situation or uses too much force in an approved situation? If you were a warden, what procedures would you put in place to hear excessive-force complaints from prisoners? What would you do if you were persuaded that excessive force had been used by one of your officers?

Who Is in Prison?

The age, education, and criminal history of the inmate population influence how correctional institutions function. What are the characteristics of inmates in our nation's prisons? Do most offenders have long records of serious offenses, or are many of them first-time offenders who have committed minor crimes? Do some inmates have special needs that dictate their place in prison? These questions are crucial to understanding the work of wardens and correctional officers.

The federal government routinely collects information on all people incarcerated in the United States. The Bureau of Justice Statistics reports that a majority of prisoners are men, aged 25 to 44, and members of minority groups. Approximately 40 percent of state prisoners have not completed high school (see Figure 11.3).

Recidivists and those convicted of violent crimes make up an overwhelming portion of the prison population. It is time-consuming to collect data on recidivism, because sufficient time has to lapse (usually several years) in order to collect reliable data on re-offending. The most recent analysis of national data indicates that 44 percent of prisoners are rearrested within the first year after release. Within three years, approximately 25 percent of all released inmates will return to prison (Langan and Levin, 2002). Many of today's prisoners have a history of persistent criminality. Four additional factors affect correctional operations: the increased number of elderly prisoners, the many prisoners with HIV/AIDS, the thousands of prisoners who are mentally ill, and the increase in long-term prisoners.

Elderly Prisoners

Correctional officials have only recently become aware of the increasing number of inmates over age 55. In 2000, approximately 42,300 inmates in U.S. prisons were 55 years or older (A. J. Beck and Harrison, 2001). By 2010, this number had increased to over 119,000 (Guerino, Harrison, and Sabol, 2011). In Florida, which defines *elderly* as over age 50, the oldest male inmate in 2010 was 90, and the oldest female inmate was 91. Prisoners over the age of 50 accounted for more than *twice* the number of sick calls as for younger inmates (State of Florida Correctional Medical Authority, 2010). A number of states have created "geriatric prisons" designed to hold older inmates classified according to need: geriatric, wheelchair users, and long-term (nursing home) care. Programs like the "True Grit" Senior Structured Living Program in Nevada is one example of a program created specifically for elderly prisoners. In this program, inmates receive programs designed to enhance their physical, mental, and spiritual health (M. T. Harrison, 2006).

To some extent, the prison population is growing older because it reflects the aging of the overall citizenry, but more so because sentencing practices have changed. Consecutive lengthy sentences for heinous crimes, long mandatory minimum sentences, and life sentences without parole mean that more people who enter prison will spend most or all of the rest of their lives behind bars.

Elderly prisoners have medical and security needs that differ from those of the average inmate. For example, they can't climb into top bunks. In many states, special sections of the institution have been designated for this older population so they will

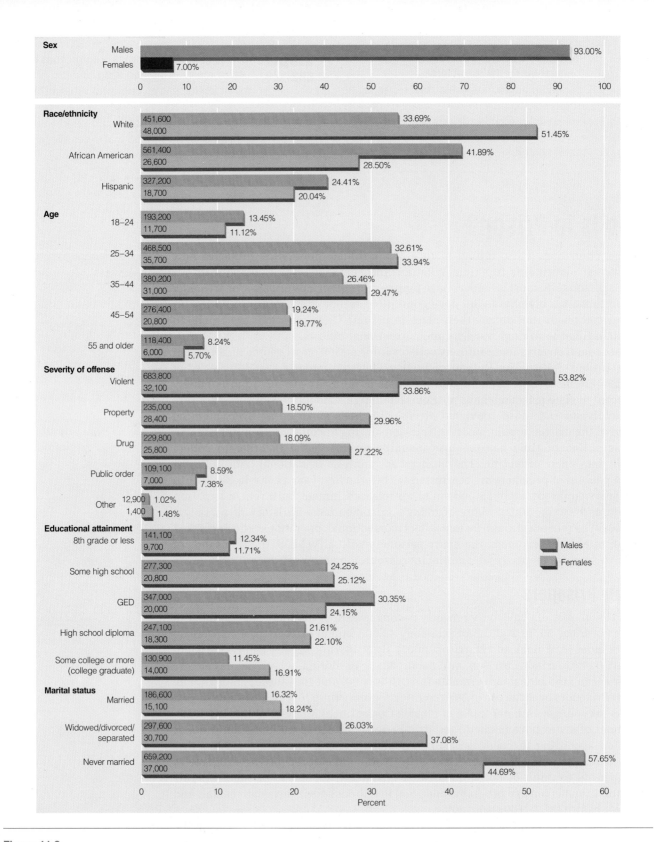

Figure 11.3

Characteristics of Male and Female Inmates in State Prisons Male and female inmates are similar in some ways, yet different in others. Use the graphs to compare the characteristics of male and female prison inmates. Why might these differences exist?

Sources: L. E. Glaze and L. M. Maruschak, "Parents in Prison and Their Minor Children," Bureau of Justice Statistics *Special Report* (Washington, DC: U.S. Department of Justice, 2008); P. Guerino, P. M. Harrison, and W. J. Sabol, "Prisoners in 2010," Bureau of Justice Statistics *Bulletin* (Washington, DC: U.S. Department of Justice, 2011); C. W. Harlow, "Education and Correctional Populations," Bureau of Justice Statistics *Special Report* (Washington, DC: U.S. Department of Justice, 2003).

not have to mix with the younger, tougher inmates. Elderly prisoners are more likely to develop chronic illnesses such as heart disease, stroke, and cancer. The costs for maintaining an elderly inmate averages about $69,000 per year, triple the average cost for a younger inmate. Ironically, while in prison, the offender will benefit from much better medical care and live a longer life than if he or she were discharged.

Prisoners with HIV/AIDS

In the coming years, AIDS is expected to be a leading cause of death among men aged 35 and younger. With 52 percent of the adult inmate population under age 35, correctional officials must cope with the problem of HIV as well as AIDS and related health issues. By the end of 2008, there were more than 20,000 HIV-positive inmates in state facilities (1.6 percent of the prison population) and 1,538 federal inmates (0.8 percent of the federal population) with AIDS or HIV-positive status (Maruschak,

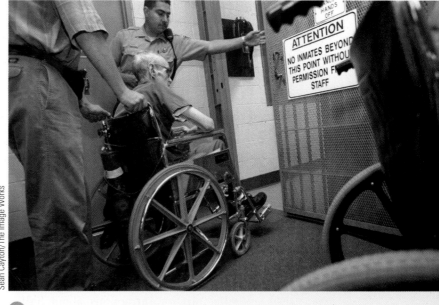

The imposition of long mandatory sentences has increased the population of elderly prisoners and also prolonged the confinement of many prisoners who need medical care. These prisoners create extra financial burdens on correctional budgets. Are there less expensive ways to punish elderly and chronically ill prisoners?

2009). The number of HIV-positive inmates is undoubtedly low because not all states conduct mandatory testing of inmates. Further, the rate of confirmed AIDS cases in state and federal prisons is two and a half times higher than in the total U.S. population. Because many inmates who are HIV infected remain undiagnosed, these numbers underestimate the scope of the problem. However, advances in treatment and improved reporting have reduced the number of AIDS-related deaths in prison significantly, from over 1,000 deaths in 1995 to 120 in 2007 (Maruschak, 2009).

To deal with offenders who have AIDS symptoms or who test positive for the virus, prison officials can develop policies on methods to prevent transmission of the disease, including the housing arrangements of those infected and medical care for inmates with the full range of symptoms. However, administrators face a host of competing pressures as they decide what actions the institution should take.

Mentally Ill Prisoners

Mass closings of public hospitals for the mentally ill began in the 1960s. At the time, new antipsychotic drugs made treating patients in the community seem a more humane and less expensive alternative to long-term hospitalization. It soon became apparent, however, that community treatment works only if the drugs are taken and that clinics and halfway houses do not exist to assist the mentally ill. Mentally ill inmates tend to follow a revolving door from homelessness to incarceration and then back to the streets, with little treatment. In Miami, for example, 97 specific mentally ill people were arrested 2,200 times and spent a combined 27,000 days in jail over a five-year period, costing taxpayers $13 million (National Public Radio [NPR], 2011). Other people with mental illness commit crimes that lead them to serve sentences in prison. Thus, there are an estimated 350,000 mentally ill offenders currently in custody in corrections institutions and the three largest in-patient psychiatric facilities in the country are inside jails in Los Angeles, New York City, and Chicago (NPR, 2011).

Correctional workers are usually unprepared to deal with the mentally ill. Cell-block officers, for instance, often do not know how to respond to disturbed inmates. Although most corrections systems have mental health units that segregate the ill, many inmates with psychiatric disorders live among other prisoners in the general population, where they are teased and otherwise exploited. Mentally ill prisoners often suffer as the stress of confinement deepens their depression, intensifies delusions, or leads to mental breakdown. Some commit suicide.

Long-Term Prisoners

More prisoners in the United States serve longer sentences than do prisoners in other Western nations. A recent survey shows that nearly 310,000 prisoners are currently serving at least 20-year sentences. Of all inmates, about 10 percent are serving "natural life," which means there is no possibility that they will be paroled, a tripling since 1992. These long-term prisoners are often the same people who will become elderly offenders, with all their attendant problems. Each life sentence costs the taxpayers over $1 million.

Severe depression, feelings of hopelessness, and other health problems are common among long-termers. Such emotional stress tends to take place earlier in the sentence as these inmates lose contact with their families. Addressing the mental health needs of this special population is critical to preventing suicide attempts.

Long-term prisoners are generally not seen as control problems. They receive disciplinary infractions about half as often as do short-term inmates. Rather, administrators must find ways to make long terms bearable. Experts suggest that administrators follow three main principles: (1) maximize opportunities for the inmate to exercise choice in his or her living circumstances, (2) create opportunities for meaningful living, and (3) help the inmate maintain contact with the outside world (Flanagan, 1995). Many long-term inmates will eventually be released after spending their prime years incarcerated. Will offenders be able to support themselves when they return to the community at age 50, 60, or 70?

The contemporary inmate population presents several challenges to correctional workers. Resources may not be available to provide rehabilitative programs for most inmates. Even if the resources exist, the goal of maintaining a safe and healthy environment may tax the staff's abilities. These difficulties are multiplied still further by AIDS and the increasing numbers of elderly and long-term prisoners. The modern corrections system must also deal with a different type of inmate, one who is more prone to violence, and with a prison society where racial tensions can soar. How well it meets this correctional challenge will greatly affect U.S. society.

check point > **6. What are the major characteristics of today's prisoners?**
Today's prisoners are largely men in their late twenties to early thirties with less than a high school education. They are disproportionately members of minority groups.

stop & analyze Draft a solution to alleviate one of the four problems discussed above: elderly prisoners, prisoners with HIV/AIDS, mental illness in prisons, or prisoners serving long sentences. In light of the budget difficulties faced by states, are there any solutions that can save money?

The Convict World

Inmates of a maximum-security prison do not serve their time in isolation. Rather, prisoners form a society with its own traditions, norms, and leadership structure. Some choose to associate with only a few close friends; others form cliques along racial or "professional" lines. Still others serve as the politicians of the convict society; they attempt to represent convict interests and distribute valued goods in return for support. Just as the free world has a social culture, the "inside" has a prisoner subculture. Membership in a group provides mutual protection from theft and physical assault, the basis of wheeling and dealing, and a source of cultural identity.

As in any society, the convict world has certain norms and values. Often described as the **inmate code**, these norms and values develop within the prison social system and help define the inmate's image of the model prisoner. As Robert Johnson notes, "The public culture of the prison has norms that dictate behavior 'on the yard' and in other public areas of the prison such as mess halls, gyms, and the larger program and work sites" (2002:100). Prison is an ultramasculine world. The culture breathes masculine toughness and insensitivity, impugning softness, and emphasizes the use of hostility and manipulation in one's relations with fellow inmates and staff. It makes caring and friendly behavior, especially with respect to the staff, look servile and silly (Sabo, Kupers, and London, 2001:7).

Reuters/Lucy Nicholson/Landov

⬆ Contemporary prison society is divided along social, ethnic, and gang subgroups. There is no longer a single inmate code to which all prisoners subscribe. As a correctional officer, how would you deal with white supremacists and other gangs based on racial and ethnic divisions within the prison population?

The code also emphasizes the solidarity of all inmates against the staff. For example, inmates should never inform on one another, pry into one another's affairs, "run off at the mouth," or put another inmate on the spot. They must be tough and trust neither the officers nor the principles for which the guards stand. Further, guards are "hacks" or "screws"; the officials are wrong and the prisoners are right.

inmate code The values and norms of the prison social system that define the inmates' idea of the model prisoner.

Some sociologists believe that the code emerges within the institution as a way to lessen the pain of imprisonment (Sykes, 1958); others believe that it is part of the criminal subculture that prisoners bring with them (Irwin and Cressey, 1962). The inmate who follows the code enjoys a certain amount of admiration from other inmates as a "right guy" or a "real man." Those who break the code are labeled "rat" or "punk" and will probably spend their prison life at the bottom of the convict social structure, alienated from the rest of the population and targeted for abuse (Sykes, 1958:84).

A single, overriding inmate code probably no longer exists in American prisons. Instead, convict society has divided itself along racial lines (Carroll, 1974; Irwin, 1980). The level of adherence to the inmate code also differs among institutions, with greater modifications to local situations found in maximum-security prisons. Still, the core code described by Sykes over 50 years ago remains.

In a changing society that has no single code of behavior accepted by the entire population, the tasks of administrators become much more difficult. They must be aware of the different groups, recognize the norms and rules that members hold in each, and deal with the leaders of many cliques rather than with a few inmates who have risen to top positions in the inmate society. In the Close Up box, TJ Granack provides "Survival Tips for Beginners."

Adaptive Roles

On entering prison, a newcomer ("fish") is confronted by the question "How am I going to do my time?" Some decide to withdraw and isolate. Others decide to become full participants in the convict social system. The choice, influenced by prisoners' values and experiences, helps determine strategies for survival and success.

Most male inmates use one of four basic role orientations to adapt to prison: "doing time," "gleaning," "jailing," and functioning as a "disorganized criminal" (Irwin, 1970:67).

Survival Tips for Beginners

TJ Granack

Okay, so you just lost your case. Maybe you took a plea bargain. Whatever. The point is you've been sentenced. You've turned yourself over to the authorities and you're in the county jail waiting to catch the next chain to the R Unit (receiving) where you'll be stripped and shaved and photographed and processed and sent to one of the various prisons in your state.

So what's a felon to do? Here are some survival tips that may make your stay less hellish:

1. Commit an Honorable Crime. Commit a crime that's considered, among convicts, to be worthy of respect. I was lucky. I went down for first-degree attempted murder, so my crime fell in the "honorable" category. Oh, goodie. So I just had to endure the everyday sort of danger and abuse that comes with prison life.

2. Don't Gamble. Not cards, not chess, not the Super Bowl, and if you do, don't bet too much. If you lose too much and pay up (don't even think of doing otherwise), then you'll be known as a rich guy who'll be very popular with the vultures. . . .

4. Never Loan Anyone Anything. Because if you do, you'll be expected to collect one way or another. If you don't collect you will be known as a mark, as someone without enough heart to take back his own. . . .

6. Make No Eye Contact. Don't look anyone in the eye. Ever. Locking eyes with another man, be he a convict or a guard, is considered a challenge, a threat, and should therefore be avoided.

7. Pick Your Friends Carefully. When you choose a friend, you've got to be prepared to deal with anything that person may have done. Their reputation is yours, and the consequences can be enormous.

8. Fight and Fight Dirty. You have to fight, and not according to the Marquis of Queensbury Rules, either. If you do it right, you'll only have to do it once or twice. If you don't, expect regular whooping and loss of possessions. . . .

10. Mind Your Own Business. Never get in the middle of anyone else's discussion/argument/confrontation/fight. Never offer unsolicited knowledge or advice.

11. Keep a Good Porn Collection. If you don't have one, the boys will think you're funny. . . .

14. Don't Talk to Staff, Especially Guards. Any prolonged discussion or associations with staff make you susceptible to rumor and suspicion of being a snitch.

15. Never Snitch. Or even appear to snitch. And above all, avoid the real thing. And if you do, you'd better not get caught.

📶 Researching the Internet

Compare this set of rules to the official information given to North Carolina prisoners to convey the rules and regulations of prison. To link to the website, visit the Criminal Justice CourseMate at cengagebrain.com, then access the web links for this chapter.

For Critical Analysis

If you were sent to prison, how would you seek to learn the code that prisoners enforce among themselves?

Source: From TJ Granack "Welcome To The Steel Hotel: Survival Tips for Beginners" in The Funhouse Mirror (pp. 6–10), edited by Robert Gordon Ellis. Copyright © 2000 by Washington State University Press. Reprinted by permission of Washington State University Press. http://wsupress.wsu .edu/recenttitles/

Doing Time   Men "doing time" view their prison term as a brief, inevitable break in their criminal careers, a cost of doing business. They try to serve their terms with the least amount of suffering and the greatest amount of comfort. They avoid trouble by living by the inmate code, finding activities to fill their days, forming friendships with a few other convicts, and generally doing what they think is necessary to survive and to get out as soon as possible.

Gleaning   Inmates who are "gleaning" try to take advantage of prison programs to better themselves and improve their prospects for success after release. They use the resources at hand: libraries, correspondence courses, vocational training, schools. Some make a radical conversion away from a life of crime.

Jailing   "Jailing" is the choice of those who cut themselves off from the outside and try to construct a life within the prison. These are often "state-raised" youths who have spent much of their lives in institutional settings and who identify little with the values of free society. These are the inmates who seek power and influence in the prison society, often becoming key figures in the politics and economy of prison life.

Disorganized Criminal A fourth role orientation—the "disorganized criminal"—describes inmates who cannot develop any of the other three orientations. They may be of low intelligence or afflicted with psychological or physical disabilities, and they find functioning in prison society difficult. They are "human putty" to be manipulated by others. These are also the inmates who cannot adjust to prison life and who develop emotional disorders, attempt suicide, and violate prison rules (K. Adams, 1992).

As these roles suggest, prisoners are not members of an undifferentiated mass. Individual convicts choose to play specific roles in prison society. The roles they choose reflect the physical and social environment they have experienced and also influence their relationships and interactions in prison. How do most prisoners serve their time? Although the media generally portray prisons as violent, chaotic places, research shows that most inmates want to get through their sentence without trouble. As journalist Pete Earley found in his study of Leavenworth, roughly 80 percent of inmates try to avoid trouble and do their time as easily as possible (1992:44).

The Prison Economy

In prison, as outside, individuals want goods and services. Although the state feeds, clothes, and houses all prisoners, amenities remain sparse. Prisoners lack everything but bare necessities. Their diet and routine are monotonous and their recreational opportunities scarce. They experience a loss of identity (due to uniformity of treatment) and a lack of responsibility. In short, the prison is relatively unique in having been deliberately designed as "an island of poverty in the midst of a society of relative abundance" (V. Williams and Fish, 1974:40).

The number of items that a prisoner can purchase or receive through legitimate channels differs from state to state and from facility to facility. For example, prisoners in some state institutions may have televisions, civilian clothing, and hot plates. Not all prisoners enjoy these luxuries, nor do these amenities satisfy the lingering desire for a variety of other goods. Some state legislatures have decreed that amenities will be prohibited and that prisoners should return to Spartan living conditions.

Recognizing that prisoners do have some basic needs that are not met, prisons have a commissary or "store" from which inmates may, on a scheduled basis, purchase a limited number of items—toilet articles, tobacco, snacks, and other food products—in exchange for credits drawn on their "bank accounts." The size of a bank account depends on the amount of money deposited at the inmate's entrance, gifts sent by relatives, and amounts earned in the low-paying prison industries.

However, the peanut butter, soap, and cigarettes of the typical prison store in no way satisfy the consumer needs and desires of most prisoners. Consequently, an informal, underground economy acts as a major element in prison society. Many items taken for granted on the outside are inordinately valued on the inside. For example, talcum powder and deodorant become more important because of the limited bathing facilities. Goods and services that a prisoner would not have consumed at all outside prison can take on an exaggerated importance inside prison. For example, unable to get alcohol, offenders may seek a similar effect by sniffing glue. Or, to distinguish themselves from others, offenders may pay laundry workers to iron a shirt in a particular way, a modest version of conspicuous consumption.

Many studies point to the pervasiveness of this economy. The research shows that a market economy provides the goods (contraband) and services not available or not allowed by prison authorities. In many prisons, inmates run private "stores." Food stolen from the kitchen for late-night snacks, homemade wine, and drugs such as marijuana are available in these stores.

As a principal feature of prison culture, this informal economy reinforces the norms and roles of the social system and influences the nature of interpersonal relationships. The extent of the underground economy and its ability to produce desired goods and services—food, drugs, alcohol, sex, preferred living conditions—

vary according to the scope of official surveillance, the demands of the consumers, and the opportunities for entrepreneurship. Inmates' success as "hustlers" determines the luxuries and power they can enjoy.

Because real money is prohibited and a barter system is somewhat restrictive, the standard currency of the prison economy is cigarettes. They are not contraband, are easily transferable, have a stable and well-known standard of value, and come in "denominations" of singles, packs, and cartons. Furthermore, they are in demand by smokers. Even those who do not smoke keep cigarettes for prison currency. As more prisons become smoke free, however, institutions that ban cigarettes have seen new forms of currency emerge, such as cans of tuna fish, postage stamps, and soap (M. Santos, 2004). At the same time, tobacco becomes more valuable because of its scarcity in the smoke-free facilities, with prisoners making efforts to persuade corrections officers to smuggle in tobacco. This issue is described in "A Question of Ethics" at the end of the chapter.

Certain positions in the prison society enhance opportunities for entrepreneurs. For example, inmates assigned to work in the kitchen, warehouse, and administrative office steal food, clothing, building materials, and even information to sell or trade to other prisoners. The goods may then become part of other market transactions. Thus, the exchange of a dozen eggs for two packs of cigarettes may result in the reselling of the eggs in the form of egg sandwiches made on a hot plate for five cigarettes each. Meanwhile, the kitchen worker who stole the eggs may use the income to get a laundry worker to starch his shirts, to get drugs from a hospital orderly, or to pay a "punk" for sex.

Participation in the prison economy can put inmates at greater risk for victimization while incarcerated (Copes et al., 2010). Economic transactions can lead to violence when goods are stolen, debts are not paid, or agreements are violated. Disruptions of the economy can occur when officials conduct periodic "lockdowns" and inspections. Confiscation of contraband can result in temporary shortages and price readjustments, but gradually, profits result. The prison economy, like that of the outside world, allocates goods and services, rewards and sanctions, and it is closely linked to the society it serves.

---

check point

7. **Why is it unlikely that a single, overriding inmate code exists in today's prisons?**
   The prison society is fragmented by racial and ethnic divisions.

8. **What are the four role orientations found in adult male prisons?**
   Doing time, gleaning, jailing, and functioning as a disorganized criminal.

9. **Why does an underground economy exist in prison?**
   To provide goods and services not available through regular channels.

stop & analyze

Is it possible to stop the underground economy in prisons? If you were a warden, what are two steps you would take to reduce the problems associated with the underground economy? (For this discussion, disregard whether you believe that you—or anyone—can completely stop it.)

Women in Prison

Most studies of prisons have focused on institutions for men. How do prisons for women differ, and what special problems do female inmates face?

Women constitute only 7.3 percent (about 105,000) of the entire U.S. prison population (Guerino, Harrison, and Sabol, 2011). However, the growth rate in the number of incarcerated women has exceeded that of men since 1981. In fact, from 2000 to 2010, the male population increased by 16 percent, whereas that of women increased by 25 percent (Guerino, Harrison, and Sabol, 2011). The increased number of women in prison has significantly affected the delivery of programs, housing conditions, medical care, staffing, and security.

Female offenders are incarcerated in 98 confinement facilities for women and 93 facilities that house men and women separately. Life in these facilities both differs from and resembles life in institutions for men alone. Women's prisons are smaller, with looser security and less structured relationships; the underground economy is not as well developed; and female prisoners seem less committed to the inmate code. Women also serve shorter sentences than do men, so their prison society is more fluid as new members join and others leave.

Many women's prisons have the outward appearance of a college campus, often seen as a group of "cottages" around a central admini-stration/dining/program building. Generally these facilities lack the high walls, guard towers, and cyclone fences found at most prisons for men. In recent years, however, the trend has been to upgrade security for women's prisons by adding barbed wire, higher fences, and other devices to prevent escapes.

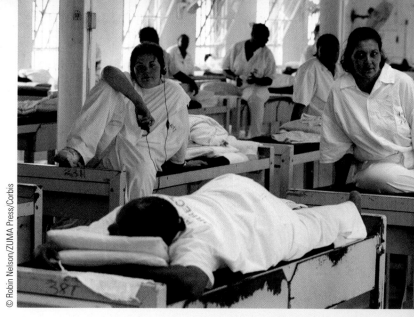

Women's experiences in prison can differ markedly from those of men. Although there is less violence between prisoners in women's institutions, women often have fewer options for educational and vocational programs. In addition, many prisons have discovered problems with male correctional officers sexually abusing women prisoners. How would you organize the selection of staff, staff training, and the development of programs to properly run a prison for women?

The characteristics of correctional facilities for women also include geographic remoteness and inmate heterogeneity. Few states operate more than one institution for women, so inmates generally live far from children, families, friends, and attorneys. In many institutions, the small numbers of inmates limit the extent to which the needs of individual offenders can be recognized and treated. Housing classifications are often so broad that dangerous or mentally ill inmates are mixed with women who have committed minor offenses and have no psychological problems. Similarly, available rehabilitative programs are often not used to their full extent, because correctional departments fail to recognize women's problems and needs.

In most respects, we can see incarcerated women, like male prisoners, as disadvantaged losers in this complex and competitive society. However, the two groups differ with regard to types of offenses and length of sentences, patterns of drug use, and criminal history. Thirty-four percent of female prisoners are sentenced for violent offenses, compared with 54 percent of male prisoners, and 27 percent for drug-related offenses, versus 18 percent of the men (Guerino, Harrison, and Sabol, 2011). Overall, women receive shorter maximum sentences than do men. Half of the women have a maximum sentence of 5 years or less, whereas half of the men have a sentence of 10 years or less (BJS, 2000a). Refer back to Figure 11.3, which summarizes some characteristics of female prisoners, and compares them to those of male prisoners.

The Subculture of Women's Prisons

Studies of the subculture of women's prisons have been less extensive than those of male convict society. Further, just as few ethnographic studies of men's prisons have taken place during the past two decades, very few of women's prisons exist.

Much early investigation of women's prisons focused on types of social relationships among female offenders. As in all types of penal institutions, same-sex relationships were found, but unlike in male prisons, such relationships among women appeared more voluntary than coerced. Perhaps more importantly, scholars reported that female inmates tended to form pseudo-families in which they adopted various roles—father, mother, daughter, sister—and interacted as a unit, rather than identifying with the larger prisoner subculture (Girshick, 1999; Propper, 1982). Esther Heffernan views these "play" families as a "direct, conscious substitution for the family relationships broken by imprisonment, or . . . the development of roles that perhaps were not fulfilled in the actual home environment" (1972:41–42). She also notes the economic aspect of the play families and the extent to which they are formed to provide for their members. Such cooperative relationships help relieve the tensions of prison life, assist the socialization of new inmates, and permit individuals to act according to clearly defined roles and rules.

In discussing the available research on women in prison, we need to consider the most recent shifts in prison life. Just as the subculture of male prisons has changed since the pioneering research of the 1950s, the climate of female prisons has undoubtedly changed. Kimberly Greer (2000) found support for the idea that, compared with male prisons, prisons for women are less violent, involve less gang activity, and lack racial tension; however, the respondents indicated that their interpersonal relationships may be less stable and less familial than in the past. They reported higher levels of mistrust among women and greater economic manipulation.

In one of the few recent studies of prison culture, Barbara Owen (1998) found that the inmates at the Central California Women's Facility developed various styles of doing time. She observed that the vast majority wanted to avoid "the mix"—"behavior that can bring trouble and conflict with staff and other prisoners." A primary feature of "the mix" is anything for which one can lose "good time" or can result in being sent to administrative segregation. Being in "the mix" was related to "'homo-secting,' involvement in drugs, fights, and 'being messy,' that is being involved in conflict and trouble." Owen found that most women want to do their time and go home, but some "are more at home in prison and do not seem to care if they 'lost time'" (Owen, 1998:179).

Male versus Female Subcultures

Comparisons of male and female prisons are complicated by the nature of the research: Most studies have been conducted in single-sex institutions, and most follow theories and concepts first developed in male prisons. However, it is important to recognize the differences between men and women who are incarcerated. Figure 11.3 contains descriptive information on the characteristics of incarcerated men and women in the United States. Based on what we know about women's prisons the following facts may explain the differences in subculture:

- Over half of male inmates but only a third of female inmates are serving time for violent offenses (Figure 11.3).
- There is less violence in prisons for women than in prisons for men.
- Women show greater responsiveness to prison programs.
- Men's prison populations are divided by security level, but most women serve time in facilities where the entire population is mixed.
- Men tend to segregate themselves by race; this is less true of women.
- Men rarely become intimate with their keepers, but many women share their lives with officers.

A major difference between the two types of prisons relates to interpersonal relationships. Male prisoners act for themselves and are evaluated by others according to how they adhere to subcultural norms. An early comparative study of one women's prison and four men's prisons found that men believe they must demonstrate physical strength and consciously avoid any mannerisms that might imply homosexuality (Fox, 1982). To gain recognition and status within the convict community, the male prisoner must strictly adhere to these values. Men form cliques, but not the family networks found in prisons for women. Male norms stress autonomy, self-sufficiency, and the ability to cope with one's own problems, and men are expected to "do their own time." Fox found little sharing in the men's prisons.

Women, on the other hand, place less emphasis on achieving status or recognition within the prisoner community. Women are also less likely "to impose severe restrictions on the sexual (or emotional) conduct of other members" (J. G. Fox, 1982:100). As noted previously, in prisons for women, close ties seem to exist among small groups akin to extended families. These family groups provide emotional support and share resources.

The differences between male and female prisoner subcultures have been ascribed to the nurturing, maternal qualities of women. Some critics charge that such an analysis stereotypes female behavior and imputes a biological basis to personality where none exists. Of importance as well is the issue of inmate–inmate violence in male and female institutions. Physical violence between female inmates occurs less often than between male inmates, but it is important to note that the violence that does exist is shaped by the different culture in women's prisons (Owen et al., 2008).

Issues in the Incarceration of Women

Under pressures for equal opportunity, states seem to believe that they should run women's prisons as they do prisons for men, with the same policies and procedures. However, advocates for female prisoners have urged governments to keep in mind that women inmates have different needs than men (Bartels and Gaffney, 2011). Understanding the pathways by which women end up incarcerated can also help prison and jail administrators manage their facilities. Many incarcerated women have been victims of physical and sexual abuse, and that history can affect their behavior while incarcerated (McCampbell, 2005).

Although correctional departments have been playing "catch up" to meet the unique needs of women offenders, sexual misconduct by officers persists, along with women prisoners' demands for education and training, medical services, and methods for dealing with the problems of mothers and their children. We next examine each of these issues and the policy implications they pose for the future.

Sexual Misconduct   When the number of female prisoners increased in the late 1990s, cases of sexual misconduct by male correctional officers escalated. After an investigation of sexual misconduct of officers in the women's prisons of five states—California, Georgia, Illinois, Michigan, and New York—Human Rights Watch reported that male officers had raped, sexually assaulted, and abused female inmates. In 2009, the state of Michigan paid over $100 million to 500 female prisoners who were raped in Michigan prisons (McFarlane, 2009).

The United States Congress signed the Prison Rape Elimination Act into law in 2003. This law requires that all state correctional systems develop standards in an effort to reduce rape in prisons, and to collect data on rape in prisons; the act also provides funding to state agencies to meet these national standards (Prison Rape Elimination Act, 117 STAT. 972). Research funded by this initiative has determined that prison inmates do not view rape in the same way that people outside prisons do. Even with protections against rape, women in prison frequently report their knowledge of "consensual" sexual relationships between inmates and guards (Fleischer and Krienert, 2006). However, because prison guards exert power and control over inmates in prisons, it is difficult to argue that sex between the two can be considered consensual. In fact, guards who have sex with inmates under their care can be charged criminally for such behavior.

Educational and Vocational Training Programs   A major criticism of women's prisons is that they lack the variety of vocational and educational programs available in male institutions. Critics also charge that programs tend to conform to sexual stereotypes of "female" occupations—cosmetology, food service, housekeeping, sewing (Morash, Haarr, and Rucker, 1994). Such training does not correspond to the wider employment opportunities available to women in today's world. Both men's and women's facilities usually offer educational programs so inmates can become literate and earn general equivalency diplomas (GEDs). Such programs matter a great deal, considering that upon release most women must support themselves, and many must support their children as well (Kruttschnitt, 2010). In addition, vocational training programs have been shown to reduce the likelihood that inmates will return to prison after being released. Female offenders in prison have different needs than male offenders, and vocational training should be designed around the specific needs of women (Holtfreter and Morash, 2003).

Medical Services   Women's prisons lack proper medical services. Yet, because of their socioeconomic status and limited access to preventive medical care, women usually have more serious health problems than do men. Compared with men, they have a higher incidence of asthma, drug abuse, diabetes, and heart disorders (T. L. Anderson, 2003). In addition, prison officials often dismiss the gynecological needs of female inmates as "unimportant" (L. Braithwaite, Treadwell, and Arriola, 2005). Although a higher percentage of women than men report receiving medical services in prison, women's institutions are less likely than men's to have a full-time medical staff or hospital facilities.

Saying that corrections must "defuse the time bomb," Leslie Acoca argues that failure to provide female inmates with basic preventive and medical treatments such as immunizations, breast cancer screenings, and management of chronic diseases "is resulting in the development of more serious health problems that are exponentially more expensive to treat" (1998:67). She says that poor medical care for the incarcerated merely shifts costs to overburdened community health care systems after release.

Mothers and Their Children   Of greatest concern to incarcerated women is the fate of their children. Over 60 percent of women inmates are mothers, with 25 percent having children aged four or younger. Especially troubling is the increase in the number of children younger than 18 with an incarcerated parent—the number of children with a mother in prison more than doubled between 1991 and 2007 (Glaze and Maruschak, 2008).

Because about 65 percent of incarcerated mothers were single caretakers of minor children before they entered prison, they do not always have partners to take care of their children. In about one-third of these cases, children are cared for by their fathers. The majority of children whose mother is incarcerated live with grandparents or other relatives, with the remaining children living with family friends or placed in foster care (Glaze and Maruschak, 2008). Due to high incarceration rates in black communities, locking up parents differentially affects black children and harms communities (Roberts, 2004). Children with incarcerated mothers are more likely to have contact with the criminal justice system as adults, and are more likely to be convicted of crimes as adults (Huebner and Gustafson, 2007).

Imprisoned mothers have difficulty maintaining contact with their children. Because most states have only one or two prisons for women, mothers may be incarcerated 150 miles or more away. This makes transportation difficult, visits short and infrequent, and phone calls uncertain and irregular. When the children do visit the prison, they face strange and intimidating surroundings. In some institutions, children must conform to the rules governing adult visitations: strict time limits and no physical contact.

Other correctional facilities, however, seek ways to help mothers maintain links to their children. For example, the Dwight Correctional Center in Illinois schedules weekend retreats, similar to camping trips, for women and their children; unfortunately, this prison may soon be closed in an attempt to reduce the correctional budget in that state (R. Miller, 2012). In some states, children can meet with their mothers at almost any time, for extended periods, and in playrooms or nurseries where contact is possible. Some states transport children to visit their mothers; some institutions even let children stay overnight with their mothers. A few prisons have family visitation programs that let the inmate, her legal husband, and her children be together, often in a mobile home or apartment, for up to 72 hours.

The future of women's correctional institutions is hard to predict. More women are being sent to prison now, and more have committed the violent crimes and drug offenses that used to be more typical of male offenders. Will these changes affect the adaptive roles and social relationships that differentiate women's prisons from men's? Will women's prisons need to become more security conscious and to enforce rules through more-formal relationships between inmates and staff? These important issues need further study.

check point

10. **What accounts for the neglect of facilities and programs in women's prisons?**
The small number of female inmates compared with the number of male inmates.

11. **How do the social relationships among female prisoners differ from those among their male counterparts?**
Men are more individualistic and their norms stress autonomy, self-sufficiency, and the ability to cope with one's own problems. Women are more sharing with one another.

12. **What problems do female prisoners face in maintaining contact with their children?**
The distance of prisons from homes, intermittent telephone privileges, and unnatural visiting environment.

stop& analyze

To what extent should society worry about, pay attention to, and spend money on programs for children whose parents are in prison? Give two arguments supporting each side of this debate.

Prison Programs

Modern correctional institutions differ from those of the past in the number and variety of programs provided for inmates. Early penitentiaries included prison industries; educational, vocational, and treatment programs were added when rehabilitation goals became prevalent. During the last 35 years, as the public called for harsher punishment of criminals, legislators have gutted prison educational and treatment programs as "frills" that only "coddled" inmates. In addition, the great increase in the number of prisoners has limited access to those programs that are still available.

Administrators argue that programs help them deal with the problem of time on the prisoners' hands. They know that the more programs prisons offer, the less likely that inmate idleness will turn into hostility; less cell time means fewer tensions. Evidence suggests that inmate education and jobs may positively affect the running of prisons, as well as reduce recidivism.

Classification of Prisoners

Determining the appropriate program for an individual prisoner usually involves a process called **classification**. A committee—often comprising the heads of the security, treatment, education, and industry departments—evaluates the inmate's security level, treatment and educational needs, work assignment, and eventually readiness for release.

Classification decisions are often based on the institution's needs rather than on those of the inmates. For example, inmates from the city may be assigned to

classification The process of assigning an inmate to a category specifying his or her needs for security, treatment, education, work assignment, and readiness for release.

farm work because that is where they are needed. Further, certain programs may remain limited, even though the demand for them is great. Thus, inmates may find that the few open seats in, for example, a computer course are filled and that there is a long waiting list. Prisoners often become angered and frustrated by the classification process and the limited availability of programs. Although release on parole can depend on a good record of participation in these programs, entrance for some inmates is blocked.

Educational Programs

Offenders constitute one of the most undereducated groups in the U.S. population. In many systems, all inmates who have not completed eighth grade are assigned full-time to prison school. Many programs provide remedial help in reading, English, and math. Nearly 80 percent of prisons offer courses to enable prisoners to earn their GED, but only 35 percent offer courses in cooperation with a college or university (Stephan, 2008). Funds have been reduced for college courses available to prisoners. The Comprehensive Crime Control Act of 1994 bans federal funding (Pell Grants) to prisoners for postsecondary education (Buruma, 2005). Studies have shown that prisoners assigned to education programs tend to avoid committing crimes after release (Andrews and Bonta, 1994). However, it remains unclear whether education helps rehabilitate these offenders or whether the types of prisoners ("gleaners") assigned to education programs tend to be those motivated to avoid further crimes.

Companies are finding that prison labor can be more efficient than outsourcing to low-wage countries elsewhere in the world. Prisoners at Wabash Valley Correctional Facility assemble yo-yos as part of a joint venture between the Indiana Department of Corrections' prison industry program and the Flambeau Products Corporation. Are these prisoners doing jobs that would otherwise provide wages for law-abiding citizens?

Vocational Education

Vocational education programs attempt to teach offenders a marketable job skill. Unfortunately, too many programs train inmates for trades that already have an adequate labor supply or in which new methods have made the skills taught obsolete.

Offenders often lack the attitudes necessary to obtain and keep a job—punctuality, accountability, deference to supervisors, cordiality to coworkers. Therefore, most prisoners need to learn not only a skill but also how to act in the work world. For example, Minnesota's "Affordable Homes Program" teaches prisoners construction skills as they build or remodel homes for low-income families. An evaluation of this program determined that prisoners who participated were more likely to be hired in construction jobs after release, and the state saved over $13 million by using inmate labor; however, graduates of this program did not have reduced rates of criminal behavior after release (Bohmert and Duwe, 2011).

Yet another problem is perhaps the toughest of all. In one state or another, the law bars ex-felons from practicing certain occupations, including nurse, beautician, barber, real estate salesperson, chauffeur, worker where alcoholic beverages are sold, cashier, and insurance salesperson. Unfortunately, some prison vocational programs actually train inmates for jobs they can never hold.

Prison Industries

Prison industries, which trace their roots to the early workshops of New York's Auburn Penitentiary, are intended to teach work habits and skills that will assist prisoners' reentry into the outside workforce. In practice, institutions rely on prison labor to provide basic food, maintenance, clerical, and other services it requires. In addition, many prisons contain manufacturing facilities that produce goods, such as office furniture and clothing, used in correctional and other state institutions.

The prison industries system carries a checkered career. During the nineteenth century, factories were established in many prisons, and inmates manufactured items that were sold on the open market. With the rise of the labor movement, however, state legislatures and Congress passed laws restricting the sale of prison-made goods so that they would not compete with those made by free workers. In 1979, Congress lifted restrictions on the interstate sale of prison-made products and urged correctional administrators to explore with the private sector possible improvements for prison industry programs. Industrial programs would relieve idleness, allow inmates to earn wages that they could save until release, and reduce the costs of incarceration. The Federal Bureau of Prisons and some states have developed industries, but generally their products are not sold on the free market and the percentage of prisoners employed varies greatly. Nonetheless, about 3.5 percent of the prisoners in the United States produced goods and services worth $1.5 billion (Swarz, 2004).

Although the idea of employing inmates sounds attractive, the inefficiencies of prison work may offset its economic value. Turnover is great, because many inmates are transferred among several institutions or released over a two-year period. Many prisoners have little education and lack steady work habits, making it difficult for them to perform many of the tasks of modern production. An additional cost to efficiency is the need to stop production periodically to count heads and to check that tools and materials have not been stolen. In addition, participation in prison industry programs may not reduce recidivism post-release for many inmates (Richmond, 2012).

Public support for rehabilitative programs (selective responses)

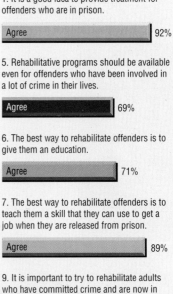

1. It is a good idea to provide treatment for offenders who are in prison.

Agree — 92%

5. Rehabilitative programs should be available even for offenders who have been involved in a lot of crime in their lives.

Agree — 69%

6. The best way to rehabilitate offenders is to give them an education.

Agree — 71%

7. The best way to rehabilitate offenders is to teach them a skill that they can use to get a job when they are released from prison.

Agree — 89%

9. It is important to try to rehabilitate adults who have committed crime and are now in the correctional system.

Agree — 88%

Critical Thinking: Should the existence and funding of rehabilitation programs in prisons be guided by public opinion or by the views of professionals who work in the field of corrections? If you were a governor, what sources of information would guide your recommendations about the allocation of resources for rehabilitation of criminal offenders?

Source: Francis T. Cullen, Jennifer A. Pealer, Bonnie S. Fisher, Brandon K. Applegate, and Shannon A. Santana, "Public Support for Correctional Rehabilitation in America: Change and Consistency?" in *Changing Attitudes to Punishment*. Edited by Julian V. Roberts and Mike Hough (Cullompton, UK: Willan, 2002), 137.

Rehabilitative Programs

Rehabilitative programs seek to treat the personal defects thought to have brought about the inmate's criminality. Most people agree that rehabilitating offenders is a desirable goal, but they disagree a great deal on the amount of emphasis that these programs should receive. Counseling and special programs are offered in 97 percent of public prisons but in only 74 percent of private institutions (Stephan, 2008).

Reports in the 1970s cast doubt on the ability of treatment programs to stem recidivism. They also questioned the ethics of requiring inmates to participate in rehabilitative programs in exchange for the promise of parole (Martinson, 1974). Supporters of treatment programs argue that certain programs, if properly run, work for certain offenders (Andrews et al., 1990; T. Palmer, 1992). Read "What Americans Think" to find out how many Americans support rehabilitative programs.

Clinical Director

Lisa Zimmer, Assistant Clinical Director,
Talbert House, Cincinnati, Ohio

Photo provided by Lisa Zimmer. © Cengage Learning

The Assistant Clinical Director assists in training clinical supervisors and other staff members who work with offenders. The position also involves developing and implementing treatment strategies and program improvements. In addition,

the position's administrative responsibilities include ensuring that the agency complies with relevant laws and policies regarding best treatment practices, clients' rights, and proper expenditure of funds. Such careers require knowledge of substance abuse and other problems affecting offenders, as well as approaches to treatment. The position requires excellent communication skills, the ability to listen carefully to staff and clients, and the capacity to solve problems.

Lisa Zimmer studied journalism and sociology in earning her undergraduate degree. After beginning a career as a professional writer creating annual reports and other publications for hospitals, she decided to shift careers so she could work at providing direct benefits to troubled people. While working full-time, she went back

to school in the evenings to earn a master's degree in social work with an emphasis on counseling. After gaining the necessary certifications and licenses, she worked as a counselor in various correctional settings. Over time, she was promoted to supervisory and administrative positions for these programs. She now works for Talbert House, a nonprofit agency that provides substance-abuse counseling, mental health treatment, and other services in jails, community corrections programs, reentry programs, and other correctional settings in Cincinnati, Ohio.

The work is challenging and rewarding at the same time. Generally, pay is not commensurate with other jobs requiring similar education, experience, and responsibility, so people who choose chemical dependency counseling or to work within the mental health or criminal justice systems aren't in it for the money. They are in it to make a difference, and they do. They help to give people back their lives.

Most corrections systems still offer a range of psychological, behavioral, and social services programs. How much they are used seems to vary according to the goals of the institution and the attitudes of the administrators. Researcher Michelle Phelps (2011) argues that while public opinion supported the "nothing works" perspective that decried rehabilitative efforts, there wasn't significant change in prison programming until the 1990s. At that point, efforts to rehabilitate inmates focused more on preparing inmates to reenter society (to be discussed in Chapter 13) than in providing them with educational programming. Incarceration's current goal of humane custody implies no effort to change inmates.

Can you imagine yourself working closely with criminal offenders to help them improve themselves? Consider the challenges of such jobs as you read "Careers in Criminal Justice."

Medical Services

Most prisons offer medical services through a full-time staff of nurses, augmented by part-time physicians under contract to the corrections system. Nurses take care of routine health care and dispense medicines from a secure in-prison pharmacy; regularly scheduled visits to the prison by doctors can enable prisoners to obtain checkups and diagnoses. For cases needing a specialist, surgery, or emergency medical assistance, prisoners must be transported to local hospitals, under close supervision by correctional staff. The aim is for the prison system to provide a range of medical assistance to meet the various needs of the population as a whole. Most states spend about $2,500 annually per inmate for health care, but some spend up to $5,000 and many under $2,000 (Pennsylvania Prison Society, 2004). Costs are also dependent on inmate age—health care costs in Oregon prisons range from $299 per inmate for those under age 30, up to $6,527 per inmate for those older than 70 (Zaitz, 2011).

Medical services in some states have not kept up with the increase in the incarcerated population. In 1976, the U.S. Supreme Court ruled that prisoners have a constitutional right to health care. In 2011, the Supreme Court's decision in *Brown v. Plata* ordered California to reduce its incarcerated population significantly to reduce overcrowding and create a healthier prison environment. The decision supported earlier findings by lower court judges that the state's failure to provide medical and mental health care was needlessly causing the death of at least one inmate every month and was subjecting prisoners to cruel and unusual punishment, which is prohibited by the Constitution (Liptak, 2011).

Although inmates' medical needs often echo those of the general population, prisoners pose two special needs, one due to poverty and the other to aging. Because prisoners as a group are very poor, they often bring to the prison years of neglect of their general health. Other consequences of being poor, such as an inadequate diet and poor hygiene, also affect the general health of the prison population.

check point >

13. **Why are prison programs important from the standpoint of prison administrators?**
Programs keep prisoners busy and reduce security problems.

14. **Why have legislators and the general public been so critical of educational and rehabilitative programs in prisons?**
Such programs are thought to "coddle" prisoners and may not reduce future criminal behavior.

stop & analyze

If budget cuts led to the elimination of all vocational training and education programs in prisons, how would that impact daily life for prisoners and corrections officers? List three possible effects from the elimination of programs.

Violence in Prison

Prisons provide a perfect recipe for violence. They confine in cramped quarters a thousand men, some with histories of violent behavior. While incarcerated, these men are not allowed contact with women and live under highly restrictive conditions. Sometimes these conditions spark collective violence, as in the riots at Attica, New York (1971), Santa Fe, New Mexico (1980), Atlanta, Georgia (1987), Lucasville, Ohio (1993), Folsom, California (2012) and Florence, Colorado (2008).

Although prison riots are widely reported in the news, few people have witnessed the level of everyday interpersonal violence that takes place in U.S. prisons. For example, each year about 34,000 inmates are physically attacked by other inmates. In 2002, 48 assault victims died. An additional 168 prisoners committed suicide (BJS, 2005:1). Great numbers of prisoners live in a state of constant uneasiness, always on the lookout for people who might demand sex, steal their few possessions, or otherwise hurt them. Some researchers suggest that the level of violence varies by offender age, institutional security designation, and administrative effectiveness (Maitland and Sluder, 1998:55). Others point out that inmates' own behavior affects their likelihood of victimization, with those who have violent prior offenses and those who participate in the prison economy more likely to be victimized in prison (Copes et al., 2010; Kerley, Hochstetler, and Copes, 2009).

When officers must remove an uncooperative or violent prisoner from a cell, trained cell-extraction teams must overwhelm the prisoner through the use of force, while also limiting the risk of injury to themselves. Such events are often filmed to prevent false claims by prisoners that officers used excessive force. Are there additional precautions that these officers should take to avoid injuries to themselves and to the prisoner?

Assaultive Behavior and Inmate Characteristics

For the person entering prison for the first time, the anxiety level and fear of violence run especially high. Gary, an inmate at Leavenworth, told Pete Earley, "Every convict has three choices, but only three. He can fight (kill someone), he can hit the fence (escape), or he can fuck (submit)" (1992:55). Even if a prisoner is not assaulted, the potential for violence permeates the environments of many prisons, adding to the stress and pains of incarceration.

Violence in correctional institutions raises serious questions for administrators, criminal justice specialists, and the general public. What causes prison violence? What can be done about it? We consider these questions by examining three main categories of prison violence: prisoner–prisoner, prisoner–officer, and officer–prisoner. First, we discuss three characteristics of prisoners that underlie these behavioral factors: age, race, and mental illness.

Age Studies have shown that young men aged 16 to 24, both inside and outside prison, are more prone to violence than are older men. Not surprisingly, 96 percent of adult prisoners are men, with an average age of 27 at time of admission. Studies also show that younger prisoners face a greater risk of being victimized than do older inmates.

Besides having greater physical strength than their elders, young men lack the commitments to career and family that can restrict antisocial behavior. In addition, many have difficulty defining their position in society. Thus, they interpret many things as challenges to their status.

Machismo, the concept of male honor and the sacredness of one's reputation as a man, requires physical retaliation against those who insult one's honor. Some inmates adopt a preventive strategy of trying to impress others with their bravado, which may result in counterchallenges and violence. The potential for violence among such prisoners is clear.

Race Race has become a major divisive factor in today's prisons. Racist attitudes, common in the larger society, have become part of the convict code. Forced association—having to live with people one would not likely associate with on the outside—exaggerates and amplifies racial conflict. Violence against members of another race may be how some inmates deal with the frustrations of their lives. The presence of gangs organized along racial lines contributes to violence in prison. White inmates may be more likely to be victimized in prison, holding constant other factors (Kerley, Hochstetler, and Copes, 2009).

Mental Illness Inmates with diagnosed mental illnesses are significantly more likely to be victims violence in prison than those not mentally ill (Blitz, Wolff, and Shi, 2008), and are also more likely to be abused sexually during incarceration (Cristanti and Frueh, 2011). Prison is a traumatic experience, and can cause mental illness to develop in individuals who were not suffering from illness when they arrived. Incarceration can also exacerbate preexisting mental conditions, leaving more inmates in need of psychological treatment (Rich, Wakeman, and Dickman, 2011). If these inmates are more likely to be victimized, their mental condition can worsen, causing even greater problems for them during their incarceration (Listwan et al., 2010).

Prisoner–Prisoner Violence

Although prison folklore may attribute violence to sadistic guards, most prison violence occurs between inmates. As Hans Toch has observed, the climate of violence in prisons has no free-world counterpart: "Inmates are terrorized by other inmates, and spend years in fear of harm. Some inmates request protective custody segregation, others lock themselves in, and some are hermits by choice" (1976:47–48). The Bureau of Justice Statistics reports that the rate of prisoner–prisoner assaults between inmates is 26 attacks per 1,000 inmates (Stephan and Karberg, 2003). But official statistics likely do not reflect the true amount of prisoner–prisoner violence, because many inmates who are assaulted do not make their victimization known to prison officials.

Prison Gangs   Racial or ethnic gangs (also referred to as "security threat groups") are now linked to acts of violence in most prison systems. Gangs make it difficult for wardens to maintain control. By continuing their street wars inside prison, gangs make some prisons more dangerous than even the worst American neighborhoods. Gangs are organized primarily to control an institution's drug, gambling, loan-sharking, prostitution, extortion, and debt-collection rackets. In addition, gangs protect their members from other gangs and instill a sense of macho camaraderie.

Prison gangs exist in the institutions of most states and the federal system, but it is sometimes difficult for management to determine the percentage of their inmates with gang affiliations. A survey of prisons in the United States found that wardens reported between 2 percent and 50 percent of their inmates were gang members, with a mean of 19 percent (Winterdyk and Ruddell, 2010). In Illinois, as much as 60 percent of the population are gang members (Hallinan, 2001:95), and the Florida Department of Corrections has identified 240 street gangs operating in their prisons (Davitz, 1998).

Many facilities segregate rival gangs by housing them in separate units of the same prison or by moving members to other prisons (sometimes even in different states), which wardens believe is an effective means of reducing gang-related violence (Winterdyk and Ruddell, 2010). Administrators have also set up intelligence units to gather information on gangs, particularly about illegal acts both inside and outside of prison. In some prisons, however, these policies create a power vacuum within the convict society that newer groups with new codes of behavior soon fill.

Prison Rape   Much of the mythology of prison life revolves around sexual assaults. Perpetrators are typically strong, experienced cons, either African American or white, who are serving sentences for violent offenses. Victims are portrayed as young, white, physically weak, mentally challenged, effeminate first-time nonviolent offenders.

Prison rape is a crime hidden by a curtain of silence. Inmate–inmate and inmate–staff sexual contact is prohibited in all prisons, yet it exists, and much of it remains hidden from authorities. Sexual violence ranges from unwanted touching to nonconsensual sex. When incidents are reported, correctional officers say that it is difficult to distinguish between rapes and consensual sex. Most officers do not catch the inmates in the act; when they do observe sexual activity, only a few officers report that they ignored the inmates' violations of prison rules (Eigenberg, 2000).

The 2004 Prison Rape Elimination Act (PREA) established a zero-tolerance standard for the incidence of rape in prison. This law requires the Bureau of Justice Statistics to conduct annual surveys in the nation's prisons and jails to measure the incidence of rape. The law also requires the attorney general to provide a list of the incidence of prison rape in each institution.

Data collected as part of PREA indicate that 7,744 allegations of inmate–inmate sexual assaults among state prisoners were reported in 2008, which is a rate of 3.1 attacks per 1,000 inmates. Perpetrators of substantial incidents of inmate-on-inmate assault tend to be male (82 percent), aged 25 to 39 and acting alone (88 percent). Victims were most likely to be male (77 percent), aged 25 to 39 (45 percent). Most incidents were found to take place between 6 P.M. and midnight, with few victims reporting physical injuries (18 percent). Offenders are most frequently punished by time in solitary or isolation (72 percent), arrest/prosecution (32 percent), transfer to a higher-security area of the prison (27 percent), or some combination of those sanctions (Guerino and Beck, 2011).

Guerino and Beck (2011) also assessed the characteristics of victims and offenders in incidents of staff-on-inmate sexual violence. Unlike inmate-on-inmate violence, a greater percentage of staff-on-inmate violence are women (37 percent), and female guards committed a majority of substantiated sexual assaults (56 percent of such assaults were by female corrections officers, compared to only 44 percent by male guards). Most of these types of incidents were committed in program service areas, such as the commissary, kitchen, storage areas, laundry, cafeteria, workshop, and hallways, between the hours of noon and 6 P.M.

Victims of prisoner–prisoner sexual victimization have few options. According to the inmate code, prisoners should "stand and fight" their own battles. For many, this is not feasible. Alternatively, some may seek the protection of a gang or a stronger inmate to whom the victim is then indebted. Others may try to fade into the shadows. Still others may seek protective custody. Each option has its pluses and minuses, but none provides victims with the ability to serve their time without constantly looking over their shoulder.

Protective Custody   For many victims of prison violence, protective custody offers the only way to escape further abuse. About 5,000 state prisoners are in protective custody. Life is not pleasant for these inmates (Browne, Cambier, and Agha, 2011). Often, they are let out of their cells only briefly to exercise and shower. Inmates who ask to "lock up" have little chance of returning to the general prison population without being viewed as a weakling—a snitch or a punk—to be preyed on. Even when they are transferred to another institution, their reputations follow them through the grapevine.

Prisoner–Officer Violence

The mass media have focused on riots in which guards are taken hostage, injured, and killed. However, violence against officers typically occurs in specific situations and against certain individuals. Yearly, inmates assault approximately 18,000 staff members (Stephan and Karberg, 2003:10). Correctional officers do not carry weapons within the institution, because a prisoner might seize them. However, prisoners do manage to obtain lethal weapons and can use the element of surprise to injure an officer. In the course of a workday, an officer may encounter situations that require the use of physical force against an inmate—for instance, breaking up a fight or moving a prisoner to segregation. Because such situations are especially dangerous, officers may enlist others to help them minimize the risk of violence. The officer's greatest fear is an unexpected attack, such as a "missile" thrown from an upper tier or an officer's "accidental" fall down a flight of stairs. The need to watch constantly against personal attacks adds stress and keeps many officers at a distance from the inmates.

Officer–Prisoner Violence

A fact of life in many institutions is unauthorized physical violence by officers against inmates. Stories abound of guards giving individual prisoners "the treatment" when supervisors are not looking. Many guards view physical force as an everyday, legitimate procedure. In some institutions, authorized "goon squads" composed of physically powerful officers use their muscle to maintain order.

Correctional officers are expected to follow departmental rules in their dealings with prisoners, yet supervisors generally cannot observe staff–prisoner confrontations directly. Further, prisoner complaints about officer brutality are often not believed until the officer involved gains a reputation for harshness. Even in this case, wardens may feel they must support their officers in order to retain their support. Research indicates that officers are more likely to victimize inmates who are male and nonwhite, and who are confined in maximum-security institutions. Inmates with a paid work assignment are less likely to be victimized by staff (Perez et al., 2009).

Decreasing Prison Violence

Five factors contribute to prison violence: (1) inadequate supervision by staff members, (2) architectural design that promotes rather than inhibits victimization, (3) the easy availability of deadly weapons, (4) the housing of violence-prone prisoners near relatively defenseless people, and (5) a general high level of tension produced by close quarters (Bowker, 1982:64). The physical size and condition of the prison and the relations between inmates and staff also affect violence.

The Effect of Architecture and Size
The fortress-like prison certainly does not create an atmosphere for normal interpersonal relationships, and the size of the larger institutions can create management problems. The massive scale of the megaprison, which may hold up to 3,000 inmates, provides opportunities for aggressive inmates to hide weapons, dispense private "justice," and engage more or less freely in other illicit activities. The size of the population in a large prison may also result in some inmates' "falling through the cracks"—being misclassified and forced to live among more-violent offenders.

Much of the emphasis on "new generation prisons"—small housing units, clear sight lines, security corridors linking housing units—is designed to limit such opportunities and thus prevent violence. However, a study of rape in Texas prisons found that cell blocks with solid doors may contribute to sexual assault (Austin et al., 2006).

The Role of Management
The degree to which inmate leaders are allowed to take matters into their own hands can affect the level of violence among inmates. When administrators run a tight ship, security measures prevent sexual attacks in dark corners, the making of "shivs" and "shanks" (knives) in the metal shop, and open conflict among inmate groups. A prison must afford each inmate defensible space, and administrators should ensure that every inmate remains secure from physical attack.

Effective management can decrease the level of assaultive behavior by limiting opportunities for attacks. Wardens and correctional officers must therefore recognize the types of people with whom they are dealing, the role of prison gangs, and the structure of institutions. John DiIulio argues that no group of inmates is "unmanageable [and] no combination of political, social, budgetary, architectural, or other factors makes good management impossible" (1991:12). He points to such varied institutions as the California Men's Colony, New York City's Tombs and Rikers Island, the Federal Bureau of Prisons, and the Texas Department of Corrections under the leadership of George Beto. At these institutions, good management practices have resulted in prisons and jails where inmates can "do time" without fearing for their personal safety. Wardens who exert leadership can manage their prisons effectively, so that problems do not fester and erupt into violent confrontations. Prisons must also be managed transparently—that is, incidents of violence in prisons must be dealt with openly and investigated by management. In addition, the public should be made aware of the nature of prison violence to better understand the challenges faced by inmates during incarceration and upon release (Byrne and Hummer, 2007).

Budget cuts in the area of corrections increasingly affect the management and organization of prisons. Reductions in the crime rate mean that fewer prisons are needed, but states are also looking to solutions that are both economical and successful in rehabilitating prisoners (Pew Center on the States, 2008). In addition, there has been increasing public concern that most states spend more on corrections than on public education. For example, in 2007 Michigan spent $1.19 on corrections for every $1.00 they spent on education. Compare this to Minnesota, which spent $.17 on corrections for every $1.00 spent on education (Pew Center on the States, 2008). Which of these institutions is more important in terms of state funding? How can states balance public safety with public education?

In sum, prisons must be made safe. Because the state uses its authority to incarcerate inmates, it has a responsibility to prevent violence and maintain order. To exclude violence from prisons, officials may have to limit movement within institutions, contacts with the outside, and the right of inmates to choose their associates. Yet, these measures may run counter to the goal of producing men and women who will be accountable when they return to society.

check point > **15. What five factors are thought to contribute to prison violence?**
Inadequate supervision, architectural design, availability of weapons, housing of violence-prone inmates with the defenseless, and the high level of tension among people living in close quarters.

stop & analyze Think about the role of architectural design in facilitating or preventing prison violence. Draw a design of a prison that would reduce the risks of and opportunities for violence. List three aspects of your design that are intended to reduce opportunities for violence.

a question of ethics

Think, Discuss, Write

In December 2011, former federal corrections officer Matthew Amos appeared in a Denver court for sentencing. He had made more than $17,000 from smuggling tobacco into a maximum-security federal prison. From 2000 to 2010, there were 272 federal corrections officers arrested, many of them for illegally smuggling tobacco and other items. Through his unethical and illegal actions, Amos added himself to that list.

In an emotional voice, he begged the judge not to sentence him to prison because of the rough treatment that any former corrections officer would face while living in the inmate population. The federal judge in Colorado was sympathetic and sentenced him to five years of probation. Not all corrections officers receive such light sentences, however. One month later, in January 2012, a former federal corrections officer in Illinois was sentenced to 30 months in prison to be followed by three years of supervised release

for engaging in the same tobacco-smuggling activities and then compounding his offense by lying to FBI agents when they began an investigation.

Discussion/Writing Assignment

If you were the warden of a prison, what steps would you take to prevent unethical activity by corrections officers, monitor the actions of officers, and create an environment in which you could stop improper conduct from taking place? Create a list of actions that you would take and explain your reasoning for each.

Sources: "Federal Correctional Officer Sentenced to Prison for Accepting Bribes and Smuggling Contraband," FBI Press Release, January 13, 2012 (www.fbi.gov); John Ingold, "Prison Black Market a Steal: Correctional Officers Get Drawn into Contraband Smuggling," *Denver Post*, December 18, 2011 (www.denverpost.com).

summary

Describe how contemporary institutions differ from the old-style "big-house" prisons

→ The typical "big-house" was a walled prison with large tiered cell blocks, a yard, and workshops.
→ Prisoners came from both rural and urban areas, were poor, and outside of the South were mainly white.
→ The prison society in the past was isolated, with restrictions on visitors, mail, and other

communications. The inmates' days were highly structured with rules enforced by the guards.

Understand the three models of incarceration that have predominated since the 1940s

→ The custodial model emphasizes the maintenance of security.
→ The rehabilitation model views security and housekeeping activities as mainly a framework for treatment efforts.

→ The reintegration model recognizes that prisoners must be prepared for their return to society.

Explain how a prison is organized

→ Most prisons are expected to fulfill goals related to keeping (custody), using (working), and serving (treating) inmates. They are organized to fulfill these goals.

Know how a prison is governed

→ The public's belief that the warden and officers have total power over the inmates is outdated.

→ Good management through effective leadership can maintain the quality of prison life as measured by levels of order, amenities, and services.

→ Four factors make managing prisons different from administering other public institutions: defects of total power, limited use of rewards and punishments, exchange relationships, and strength of inmate leadership.

Understand the role of correctional officers in a prison

→ Because they remain in close contact with the prisoners, correctional officers are the linchpins of the prison system. The effectiveness of the institution rests on their shoulders.

Explain the characteristics of the incarcerated population

→ Most prisoners are male, young, members of minority groups, with low education levels.

→ Prison administrators must deal with the special needs of some groups, including elderly prisoners, prisoners with HIV/AIDS, mentally ill prisoners, and long-term prisoners.

Discuss what prison is like for men and for women

→ Inmates do not serve their time in isolation but are members of a subculture with its own traditions, norms, and leadership structure. Such norms are often described as the inmate code.

→ Today's prisons, unlike those of the past, do not have a uniform inmate code but several, in part because of the influence of gangs.

→ Inmates deal with the pain of incarceration by assuming an adaptive role and lifestyle.

→ Male inmates are individualistic, and their norms stress autonomy, self-sufficiency, and the ability to cope with one's own problems. Female inmates share with one another and place less emphasis on achieving status or recognition within the prisoner community. There is less violence in female prisons than in male ones.

List some of the programs and services available to prisoners

→ Educational, vocational, industrial, and rehabilitative programs are available in prisons. Administrators believe that these programs are important for maintaining order.

→ Medical services are provided to all inmates.

Describe the nature of prison violence

→ Violence occurs between prisoners and between prisoners and guards.

→ Violence in prison depends on such things as administrative effectiveness, the architecture and size of prisons, and inmate characteristics such as age, attitudes, and race. Prison gangs play an increasing role in causing prison violence.

Questions for Review

1. How do modern prisons differ from those in the past?
2. What characteristics of prisons distinguish them from other institutions?
3. What must a prison administrator do to ensure successful management?
4. What is meant by an adaptive role? Which roles are found in male prison society? In female prison society?
5. How does the convict society in institutions for women differ from that in institutions for men?
6. What are the main forms of prison programs, and what purposes do they serve?
7. What are forms and causes of prison violence?

Key Terms and Cases

classification (p. 367)

custodial model (p. 347)

inmate code (p. 359)

rehabilitation model (p. 347)

reintegration model (p. 347)

12

Probation and Intermediate Sanctions

Learning Objectives

→ Describe the philosophical assumptions that underlie community corrections

→ Explain how probation evolved and how probation sentences are implemented today

→ List the types of intermediate sanctions and how they are administered

→ Discuss the key issues faced by community corrections at the beginning of the twenty-first century

Fresh out of rehab, On February 8, 2009, R&B singer Chris Brown assaulted his then-girlfriend, singer Rihanna. During an argument in Brown's car, he attempted to force Rihanna out of the car while it was moving. After she called her assistant for help, he punched and bit her. Tabloid photos of Rihanna after the assault revealed extensive bruising and bleeding on her face. Brown was later arrested and pleaded guilty to a charge of felony assault, thereby avoiding jail time (Duke and Rowlands, 2009).

A number of sanctions were placed on Brown as part of his punishment. Even though he avoided jail by accepting a plea agreement, he was sentenced to 180 days of community labor near his home in Virginia. He was also required to complete a one-year class focused on issues of domestic violence and was placed on probation for five years (Hutchinson, 2009). This combination of alternative sanctions was thought to be "the equivalent" of 180 days in jail for Brown, who had no criminal record prior to this incident (Duke and Rowlands, 2009).

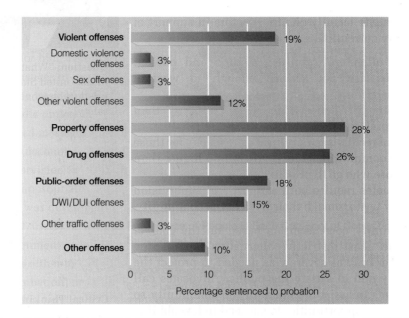

Figure 12.2

Most Serious Offense Committed by Offenders Sentenced to Probation Most probationers are serving their sentence because they committed property or drug offenses, but almost 20 percent of probationers have been convicted of violent offenses. Sex offenders comprise the smallest category of people sentenced to probation.

Source: Lauren E. Glaze and Thomas P. Bonczar, 2011, "Probation and Parole in the United States, 2010," Bureau of Justice Statistics *Bulletin* (December) NCJ 231674. Detail may not sum to total due to rounding.

another crime, the judge can order the entire sentence to be served in prison. Although probation offers many benefits over incarceration, the public often sees it as a "slap on the wrist" for offenders (Public Opinion Strategies, 2010).

Today, although more than 4.1 million offenders are on probation, probation budgets in many states have been cut and caseloads increased as lawmakers struggle with shrinking resources. In 2012, for example, the Florida Department of Corrections attempted to address a $79 million budget deficit, in part, by cutting funds for probation (Campbell, 2012). Given that caseloads in some urban areas reach 300 offenders per officer, probation officers often cannot provide the level of supervision necessary.

Origins and Evolution of Probation

Probation first developed in the United States when John Augustus, a Boston boot maker, persuaded a judge in the Boston Police Court in 1841 to give him custody of a convicted offender for a brief period, and then helped the man appear rehabilitated by the time of sentencing.

Massachusetts developed the first statewide probation system in 1880; by 1920, another 21 states had followed suit. The federal courts were authorized to hire probation officers in 1925. By the beginning of World War II, probation systems had been established in 44 states.

Probation began as a humanitarian effort to allow first-time and minor offenders a second chance. Early probationers were expected not only to obey the law but also to behave in a morally acceptable fashion. Officers sought to provide moral leadership to help shape probationers' attitudes and behavior with respect to family, religion, employment, and free time.

By the 1940s, the development of psychology led probation officers to shift their emphasis from moral leadership to therapeutic counseling. This shift brought three important changes. First, the officer no longer acted primarily as a community supervisor charged with enforcing a particular morality. Second, the officer became more of a clinical social worker who aimed at helping the offender solve psychological and social problems. Third, the offender was expected to become actively involved in the treatment. The pursuit of rehabilitation as the primary goal of probation gave the officer extensive discretion in defining and treating the offender's problems. Officers used their judgment to evaluate each offender and develop a treatment approach to the personal problems that presumably had led to crime.

During the 1960s, probation moved in another direction. Rather than counseling offenders, probation officers provided them with concrete social services such as assistance with employment, housing, finances, and education. This emphasis on reintegrating offenders and remedying the social problems they faced fit with federal efforts to wage a war on poverty. Instead of being a counselor or therapist, the probation officer served as an advocate, dealing with private and public institutions on the offender's behalf.

In the late 1970s, the orientation of probation changed again as the goals of rehabilitation and reintegration gave way to "risk management." This approach, still dominant today, seeks to minimize the probability that an offender will commit a new offense. Risk management reflects two basic goals. First, in accord with the deserved-punishment ideal, the punishment should fit the offense, and correctional intervention should neither raise nor lower the level of punishment. Second, according to the community-protection criterion, the degree of risk that the probationer will return to crime determines the amount and type of supervision.

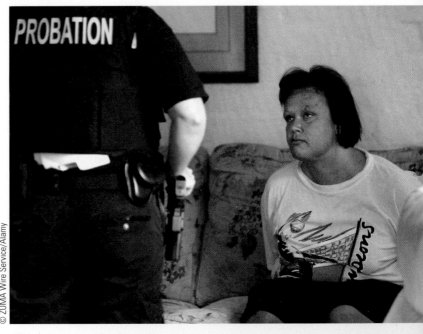

© ZUMA Wire Service/Alamy

Probation officers often handle large caseloads of offenders who must be monitored through drug testing, curfew checks, and other means to ensure that they are fulfilling the court-mandated conditions of probation. How difficult is it to monitor the behavior of offenders in the community?

Organization of Probation

As a form of corrections, probation falls under the executive branch, and people usually see it as a concern of state government. However, in about 25 percent of the states, probation falls to county and local governments. Further, in many states the judiciary administers it locally. The state sets the standards and provides financial support and training courses, but locally administered programs handle about two-thirds of all people under probation supervision.

In many jurisdictions, although the state is formally responsible for all probation services, the locally elected county judges are in charge. This seemingly odd arrangement produces benefits as well as problems. On the positive side, having probationers under the supervision of the court permits judges to keep closer tabs on them and to order incarceration if the conditions of probation are violated. On the negative side, some judges know little about the goals and methods of corrections, and the probation responsibility adds to the administrative duties of already overworked courts.

Judicially enforced probation seems to work best when the judges and the supervising officers have close relationships. Proponents of this system say that judges need to work with probation officers whom they can trust, whose presentence reports they can accurately evaluate, and on whom they can rely to report the success or failure of individual cases.

For the sake of their clients and the goals of the system, probation officers need direct access to corrections and other human services agencies. However, these agencies are located within the executive branch of government. Several states have combined probation and parole services in the same agency to coordinate resources and services better. Others point out, however, that probationers differ from parolees. Parolees already have served prison terms, frequently have been involved in more-serious crimes, and often have been disconnected from mainstream society. By contrast, most probationers have not developed criminal lifestyles to the same degree and do not have the same problems of reintegration into the community.

Probation Officer Assistant

Scott Lopofsky, U.S. Probation Officer Assistant,
U.S. Probation Office, Northern District of Illinois

Photo provided by Scott Lopofsky. © Cengage Learning

The duties of a U.S. probation officer assistant vary by district and by the need or mission of each office. In the Northern District of Illinois, officer assistants are responsible for conducting collateral criminal-history investigations and home visits; they also monitor Immigration and Naturalization Service cases and perform various tasks in the offender urinalysis lab. Collateral criminal-history investigations consist of analyzing a defendant's criminal-history report and collecting all necessary documents for disposition information. When the complete past criminal history is collected, the officer writes a report to present his or her findings. The report is used in presentence investigation reports as a tool for judges and probation officers to determine the number of criminal-history points a defendant will receive when sentencing guidelines are applied by the judge. Home visits require face-to-face contact with the defendant, or with a family member of the defendant, for residential verification. A probation officer assistant also has the task of conducting presentence interviews when the defendant resides within the district but is being sentenced in a different district.

The qualifications for this position vary for each district. The majority of districts require a bachelor's degree, as well as strong writing skills and effective case-management abilities. An applicant must also pass a full government background investigation. The majority of probation office assistants have criminal justice or social work backgrounds.

In preparing for his career as a probation officer assistant, Scott Lopofsky earned a bachelor's degree in criminal justice. He then worked for one year as an investigator conducting background investigations for a government contractor that developed reports on applicants for federal law enforcement positions. He is currently enrolled part-time in a criminal justice graduate program.

The biggest challenge I face as a probation officer assistant is producing accurate and thorough reports while adhering to strict deadlines. Criminal-history reports can be complex and require numerous follow-ups with different law enforcement agencies. This is a challenging task because my caseload is high and the turnaround time to complete the investigation is short.

Probation Services

Probation officers play roles similar to both the police and social workers. In addition to assisting the judiciary with presentence investigations (see Chapter 9), probation officers supervise clients to keep them out of trouble and enforce the conditions of the sentence. This law enforcement role involves discretionary decisions about whether to report violations of probation conditions. Probation officers are also expected to act like social workers by helping clients obtain the housing, employment, and treatment services they need. The potential conflict between the roles is great. Not surprisingly, individual officers sometimes emphasize one role over the other. As you read about the job of a probation officer in "Careers in Criminal Justice," consider whether you would be interested in supervising offenders in the community.

A continuing issue for probation officers is the size of their caseloads. How many clients can one officer effectively handle? In the 1930s, the National Probation Association recommended a 50-unit caseload; in 1967, the U.S. President's Commission on Law Enforcement and Administration of Justice reduced it to 35. However, today the national average for adult supervision is about 150, with some urban caseloads exceeding 300, as we have seen. The oversized caseload is usually cited as one of the main obstacles to successful probation. In San Diego County, after a budget cut of $17 million led to the elimination of nearly 150 positions in probation, there were only 76 probation officers to monitor 18,000 adults on probation in that county. Chief Probation Officer Mack Jenkins hoped to keep the caseload at 50 for officers handling high-risk probationers, but feared that budget cuts could force officers supervising medium-risk probationers to handle more than 300 cases (Orr, 2009). For probation officers in the field, these caseload concerns are very real because they affect how often the officers can see each probationer. However, the field's most effective advocate for probation and parole supervision, the American Probation and Parole Association, has been unable to uncover a link between caseload size and the effectiveness of supervision (Papparozzi and Hinzman, 2005).

During the past decade, probation officials have developed methods of classifying clients according to their service needs, the element of risk they pose to the community, and the chance that they will commit another offense. Risk classification fits the deserved-punishment model of the criminal sanction in that the most serious cases receive the greatest restrictions and supervision. If probationers live according to the conditions of their sentence, the level of supervision is gradually reduced.

Several factors affect how much supervision serious cases actually receive. Consider the war on drugs. It has significantly increased probation levels in urban areas, because large numbers of people convicted of drug sales or possession are placed on probation. Many of these offenders have committed violent acts and live in inner-city areas marked by drug dealing and turf battles to control drug markets. Under these conditions, direct supervision can place the probation officer in danger. In some urban areas, probationers are merely required to telephone or mail reports of their current residence and employment. In such cases, it is hard to see how any goal of the sanctions—deserved punishment, rehabilitation, deterrence, or incapacitation— is being realized. If none of these objectives is being met, the offender is "getting off."

In some cities, budget cuts have led to the expanded use of volunteers to assist in probation functions. These programs operate according to at least two different models. In one model, the volunteers actually act as unpaid probation officers. After receiving training, they carry out the duties of professionals, enabling their cities and counties to administer probation programs less expensively. For example, the website of the city of Westminster, Colorado, insists that "volunteers do not do 'social' type activities with the clients" and describes the responsibilities carried out by volunteers: enforce court orders; provide mentoring; monitor compliance with probation terms; write monthly reports on each offender; attend probation court hearings; and attend monthly training sessions (City of Westminster website, 2011). In the second model, volunteers conduct a wider array of activities in support of the probation office. For example, in San Diego, the Volunteers in Probation program carries out fundraising activities and clothing drives to provide clothing, eye exams, scholarships, emergency funds, and bus passes for probationers who are fulfilling the conditions of probation (www.volunteersinprobation.org, 2011).

Revocation and Termination of Probation

Probation ends in one of two ways: (1) the person successfully completes the period of probation, or (2) the probationary status is revoked because of misbehavior. Revocation of probation typically occurs for either a **technical violation** or a new arrest.

Technical violations occur when a probationer fails to meet the conditions of a sentence by, for instance, violating curfew, failing a drug test, or using alcohol. Officers have discretion as to whether or not they bring this fact to the attention of the judge. In making these discretionary decisions, they must be professional, ethical, and fair. Read "A Question of Ethics" at the end of the chapter to consider ethical issues, including the problem of probation officers who improperly engage in favoritism when making decisions related to probation violations.

As indicated by Table 12.1, probation revocations in New York counties outside of New York City were triggered by technical violations in 54 percent of cases and by arrests in 23 percent of cases (New York State Division of Criminal Justice Services, 2008).

Probation officers and judges have widely varying notions of what constitutes grounds for revoking probation. When encountering technical violations, probation officers may first try to impose stricter rules, sternly lecture the probationer, and

technical violation The probationer's failure to abide by the rules and conditions of probation (specified by the judge), resulting in revocation of probation.

TABLE 12.1 Probation Revocation Hearings: Justifications and Outcomes

This is a snapshot of the reasons for outstate New York probation officers' recommendations for revocation and the outcomes when probationers were resentenced as a result of revocation.*

Violation Reasons	
Technical violations	54%
Arrest	23
New conviction	13
Abscond (go missing)	11
Total†	100%
Resentence after Probation Revocation	
Local jail	74%
State prison	15
Probation	4
Intermittent imprisonment	4
Unconditional discharge	2
Fine	1
Total	100%

Note: Two additional offenders were sent to juvenile detention facilities.

*The data present reasons and outcomes for the 57 counties outside of New York City. New York City's probation population is much more heavily composed of convicted felons. The outstate counties' mix of misdemeanants and felons on probation may be more similar to the probation populations throughout the country.

†Total does not equal 100% due to rounding.

Source: *New York State Probation Population: 2007 Profile*, Albany: New York State Division of Criminal Justice Services, June 2008.

increase the frequency of contacts with the probationer. Yet, the probation officer may face special challenges if the probationer does not take seriously the likelihood of consequences for technical violations. Indeed, a study in Wisconsin found that 68 percent of probationers failed on at least one occasion to report as required to the probation officer, in contrast to only 42 percent of parolees committing the same technical violation (Van Stelle and Goodrich, 2009). Unlike parolees who, as we will see in Chapter 13, have already been to prison and therefore may be more likely to fear being sent back, many probationers are young and less experienced with the system. This failure to fulfill probation conditions may demonstrate their greater immaturity as well as their failure to recognize that technical violations could actually lead to incarceration if their probation officer seeks revocation.

Once the officer calls a violation to the attention of the court, the probationer may be arrested or summoned for a revocation hearing. The Legislative Analyst's Office for the State of California calculates that it costs taxpayers an extra $50,000, on average, each time an offender is sent to prison for a probation revocation. That amount includes not only the marginal cost of sending an offender to prison, but also the average length of the probationer's sentence (17 months), the subsequent cost of parole supervision, and the likelihood that some percentage of these offenders will be sent to prison again for parole violations (Taylor, 2009). Because of the contemporary emphasis on avoiding the expense of incarceration except for flagrant and continual violations of the conditions of probation, revocations increasingly rest on a new arrest or multiple violations of rules rather than on a small number of technical violations.

As discussed in Chapter 10, the U.S. Supreme Court extended due process rights to probationers by ruling that, before probation can be revoked, the offender is entitled to both a preliminary and a final hearing, and a right to counsel in some cases. When a probationer is taken into custody for violating the conditions of probation, a preliminary hearing must be held to determine whether probable cause exists to believe that the incident occurred. If there is a finding of probable cause, a final hearing, where the revocation decision is made, is mandatory. At these hearings, the probationer has the right to cross-examine witnesses and to receive notice of the alleged violations and receive a written report of the proceedings. The Court ruled, though, that the probationer does not have an automatic right to counsel; this decision is to be made on a case-by-case basis. At the final hearing, the judge decides whether to continue probation or to impose tougher restrictions, such as incarceration.

For those who successfully complete probation, the sentence ends. Ordinarily, the probationer is then a free citizen again, with obligation neither to the court nor to the probation department.

Probation officers make decisions about whether probationers should be taken into custody for violating the terms of probation. After the decision is made, they often require police assistance for this task. Do probation officers need the same training as police officers, or should they receive a different kind of training in order to do their jobs effectively?

Assessing Probation

As states deal with continuing budget difficulties, the use of probation is certain to expand. Yet, critics see probation as nothing more than a slap on the wrist, an absence of punishment. The importance of probation for public safety has never been greater: At the end of 2010, studies indicated that 50 percent of those sentenced to probation had been assigned that punishment upon conviction for a felony (Glaze and Bonczar, 2011). This statistic is striking because many people assume that probationers have typically only committed misdemeanors. Despite the fact that many probationers have been convicted of serious crimes, caseload burdens and limited resources lead many probation officers to meet with individual offenders little more than once a month. Such limited contact raises questions about whether convicted felons receive adequate supervision and monitoring in the community. Yet, as budget cuts aimed at the expense of imprisonment increase the number of offenders assigned to community sanctions, contact between officers and probationers may be further reduced in many jurisdictions that cannot afford to simultaneously increase the number of probation officers.

The 2009 report of the Pew Center on the States presents research-based recommendations designed to strengthen community corrections systems, saving money and reducing crime (Pew Center on the States, 2009). These recommendations include the following:

- Sort offenders by risk to public safety to determine appropriate levels of supervision
- Base intervention programs on sound research about what works to reduce recidivism
- Harness advances in supervision technology such as electronic monitoring and rapid-result alcohol and drug tests
- Impose swift and certain sanctions for offenders who break the rules of their release but who do not commit new crimes
- Create incentives for offenders and supervision agencies to succeed, and monitor their performance

Although the recidivism rate for probationers is lower than the rate for those who have been incarcerated, researchers question whether this is a direct result of supervision or an indirect result of the maturing of the offenders. Most offenders placed on probation do not become career criminals—their criminal activity is short lived, and they become stable citizens as they obtain jobs and get married. Most of those who are arrested a second time do not repeat their mistake again.

To offer a viable alternative to incarceration, probation services need the resources to supervise and assist their clients appropriately. The new demands on probation have brought calls for increased electronic monitoring and for risk-management systems that provide different levels of supervision for different kinds of offenders.

check point >

1. **What are the four main assumptions underlying community corrections?**
   Many offenders' crimes and records do not warrant incarceration; community supervision is cheaper; recidivism rates for those supervised in the community are no higher than for those who serve prison time; incarceration is more destructive to the offender and society.

2. **What are the main tasks of the probation officer?**
   To assist judges by preparing presentence reports and to provide assistance and supervision to offenders in the community.

3. **What are the grounds for revocation of probation?**
   An arrest for a new offense or a technical violation of the conditions of probation that were set by the judge.

stop& analyze

Why would a probation officer decline to seek revocation for every technical violation? Does the criminal justice system benefit from such decisions? Give two arguments for each side of this question.

Intermediate Sanctions in the Community

Dissatisfaction with the traditional means of probation supervision, coupled with the crowding and high cost of prisons, has resulted in the expansion of intermediate sanctions. These sanctions are more restricting than simple probation and, therefore, constitute a greater degree of actual punishment, especially for those who have committed more-serious offenses.

Many experts support the case for intermediate sanctions. For example, Norval Morris and Michael Tonry say, "Prison is used excessively; probation is used even more excessively; between the two is a near vacuum of purposive and enforced punishments" (1990:3). Sixty-nine percent of convicted felons are incarcerated, the severest sentence, whereas 27 percent receive probation, the least severe. Hence, nearly all convicted felons receive either the severest or the most lenient of possible penalties (Rosenmerkel, Durose, and Farole, 2009). Morris and Tonry have urged that punishments be created that are more restrictive than probation yet match the severity of the offense and the characteristics of the offender, and that can be carried out while still protecting the community. In addition, they emphasize that intermediate punishments must be supported and enforced by mechanisms that take any breach of the conditions of the sentence seriously.

We can view intermediate sanctions as a continuum—a range of punishments that vary in levels of intrusiveness and control, as shown in Figure 12.3. Corrections employs many types of intermediate sanctions. They can be divided into (1) those

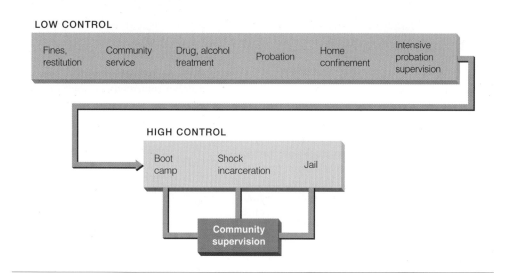

Figure 12.3
Continuum of Intermediate Sanctions Judges may use a range of intermediate sanctions, from those imposing a low level of control to those imposing a high level.

© Cengage Learning

administered primarily by the judiciary (fines, restitution, and forfeiture), (2) those administered primarily in the community with a supervision component (home confinement, community service, day reporting centers, and intensive probation supervision), and (3) those administered inside institutions and followed by community supervision. Furthermore, sanctions may be imposed in combination—for example, a fine and probation, or boot camp with community service and probation.

Intermediate Sanctions Administered Primarily by the Judiciary

The judiciary administers many kinds of intermediate sanctions. Here, we discuss three of them—fines, restitution, and forfeiture. Because all three involve the transfer of money or property from the offender to the government or crime victim, the judiciary is considered the proper body not only to impose the sanction but also to collect what is due.

Fines   **Fines** are routinely imposed for offenses ranging from traffic violations to felonies. Studies have shown that the fine is used widely as a criminal sanction and that nationally well over $1 billion in fines has been collected annually. Yet, judges in the United States make little use of fines as the *sole* punishment for crimes more serious than motor vehicle violations. Instead, they typically use fines in conjunction with other sanctions, such as probation and incarceration, for example, two years of probation and a $500 fine.

  Many judges cite the difficulty of collecting fines as the reason that they do not make greater use of this punishment. They note that offenders tend to be poor, and many judges fear that fines will be paid from the proceeds of additional illegal acts. Other judges are concerned that relying on fines as an alternative to incarceration will let affluent offenders "buy" their way out of jail while forcing the poor to serve time.

  Fines are used extensively in Europe. There, they are enforced and are normally the sole sanction for a wide range of crimes. To deal with the concern that fines exact a heavier toll on the poor than on the wealthy, Finland, Sweden, and Germany have developed the "day fine," which bases the penalty on offenders' daily income and the gravity of the offense. The day fine has been tested in Arizona, Connecticut, Iowa, New York, and Washington (Zedlewski, 2010). As you read the "Comparative Perspective," consider the philosophical and practical difficulties involved in the use of the day fine as a sanction.

Restitution   **Restitution** is repayment by an offender to a victim who has suffered some form of financial loss from the crime. It is *reparative* in that it seeks to repair the harm done. In the Middle Ages, restitution was a common way to settle a criminal case (Karmen, 2001). The offender was ordered to pay the victim or do the victim's

fine A sum of money to be paid to the state by a convicted person as punishment for an offense.

restitution Repayment—in the form of money or service—by an offender to a victim who has suffered some loss from the offense.

The Day Fine: Questions and Challenges from a European Punishment

Northern European countries began to develop the day fine as a criminal punishment in the 1920s. Now it is a primary form of punishment for various offenses in countries such as Sweden, Finland, and Germany. In Germany, 80 percent of criminal sentences are day fines. Such fines are intended to reduce the use of expensive imprisonment and make more-affluent offenders feel the punitive effects of fines to the same degree as those less affluent offenders who would have difficulty paying any fine.

The formulation of the day fine depends on the seriousness of the offense and the income of the offender. The fine is stated as a number of days' worth of income for the particular offender, with allowances for offenders' need to retain money for their families' daily living expenses. As a result, wealthy people can receive eye-popping fines for relatively minor offenses. Periodically, news reports will note, for example, that a multimillionaire in Finland or elsewhere received a fine of $200,000 for driving 25 miles per hour over the speed limit. An individual with a modest income would have received a much lower fine for the same offense.

The unequal results of day fines are intended to advance the goal of equity by making offenders experience comparable severity. Otherwise, wealthy people might just pay fines and continue to break the same laws with impunity because their checkbooks would permit them to pay standardized fines without feeling any "pain." Yet, important philosophical and practical challenges lurk within the day-fine system—challenges that Americans would need to confront before widely adopting this form of punishment that is currently used in relatively few American jurisdictions.

Is it fair to impose a harsher punishment on offenders who are more wealthy? The underlying purpose is to make punishments equitable and impactful, but the effect is to make punishments unequal. Would this form of inequality be less acceptable to Americans than it is to Europeans?

Should the formulation of the day fine take account of an individuals' monthly debts—credit cards, car payments, and student loans? In addition, should the formulation take account of assets? If not, wealthy people with large bank accounts might be able to easily pay substantial fines without noticing any meaningful effect on their incomes.

What should happen to people who cannot or do not pay their mandated day fines? Should people be jailed or should courts use community service or another intermediate sanction as an alternative?

Day fines have been used in many European countries for decades. The United States can consider expanded use of this punishment as a means to reduce the costs of jail and other sanctions. However, as with other punishments, the choice to use this sanction brings with it complications and potential problems.

For Critical Analysis

Would you support the use of day fines in the United States? If not, why not? If so, for which offenses should it apply and how many days' worth of fines should be imposed for each offense?

Sources: Hans-Joerg Albrecht, "Sentencing in Germany—Explaining Long Term Stability in the Structure of Criminal Sanctions and Sentencing," unpublished paper presented at University of Haifa, 2011; Lina Eriksson and Robert E. Goodin, "The Measuring Rod of Time: The Example of the Swedish Day-fines," *Journal of Applied Philosophy* 24 (2007): 125–36; Craig Howie, "The World's Highest Speeding Fines," AOL Autos News, January 7, 2011 (http://autos.aol.com); Justice Policy Institute, "Fact Sheet: Sentencing," *Finding Direction: Expanding Criminal Justice Options by Considering Policies of Other Nations*, April 2011; Edwin Zedlewski, "Alternatives to Custodial Supervision: The Day Fine," National Institute of Justice Discussion Paper, April 2010.

---

work. The growth of the modern state saw the decline of such punishments based on "private" arrangements between offender and victim. Instead, the state prosecuted offenders, and punishments focused on the wrong the offender had done to society.

Though largely unpublicized, victim restitution has remained a part of the U.S. criminal justice system. In many instances, restitution derives from informal agreements between the police and offenders at the station, during plea bargaining, or in the prosecutor's sentence recommendation. Only since the late 1970s has restitution been institutionalized, usually as one of the conditions of probation.

As with fines, convicted offenders differ in their ability to pay restitution, and the conditions inevitably fall more harshly on less affluent offenders. Someone who has the "good fortune" to be victimized by an affluent criminal might receive full compensation, whereas someone victimized by a poor offender might never receive a penny.

In Colorado, a corps of investigators work with probation officers to monitor cases, collecting restitution, and working out payment plans if necessary. As a result, collections in Colorado counties have increased by 25 to 50 percent since the late 1980s. However, even in a well-organized system, it can be difficult to collect from many offenders. In 2009, offenders in Colorado still owed an uncollected $563 million in restitution and $215 million in court fines and costs. Pennsylvania, which was less active and organized in collecting from offenders, was owed $1.5 billion by criminal offenders (Crummy, 2009).

Restitution is more easily imposed when the "damage" inflicted can be easily measured—value of property destroyed or stolen, or medical costs, for instance. Thus restitution is most frequently ordered for property crimes.

Forfeiture   With the passage of two laws in 1970—the Racketeer Influenced and Corrupt Organizations Act (RICO) and the Continuing Criminal Enterprise Act (CCE)—Congress resurrected forfeiture, a criminal sanction that had lain dormant since the American Revolution. Through amendments in 1984 and 1986, Congress improved ways to implement the law. Most states now have similar laws, particularly to deal with organized crime and with trafficking in controlled substances.

A potential buyer examines property seized by federal officials from Congressman Randy "Duke" Cunningham after his conviction for taking bribes. Presumably obtained through illegal funds, the property items were to be sold at auction. Should law enforcement agencies be permitted to keep or sell the property that they seize from criminal offenders?

Forfeiture is government seizure of property and other assets derived from or used in criminal activity. Assets seized by federal and state agencies through forfeiture can be quite considerable, and have increased significantly in the past 30 years. For example, in 1989, U.S. attorneys seized $285 million in assets—by 2010, that amount had increased to $1.8 billion (BJS, 2011b).

Forfeiture is controversial. Critics argue that confiscating property without a court hearing violates citizens' constitutional rights. They have also raised concerns about the excessive use of this sanction, because forfeited assets often go into the budget of the law enforcement agency taking the action (Witt, 2009).

Those in opposition further argue that ownership of the seized property is often unclear. For example, in Hartford, Connecticut, a woman's home was seized because her grandson, unbeknownst to her, was using it as a base for selling drugs. Under a law passed by Congress in 2000, owners' property cannot be seized if they can demonstrate their innocence by a preponderance of evidence.

forfeiture Government seizure of property and other assets derived from or used in criminal activity.

Intermediate Sanctions Administered in the Community

One argument for intermediate sanctions is that probation, as traditionally practiced, cannot accommodate the large numbers of offenders whom probation officers must supervise today. Probation leaders have responded to this criticism by developing new intermediate sanction programs and expanding old ones. Four of these are home confinement, community service, day reporting centers, and intensive supervision probation.

Home Confinement   With technological innovations that provide for electronic monitoring, **home confinement**, in which offenders must remain at home during specific periods, has gained attention. Offenders under home confinement (often called "house arrest") may face other restrictions, such as the usual probation rules against the use of alcohol and drugs, as well as strictly monitored curfews and check-in times.

Some offenders are allowed to go to a place of employment, education, or treatment during the day but must return to their homes by a specified hour. Those supervising home confinement may telephone offenders' homes at various times of the day or night to speak personally with offenders to make sure they are complying.

home confinement A sentence requiring the offender to remain inside his or her home during specified periods.

© Jim West/Alamy

⬆ Probation officers are responsible for offenders who are subject to home confinement and other forms of electronic monitoring, such as GPS (global positioning systems) to keep track of a probationer's movements. Do home confinement and monitoring actually impose punishment on offenders?

Home confinement offers a great deal of flexibility for judges and corrections officials. It can be used as a sole sanction or in combination with other penalties. It can be imposed at almost any point in the criminal justice process: during the pretrial period, after a short term in jail or prison, or as a condition of probation or parole. In addition, home confinement relieves the government of the responsibility of providing the offender with food, clothing, and housing, as it must do in prisons. For these reasons, home confinement programs have grown and proliferated.

The development of electronic monitoring equipment has made home confinement an enforceable sentencing option. The number of offenders currently being monitored is difficult to estimate, because the equipment manufacturers consider this confidential information. However, the best estimates say approximately 17 different companies provide electronic monitoring of nearly 100,000 offenders (Conway, 2001).

Two basic types of electronic monitoring devices exist. Passive monitors respond only to inquiries; most commonly, the offender receives an automated telephone call from the probation office and is told to place the device on a receiver attached to the phone. Active monitors send continuous signals that a receiver picks up; a computer notes any break in the signal.

Despite favorable publicity, home confinement with electronic monitoring poses certain legal, technical, and correctional issues that must be addressed before it can become a standard punishment. First, some criminal justice scholars question its constitutionality. Monitoring may violate the Fourth Amendment's protection against unreasonable searches and seizures. At issue is a clash between the constitutionally protected reasonable expectation of privacy and the invasion of one's home by surveillance devices. Second, the monitoring devices still have extensive technical problems, such as frequently giving erroneous reports that the offender is home. Third, offender failure rates may prove to be high. There is little evidence that electronic monitoring reduces recidivism rates (Renzema and Mayo-Wilson, 2005). Being one's own warden is difficult, and visits by former criminal associates and other negative enticements may become problematic for many offenders. Anecdotal evidence suggests that four months of full-time monitoring is about the limit before a violation will occur. Fourth, an additional issue is that some crimes—such as child abuse, drug sales, and assaults—can be committed while the offender is at home. Finally, observers point out that the only offenders eligible for this type of program are those who own telephones and can afford the weekly rental rates of $35–$120 for the electronic system and components. Clark County, Washington, informs offenders that they must meet three specific conditions in order to be eligible for home confinement: " [1] A stable and approved residence; [2] A dedicated phone line for the EHC equipment (no options like call-waiting or call forwarding); [3] Ability to pay $15.00 per EHC day plus a $40.00 hookup fee" (www.clark.wa.gov, 2010). As indicated by these requirements, home confinement seems best suited to low-risk offenders who have relatively stable residences. As you read the "Close Up," consider whether home confinement is either too soft as a punishment or, alternatively, is too frequently violated to serve as an appropriate intermediate sanction.

community service A sentence requiring the offender to perform a certain amount of unpaid labor in the community.

Community Service   A **community service** sentence requires the offender to perform a certain amount of unpaid labor in the community. As indicated in the chapter opening, singer Chris Brown was required to perform community labor as part of his sentence.

Life under Home Confinement

As government officials struggle to deal with budget cuts, cost-saving measures, such as electronic monitoring and home confinement, become more attractive. In Rock County, Wisconsin, it costs $64 per day to hold an offender in jail. By contrast, it costs only $9 per day for an electronic monitoring device that is used in conjunction with home confinement. The offenders and their families handle their own living expenses during home confinement. Moreover, many counties charge the offenders a fee to cover the costs of electronic monitoring. Sheriffs can save their jail space and resources for offenders with records of violence. Low-risk offenders can be punished in their homes without expending scarce resources.

For many offenders, home confinement is a desirable alternative to jail. They are in familiar surroundings with control over their own indoor activities and meals. They are also removed from the changing array of threatening characters with whom they may end up sharing cells at jail. From the perspective of a sheriff, police chief, or judge, home confinement also can create an incentive for good behavior by those low-risk offenders who wish to avoid jail. Thus society can benefit from using this form of community corrections.

Critics believe that home confinement is not really punishment because offenders enjoy too much freedom. Yet offenders often discover that home confinement actually creates more pressure and control than they anticipated. They are kept on rigid schedules that define when they can go to work, when they can go grocery shopping, and when they must be at home. They may live in fear that if they open the front door to get the newspaper, their device will record a violation. In 2011, when actress Lindsay Lohan served 35 days of electronic monitoring and home confinement after conviction for shoplifting from a jewelry store, her ankle monitor notified police that she had left the house without authorization. Authorities found her at home reading scripts and she claimed that her monitor experienced a mechanical malfunction. Her example illustrates another source of worry for offenders who are concerned about being wrongly blamed for violating the requirements of home confinement.

Another source of pressure is the experience of being so close to people in free society—watching them pass by the window every day—but not being able to enjoy freedom. Johnnie Whichard, a man who served home confinement in Montgomery Country, Maryland, was permitted to leave home at certain times in order to go to his job. He noted, however, that he gave up on using his six allotted hours to leave home each week for other purposes because there was so much planning involved as well as a two-day wait for approval of the detailed itineraries that were required. Kerry Wehrwein, a Wisconsin woman sentenced to home confinement for multiple drunk-driving convictions, was not allowed to have visitors and was tested regularly by a deputy sheriff who arrived to give her breathalyzer tests. Because she also wore an alcohol monitor, she had to avoid cosmetics and cleaning products for fear that exposure to chemicals would make the monitor register a false reading for consumption of alcohol.

There are some offenders who will repeatedly violate home confinement rules when, for example, they know that the jail is full and that the police really cannot take them into custody. Such offenders are obviously not good candidates for electronic monitoring and eventually they will be carted off to jail. For low-risk offenders who are fearful of jail, however, home confinement can be an inexpensive means of control and punishment.

Researching the Internet

Michigan's system of electronically monitoring offenders in the community is described online. To link to the website, visit the Criminal Justice Course-Mate at cengagebrain.com, then access the web links for this chapter.

For Critical Analysis

Electronic monitoring makes the lives of Johnnie Whichard and Kerry Wehrwein different than they would like, yet they are allowed to live at home and move about the community at approved times. Thus their loss of liberty is not nearly as severe as it would have been in prison or jail. In fact, some observers may believe that this isn't much of a punishment. List three crimes for which electronic monitoring would be appropriate. What is the most serious offense for which you would consider a sentence of home confinement? If you believe that electronic monitoring is not appropriate for any offenses, give three reasons for your conclusion.

Sources: Paul Duggan, "Long Arm of the Law Has Man by the Ankle," *Washington Post*, March 28, 2005, p. B1; Lauren Kravets, "Electronic Monitoring Reducing Recidivism in Rock County," WIFR.com, February 17, 2011 (www.wifr.com); Tracy Pepey, "Lindsay Lohan's Electronic Monitoring Device Goes Off," iVillage.com, June 3, 2011 (www.ivillage.com); Ted Sullivan, "Life Under Surveillance," *Janesville Gazette*, January 4, 2009 (http://gazettextra.com).

Community service can take a variety of forms, including assisting in social-service agencies, cleaning parks and roadsides, or helping the poor. The sentence specifies the number of hours to be worked and usually requires supervision by a probation officer. Judges can tailor community service to the skills and abilities of offenders. For example, less educated offenders might pick up litter along the highway, whereas those with schooling might teach reading in evening literacy classes. Many judges order community service when an offender cannot pay a fine. The offender's effort to make reparation to the community harmed by the crime also serves a symbolic function.

Common Belief: Community service does not punish those who receive the sanction.

- There are elements of punishment in the community service sanction.
- Individuals suffer a partial loss of liberty as they must report to specific locations, surrender their time and freedom of movement, and obey authorities' orders to complete tasks that they would otherwise not do.
- They also risk feeling the shame and embarrassment of being seen doing tasks, such as collecting trash along a highway, that indicates to other people that they have gotten into trouble with the law.
- Does this mean that community service is sufficiently severe to serve as a punishment for all kinds of nonviolent offenses? No. Society may legitimately conclude that greater restrictions on liberty and behavior, such as those associated with home confinement, may be appropriate for some offenses and repeat offenders.
- We should recognize, however, that community service carries sanctioning elements while simultaneously avoiding the high costs of more-expensive sanctions and permitting minor offenders to stay connected to their families and communities by retaining their jobs or continuing in school.

Although community service has many supporters, some labor unions and workers criticize it for possibly taking jobs away from law-abiding citizens. In addition, some experts believe that if community service is the only sanction, it may be too mild a punishment, especially for upper-class and white-collar criminals. Examine your own views about community service as a punishment when you read "Criminal Justice: Myth & Reality."

Day Reporting Centers Another intermediate sanction is the **day reporting center**—a community correctional center to which the offender must report each day to carry out elements of the sentence. Designed to ensure that probationers follow the employment and treatment stipulations attached to their sentence, day reporting centers also increase the likelihood that offenders and the general public will consider probation supervision to be credible.

Most day reporting centers incorporate multiple correctional methods. For example, in some centers offenders must remain in the facility for eight hours or report for drug-related urine checks before going to work. Centers with a rehabilitation component carry out drug and alcohol treatment, literacy programs, and job searches. Others provide staff–offender contact levels equal to or greater than those in intensive supervision programs.

day reporting center A community correctional center where an offender reports each day to comply with elements of a sentence.

So far, there are few evaluations of these programs. As with many newly established criminal justice programs, strict eligibility requirements result in small numbers of cases actually entering the program; but even with the limited number of participants under day reporting center supervision, there is evidence that recidivism rates can be reduced (Ostermann, 2009). Evaluations of jail-run day reporting centers find that the participants have lower levels of drug use and absconding. However, because participants were carefully screened for acceptance, applicability may be limited to low-risk cases (Porter, Lee, and Lutz, 2002).

intensive supervision probation (ISP) Probation granted under conditions of strict reporting to a probation officer with a limited caseload.

Intensive Supervision Probation (ISP) Intensive supervision probation (ISP) is a means of dealing with offenders who need greater restrictions than traditional community-based programs can provide. Jurisdictions in every state have programs to intensively supervise such offenders. ISP uses probation as an intermediate form of punishment by imposing conditions of strict reporting to a probation officer who has a limited caseload.

There are two general types of ISP programs. *Probation diversion* puts under intensive surveillance those offenders thought to be too risky for routine supervision. *Institutional diversion* selects low-risk offenders already sentenced to prison and provides supervision for them in the community. Daily contact between the probationer and the probation officer may cut rearrest rates. Such contact also gives the probationer greater access to the resources the officer can provide, such as treatment services in the community. Offenders have incentives to obey rules, knowing that they must meet with their probation officers daily and, in some cases, must speak with them even more frequently. Offenders often face additional restrictions as well, such as electronic monitoring, alcohol and drug testing, community service, and restitution.

ISP programs have been called "old-style" probation because each officer has only 20 clients and requires frequent face-to-face contact. Nonetheless, some people question how much of a difference constant surveillance can make to probationers with numerous problems. Such offenders frequently need help to get a job, counseling to deal with emotional and family situations, and a variety of supports to avoid drug or alcohol problems that may have contributed to their criminality. Yet, ISP may be a way of getting the large number of drug-addicted felons into treatment.

Because it presents a "tough" image of community supervision and addresses the problem of prison crowding, ISP has become popular among probation administrators, judges, and prosecutors. Most ISP programs require a specific number of monthly contacts with officers, performance of community service, curfews, drug and alcohol testing, and referral to appropriate job-training, education, or treatment programs.

Some observers warn that ISP is not a "cure" for the rising costs and other problems facing corrections systems. Ironically, ISP can increase the number of probationers sent to prison. All evaluations of ISP find that, probably because of the closer contact with clients, probation officers uncover more violations of rules than they do in regular probation. Therefore, ISP programs often have higher failure rates than do regular probation, even though their clients produce fewer arrests. Recent analyses of recidivism post-ISP indicate that it can be successful, particularly if combined with rewards for noncriminal behavior (Wodahl et al., 2011).

Brandon Todd/Splash News/Newscom

↑ Singer Chris Brown did physical labor outdoors at a police horse stable and elsewhere along roads in fulfillment of his community service sentence. Such sanctions can provide benefits to the community. There may also be a "shaming" effect if offenders are embarrassed to be seen in public fulfilling a criminal punishment. Can you think of creative and effective ways to expand the use of community services sanctions?

One surprising finding is that, when given the option of serving prison terms or participating in ISP, many offenders choose prison. In New Jersey, 15 percent of offenders withdrew their applications for ISP once they learned the conditions and requirements. Similarly, when offenders in Marion County, Oregon, were asked if they would participate in ISP, one-third chose prison instead (Petersilia, 1990). Apparently, some offenders would rather spend a short time in prison, where tough conditions may differ little from their accustomed life, than a longer period under demanding conditions in the community. To these offenders, ISP does not represent freedom, because it is so intrusive and the risk of revocation seems high.

Despite problems and continuing questions about its effectiveness, ISP has rejuvenated probation. Many of these programs have demonstrated especially effective supervision of offenders. As with regular probation, the size of a probation officer's caseload, within reasonable limits, often matters less in preventing recidivism than does the quality of supervision and assistance provided to probationers. If properly implemented, ISP may improve the quality of supervision and services that foster success for more kinds of offenders.

Intermediate Sanctions Administered in Institutions and the Community

Among the most publicized intermediate sanctions are **boot camps**. Often referred to as "shock incarceration," these programs vary; however, all stem from the belief that young offenders (usually 14- to 21-year-olds) can be "shocked" out of their criminal ways. Boot camps put offenders through a 30- to 90-day physical regimen designed to develop discipline and respect for authority. Like the Marine Corps, most programs emphasize a spit-and-polish environment and restrict the offenders to a disciplined and demanding routine that seeks ultimately to build self-esteem. Most camps also include education, job-training programs, and other rehabilitation services. On successful completion of the program, offenders are released to the community. At this point, probation officers take over, and the conditions of the sentence are imposed.

Boot camps proliferated in the 1980s. By 1995, some states and the Federal Bureau of Prisons operated 93 camps for adults and 30 for juveniles. At their peak, boot

boot camp A short-term institutional sentence, usually followed by probation, that puts the offender through a physical regimen designed to develop discipline and respect for authority. Also referred to as shock incarceration.

13

Reentry into the Community

Learning Objectives

➡ Understand what is meant by the "reentry problem"

➡ Explain the origins of parole and how it operates today

➡ Identify the mechanisms for the release of felons to the community

➡ Describe how ex-offenders are supervised in the community

➡ Understand the problems that parolees face during their reentry

Newspaper headlines regularly remind us about the risks posed by offenders who are released from prison: "Parolee Arrested in Drug Bust" (Handy, 2012); "Parolee Arrested after Attacking Former Girlfriend" (Valenzuela, 2012); "Parolee Arrested in Pimping of 15-Year-Old Girl" (Emery, 2012). With nearly 700,000 people released from state and federal prisons each year, such events can make people understandably fearful about the return of convicted offenders to society. Yet, society must become ready for the return of these offenders and, more importantly, have developed programs to prepare these offenders for successful reentry into the community. Only a small percentage of imprisoned offenders are serving life sentences, as illustrated by a description of the Montana Women's Prison: "Only one inmate . . . is currently serving a life sentence. That means at some point roughly 265 offenders will be released back into society" (Wooley, 2011). Reentry issues are important as an inevitable component of the corrections process, and they have become even more important as budget crises push states to reduce prison populations by moving offenders back into society more quickly.

Offenders who leave prison, either under parole supervision or after the completion of their sentences, face serious difficulties. Many of them were never successful in mainstream society prior to incarceration, so they are in greater need than average Americans for education, job training, and a reorientation to values and proper behavior. Moreover, many offenders will be returning to the community environment in which their problems with drugs and alcohol may be renewed. These newly released individuals will seek jobs in a sluggish economy that makes finding jobs difficult, even for those who do not have criminal records. If a criminal record does not stop an employer from considering a former prisoner as a potential employee, many of those leaving prison are further hindered by their limited education and lack of legitimate employment experience and weak skills that do not match up to those of other job applicants.

Less visible to the public are news accounts that highlight success stories, such as Jarrett McCormick, a convicted armed robber in Michigan who, after serving two prison terms, now builds houses for Habitat for Humanity and takes online college courses to prepare himself to compete in the job market (Dickson, 2011). In recent years, many programs have been introduced to teach prisoners the skills they need to reenter society. Some programs are conducted inside prisons and others involve supervision and instruction in the community. A major challenge facing the criminal justice system is to develop and evaluate effective programs to help parolees and ex-offenders turn out like McCormick rather than appear in jarring news headlines as perpetrators of frightening crimes.

Many offenders stumble when they initially reenter society by failing to obey their conditions of parole, returning to drug use, or quitting education and job-training programs. Some of these offenders will overcome these stumbles, perhaps after a stint in jail awakens them to the looming prospect of a return to prison. Although numerous offenders will fail and be returned to prison for parole violations or the commission of new crimes, American society has a great interest in finding ways to reduce the number returned to prison and to increase the numbers of those who achieve successful reentry.

A newspaper article in 2011 described Danny Bell, a man just released from a Texas prison after serving 21 years for murder. At the bus station a block away from the prison, Bell waited with the other 130 offenders released from the prison that day as they spent their $100 "gate money"—money given to them by the state upon release—on soda pop, snacks, and bus tickets. In the words of the reporter who observed the scene, "Mr. Bell had only a vague notion of how to re-enter the free world. He would stay with his grandmother [and] take any job he could find" (Grissom, 2011). For American society, a question looms about whether he—and each year's other 700,000 releasees—will commit new crimes. For releasees like Bell, who had little preparation for the day he left prison, the risks seem very high.

In this chapter, we examine the mechanisms by which prisoners are released from incarceration; we also look at their supervision in the community. Finally, we discuss the many problems facing parolees as they reenter society.

Prisoner Reentry

Reentry has been described as a "transient state between liberty and recommitment" (A. Blumstein and Beck, 2005:50). It is a limited period of supervision whereby an inmate either moves to full liberty in the community or returns to prison for committing a new crime or for violating the terms of parole. Prisoner reentry has become an important public issue. As indicated in "What Americans Think," many Americans believe there are too many people in prison, yet the sudden flood of offenders leaving prison raises serious questions as to how the criminal justice system deals with the reentry of ex-felons. What is the crux of this problem?

Jeremy Travis and Joan Petersilia (2001) point to several factors contributing to the reentry problem. They argue that, beginning in the 1970s, the power of parole boards to make release decisions was abolished in mandatory release states and severely restricted in discretionary release states. This means that more inmates are automatically leaving prison, ready or not, when they meet the requirements of their sentence. It also means that there has been little or no prerelease planning to ensure that the new parolee has a job, housing, and a supportive family when he or she hits the streets.

A second factor they believe contributes to the reentry problem is the uneven commitment of resources for prison education, job training, and other rehabilitation programs designed to prepare inmates for their return to the community. States developed programs in an effort to reduce expensive prison populations, but across-the-board budget cuts often created pressure to cut funding for all aspects of corrections, including reentry programs (Bousequet, 2012a).

Finally, Travis and Petersilia note that the profile of returning prisoners has changed in ways that pose new challenges to successful reentry. In particular, the conviction offense and time served differ from what they were 20 years ago. Now, more than a third of prisoners released to parole are incarcerated for a drug offense—up from 12 percent in 1985. The average time served has also increased by almost a half year since 1990. Further, some drug and violent offenders are exiting prison after very long terms, perhaps 20 or more years. The longer time in prison means a longer period the prisoner has lived apart from family and friends.

Many have expressed concern regarding how the corrections system prepares prisoners to live as law-abiding citizens. Successful prisoner reentry requires that parole and post-release services focus on linking offenders with community institutions—churches, families, self-help groups, and nonprofit programs.

what americans think

Question: "Do you believe there are too many people in prison in the United States, not enough people in prison, or is the number of people in prison about right?"

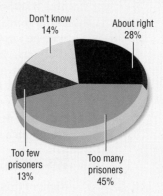

Don't know 14%
About right 28%
Too few prisoners 13%
Too many prisoners 45%

Critical Thinking: Can government officials use these opinions to convince voters to invest more money in reentry programs? What factors might hinder the ability of officials to persuade the public to spend more government funds on reentry?

Source: Pew Center on the States, "Public Opinion on Sentencing and Corrections Policy in America." National poll conducted by Public Opinion Strategies and The Mellman Group, January 2012.

Research indicates that the prisoners most likely to succeed in the job market are those that had work experience prior to prison, connected to employers prior to release, and had conventional family relationships (Visher, Debus-Sherill, and Yahner, 2011). Many prisoners do not have these assets as they exit prison. Thus efforts must be made to improve their chances for success in free society. According to Joan Petersilia (2003), because public safety and neighborhood stability depend on successful reentry, communities must share with corrections officials the responsibility for transitioning offenders to the community.

Contemporary Budget Cuts and Prisoner Release

The economic recession of 2008 and its lingering aftermath produced a drop in employment rates and created difficulties for many American businesses and families. When the incomes of families fall and businesses are less profitable, the government receives less tax revenue to fund needed programs, including corrections. Because incarceration is such an expensive form of punishment, with states and counties paying $25,000 or more annually to cover the costs of holding each prisoner in a secure facility, government officials began to rethink sentencing policies that caused prison populations to skyrocket since the 1980s. In particular, they gave consideration to greater utilization of probation and community corrections for nonviolent and drug offenders. In addition, many states sought ways to reduce their prison populations by accelerating the release into the community of nondangerous offenders and those nearing the completion of their sentences. For example, Michigan, a state with budget problems stemming from one of the nation's highest unemployment rates, reduced its prison population from a peak of 51,554 in March 2007 to 42,940 in December 2011 (Deng, 2012). The reductions enabled the state to save money by closing several prisons. These developments were facilitated, in part, by Michigan's effort to develop reentry programs that would help prisoners become prepared to move back into the community (Pew Center, 2011).

Such efforts to reduce prison populations can be affected by continuing budget difficulties that lead to cuts in reentry programs, thereby diminishing the state's ability to prepare offenders for effective reentry. The state of California, for example, cut $250 million from educational, training, and substance-abuse programs in 2009 and 2010, with additional significant cuts in 2011 (*Corrections Reporter,* 2011). In Ohio, funding was cut for a community rehabilitation center, meaning more inmates will be kept in prison because there are fewer community-based placement options (Balmert, 2011). The Oklahoma Department of Corrections recently eliminated treatment programs for sex offenders, which experts regard as essential to keeping them from re-offending in the future (Doney, 2011). Thus, in the second decade of the twenty-first century, states face problems from cutting corrections budgets by reducing prison populations. Those state budget cuts also often terminate programs and reduce services that help to prepare early release prisoners for reentry into society.

Institutional Reentry Preparation Programs

Most of this chapter discusses post-release community corrections, especially issues involving parole. As you read "Careers in Criminal Justice," about the job of a reentry specialist in the Indiana corrections system, you will see that states are increasingly developing programs within prisons as the first step to begin offenders' preparation for reentry. The career description illustrates the effort to create an institution dedicated to preparing offenders for reentering society, so that they can spend the last portion of their sentences in a special prison among other prisoners who are also focused on taking classes to prepare for release. Some correctional officials argue that preparation for reentry should begin at an even earlier point in the prison sentence. As one prison warden said,

> Instead of waiting until the last few months, or when we know they had parole, to start this re-entry, we're trying to start the day they come in [to the prison]. I want you to start looking at what do you need to do here to prepare yourself when you go. We try to get that into their minds immediately. (Wooley, 2011).

In 2011, the Pew Center on the States issued a report, entitled *State of Recidivism: The Revolving Door of America's Prisons*, which noted that nationwide a consistent percentage of offenders—40 percent—was reimprisoned within three years of release. This percentage remained steady throughout the study period of 1999–2007 (Pew Center, 2011). The Pew Center report pointed out that the recidivism rate actually varied by state and that some individual states had seen declines in recidivism even as the national rate hovered at the same level. After examining approaches taken by different states, one of the Pew Center report's recommendations was "begin preparation for release at time of prison admission" (Pew Center, 2011). The report highlighted the need to see the period of imprisonment as a time in which efforts can be made to address offenders' problems and needs. This is contrary to the traditional practice of using prisons for custody, a practice that typically gives little attention to preparing inmates for reentry into the community at the time of release. The perspective presented in the report is not advocating treating offenders as "victims of society" who deserve attention and care. Instead, it reflects merely the practical recognition that society benefits from thinking in advance about the reality that most offenders will eventually be released back into the community. Critics of the prison system have raised this question: If we treat offenders as "monsters" while they are in prison, shouldn't we expect that they will inevitably affect society by acting as "monsters" when they again live among us?

South Carolina, Florida, Indiana, and other states developed reentry preparation programs within prisons to assist offenders with the transition back to society. These programs are often in special facilities and involve spending a specific period of months in the programs just prior to release. Indiana developed an innovation by creating the nation's first prison dedicated to preparation for reentry. The Indianapolis Re-entry

Reentry Specialist

Richard Rosales, Reentry Specialist,
Indiana Department of Correction, Indianapolis Re-Entry Educational Facility

Photo provided by Lindsey Murray. © Cengage Learning

The position of reentry specialist is unique in the field of corrections because it exists only at the Indianapolis Re-Entry Educational Facility (IREF), which is, in turn, the only "application facility" in the United States. Offenders must apply from another facility in Indiana; if they meet the criteria for admittance, they are then transferred to IREF. At IREF, offenders are called "residents" to facilitate a different atmosphere. Residents dress in civilian clothes, live in dormitory-style housing, and manage their own daily schedule. IREF has numerous programs designed to assist successful reentry; these include educational, vocational, substance-abuse, and spiritual programs.

A reentry specialist is responsible for fulfilling three different roles: case manager, counselor, and custody officer. Specialists manage a caseload of residents, including every aspect of their reentry preparation. Their reentry accountability plan, for instance, details everything—the programs and plans for self-improvement and preparation—that will facilitate a successful reentry into society. Residents who need counseling for personal problems and other matters rely on their specialist for assistance. Specialists also handle the custody functions that are necessary for safety and security in any correctional institution. Among other duties, they conduct counts and shakedowns and monitor residents' compliance with rules.

A reentry specialist must have thorough knowledge of the criminal justice system in order to understand the documents and procedures. They must have thorough knowledge of the processes that lead an offender to incarceration and also of the challenges that confront parolees on their return to the community. Superior communication skills are essential to working with both offenders and staff. Anyone in corrections can expect to be manipulated and tested and therefore must maintain constant vigilance regarding their surroundings and interactions. A reentry specialist is also expected to prepare numerous reports, both in-house and for outside criminal justice agencies such as the courts and those dealing with probation and parole.

Richard Rosales prepared for this position by obtaining undergraduate and graduate degrees in criminal justice. During college and graduate school, he completed internships with a state police agency. He first worked with the Indiana Department of Correction through the AmeriCorps*VISTA program, a public-service program funded by the federal government. At the conclusion of his year of service, he applied and was accepted for his current position.

The best part of my position in the field of corrections is that every day I have the chance to make a difference in the lives of my residents. The work I do today can prevent someone from returning to prison tomorrow and, in turn, make the community safer for the citizens of Indiana. We are seeing the direction of corrections shift to reentry, and IREF is at the forefront of this exciting movement.

Education Facility, previously located at the Plainfield, Indiana, corrections facility, is small—it houses only 350 prisoners who are nearing their release date—and focuses on providing a range of programs that cover job readiness, business ownership, fatherhood, conflict resolution, financial knowledge, and other concrete subjects (Indiana Department of Corrections, 2009). By establishing these programs, criminal justice officials are acknowledging that successful reentry does not depend merely on gaining employment, but also on having sufficient knowledge about finances and asset management to use money wisely for expenses and family responsibilities (Martin, 2011).

The concept of prerelease facilities and programs has gained the support of those people, including legislators, who recognize that society benefits in many ways, including cost savings, by helping offenders avoid a return to the expensive environment of prison. In 2012, the Florida Department of Corrections announced that it would close two reentry facilities as part of an effort to solve a $79 million budget deficit. Closing the centers would result in cutting 300 prisoners from job-training and life-skills courses and returning them to the general inmate population at other prisons. State legislators and newspaper editorial writers complained that it was shortsighted to target reentry programs for cuts. They argued that in closing the two centers, the short-term budget savings would only amount to $1 million, which would barely affect the overall corrections budget deficit. Ultimately, the political pressure and public outcry led Florida's corrections officials to decide keep the reentry facilities in operation (Bousquet, 2012a, 2012b). In other states, however, budget pressures have led to a reduction in reentry programs.

check point ⟩ 1. **How have government budget problems contributed to challenges in prisoner reentry?** States seek to reduce expensive prison populations, yet continuing budget difficulties can hamper efforts to develop and sustain programs to facilitate offenders' successful return to society.

stop& analyze Take note of Professor Petersilia's argument that communities must share with corrections officials the responsibility for transitioning offenders into society. What are two things that community members can do to help parolees stay away from criminal activities and succeed in reentry?

Release and Supervision

Except for the less than 7 percent of inmates who die in prison, all will eventually be released to live in the community. Currently about 77 percent of felons will be released on parole and will remain under correctional supervision for a specific period. About 19 percent will be released at the expiration of their sentence, having "maxed out" and earned the freedom to live in the community without supervision.

parole The conditional release of an inmate from incarceration, under supervision, after part of the prison sentence has been served.

Parole is the *conditional* release of an offender from incarceration but not from the legal custody of the state. Thus, offenders who comply with parole conditions and do not have further conflict with the law receive an absolute discharge from supervision at the end of their sentences. If a parolee breaks a rule, parole can be revoked and the person can be returned to a correctional facility. Parole rests on three concepts:

1. *Grace.* The prisoner could be kept incarcerated, but the government extends the privilege of release.
2. *Contract.* The government enters into an agreement with the prisoner whereby the prisoner promises to abide by certain conditions in exchange for being released.
3. *Custody.* Even though the offender is released from prison, he or she remains a responsibility of the government. Parole is an extension of correctional programs into the community.

Only felons are released on parole; adult misdemeanants are usually released immediately after they have finished serving their sentences. Today, about 850,000 people are under parole supervision, a fourfold increase since 1980 (Glaze and Bonczar, 2011).

The Origins of Parole

Parole in the United States evolved during the nineteenth century from the English, Australian, and Irish practices of conditional pardon, apprenticeship by indenture, transportation of criminals from one country to another, and issuance of "tickets of leave." These were all methods of moving criminals out of prison as a response to overcrowding, unemployment, and the cost of incarceration.

A key figure in developing the concept of parole in the nineteenth century was Captain Alexander Maconochie, an administrator of British penal colonies in Tasmania and elsewhere in the South Pacific. A critic of definite prison terms, Maconochie devised a system of rewards for good conduct, labor, and study. Under his classification procedure, prisoners could pass through stages of increasing responsibility and freedom: (1) strict imprisonment, (2) labor on government chain gangs, (3) freedom within a limited area, (4) a ticket of leave or parole resulting in a conditional pardon, and (5) full restoration of liberty. Like modern correctional practices, this procedure assumed that prisoners should be prepared gradually for release. The roots of the American system of parole lie in the transition from imprisonment to conditional release to full freedom.

Maconochie's idea of requiring prisoners to earn their early release caught on first in Ireland. There, Sir Walter Crofton built on Maconochie's idea to link an offender's progress in prison to a ticket of leave. Prisoners who graduated through Crofton's three successive levels of treatment were released on parole under a series of conditions. Most significant was the requirement that parolees submit monthly reports to the police. In Dublin, a special civilian inspector helped releasees find jobs, visited them periodically, and supervised their activities.

The Development of Parole in the United States

In the United States, parole developed during the prison reform movement of the latter half of the nineteenth century. Relying on the ideas of Maconochie and Crofton, American reformers such as Zebulon Brockway of the Elmira State Reformatory in New York began to experiment with the concept of parole. After New York adopted indeterminate sentences in 1876, Brockway started to release prisoners on parole. Under the new sentencing law, prisoners could be released when their conduct showed they were ready to return to society. This idea spread, so that 20 states had parole systems by 1900, and 44 states and the federal government had them by 1932 (Friedman, 1993). Today, every state has some procedure for the release of offenders before the end of their sentences.

Although it has been used in the United States for more than a century, parole remains controversial. To many people, parole allows convicted offenders to avoid serving the full sentence they deserve. The public hue and cry following commission of a particularly heinous act by a parolee creates pressure for authorities to limit release. For example, when two parolees in Michigan were accused of committing home invasions and murdering a senior citizen, media attention and public outcry contributed to an audit of prisoner release programs, a report criticizing aspects of parole supervision, and the suspensions of two parole officials (Martindale, 2012). On the other hand, public officials are obligated to balance shrinking corrections budgets, so they feel countervailing pressures to find ways to reduce the number of offenders in prison through increased parole releases.

 2. In what countries did the concept of parole first develop?
England, Australia, Ireland.

 If you were placed in charge of a state's parole system, what are three steps that you would take to diminish the likelihood that parolees would commit crimes?

Release Mechanisms

From 1920 to 1973, there was a nationwide sentencing and release policy. During this period, all states and the federal government used indeterminate sentencing, authorized discretionary release by parole boards, and supervised prisoners after release—and they did this all in the interest of the rehabilitation of offenders.

With the 1970s came critiques of rehabilitation, the move to determinate sentencing, and the public's view that the system was "soft" on criminals. By 2002, 16 states and the federal government had abolished discretionary release by parole boards. Another 5 states had abolished discretionary parole for certain offenses (Petersilia, 2003:65). Further, in some of the states that kept discretionary release, parole boards have been reluctant to grant it.

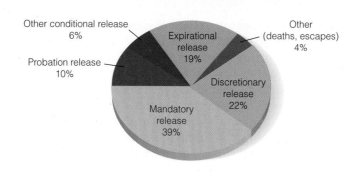

Figure 13.1

Methods of Release from State Prison Felons are released from prison to the community, usually under parole supervision, through various means depending on the law.

Source: Bureau of Justice Statistics *Bulletin*, November 2006, p. 8.

There are now four basic mechanisms for people to be released from prison: (1) expiration release, (2) mandatory release, (3) other conditional release, and (4) discretionary release. Figure 13.1 shows the percentage of felons released by the various mechanisms.

Expiration Release

expiration release The release of an inmate from incarceration, without further correctional supervision; the inmate cannot be returned to prison for any remaining portion of the sentence for the current offense.

An increasing percentage of prisoners receive an **expiration release**. As noted earlier, such offenders have served the maximum court sentence, minus good time—they have "maxed out." These inmates are released from any further correctional supervision and cannot be returned to prison for their current offense because they are not on parole and thereby not subject to parole restrictions.

Mandatory Release

mandatory release The required release of an inmate from incarceration to community supervision upon the expiration of a certain period, as specified by a determinate-sentencing law or parole guidelines.

Mandatory release occurs after an inmate has served time equal to the total sentence minus good time, if any, or to a certain percentage of the total sentence as specified by law. Mandatory release is found in federal jurisdictions and states with determinate sentences and good-time provisions (see Chapter 9). Without a parole board to make discretionary decisions, mandatory release is a matter of bookkeeping to check the correct amount of good time and other credits and make sure the sentence has been accurately interpreted. The prisoner is conditionally released to parole supervision for the rest of the sentence.

Other Conditional Release

other conditional release A term used in some states to avoid the rigidity of mandatory release, by placing convicts in various community settings, under supervision.

Because of the growth of prison populations, many states have devised ways to get around the rigidity of mandatory release, by placing inmates in the community through furloughs, home supervision, halfway houses, emergency release, and other programs (BJS, 2000b; Griset, 1995). These types of **other conditional release** also avoid the appearance of the politically sensitive label "discretionary parole."

Circumstances may also arise in which prison officials use their discretion to release offenders early instead of going through the usual parole process. In order to close a budget deficit in 2002, Montana corrections officials released nonviolent offenders early from prison and placed them under the supervision of community corrections authorities. An important study of the results of that release showed that those offenders who received this conditional release from prison, instead of going through the usual parole decision process, had higher levels of recidivism (Wright and Rosky, 2011). As in other states, a significant portion of admissions to prison are composed of offenders returning to prison for violating conditions of release or for committing new crimes while under the supervision of community corrections. According to Wright and Rosky (2011:901), "Montana, in particular, experienced a significant increase in the annual 3-year recidivism rate as a result of the early release program." Thus, when undertaking conditional releases, states need to be aware of preparing prisoners for release and of the supervision capabilities of community corrections officials. Inadequate preparation and oversight may result in returning many offenders to the expensive environment of imprisonment, thereby undercutting the intended financial benefits of reducing prison populations through this mechanism.

The situation faced by Montana is reflected in larger debates about the proper course of action, just as it reflected specific debates within Montana itself. As the authors of the study observed, "Not surprisingly, a public battle among the [Montana Department of Corrections] and legislators, judges, and prosecutors ensued over the appropriateness of the early release program in Montana" (Wright and Rosky, 2011:887). Although there has been a growing consensus among liberal and conservative politicians about rethinking the costs of using incarceration to punish nonviolent offenders (Savage, 2011b), there are debates about the wisdom of releasing prisoners as opposed to a more gradual approach of simply changing sentencing policies as they affect certain offenders ("Our View," 2011; Mauer, 2011). As you read "The Policy Debate" on this issue, consider which side has the more compelling argument.

Litigation can also create pressure to reduce prison populations through releases outside the usual parole process if overcrowding causes constitutional violations. In the provisions of the Prison Litigation Reform Act of 1996, Congress had attempted to limit the ability of judges to order the release of prisoners by mandating that any such decisions be made by three-judge panels rather than by a single judge. However, as the Supreme Court decided with respect to overcrowding and the lack of medical services in California's prisons in *Brown v. Plata* (2011), circumstances can arise in which states may be forced to quickly and creatively find ways reduce prison populations. Because most states are currently seeking ways to save money by reducing prison populations, the prospect for more litigation affecting releases seems unlikely during the current era.

Discretionary Release

States retaining indeterminate sentences allow **discretionary release** by the parole board within the boundaries set by the sentence and the penal law. This is a conditional release to parole supervision. This approach, as discussed in the next section, lets the board members assess the prisoner's readiness for release within the minimum and maximum terms of the sentence. In reviewing the prisoner's file and asking questions, the parole board focuses on the nature of the offense, the inmate's behavior, and his or her participation in rehabilitative programs. This process places great faith in the ability of parole board members to predict the future behavior of offenders.

discretionary release The release of an inmate from prison to conditional supervision at the discretion of the parole board within the boundaries set by the sentence and the penal law.

The Parole Board Process

State parole boards are typically composed of citizens who are appointed for fixed terms in office by the governor. For example, the Vermont Parole Board consists of five regular members and two alternates who are appointed for three-year terms by the governor. The Texas Board of Pardons and Paroles consists of seven members who receive appointments by the governor for renewable six-year terms. The people on the current Texas board include: a former city attorney; a former county attorney; a former juvenile probation officer; a former county sheriff; an individual with experience in business and government; a former military officer; and an individual with experience in education and criminal justice—who is also the spouse of a former top official in the Texas corrections system (Texas Board of Pardons and Parole website, 2011). Obviously, the members bring with them values, perspectives, and experiences that inform their judgments about whether offenders should be released on parole. It is possible that the governor's decision to appoint board members with prior connections to the criminal justice system may be an effort to ensure there is caution and skepticism about prisoners' claims of self-improvement during incarceration. The Texas structure also includes 11 commissioners, all of whom are experienced criminal justice professionals, who join with the parole board members in making decisions about parole.

Should Prison Populations Be Reduced through the Accelerated Release of Offenders?

States throughout the country currently face budget pressures as their tax revenues remain uncertain during a period when the national economy is slowly recovering from the recession of 2008. Because incarceration is an especially expensive form of punishment, with each imprisoned offender costing the state tens of thousands of dollars each year, many state governments have sought to reduce their prison populations through accelerated releases.

For Accelerated Release of Offenders

Those who support the accelerated release of offenders find fault in the overuse of expensive incarceration during the past three decades. They point to the many nonviolent and drug offenders who, through needlessly long prison sentences, had no hope of being rehabilitated or of regaining a productive place in the community. As a result of these long incarcerations, families and specific neighborhoods suffered financial declines and devastation that affected children, as well as the quality of life in those communities. Moreover, taxpayers needlessly paid high bills for expensive punishments when cheaper approaches within the community would have been a more effective mechanism to simultaneously punish offenders as well as to support and guide their reentry into the community.

The arguments for accelerating the release of offenders from prison include these:

- Imprisonment has been overused through application to thousands of nonviolent offenders.
- State budget difficulties require the immediate reduction of prison populations in favor of less expensive approaches to punishment within the community.

- Moving offenders from prison to community settings or early release will assist in their successful reentry into the community and permit them to reestablish relationships with family members, thereby providing support to children and needed contributions to families' financial support.
- Community-based programs are more effective in rehabilitating offenders.

Against Accelerated Release of Offenders

Opponents of accelerated release worry that offenders released early from prison are likely to commit new crimes or otherwise violate the conditions of their release. They also worry that the focus on saving money through releases often outweighs careful examination of which offenders should be released. This focus also ignores the inadequate resources and unproven effectiveness of many community-based programs, thus leading to troubling recidivism rates in many states. They also worry that shortened prison sentences will mean that some offenders do not receive appropriately severe punishment.

The arguments against accelerated release of offenders include these:

- Excessive focus on saving money through accelerated prison releases can lead to inadequate evaluation of early release candidates and insufficient supervision of these offenders once they are in the community.
- Because studies present evidence of troubling recidivism rates in many states, the release of offenders places citizens under unnecessary risk of crime victimization from these offenders who would otherwise be behind bars.

- Early releases mean that some offenders do not receive appropriately severe punishments for their crimes.
- Community-based programs have not proven their effectiveness in lowering the recidivism rates of those offenders released early from prison.

What Should U.S. Policy Be?

The massive increase in incarceration since the 1980s has been very costly in both financial and human terms. Because of budget pressures, states have accelerated efforts to reduce their prison populations, including the use of early release for many offenders. Have enough resources been devoted to community programs to feel confident that society is prepared to assist in the reentry of increasing numbers of released offenders? Do persistent recidivism rates in many states indicate that the releases pose risks to society? Alternatively, do recidivism rates merely show that some states have not prepared adequate programs for education and supervision of offenders released from prison? Does the weight of budget pressures lead policy makers to engage in wishful thinking about the effectiveness of less expensive community corrections?

Researching the Internet

To see the 2011 report, *State of Recidivism: The Revolving Door of America's Prisons* issued by the Pew Center on the States, visit the Criminal Justice CourseMate at cengagebrain.com, then access the web links for this chapter.

For Critical Analysis

What are the consequences of choosing not to accelerate the release of offenders? What steps could be taken to reduce the concerns expressed by the opponents of accelerated release?

Parole boards are often described as if the governors' appointees sit together as they question and listen to the parole-eligible prisoner and also hear arguments from the prisoner's attorney. In fact, there are differences in the parole processes in various states. For example, parole-eligible prisoners in California, all of whom are serving life sentences, have attorneys at parole hearings, either one that they hire or one that is appointed for them. In other states, parole board members simply interview the prisoner. Elsewhere, the parole board may simply review the written file on the prisoner's progress in prison. There is no single model for what "the parole board process" looks like.

As indicated by the great increase in prison populations in the last few decades, large numbers of prisoners become parole eligible each year—too many to have hearings in front of a state's full parole board. Thus parole processes involve hearings or interviews conducted by only a portion of a parole board,

⬆ Parole hearings are often brief proceedings in which board members ask questions of the prisoner who is eligible for parole. In many places, the crime victim or the victim's family are permitted to communicate with the board, in writing or in person, to express their views about the prospect of the offender's early release from prison. How much influence should crime victims have over parole decisions?

often with other members of the board making decisions based on the report written by their colleague. In some circumstances, if a panel of a board is divided on a decision, the full board may examine the records in the case and make a decision.

In California, for example, each parole hearing is conducted by a 2-member panel. At least 1 of the 2 members is a "commissioner," the title used in that state for the 12 parole board members appointed by the governor. The other member is either a second commissioner or a "deputy commissioner," which is a state employee who works in the parole process. Immediately after the hearing, the two decision makers leave the hearing room and finalize their decision. If they disagree about whether to recommend parole, then there will be a second hearing in front of the full 12-member California Board of Parole Hearings. After a unanimous decision by the 2-member panel or a vote by the full board, the decision goes to the staff of the board to make sure that there were no errors of law or fact in the process. The decision is then submitted to the governor who can approve the parole, add a condition to the parole release, refer a panel decision to the full board, or reverse the decision to grant parole in cases of convicted murderers (California Department of Corrections and Rehabilitation, 2010).

By using only a portion of the parole board for interviews and hearings, states can conduct many interviews and hearings simultaneously. This is the only way that they can handle the large volume of cases. Texas uses a different procedure to process the 77,540 prisoners who were considered for parole in 2010. The Texas Board of Pardons and Paroles operates out of six different offices around the state, each with three-member panels composed of one board member and two "commissioners." For each parole-eligible prisoner, one member of the panel interviews the prisoner and writes a report while the other two members review that report and the written file. If two of the three members approve, then the prisoner gains release under parole supervision (Texas Board of Pardons and Paroles, 2012).

Even small states divide their parole boards for hearings. In Wyoming, the least populous state in the country, a seven-member board sits in three-member hearing panels and conducts some hearings by telephone and video conference (Wyoming Board of Parole website, 2011). In Vermont, another of the least-populous states, hearings and interviews are conducted by a minimum of three of the parole board's five members and two alternates (Vermont Parole Board, 2010).

Parole board hearings and interviews are much less formal than court proceedings. Board members want the opportunity to ask prisoners about their crimes,

A Personal Encounter with the Parole Process in Michigan

Note: *Dr. Christopher Smith, one of the coauthors of this textbook, served as the "representative" for Christopher Jones (whose story of arrest and imprisonment appears in Chapter 1) at the parole board interview that ultimately led to Jones's release on parole. This is a first-person account of that process.*

I agreed to serve as the "representative" for Christopher Jones at the parole interview because I had known him and his family since he was a teenager. As an outside observer, I had seen his self-destruction through drugs and theft crimes as well as his gradual self-rehabilitation, as I corresponded with him and occasionally visited him during his ten years behind bars. Moreover, I was grateful for his eagerness to present his story in this book so that college students could learn about the justice process through his mistakes and experiences. In Michigan, a parole interview representative is typically a family member or someone else who can vouch for the prisoner's progress and good qualities. In speaking with a former parole board member

prior to the interview, I knew that prisoners often had their mothers appear as their representatives. However, this was often counterproductive because mothers too often made excuses for their children or displayed emotion rather than providing information that would be useful in the parole decision. Although I am trained as a lawyer, prisoners are not represented by lawyers to make arguments on their behalf (unlike in California parole hearings). In Michigan, they each have only one representative present to provide personal endorsement and information.

After spending nearly an hour in the prison's visitor waiting room, I was searched and led through several sets of locked doors to a small office. Outside of the office, I came upon a dozen or more prisoners fidgeting nervously in a long line of chairs as they waited to be called one-by-one into the interview room. Mr. Jones was in the first chair. He rose to greet me and we were immediately ushered into the office together.

I had driven nearly 250 miles from Lansing in the middle of Michigan's Lower Peninsula to a low-security prison

in the Upper Peninsula to be present for the interview. Ironically, the interview was conducted via video conference by one of the ten members of the Michigan parole board who was physically back in Lansing—the very place I had left the day before and to which I would return later that day. We saw him live on a television screen in the prison up north while he saw us on a screen in his office in Lansing. Video technology permits Michigan to save a substantial amount of money that previously would have been spent for the parole board members to travel to prisons throughout the state to conduct interviews.

After Mr. Jones introduced me as his representative, the parole board member introduced himself and informed me that he had many questions for Mr. Jones and that I should refrain from speaking until questions were directed to me. The parole board member noted that Mr. Jones had participated in many prison programs and that the file contained an impressive number of letters of support from family members and a minister. The board member asked Mr. Jones about his plan to live with his parents and work for his father's home inspection business. Mr. Jones was asked about how he had changed from when

their remorse, their attitudes, their disciplinary records and their participation in programs in prison, and their concrete plans for where they will live and work if they are granted parole. Prisoners are typically nervous because they do not know exactly what will be asked. They may quickly discover that the board members seem very skeptical about what they say. They may also find that board members lecture them about what they have done wrong in life and issue stern warnings to them about what will happen if they are released and then violate conditions of parole. Because board panels must necessarily schedule back-to-back-to-back interviews or hearings with numerous parole-eligible prisoners on any given day, each individual prisoner may leave the brief encounter feeling very dissatisfied and disappointed; as if he or she did not have a full opportunity to explain how much change has occurred in attitude and behavior since entering prison. When a prisoner feels as if there was no complete opportunity to make a good, persuasive presentation about being reformed, there is likely to be great anxiety about whether the long-awaited opportunity to speak to a parole board member or panel will actually lead to release.

Crime victims have become much more important participants in the parole decision process in recent decades. Many states have victims' rights laws that require officials to keep victims informed of offenders' upcoming parole consideration and to invite victims to provide input in the process. In California, crime victims and their families are invited to parole hearings where they are permitted to speak or they he committed his crimes. The board member pressed Mr. Jones about how he would respond to the availability of drugs and alcohol if he was on parole back in his hometown. Predictably, Mr. Jones, who had spent years looking forward to the chance to have a parole interview, provided reassuring responses and pledged to stay away from the people, places, and substances that had been his downfall in the past. The board member spoke sternly to him about the consequences of violating the conditions of parole or committing new crimes. During this lecture, Mr. Jones nodded his head and repeatedly said, "yes, sir, yes, sir."

Throughout the interview with Mr. Jones, I restrained myself from speaking as I thought of many helpful things to say. I kept quiet, however, and then the board member turned to me to ask what I had to add as information for the board's consideration. I gave a brief endorsement of the changes that I had observed over the years Mr. Jones had been in prison and described his participation in education and substance-abuse recovery programs. And then the interview was over. It was obvious that the board member

had many other interviews that he needed to do, so he could not spend more than 15 minutes or so on any individual interview.

I came away from the brief experience without any strong sense about what the decision would be. The interview seemed to go as well as it could have gone, but it was so short that there was not much information exchanged. Moreover, I wondered whether a parole board member could really trust reassurances from a parole-eligible prisoner, especially a former drug user, when the board member obviously knew that a notable percentage of such offenders return to drugs, violate parole conditions, or commit new crimes once back in the community. Obviously, the most significant information for the decision came from the reports and prison disciplinary records in the file. The quick interview gave the board member an opportunity to gain a brief impression of the prisoner's attitude and demeanor. Moreover, it was an opportunity to issue stern warnings to the prisoner about returning to prison for any failure to behave properly on parole. The release decision hinged on this board member's recommendation and report that would be significant

factors in determining whether at least two of the three board members (including himself) assigned to the case would vote to grant parole.

Ultimately, the parole decision is shaped by impressions and judgments, not just those of the board members, but also those of the prison counselors who wrote evaluative reports for the file and thereby shaped the impressions of the board members. No one can make an absolutely certain prediction about whether a specific prisoner will commit future violations or crimes on parole—not even the prisoner himself. The prisoner may feel determined to succeed, but he does not yet know the practical challenges of parole that await in being offered drugs, feeling frustrated by unemployment, or having conflicts with friends and family who have become, in some sense, strangers after years of separation.

For Critical Analysis
Does this parole interview process, as described, provide enough information to make a decision about whether or not to grant parole? Should the process be changed in any way? Provide three arguments either supporting the interview process as adequate or supporting specific changes in the process.

can bring a representative to speak for them about the impact of the crime and their concerns about the offender being granted parole. Alternatively, they can submit written statements or audio or video statements for consideration by the board members. At the hearing, the victim is accompanied by a victim services representative from the state's Office of Victim and Survivor Rights and Services. A prosecutor also attends the hearing and may speak about the offender who is being considered for parole. In addition, news reporters may be permitted to attend California parole hearings (California Department of Corrections and Rehabilitation, 2010).

In Wyoming, crime victims are invited to meet with the board separately from the prisoner's hearing. Similarly, in Vermont the victim can testify prior to the scheduled appearance of the prisoner before the board. In both of these states, the interviews or hearings are held in private and the policies about victims' participation are designed to prevent the victim from having a face-to-face encounter with the offender. By contrast, Connecticut is more like California in that the victim is invited to speak at hearings that, while not open to the public, are more available to the public in the sense that they can be recorded and broadcast on public television, just as California's hearings may be covered by the news media in some cases. In all of these states, victims have the option of submitting written statements to be added to the file that is reviewed by the board members. Read the "Close Up" for a personal account of the parole process in Michigan.

Figure 13.2

Estimated Time to be Served by Adults Convicted of Selected Crimes The data indicate that the average felony offender going to prison for the first time spends about two years in prison. How would you expect the public to react to that fact?

Source: Thomas P. Bonczar, *National Corrections Reporting Program— Statistical Tables*, May 5, 2011, Table 9 (http://bjs.ojp.usdoj.gov /index.cfm?ty=pbdetail&iid=2174).

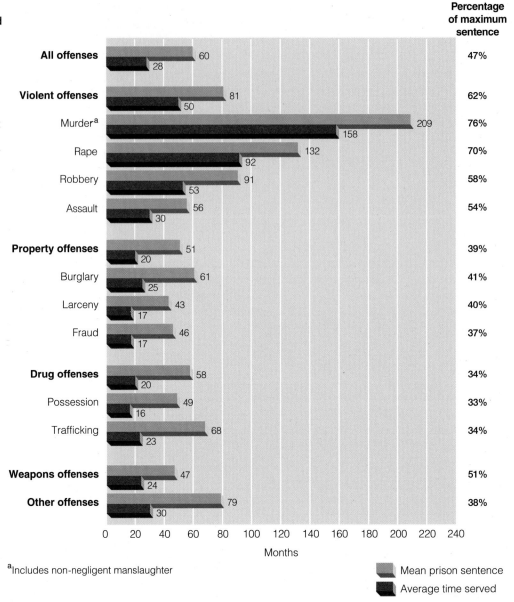

	Percentage of maximum sentence
All offenses 60 / 28	47%
Violent offenses 81 / 50	62%
Murder[a] 209 / 158	76%
Rape 132 / 92	70%
Robbery 91 / 53	58%
Assault 56 / 30	54%
Property offenses 51 / 20	39%
Burglary 61 / 25	41%
Larceny 43 / 17	40%
Fraud 46 / 17	37%
Drug offenses 58 / 20	34%
Possession 49 / 16	33%
Trafficking 68 / 23	34%
Weapons offenses 47 / 24	51%
Other offenses 79 / 30	38%

Months

[a]Includes non-negligent manslaughter

■ Mean prison sentence
■ Average time served

Impact of Release Mechanisms

Parole release mechanisms do more than simply determine the date at which a particular prisoner will be sent back into the community. Parole release also greatly affects other parts of the system, including sentencing, plea bargaining, and the size of prison populations.

One important effect of discretionary release is that an administrative body—the parole board—can shorten a sentence imposed by a judge. Even in states that have mandatory release, various potential reductions built into the sentence mean that the full sentence is rarely served. Good time, for example, can reduce punishment even if there is no eligibility for parole.

To understand the impact of release mechanisms on criminal punishment, we must compare the amount of time actually served in prison with the sentence specified by the judge. In most states, good time and jail time are the main factors that reduce the time actually served. On a national basis, felony inmates serve an average of two and a half years before release. Figure 13.2 shows the average time served for selected offenses.

Supporters of discretion for the paroling authority argue that parole benefits the overall system. Discretionary release mitigates the harshness of the penal code. If the legislature must establish exceptionally strict punishments as a means of conveying a "tough on crime" image to frustrated and angry voters, parole can effectively permit sentence adjustments that make the punishment fit the crime. Not everyone convicted of larceny has done equivalent harm, yet some legislatively mandated sentencing schemes impose equally strict sentences. Early release on parole can be granted to an offender who is less deserving of strict punishment, such as someone who voluntarily makes restitution, cooperates with the police, or shows genuine regret.

A major criticism of discretionary release is that it shifts responsibility for many primary criminal justice decisions from a judge, who holds legal procedures uppermost, to an administrative board, where discretion rules. Judges know a great deal about constitutional rights and basic legal protections, but parole board members may not have such knowledge. In most states with discretionary release, parole hearings are secret, with only board members, the inmate, and correctional officers present. Often, no published criteria guide decisions, and prisoners receive no reason for denial or granting of parole. However, an increasing number of states permit oral or written testimony by victims and by members of the offender's family.

check point > **3. What are the four release mechanisms for prisoners?**
Discretionary release, mandatory release, other conditional release, and expiration release.

stop & analyze In light of the differences in parole processes used in different states, how do you see the importance (or lack thereof) of involvement by defense attorneys and crime victims in parole hearings? Do they provide helpful information about whether an offender is reformed enough for release? Provide two advantages and two risks from permitting attorneys to represent prisoners at parole hearings. Provide two advantages and two risks from allowing victims to provide input.

Parole Supervision in the Community

Parolees are released from prison on condition that they abide by laws and follow rules, known as **conditions of release**, designed to aid their readjustment to society and control their movement. As in probation, the parolee may be required to abstain from alcohol, keep away from undesirable associates, maintain good work habits, and not leave the state without permission. If they violate any of these conditions, they could be returned to prison to serve out the rest of their sentence. Nearly 80 percent of released prisoners are subject to some form of community supervision. Only those who have served their full sentence minus good time ("maxed out") are free from supervision.

conditions of release
Conduct restrictions that parolees must follow as a legally binding requirement of being released.

The restrictions are justified on the ground that people who have been incarcerated must readjust to the community so that they will not fall back into preconviction habits and associations. The strict enforcement of these rules may create problems for parolees who cannot fulfill all the demands placed on them. For example, a parolee may find it impossible to be tested for drugs, attend an Alcoholics Anonymous meeting, and work full-time while also meeting family obligations.

The day they come out of prison, parolees face a staggering array of problems. In most states, they receive only clothes, a token amount of money, a list of rules governing their conditional release, and the name and address of the parole officer to whom they must report within 24 hours. Although a promised job is often required for release, an actual job may be another matter. Most former convicts are unskilled

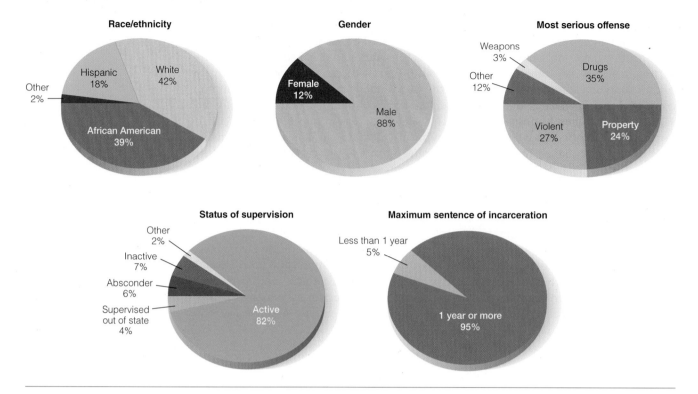

Figure 13.3

Personal Characteristics of Parolees Prison releasees tend to be men in their thirties who have an inadequate education and were incarcerated for a nonviolent offense.

Source: Lauren E. Glaze and Thomas P. Bonczar, "Probation and Parole in the United States, 2010," Bureau of Justice Statistics *Bulletin*, November 2011, NCJ 236019.

or semiskilled, and the conditions of release may prevent them from moving to areas where they could find work. If the parolee is African American, male, and under 30, he joins the largest demographic group of unemployed people in the country. Figure 13.3 shows the personal characteristics of parolees.

Parolees bear the added handicap of former-convict status. In most states, laws prevent former prisoners from working in certain types of establishments—where alcohol is sold, for example—thus ruling out many jobs. In some states, those who have served time are assumed to have "a lack of good moral character and trustworthiness," a condition required to acquire a license to be a barber, for example. Finally, ex-convicts face a significant dilemma. If they are truthful about their backgrounds, many employers will not hire them. If they are not truthful, they can be fired for lying if the employer ever learns about their conviction.

Other reentry problems plague parolees. For many, the transition from the highly structured life in prison to open society is too difficult to manage. Many just do not have the social, psychological, and material resources to cope with the temptations and complications of modern life. For these parolees, freedom may be short-lived as they fall back into forbidden activities such as drinking, using drugs, and stealing.

Community Programs following Release

There are various programs to assist parolees. Some help prepare offenders for release while they are still in prison; others provide employment and housing assistance after release. Together, the programs are intended to help the offender progress steadily toward reintegration into the community. Almost all penologists agree that there should be pre- and post-release programs to assist reentry, yet many prisoners do not now participate in such programs. Although all states offer reentry programs, relatively few prisoners have access to them.

Among the many programs developed to help offenders return to the community, three are especially important: work and educational release, furloughs, and halfway houses. Although similar in many ways, each offers a specific approach to helping formerly incarcerated individuals reenter the community.

Work and Educational Release Programs of **work and educational release**, in which inmates are released from correctional institutions during the day to work or attend school, were first established in Vermont in 1906. However, the Huber Act, passed by the Wisconsin legislature in 1913, is usually cited as the model on which such programs are based. By 1972, most states and the federal government had instituted these programs. Nonetheless, by 2002, only about one-third of prisons operated them for fewer than 3 percent of U.S. inmates (Petersilia, 2009).

Although most work and educational release programs are justifiable in terms of rehabilitation, many correctional administrators and legislators also like them because they cost relatively little. In some states, a portion of the inmate's earnings from work outside may be deducted for room and board. One problem with these programs is that they allegedly take jobs from free citizens, a complaint often given by organized labor.

Grace Bernstein, an administrative law judge at the Harlem Parole Reentry Court in New York City, conducts a hearing to discuss and resolve issues related to parolees under supervision in the community. Should parolees be given second chances if they violate conditions of release, such as rules about curfews or consumption of alcohol?

work and educational release The daytime release of inmates from correctional institutions so they can work or attend school.

Furloughs Isolation from loved ones is one of the pains of imprisonment. Although correctional programs in many countries include conjugal visits, only a few U.S. corrections systems have used them. Many penologists view the **furlough**—the temporary release of an inmate from a correctional institution for a visit home—as a meaningful approach to inmate reintegration.

Furloughs are thought to offer an excellent means of testing an inmate's ability to cope with the larger society. Through home visits, the inmate can renew family ties and relieve the tensions of confinement. Most administrators also feel that furloughs increase prisoners' morale. The general public, however, does not always support the concept. Public outrage is inevitable if an offender on furlough commits another crime or fails to return. Correctional authorities are often nervous about using furloughs, because they fear being blamed for such incidents.

furlough The temporary release of an inmate from a correctional institution for a brief period, usually one to three days, for a visit home. Such programs help maintain family ties and prepare inmates for release on parole.

Halfway Houses As its name implies, the **halfway house** is a transitional facility for soon-to-be-released inmates that connects them to community services, resources, and support. Usually, felons work in the community but reside in the halfway house during nonworking hours. Halfway houses range from secure institutions in the community, with programs designed to assist inmates who are preparing for release on parole, to group homes where parolees, probationers, or others diverted from the system live with minimal supervision and direction. Some halfway houses deliver special treatment services, such as programs designed to deal with alcohol, drug, or mental problems.

Residential programs face specific problems. Few neighborhoods want to host halfway houses or treatment centers for convicts. Community resistance has significantly impeded the development of community-based correctional facilities and has even forced some successful facilities to close. Many communities, often

halfway house A correctional facility housing convicted felons who spend a portion of their day at work in the community but reside in the halfway house during nonworking hours.

Commercial Appeal/Nikki Boertman/Landov

↑ Community-based corrections facilities, such as halfway houses, provide opportunities for offenders to gradually transition back into the community. How would you react if someone proposed placing a halfway house in your neighborhood? If you would oppose such a facility near your home, where do you think such facilities should be located?

wealthier ones, have blocked the placement of halfway houses or treatment centers within their boundaries. For example, a suburban city council near Grand Rapids, Michigan, considered a new ordinance in 2012 that would limit future housing facilities for parolees to locations in the industrial area of the city (L. Smith, 2012). One result of the NIMBY ("not in my backyard") attitude is that many centers are established in deteriorating neighborhoods inhabited by poor people, who lack the political power and resources to block unpopular programs.

Nonetheless, a survey found a striking increase in the number of community-based residential corrections facilities. Such facilities were defined as those in which 50 percent or more of residents regularly leave unaccompanied for work or study in the community, thus including halfway houses and similar programs that provide substance-abuse treatment. What was most striking about the survey was the decrease in the number of public facilities from 297 to 221 between 2000 and 2005 at the same time that private facilities increased from 163 to 308 (Stephan, 2008). These private facilities undoubtedly rely on contracts from state governments to provide services that the state believes are less expensive in the private sector. The interesting question for contemporary times is whether, in an atmosphere of budget cuts, state governments will find money for the use of such facilities to assist in the reentry of prisoners. Budget reductions can eliminate the availability of funds for outside contracts but, alternatively, such cuts can also lead to increased reliance on private facilities if their use is viewed as means of saving money (S. Davis, 2012).

Parole Officer: Cop or Social Worker?

After release, a parolee's principal contact with the criminal justice system is the parole officer, who must provide both surveillance and assistance. Thus, parole officers are asked to play two different, some might say incompatible, roles: cop and social worker. Whereas parole was originally designed to help offenders make the transition from prison to the community, supervision has shifted ever more toward surveillance, drug testing, monitoring curfews, and collecting restitution. Safety and security have become major issues in parole services.

The Parole Officer as Cop   In their role as cop, parole officers have the power to restrict many aspects of the parolee's life, to enforce the conditions of release, and to initiate revocation proceedings if parole conditions are violated. Like other officials in the criminal justice system, the parole officer has extensive discretion in low-visibility situations. In many states, parole officers have the authority to search the parolee's house without warning; to arrest him or her, without the possibility of bail, for suspected violations; and to suspend parole pending a hearing before the board. This authoritarian component of the parole officer's role can give the ex-offender a sense of insecurity and hamper the development of mutual trust.

The parole officer is responsible for seeing that the parolee follows the conditions imposed by the parole board or department of corrections. Typically, the conditions require the parolee to follow the parole officer's instructions; to permit the officer to visit the home and place of employment; to maintain employment; not to leave the state without permission; not to marry without permission; not to own a firearm; not to possess, use, or traffic in narcotics; not to consume alcohol to excess; and to comply with all laws and be a good citizen.

Parole officers are granted law enforcement powers in order to protect the community from offenders coming out of prison. However, because these powers diminish the possibility for the officer to develop a close relationship with the client, they can weaken the officer's ability to help the parolee adjust to the community. Read "A Question of Ethics" at the end of the chapter to consider how training might be developed to avoid the risk that parole officers will exceed their authority in carrying out law enforcement functions.

The Parole Officer as Social Worker Parole officers must act as social workers by helping the parolee find a job and restore family ties. Officers channel parolees to social agencies, such as psychiatric, drug, and alcohol clinics, where they can obtain help. As caseworkers, officers try to develop a relationship that allows parolees to confide their frustrations and concerns.

Because parolees may not talk honestly if they are constantly aware of the parole officer's ability to send them back to prison, some researchers have suggested that parole officers' conflicting responsibilities of cop and social worker should be separated. Parole officers could maintain the supervisory aspects of the position, and other personnel—perhaps a separate parole counselor—could perform the casework functions. Another option would be for parole officers to be charged solely with social work duties, while local police check for violations.

The Parole Bureaucracy

Although parole officers have smaller caseloads than do probation officers, parolees require more-extensive services. One reason is that parolees, by the very fact of their incarceration, generally have committed more-serious crimes than those perpetrated by probationers. Another reason is that parolees must make a difficult transition from the highly structured prison environment to a society in which they have previously failed to live as law-abiding citizens. It is exceptionally difficult for a parole officer to monitor, control, and assist clients who may have little knowledge of or experience with living successfully within society's rules.

The parole officer works within a bureaucratic environment. Like most other human services organizations, parole agencies are short on resources and expertise. Because the difficulties faced by many parolees are so complex, the officer's job is almost impossible. As a result, parole officers frequently must classify parolees and give priority to those most in need. For example, most parole officers spend extra time with the newly released. As the officers gain greater confidence in the parolees, they can adjust their level of supervision to "active" or "reduced" surveillance. Depending on how the parolees have functioned in the community, they may eventually be allowed to check in with their officers periodically instead of submitting to regular home visits, searches, and other intrusive monitoring.

Adjustment to Life Outside Prison

With little preparation, the ex-offender moves from the highly structured, authoritarian life of the institution into a world filled with temptations and complicated problems. Suddenly, ex-convicts who are unaccustomed to undertaking even simple tasks such as going to the store for groceries are expected to assume pressing, complex responsibilities. Finding a job and a place to live are not the only problems the newly released person faces. The parolee must also make significant social and psychological role adjustments. A male ex-convict, for example, must suddenly become not only a parolee but also an employee,

Common Belief: Offenders who never qualify for parole will still inevitably be returned to society upon completion of their sentences.

- The foregoing statement is generally true for those offenders who are not serving life sentences. However, some states, such as Kansas and Washington, enacted laws to prolong the detention of offenders whom officials regard as especially dangerous: predatory sex offenders.

- Under these laws, offenders who are diagnosed with mental conditions that make them highly likely to commit further sex crimes are transported to secure mental facilities upon the completion of their prison sentences. In other words, even after serving their full prison sentences, they remain locked up in state facilities.

- The U.S. Supreme Court ruled that such indefinite detention statutes are permissible as long as the purpose of the laws is treatment rather than punishment (*Kansas v. Hendricks, 1997*).

- In theory, these individuals will be released when psychiatrists conclude that they can safely reenter society. In practice, they may never receive such approval.

- One of the most significant risks of such laws is that they will be applied to people who actually do not pose a significant risk of re-offending. This is especially true because the psychiatric conditions that justify post-sentence detentions are vaguely defined and difficult to diagnose accurately.

a neighbor, a father, a husband, and a son. The expectations, norms, and social relations in the free world differ greatly from those learned in prison. The relatively predictable inmate code gives way to society's often unclear rules of behavior—rules that the offender had failed to cope with during his previous life in free society.

In terms of living a crime-free life, today's parolees face even greater obstacles than did those released prior to 1990. Since that time, Congress and many state legislatures have imposed new restrictions on ex-felons. These include denial of many things, including welfare benefits such as food stamps, for those convicted of even minor drug crimes; access to public housing; receipt of student loans; and in some states voting rights. Studies have found that returning inmates often face so many restrictions after long periods of incarceration that the conditions amount to years of "invisible punishment" (Mauer and Chesney-Lind, 2002:1). The effects of these policies impact not only the individual parolee, but also their families and communities (Travis, 2002).

News accounts of brutal crimes committed by ex-offenders on parole fuel a public perception that parolees pose a threat to the community. The murder of 12-year-old Polly Klaas by a parolee and the rape and murder of 7-year-old Megan Kanka by a paroled sex offender spurred legislators across the nation to enact "sexual offender notification" laws. These laws require that the public be notified of the whereabouts of "potentially dangerous" sex offenders. In some states, paroled sex offenders must register with the police, whereas in others, the immediate neighbors must be informed. Many states now have publicly accessible sex offender websites listing the names and addresses of those registered. The state of Washington created a statewide online database that not only lets you see which sex predators are in your midst, but also can alert you by email if an offender moves close by (J. Sullivan, 2009).

These laws have generated several unintended consequences. For example, parolees have been "hounded" from communities, the media have televised the parolees' homecomings, homes have been burned, parolees have been killed, and neighbors have assaulted parolees they erroneously thought were sex offenders. In some states, legislators wrote laws so broadly that consensual sex between teenagers and third-degree assault that might constitute inappropriate touching or sexual contact are included in the notification mandate. In 2006, two Maine parolees were shot by a man intent on killing registered sex offenders. One of those killed was on the list because, at age 19, he had been convicted of having consensual sex with his underage girlfriend. His murder heightened national debate as to whether the online registries put those who are listed at risk (G. Adams, 2006).

The fact of repeat violence fuels a public perception that parolees represent a continuing threat to the community. Although the new laws primarily focus on people who have committed sex offenses against children, some fear that the community will eventually target all parolees. This preoccupation with potential parolee criminality makes successful reentry even more difficult for ex-offenders. Read "Criminal Justice: Myth & Reality" and consider your views on the policies adopted by some states to control the offenders whom they fear most.

Revocation of Parole

The potential revocation of parole, for committing a new crime or violating the conditions of release, hangs constantly over the ex-inmate's head. The public tends to view the high number of revocations as a failure of parole. Correctional officials point to the great number of parolees who are required to be drug free, be employed, and pay restitution—conditions that many find difficult to fulfill.

As discussed in Chapter 10, the Supreme Court ruled in *Morrissey v. Brewer* (1972) that if the parole officer alleges a technical violation, a two-step revocation proceeding is required. In the first stage, a hearing determines whether there is probable cause to believe the conditions have been violated. The parolee has the right to be notified of the charges, to be informed of the evidence, to present witnesses, and to confront the witnesses. In the second stage, the parole authority decides if the violation is severe enough to warrant the return to prison.

Despite the increase in the number of parolees supervised, the percentage of those who are returned to prison because of a technical violation or conviction for a new offense has remained at about 39 percent (BJS 2007:7). However, the percentage of violators returned to prison varies by state, accounting for more than half of prison admissions in California (67 percent), Utah (55 percent), and Louisiana (53 percent), but less than 10 percent in Alabama and Florida. The percentage of parolees returned for technical violations also varies. For example, 17 percent of California's prison population consists of inmates who were returned for a technical violation, whereas in the state of Washington, only 1 percent were (Austin, 2001:319). As shown in Table 13.1, of those returned to prison, 70 percent had been arrested or convicted of a new offense.

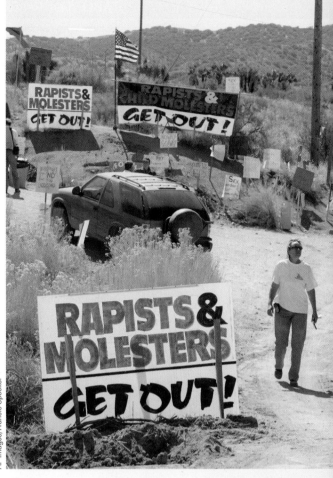

AP Images/Francis Specker

Sex offender registration laws have made adjustment to the community difficult for many parolees. Residents of some neighborhoods, such as these in Placentia, California, have protested the renting or sale of property to paroled sex offenders. To what extent have these laws resulted in all parolees being labeled as "dangerous"?

check point

4. **What are three programs designed to ease the reentry of offenders into the community?**
   Work and educational release programs, furlough programs, and halfway houses.

5. **What are the main tasks of parole officers?**
   Surveillance and assistance.

6. **What two conditions can result in the revocation of parole?**
   Arrest for a new crime, or a technical violation of one or more of the conditions of parole.

stop & analyze Should criminal justice officials be able to revoke parole without a hearing? Alternatively, should parolees be entitled to a full trial and representation by counsel before parole is revoked, since the revocation decision has such a huge impact on their personal liberty? Give three reasons for your responses to these two questions.

TABLE 13.1 Reasons for Revocation among Parole Violators in State Prison

An increasing number of parolees are being returned to prison because of new arrests or technical violations. What factors might be causing this increase?

Reason for Revocation	Percentage of Parolees Returned
Arrest/conviction for new offense	69.9%
Drug-related violations	16.1%
Positive test for drug use	7.9
Possession of drugs	6.6
Failure to report for drug testing	2.3
Failure to report for drug treatment	1.7
Absconders	22.3%
Failure to report/absconded	18.6
Left jurisdiction without permission	5.6
Other reasons	17.8%
Possession of gun(s)	3.5
Failure to report for counseling	2.4
Failure to meet financial obligations	2.3
Failure to maintain employment	1.2
Maintained contact with known offenders	1.2

Detail adds to more than 100 percent because some inmates may have had more than one violation of parole.

Source: Timothy A. Hughes, Doris James Wilson, and Allen J. Beck, "Trends in State Parole, 1990–2000," Bureau of Justice Statistics, *Special Report*, October 2001, NCJ 184735, p. 14.

The Future of Prisoner Reentry

The rising number of offenders returning to the community has new importance to policy makers. Large numbers of offenders are gaining release each year as a natural consequence of the nation's significant expansion of its prison population in the past few decades. Moreover, many states are attempting to increase the number of offenders released from prison as a means to cut costs amid the contemporary budget crisis affecting all levels of government. These factors increase the necessity of looking closely at ways to make reentry effective for offenders and society.

The likelihood of rules violations by released offenders is affected not only by the kinds of crimes for which they were convicted, but also by the intensity and duration of their supervision (Grattet, Lin, and Petersilia, 2011). The longer the period of time under a strict set of rules, the greater the likelihood that some rules will be broken, and then states are faced with the question of whether to send an offender back to prison, even if the offender has not committed a new crime. The 2011 report by the Pew Center on the States highlighted Oregon as a place where great efforts are made to respond to violations by parolees without sending them back to the expensive and unproductive environment of prison. For example, research has shown that using community-based sanctions for parole violations can be an effective and less costly approach to combatting recidivism (Steiner et al., 2012). States can also benefit from proactively reaching out to employers and, in cooperation with employers, develop transitional job programs that provide financial and personal support as well as the necessary training and supervision for parolees and ex-offenders (Rosenberg, 2012). Successful entry into the workforce can have substantial beneficial effects for offenders, although this important step can contain numerous obstacles for the many offenders who lack meaningful prior work experience or the commitment to fulfill the responsibilities of a job.

An additional challenge facing reentry is the maintenance of budgets for programs that facilitate reintegration into the community even as states are cutting funds elsewhere in corrections. For example, some cities have used reentry courts with judges dedicated to overseeing the progress of parolees (Hamilton, 2010). Yet, in San Francisco in 2011, budget cuts eliminated the Parole Reentry Court, despite its record of helping parolees avoid recidivism, leading Judge Jeffrey Tauber to apologize to parolees in the courtroom by saying, "I'm truly apologizing that I've not been able to fulfill my commitment and promise to you" (Bundy, 2011). Elsewhere in the country, other parole and reentry programs have shared the burden of budget cuts. The need to facilitate the successful reentry of a large number of parolees and ex-offenders will lead to hard questions and difficult choices about how to allocate resources in the justice system.

Legislators and correctional officials increasingly recognize that government lacks the money and facilities to incarcerate all offenders for the sentence lengths that had been imposed in recent decades. Alternative approaches will affect not only sentencing decisions for nonviolent and drug offenders, but also efforts to increasingly reduce prison populations through various release mechanisms. Parole and other community programs represent an effort to address the inevitability of prison reentry. Even if such programs do not prevent all offenders from returning to crime, they do help some to turn their lives around.

a question of ethics

Writing Assignment: Think, Discuss, Write

For parole officers, as well as for other criminal justice officials, it is important to behave professionally in all circumstances and avoid any temptation to abuse authority based on feelings of anger or contempt for parolees and their families. A U.S. Court of Appeals decision described the behavior of a parole officer and several police officers who were instructed to conduct searches of parolees' homes, including parolees not under the supervision of this particular parole officer. The manner in which they conducted the search raises troubling questions about their attitudes and behavior.

The officers who searched Motley's residence for purported parolee Janae Jamerson conducted the search in a harassing manner. When [the parolee's girlfriend] Motley came to the door in her pajamas, the officers told her several falsehoods. Kading said that he was there with Jamerson's [actual supervising] parole officer and that they had a warrant to search the apartment, neither of which was true. Motley told the searching officers that [the parolee] Jamerson did not live there and was in custody. One of the officers then told her that Jamerson had been released three days earlier, another lie. When

the officers then asked Motley who else was inside the house with her, she said that only she and her five-week-old son were there. Kading told Motley that if she did not let them in, they would arrest her and put her son in foster care. Faced with Kading's threat to take her son away, Motley unlocked the security gate. Kading pushed her out of the way and against the wall with his forearm as he went into the house. The officers all entered the apartment with their guns drawn. During the search, the officers were "going through things," including closets and a file box, a search that was completely unauthorized.

Kading knew that the baby was in the back bedroom, and as soon as he entered that room he pointed his gun directly at the five-week-old infant. The baby was on his back on the bed looking toward the bedroom door. The baby began screaming as soon as Kading entered, and so Motley ran to the room, where Kading was still pointing the gun at the baby. Kading did not move his gun when Motley entered, and he kept it pointed at Motley's tiny son while he searched the room.

Technology and Criminal Justice

Learning Objectives

→ Understand how adaptation and belief in science can affect the use of technology

→ Recognize the many aspects of cyber crime and counterfeiting

→ Analyze the role of communications, computers, and databases in policing

→ Describe developments and problems in DNA testing and new weapons technologies

→ Understand the use of technology in courts and corrections

→ Recognize the continuing questions about the effects of technology on civil liberties

n a small, five-member police department in Pennsylvania in 2009, an officer sat down at a computer and entered an adults-only, online chat room. His objective was to detect whether there were sexual predators online seeking to victimize children. During a conversation with one participant in the chat room, the male officer, who had identified himself online as "Emily," was asked his age. "I'm 15," the officer replied. The participant with whom the officer chatted said that he "didn't want any trouble," yet he continued to converse with "Emily." Eventually, the middle-aged man in another state with whom "Emily" engaged in flirtatious conversation exposed himself to his webcam and performed a sex act for "Emily" to view (Bai, 2012). These

429

actions ultimately led to the prosecution and conviction of the man on six criminal charges, including unlawful contact with a minor (Demare, 2011).

Every day across the country, law enforcement officers use computers to investigate crimes. Special agents in the FBI attempt to discover whether online communications contain evidence about impending terrorism attacks on the United States. DEA agents monitor communications concerning drug trafficking. Police at all levels of government seek to discover the transmission of child pornography. And, as in the Pennsylvania case, officers seek to identify online sexual predators before they can do harm to unsuspecting victims, especially young people who are trusting and easily misled.

The most shocking aspect of the Pennsylvania case was the identity of the man convicted of the crimes: Scott Ritter, a former U.S. Marine Corps major and United Nations weapons inspector, who rose to international prominence for publicly challenging President Bush's claim in 2003 that Iraq possessed weapons of mass destruction (WMD) and thus was a threat to U.S. security. After the U.S. military forces invaded Iraq, it became clear that Ritter's report discounting Iraqi WMDs was confirmed to be totally accurate (Scott, 2011). Ritter was sentenced to 18 to 66 months in state prison and was designated as a "sexually violent predator," in part because he had been caught in two prior police sting operations in New York in which he thought he had arranged meetings with teenage girls when he was actually communicating with police officers in online chat rooms (Scott, 2011). In the prior cases, prosecutors dismissed charges in exchange for Ritter's agreement to enter counseling programs (Bai, 2012). Ritter is not the only prominent person whose private activities led to a criminal conviction through police investigations using computers. In 2006, for example, Brian Doyle, the deputy press secretary for the U.S. Department of Homeland Security, was convicted and sentenced to prison for online sexual conversations with what he erroneously believed was a teenager (T. Fields, 2011). These examples help to demonstrate how technological developments create opportunities for new kinds of crimes but also provide law enforcement officials with new tools for gathering criminal evidence.

Contemporary Americans take for granted the availability and usefulness of technology. American television viewers are fascinated by the CBS television network's *CSI: Crime Scene Investigation* dramas and other networks' programs that show the impressive ability of scientists to identify criminal suspects by examining microscopic bits of evidence. Because the United States is a relatively wealthy and technologically sophisticated country, it can fund and benefit from the development of new technologies that provide crucial assistance in various operations of the criminal justice system. However, the invention of a new device or the development of new software, no matter how potentially useful, does not automatically benefit actors in the criminal justice system. Agencies must have enough money to acquire new technology, and their personnel must have expertise and resources for training in order to make effective use of it.

Further, Americans readily recognize that many countries in the world are too poor and their infrastructure resources, such as electricity, are too unreliable to use some of the varied technologies that benefit the criminal justice system. Less recognized, but equally important, is that the benefits of technology are not distributed equally across the United States because of fragmentation and limited local resources. For example, some cities' police departments can afford to put computers into all police patrol cars, but others cannot. As we learn about the role of technology in criminal justice, we must remember that existing technological resources are not universally available, even in the United States.

In this chapter, we examine the role of technology in criminal justice. Each year brings new inventions—as well as improvements to existing technologies—that affect crime and justice. As we shall see, technological change affects the nature of crime even as it boosts the capacity of law enforcement officials to prevent criminal acts and apprehend criminal offenders. Technology also impacts the processing of criminal cases in courts and the monitoring and control of convicted offenders in correctional settings. The use of technology increases the capability of criminal justice officials to perform their vital functions effectively. Simultaneously, however, technology creates its own issues and problems, including concerns about the ways in which it may collide with citizens' expectations about their privacy and other constitutional rights.

Technological Development and Criminal Justice

Throughout history, humans have sought to invent tools to advance their goals. The invention of early tools and wheels, for example, promoted agriculture and transport. Over time, simple farming tools have given way to gigantic tractors and other farm machinery. The wheel has similarly been updated through advancing transportation mechanisms—from horse-drawn wagons through steam trains to jet planes. The appreciation for the advantages of technology naturally leads to inventive developments affecting all areas of human experience, including criminal justice.

However, the use of technology in criminal justice differs from its use in many other areas of human activity. Technology in this case is not merely an effort to overcome the natural environment by increasing productivity, easing daily life, and expanding the range of travel. In criminal justice, as in military affairs, technology becomes an element in the interaction, competition, and conflict among human beings who have opposing objectives. In this case, the clash is between those who would seek to profit or cause harm by breaking society's laws (as in theft or murder) and those who seek to stop, identify, apprehend, process, and punish criminals. This observation highlights two important points about technological development in criminal justice. First, new developments that benefit one side in this competition, whether lawbreaker or law enforcer, will lead to adjustments and adaptations by the other. Second, the pressure to find new and better devices to combat crime can lead to excessive faith in the effectiveness of technology; this can lead to problems when people do not stop to examine the consequences of new technology. After we briefly examine each of these points, keep them in mind to see how they relate to the topics discussed in the rest of this chapter.

Competition and Adaptation

Throughout history, the development of both weapons and protective devices affected the preservation of persons and property, which is one of the fundamental goals of criminal justice. As weaponry advanced from daggers and swords to firearms and then later to multishot pistols that could be concealed inside pockets, the threats posed by robbers increased. Thus, when American policing expanded in the nineteenth century, law enforcement officers in the western frontier, and later throughout the country, armed themselves in a way that would help them deal with pistol-toting criminals. These developments continue. News reports have made contemporary Americans well aware that many police departments now struggle to match the firepower of the automatic weapons possessed by some criminal offenders and organized-crime groups (A. Klein, 2008).

Similarly, the development of fortified walls, door locks, and safes led to criminals' adaptive strategies for overcoming these barriers. For example, the creation of locks spawned devices and techniques for picking locks. So, too, the creation of safes led to the birth of professional safecrackers. Later, the introduction of police radar to detect speeders led to a profitable industry selling radar detectors to motorists who wanted to drive at excessive speeds without paying fines. Today, criminals' efforts to overcome residential burglar alarms, as well as cyber criminals' creativity in overcoming security software, illustrate the interactions among technological development, criminals' adaptive behavior, and society's efforts to counteract new forms of criminality.

Fundamentally, these examples should remind us that technological developments do not always help criminal justice officials. New technologies can be developed and used by those who seek to violate criminal laws. Moreover, new devices designed specifically to protect property or to assist police officers will generate adaptive behavior by would-be lawbreakers who adjust their behavior, invent their own devices, or otherwise develop strategies to overcome new barriers to the attainment of their goals. James Byrne summarizes the overall impact of technology:

© Lake County Museum/CORBIS

Advances...in technology have resulted in new opportunities for crime (through the Internet), new forms of criminality (e.g., Internet scams...), new techniques for committing crimes (e.g., computer software programs,...the use of [T]asers as weapons in robberies), and new categories of offenders and victims (such as online predators and identity theft victims) (2008:10–11).

Science and the Presumption of Progress

From the mid-nineteenth century through today, Americans have benefited from industrialization, the development of electricity, the rise of the scientific method, and advances in various scientific fields, such as medicine and engineering. In light of the extraordinary advancements in human knowledge and the new inventions that have dramatically altered the nature of American society, it is not surprising that many people equate technological advancements with "progress." However, contemporary Americans are regularly reminded that new developments can produce consequences, such as side effects from new medicines, that are unexpected and undesirable. Thus, in the field of criminal justice, as in other fields, we need to guard against the assumption that new technologies will always be better than older techniques and devices. Similarly, even when the benefits of new technologies are clear, we need to consider the possibility of undesirable risks and consequences that have not yet been discovered.

In the late nineteenth century, the development of electricity brought with it efforts to apply this "miracle" resource to various societal needs. One idea applied to criminal justice was the invention of the electric chair as a modern method to produce an instantaneous and presumably humane execution for criminals sentenced to death. At that time, most executions were carried out through hanging. This "old-fashioned" execution method had been used for centuries, with little change in its use of rope and a means to drop the condemned person's body so that the neck would break or the person would be strangled.

Many people presumed that the electric chair provided a quicker, more humane way to execute criminals because the use of electricity was developed as an amazing innovation that was the product of science. In fact, many such executions seemed to be far more painful and prolonged than the traditional use of hanging. Are there any new technologies in criminal justice that are likely to have unexpected and undesirable consequences?

The first man condemned to execution by electric chair was William Kemmler, a convicted murderer in New York. Kemmler challenged his sentence through the court system, eventually presenting to the U.S. Supreme Court a claim that execution by electricity constituted "cruel and unusual punishment" in violation of Kemmler's constitutional rights. After all, what could be more "unusual" than to be the first person executed through the use of a newfangled invention?

In rejecting Kemmler's claim in 1890, the U.S. Supreme Court noted that the New York statute permitting execution by electric chair "was passed in the effort to devise a more humane method of reaching the result [of extinguishing life and] that courts were bound to presume that the legislature was possessed of the facts upon which it took action" (*In re Kemmler*, 1890). Thus, there was acceptance of the idea that this new scientific method would be more effective and humane than hanging. When Kemmler was actually executed, however, the first jolt of 1,000 volts did not kill him, and witnesses saw that he was still breathing despite the attending physician's initial declaration that he was dead (Moran, 2002). The wires were reattached to his head, and the chair was revved up to 2,000 volts for an extended period.

> Froth oozed out of Kemmler's strapped mouth. The small blood vessels under his skin began to rupture. Blood trickled down his face and arms.... The awful smell of burning flesh filled the death chamber. Kemmler's body first smoldered and then caught fire.... From the moment he first sat down on the chair until the electricity was shut off the second time, eight minutes had elapsed. (Moran, 2002:15–19)

Did the electric chair fulfill its presumed function of using science to provide instantaneous, humane executions? Although it was used in two thousand executions in the century after Kemmler's death, highly publicized instances of other gruesome death-chamber scenes eventually led to a complete reconsideration of its use. In 2001, Georgia's Supreme Court declared that this method of execution imposed unconstitutional "cruel and unusual punishment" on condemned offenders (H. Weinstein, 2001). By the time that the Nebraska Supreme Court made an identical ruling in 2008, all states had moved toward the use of lethal injection as the method of execution for new capital murder convictions. Clearly, the original presumptions about the humane scientific "progress" represented by the electric chair had been rejected nationwide (Mears, 2008).

The story of the electric chair provides a graphic example of slow reconsideration of the effects of one particular technological invention. Today we see similar examples concerning the actual risks and consequences of certain technologies. For example, in 2009, the National Academy of Sciences (2009) produced a report that questioned the validity and accuracy of many forensic science methods used by police and prosecutors. In one section, the report said that forensic science "analyses are often handled by poorly trained technicians who then exaggerate the accuracy of their methods in court" (S. Moore, 2009). Obviously, the effectiveness of technology is limited by the errors made by the human beings who use that technology, despite the seeming infallibility of forensic techniques dramatized in *CSI : Crime Scene Investigation* and other popular shows. Indeed, even the use of a simple photo from a surveillance camera can cause problems when people make mistakes. This point was experienced by Cornell University sociology professor Stephen Morgan in New York, when he saw that his old driver's license photo was being mistakenly circulated on the Internet—instead of a photo of the actual Stephen Morgan being sought for a fatal shooting in Connecticut at Wesleyan University's student bookstore in 2009—as officials sought the public's help in finding the shooter (M. Spencer, 2009). In addition, the technology itself, even when properly used, may also produce unanticipated risks and consequences. An accurate understanding of the role of technology in criminal justice requires recognition of the potential for undesirable results. Think about your own perceptions of the scientific testing of criminal evidence as you read "Criminal Justice: Myth & Reality."

criminal justice | myth & reality

Common Belief: As long as forensic scientists do not mishandle evidence, modern scientific methods ensure that reliable conclusions can be drawn after the laboratory testing of various forms of evidence, including fingerprints, hair, soil, handwriting, and bite marks.

- In reality, the National Academy of Sciences concluded that "many forensic disciplines—including analysis of fingerprints, bite marks, and the striations and indentations left by a pry bar or a gun's firing mechanism—were not grounded in the kind of rigorous, peer-reviewed research that is the hallmark of classic science" (Fountain, 2009).
- Major scandals have emerged when experts purported to state definitive conclusions about bite marks, handwriting analysis, and other forms of evidence after scientific testing, only to discover later that these conclusions were incorrect and had led to the conviction of innocent people (F. Santos, 2007).
- DNA analysis is the only form of scientific evidence that has been subjected to rigorous testing through the methods of science.
- Although courts admit into evidence other forms of scientific testing, as well as conclusions drawn about such evidence by scientists, many of these other tests have not been validated through rigorous research. Thus, judges and attorneys should display caution in examining and accepting such evidence.

---

check point ▷ 1. **What are two reasons to be cautious about assuming that new technological developments automatically provide benefits for the criminal justice system?**

Lawbreakers can develop and use technology for the purpose of committing crimes; new technologies produce the risks of unanticipated, undesirable risks and consequences.

stop & analyze What steps do you take to avoid victimization by technology-based crimes? Which technology-based crimes do you fear most?

Crime and Technology

As new technologies emerge, so do people who take advantage of them for their own gain. One has only to think of how the invention of the automobile enhanced criminals' mobility to realize the extent to which computers and other new technologies will enhance existing criminal enterprises. For example, the acquisition of automatic weapons can make drug traffickers more dangerous in battling their rivals and threatening witnesses. Instantaneous transfers of funds between banks via computer networks can make it easier for criminals to move money in order to purchase weapons, drugs, and other contraband, as well as to hide assets from government agencies responsible for law enforcement and tax collection. Computers and other technologies also create opportunities to commit new kinds of crimes, such as cyber crime and counterfeiting. We should note as well that individual citizens can respond by using technology themselves to thwart crime through improved lighting and alarm systems in their homes, security software on their computers, and pepper-spray canisters and other weapons for personal protection.

Cyber Crime

As we saw in Chapter 2, cyber crimes involve the use of computers and the Internet to commit acts against people, property, public order, or morality. Cyber criminals use computers to steal information, resources, or funds. These thefts can be aimed at simply stealing money or they can involve the theft of companies' trade secrets, chemical formulas, and other valuable information. Others use computers for malicious, destructive acts, such as releasing Internet viruses and "worms" to harm computer systems. They may also use innocent victims' computers, via remote commands, to assist in crimes such as the dissemination of child pornography (Kravets, 2011). In 2012, the countries in the European Union announced that they would open a new anticrime center in the Netherlands dedicated to combatting cyber crimes, many of which are increasingly perpetrated by organized-crime groups. The European Union has estimated that organized-crime groups gained $388 billion annually from cyber crime, an amount greater than the total profits produced through global trade in marijuana, cocaine, and heroin (H. Morris, 2012).

In addition, the illegal downloading of software, music, videos, and other copyrighted materials is widespread (Hinduja, 2007). Doing so is a federal crime. However, although millions of Americans perform illegal downloads every day, they are seldom prosecuted unless the government identifies individuals or organizations with substantial involvement in such activities. The government has acted to shut down large operations engaged in illegally disseminating movies and other copyrighted entertainment media. In 2012, for example, the FBI, in cooperation with officials in nearly a dozen countries, gained the arrests of three individuals in New Zealand and sought three other suspects abroad for gaining more than $175 million in illegal profits from posting movies and other copyrighted works online (U.S. Department of Justice, 2012).

New issues continually arise that produce suggestions about criminalizing new forms of cyber behavior, such as cyber bullying among teens that may lead to psychological harms and behavioral problems (Patchin and Hinduja, 2012).

Identity theft has become a huge problem affecting many middle-class and affluent Americans who would otherwise seldom find themselves victimized by criminals (J. Collins, 2005). Perpetrators of identity theft use other people's credit card numbers and social security numbers to secure fraudulent loans and steal money and merchandise. In December 2011, for example, 55 people in New York City were charged with being part of a cyber-crime ring in which one person stole financial information from donors to a philanthropic foundation and then supplied that information to crime partners who opened bank accounts and created counterfeit checks in the names of the donors (Nir, 2011). According to the National Crime Victimization Survey, 8.6 million American households

identity theft The theft of social security numbers, credit card numbers, and other information in order to secure loans, withdraw bank funds, and purchase merchandise while posing as someone else: the unsuspecting victim who will eventually lose money in these transactions.

TABLE 14.1 Type of Identity Theft Experienced by Households, and Total Financial Loss Attributed to Each Type of Identity Theft in 2010

Types of Identity Theft	Percent of Victimizations	Total Loss	Percent of Total Loss
All types	100%	$13.3 billion	100%
Existing credit card	54.0%	$4.2 billion	31.8%
Other existing account	25.6%	$2.3 billion	17.4%
Personal information	9.0%	$3.9 billion	29.4%
Multiple types	11.4%	$2.8 billion	21.4%

Source: Lynn Langton, "Identity Theft Reported by Households, 2005–2010," Bureau of Justice Statistics *Crime Data Brief*, November 2011, p. 5.

were victimized by identity theft in 2010 with losses totaling more than $13.3 billion (Langton, 2011). For many Americans, identity theft can occur without any financial loss if, for example, they are reimbursed by a bank or credit card company for their losses. Yet they still suffer victimization from computer crime since they may go through lengthy hassles in changing online financial records, getting new credit cards, or straightening out government records (Florencio and Herley, 2012).

As indicated by Table 14.1 the theft of existing credit card information is the most common form of identity theft, although other thefts involve existing bank accounts, PayPal accounts, and personal information used by thieves to set up fraudulent new accounts or file for fraudulent tax refunds (Langton, 2011). Credit card numbers are often stolen by dishonest restaurant servers and retail clerks who use electronic "skimmer" devices to quickly record the magnetic strip on the back of the card so that the information can be sold to organized-crime gangs or used to purchase items and manufacture counterfeit credit cards (Conte, 2012).

Other offenders use the Internet to disseminate child pornography, to advertise sexual services, or to stalk the unsuspecting. As illustrated by the chapter opening example of Scott Ritter's prosecution, police departments have given special emphasis to stopping computer predators who establish online relationships with juveniles in order to manipulate those children into sexual victimization. Thus, officers often pose as juveniles in "chat rooms" to see if sexual predators will attempt to cultivate a relationship and set up a personal meeting (Bai, 2012; Eichenwald, 2006).

The various forms of cyber crime present a serious concern to Americans. See "What Americans Think" and compare your own concerns and awareness with those of the rest of the country.

In attacking these problems, the FBI's National Computer Crime Squad lists its responsibilities as covering the following:

- Intrusions of the public switched network (the telephone company)
- Major computer network intrusions
- Network integrity violations
- Privacy violations
- Industrial espionage
- Pirated computer software
- Other crimes where the computer is a major factor in committing the criminal offense

The global nature of the Internet presents new challenges to the criminal justice system. For example, in 2011, the FBI, in cooperation with other countries' law enforcement agencies, announced criminal charges against two individuals

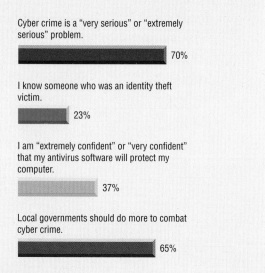

Question: "What do you know and believe about cyber crime?"

Cyber crime is a "very serious" or "extremely serious" problem.

70%

I know someone who was an identity theft victim.

23%

I am "extremely confident" or "very confident" that my antivirus software will protect my computer.

37%

Local governments should do more to combat cyber crime.

65%

Critical Thinking: In the current era of government budget cuts, do you believe that Americans' expressed concern about the growing problem of cyber crime will lead to increased funding for efforts to catch and punish cyber criminals? Why or why not?

Source: Kelly Jackson Higgins, "Poll: 65% of Consumers Want Local Government to Do More about Cybercrime," April 23, 2009, national poll by Competitive Edge Research and Communication (http://cerc.net).

in Latvia for leading an international cyber-crime operation that stole more than $70 million. The operation sent hundreds of thousands of computer "scareware" messages that warned people of serious virus infections and then offered to sell them fake software to remedy the nonexistent virus infections. In disrupting this operation, law enforcement officials also shut down computers and servers in seven European countries (U.S. Department of Justice, 2011). Nigerian thieves have become well known for their "419 scams," named after a section of their country's criminal code, in which they send email messages to Americans and people in other countries offering large sums of money in exchange for payments from these targeted fraud victims that will enable the thieves to unfreeze these actually nonexistent assets in banks and trust funds. For example, they falsely claim that if the individual would simply send $5,000 to cover an overdue fee owed to a bank, then the bank will unfreeze an account containing a multimillion-dollar inheritance that will be split with the investor-scam victim (Bjelopera and Finklea, 2012). Unfortunately, many gullible Americans have fallen prey to such fraudulent offers through which the $5,000 or other fee sent to Nigeria simply disappears because the frozen bank account and fortune in question do not actually exist. In another example, stolen credit card numbers are sold on the Internet, primarily by dealers based in states that were formerly part of the Soviet Union. Computer hackers steal thousands of credit card numbers from the computer systems of legitimate businesses and sell them in bulk to dealers who market them throughout the world via members-only websites. Credit card fraud costs online merchants more than $1 billion each year (Richtel, 2002; Segal, Ngugi, and Mana, 2011).

It is extremely difficult to know how many cyber crimes occur and how much money is lost through identity theft, auction fraud, investment fraud, and other forms of financial computer crime. Unfortunately for businesses, many harmful attacks and thefts carried out by computer are done by people inside a company. Moreover, many of these events are not reported to the police. The federal government's Internet Crime Complaint Center (IC3) publishes an annual report that provides perspective on the question by compiling information on complaints filed each year. In 2010, the IC3 received nearly 304,000 complaints about cyber crimes, up from 207,000 complaints in 2007 (Internet Crime Complaint Center, 2011). These cyber crimes primarily were committed by perpetrators in the United States (66 percent), but thieves in other countries also victimized Americans regularly. The other leading country of origin for cyber criminal enterprises were Great Britain (10 percent), Nigeria (6 percent), China (3 percent), and Canada (2 percent) (Internet Crime Complaint Center, 2011).

Efforts to create and enforce effective laws that will address such activities have been hampered by the international nature of cyber crime. Agencies in various countries are seeking to improve their ability to cooperate and share information. However, not all law enforcement officials throughout the world are equally committed to, nor capable of, catching cyber thieves and hackers. Criminals in some countries may have better computer equipment and expertise than do the officials trying to catch them. However, the FBI and other law enforcement agencies have made a concerted effort to improve their equipment, hire computer experts, and train their officers to investigate cyber crime. The FBI uses Cyber Action Teams or CATs to act quickly in addressing large-scale or very damaging cyber crimes. The FBI describes CATs as "small, highly trained teams of FBI agents, analysts, and computer forensics and malicious code experts who travel around the world on a moment's notice to respond to cyber intrusions" (FBI, 2006). For example, in 2006 an FBI CAT team traveled to Morocco and Turkey to help those governments apprehend cyber criminals who were unleashing malicious codes on the Internet and stealing credit card numbers (FBI, 2006).

Since the events of September 11, many countries' law enforcement agencies have increased their communication and cooperation in order to thwart terrorist activities. As these countries cooperate in investigating and monitoring the financial transactions of groups that employ terror tactics, it seems likely that they will also improve their capacity to discover and pursue cyber criminals. For example, the FBI has also joined forces with the national police agencies of Australia, Canada, New Zealand, and the United Kingdom to form the Strategic Alliance Cyber Crime Working Group, an international organization for sharing information and cooperating in cyber crime investigations (FBI, 2008).

Law enforcement agencies cannot prevent cyber crimes from occurring. Generally, they react to such harmful activities in order to limit theft and damage. People cannot rely on law enforcement efforts to protect them from such harms. The first defense against some forms of cyber crime is citizen awareness and caution. Do you think most people know enough about cyber crime to protect themselves from becoming victims?

Law enforcement officers need up-to-date knowledge and equipment to have any hope of pursuing cyber criminals on the Internet. Local police officers often successfully pretend to be teenagers in chat rooms, drawing out people who would sexually abuse children. Local officials cannot usually maintain the expertise to counteract international cyber crime operations, so the FBI takes the lead in those efforts. Should computer courses become a required component of every college criminal justice program?

Counterfeiting

Traditional counterfeiting involves the creation of fake currency that can be used for illegal profit. Counterfeiting not only constitutes theft by permitting criminals to exchange fake bills for actual products and services; it also harms the economy by placing into circulation bills that have no monetary value. Additional victims may receive the worthless paper as change in a purchase transaction or in payment for products and services. Historically, currency counterfeiters in the United States had difficulty matching the paper, ink, and intricate designs of real currency. While they could produce counterfeit bills that might fool individual clerks in stores, restaurants, and banks, criminals rarely avoided the eventual discovery that the bills were fakes. As image-reproduction technology developed, especially photocopiers and scanners, criminals found new ways of counterfeiting. Among the reasons that it is a crime to make any reproduction of U.S. currency is that counterfeiters initially found ways to photocopy currency images and feed those images into change machines. In went the fake paper currency and out came an equal amount of coins with real monetary value that the counterfeiters could then take to a bank and exchange for real paper money.

Continued improvements in computer and printing technology permitted counterfeiters to produce fake currency of increasing quality (Lazarus, 2010). Thus, in 1996, the United States began to redesign American currency and employ new technological techniques in order to make imitation more difficult:

Counterfeiting poses serious problems for the American economy through the production of phony currency and bogus consumer products. What should the United States government do to stop the importation of counterfeit currency, such as high-quality fake bills produced by North Korea to harm the American economy?

Almost everything about the new design was aimed at frustrating potential counterfeiters, including a security thread embedded in the paper, a watermark featuring a shadow portrait of the figure on the bill and new "microprinting," tiny lettering that is hard to imitate. The most significant addition was the use of optically variable ink, better known as O.V.I. Look at the bills in circulation today: all 10's, 20's, 50's and 100's now feature this counterfeiting deterrent in the denomination number on the lower-right-hand corner. Turn the bill one way, and it looks bronze-green; turn it the other way, and it looks black. O.V.I is very expensive, costing many times more than conventional bank-note ink. (Mihm, 2006)

Despite the effort to prevent counterfeiting, in 2004 and 2005, FBI and Secret Service agents began to intercept large shipments of "supernotes" that featured the same color-shifting ink and paper as real American currency. Apparently, the government of North Korea had purchased the same currency-printing technology that a Swiss company had sold to the U.S. Department of Treasury (Rose, 2009). North Korean defectors claimed that the country's dictator, Kim Jong-il, had ordered his scientists to counterfeit U.S. money as a means to generate income for the isolated, impoverished country and with the specific intention to "fight America, and screw up the American economic system" (Mihm, 2006). Although U.S. officials believe that too few fake bills have made it into the United States to adversely affect the U.S. economy, they have serious concerns about how the bills are used elsewhere in the world to purchase weapons for terrorist activities.

Currency is not the only product susceptible to counterfeiting through the use of available reproduction technologies. For example, legitimate businesses lose billions of dollars in potential sales each year when consumers purchase illegally copied, or "pirated," Hollywood DVDs, as well as counterfeit luxury products that purport to be from name brands such as Gucci, Chanel, Louis Vuitton, and Prada. The pirated American movies, music, and computer software produced in China alone cost legitimate businesses more than $2 billion in sales each year (LaFraniere, 2009). Although American law enforcement agencies can attempt—with limited success—to prevent the importation of counterfeit and pirated products, they can do little to prevent the manufacture of such products without the cooperation of authorities in the countries where the counterfeiters are located.

Although counterfeit consumer products impose significant costs on American businesses, far worse human costs result from the counterfeiting of another product: prescription drugs (Toscano, 2011). Technological advancements produced a sharp increase in counterfeit medications during the first decade of the twenty-first century. The discovery of counterfeit versions of specific medications increased from 5 different prescription and over-the-counter drugs per year in the late 1990s to more than 20 new counterfeit drugs per year beginning in 2000 (Grady, 2003). The dangers of counterfeit drugs are obvious: They can cause the deaths of patients who believe that they are taking genuine drugs, or prevent patients from recovering appropriately from nonfatal illnesses. In 2008, a counterfeit version of the blood-thinning drug heparin came to the United States from China and led to the deaths of 19 Americans as well as causing hundreds of serious allergic reactions (Bogdanich, 2008). The serious risks from counterfeit drugs include the following:

> Counterfeit drugs are worthless fakes passed off as genuine. They may contain inactive substances like tap water or chalk, wrong ingredients, incorrect dosages or contaminants. Expensive drugs for severe cases of cancer and AIDS have been among the targets. In one case, aspirin tablets were substituted for the schizophrenia drug, Zyprexa. (Grady, 2003)

Imagine needing immediate medications to fight a dangerous illness, but unknowingly receiving counterfeit drugs that will have no effect on the illness. This kind of illegal activity can easily kill vulnerable people. In 2012, a warning was issued that counterfeit vials of the best-selling cancer drug Avastin were turning up in hospital pharmacies (Associated Press, 2012b). These drugs represented exactly the type of worst-case situation in which a counterfeit product could lead to the deaths of people receiving medical treatments.

Because counterfeiting prescription drugs can be quite profitable, it has attracted organized-crime groups. In one case, criminals in Florida copied the packaging and labels of the anemia drug Procrit, which is used to treat people with cancer and AIDS. They diluted the dosages in some bottles and filled other bottles with water. Because Procrit sells for $500 per dosage bottle, the criminals gained an estimated $46 million in profit before the scheme was discovered (Grady, 2003).

The U.S. Food and Drug Administration (FDA) and other government agencies face significant challenges in finding and seizing counterfeit drugs. New efforts to inspect and supervise pharmaceutical production facilities in the United States and abroad and to track individual medications as they move from factory to pharmacy have sought to reduce the risks for the American public. Unfortunately, profit-seeking criminals are working just as hard to defeat any new monitoring systems that are developed to intercept counterfeits. The proliferation of Internet pharmacies, which sell prescription medications online, has presented new challenges. Such enterprises may be located outside the borders of the United States. FDA officials have worked to warn Americans against purchasing medications from online sources other than the websites of established pharmacy retail chains. However, because many Americans do not have medical insurance or have incomplete prescription drug coverage, some people will purchase medications inexpensively over the Internet, without being aware that they may be purchasing counterfeit drugs. Other people use online sources to seek medications, such as painkillers, for which they do not have legal prescriptions. These people face the potentially grave risks of ingesting fake medications.

check point 2. **What actions have been taken to combat counterfeit currency in the United States?**
Redesign of U.S. currency; efforts to detect counterfeit currency from the level of individual cashiers at stores to international investigations leading to the seizure of large quantities of fake currency.

3. **What harms are caused by counterfeit products in the United States?**
Billions of dollars in losses for American businesses because of counterfeit and pirated products; deaths and other harmful health consequences from counterfeit medications.

stop& analyze If you were the director of the U.S. Food and Drug Administration, what steps would you recommend to diminish the likelihood that counterfeit prescription drugs would reach American patients?

Policing and New Technology

Policing has long made use of technological developments. Twentieth-century police departments adopted the use of automobiles and radios in order to increase the effectiveness of their patrols, including better response time to criminal events and emergencies. Over time, technological advances also helped to provide better protection for police officers, including stronger, lighter bulletproof vests and protective features of patrol cars. Technology has affected the investigation of crime as well. As early as 1911, fingerprint evidence was used to convict an offender. Police officers have collected fingerprints, blood, fibers, and other crime-scene materials to be analyzed through scientific methods in order to identify and convict criminal offenders.

Police officers also use polygraphs, the technical name for lie detectors, that measure people's heart rates and other physical responses as they answer questions. Although polygraph results are typically not admissible as evidence, police officers have often used these examinations on willing suspects and witnesses as a basis for excluding some suspects or for pressuring others to confess.

Several issues arise as police adopt new technologies. First, questions about the accuracy and effectiveness of technological developments persist, even though the developments were originally embraced with great confidence. For example, despite the long and confident use of fingerprint evidence by police and prosecutors, its accuracy has been questioned. In 2002, a federal judge ruled that expert witnesses could compare crime-scene fingerprints with those of a defendant, but they could not testify that the prints definitely matched. The judge pointed out that fingerprint evidence processes have not been scientifically verified, the error rate for such identifications has never been measured, and there are no scientific standards for determining when fingerprint samples match (Loviglio, 2002). Prosecutors later persuaded the judge to reverse his original decision and admit the expert testimony about a fingerprint match, but the judge's first decision raises the possibility that other judges will scrutinize fingerprint evidence more closely.

Second, some worry that innovative technologies will create new collisions with citizens' constitutional rights. As police gain greater opportunities for sophisticated electronic surveillance, for example, new questions arise about what constitutes a search that violates citizens' reasonable expectations of privacy. For example, a technology that allows law enforcement agencies to intercept email messages raises questions about privacy that were not foreseeable in prior decades. Similarly, in several cities, police officers with DNA evidence from a rape have asked all of the men in a particular community to submit a DNA sample from inside the cheek in order to find a match with DNA of the perpetrator. Many critics believe that innocent citizens who have done nothing suspicious should not be pressured to provide the government with a sample of their DNA.

Communications and Computer Technology

Communications and the exchange of information serve as central elements in effective law enforcement. Dispatchers receive calls for service and bear responsibility for communicating citizens' immediate needs to patrol officers. In addition, police officers have traditionally relied on communication with dispatchers to obtain essential information, such as whether a particular car was stolen or whether a particular individual is being sought under an arrest warrant. New computer technology has altered both citizens' communications with dispatchers and police officers' reliance on their central headquarters. In addition, the use of computers and databases has enhanced the ability of law enforcement officers to investigate many kinds of crimes.

Communications   In many places, the number of calls to 911 emergency operators increased significantly as the spread of cell phones made it easier for people to call as incidents arose. In 1997, the Federal Communications Commission (FCC) set aside "311" as an option for cities to use as a nonemergency number. First Baltimore, then Detroit and New York, implemented the 311 call system, but many cities have not done so. The FCC later set aside "211" for social services information and "511" for traffic information, but relatively few cities have implemented call centers to use these numbers (McMahon, 2002). Although 911 systems can automatically trace the location of calls made from landlines, many cities are struggling to upgrade their 911 systems so that they can trace wireless calls to the vicinity of the nearest cell-phone tower (Reaves, 2010; Dewan, 2007). Such efforts to upgrade equipment, procedures, and training become more visible in the aftermath of tragedies. One such example is the murder of a University of Wisconsin student in 2008 who dialed 911 from her cell phone, apparently when confronted by an intruder in her apartment; the operator did not know her precise location or the nature of the emergency (Arnold, 2008). The 911 system remains the primary means for callers to reach their local government, but there are always concerns that those lines may become too tied up with emergency calls and thereby disrupt the ability of police and other emergency responders to receive quick reports about urgent situations.

Computers   The use of computers inside patrol cars has improved police efficiency and reduced officers' demands on central office dispatchers. Computers enable instant electronic communication that permits the radio airwaves to be reserved for emergency calls rather than being used for requests to check license numbers and other routine matters. Computer programs permit officers to type information about traffic violations, crime suspects, and investigations directly into central computers without filling out numerous, separate forms by hand. For example, new computers in the Lansing, Michigan, police department patrol cars permit officers to swipe the bar code on Michigan drivers' licenses to call up a driver's record instantly (M. Miller, 2009).

Officers can also gain quick access to information about automobile license plates and pending warrants (J. Fields and Peveto, 2008). For example, computer technology can reduce the time required for an officer to process a drunken-driving arrest from four hours to less than one hour and enable officers to ticket twice as many speeders. The computer-connected officers also made more felony and misdemeanor arrests, presumably because paperwork absorbed less of their time.

The increase in efficiency gained through the use of computers may give police administrators greater flexibility in deciding how to deploy officers on patrol. However, the new technology has its costs and consequences. Patrol-car computers can require increased time and money for training officers. They also raise safety issues in that the computers become dangerous projectiles within the vehicles during

Population Served	Percentage of Agencies Using Computers for:			
	Crime Analysis	Intelligence Gathering	Crime Mapping	Hot Spot Identification
All sizes	38%	40%	27%	13%
1,000,000 or more	100%	85%	100%	92%
500,000–999,999	100	90	100	100
250,000–499,999	100	93	100	80
100,000–249,999	96	82	94	66
50,000–99,999	88	72	82	56
25,000–49,999	69	63	60	31
10,000–24,999	53	49	41	19
2,500–9,999	37	42	23	9
Under 2,500	21	26	11	5

Source: Brian A. Reaves, *Local Police Departments, 2007* (Washington, DC: Bureau of Justice Statistics, December 2010), 22.

high-speed pursuits or collisions. In addition, because local police departments are under the control of local governments that do not possess equal resources, some departments cannot afford to purchase computers for patrol cars.

By 2007, more than 90 percent of departments in cities with 25,000 or more inhabitants used in-vehicle computers. A survey by the U.S. Bureau of Justice Statistics found that

> From 2003 to 2007, there was an increase in the percentage of local police officers employed by a department with in-field computer access to vehicle records (78% to 86%), driving records (71% to 80%), calls-for-service histories (39% to 65%), and criminal histories (39% to 56%) (Reaves, 2010:7).

From these figures, we can see that the availability of communications and information technology is expanding, yet it still varies depending on departmental resources. Table 14.2 shows how differences in resources affect police officers' computer access and capabilities. These categories focus on police departments' computer usage and is not limited to in-vehicle computers.

As mentioned, patrol-car computers enhance police officers' investigative capabilities through quick access to databases and other sources of information that help identify suspects. Depending on the software used and the organization of databases, many officers can make quick checks of individuals' criminal histories, driving records, and outstanding warrants (Reaves, 2010). With more-advanced computers and software, some officers can even receive mug shots and fingerprint records on their computer screens. Advances in technology provide a variety of possibilities for improving officers' ability to evaluate evidence at the scene of an event. With mobile scanners, officers can potentially run a quick check of an individual's fingerprints against the millions of fingerprint records stored in the FBI's database (Pochna, 2002). The Seal Beach, California, Police Department has worked with high-tech companies to develop streaming video capabilities that can permit officers to view live video from crime-scene cameras as they approach the location of an incident. For example, officers using their computers to access surveillance cameras in banks and convenience stores can see the details of a robbery in progress

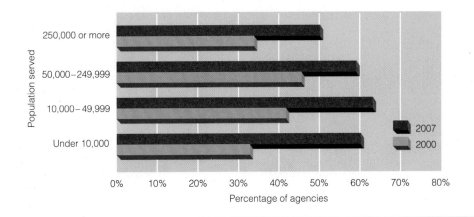

Figure 14.1
**Local Police Departments
Using Video Cameras in
Patrol Cars, 2000 and 2007**
Source: Brian A. Reaves, *Local Police
Departments, 2007* (Washington,
DC: Bureau of Justice Statistics,
December 2010), 21.

as they approach the scene (Cisco Systems, 2002). Thus, technology can improve the safety and effectiveness of police officers, especially in their crime-fighting role.

One snapshot of the speed with which the use of Patrol-car technology is expanding is represented in Figure 14.1. Note how rapidly video cameras came into use in more and more patrol cars when this study was conducted a few years ago. Just imagine how much more technology has been put into use today.

Computers have become very important for investigating specific types of crimes, especially cyber crimes (Hinduja, 2004). Many police departments have begun to train and use personnel to investigate people who use computers to meet children online with the intention of luring them into exploitative relationships (Bundy, 2012). As we have seen, computer investigations also involve pursuing people who commit identity theft, steal credit card numbers, and engage in fraudulent financial transactions using computers (J. Collins, 2005). At the national level, federal officials must use computers to detect and prevent sophisticated efforts to hack into government and corporate computer systems in order to steal secrets or harm critical infrastructures, such as regional electrical systems and emergency warning systems (Kilgannon and Cohen, 2009; Markoff, 2009).

Computers are also essential for crime analysis and crime mapping, methods used with increasing frequency by local police departments. Through the use of **Geographic Information System (GIS)** technology and software, police departments can analyze hot spots, crime trends, and other crime patterns with a level of sophistication and precision that was previously unavailable (Ratcliffe, 2010). By analyzing the locations and frequencies of specific crimes, such as burglary, or the nature of calls for service in various neighborhoods, police are better able to deploy their personnel effectively and plan targeted crime-prevention programs (Stroshine, 2005).

Another promising computerized tool for police is a system for detecting gunshots, quickly analyzing their location, and instantly communicating the information to police without reliance on human witnesses to dial the phone and guess where a shooting took place. These systems were originally developed for the military in order to identify the location of snipers. They operate through the use of sensors, installed in a neighborhood, that can distinguish gunshots from other sounds and detect the location of the gunshots through interaction with other sensors. The expensive systems have been used in specific neighborhoods within such cities as East Orange, New Jersey; Newport News, Virginia; and Roosevelt, New York (Domash, 2008; Holl, 2005).

Databases Computer technology permits law enforcement officials to gather, store, and analyze data. In minutes, or even seconds, computers can sort through data with the effectiveness that spares a user from spending hours combing through papers stored in a filing cabinet. For example, New York City detectives solved an armed robbery case in 2005 by taking a witness's description of the robber's tattoo and running it through the police department's computerized tattoo database. Very quickly, the detectives identified a suspect, showed his mug shot to the robbery victim, and tracked him down to make the arrest. The New York Police Department's database

Geographic Information System (GIS) Computer technology and software that permits law enforcement officials to map problem locations in order to understand calls for service and the nature and frequency of crimes and other issues within specific neighborhoods.

The development of databases and improvements in nationwide computer access to them help investigators identify suspects through DNA samples, fingerprints, tattoos, and other markers. Is there any information about Americans that should not be recorded in a centralized database?

MACON VALERIE/SIPA/Newscom

contains records on criminal complaints, warrants, 911 calls, individuals' criminal and parole records, and other kinds of property and public records (Hays, 2006).

In the discussion that follows, keep in mind that the accuracy and usefulness of any database, including that of New York, depend on the accurate input of correct information and methods to permit the information to be accessed efficiently by police officers. Human errors in database development and management can not only limit the usefulness of this technology but also wreak havoc on the lives of people whose information is misclassified. For example, since 9/11, many innocent people, including small children, have faced problems trying to board airplanes because their names were among the thousands on the Transportation Safety Agency's overly broad terrorist watch list. Even the late Senator Edward Kennedy of Massachusetts found himself denied plane tickets when the name "Edward Kennedy" appeared on the list (Sharkey, 2008; Swarns, 2004).

One of the largest and historically most important criminal justice databases is the fingerprint database. Police departments throughout the country can submit fingerprints from a crime scene in the hope of finding the criminal's identity from among the more than 47 million sets of fingerprints stored in the FBI computers. Local and federal law enforcement officials routinely submit the fingerprints of everyone arrested for a serious charge so that the prints can be added to the database. If a suspect is found not guilty, the prints are supposed to be removed from the system. These databases may also be used for background checks on people who work in regulated industries such as casinos and banks (Engber, 2005).

A few years ago, matching fingerprints was time consuming because fingerprints had to be sent to the FBI on cards. Since 1999, however, the Integrated Automated Fingerprint Identification System (IAFIS) has enabled police to send fingerprints electronically and then have those prints matched against the millions of prints in the database. The FBI can also provide electronic images of individuals' fingerprints to local law enforcement agencies upon request. Finally, the FBI provides training for state and local police on taking fingerprints and transmitting those prints to the IAFIS for evaluation.

The Department of Homeland Security has developed its own fingerprint database from two primary sources. New post-9/11 rules require the collection of fingerprints from every noncitizen entering the United States. This has created a database of more than 64 million fingerprints, which can be linked to the FBI database containing an additional 40 million sets. Military and intelligence officials are also collecting unidentified **latent fingerprints** from cups, glasses, firearms, ammunition, doorknobs, and any other objects that they find overseas in abandoned al-Qaeda training camps, safe houses, and battle sites. These prints are the patterned residue of natural skin secretions or contaminating materials such as ink, blood, or dirt that were present on the fingertips at the time of their contact with the objects. The hope is that terrorists will be identified if their fingerprints match those of visitors to the United States (Richey, 2006). As we shall see later in this chapter, DNA databases present similar hopes for identifying perpetrators, especially in domestic criminal cases (Eligon and Kaplan, 2012).

New debates have emerged about whether there should be a national database of ballistic evidence. Advocates argue that every gun sold should undergo a firing test so that its ballistic fingerprint can be stored in the database, just in case the weapon is later used in a crime. Opponents claim that this is an undesirable step toward national gun registration and that such a database would be useless because the ballistic characteristics of a gun's fired bullets change as the gun is used over time (Chaddock, 2002). The usefulness of these databases depends on the accuracy of technology to match evidence with stored information and the accessibility of database information to police departments and individual officers (M. A. Johnson, 2010). In addition, as indicated by the debate about ballistic evidence, the nature and use of evidence databases rely in part on public-policy debates about what information can be gathered and how it will be used.

check point

4. **How do computers in patrol cars aid officers in communication issues?**
   Officers do not need to tie up the radio airwaves and the attention of dispatchers to check on stolen cars, drivers' records, and other important information that can be accessed via computer.

5. **How can the use of Geographic Information Systems (GIS) assist criminal justice officials?**
   They can create sophisticated maps for the analyses of crime patterns and other problems in neighborhoods.

6. **What kinds of information can be collected in law enforcement databases?**
   Fingerprints, tattoos, DNA samples, gun/ballistics records.

stop & analyze

Are there other kinds of information that could be usefully stored in databases to help solve crimes? Are there any kinds of information that pose risks of error or risks to people's rights if kept in databases and used by the police?

DNA Analysis

In recent years, scientific advances have enabled police and prosecutors to place greater reliance on **DNA analysis**. This technique identifies people through their distinctive gene patterns (also called genotypic features). DNA, or deoxyribonucleic acid, is the basic component of all chromosomes; all the cells in an individual's body, including those in skin, blood, organs, and semen, contain the same unique DNA. The characteristics of certain segments of DNA vary from person to person and thus form a genetic fingerprint. Forensic labs can analyze DNA from, for example, samples of hair and compare them with those of suspects. As described by several law enforcement officials, the increasing effectiveness of DNA testing as an investigative tool has stemmed from "improved technology, better sharing of DNA databases among states and a drop in crime . . . that allowed detectives more

DNA analysis A scientific technique that identifies people through their distinctive gene patterns (also called genotypic features). DNA, or deoxyribonucleic acid, is the basic component of all chromosomes; all the cells in an individual's body, including those in skin, blood, organs, and semen, contain the same unique DNA.

Forensic Function	Total[a]	State	County	Municipal
Controlled substances	89%	88%	94%	85%
Firearms/toolmarks	59	60	59	56
Biology screening	57	58	61	51
Latent prints	55	50	51	76
Trace evidence	55	57	59	44
DNA analysis	53	55	61	42
Toxicology	53	57	49	47
Impressions	52	50	53	56
Crime scene	40	36	46	56
Questioned documents	20	18	22	24
Computer crimes	12	9	16	15
Number of labs reporting	351	207	79	55

[a] Includes federal labs, not shown separately

Source: Matthew R. Durose, "Census of Publicly Funded Forensic Crime Laboratories, 2005" Bureau of Justice Statistics *Bulletin*, July 2008, p. 3.

time to work on unsolved cases" (Yardley, 2006). Although fingerprint evidence is still used, advances in DNA technology have greatly reduced any reliance on the less-precise testing of blood and hair evidence as the sole means of identifying suspects.

Forensic science laboratories perform many kinds of scientific tests. As indicated in Table 14.3, many of these labs examine narcotics, firearms, and fingerprints as well as DNA. The information in Table 14.3 is from 2005, the last year for which the Bureau of Justice Statistics has data, so one might presume that the capacity of crime labs to do additional tests has expanded over time. However, the impact of government budget cuts has affected crime labs and led to reduced capability and longer delays in processing evidence for testing (M. A. Johnson, 2010). Alabama, for example, cut the annual funding for crime labs from $15 million to $9 million over the period of 2009 to 2012. Several crime labs were closed and toxicology tests statewide were directed to a single lab, leading to 90-day waiting periods for police departments to obtain results (Malone, 2012).

Although many publicly funded labs are not equipped to do DNA testing, DNA analysis has become especially important in criminal justice. It is revolutionizing the use of science for the investigation of crimes. Because scientists are increasing their capacity to extract testable DNA samples from tiny samples of biological material, law enforcement officials are increasingly able to tie specific individuals to a location or piece of evidence. When the local government lab is not able to conduct DNA tests, agencies hire private labs to do the analysis.

DNA Databases In spite of questions about which offenders should be required to submit DNA samples, many states and the federal government are building a national database of DNA records that is maintained by the FBI. Known as CODIS, which stands for Combined DNA Index System, the project began in 1990 as a pilot project serving a few state and local laboratories. CODIS has now grown to include 137 laboratories in 47 states and the District of Columbia.

The federal Justice for All Act, enacted in October 2004, greatly expanded the number of offenders in the federal justice system who must submit DNA samples. Previously, samples were taken only from those who had committed specific violent crimes. Later, collection expanded to federal offenders convicted of any felony, violent act, or conspiracy. In 2009, collection of DNA samples expanded further to all people arrested for federal crimes and all noncitizens who are detained (Weiss, 2008). The Federal Bureau of Prisons obtains DNA through blood samples from *all* incoming offenders. In addition, federal probation offices must now obtain samples under the newer law. Federal probation offices are scrambling to find qualified phlebotomists (people trained to draw blood samples), as well as to acquire enough test kits for thousands of additional offenders. Moreover, Congress mandated that the samples be collected but did not provide any funds for the probation offices within federal courts to collect these samples (Administrative Office of the U.S. Courts, 2005). Thus, the new requirement is causing budget problems in the justice system.

States have their own laws governing DNA and which people are required to submit a sample. Efforts are underway to expand the collection of samples. In 2012, for example, New York officials began to collect samples from all convicted offenders; previously the state's law mandated collection only for those convicted of specific offenses (Eligon and Kaplan, 2012). In 2008, Maryland joined a dozen other states in collecting samples from people arrested, but not yet convicted, for murder, rape, and assault (Arena and Bohn, 2008). California began taking samples from everyone arrested on felony charges in 2009, whether or not they are ultimately convicted of a crime (Felch and Dolan, 2008). Georgia instituted a new law in 2008 to permit investigators to compare DNA evidence with samples collected from suspects when a search warrant is obtained to require a subject to provide a sample. Previously, DNA evidence in Georgia could only be compared with samples taken from convicted felons (Armstrong, 2008). One southern California prosecutor regards DNA databases as such a useful resource for solving serious crimes that he began to dismiss some misdemeanor and drug charges against defendants if they would agree to provide a DNA sample. Skeptics questioned whether the so-called "spit and acquit" program was appropriate, because it permitted drug offenders to go free without any treatment (Weiss, 2009a). By 2009, every state except Idaho, Nebraska, and New Hampshire collected DNA samples from all convicted felons. An additional 15 states collected samples from people arrested, even if they have not been convicted of any crime, and 19 more had pending proposals in their legislatures to do the same (Protess, 2009).

Another proposal to expand the use of DNA testing and evidence concerns searches that look for relatives rather than the exact person whose DNA was left at the crime scene. Although only exact matches of crime-scene evidence and an individual's DNA are supposed to be used in court, it is possible to identify other suspects through wider comparisons. For example, DNA comparisons may indicate that a convicted felon whose sample is in the database is not the perpetrator of a rape, but that he is a relative of the rapist. Thus, police would have reason to undertake further investigations of the convicted felon's close male relatives. So-called "kinship-based DNA searching" is already used in Great Britain but is not used as widely in the United States (Wade, 2006).

By taking samples from people convicted of specific crimes in the state and federal systems, officials hope that CODIS will enable them to close unsolved crimes that involve DNA evidence. Unfortunately, problems and delays in collecting and processing the samples persist. Nonetheless, the use of DNA testing and databases has led to arrests in a growing number of unsolved cases.

Many examples illustrate the use of DNA identification to close cold cases. In March 2011, DNA tests on a discarded cigarette butt led to the arrest of a Connecticut man who was tied through DNA testing to 17 rapes in various eastern states from 1997 through 2009 (T. Moore, 2011). In April 2005, DNA tests linked a man in Georgia with 25 unsolved rapes in three states, including a rape committed in New York in 1973. The man had fled New York nearly 20 years earlier when facing different rape charges. He was eventually located when Georgia conducted a routine background

↑ Conducted-energy devices, such as Tasers, now give police officers the opportunity to subdue threatening people by using less-than-lethal force, when in prior years they might have used firearms. Because some people have died after being subjected to these alternative weapons, controversies exist about whether their use should be strictly limited to truly dangerous situations. Are there risks that new weapons technology will be used in the field without a full understanding of the harms that may be inflicted on people with specific medical conditions or other vulnerabilities?

pellets with green dye in order to mark and later arrest individuals in an out-of-control crowd (Randolph, 2001). Other weapons under development include one that shoots nets that wrap around individual suspects and another that sprays a fountain of foam that envelops the suspect in layers of paralyzing ooze. Law enforcement agencies may also eventually have versions of new weapons being developed for the military, such as devices that send out incapacitating blasts of heat or blinding flash explosions (Hambling, 2005). For example, a new military weapon called "Silent Guardian" shoots a focused beam of radiation that is tuned precisely to stimulate human pain nerves. It inflicts unbearable, incapacitating pain but, according to the inventors, does not cause injuries (Hanlon, 2007). A law enforcement version, if it worked as intended, could be an alternative to using lethal firearms in some situations.

For suspects who are close at hand, many police departments use CEDs—conducted energy devices—the most well-known of which is the Taser, a weapon with prongs that sends an incapacitating electric jolt of 50,000 volts into people on contact (Ith, 2001). Recent research found a rise in citizen injuries from the use of CEDs and urged greater attention to their use and their consequences (Terrill and Paoline, 2012). More than 12,000 law enforcement agencies in the United States use these devices. As a result, there is great potential for the devices to be used frequently. However, a study by Amnesty International found that more than 330 people died in the United States between 2001 and 2008 after being shocked by Tasers (Ferretti and Feighan, 2009). Nearly all of them were unarmed. Some of those who received shocks for failing to obey police commands reportedly suffered from mental or physical disabilities that impeded their ability to cooperate. The manufacturer of Tasers as well as some researchers dispute whether the device actually caused the deaths. Issues have also arisen about whether officers are too quick to use Tasers when they could use persuasion or other means to calm agitated or uncooperative people. The controversy reached a high point when Miami police officers used a Taser on a six-year-old child who was threatening to harm himself (CNN, 2004b). Thus, debates about Tasers and other electroshock devices will likely persist in the future, as when two unarmed teenagers in Michigan died after being tasered in separate incidents within a one-month period in 2009 (Ferretti and Feighan, 2009). A related controversy expanded in 2008 when lawsuits by Taser International, the device's manufacturer, succeeded in persuading a judge to throw out a county medical examiner's conclusion that the device had caused the death of a jail inmate. Some critics fear that such lawsuits may have a chilling effect on doctors and deter them from reporting findings about any links between the Taser and injuries or deaths experienced by those who receive electrical shocks from the device (Anglen, 2008).

The development of less-lethal weapons has undoubtedly saved officers from firing bullets in many situations in which they previously would have felt required to shoot threatening suspects. The use of CEDs may reduce overall injuries to officers and citizens (Bulman, 2010). However, as with all technologies, these weapons do not magically solve the problem of incapacitating suspects safely. Mechanical problems or misuse by the officer may make the new weapons ineffectual. In addition, officers may act too quickly in firing a less-lethal weapon during inappropriate situations. In such circumstances, needless minor injuries may be inflicted, or the targeted person may become more enraged and thus more threatening to the officers who later must transport the person to jail. Moreover, an officer can carry only so many weapons in his or her arms. The existence of less-lethal weapons will not ensure that such weapons are actually handy when officers must make difficult, on-the-spot decisions about how to handle a threatening situation.

check point 10. **What kinds of new weaponry have police employed?**
Less-lethal weapons including bean-bag projectiles, CEDs, and PepperBall projectiles.

stop& analyze Should all police officers submit themselves during training to receive the application of any less-than-lethal weapons that they might be called upon to use? Why or why not?

Technology in Courts and Corrections

Much of the investment in new technology has been directed toward surveillance equipment and investigation techniques, including DNA analysis, that will assist law enforcement officers in identifying and convicting criminal offenders. Although fewer resources have been directed toward technology in other segments of the criminal justice system, courts and corrections both face new issues and opportunities stemming from the use of technology.

Courts

Many local courthouses struggle to keep up with the processing of cases and the attendant consequences of case backlogs. One of the central issues for many busy courthouses is simply the matter of having case files up-to-date and readily available for judges, prosecutors, and defense attorneys. The volume of files in many courthouses can create storage and accessibility problems. There are only so many rooms and filing cabinets available for storing files in any building. Thus, older files may be moved to remote locations where they are not easily accessible and must be retrieved if a case is reexamined on appeal or through later motions concerning the discovery of new evidence and other matters.

Technology provides a mechanism for reducing the problems of "too much paper" in courthouse files. Many courts have moved toward **electronic file management** systems in which records are digitized and made available as computer files. Such systems typically also use electronic filing systems in which attorneys file motions and other documents via email rather than as traditional paper documents.

One example of a court moving toward a reduction in paper used for case processing is the state circuit court in Eaton County, Michigan. The prosecutors carry into the courtroom laptops that can wirelessly access police reports, 911 calls, court orders, and crime-scene photos. As noted by the county prosecutor, "We go to court with much more information than a prosecutor carrying a stack of files" (Grasha, 2009a). Gradually, other courts throughout the country are purchasing equipment and software to enable efficient access to information and to reduce the costs of producing and storing paper documents (Richter and Humke, 2011).

Computers can also help increase efficiency in judges' calculation of possible sentencing options. The development of sentencing guidelines has reduced judges' discretion for determining appropriate sentences. Instead, judges add up points, based on the offense and the prior record, to determine the sentence range mandated by the legislature. Private computer companies have developed software that will do sentencing calculations quickly for judges and for the probation officers who write presentence reports.

electronic file management Computerization of court records, done to reduce reliance on paper documents and make documents easily accessible to the judge and attorneys via computer.

Does relying on computer calculations pose any risks? Most basically, if incorrect numbers are included in the calculations, an improper sentence will be produced. For defendants with complex records, such as numerous arrests and probation violations, the person inputting the data could easily miscount arrests and reported probation violations in the score, even though the sentence is supposed to be based on the number of actual criminal convictions. More importantly, does the software program diminish the image of justice, giving the impression that sentencing occurs by machine? State judges are supposed to represent the community, delivering messages about justice on the community's behalf as they make rulings.

The presentation of evidence in court is changing through the introduction of new technology. Previously, lawyers presenting documents and objects as evidence often needed to carry them in front of jurors or have jurors pass them through the jury box. This meant that jurors often got only a fleeting glimpse of specific pieces of evidence. Now, many courthouses are developing electronic courtrooms, using presentation technologies that have long been used in business meetings. These mechanisms include projection screens or multiple monitors that permit jurors to study documents and photographs simultaneously. Websites of U.S. district courts often list the equipment available in each courtroom and instruct attorneys on how to use the equipment. For example, a partial list of equipment presented on one district court's website includes the following:

- *Evidence presentation cart,* containing
  Evidence camera
  Annotation monitor
  Microphone
  VCR
  Auxiliary connections
- *Counsel table,* containing
  PC connection
  Internet access
  Real-time court reporting connection

- *Jury box/plasma screen.* A 50-inch retractable plasma screen over the jury box can be lowered when needed.
- *Gallery.* Two monitors are located on the sides of the gallery to allow spectators to see evidence being presented during a court proceeding.
- *Side camera.* A side camera is located near the ceiling above the jury box. It is used to display demonstrative exhibits which may be placed on a tripod easel in front of the jury box or by the witness stand. Use of the side camera allows the judge, the witness, the jury, all counsel and those seated in the gallery to view the exhibit with ease.
- *Hearing assistance system.* Wireless headphones are available for use by the hearing impaired, or for language interpretation.
- *Color video printer.* The printer is available should counsel wish to print a displayed image for admission into evidence.

Such technologies are obviously useful in communicating more effectively to everyone in the courtroom. There are risks, however, that some uses of technology may distort rather than clarify an accurate understanding of the evidence. For example, the use of computer simulations raises issues about the accurate presentation of evidence.

Attorneys have traditionally attempted to use their words to "paint a picture" for the jurors. In a criminal case, the prosecutor and defense each presents their own version of a chain of events or the circumstances under which a crime allegedly occurred. It is entirely possible that, after hearing the same presentations, individual jurors will leave the courtroom with very different perceptions about what happened at the crime scene (McCormick, 2000). Contemporary attorneys have attempted to use computer technology to advance an image of their version of events. Much like realistic video games, similar realism has now been developed in computer-generated re-creations of crime scenes (McCormick, 2000). The jury may see, for example, a computer-generated film of a person being struck from behind or falling in a manner consistent with the victim's injuries. Yet, this film will be prepared in accordance with a particular version of events, the prosecutor's or the defendant's. There are risks that the realism of the re-created events on the screen will stick in the minds of jurors, even if the presentation is not an objective interpretation of the facts in the case (Schofield, 2011). Judges and attorneys must be wary about the use of such technologies if they may distort perceptions rather than contribute to accurate fact-finding.

Problems also arise through jurors' use of technology. Typically, a judge will tell jurors that they cannot investigate the facts of a case on their own. They are sometimes instructed not to read any articles in a newspaper about the case being presented before them. The widespread use of the Internet, however, makes seeking information about a case not only easy, but also quite tempting for some jurors. While a judge may hear if a juror attempted to visit a crime scene and thereby exclude the juror from the trial for misconduct, it is much more difficult to know whether jurors have sought information about a case through an Internet search. The use of such devices as iPhones and BlackBerrys has even enabled disobedient jurors to do their own research on a case during a lunch break in the middle of the attorneys' arguments. In one case in Florida, 8 out of 12 jurors eventually admitted that they had done their own Internet research on the case, including finding information that was excluded from presentation at trial through the rules of evidence. Thus, the judge had to declare a mistrial, and eight weeks of work by prosecutors and defense attorneys went to waste and the long, complex trial had to begin again after the selection of a new jury (Schwartz, 2009).

Problems have also arisen as jurors use blogs and social media sites to post announcements about the progress of a case or about jury deliberations. There is evidence that some jurors even send out messages by cell phone during breaks in the trial (Schwartz, 2009). Thus, judges have become more keenly aware of the need

CBS via Getty Images

↑ Many prosecutors and judges worry that the *CSI* effect may help guilty defendants go free if there is no DNA or other scientific evidence to use against them. Critics claim that the *CSI* effect is a myth that is perpetuated by prosecutors and the media. What evidence would you want to see in order to conclude whether or not the *CSI* effect exists?

CSI effect A widely discussed but unproved belief that television dramas revolving around forensic science raise jurors' expectations about the use of scientific evidence in criminal cases and thereby reduce the likelihood of "guilty" verdicts in trials that rely solely on witness testimony and other forms of nonscientific evidence.

to bar jurors from bringing cell phones to court as well as the need to give thorough and stern warnings about the rule against jurors conducting their own investigations. Under the adversary system, evidence is presented by the opposing attorneys who have been trained to respect the rules of evidence. Independent examinations of evidence by jurors acting as amateur detectives can enhance risks of inaccurate conclusions about facts. Because of media attention directed at the misbehavior of jurors in San Francisco, starting in 2012 California implemented a new law that authorized judges to impose jail sentences on jurors who used cell phones or other devices to either research a case or provide information to others about a case (Ward, 2011).

As described in the "Close Up" in Chapter 8, another potential impact of technology on jury trials is the so-called **CSI effect** that makes jurors unwilling to render "guilty" verdicts unless there is scientific evidence to link the defendant to the crime. Americans are fascinated by dramatized television programs that show the use of science for solving crimes and medical mysteries. According to a 2009 Harris Poll, the television show *CSI: Crime Scene Investigation* set in Las Vegas is Americans' all-time, favorite television series (Harris Poll, 2009). The show was so popular that the CBS network created two *CSI* spin-off shows, set in Miami and New York, respectively. The fourth most-popular show is *NCIS*, a parallel drama about the U.S. Navy's Criminal Investigative Service, which also portrays the use of forensic science. The third most-popular program, *House*, shows the use of science to solve medical mysteries (Harris Poll, 2009). Because these popular programs portray specialists using science to make definitive conclusions, many judges and prosecutors believe jurors now erroneously think that there should be DNA evidence, soil sample testing, and other scientific evidence in every criminal case (Toobin, 2007). In fact, the evidence in many cases consists of witness testimony, circumstantial evidence, and objects with no fingerprints or DNA on them. Moreover, the television programs show fictional situations in which experts instantly make accurate and definitive conclusions about a "match" between hair samples, fiber samples, handwriting samples, or other materials for which real forensic scientists have grave doubts about anyone's ability to make definitive identifications of suspects.

Students of criminal justice should regard claims about the *CSI* effect with caution. The claims emerge from individual prosecutors' and judges' feelings of surprise or disappointment with the decisions and questions of juries in particular cases. Moreover, because news stories have presented the *CSI* effect as if it were a real phenomenon, prosecutors and judges may merely assume that it has an impact when, in fact, it may not even exist.

In reality, the existence of any actual *CSI* effect remains the subject of debate (S. Stephens, 2007). Actual research on the *CSI* effect calls its existence into question (Podlas, 2006). Surveys indicate that jurors may expect to see specific kinds of scientific evidence, but this expectation may be related to a more general "tech effect" of American using technology in their daily lives rather than watching specific television shows. Moreover, the increased expectation for scientific evidence does not necessarily mean that jurors will not vote to convict a defendant without it (Huey, 2010). The debate about the *CSI* effect illustrates the possibility that decision making within the criminal justice system can be affected by popular perceptions and assumptions about the role of technology and science in the investigation of criminal cases.

11. How is technology employed in courthouses?
Electronic file management for records and presentation technology in courtrooms for displaying evidence.

12. How can technology disrupt jury trials?
Jurors using the Internet to investigate cases or use blogs and social media sites to reveal information about jury deliberations; risks of the so-called *CSI* effect.

stop& analyze Should one side in a case be permitted to present computer simulations in the courtroom if the other side—such as a poor defendant represented by a public defender—cannot afford to hire consultants who are experts in using technology?

Corrections

Many of the technologies previously discussed for policing and courts also have applications in corrections. Computerized record-keeping and statewide databases can reduce the burden of maintaining, storing, and transporting paper files on each prisoner. Instead, officials throughout the state can access records instantly via computer. In fact, many states have set up online records-retrieval systems that are accessible to the public. Often called OTIS (Offender Tracking Information Systems), these accessible databases permit crime victims to keep track of when specific offenders gain release on parole. They can also help employers to do background checks on job applicants. Separate public-access information systems often provide specific information on the residences of convicted sex offenders. Typically, members of the public can use the state correctional department's website to discover the identities and home addresses of sex offenders within a specific zip code. These databases are intended to warn people about the presence of a specific category of ex-convicts in their neighborhoods.

Public access to information about ex-offenders can cause serious problems. In Maine, Washington, and New Hampshire, individuals looked up the names and addresses of released sex offenders on a state database, then hunted them down and shot them. As we saw in Chapter 13, one of the murder victims in Maine was on the sex offender registry for the "sex crime" of misdemeanor sexual abuse because, as a 19-year-old youth, he had consensual sex with his girlfriend who was two weeks shy of making their sexual contact legal by reaching her sixteenth birthday (Ellement and Smalley, 2006). These crimes led to debates about which offenders should actually be listed in databases and whether such databases should be open to the public.

In correctional institutions, technology enhances safety and security through the use of such developments as electronically controlled cell doors and locks, motion sensors, surveillance cameras, and small radios attached to the shirts of correctional officers. Note that surveillance cameras are not always popular with correctional officers, because cameras also reveal whether officers are doing their jobs conscientiously and properly. There is also a big push in many prisons to provide body armor for correctional officers. Although the stiff vests may be uncomfortable and make upper-body movements less free and easy, they can save lives by protecting officers against being stabbed by inmates' homemade knives (U.S. Government Accountability Office, 2011).

Because security is the top priority for correctional institutions, most technology resources are devoted to this goal rather than on prisoners' vocational training and rehabilitation. In a fast-changing world, prisoners who face the challenges of reentry are often like Rip Van Winkle, the character in the Washington Irving short story who awakens after sleeping for 20 years and discovers many changes in the world. For a contemporary inmate emerging from prison after serving a long sentence, basic facts of modern life, such as email and cell phones, may be completely unknown or baffling. Released prisoners may also lack basic skills for modern employment, such as the rudimentary use of computers, word processing, and spreadsheet programs. Although new technologies change modern life, limited resources cause correctional officials to focus on improvements in security rather than on a fuller range of goals serving prisoners.

As in policing, technological developments increase the variety of less-lethal weapons that are available for correctional officers to use in subduing and controlling offenders who pose a threat to institutional safety or who attempt to escape. Corrections officers typically do not have weapons when they are working within the prison population because they can have weapons taken away from them as they are so outnumbered by the prisoners. In 2012, however, Michigan began issuing Tasers for corrections officers to improve safety by enabling officers to break up fights without putting themselves at risk by becoming physically involved in the conflict (Kloepfer, 2012). It remains to be seen if there are adverse consequences from the presence of the CED less-lethal weapons within the yard and cell blocks that are numerically dominated by prisoners.

The transportation of prisoners presents a daily challenge for officials at courts, jails, and prisons. People in custody must be moved from jails and prisons to courts for hearings. They must be transferred from jails to prisons and moved between different prisons when they begin to serve their sentences. New technologies have been developed to prevent prisoners from attempting to escape or otherwise misbehaving while being transported. The most controversial device is the remote-controlled stun belt that prisoners may be required to wear while being transported. The deputy or bailiff in control of the belt can deliver an excruciating 8-second, 50,000-volt jolt of electricity to prisoners. Americans became aware of the belts when a California prisoner, who was zapped in a courtroom at the order of a judge, filed a $50 million lawsuit. The prisoner had not attempted to escape or threaten anyone; he had merely talked too much when the judge had told him to be silent (Canto, 1998). The international human rights organization Amnesty International mounted a campaign to have the devices banned as torture (Amnesty International, 1999). Although the New York Corrections Department canceled an order for the devices, 25 state correctional departments and 100 county jails reportedly still use them.

Such devices may reduce the number of officers required to escort a prisoner, and they deter prisoners from misbehaving. However, such a jolt of electricity may kill some people if their heart rhythm is susceptible to disruption or if they hit their heads when they fall during the electric shock. There are also issues about whether officers will limit their use to appropriate circumstances.

One particularly important and expanding use of technology is the electronic monitoring of offenders within the community. Offenders in home confinement or "on tether" in the community wear various electronic devices that help monitor whether they obey curfews, remain at home, or otherwise fulfill restrictions about where they are permitted to be. Increasingly, local jails save money by charging fees to nonviolent offenders who choose to pay for electronic monitoring and home confinement rather than imposing expenses on the county for food and supervision by serving their misdemeanor sentences in jail (Grasha, 2009b). There is also expanded use of monitors with GPS capability to track the movements of criminal stalkers and perpetrators of domestic violence. Thus, law enforcement officials can be warned if individuals under restraining orders attempt to approach the homes of their victims (A. Green, 2009).

One aspect of technology that has created difficulties for corrections officials is the presence of smuggled cell phones in the possession of prisoners. Read the "Close Up" and consider the difficulties faced by corrections officials in stopping this prohibited use of technology by prisoners.

Cell Phones in Prisons

Correctional administrators throughout the United States face a significant problem involving technology: prisoners acquiring and using cell phones. Some prisoners argue that cell phones have a positive influence by permitting them to stay in close touch with their families. However, prison administrators ban cell phones because of major problems that have arisen with them, including prisoners communicating with associates outside the walls to arrange the murder of witnesses or to plan other crimes. There have also been issues involving prisoners calling victims and witnesses to threaten and harass them. Prisoners in Georgia used cell-phone communications to plan, coordinate, and carry out a prisoners' work stoppage at several facilities simultaneously.

The cell-phone problem is widespread. California confiscated 2,800 cell phones inside prison walls in 2008 and the number rose to 9,000 in 2010. The Federal Bureau of Prisons confiscated 1,188 cell phones in the first four months of 2010. Most cell phones that enter prisons are smuggled by corrections officers in exchange for money. One corrections officer in California admitted that he made more $100,000 in one year by selling cell phones to prisoners. Other cell phones are smuggled in by family members and other visitors. Family members pay the monthly charges that enable the cell phones to be

used. In some prisons, cell phones are thrown over prison fences at planned moments by outside accomplices, sometimes wrapped in a bundle of dirt and grass so that they will not be noticed in the prison yard. In 2010, President Obama signed a new law making it a crime punishable by one year in prison for an offender to possess a cell phone inside a federal prison.

Officials are developing new techniques to find illegal cell phones, in addition to old-fashioned physical searches of prisoner's personal possessions and bunk areas. In some states, dogs are being trained to sniff for cell-phone batteries during searches. Many corrections officials would like to use jamming technology to prevent cell phones from being used in prisons, but jamming violates federal law and could affect the phones of people living near prisons. Mississippi implemented a system that detects calls and texts going into and out of prisons. With the cooperation of cell-phone companies, a message is sent to the phone announcing that the device will be shut off and made unusable.

California officials believe that course of action could significantly reduce the cell-phone problem, combined with thorough searches of corrections officers as they enter the prison for each shift. However, employee searches would cost

millions of dollars in additional wages for corrections officers because the thousands of officers would have to be paid for several additional minutes each day as they remove their shoes and equipment in order to be searched.

Researching the Internet
Read the report submitted to Congress by the National Telecommunications and Information Administration concerning the problem of cell phones in prisons. To link to the website, visit the Criminal Justice CourseMate at cengagebrain.com, then access the web links for this chapter.

For Critical Analysis
In times of budget cuts, how will corrections officials be able to keep up with smuggled technology in prisons? Even if Mississippi's system proves to be effective, can other states afford to purchase new technology in order to combat prisoners' illegal cell phones? List three things you would do if you were in charge of solving the cell-phone problem.

Sources: Jack Dolan, "California Prison Guards Union Is Called Main Obstacle to Keeping Cellphones Away from Inmates," *Los Angeles Times*, February 4, 2011 (www.latimes.com); Tom McNichol, "Prison Cell-Phone Use a Growing Problem," *Time*, May 26, 2009 (www.time.com); Kim Severson and Robbie Brown, "Outlawed, Cellphones Are Thriving in Prisons," *New York Times*, January 2, 2011 (www.nytimes .com).

check point 13. **Corrections has several goals. Which of these goals is advanced by the use of technology?**
Technology is used for security, control surveillance, and record keeping, but technology resources are less likely to be devoted to rehabilitation.

stop & analyze If you were a prison warden, would you require corrections officers to wear body armor? How would you respond to their complaints that the vests are too hot in the summer and interfere with their mobility if they need to run to another part of the prison to respond to an urgent situation?

Current Questions and Challenges for the Future

As we have just seen, technological changes have affected nearly every agency and process within the criminal justice system. Most of this chapter's discussion has focused on new technological devices designed to assist officials with specific tasks. James Byrne (2008) classifies these devices as "hard technology" and contrasts them with the development of "soft technology," such as computer software for crime mapping and sentencing calculations. Both categories of technology are important for criminal justice. In some respects, the soft technology may present especially significant possibilities for affecting the performance of criminal justice officials, as computer experts invent new ways to gather and evaluate information that can be used for training, classification of offenders, assessing risk, and other important purposes. Table 14.4 shows examples of various hard and soft technological innovations that have affected each institutional segment of the criminal justice system.

There is no doubt that the desire for efficiency and effectiveness will lead to continued efforts to create new technologies and refine existing technologies to assist the police in their tasks. One can easily envision increased access to information through computers, better surveillance cameras and body scanners, and expanded use of GPS devices. In addition, there will be continued development and experimentation with less-lethal weapons, some of which are likely to be borrowed from those being developed by the U.S. military, including devices that rely on heat or light or sound to incapacitate threatening individuals.

In light of financial problems affecting state and local correctional budgets, there will inevitably be efforts to refine and expand the use of surveillance and monitoring technology to reduce the costs associated with confining lesser offenders. For example, the future will likely see the expanded use of ignition interlock systems for convicted drunken drivers. In this system, drivers blow into a tube set up in their car, and the engine starts only if they have not consumed alcohol. This can help prevent drunken driving without relying so heavily on incarceration for first offenders. New and expanded use of surveillance and control mechanisms may also improve officials' ability to monitor probationers, parolees, and other offenders under correctional supervision in the community.

As noted, technological developments produce risks, questions, and consequences beyond increased efficiency in carrying out tasks. Technological devices are operated by human beings who can make errors that affect the lives of others. What happens when a forensic scientist makes an error in conducting a test? What happens when incorrect information about an individual is entered into a database? With a perception that new weapons will not cause serious injury or death, are police officers more inclined to use CEDs, PepperBalls, and other less-lethal weapons in situations that might otherwise have been resolved through determined use of verbal warnings and other communications? These are important questions that arise with increasing frequency as we analyze events in which technology produced unintended and undesirable results.

Equally important are concerns about the impact of technology on the civil rights and liberties of individual Americans. In the post-9/11 era, there are already indications that some government officials will react to perceived threats by making use of available technology without necessarily planning for the protection of civil liberties or adherence to existing law. The administration of President George W. Bush, for example, secretly intercepted Americans' phone calls and emails without the court authorizations required under federal law (Sanger and Lichtblau, 2006). When Congress later granted limited authority to undertake such electronic surveillance of communications, the National Security Agency violated the law by intercepting calls that did not fall within the scope of the law (Lichtblau and Risen, 2009). Similar complaints arose concerning actions in the Obama administration

	Hard Technology	Soft Technology
Crime prevention	• CCTV • Street lighting • Citizen protection devices (e.g., Mace, Tasers) • Metal detectors • Ignition interlock systems (drunk drivers)	• Threat assessment instruments • Risk assessment instruments • Bullying ID protocol • Sex offender registration • Risk assessment prior to involuntary civil commitment • Profiling
Police	• Improved police protection devices (helmets, vests, cars, buildings) • Improved/new weapons • Less-than-lethal force (mobile/riot control) • Computers in squad cars • Hands-free patrol car control (Project 54) • Offender and citizen IDs via biometrics/fingerprints • Gunshot location devices	• Crime mapping (hot spots) • Crime analysis (e.g., COMPSTAT) • Criminal history data systems enhancement • Info sharing within CJS and private sector • New technologies to monitor communications (phone, mail, Internet) to/from targeted individuals • Amber alerts
Court	• The high-tech courtroom (computers, video, cameras, design features of buildings) • Weapon detection devices • Video conferencing • Electronic court documents • Drug testing at pretrial stage	• Case flow management systems • Radio frequency identification technology • Data warehousing • Automation of court records • Problem-oriented courts
Institutional corrections	• Contraband detection devices • Duress alarm systems • Language translation devices • Remote monitoring • Perimeter screening • Less-than-lethal force in prison • Prison design (supermax) • Expanded use of segregation units	• Use of simulations as training tools (mock prison riots) • Facial recognition software • New inmate classification systems (external/internal) • Within-prison crime analysis (hot spots; high-rate offenders) • Information sharing with police, community, victims, and community-based corrections (reentry)
Community corrections	• GPS for offender monitoring and location restriction enforcement • New devices (breathalyzers, instant drug tests, language translators, plethysmographs) • Polygraph tests (improved) • Laptops/GPS for line staff • Reporting kiosks	• New classification devices for sex, drugs, and MI [mentally ill] offenders • New workload software • New computer monitoring programs for sex offenders • Information with community police, treatment providers (for active offender supervision and for absconder location)

Source: James M. Byrne, "The Best Laid Plans: An Assessment of the Varied Consequences of New Technologies for Crime and Social Control," *Federal Probation* 72 (no. 3, 2008): 11.

after the PATRIOT Act was extended (Savage, 2011). As with other technologies, the means available could be misused in ways that violate Fourth Amendment restrictions on unreasonable searches and other rights under the Constitution. Read "A Question of Ethics" at the end of the chapter to consider what policies you would develop to address these issues.

Another large question looms. Have new technologies been effective in preventing crime and catching criminals? We know that certain technologies, such as DNA testing, have been highly effective in identifying individuals whose biological matter, such as blood or tissue, is found at a crime scene or on a weapon. It is less clear, however, that all of the surveillance, communications, and search technologies have produced entirely desirable benefits. For example, in pointing to declining clearance rates for homicide crimes, James Byrne concludes, "I would be hard pressed to offer an assessment of the positive effect of new technological innovations during this period given these data on police performance" (2008:14). The underlying point is that we know many new technologies expand the scope of social control by government through collecting information, watching and searching the citizenry, and providing new tools for police to use in coercing compliant behavior (as in CEDs). Are the costs of this social control justified? Can we use the benefits of technology without reducing the extent of Americans' freedom and privacy? These are questions that future criminal justice officials and policy makers must continually reexamine. They can do this through the systematic study of the performance of police, courts, and corrections as well as by evaluating the consequences for Americans' civil liberties.

check point ▷ **14. What questions about technology will bear watching in the future?**
How will government budget problems affect the use of technology? How will the risk of human errors affect the use of technology? How will technology impact civil rights and liberties? Are new technologies actually effective in preventing crime and catching criminals?

stop & analyze
If you were a governor or mayor struggling with difficult budget choices as tax revenues decline, what decisions would you make about technology affecting criminal justice? Would increasing the use of technology be a high priority for you? If so, what other aspects of the government budget would you cut to advance this priority? Among the various technologies currently available, which ones would you regard as especially worthy of additional expenditures from your budget? Why?

a question of ethics

Think, Discuss, Write

In 2011, newspaper stories described a dispute between the Michigan State Police and the American Civil Liberties Union (ACLU) over state troopers' reported use of forensic cell-phone analysis devices that can extract information from cell phones. The ACLU became aware that troopers used the devices to obtain information from drivers' cell phones at traffic stops, and the organization complained that such actions could constitute a violation of drivers' Fourth Amendment right against unreasonable seizures. Many members of the public did not know that such devices existed, let alone that the police could use them to quickly copy phone numbers, text messages, photos, and other information stored in people's cell phones and smartphones.

The State Police initially refused to provide information to the ACLU about their use of the devices. Amid growing public attention, the agency issued a statement saying that the devices are only used when they have a search warrant or when the cell-phone owner consents to the search of the phone.

Discussion/Writing Assignment

Cell phones and smartphones may contain evidence of crimes, such as messages about drug trafficking or child pornography; thus law enforcement officials may be tempted to find out what information people have in their phones. However, the phones may also contain very personal messages and photos owned by innocent people who have no connection to crime. If you were the commander of the Michigan State Police, what policies would you put in place to ensure that your officers were not tempted to use the devices merely to undertake "fishing expeditions" on drivers' phones during traffic stops or other encounters with the public. Describe at least four policies and practices that you would recommend and explain your reasons for each one.

Source: "ACLU Concerned over Michigan State Police Extracting Data from Cellphones," *Los Angeles Times*, April 21, 2011 (www.latimes.com).

Understand how adaptation and belief in science can affect the use of technology

→ New technology can be employed by criminals as well as by criminal justice officials.

→ Criminal justice officials and the public must be wary of automatically assuming that new scientific developments will achieve their intended goals or will produce only desirable consequences.

Recognize the many aspects of cyber crime and counterfeiting

→ Cyber crime includes identity theft, Internet child pornography, hackers' theft of trade secrets, and destruction of computer networks.

→ Counterfeiting extends beyond currency and consumer goods to include dangerous and worthless fake prescription drugs.

Analyze the role of communications, computers, and databases in policing

→ Calls for service to police have expanded from 911 numbers to 311 and 211 for nonemergency purposes.

→ Computers in patrol cars have expanded police officers' access to information.

→ Police also use computers in crime mapping, gunshot detection systems, and investigation of cyber crimes.

→ Databases permit the collection and matching of information concerning fingerprints, DNA, tattoos, criminal records, and other useful data.

Describe developments and problems in DNA testing and new weapons technologies

→ DNA testing permits scientists to identify the source of biological material with a high degree of certainty.

→ Some crime labs have been careless and unethical in testifying about DNA results, and some prosecutors have opposed DNA testing that might benefit criminal defendants.

→ New less-lethal weapons such as CEDs (e.g., Tasers), PepperBalls, and other projectiles are used by police.

→ Less-lethal weapons have been involved in incidents that led to the deaths of individuals against whom the police used these weapons.

Understand the use of technology in courts and corrections

→ Courts use technology in computerized record-keeping and presentation of evidence.

→ Jurors' perceptions about forensic science and use of technology during trials may cause problems.

→ Correctional officials use technology for security purposes and for monitoring offenders in the community.

Recognize the continuing questions about the effects of technology on civil liberties

→ The expanded use of technology by government raises questions about the protection of Americans' rights.

→ There are questions about the extent to which many new technologies advance criminal justice goals and do not merely expand mechanisms for societal surveillance and control.

Questions for Review

1. How have criminals adapted to changes in technology?
2. How are computers used to investigate crimes?
3. What questions and problems arise from the development of new weapons for police?
4. What undesirable effects can science and technology have on jury trials?
5. How can GPS devices assist correctional officials?
6. How can the use of technology clash with Americans' expectations about rights, liberty, and privacy?

Key Terms and Cases

CSI effect (p. 458)

DNA analysis (p. 445)

electronic file management (p. 455)

Geographic Information System (GIS) (p. 443)

identity theft (p. 434)

latent fingerprints (p. 445)

less-lethal weapons (p. 453)

Kyllo v. United States (2001) (p. 452)

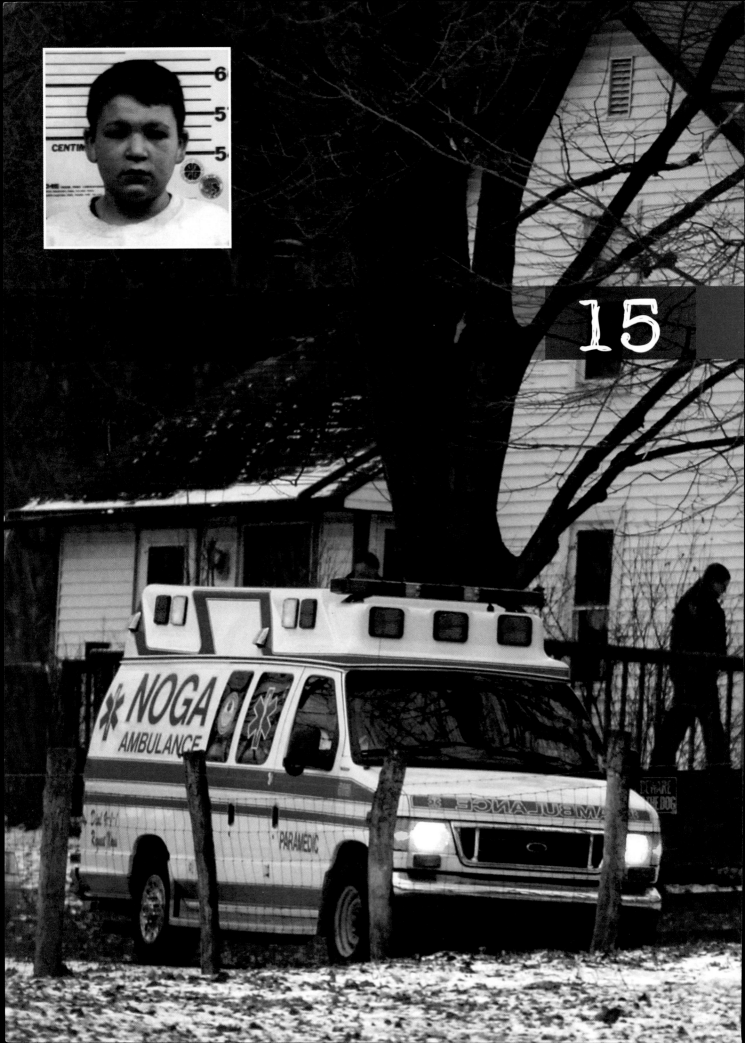

15

Juvenile Justice

Learning Objectives

→ Recognize the extent of youth crime in the United States

→ Understand how the juvenile justice system developed and the assumptions on which it was based

→ Identify what determines the jurisdiction of the juvenile justice system

→ Understand how the juvenile justice system operates

→ Analyze some of the issues facing the American system of juvenile justice

Jordan Brown's father gave him a shotgun on Christmas Day 2008, in the hopes of teaching the 11-year-old how to hunt. Two months later, Jordan used that shotgun to kill his father's fiancée, 26-year-old Kenzie Houk, in their home in New Bethlehem, Pennsylvania. At the time of the murder, Ms. Houk was eight months pregnant (J. L. Sherman, 2009).

The age of the alleged offender in this case is not the only reason for concern. After committing the murder, Jordan boarded the school bus and attended class as if it were a typical day. In addition, he left Houk's 4-year-old daughter behind to find her mother's body (Canning and Burbank, 2010).

Most states can choose to try juvenile offenders in either the juvenile court or adult courts, depending on the severity of their offense. In Pennsylvania, juveniles who commit murder are automatically charged as adults, but Brown's attorneys were able to move the case back to juvenile

court. In April 2012 Brown was found guilty as a juvenile, so he can only be incarcerated until the age of 21 (Associated Press, 2012a). If he had been tried in the adult court system, he could have received a life sentence for each murder (for both Kenzie Houk and her unborn child) with no possibility of parole (Poole, 2011).

Was this the best outcome for this case? Should a double murderer walk free after only ten years of incarceration? Or, should he have been incarcerated for the rest of his natural life? At 21 years old, will he still pose a danger to the community in which he lives? Alternatively, was the murder a one-time occurrence that would not be repeated? Should the justice system hold a juvenile to the same level of responsibility as an adult?

Although the juvenile justice system is separate from the adult criminal justice system, the key values of freedom, fairness, and justice undergird both systems. The formal processes of each differ mainly in emphasis, not in values. Although different, the systems are interrelated. One cannot separate the activities and concerns of policing, courts, and corrections from the problems of youth. With juveniles committing a significant portion of criminal offenses, officials in the adult system must pay serious attention to the juvenile system as well.

Youth Crime in the United States

In Nashville, a 16-year-old girl doing homework in her bedroom was hit by a bullet fired by another teenager, who was aiming for a pedestrian. Fifteen-year-old Michael Phelps shot a classmate at his middle school in Martinsville, Indiana. Police in Rimrock, Arizona, arrested five people running a methamphetamine lab, three of whom were juveniles. Such dramatic criminal acts make headlines. Are these only isolated incidents, or is the United States facing a major increase in youth crime?

The juvenile crime incidents just described are rare. In a nation with 74 million people under age 18, about 1.3 million arrests of juveniles occur each year, 59,000 of which (just over 4.5 percent) are for violent crimes (FBI, 2011a: Table 41). Murders committed by juveniles have decreased dramatically since 1993, when juveniles were responsible for 16 percent of all murder arrests; in 2009, this fell to 9 percent of all arrests for murder, which represents a record low for juvenile homicide (Snyder, 2011).

Youth crimes range from UCR Index Crimes (for example murder, rape, robbery, assault) to "youthful crimes" such as curfew violations, loitering, and being a runaway (see Figure 15.1). Consistent with the trends discussed above, although about 1.7 million delinquency cases were handled in the juvenile court in 2007, the decline in caseloads since the mid-1990s is the largest since 1960. Most juvenile crimes are committed by young men, but young women make up an increasing percentage of juveniles appearing in court. Between 1985 and 2007, the percentage of young women appearing in juvenile courts increased from 19 percent to 27 percent of all cases heard (Knoll and Sickmund, 2010).

Criminologists have tried to explain the rise of the "epidemic" of violent youth crime that erupted in the mid-1980s, reaching its peak in 1993. Among the explanations, two seem the most promising. One explanation uses a "cohort" approach, arguing that during the 1980s the increase in violence was due to an increase in the prevalence of exceptionally violent individuals—so-called "super predators." Critics of this approach, however, say that the birth cohort that peaked during the early 1990s was not at all exceptional with respect to involvement in violence in their younger years (P. J. Cook and Laub, 2002:2).

A second explanation focuses on environmental factors that influenced the rise in violent youth crime. Scholars holding this position point to the impact of the drug trade, especially crack cocaine and the related increase in gun use and possession by

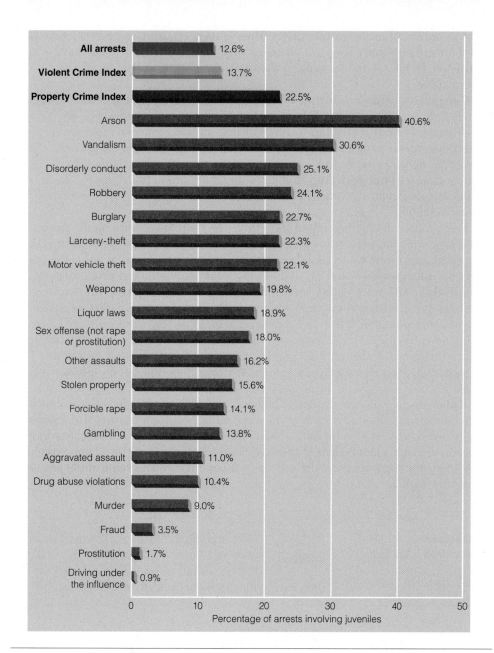

Figure 15.1

Percentage of Arrests of People under 18 Years Old (rounded) Juveniles are arrested for a wide range of offenses. For some offenses—such as arson, vandalism, motor-vehicle theft, and burglary—juveniles account for a larger proportion of arrests than the percentage of juveniles in the general population would suggest.

Source: Federal Bureau of Investigation, *Crime in the United States, 2010* (Washington, DC: U.S. Government Printing Office, 2011), Table 41.

youths. Alfred Blumstein (2002) suggests that as more juveniles, particularly inner-city minorities, were recruited into the drug trade, they armed themselves with guns and used those firearms in battles over market turf. Other factors may have also played a role—violent crime by youth was most prevalent in neighborhoods with deteriorating social and economic conditions. These changes led to increases in family instability and reductions in shared social expectations about behavior, particularly in minority neighborhoods (Strom and MacDonald, 2007).

Certainly, drug use by juveniles has significantly affected the juvenile justice system. From 1985 to 2009, the number of drug offense cases processed by juvenile courts increased from about 75,000 cases to almost 170,000 cases per year (Sickmund, Sladky, and Kang, 2012). In addition, drug use cases have skyrocketed for white juveniles, increasing 341 percent from 1984 to 2004 (compared with a 32 percent increase for African American juveniles). This has resulted in higher caseloads handled by juvenile courts in the past 20 years (Stahl, 2008).

Youth gangs are another factor explaining violent youth crime. Gangs such as the Black P. Stone Nation, CRIPS (Common Revolution in Progress), and Bloods first came to police attention in the 1970s. The National Youth Gang Survey estimates that there are now more than 27,900 gangs with 774,000 members, and that the most significant factor related to gang violence is drug activity (National Youth Gang Center, 2009).

Gangs are a primary source of fear and peril in many neighborhoods. A gang can destabilize neighborhood life, especially when gang members are armed. Youth gangs are not restricted to large cities—crackdowns on violence in cities sometimes force gangs into suburban areas (Sanchez and Giordano, 2008). Fear of being a crime victim can lead youths to seek protection through gang membership without realizing that gang members are actually more likely than other juveniles to be victims of violence and property crimes (Melde, Taylor, and Esbensen, 2009).

Many cities have developed programs to help deal with gang problems. Some programs focus on preventing youth from joining gangs, such as the GRYD (Gang Reduction and Youth Development) program in Los Angeles. Other programs focus on intervention—that is, identifying gang members and attempting to get them to leave the gang. Some researchers suggest that targeting the "core" gang members and limiting their involvement will result in the greatest decreases in gang violence (Maxson, 2011). Other programs focus on the community. In Chicago, "violence interrupters" get involved when gang violence erupts, attempting to reduce further violence and decreasing the risk of gang-related homicide. This program has been successful in several Chicago neighborhoods (Skogan et al., 2008).

Although juvenile delinquency, neglect, and dependency have been concerns since the nation's earliest years, not until the early twentieth century did a separate system to deal with these problems evolve. The contemporary juvenile justice system has gone through a major shift of emphasis as well. The rest of this chapter explores the history of juvenile justice, the process it follows today, and some of the problems associated with it.

check point > 1. **What might explain the epidemic of violent crime committed by juveniles in the 1990s?** Large youth cohorts, gun use related to drug sales, and gangs.

stop & analyze There appears to be a strong link between drug use and delinquency rates. What might you recommend to lawmakers to help reduce juvenile drug use, so that delinquency rates can be decreased?

The Development of Juvenile Justice

The system and philosophy of juvenile justice that began in the United States during the social reform period of the late nineteenth century was based on the idea that the state should act as a parent would in the interest of the child. This view remained unchallenged until the 1960s, when the Supreme Court ushered in the juvenile rights period. With the rise in juvenile crime in the 1980s, the juvenile justice system shifted again to one focusing on the problem of controlling youth crime. Today, people are again reexamining the philosophy and processes of the juvenile justice system.

The idea that children should be treated differently from adults originated in the common law and in the chancery courts of England. The common law had long prescribed that children under seven years of age were incapable of felonious intent and were therefore not criminally responsible. Children aged 7 to 14 could be held accountable only if it could be shown that they understood the consequences of their actions.

The English chancery courts, established during the Middle Ages, heard only civil cases, mainly concerning property. However, under the doctrine of ***parens patriae***, which held the king to be the father of the realm, the chancery courts exercised

parens patriae The state as parent; the state as guardian and protector of all citizens (such as juveniles) who cannot protect themselves.

TABLE 15.1 Juvenile Justice Developments in the United States

Period	Major Developments	Causes and Influences	Juvenile Justice System
Puritan 1646–1824	Massachusetts Stubborn Child Law (1646)	A. Puritan view of child as evil B. Economically marginal agrarian society	Law provides A. Symbolic standard of maturity B. Support for family as economic unit
Refuge 1824–1899	Institutionalization of deviants; House of Refuge in New York established (1825) for delinquent and dependent children	A. Enlightenment B. Immigration and industrialization	Child seen as helpless, in need of state intervention
Juvenile court 1899–1960	Establishment of separate legal system for juveniles; Illinois Juvenile Court Act (1899)	A. Reformism and rehabilitative ideology B. Increased immigration, urbanization, large-scale industrialization	Juvenile court institutionalized legal irresponsibility of child
Juvenile rights 1960–1980	Increased "legalization" of juvenile law; Gault decision (1967); Juvenile Justice and Delinquency Prevention Act (1974) calls for deinstitutionalization of status offenders	A. Criticism of juvenile justice system on humane grounds B. Civil rights movement by disadvantaged groups	Movement to define and protect rights as well as to provide services to children
Crime control 1980–2005	Concern for victims, punishment for serious offenders, transfer to adult court of serious offenders, protection of children from physical and sexual abuse	A. More-conservative public attitudes and policies B. Focus on serious crimes by repeat offenders	System more formal, restrictive, punitive; increased percentage of police referrals to court; incarcerated youths stay longer periods
"Kids are different" 2005–present	Elimination of death penalty for juveniles, focus on rehabilitation, states increasing age of transfer to adult court	A. *Roper v. Simmons* (2005) B. Scientific evidence on youth's biological, emotional, and psychological development	Recognition that juveniles are less culpable than adults

Sources: Portions adapted from Barry Krisberg, Ira M. Schwartz, Paul Litsky, and James Austin, "The Watershed of Juvenile Justice Reform," *Crime and Delinquency* 32 (January 1985): 5–38; U.S. Department of Justice, *A Preliminary National Assessment of the Status Offender and the Juvenile Justice System* (Washington, DC: U.S. Government Printing Office, 1980), 29.

protective jurisdiction over all children, particularly those involved in questions of dependency, neglect, and property. At this time, the criminal courts, not a separate juvenile court, dealt with juvenile offenders. In legitimizing the actions of the state on behalf of the child, however, the concept of *parens patriae* laid the groundwork for the development of juvenile justice.

Table 15.1 outlines the shifts in how the United States has dealt with the problems of youth. These shifts fall into six periods of American juvenile justice history. Each was characterized by changes in juvenile justice that reflected the social, intellectual, and political currents of the time. During the past 200 years, population shifts from rural to urban areas, immigration, developments in the social sciences, political reform movements, and the continuing problem of youth crime have all influenced how Americans have treated juveniles.

During the nineteenth century, reformers were alarmed by the living conditions of inner-city youths. Reformers in Chicago ushered in the juvenile justice system. Why should juveniles be treated differently than adults when they commit the same criminal acts?

The Puritan Period (1646–1824)

The English procedures were maintained in the American colonies and continued into the nineteenth century. The earliest attempt by a colony to deal with problem children was passage of the Massachusetts Stubborn Child Law in 1646. With this law, the Puritans of the Massachusetts Bay Colony imposed the view that the child was evil, and they emphasized the need of the family to discipline and raise youths. Those who would not obey their parents were dealt with by the law.

The Refuge Period (1824–1899)

As the population of American cities began to grow during the early 1800s, the problem of youth crime and neglect became a concern for reformers. Just as the Quakers of Philadelphia had been instrumental during the same period in reforming correctional practices, other groups supported changes concerning the education and protection of youths. These reformers focused their efforts primarily on the urban immigrant poor, seeking to have parents declared "unfit" if their children roamed the streets and were apparently "out of control." Not all such children were engaged in criminal acts, but the reformers believed that children whose parents did not discipline and train them to abide by the rules of society would end up in prison. The state would use its power to prevent delinquency. The solution was to create institutions where these children could learn good work and study habits, live in a disciplined and healthy environment, and develop "character."

The first of these institutions was the House of Refuge of New York, which opened in 1825. This half-prison, half-school housed destitute and orphaned children as well as those convicted of crime (Friedman, 1993:164). Similar facilities followed in Boston, Philadelphia, and Baltimore. Children were placed in these homes by court order usually because of neglect or vagrancy. They often stayed until they were old enough to be legally regarded as adults. The houses were run according to a strict program of work, study, and discipline.

Some states created "reform schools" to provide the discipline and education needed by wayward youth in a "homelike" atmosphere, usually in rural areas. The first, the Lyman School for Boys, opened in Westboro, Massachusetts, in 1848. A similar Massachusetts reform school for girls opened in 1855 for "the instruction . . . and reformation, of exposed, helpless, evil disposed and vicious girls" (Friedman, 1993:164). Institutional programs began in New York in 1849, Ohio in 1850, and Maine, Rhode Island, and Michigan in 1906.

Despite these reforms, children could still be arrested, detained, tried, and imprisoned. Even in states that had institutions for juveniles, the criminal justice process for children was the same as that for adults.

The Juvenile Court Period (1899–1960)

With most states providing services to neglected youth by the end of the nineteenth century, the problem of juvenile criminality became the focus of attention. Progressive reformers pushed for the state to provide individualized care and treatment to deviants of all kinds—adult criminals, the mentally ill, juvenile delinquents. They urged adoption of probation, treatment, indeterminate sentences, and parole for adult offenders and succeeded in establishing similar programs for juveniles.

Referred to as the "child savers," these upper-middle-class reformers sought to use the power of the state to save children from a life of crime (Platt, 1977). They shared a concern about the role of environmental factors on behavior and a belief that benevolent state action could solve social problems. They also believed the claim of the new social sciences that they could treat the problems underlying deviance.

Reformers wanted a separate juvenile court system that could address the problems of individual youths by using flexible procedures that, as one reformer said, "banish entirely all thought of crime and punishment" (Rothman, 1980:213). They put their idea into action with the creation of the juvenile court.

Passage of the Juvenile Court Act by Illinois in 1899 established the first comprehensive system of juvenile justice. The act placed under one jurisdiction cases of dependency, neglect, and delinquency ("incorrigibles and children threatened by immoral associations as well as criminal lawbreakers") for children under 16. The act had four major elements:

1. A separate court for delinquent, dependent, and neglected children
2. Special legal procedures that were less adversarial than those in the adult system
3. Separation of children from adults in all portions of the justice system
4. Programs of probation to assist the courts in deciding what the best interest of the state and the child entails

Activists such as Jane Addams, Lucy Flower, and Julia Lathrop, of the settlement-house movement; Henry Thurston, a social work educator; and the National Congress of Mothers successfully promoted the juvenile court concept. By 1904, ten states had implemented procedures similar to those of Illinois. By 1917, all but three states provided for a juvenile court.

The philosophy of the juvenile court derived from the idea that the state should deal with a child who broke the law much as a wise parent would deal with a wayward child. The doctrine of *parens patriae* again helped legitimize the system. Procedures would be informal and private, records would be confidential, children would be detained apart from adults, and probation and social workers would be appointed. Even the vocabulary and physical setting of the juvenile system were changed to emphasize diagnosis and treatment instead of findings of guilt. The term *criminal behavior* was replaced by *delinquent behavior* when referring to the acts of children. The terminology reflected the underlying belief that these children could be "cured" and returned to society as law-abiding citizens.

Because procedures were not to be adversarial, lawyers were unnecessary. The main professionals attached to the system were psychologists and social workers, who could determine the juvenile's underlying behavioral problem. These reforms, however, took place in a system in which children lacked the due process rights held by adults.

While the creation of the juvenile court was a positive development for juveniles in general, some contemporary researchers criticize the tendency for these reformers to hold different standards for girls and boys. For example, girls found guilty of the status offense of "promiscuity" were frequently incarcerated until adulthood (age 18) for their own protection. Boys were rarely charged with this type of offense.

The Juvenile Rights Period (1960–1980)

Until the early 1960s, few questioned the sweeping powers of juvenile justice officials. When the U.S. Supreme Court expanded the rights of adult defendants, however, lawyers and scholars began to criticize the extensive discretion given to juvenile justice officials. In a series of decisions (see Figure 15.2), the U.S. Supreme Court expanded the rights of juveniles.

In the first of these cases, *Kent v. United States* (1966), the Supreme Court ruled that juveniles had the right to counsel at a hearing at which a juvenile judge may waive jurisdiction and pass the case to the adult court.

In re Gault (1967) extended due process rights to juveniles. Fifteen-year-old Gerald Gault had been sentenced to six years in a state training school for making a prank phone call. Had he been an adult, the maximum punishment for making such a call

In re Gault (1967) Juveniles have the right to counsel, to confront and examine accusers, and to have adequate notice of charges when confinement is a possible punishment.

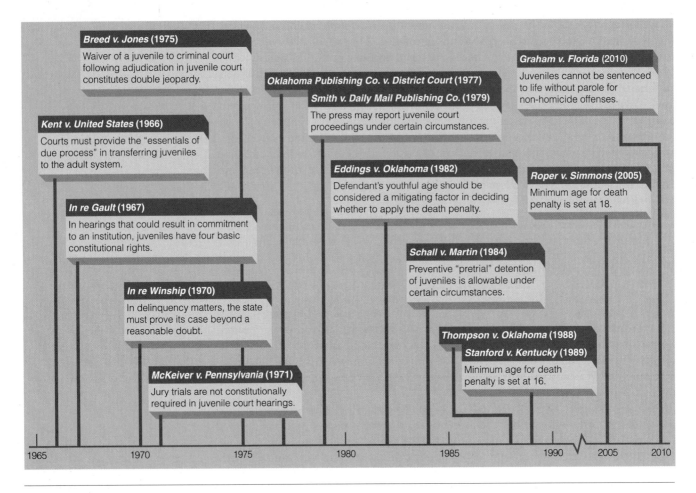

Figure 15.2

Major Decisions by the U.S. Supreme Court Regarding the Rights of Juveniles Since the mid-1960s, the Supreme Court has gradually expanded the rights of juveniles but has continued to recognize that the logic of the separate system for juvenile offenders justifies differences from some adult rights.

Note: For discussion of death penalty cases, see Chapter 9.

Sources: Office of Juvenile Justice and Delinquency Prevention, *1999 National Report* (Washington, DC: U.S. Government Printing Office, 1999), 90–91; *Roper v. Simmons*, 543 U.S. 551 (2005); *Graham v. Florida*, 130 S. Ct. 2011 (2010).

***In re Winship* (1970)** The standard of proof beyond a reasonable doubt applies to juvenile delinquency proceedings.

***McKeiver v. Pennsylvania* (1971)** Juveniles do not have a constitutional right to a trial by jury.

***Breed v. Jones* (1975)** Juveniles cannot be found delinquent in juvenile court and then transferred to adult court without a hearing on the transfer; to do so violates the protection against double jeopardy.

would have been a fine of $5 to $50 or imprisonment for two months at most. Gault was convicted and sentenced in an informal proceeding without being represented by counsel. The justices held that a child in a delinquency hearing must be given certain procedural rights, including notice of the charges, right to counsel, right to confront and cross-examine witnesses, and protection against self-incrimination. Writing for the majority, Justice Abe Fortas emphasized that due process rights and procedures have a place in juvenile justice: "Under our Constitution the condition of being a boy does not justify a kangaroo court."

The precedent-setting *Gault* decision was followed by a series of cases further defining the rights of juveniles. In the case of ***In re Winship* (1970)**, the Court held that proof must be established "beyond a reasonable doubt" and not on "a preponderance of the evidence" before a juvenile may be classified as a delinquent for committing an act that would be a crime if it were committed by an adult. The Court was not willing to give juveniles every due process right, however: It held in ***McKeiver v. Pennsylvania* (1971)** that "trial by jury in the juvenile court's adjudicative stage is not a constitutional requirement." But in ***Breed v. Jones* (1975)**, the Court extended the protection against double jeopardy to juveniles by requiring that, before a case is adjudicated in juvenile court, a hearing must be held to determine if it should be transferred to the adult court.

Another area of change concerned **status offenses**—acts that are not illegal if committed by an adult; these include skipping school, running away from home, and living a "wayward, idle or dissolute life" (Feld, 1993:203). In 1974, Congress passed the Juvenile Justice and Delinquency Prevention Act, which included provisions for taking status offenders out of correctional institutions. Since then, people have worked on diverting such children out of the system, reducing the possibility of incarceration, and rewriting status offense laws.

As juvenile crime rates continued to rise during the 1970s, the public began calling for tougher approaches in dealing with delinquents. In the 1980s, at the same time that stricter sanctions were imposed on adult offenders, juvenile justice policies shifted to crime control.

Although the courts expanded the definition of rights for juveniles, consider the state of teenagers' rights today as you read "Criminal Justice: Myth & Reality."

The Crime Control Period (1980–2005)

The public demand to "crack down on crime" began in 1980. Legislators responded in part by changing the juvenile system. Greater attention began to be focused on repeat offenders, with policy makers calling for harsher punishment for juveniles who commit crimes.

In **Schall v. Martin (1984)**, the Supreme Court significantly departed from the trend toward increased juvenile rights. The Court confirmed that the general notion of *parens patriae* was a primary basis for the juvenile court, equal in importance to the Court's desire to protect the community from crime. Thus, juveniles may be held in preventive detention before trial if they are deemed a "risk" to the community.

The *Schall* decision reflects the ambivalence permeating the juvenile justice system. On one side are the liberal reformers, who call for increased procedural and substantive legal protections for juveniles accused of crime. On the other side are conservatives, who are devoted to crime control policies and alarmed by the rise in juvenile crime.

Crime control policies resulted in many more juveniles being tried in adult courts. As noted by Alex Kotlowitz, "the crackdown on children has gone well beyond those accused of violent crimes" (1994:40). Data from the National Juvenile Court Data Archive show that delinquency cases waived to the adult criminal courts increased 83 percent from 1987 to 1994 (Snyder and Sickmund, 2006:186). In addition, some claim that increased penalties on juvenile offenders affect minority youth more than they do those who are white (Feld, 1999, 2003).

The "Kids Are Different" Period (2005–Present)

Some observers believe that a new period in juvenile justice may be developing. In *Roper v. Simmons* (2005), discussed in Chapter 9, the United States Supreme Court ruled that executions were unconstitutional for crimes committed by those younger than 18 years of age. This important ruling shepherded in a new era of juvenile justice. In *Roper*, the Court focused on the issue of culpability. The justices ruled that juveniles were less culpable than adults because of factors related to physical and emotional development that result from the growth and maturation process of the human brain (MacArthur Foundation, 2007c). Additional research

criminal justice **myth & reality**

Common Belief: With the exception of convicted criminal offenders, who have limited constitutional rights, all other Americans receive identical protections from the rights contained in the Constitution.

- The recognition and expansion of rights for youths in the justice system did not lead to equal application of rights for juveniles and adults.
- Some of the most obvious differences concern protections against unreasonable searches and seizures, especially in the context of public schools.
- The U.S. Supreme Court has approved school policies that mandate random drug testing for student athletes (*Vernonia School District v. Acton*, 1995) and for all other students participating in extracurricular activities (*Board of Education v. Earls*, 2002).
- Schools can mandate drug tests, which are considered searches under the Fourth Amendment, even if there is no reason to suspect wrongdoing by a student. By contrast, the Supreme Court forbade the state of Georgia from requiring drug testing of adult candidates for political office (*Chandler v. Miller*, 1997).
- Students possess some protections in schools. In 2009, the Supreme Court declared constitutional rights were violated when school officials strip-searched a teenage girl based on the false claim by another student that the student was carrying prescription-strength painkillers (*Safford Unified School District #1 v. Redding*, 2009).

status offense Any act committed by a juvenile that is considered unacceptable for a child, such as truancy or running away from home, but that would not be a crime if it were committed by an adult.

Schall v. Martin (1984) Juveniles can be held in preventive detention if there is concern that they may commit additional crimes while awaiting court action.

During the final decades of the twentieth century, the police and courts followed crime control policies in reacting to juvenile crime. Many legislators favor severe sentences for juveniles who commit serious crimes. Can the threat of long prison sentences deter juveniles from committing crimes?

JOE CAVARETTA/MCT/Landov

indicates that intellectual maturity occurs at age 16, but other factors (such as control over impulsiveness) are not fully developed until age 24 to 26. This growing recognition of teenage development provides a basis for new programs and proposed laws designed to treat juveniles differently than adults for purposes of treatment and punishment.

Emotional and intellectual development also plays a role in how juveniles understand (or fail to understand) their rights according to the Constitution, particularly with regard to their rights during questioning by police. As you can read in the "Close Up" feature, in 2011 a divided Court decided (*J. D. B. v. North Carolina*) that police must take age into account when explaining *Miranda* rights to juveniles. As stated by Justice Sotomayor, "[t]he law has historically reflected the same assumption that children characteristically lack the capacity to exercise mature judgment and possess only an incomplete ability to understand the world around them."

Current program trends aim at helping juvenile offenders through rehabilitation and the prevention of delinquency. Such programs are not yet widespread or fully developed. For example, there are few free substance-abuse programs for juveniles outside of correctional institutions. This means that a juvenile must be incarcerated to receive such assistance. Reducing drug use before it increases delinquency is important for limiting criminal behavior, so there is increasing interest in developing more programs that are accessible to youths in the community. Research is also focusing on the relationship between parents and children, and how parenting programs may help to keep kids out of juvenile court (MacArthur Foundation, 2007b).

waiver Procedure by which the juvenile court waives its jurisdiction and transfers a juvenile case to the adult criminal court.

Once popular, the use of judicial **waiver**, the process to waive juvenile court jurisdiction in order to move juveniles into adult court for prosecution and punishment, declined dramatically from 1994 to 2001, and has remained stable since then. This decrease in waiver mirrors the decrease in violent juvenile crime during that period (Adams and Addie, 2011). Recent changes in a few states indicate that waiver is becoming less popular. Several states are considering the abolition of juvenile waiver by increasing their minimum age for adult trial to 18. Research on public attitudes also indicates that U.S. citizens are becoming less supportive of waiver, and believe it should be used "sparingly and selectively" and only when the adult justice system is able to provide a rehabilitative component to punishment for juveniles (Applegate, Davis, and Cullen, 2009).

Courts are beginning to focus on the use of Life Without Parole, or LWOP, for juvenile offenders. In 2010, the Supreme Court decided in *Graham v. Florida* that the use of LWOP was unconstitutional for juveniles convicted of *non-homicide* offenses; however, only a small percentage of juveniles were then serving life sentences for non-homicide crimes (Graham himself was convicted of armed burglary and later violated the terms of his probation). Some legal scholars have argued that the "Kids are Different" philosophy should apply to all juveniles, even those convicted of serious crimes (Berkheiser, 2011). In 2012, the Court placed another limitation on sentences. In *Miller v. Alabama*, the majority ruled that juveniles cannot be subject to a mandatory LWOP sentence for *homicide* offenses.

In spite of the increasingly tough policies directed at juvenile offenders in the late twentieth century, changes that occurred during the juvenile rights period continue

J. D. B. v. North Carolina (2011)

Justice Sonia Sotomayor wrote the majority opinion on behalf of a narrow five-justice majority. Four dissenting justices, led by Justice Samuel Alito, strongly disagreed with the majority's treatment of juveniles as different than adult suspects for purposes of Miranda *warnings in this case. An early portion of Justice Sotomayor's opinion described the circumstances of the case:*

Petitioner J. D. B. was a 13-year-old, seventh-grade student attending class at Smith Middle School in Chapel Hill, North Carolina, when he was removed from his classroom by a uniformed police officer, escorted to a closed-door conference room, and questioned by police for at least half an hour.

This was the second time that police questioned J. D. B. in the span of a week. Five days earlier, two home break-ins occurred, and various items were stolen. Police stopped and questioned J. D. B. after he was seen behind a residence in the neighborhood where the crimes occurred. That same day, police also spoke to J. D. B.'s grandmother—his legal guardian—as well as his aunt.

Police later learned that a digital camera matching the description of one of the stolen items had been found at J. D. B.'s middle school and seen in J. D. B.'s possession. . . . [When the police arrived at the school to question J. D. B.,] neither the police officers nor the school administrators contacted J. D. B.'s grandmother. . . .

. . . The door to the conference room was closed. With the two police officers and the two administrators present, J. D. B. was questioned for the next 30 to 45 minutes. Prior to the commencement of questioning, J. D. B. was given neither *Miranda* warnings nor the opportunity to speak to his grandmother. Nor was he informed that he was free to leave the room.

Questioning began with small talk—discussion of sports and J. D. B.'s family life. [Officer] DiCostanzo asked, and J. D. B. agreed, to discuss the events of the prior weekend. Denying any wrongdoing, J. D. B. explained that he had been in the neighborhood where the crimes occurred because he was seeking work mowing lawns. DiCostanzo pressed J. D. B. for additional detail about his efforts to obtain work; asked J. D. B. to explain a prior incident, when one of the victims returned home to find J. D. B. behind her house; and confronted J. D. B. with the stolen camera. The assistant principal urged J. D. B. to "do the right thing," warning J. D. B. that "the truth always comes out in the end."

Eventually, J. D. B. asked whether he would "still be in trouble" if he returned the "stuff." In response, DiCostanzo explained that return of the stolen items would be helpful, but "this thing is going to court" regardless. ("[W]hat's done is done[;] now you need to help yourself by making it right"); DiCostanzo then warned that he may need to seek a secure custody order if he believed that J. D. B. would continue to break into other homes. When J. D. B. asked what a secure custody order was, DiCostanzo explained that "it's where you get sent to juvenile detention before court." (*Id.* , at 112a).

After learning of the prospect of juvenile detention, J. D. B. confessed that he and a friend were responsible for the break-ins. DiCostanzo only then informed J. D. B. that he could refuse to answer the investigator's questions and that he was free to leave. Asked whether he understood, J. D. B. nodded and provided further detail, including information about the location of the stolen items. Eventually J. D. B. wrote a statement, at DiCostanzo's request. When the bell rang indicating the end of the schoolday, J. D. B. was allowed to leave to catch the bus home.

A central issue in standard Miranda *warning cases is whether the suspect is "in custody" and not free to leave and therefore entitled to be given the warnings prior to questioning. Generally, adults are presumed to know that when they are not under arrest, they are generally free to leave. Justice Sotomayor addressed this issue with respect to J. D. B. in a decision that will affect how police are required to treat other juvenile suspects:*

Justice Sotomayor Delivered the Opinion of the Court.

This case presents the question whether the age of a child subjected to police questioning is relevant to the custody analysis of *Miranda v. Arizona*, 384 U.S. 436 (1966) . It is beyond dispute that children will often feel bound to submit to police questioning when an adult in the same circumstances would feel free to leave. Seeing no reason for police officers or courts to blind themselves to that commonsense reality, we hold that a child's age properly informs the *Miranda* custody analysis.

***

In some circumstances, a child's age "would have affected how a reasonable person" in the suspect's position "would perceive his or her freedom to leave." . . . That is, a reasonable child subjected to police questioning will sometimes feel pressured to submit when a reasonable adult would feel free to go. We think it clear that courts can account for that reality without doing any damage to the objective nature of the custody analysis.

. . . Such conclusions apply broadly to children as a class. And, they are self-evident to anyone who was a child once himself, including any police officer or judge.

Time and again, this Court has drawn these commonsense

(continued)

J. D. B. v. North Carolina (2011)

conclusions for itself. We have observed that children "generally are less mature and responsible than adults," . . . ; that they "often lack the experience, perspective, and judgment to recognize and avoid choices that could be detrimental to them," . . . ; that they "are more vulnerable or susceptible to . . . outside pressures" than adults, *Roper*, 543 U.S., at 569; and so on. . . . Addressing the specific context of police interrogation, we have observed that events that "would leave a man cold and unimpressed can overawe and overwhelm a lad in his early teens." *Haley v. Ohio*, 332 U.S. 596, 599 (1948) (plurality opinion); see also *Gallegos v. Colorado*, 370 U.S. 49, 54 (1962) ("[N]o matter how sophisticated," a juvenile subject of police interrogation "cannot be compared" to an adult subject). . . .

Our various statements to this effect are far from unique. The law has historically reflected the same assumption that children characteristically lack the capacity to exercise mature judgment and possess only an incomplete ability to understand the world around them. . . .

Justice Alito, with Whom the Chief Justice Roberts, Justice Scalia, and Justice Thomas Join, Dissenting

The Court's decision in this case may seem on first consideration to be modest and sensible, but in truth it is neither. It is fundamentally inconsistent with one of the main justifications for the *Miranda* rule: the perceived need for a clear rule that can be easily applied in all

cases. And today's holding is not needed to protect the constitutional rights of minors who are questioned by the police. . . .

. . . [T]here is no need to go down this road. First, many minors subjected to police interrogation are near the age of majority, and for these suspects the one-size-fits-all *Miranda* custody rule may not be a bad fit. . . .

***

The Court's rationale for importing age into the custody standard is that minors tend to lack adults' "capacity to exercise mature judgment" and that failing to account for that "reality" will leave some minors unprotected under *Miranda* in situations where they perceive themselves to be confined. I do not dispute that many suspects who are under 18 will be more susceptible to police pressure than the average adult. As the Court notes, our pre-*Miranda* cases were particularly attuned to this "reality" in applying the constitutional requirement of voluntariness in fact. It is no less a "reality," however, that many persons *over* the age of 18 are also more susceptible to police pressure than the hypothetical reasonable person. See *Payne,* 356 U.S., at 567 (fact that defendant was a "mentally dull 19-year-old youth" relevant in voluntariness inquiry). Yet the *Miranda* custody standard has never accounted for the personal characteristics of these or any other individual defendants.

Indeed, it has always been the case under *Miranda* that the unusually meek or compliant are subject

to the same fixed rules, including the same custody requirement, as those who are unusually resistant to police pressure. . . .

***

Researching the Internet

At the website of the Supreme Court of the United States blog (SCOTUS blog), read the arguments and research presented to the Supreme Court by the psychologists, psychiatrists, and social workers to demonstrate that "kids are different" and should be treated differently for purposes of criminal punishment. To link to this website, visit the Criminal Justice CourseMate at cengagebrain.com, then access the web links for this chapter.

For Critical Analysis

Justice Sotomayor's opinion now requires police officers to take into consideration the age of each juvenile suspect in deciding whether to provide *Miranda* warnings in situations where such warnings would not be required of adults. Justice Alito argued that there are many individuals, in addition to juveniles, who understand their rights less clearly than does the typical adult. He noted that the Court has never made exceptions before and that this new exception places officers in the difficult position of not knowing exactly when to provide the warnings. Alito believes that police officers can function more effectively with a single, clear rule that applies in all situations. Which opinion presents the strongest argument? Should juveniles be treated differently in these situations? Give three reasons why you believe one opinion is stronger than the other opinion.

to affect the system profoundly. Lawyers are now routinely present at court hearings and other stages of the process, adding a note of formality that was not present 30 years ago. Status offenders seldom end up in secure, punitive environments such as training schools. The juvenile justice system looks more like the adult justice system than it did, but it remains less formal. Its stated intention is also less harsh: to keep juveniles in the community whenever possible. The rulings in *Roper v. Simmons* and *Graham v. Florida* may indicate further changes away from tough policies.

check point

2. **What were the major elements of the Illinois Juvenile Court Act of 1899?**

A separate court for delinquent, dependent, and neglected children; special legal procedures that were less adversarial than in the adult system; separation of children from adults throughout the system; programs of probation to assist judges in deciding what is in the best interests of the child.

3. **What was the main point of the *In re Gault* decision?**

Procedural rights for juveniles, including notice of charges, right to counsel, right to confront and cross-examine witnesses, and protection against self-incrimination.

stop & analyze

The Supreme Court has been deeply divided over the issue of whether sentences of death for murder and life without parole for non-homicide offenses are out of step with the values of contemporary society. Do you think modern society values would reject such sentences for juveniles? If you were a lawyer, what evidence could you use to attempt to demonstrate that current values either reject or accept such harsh sentences for juveniles?

The Juvenile Justice System

Juvenile justice operates through a variety of procedures in different states; even different counties within the same states vary. Because the offenses committed by juveniles are mostly violations of state laws, there is little federal involvement in the juvenile justice system. Despite internal differences, the juvenile justice system is characterized by two key factors: (1) the age of clients and (2) the categories of cases under juvenile instead of adult court jurisdiction.

Age of Clients

Age normally determines whether a person is processed through the juvenile or adult justice system. The upper age limit for original juvenile court jurisdiction varies from 16 to 18. In 39 states and the District of Columbia, it is the 18th birthday; in 10 states, the 17th; and in the remaining 2 states, the 16th. In 45 states, judges have the discretion to transfer juveniles to adult courts through a waiver hearing. Figure 15.3 shows the age at which juveniles can be transferred to adult court.

Categories of Cases under Juvenile Court Jurisdiction

Four types of cases fall under the jurisdiction of the juvenile justice system: delinquency, status offenses, neglect, and dependency. Mixing together young criminals and children who suffer from their parents' inadequacies dates from the earliest years of juvenile justice.

Delinquent children have committed acts that if committed by an adult would be criminal—for example, auto theft, robbery, or assault. Juvenile courts handle about 1.6 million delinquency cases each year. Males are most frequently in court, representing 73 percent of delinquency cases. Among the criminal charges brought before the juvenile court, 24 percent are for crimes against the person, 37 percent for property offenses, 11 percent for drug law violations, and 27 percent for public-order offenses (Knoll and Sickmund, 2011).

Recall that status offenses are acts that are illegal only if they are committed by juveniles. Status offenders have not violated a penal code; instead, they are charged with being ungovernable or incorrigible: as runaways, truants, or **PINS** (persons in need of supervision). Status offenders make up about 10 percent of the juvenile court caseload. Although female offenders account for only 27 percent of delinquency cases, they make up 42 percent of the status offense cases (Puzzanchera, Adams, and Sickmund, 2011).

delinquent A child who has committed an act that if committed by an adult would be a criminal act.

PINS Acronym for *person(s) in need of supervision*, a term that designates juveniles who are either status offenders or thought to be on the verge of trouble.

Figure 15.3
The Youngest Age at Which Juveniles May Be Transferred to Adult Criminal Court by Discretionary Waiver of Juvenile Jurisdiction The waiver provisions of states vary greatly, and no clear regional or other factor explains the differences.

Source: Patrick Griffin, "Transfer Provisions," *State Juvenile Justice Profiles* (Pittsburgh: National Center for Juvenile Justice, 2010).

neglected child A child who is receiving inadequate care because of some action or inaction of his or her parents.

dependent child A child who has no parent or guardian or whose parents cannot give proper care.

Some states do not distinguish between delinquent offenders and status offenders; they label both as juvenile delinquents. Those judged to be ungovernable and those judged to be robbers may be sent to the same correctional institution.

Beginning in the early 1960s, many state legislatures attempted to distinguish status offenders and to exempt them from a criminal record. In states that have decriminalized status offenses, juveniles who participate in these activities may now be classified as dependent children and placed in the care of child-protective agencies.

Juvenile justice also deals with problems of neglect and dependency. Some children are hurt through no fault of their own because their parents have failed to provide a proper environment for them. People see the state's proper role as acting as a parent to a child whose own parents are unable or unwilling to provide proper care. Illinois, for example, defines a **neglected child** as one who is receiving inadequate care because of some action or inaction of his or her parents. This may include not being sent to school, not receiving medical care, being abandoned, living in an injurious environment, or not receiving some other care necessary for the child's well-being. A **dependent child** either has no parent or guardian or is receiving inadequate care because of the physical or mental disability of the parent. The law governing neglected and dependent children is broad and includes situations in which the child is viewed as a victim of adult behavior.

Nationally, about 75 percent of the cases referred to the juvenile courts are delinquency cases; one-fifth of these are for status offenses. Twenty percent are dependency and neglect cases, and about 5 percent involve special proceedings, such as adoption. The system, then, deals with both criminal and noncriminal cases. Often, juveniles who have done nothing wrong are categorized, either officially or in the public mind, as delinquents. In some states, little effort is made in pre-judicial detention facilities or in social service agencies to separate the classes of juveniles.

4. What are the jurisdictional criteria for the juvenile court?

The age of the youth, usually under 16 or 18, and the type of case—delinquency, status offense, neglect, or dependency.

stop& analyze

Why do most state laws use 18 as the age of majority? Is there something special that occurs at age 18 that indicates a shift from "juvenile" to "adult"? Would you use a specific age, or design some tests of knowledge and maturity or some other basis for deciding whether to try an older teen as a juvenile or adult? Why?

The Juvenile Justice Process

Underlying the juvenile justice system is the philosophy that police, judges, and correctional officials should focus primarily on the interests of the child. Prevention of delinquency is the system's justification for intervening in the lives of juveniles who are involved in either status or criminal offenses.

In theory at least, juvenile proceedings are to be conducted in a nonadversarial environment. The juvenile court is to be a place where the judge, social workers, clinicians, and probation officers work together to diagnose the child's problem and select a treatment program to attack that problem.

Juvenile justice is a bureaucracy based on an ideology of social work. It is staffed primarily by people who think of themselves as members of the helping professions. Not even the recent emphasis on crime control and punishment has removed the treatment philosophy from most juvenile justice arenas. However, political pressures and limits on resources may stymie the implementation of this philosophy by focusing on the punishment of offenders rather than the prevention of delinquency. Politicians may view increased spending for rehabilitative programs as being "soft on crime," even though the public is more supportive of using money for prevention programs and rehabilitation than for funding continued use of incarceration (Nagin et al., 2006).

Like the adult system, juvenile justice functions within a context of exchange relationships between officials of various government and private agencies that influence decisions. The juvenile court must deal not only with children and their parents, but also with patrol officers, probation officers, welfare officials, social workers, psychologists, and the heads of treatment institutions, all of whom have their own goals, perceptions of delinquency, and concepts of treatment.

Figure 15.4 outlines the sequence of steps that are taken from police investigation to correctional disposition. As you examine this figure, compare the procedures with those of the criminal justice system for adults. Note the various options available to decision makers and the extensive discretion that they can exercise.

Police Interface

Many police departments, especially in cities, have special juvenile units. The juvenile officer is often selected and trained to relate to youths, knows much about relevant legal issues, and is sensitive to the special needs of young offenders. This officer also serves as an important link between the police and other community institutions, such as schools and other organizations serving young people. As discussed in Chapter 5, some communities hire *school resource officers* (SROs), who provide counseling and a security presence in school buildings. There is debate about whether SROs actually reduce crime in schools (Na and Gottfredson, 2011), but some research reports that SROs provide students with a positive image of police and increase student likelihood of reporting problems (Finn and McDevitt, 2005).

Most complaints against juveniles are brought by the police, although an injured party, school officials, and even the parents can initiate them as well. The police must make three major decisions with regard to the processing of juveniles:

Figure 15.4

The Juvenile Justice System

Decision makers have more options for the disposition of juvenile offenders, compared with options in the criminal justice system for adults.

Source: National Advisory Commission on Criminal Justice Standards and Goals, *Report of the Task Force on Juvenile Justice and Delinquency Prevention* (Washington, DC: Law Enforcement Assistance Administration, 1976).

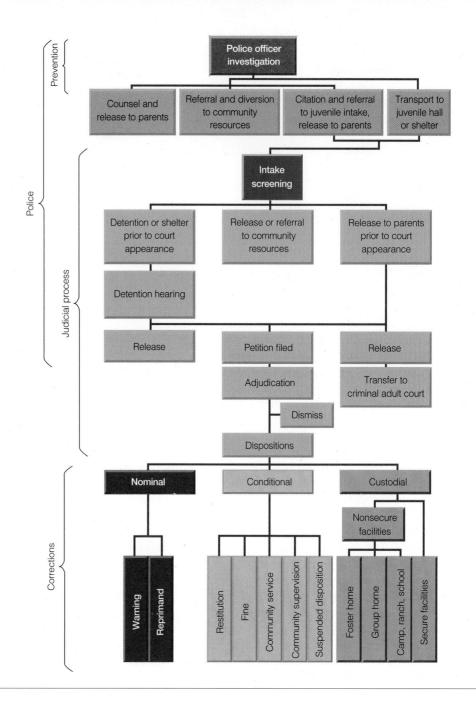

1. Whether to take the child into custody
2. Whether to request that the child be detained following apprehension
3. Whether to refer the child to court

The police exercise enormous discretion in these decisions. They do extensive screening and make informal adjustments in the street and at the station house. In communities and neighborhoods where the police have developed close relationships with the residents or where policy dictates, the police may deal with violations by giving warnings to the juveniles and notifying their parents. Figure 15.5 shows the disposition of juveniles taken into police custody.

Initial decisions about what to do with a suspected offender are influenced by such factors as the predominant attitude of the community; the officer's attitude toward the juvenile, the juvenile's family, the offense, and the court; and the officer's conception of his or her own role. The disposition of juvenile cases at the arrest stage also relies on the seriousness of the offense, the child's prior record, and his or her

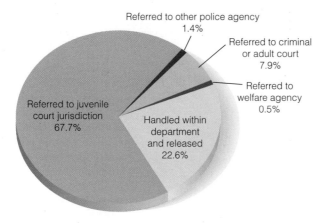

Referred to other police agency
1.4%

Referred to criminal
or adult court
7.9%

Referred to
welfare agency
0.5%

Referred to juvenile
court jurisdiction
67.7%

Handled within
department
and released
22.6%

Figure 15.5
Disposition of Juveniles Taken into Police Custody
The police have discretion in the disposition of juvenile arrest cases. What factors can influence how a case is disposed?
Source: Federal Bureau of Investigation, *Uniform Crime Reports, 2010* (Washington, DC: U.S. Government Printing Office, 2011), Table 68.

demeanor. To summarize, several key factors influence how the police dispose of a case of juvenile delinquency:

1. The seriousness of the offense
2. The willingness of the parents to cooperate and to discipline the child
3. The child's behavioral history as reflected in school and police records
4. The extent to which the child and the parents insist on a formal court hearing
5. The local political and social norms concerning dispositions in such cases
6. The officer's beliefs and attitudes

Although young people commit many serious crimes, the juvenile function of police work is concerned largely with order maintenance. In most incidents of this sort, the law is ambiguous, and blame cannot easily be assigned. Many offenses committed by juveniles that involve physical or monetary damage are minor infractions: breaking windows, hanging around the business district, disturbing the peace, public sexual behavior, and shoplifting. Here, the function of the investigating officer is not so much to solve crimes as to handle the often legally uncertain complaints involving juveniles. The officer seeks both to satisfy the complainant and to keep the youth from future trouble. Given this emphasis on settling cases within the community instead of strictly enforcing the law, the threat of arrest can be used as a weapon to deter juveniles from criminal activity and to encourage them to conform to the law.

diversion The process of screening children out of the juvenile justice system without a decision by the court.

Intake Screening at the Court

The juvenile court processing of delinquency cases begins with a referral in the form of a petition, not an arrest warrant as in the adult system. When a petition is filed, an intake hearing is held, over which a hearing officer presides. During this stage, the officer determines whether the alleged facts are sufficient for the juvenile court to take jurisdiction or whether some other action would be in the child's best interest.

Nationally, 44 percent of all referrals are disposed of at this stage, without formal processing by a judge. **Diversion** is the process of screening children out of the system without a decision by the court, thereby limiting their involvement in the formal juvenile justice system (Hamilton et al., 2007). In 42 percent of these cases, the charges are dismissed; another 23 percent are diverted to an informal probation, and 35 percent are dealt with through some agreed-on alternative sanction (Puzzanchera and Kang, 2011).

© Joe Tabacca

↑ The concept of restorative justice has been extended to juveniles. At the Red Hook Youth Court in New York, a 15-year-old arrested for spraying graffiti sits before a jury of his peers with a 16-year-old acting as the judge. The court deals with minor offenses, often where formal charges have not yet been brought. Officials say that 85 percent of the offenders complete restitution, ranging from community service to letters of apology. Is this an effective way to deal with youthful offenders?

Intake Referee

Kia Loggins, Intake Referee, Circuit Court—Family Division, Lansing, Michigan

Photo provided by Kia Loggins. © Cengage Learning

An intake referee conducts preliminary inquiries and preliminary hearings regarding juvenile delinquency petitions, traffic violations (such as "minor in possession of alcohol" or "no operator's license"), and abuse and neglect matters. An intake referee takes testimony, investigates family situations, determines probable cause, and decides appropriate legal action. In a hearing, a referee might have to determine the custody of minors, prepare preliminary orders, or assign the case to a juvenile court officer for further investigative work or supervision. When a case is resolved informally, the intake referee must recommend appropriate community-based services such as counseling, community service, behavioral groups, or other diversion programs.

Kia Loggins studied criminal justice as an undergraduate and counseling as a graduate student. In college, she sought out a wide range of volunteer and internship opportunities to gain experience in juvenile justice. For example, she served as a juvenile court tutor and as an intern in a residential program for troubled boys. After college, she worked in a juvenile detention facility before becoming a juvenile probation officer. She subsequently spent several years working for a nonprofit organization that provides training and consulting services for staff members at juvenile detention facilities throughout the country. By the time she had the opportunity to become an intake referee, Loggins had gained professional experience in many aspects of the juvenile justice system.

The most challenging aspect of my job is working with parents or teens who are not willing to improve themselves but are quick to blame the system. In that situation, I must make the best decision possible while hoping that some positive seeds of change will be planted in the process.

Would you want to undertake the important and difficult responsibility of determining what should be done with juveniles taken into custody by the police? Consider this question as you read "Careers in Criminal Justice."

Pretrial Procedures

When a decision is made to refer the case to the court, the court holds an initial hearing. Here, the juveniles are informed of their rights and told that if a plea is given it must be voluntary.

detention hearing A hearing by the juvenile court to determine if a juvenile is to be detained or released prior to adjudication.

If the juvenile is to be detained pending trial, most states require a **detention hearing**, which determines if the youth is to be released to a parent or guardian or to be held in a detention facility until adjudication. Some children are detained to keep them from committing other crimes while awaiting trial. Others are held to protect them from the possibility of harm from gang members or parents. Still others are held because, if released, they will likely not appear in court as required. Nationally, about 20 percent of all delinquency cases involve detention between referral to the juvenile court and disposition of the case (Sickmund, Sladky, and Kang, 2012).

The conditions in many detention facilities are poor; abuse is often reported. In some rural areas, juveniles continue to be detained in adult jails even though the federal government has pressed states to hold youths in separate facilities. In 2003, the city of Baltimore unveiled a new juvenile detention facility, meant to expedite juvenile cases and centralize services to delinquent youth. After its opening, the facility was called a "monstrosity," with poor lines of sight (officers cannot easily observe and supervise the juvenile detainees), overcrowding, and increasing rates of violence within its walls (Bykowicz, 2008). Independent evaluations have determined that the high rates of violence in the facility have begun to decrease, but slowly (Dedel, 2010). Baltimore is considering the construction of another facility designed to hold juveniles charged as adults, but this effort has been met with controversy (Fujii, 2012).

Believing that detaining youths accelerates their delinquent behaviors, some jurisdictions have attempted to stem the tide of rising numbers of juveniles in detention. Indianapolis has implemented a program to increase the use of diversion and send more youths home to live with their families while awaiting trial. This attempt has reduced both the number of incarcerated youths and delinquency rates (Murray, 2008).

Transfer (Waiver) to Adult Court

One of the first decisions to be made after a juvenile is referred is whether a case should be transferred to the criminal (adult) justice system. In 45 states, juvenile court judges may waive their jurisdiction. This means that, after considering the seriousness of the charge, the age of the juvenile, and the prospects of rehabilitation, the judge can transfer the case to adult court. In 29 states, certain violent crimes such as murder, rape, and armed robbery are excluded by law from the jurisdiction of the juvenile courts. In 1970, only three states allowed prosecutors the authority to decide whether to file in adult or juvenile court. Today, 15 states give prosecutors the authority to do so (P. Griffin, 2011). Critics question whether prosecutors will "make better informed and more appropriate 'criminal adulthood' decisions than would judges in an adversarial waiver hearing" (Feld, 2004:599). See "What Americans Think" for a look at public attitudes about transferring juveniles to the adult court.

After a "tougher" approach to juvenile crime took hold in the 1970s, the number of cases transferred increased dramatically. Several states expanded their ability to transfer juveniles by excluding certain crimes from juvenile court jurisdiction, or lowering the minimum age for transfer to adult court. The likelihood of waiver varies by seriousness of offense, offender age, and offender race. African American youths are more likely to be waived than are white youths (Sickmund, Sladky, and Kang, 2012). This disparity can be affected by offending patterns (that is, which offenses are more frequently committed by which youths) as well as by the risk of biased decision making.

One result of the increased use of the waiver was that more juveniles were being sent to adult state prisons. Between 1985 and 1997, the number doubled from 3,400 to 7,400 (Austin, Johnson, and Gregoriou, 2000). As the use of waiver subsequently declined, so, too, did the number of juveniles sent to prison. From 1997 to 2002, there was a 45 percent decline in the number of new admissions of offenders under age 18 into state prisons (Snyder and Sickmund, 2006). Critics of the policies claim that waiver subverts the intent of the juvenile justice system and exposes juvenile offenders to harsh conditions in adult prisons—where they are susceptible to physical and sexual victimization (DeJong and Merrill, 2000). In addition, those juveniles tried in adult courts are more likely to reoffend after release (MacArthur Foundation, 2007a). There is also evidence that increased use of waiver has had no effect on juvenile crime rates (Steiner, Hemmens, and Bell, 2006; Steiner and Wright, 2006). Transferring juveniles to be tried in the adult courts remains controversial, as outlined in "The Policy Debate."

what americans think

Question: "Currently, most juvenile offenders are handled in the juvenile justice system. How much would you approve of eliminating this system and handling all juvenile offenders in the same system used for adults?"

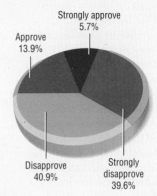

Strongly approve
5.7%

Approve
13.9%

Disapprove
40.9%

Strongly disapprove
39.6%

Critical Thinking: If Americans overwhelming believe that there should be separate justice processes for juveniles, do you believe that they would also support investing more resources in the *prevention* of delinquency by juveniles? What are two examples of programs for which taxpayers might support additional investment? What are two programs that are unlikely to gain public support? Is the key to public support the cost of the program? The effectiveness of the program? Or some other factor?

Source: Dan Mears, Carter Hay, Marc Gertz, and Christina Mancini, "Public Opinion and the Foundation of the Juvenile Court," *Criminology* 45 (2007): 223–57.

⬆ The juvenile waiver process permits juveniles to be sent to adult court and receive the same punishments as adults for serious crimes—except for the death penalty and life without parole for non-homicide offenses. Here a juvenile suspect is led from the courthouse after being charged with murder.

Should Juvenile Offenders Be Tried as Adults?

Arrests of juveniles for violent crimes more than doubled between 1988 and 1994. Since their peak in 1994, juvenile violent-crime arrests have declined, yet cases still come up that are so serious that the public demands severe punishment. Youths are also the primary victims of violent crime. Experts cite the availability of guns, the prevalence of urban youth gangs, and the problem of drugs as the causes of violent youth crimes.

In the face of crimes such as schoolyard shootings, the public has loudly called for "getting tough with these young hoods." Politicians and criminal justice planners have urged that steps be taken to ensure that juveniles accused of serious crimes be dealt with in the adult courts.

For Trying Juveniles as Adults

Those who want to make trying juveniles as adults easier point not only to the high levels of violence but also to the heinous nature of some crimes committed by youths. They see the juvenile courts as "coddling" these young predators. Often, only when a youth is transferred to the adult system is his or her long record of felonies revealed—felonies for which the juvenile court ordered little punishment. They say that criminal acts of violence by juveniles requires that offenders be dealt with swiftly and quickly so as to deter the upcoming generation from following in the footsteps of their older siblings.

The arguments for trying serious juvenile offenders in the adult criminal justice system include these:

- Violence by juveniles is a serious problem and must be dealt with in a swift and certain manner.
- Juvenile courts have not been effective in stemming the tide of violence by young people.
- Procedures for waiving juvenile jurisdiction are cumbersome in many states.
- Justice demands that heinous crimes, regardless of the age of the accused, be dealt with to the full extent the law provides.

Against Trying Juveniles as Adults

Although they recognize that serious youth crime is a problem, many experts believe that trying juveniles as adults only makes things worse. They point out that treating adolescents as adults ignores the fact that they are at a different stage of social and emotional development. They argue that children should not be held to the same standards as adults. In an increasingly violent world, children need help to navigate the temptations and threats of adolescence.

The arguments against trying serious juvenile offenders in the adult criminal justice system include these:

- The juvenile justice system is better able to deal with the social and emotional problems of young offenders.

- The basic foundations of criminal law recognize that children carry diminished responsibility for their acts.
- Punishing juveniles in adult institutions robs them of their childhood and threatens their future.
- The problem of violent crime by juveniles must be dealt with by changing the environment within which they live.

What Should U.S. Policy Be?

Under pressure to "do something" about violent juvenile crime, legislators have proposed that the age of adulthood be lowered and that the cases of serious offenders be tried in the adult criminal justice system. Is this the best way to protect community safety—to punish youthful offenders in the adult criminal justice system? Is the juvenile corrections system equipped to treat and guide juvenile offenders in a way that will return them to their communities as productive people?

 Researching the Internet

You can read the article "Delinquents or Criminals: Policy Options for Young Offenders" by visiting the Criminal Justice CourseMate at cengagebrain.com, and then accessing the web links for this chapter.

For Critical Analysis

What are the likely consequences—for both the individual offender and society—of trying juveniles as adults? What are the likely consequences of trying these offenders in the juvenile courts?

Adjudication

Juvenile courts deal with almost 1.6 million delinquency cases a year (Knoll and Sickmund, 2011). *Adjudication* is the trial stage of the juvenile justice process. If the child has not admitted to the charges and the case has not been transferred to the adult court, an adjudication hearing is held to determine the facts in the case and, if appropriate, label the juvenile as a "delinquent."

The Supreme Court's decision in *Gault* and other due process rulings mandated changes that have altered the philosophy and actions of the juvenile court. Contemporary juvenile proceedings are more formal than those of the past, although still more informal than adult courts. The parents and child must receive copies of petitions with specific charges; counsel may be present, and free counsel can be appointed if the juvenile cannot pay; witnesses can be cross-examined; and a transcript of the proceedings must be kept.

TABLE 15.2 The Adult and Juvenile Criminal Justice Systems

Compare the basic elements of the adult and juvenile systems. To what extent does a juvenile have the same rights as an adult? Are the different decision-making processes necessary because a juvenile is involved?

	Adult System	Juvenile System
Philosophical assumptions	Decisions made as a result of adversarial system in context of due process rights	Decisions made as a result of inquiry into needs of juvenile within context of some due process elements
Jurisdiction	Violations of criminal law	Violations of criminal law, status offenses, neglect, dependency
Primary sanctioning goals	Retribution, deterrence, rehabilitation	Retribution, rehabilitation
Official discretion	Widespread	Widespread
Entrance	Official action of arrest, summons, or citation	Official action, plus referral by school, parents, other sources
Role of prosecuting and defense attorneys	Required and formalized	Sometimes required; less structured; poor role definition
Adjudication	Procedural rules of evidence in public jury trial required	Less formal structure to rules of evidence and conduct of trial; no right to public trial or jury in most states
Treatment programs	Run primarily by public agencies	Broad use of private and public agencies
Terminology	Arrest	Referral
	Preliminary hearing	Intake
	Prosecution	Adjudication
	Sentencing	Disposition
	Parole	Aftercare

Application of Bill of Rights amendments

		Adult System	Juvenile System
Fourth	Unreasonable searches and seizures	Applicable	Applicable
Fifth	Double jeopardy	Applicable	Applicable (re: waiver to adult court)
	Self-incrimination	Applicable (*Miranda* warnings)	Applicable
Sixth	Right to counsel	Applicable	Applicable
	Public trial	Applicable	Applicable in less than half of states
	Trial by jury	Applicable	Applicable in less than half of states
Fourteenth	Right to treatment	Not applicable	Applicable

© Cengage Learning

As with other Supreme Court decisions, local practice may differ sharply from the procedures spelled out in the high court's rulings. Juveniles and their parents often waive their rights in response to suggestions from the judge or probation officer. The lower social status of the offender's parents, the intimidating atmosphere of the court, and judicial hints that the outcome will be more favorable if a lawyer is not present are reasons the procedures outlined in *Gault* might not be followed. The litany of "getting treatment," "doing what's right for the child," and "working out a just solution" may sound enticing, especially to people who are unfamiliar with the intricacies of formal legal procedures. In practice, then, juveniles still lack many of the protections given to adult offenders. Some of the differences between the juvenile and adult criminal justice systems are listed in Table 15.2.

The increased concern about crime has given prosecuting attorneys a more prominent part in the system. In keeping with the traditional child-saver philosophy,

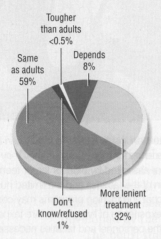
Institutions for juvenile offenders are classified as either nonsecure or secure. *Nonsecure* placements (foster homes, group homes, camps, ranches, or schools) include a significant number of nonoffenders—youths referred for abuse, neglect, or emotional disturbance. *Secure* facilities, such as reform schools and training schools, deal with juveniles who have committed crimes and have significant personal problems. Most secure juvenile facilities are small, designed to hold 40 or fewer residents. However, many states have at least one facility holding 200 or more hard-core delinquents who are allowed limited freedom. Because the residents are younger and somewhat more volatile than adults, behavioral control is often an everyday issue, and fights and aggression are common. Poor management practices can lead to difficult situations.

Boot camps for juvenile offenders saw a growth spurt in the early 1990s. By 1997, more than 27,000 teenagers were passing through 54 camps in 34 states annually. However, as with boot camps for adults, the results have not been promising. A national study shows that recidivism among boot camp attendees ranges from 64 percent to 75 percent, slightly higher than for youths sentenced to adult prisons (Blair, 2000). Additionally, reports of mistreatment of inmates at juvenile boot camps prompted the U.S. House of Representatives to develop standards of care for such inmates (J. Abrams, 2008). States are rethinking their policies, with many closing their programs.

The Survey of Youth in Residential Placement (SYRP), conducted in 2003, showed that 43 percent of juveniles were incarcerated for violent offenses, 44 percent were under the influence of alcohol or drugs at the time of their arrest, and 45 percent were living with only one parent when they were taken into custody. Also, 85 percent of the residents were male, the percentages of African Americans (32 percent) and Hispanics (24 percent) were greater than the percentages of those groups in the general population, and the majority (57 percent) had been suspended from school in the same year of their entry into the juvenile justice system (Snyder and Sickmund, 2006). Figure 15.6 shows the types of offenses of juveniles in public correctional facilities.

The contemporary budget crises led to major funding cuts for state juvenile justice agencies around the United States. For example, the state of New York cut 371 juvenile justice workers from its payroll in 2011 (J. Campbell, 2011); New Hampshire cut the majority of funding for its CHINS (Children in Need of Services) program (Fahey, 2011); and Fresno County, California, is considering the partial closure of a juvenile facility built only five years ago (K. Alexander, 2011). It is unclear how these cuts will impact the rate of juvenile delinquency in these areas, but the lack of treatment options for juveniles does not bode well for their ability to avoid criminal behavior as adults.

Institutional Programs Because of the emphasis on rehabilitation that has dominated juvenile justice for much of the past 50 years, a wide variety of treatment programs has been used. Counseling, education, vocational training, and an assortment of psychotherapeutic methods have been incorporated into the juvenile correctional programs of most states. Unfortunately, research has raised many questions about the effectiveness of rehabilitation programs in juvenile corrections. For example, incarceration in a juvenile training institution primarily seems to prepare many offenders for entry into adult corrections. John Irwin's (1970) concept of the state-raised

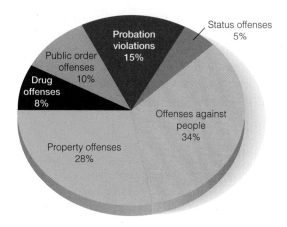

Figure 15.6
Juveniles in Public Facilities: Types of Offenses and Nondelinquent Reasons for Placement

Source: H. N. Snyder and M. Sickmund, *Juvenile Offenders and Victims: 2006 National Report* (Washington, DC: U.S. Office of Juvenile Justice and Delinquency Prevention, 2006), 198.

youth is a useful way of looking at children who come in contact with institutional life at an early age, lack family relationships and structure, become accustomed to living in a correctional facility, and cannot function in other environments. Current recommendations focus on the importance of prevention and keeping juvenile offenders from incarceration at the first signs of problem behavior (Hoge, Guerra, and Boxer, 2008).

Aftercare   The juvenile equivalent of parole is known as **aftercare**. Upon release, the offender is placed under the supervision of a juvenile parole officer who assists with educational, counseling, and treatment services. Quality aftercare is associated with lower rates of recidivism after release from incarceration, and many have blamed the failure of boot camps on poor aftercare (Kurlychek and Kempinen, 2006). As with the adult system, juveniles may be returned to custodial care should they violate the conditions of their parole.

aftercare Juvenile justice equivalent of parole, in which a delinquent is released from a custodial sentence and supervised in the community.

Community Treatment   In the past decade, treatment in community-based facilities has become much more common. Today many private, nonprofit agencies contract with states to provide services for troubled youths. Community-based options include foster homes, in which juvenile offenders live with families, usually for a short period, and group homes, often privately run facilities for groups of 12 to 20 juvenile offenders. Each group home has several staff personnel who work as counselors or houseparents during 8- or 24-hour shifts. Group-home placements provide individual and group counseling, allow juveniles to attend local schools, and offer a more structured life than most of the residents have received in their own homes. These programs must be adequately funded and staffed with trained professionals in order to be effective. However, critics suggest that group homes often are mismanaged and may do little more than "warehouse" youths.

Reforms developed to increase the use of community treatment can also have unintended effects elsewhere in the system. For example, a 2012 report on the Texas juvenile corrections system found that as more offenders were diverted to community programs, the secure institutional settings were left with higher concentrations of the most difficult offenders. In the wake of these changes, youth-on-youth assaults increased from

© Joel Gordon

Many courts develop community programs in an effort to avoid confining youthful offenders in juvenile institutions. Here a juvenile offender meets with a councelor for monitoring, guidance, and support. What are the potential advantages and benefits of emphasizing community-based programs?

17 assaults per 100 detained youths in 2007 to 54 assaults per 100 youths in 2011. The institutions also experienced a similar rise in assaults against staff by youths (Grissom, 2012). Criminal justice planners think very carefully about the impacts of new policies, yet it can be very difficult to anticipate what issues may arise. Read "A Question of Ethics" at the end of the chapter to consider what recommendations you would make to address problems in correctional settings for juveniles.

check point > 5. **What three discretionary decisions do the police make with regard to processing juveniles?**
Whether to take the child into custody, whether to request that the child be detained, whether to refer the child to court.

6. **What is the purpose of diversion?**
To avoid formal proceedings when the child's best interest can be served by treatment in the community.

7. **What sentencing dispositions are available to the judge?**
Probation, intermediate sanctions, custodial care, community treatment.

stop& analyze Juvenile records are sealed and generally cannot be used against adult offenders. Why would such a policy exist? Would it make more sense to allow juvenile records to be used routinely in adult criminal proceedings? State your view and give two reasons to support your position.

Problems and Perspectives

Much of the criticism of juvenile justice has emphasized the disparity between the treatment ideal and the institutionalized practices of an ongoing bureaucratic system. Commentators have focused on how the language of social reformers has disguised the day-to-day operations that lack the elements of due process and in which custodial incarceration is all too frequent. Other criticisms claim that the juvenile justice system does not control juvenile crime.

The juvenile court, in both theory and practice, is a remarkably complex institution that must perform a wide variety of functions. The juvenile justice system must play such a range of roles that goals and values will inevitably collide.

In many states, the same judges, probation officers, and social workers are asked to deal with both neglected children and young criminals. Although departments of social services usually deal primarily with cases of neglect, the distinction between the criminal and the neglected child is often not maintained.

In addition to recognizing that the juvenile system has organizational problems, society must acknowledge that little is known about the causes of delinquency and its prevention or treatment. Over the years, people have advanced various social and behavioral theories to explain delinquency. One generation looked to slum conditions as the cause of juvenile crime, and another pointed to the affluence of the suburbs. Psychologists sometimes point to masculine insecurity in a matriarchal family structure, and some sociologists note the peer-group pressures of the gang. This array of theories has led to a variety of proposed and often contradictory treatments. In such confusion, those interested in the problems of youth may despair. What is clear is that we need additional research on the causes of delinquency and the treatment of juvenile offenders.

Youth gangs pose unique problems to those making decisions in the juvenile justice system. Gangs are responsible for a significant amount of delinquency in communities, and these gangs also thrive in correctional institutions (particularly, adult institutions). How does the presence and behavior of youth gangs affect

Gang Behavior and the Criminal Justice Response in Europe: Eurogang

The problem of youth gangs is not unique to the United States. Researchers in the United States and Europe have been collaborating for the past 15 years to determine whether and how youth gangs differ across cultures. Called "The Euro-gang Project," this group of researchers has created the following goals:

- To build a foundation of knowledge regarding the European socio-economic conditions and institutional processes that foster or curtail the social exclusion and subsequent emergence and persistence/dissolution of youth gangs and problematic groups;
- To construct an infrastructure for comparative, multi-method, cross-national research on youth violence in group contexts; and
- To disseminate and effectively utilize knowledge to inform the development of effective local, national and international responses to emerging youth crime and violence issues.

(From Eurogang home page: http:// www.umsl.edu/ccj/eurogang /euroganghome.html)

In short, they desire to increase knowledge about gangs in the United States and Europe, conduct research in this area, and use that knowledge to generate potential solutions to gang-related problems.

Working together, this group has formulated a concise definition of the word *gang* for their purposes: "A street gang . . . is any durable, street-oriented youth group whose involvement in illegal activity is part of its group identity." This definition contains several important characteristics:

- *Number of members*: A "group" is defined as more than two people, so youth gangs (as defined here) must have more than two members.
- *Age*: The definition includes the word "youth," which means members must be young.
- *Location*: Youth gangs are defined as "street-oriented" to imply that these groups of young people are out walking the streets, not sitting home in groups. This image frequently instills fear in members of the community.
- *Stability*: Gangs are durable—members join for long periods of time and are committed to the group.
- *Group identity*: Gang members feel that they are part of a group and not simply a collection of individuals.
- *Illegal activity*: Youth gangs that do not engage in illegal activity are not generally a concern for law enforcement. Also, to be considered a "street gang," the group must feel that illegal activity is an important part of how they define the activities of their group.

While this definition might fit with the United States version of youth gangs, some research of gangs in European countries indicates important differences. For example, in the United Kingdom, street gangs tend to be more disorganized with no strong leadership. In fact, some gang members report that they are "simply a group of friends doing what they choose to do." In the Netherlands, problematic youth groups are referred to as *jeugdbendes*, but officials take care to distinguish these groups from the stereotypical view of violent American youth gangs.

Studying youth gangs in a non-American context helps to clarify why young people join gangs. Some researchers hypothesize that young men and women join gangs due to a shared set of circumstances or experiences. For example, young men of German ancestry living in Russia have formed youth gangs, and may have a common feeling of being "outsiders" in their country. One in-depth study of an Italian youth gang found that they all came from families in southern Italy, and shared values and a language common to their ancestry.

The importance of understanding immigration issues has been underscored in research as well. In the United States, early gangs were comprised of immigrant youth whose parents had come to America in search of a better life than they experienced in their home countries. This phenomenon is not specific to the United States—there have been extensive studies of Moroccan youth forming gangs in the Netherlands and Pakistani immigrants forming gangs in Norway.

Based on the work of Eurogang and other international researchers, the patterns found in gang membership share many common traits, even if researchers have had difficulty creating a common definition of what constitutes a "youth gang."

Sources: Information taken from Scott Decker and Frank M. Weerman, *European Street Gangs and Troublesome Youth Groups* (Lanham, MD: AltaMira, 2005); Finn-Aage Esbensen and Cheryl L. Maxson, *Youth Gangs in International Perspective* (New York: Springer, 2012); Frank van Gemert, Dana Peterson, and Inger-Lise Lien, *Street Gangs, Migration and Ethnicity* (Portland, OR: Willan, 2008). More information on the Eurogang program can be found on their web page at: http://www.umsl.edu/ccj/eurogang /euroganghome.html.

juvenile justice policy? Recent research has indicated that gang members are more likely than nongang members to carry guns, thereby also increasing the likelihood of severe or lethal violence among these groups. Gang members are also more likely to receive longer sentences, given that gang membership and weapon ownership can increase the severity of punishment for juveniles (Melde, Esbensen, and Taylor, 2009). Youth gangs are also a problem outside of the United States. Review the "Comparative Perspective" to learn more about the EuroGang project, in which

American researchers work with colleagues in Europe to study and formulate solutions to youth gang problems.

In recent years, juveniles have been engaging in delinquent behavior online. The phenomenon of "cyber bullying" involves the use of computers, cell phones, and other electronic devices by youths to mistreat and harm their peers. Approximately one-third of adolescents have been bullied online, while approximately 20 percent of youth admit to cyber bullying others (Hinduja and Patchin, 2009; Patchin and Hinduja, 2012). While additional inquiry is necessary, cyber bullying has been correlated with traditional bullying and various forms of school violence (Hinduja and Patchin, 2007).

What trends foretell the future of juvenile justice? The conservative crime control policies that hit the adult criminal justice system with their emphasis on deterrence, retribution, and getting tough have also influenced juvenile justice in the past 20 years. One can point to growing levels of overcrowding in juvenile institutions, increased litigation challenging the abuse of children in training schools and detention centers, and higher rates of minority youth incarceration. All of these problems have emerged during a period of declining youth populations and fewer arrests of juveniles. With a renewed focus on juvenile crime under the philosophy that "kids are different," the juvenile justice system may be embarking on a less severe path to dealing with juvenile offenders.

On the other hand, future developments and events might ultimately lead to a continuation of the crime control orientation in many states. We must wait to see if we are truly moving into a new era that recognizes and focuses on the vast developmental differences between juveniles and adults. For example, the Supreme Court's ban on the execution of offenders for crimes committed prior to the age of 18 is not necessarily permanent. *Roper v. Simmons* was decided on a 5-to-4 vote of the Supreme Court's justices. Thus a change in the Court's composition may lead to the reinstatement of the death penalty for juveniles in some states if a newly appointed future justice replaces a supporter of the *Roper* majority and votes to reverse the decision when the issue arises in a new case.

a question of ethics

Think, Discuss, Write

In 2007, Texas initiated reforms of its secure detention facilities for juveniles in light of a scandal concerning the number of sexual and physical assaults by staff members against juvenile offenders under their supervision and care. When the diversion of many offenders to community programs left the institutions with higher concentrations of the most difficult offenders, there was an increase in assaults by juvenile offenders against each other and against staff. A report on these problems also raised questions about whether staff members were too quick to use pepper spray as a means to prevent and stop violent incidents. In one secure detention facility, staff members used pepper spray on youths 74 times in 2007, but then used this less-than-lethal weapon 216 times in 2011. The facility was attempting to develop a plan to reduce the use of pepper spray.

Discussion/Writing Assignment

What ethical considerations arise when staff members of a juvenile corrections facility choose to pepper spray rather than physically restraining a violent or out-of-control teenager? Are there risks that staff will use such weapons too quickly without attempting to understand the nature and source of the problem? Does the use of such weapons communicate to the juvenile offenders that it is legitimate to use weapons and violence to solve conflicts? Might such weapons be used inconsistently or in discriminatory ways when deciding which juveniles to spray rather than restrain? Describe the policies and training that you would develop for instructing staff members on when to use pepper spray—if at all—and when to use physical restraint.

Source: Brandi Grissom, "More Inmates Attack One Another," *New York Times*, February 11, 2012 (www.nytimes.com).

Recognize the extent of youth crime in the United States

→ Crimes committed by juveniles remain a serious concern even though crimes of violence in general have decreased.

Understand how the juvenile justice system developed and the assumptions on which it was based

→ The history of juvenile justice comprises six periods: Puritan, refuge, juvenile court, juvenile rights, crime control, and "kids are different."

→ Creation of the juvenile court in 1899 established a separate juvenile justice system.

→ The *In re Gault* decision by the U.S. Supreme Court in 1967 brought due process to the juvenile justice system.

Identify what determines the jurisdiction of the juvenile justice system

→ The juvenile system handles cases based on the ages of youths.

→ Juvenile cases fall into one of four categories: delinquency, status offenses, neglect, or dependency.

Understand how the juvenile justice system operates

→ Decisions by police officers and juvenile intake officers dispose of a large portion of the many cases that are never referred to the court.

→ In juvenile court, most cases are settled through a plea agreement.

→ After conviction or plea, a disposition hearing is held. Before passing sentence, the judge reviews the offense and the juvenile's social history.

→ Possible dispositions of a juvenile case include probation, intermediate sanctions, custodial care, and community treatment.

→ Juvenile court jurisdiction may be waived so that youths can be tried in the adult criminal justice system, but such waivers have decreased since the mid-1990s.

Analyze some of the issues facing the American system of juvenile justice

→ Juvenile justice faces issues of racial disparities in punishment, criminal activity by gangs, and new behavioral problems, such as cyber bullying, that involve computers and other electronic devices.

→ It remains to be seen whether the current move toward increased rehabilitation will continue or whether crime control policies will remain a priority.

Questions for Review

1. What are the major historical periods of juvenile justice in the United States?
2. What is the jurisdiction of the juvenile court system?
3. What are the major processes in the juvenile justice system?
4. What are the sentencing and institutional alternatives for juveniles who are judged delinquent?
5. What due process rights do juveniles have?

Key Terms and Cases

aftercare (p. 491)

delinquent (p. 479)

dependent child (p. 480)

detention hearing (p. 484)

diversion (p. 483)

neglected child (p. 480)

parens patriae (p. 470)

PINS (p. 479)

status offense (p. 475)

waiver (p. 476)

Breed v. Jones (1975) (p. 474)

In re Gault (1967) (p. 473)

In re Winship (1970) (p. 474)

McKeiver v. Pennsylvania (1971) (p. 474)

Schall v. Martin (1984) (p. 475)

Reflections

The other day, while stopped at a red light, I suddenly thought about all the years I spent in "those places." Cells, segregated chow halls, racial tension, monotony, overcrowded conditions. All the years spent being ordered around by judges, guards, and parole officers. And then I thought about all the people who are there right now. Not only are there many more people doing it than before, but they are doing it for extensively longer periods of time. The thought chilled me to the bone. It hasn't always been like this.

People used to consider rehabilitation as a valid justification for imprisonment. Those who broke the law were seen as less fortunate and in need of help. This was when societal goals included using the law to even up the socioeconomic playing field for women and minorities, when social programs designed to fight poverty were being implemented rather than cut, and when popular enemies included communists and crooked politicians. Now many dwell on the harm created by "single-parent families," "illegal immigrants," "welfare dependency," and the evils of affirmative action. And now we have the perfect scapegoat, someone everyone can hate—the criminal.

Today "criminals" are depicted as inherently "bad" people. They are blamed for, among other things, our economic problems, fear of going out at night, dilapidated schools, rundown neighborhoods, and our children's unhappiness. Prisons and all the things that go along with "protecting" the public (alarm systems, more prisons, gated communities, increased budgets for policing, new laws) are "sold" and "bought" as essential mechanisms of control. By keeping "these people" in their place "we" can live "normal," safe lives.

Our aim now is to punish instead of rehabilitate. Increasing levels of formal social control are the means by which crime is "fought." We seldom address crime-generating factors like our market mentality, which revolves around the need to have, to get, and to have yet more; the increasing economic gap between the "haves" and "have-nots"; capital flight; racism; child abuse; homophobia; chronic unemployment; rampant inequality; economic insecurity; and the desperation that leads to drug addiction and other social ills. Instead, our attention is diverted toward individuals. We seem to blindly accept the sanity of draconian sentencing policies such as mandatory minimum laws that require prison time for selling crack cocaine, even for first-time offenders. Or the "Three Strikes and You're Out Law" in California that, though designed to imprison violent offenders, has been twisted and reshaped so that today roughly 70 percent of those going to prison under this law do so for a non-violent crime. After spending so many years in "those places," I find what I see today difficult to accept.

Today I find myself around academics and "experts" in the field of criminal justice. I hope that we can learn from each other. I am given the opportunity to write papers like this and speak in front of hundreds of students in undergraduate classes. I feel fortunate to be doing all this, and more than grateful to be free from the grips of addiction and the criminal justice system.

Yet the story is far from over. The nightmare continues. "Those places" are being jammed with bodies faster than they can be built. Prisons and jails become home to the unemployable, addicts, the underprivileged, and outcasts of society. And rather than help, or even punish, doing time on such a massive scale will likely have disastrous effects on individuals, families, and communities that will last lifetimes and beyond. Can it be that we are crippling or incapacitating "those people"? After being oppressed, controlled, and degraded (especially for long periods of time), inmates turn into angry, fearful human beings who are unable to cope with things that people out here deal with all the time. The difficulty of participating in interpersonal relationships, finding and retaining employment, controlling anger, and "fitting in," to name a few, can become insurmountable obstacles. Yet most of our efforts to do anything about the situation only worsens it.

Efforts to improve sophisticated techniques of identifying, labeling, and monitoring parolees, "gang" members, and other "miscreants" are continually being developed. The school I attended inside no longer offers college classes—funding was pulled. Lifting weights—a positive, healthy way to release energy—is no longer allowed in many prisons: can't let "them" get too strong.

Today I have a friend in the county jail facing sixty years to life under California's three-strikes law for possession of less than a gram of cocaine. He is an addict, 48 years old, and if convicted will probably never get out. His first two strikes were for burglaries in the 1970s. Over the last few years he has battled with his addiction and, at one time, made it nearly two years without using. If the laws would have been the way they are today before I got clean, I would have been "striked out" myself. Is there anything wrong with all this?

My hope is that we are entering a new era, one in which we work on replacing blame and increasing levels of social control with understanding and compassion. An era in which we acknowledge the reality of contemporary life, its horrors, and its injustices as well as its joys. And I hope we can begin to alter the way we view those we perceive as being different from ourselves. All of us have fears. All of us need to belong and fit in somewhere. Oppression, hatred, and blame do not build better lives for anyone. We all need hope.

Reducing violence and crime requires lessening the harm we do to one another—including criminals. I know that, for me, the way I lived for so many years in "those places" affected my self-image, outlook, and actions in such a way that I had become almost completely alienated from everything in the outside world. Luckily, education and my motivation to learn gave me a new perspective and some hope. It helped me see more clearly. I was lucky to make it. Maybe it's time that people out here begin to imagine what it's like to be locked up. What it's like to be pushed into a life of crime, addiction, desperation, and hopelessness. Maybe by taking a closer look at the real factors associated with crime, and by changing the way we "see" those who get caught up in the criminal justice system, we can begin to end the nightmare.

Glossary

accusatory process The series of events from the arrest of a suspect to the filing of a formal charge (through an indictment or information) with the court.

adjudication The process of determining whether the defendant is guilty.

adversarial process Court process, employed in the United States and other former British colonies, in which lawyers for each side represent their clients' best interests in presenting evidence and formulating arguments as a means to discover the truth and protect the rights of defendants.

affidavit Written statement of fact, supported by oath or affirmation, submitted to judicial officers to fulfill the requirements of probable cause for obtaining a warrant.

aftercare Juvenile justice equivalent of parole, in which a delinquent is released from a custodial sentence and supervised in the community.

aggressive patrol A patrol strategy designed to maximize the number of police interventions and observations in the community.

anomie A breakdown or disappearance of the rules of social behavior.

appeal A request to a higher court that it review actions taken in a trial court.

appellate courts Courts that do not try criminal cases but hear appeals of decisions of lower courts.

arraignment The court appearance of an accused person in which the charges are read and the accused, advised by a lawyer, pleads guilty or not guilty.

arrest The physical taking of a person into custody on the grounds that there is reason to believe that he or she has committed a criminal offense. Police may use only reasonable physical force in making an arrest. The purpose of the arrest is to hold the accused for a court proceeding.

assigned counsel An attorney in private practice assigned by a court to represent an indigent. The attorney's fee is paid by the government with jurisdiction over the case.

Atkins v. Virginia (2002) Execution of developmentally disabled offenders is unconstitutional.

bail An amount of money, specified by a judge, to be paid as a condition of pretrial release to ensure that the accused will appear in court as required.

bench trials Trials conducted by a judge who acts as fact finder and determines issues of law. No jury participates.

Bill of Rights The first ten amendments added to the U.S. Constitution to provide specific rights for individuals, including criminal justice rights concerning searches, trials, and punishments.

biological explanations Explanations of crime that emphasize physiological and neurological factors that may predispose a person to commit crimes.

boot camp A short-term institutional sentence, usually followed by probation, that puts the offender through a physical regimen designed to develop discipline and respect for authority. Also referred to as shock incarceration.

Bordenkircher v. Hayes (1978) A defendant's rights were not violated by a prosecutor who warned that refusing to enter a guilty plea would result in a harsher sentence.

Boykin v. Alabama (1969) Before a judge may accept a plea of guilty, defendants must state that they are making the plea voluntarily.

Breed v. Jones (1975) Juveniles cannot be found delinquent in juvenile court and then transferred to adult court without a hearing on the transfer; to do so violates the protection against double jeopardy.

chain of command Organizational structure based on a military model with clear definition of ranks to indicate authority over subordinates and obligations to obey orders from superiors.

challenge for cause Removal of a prospective juror by showing that he or she has some bias or some other legal disability. The number of such challenges available to attorneys is unlimited.

Chimel v. California (1969) Supreme Court decision that endorsed warrantless searches for weapons and evidence in the immediate vicinity of people who are lawfully arrested.

circumstantial evidence Evidence provided by a witness from which a jury must infer a fact.

citation A written order or summons, issued by a law enforcement officer, directing an alleged offender to appear in court at a specific time to answer a criminal charge.

civil infractions Minor offenses that are typically punishable by small fines and that produce no criminal record for the offender.

civil law Law regulating the relationships between or among individuals, usually involving property, contracts, or business disputes.

civilian review board Citizens' committee formed to investigate complaints against the police.

classical criminology A school of criminology that views behavior as stemming from free will, demands responsibility and accountability of all perpetrators, and stresses the need for punishments severe enough to deter others.

classification The process of assigning an inmate to a category specifying his or her needs for security, treatment, education, work assignment, and readiness for release.

clearance rate The percentage of crimes known to the police that they believe they have solved through an arrest; a statistic used to measure a police department's productivity.

Commission on Accreditation for Law Enforcement Agencies (CALEA) Nonprofit organization formed by major law enforcement executives' associations to develop standards for police policies and practice; on request, will review police agencies and award accreditation upon meeting those standards.

community corrections A model of corrections based on the goal of reintegrating the offender into the community.

community crime prevention Programs through which criminal justice officials cultivate relationships with and rely on assistance from citizens in preventing crime and apprehending offenders within neighborhoods.

community policing Approach to policing that emphasizes close personal contact between police and citizens and the inclusion of citizens in efforts to solve problems, including vandalism, disorder, youth misbehavior, and crime.

community service A sentence requiring the offender to perform a certain amount of unpaid labor in the community.

CompStat Approach to crime prevention and police productivity measurement pioneered in New York City and then adopted in other cities that involves frequent meetings among police supervisors to examine detailed crime statistics for each precinct and develop immediate approaches and goals for problem solving and crime prevention.

conditions of release Conduct restrictions that parolees must follow as a legally binding requirement of being released.

congregate system A penitentiary system, developed in Auburn, New York, in which each inmate was held in isolation during the night but worked and ate with other prisoners during the day under a rule of silence.

consent search A permissible warrantless search of a person, vehicle, home, or other location based on a person with proper authority or the reasonable appearance of proper authority voluntarily granting permission for the search to take place.

continuance An adjournment of a scheduled case until a later date.

contract counsel An attorney in private practice who contracts with the government to represent all indigent defendants in a county during a set period of time and for a specified dollar amount.

contract labor system A system under which inmates' labor was sold on a contractual basis to private employers who provided the machinery and raw materials with which inmates made salable products in the institution.

control theories Theories holding that criminal behavior occurs when the bonds that tie an individual to society are broken or weakened.

Cooper v. Pate (1964) Prisoners are entitled to the protection of the Civil Rights Act of 1871 and may challenge in federal courts the conditions of their confinement.

corrections The variety of programs, services, facilities, and organizations responsible for the management of people who have been accused or convicted of criminal offenses.

count Each separate offense of which a person is accused in an indictment or an information.

crime control model A model of the criminal justice system that assumes freedom is so important that every effort must be made to repress crime; it emphasizes efficiency, speed, finality, and the capacity to apprehend, try, convict, and dispose of a high proportion of offenders.

crime control model of corrections A model of corrections based on the assumption that criminal behavior can be controlled by more use of incarceration and other forms of strict supervision.

crimes Actions that violate laws defining which socially harmful behaviors will be subject to the government's power to impose punishments.

criminogenic Having factors thought to bring about criminal behavior in an individual.

critical criminology Theories that assume criminal law and the criminal justice system are primarily a means of controlling the lower classes, women, and minorities.

CSI effect A widely discussed but unproved belief that television dramas revolving around forensic science raise jurors' expectations about the use of scientific evidence in criminal cases and thereby reduce the likelihood of "guilty" verdicts in trials that rely solely on witness testimony and other forms of nonscientific evidence.

custodial model A model of incarceration that emphasizes security, discipline, and order.

cyber crimes Offenses that involve the use of one or more computers.

dark figure of crime A metaphor that emphasizes the dangerous dimension of crimes that are never reported to the police.

day reporting center A community correctional center where an offender reports each day to comply with elements of a sentence.

defense attorney The lawyer who represents accused offenders and convicted offenders in their dealings with criminal justice.

delinquent A child who has committed an act that if committed by an adult would be a criminal act.

demonstrative evidence Evidence that is not based on witness testimony but that demonstrates information relevant to the crime, such as maps, X-rays, and photographs; includes real evidence involved in the crime.

dependent child A child who has no parent or guardian or whose parents cannot give proper care.

detectives Police officers, typically working in plainclothes, who investigate crimes that have occurred by questioning witnesses and gathering evidence.

detention hearing A hearing by the juvenile court to determine if a juvenile is to be detained or released prior to adjudication.

determinate sentence A sentence that fixes the term of imprisonment at a specific period.

differential response A patrol strategy that assigns priorities to calls for service and chooses the appropriate response.

direct evidence Eyewitness accounts.

directed patrol A proactive form of patrolling that directs resources to known high-crime areas.

discovery A prosecutor's pretrial disclosure to the defense of facts and evidence to be introduced at trial.

discretion The authority to make decisions without reference to specific rules or facts, using instead one's own judgment; allows for individualization and informality in the administration of justice.

discretionary release The release of an inmate from prison to conditional supervision at the discretion of the parole board within the boundaries set by the sentence and the penal law.

discrimination Differential treatment of individuals or groups based on race, ethnicity, gender, sexual orientation, or economic status, instead of on their behavior or qualifications.

disparity A difference between groups that may either be explained by legitimate factors or indicate discrimination.

diversion The process of screening children out of the juvenile justice system without a decision by the court.

DNA analysis A scientific technique that identifies people through their distinctive gene patterns (also called genotypic features). DNA, or deoxyribonucleic acid, is the basic component of all chromosomes; all the cells in an individual's body, including those in skin, blood, organs, and semen, contain the same unique DNA.

domestic violence The term commonly used to refer to intimate partner violence or violent victimizations between spouses, boyfriends, and girlfriends, or those formerly in intimate relationships. Such actions account for a significant percentage of the violent victimizations experienced by women.

double jeopardy The subjecting of a person to prosecution more than once in the same jurisdiction for the same offense; prohibited by the Fifth Amendment.

dual court system A system consisting of a separate judicial system for each state in addition to a national system. Each case is tried in a court of the same jurisdiction as that of the law or laws broken.

due process model A model of the criminal justice system that assumes freedom is so important that every effort must be made to ensure that criminal justice decisions are based on reliable information; it emphasizes the adversarial process, the rights of defendants, and formal decision-making procedures.

earned time Reduction in a prisoner's sentence as a reward for participation in educational or other rehabilitation programs, and for work assignments, such as disaster relief and conservation projects.

electronic file management Computerization of court records, done to reduce reliance on paper documents and make documents easily accessible to the judge and attorneys via computer.

Enlightenment A movement during the eighteenth century in England and France in which concepts of liberalism, rationalism, equality, and individualism dominated social and political thinking.

entrapment The defense that the individual was induced by the police to commit the criminal act.

evidence-based policing The deployment of police personnel and development of police strategies based on the utilization of results from social science studies on the nature of crime and other social problems and the effectiveness of past efforts to address these problems.

excessive use of force Applications of force against individuals by police officers that violate either departmental policies or constitutional rights by exceeding the level of force permissible and necessary in a given situation.

exchange A mutual transfer of resources: a balance of benefits and deficits that flow from behavior based on decisions about the values and costs of alternatives.

exclusionary rule The principle that illegally obtained evidence must be excluded from trial.

exigent circumstances When there is an immediate threat to public safety or the risk that evidence will be destroyed, officers may search, arrest, or question suspects without obtaining a warrant or following other usual rules of criminal procedure.

expiration release The release of an inmate from incarceration, without further correctional supervision; the inmate cannot be returned to prison for any remaining portion of the sentence for the current offense.

FBI special agents The sworn law enforcement officers in the FBI who conduct investigations and make arrests.

federalism A system of government in which power is divided between a central (national) government and regional (state) governments.

felonies Serious crimes usually carrying a penalty of death or of incarceration for more than one year in prison.

feminist theories Theories that criticize existing theories for ignoring or undervaluing women's experiences as offenders, victims, and people subjected to decision making by criminal justice officials. These theories seek to incorporate an understanding of differences between the experiences and treatment of men and women while also integrating consideration of other factors, such as race and social class.

filtering process A screening operation; a process by which criminal justice officials screen out some cases while advancing others to the next level of decision making.

fine A sum of money to be paid to the state by a convicted person as punishment for an offense.

forfeiture Government seizure of property and other assets derived from or used in criminal activity.

frankpledge A system in old English law in which members of a tithing (a group of ten families) pledged to be responsible for keeping order and bringing violators of the law to court.

fundamental fairness A legal doctrine supporting the idea that so long as a state's conduct maintains basic standards of fairness, the Constitution has not been violated.

furlough The temporary release of an inmate from a correctional institution for a brief period, usually one to three days, for a visit home. Such programs help maintain family ties and prepare inmates for release on parole.

Furman v. Georgia (1972) The death penalty, as administered, constitutes cruel and unusual punishment.

fusion centers Centers run by states and large cities that analyze and facilitate sharing of information to assist law enforcement and homeland security agencies in preventing and responding to crime and terrorism threats.

Gagnon v. Scarpelli (1973) Before probation can be revoked, a two-stage hearing must be held and the offender provided with specific elements of due process. Requested counsel will be allowed on a case-by-case basis.

general deterrence Punishment of criminals that is intended to be an example to the general public and to discourage the commission of offenses.

Geographic Information System (GIS) Computer technology and software that permits law enforcement officials to map problem locations in order to understand calls for service and the nature and frequency of crimes and other issues within specific neighborhoods.

Gideon v. Wainwright (1963) Indigent defendants have a right to counsel when charged with serious crimes for which they could face six or more months of incarceration.

going rate Local court officials' shared view of the appropriate sentence, given the offense, the defendant's prior record, and other case characteristics.

"good faith" exception Exception to the exclusionary rule that permits the use of improperly obtained evidence when police officers acted in honest reliance on a defective statute, a warrant improperly issued by a magistrate, or a consent to search by someone who lacked authority to give such permission.

good time A reduction of an inmate's prison sentence, at the discretion of the prison administrator, for good behavior or participation in vocational, educational, or treatment programs.

grand jury Body of citizens drawn from the community to hear evidence presented by the prosecutor in order to decide whether enough evidence exists to file charges against a defendant.

Gregg v. Georgia (1976) Death penalty laws are constitutional if they require the judge and jury to consider certain mitigating and aggravating circumstances in deciding which convicted murderers should be sentenced to death. Proceedings must also be divided into a trial phase and a punishment phase, and there must be opportunities for appeal.

habeas corpus A writ or judicial order requesting the release of a person being detained in a jail, prison, or mental hospital. If a judge finds the person is being held improperly, the writ may be granted and the person released.

halfway house A correctional facility housing convicted felons who spend a portion of their day at work in the community but reside in the halfway house during nonworking hours.

hands-off policy Judges should not interfere with the administration of correctional institutions.

home confinement A sentence requiring the offender to remain inside his or her home during specified periods.

Hudson v. Palmer (1984) Prison officials have the authority to search cells and confiscate any materials found.

identity theft The theft of social security numbers, credit card numbers, and other information in order to secure loans, withdraw bank funds, and purchase merchandise while posing as someone else: the unsuspecting victim who will eventually lose money in these transactions.

Illinois v. Gates (1983) U.S. Supreme Court decision that established the flexible totality of circumstances test for determining the existence of the probable cause needed for obtaining a search warrant.

In re Gault (1967) Juveniles have the right to counsel, to confront and examine accusers, and to have adequate notice of charges when confinement is a possible punishment.

In re Winship (1970) The standard of proof beyond a reasonable doubt applies to juvenile delinquency proceedings.

incapacitation Depriving an offender of the ability to commit crimes against society, usually by detaining the offender in prison.

inchoate or **incomplete offenses** Conduct that is criminal even though the harm that the law seeks to prevent has not been done but merely planned or attempted.

incident-driven policing Policing in which calls for service are the primary instigators of action.

incorporation The extension of the due process clause of the Fourteenth Amendment to make binding on state governments the rights guaranteed in the first ten amendments to the U.S. Constitution (the Bill of Rights).

indeterminate sentence A period, set by a judge, that specifies a minimum and a maximum time to be served in prison. Sometime after the minimum, the offender may be eligible for parole.

indictment A document returned by a grand jury as a "true bill" charging an individual with a specific crime on the basis of a determination of probable cause as presented by a prosecuting attorney.

inevitable discovery rule Supreme Court ruling that improperly obtained evidence can be used when it would later have been inevitably discovered by the police.

information A document charging an individual with a specific crime. It is prepared by a prosecuting attorney and presented to a court at a preliminary hearing.

inmate code The values and norms of the prison social system that define the inmates' idea of the model prisoner.

inquisitorial process Court process, employed in most countries of the world, in which the judge takes an active role in investigating the case and examining evidence by, for example, questioning witnesses.

integrated theories Theories that combine differing theoretical perspectives into a larger model.

intensive supervision probation (ISP) Probation granted under conditions of strict reporting to a probation officer with a limited caseload.

intermediate sanctions A variety of punishments that are more restrictive than traditional probation but less severe and less costly than incarceration.

internal affairs unit A branch of a police department that receives and investigates complaints alleging violation of rules and policies on the part of officers.

Interpol The International Criminal Police Organization formed in 1946 and based in France with the mission of facilitating international cooperation in investigating transnational criminal activities and security threats.

inventory search Permissible warrantless search of a vehicle that has been "impounded"— meaning that it is in police custody—so that police can make a record of the items contained in the vehicle.

jail An institution authorized to hold pretrial detainees and sentenced misdemeanants for periods longer than 48 hours.

jurisdiction The geographic territory or legal boundaries within which control may be exercised; the range of a court's authority.

jury A panel of citizens selected according to law and sworn to determine matters of fact in a criminal case and to deliver a verdict of guilty or not guilty.

Kyllo v. United States (2001) Law enforcement officials cannot examine a home with a thermal-imaging device unless they obtain a warrant.

labeling theories Theories emphasizing that the causes of criminal behavior are not found in the individual but in the social process that labels certain acts as deviant or criminal.

latent fingerprints Impressions of the unique pattern of ridges on the fingertip that are left behind on objects; these impressions are the residue of natural skin secretions or contaminating materials such as ink, blood, or dirt that were present on the fingertips at the time of their contact with the objects.

law enforcement The police function of controlling crime by intervening in situations in which the law has clearly been violated and the police need to identify and apprehend the guilty person.

law enforcement certification Preservice training required for sworn officers in many states includes coursework on law, use of weapons, psychology, and police procedures. Police departments for state and large cities often run training programs, called police academies, for their own recruits.

law enforcement intelligence Information, collected and analyzed by law enforcement officials, concerning criminal activities and organizations, such as gangs, drug traffickers, and organized crime.

learning theories Theories that see criminal behavior as learned, just as legal behavior is learned.

lease system A system under which inmates were leased to contractors who provided prisoners with food and clothing in exchange for their labor.

legal responsibility The accountability of an individual for a crime because of the perpetrator's characteristics and the circumstances of the illegal act.

legalistic style Style of policing that emphasizes strict enforcement of laws and reduces officers' authority to handle matters informally.

less-lethal weapons Weapons such as pepper spray and air-fired beanbags or nets that are meant to incapacitate a suspect without inflicting serious injuries.

life course theories Theories that identify factors affecting the start, duration, nature, and end of criminal behavior over the life of an offender.

local legal culture Norms shared by members of a court community as to how cases should be handled and how a participant should behave in the judicial process.

mala in se Offenses that are wrong by their very nature.

mala prohibita Offenses prohibited by law but not wrong in themselves.

mandatory release The required release of an inmate from incarceration to community supervision upon the expiration of a certain period, as specified by a determinate-sentencing law or parole guidelines.

mandatory sentence A sentence determined by statutes and requiring that a certain penalty be imposed and carried out for convicted offenders who meet certain criteria.

Mapp v. Ohio **(1961)** Supreme Court decision that applied the exclusionary rule as the remedy for improper searches by state and local officials.

mark system A point system in which prisoners can reduce their term of imprisonment and gain release by earning "marks" or points through labor, good behavior, and educational achievement.

McCleskey v. Kemp **(1987)** The Supreme Court rejects a challenge of Georgia's death penalty on grounds of racial discrimination.

McKeiver v. Pennsylvania **(1971)** Juveniles do not have a constitutional right to a trial by jury.

medical model A model of corrections based on the assumption that criminal behavior is caused by biological or psychological conditions that require treatment.

mens rea "Guilty mind" or blameworthy state of mind, necessary for legal responsibility for a criminal offense; criminal intent, as distinguished from innocent intent.

merit selection A reform plan by which judges are nominated by a commission and appointed by the governor for a given period. When the term expires, the voters approve or disapprove the judge for a succeeding term. If the judge is

disapproved, the committee nominates a successor for the governor's appointment.

Miranda v. Arizona U.S. Supreme Court decision declaring that suspects in custody must be informed of their rights to remain silent and be represented during questioning.

misdemeanors Offenses less serious than felonies and usually punishable by incarceration of no more than one year in jail, probation, or intermediate sanction.

Missouri v. Frye **(2012)** Criminal defendants' Sixth Amendment right to counsel includes protection against ineffective assistance of counsel in the plea bargaining process, such as defense attorneys' failures to inform their clients about plea bargain offers.

money laundering Moving the proceeds of criminal activities through a maze of businesses, banks, and brokerage accounts so as to disguise their origin.

Morrissey v. Brewer **(1972)** Due process rights require a prompt, informal, two-stage inquiry before an impartial hearing officer before parole may be revoked. The parolee may present relevant information and confront witnesses.

motion An application to a court requesting that an order be issued to bring about a specific action.

National Crime Victimization Surveys (NCVS) Interviews of samples of the U.S. population conducted by the Bureau of Justice Statistics to determine the number and types of criminal victimizations and thus the extent of unreported as well as reported crime.

National Incident-Based Reporting System (NIBRS) A reporting system in which the police describe each offense in a crime incident, together with data describing the offender, victim, and property.

neglected child A child who is receiving inadequate care because of some action or inaction of his or her parents.

net widening Process in which new sentencing options increase rather than reduce control over offenders' lives.

Nix v. Williams **(1984)** Legal decision in which the Supreme Court created the "inevitable discovery" exception to the exclusionary rule.

nolle prosequi An entry, made by a prosecutor on the record of a case and announced in court, indicating that the charges specified will not be prosecuted. In effect, the charges are thereby dismissed.

nonpartisan election An election in which candidates' party affiliations are not listed on the ballot.

North Carolina v. Alford **(1970)** A plea of guilty by a defendant who maintains his or her innocence may be accepted for the purpose of a lesser sentence.

occupational crimes Criminal offenses committed through opportunities created in a legal business or occupation.

order maintenance The police function of preventing behavior that disturbs or threatens to disturb the public peace or that involves face-to-face conflict between two or more people. In such situations, the police exercise discretion in deciding whether a law has been broken.

organized crime A framework for the perpetuation of criminal acts—usually in fields

such as gambling, drugs, and prostitution—providing illegal services that are in great demand.

other conditional release A term used in some states to avoid the rigidity of mandatory release, by placing convicts in various community settings, under supervision.

parens patriae The state as parent; the state as guardian and protector of all citizens (such as juveniles) who cannot protect themselves.

parole The conditional release of an inmate from incarceration, under supervision, after part of the prison sentence has been served.

partisan election An election in which candidates openly endorsed by political parties are presented to voters for selection.

patrol units The core operational units of local police departments that deploy uniformed officers to handle the full array of police functions for service, order maintenance, and law enforcement.

penitentiary An institution intended to punish criminals by isolating them from society and from one another so they can reflect on their past misdeeds, repent, and reform.

percentage bail Defendants may deposit a percentage (usually 10 percent) of the full bail with the court. The full amount of the bail is required if the defendant fails to appear. The percentage of bail is returned after disposition of the case, although the court often retains 1 percent for administrative costs.

peremptory challenge Removal of a prospective juror without giving any reason. Attorneys are allowed a limited number of such challenges.

PINS Acronym for *person(s) in need of supervision*, a term that designates juveniles who are either status offenders or thought to be on the verge of trouble.

plain view doctrine Officers may examine and use as evidence, without a warrant, contraband or evidence that is in open view at a location where they are legally permitted to be.

plea bargain A defendant's plea of guilty to a criminal charge with the reasonable expectation of receiving some consideration from the state for doing so, usually a reduction of the charge. The defendant's ultimate goal is a penalty lighter than the one formally warranted by the charged offense.

police bureaucracy The organizational description of police departments' design and operations that seek to achieve efficiency through division of labor, chain of command, and rules to guide staff.

police corruption Police officers' violations of law and departmental policy for personal gain or to help their family and friends.

political crime An act, usually done for ideological purposes, that constitutes a threat against the state (such as treason, sedition, or espionage); also describes a criminal act by the state.

positivist criminology A school of criminology that views behavior as stemming from social, biological, and psychological factors. It argues that punishment should be tailored to the individual needs of the offender.

Powell v. Alabama **(1932)** An attorney must be provided to a poor defendant facing the death penalty.

Powell v. Alabama (1932) An attorney must be provided to a poor defendant facing the death penalty.

presentence report A report, prepared by a probation officer, that presents a convicted offender's background and is used by the judge in selecting an appropriate sentence.

presumptive sentence A sentence for which the legislature or a commission sets a minimum and maximum range of months or years. Judges are to fix the length of the sentence within that range, allowing for special circumstances.

preventive detention Holding a defendant for trial, based on a judge's finding that if the defendant were released on bail, he or she would endanger the safety of any other person and the community or would flee.

preventive patrol Making the police presence known, to deter crime and to make officers available to respond quickly to calls.

prison An institution for the incarceration of people convicted of serious crimes, usually felonies.

proactive Acting in anticipation, such as an active search for potential offenders that is initiated by the police without waiting for a crime to be reported. Arrests for victimless crimes are usually proactive.

probable cause An amount of reliable information indicating that it is more likely than not that evidence will be found in a specific location or that a specific person is guilty of a crime.

probation A sentence that the offender is allowed to serve under supervision in the community.

problem-oriented policing An approach to policing in which officers routinely seek to identify, analyze, and respond to the circumstances underlying the incidents that prompt citizens to call the police.

problem-solving courts Lower-level local courts dedicated to addressing particular social problems or troubled populations. Examples of such courts include drug courts, domestic violence courts, and mental health courts.

procedural criminal law Law defining the procedures that criminal justice officials must follow in enforcement, adjudication, and corrections.

prosecuting attorney A legal representative of the state with sole responsibility for bringing criminal charges. In some states, this person is referred to as the district attorney, state's attorney, commonwealth attorney, or county attorney.

psychological explanations Explanations of crime that emphasize mental processes and behavior.

public defender An attorney employed on a full-time, salaried basis by a public or private nonprofit organization to represent indigents.

"public safety" exception Exception to Miranda requirements that permits police to immediately question a suspect in custody without providing any warnings, when public safety would be jeopardized by their taking the time to supply the warnings.

reactive Occurring in response, such as police activity in response to notification that a crime has been committed.

real evidence Physical evidence—such as a weapons, records, fingerprints, and stolen property—involved in the crime.

reasonable doubt The standard used by a jury to decide if the prosecution has provided enough evidence for conviction.

reasonable expectation of privacy The objective standard developed by courts for determining whether a government intrusion into an individual's person or property constitutes a search because it interferes with the individual's interests that are normally protected from government examination.

reasonable suspicion A police officer's belief based on articulable facts that would be recognized by others in a similar situation as indicating that criminal activity is afoot and necessitates further investigation that will intrude on an individual's reasonable expectation of privacy.

recidivism A return to criminal behavior.

reformatory An institution for young offenders that emphasizes training, a mark system of classification, indeterminate sentences, and parole.

rehabilitation model A model of corrections that emphasizes the need to restore a convicted offender to a constructive place in society through some form of vocational or educational training or therapy.

rehabilitation The goal of restoring a convicted offender to a constructive place in society through some form of vocational or educational training or therapy.

reintegration model A model of a correctional institution that emphasizes maintaining the offender's ties to family and community as a method of reform, recognizing that the offender will be returning to society.

release on recognizance (ROR) Pretrial release granted, on the defendant's promise to appear in court, because the judge believes that the defendant's ties to the community guarantee that he or she will appear.

restitution Repayment—in the form of money or service—by an offender to a victim who has suffered some loss from the offense.

restorative justice Punishment designed to repair the damage done to the victim and community by an offender's criminal act.

retribution Punishment inflicted on a person who has harmed others and so deserves to be penalized.

Ricketts v. Adamson (1987) Defendants must uphold the plea agreement or suffer the consequences.

Roper v. Simmons (2005) Execution of offenders for crimes committed while under the age of 18 is unconstitutional.

Santobello v. New York (1971) When a guilty plea rests on a promise of a prosecutor, the promise must be fulfilled.

Schall v. Martin (1984) Juveniles can be held in preventive detention if there is concern that they may commit additional crimes while awaiting court action.

school resource officer (SRO) Police officers assigned for duty in schools to assist in order maintenance while also developing positive relationships with students that may assist in delinquency prevention.

search Government officials' examination of and hunt for evidence on a person or in a place in a manner that intrudes on reasonable expectations of privacy.

Section 1983 lawsuits Civil lawsuits authorized by a federal statute against state and local officials and local agencies when citizens have evidence that these officials or agencies have violated their federal constitutional rights.

seizures Situations in which police officers use their authority to deprive people of their liberty or property and which must not be "unreasonable" according to the Fourth Amendment.

selective incapacitation Making the best use of expensive and limited prison space by targeting for incarceration those individuals whose incapacity will do the most to reduce crime in society.

self-incrimination The act of exposing oneself to prosecution by being forced to respond to questions when the answers may reveal that one has committed a crime. The Fifth Amendment protects defendants against compelled self-incrimination.

sentencing guidelines A mechanism to indicate to judges the expected sanction for certain offenses, in order to reduce disparities in sentencing.

separate confinement A penitentiary system, developed in Pennsylvania, in which each inmate was held in isolation from other inmates. All activities, including craft work, took place in the cells.

service The police function of providing assistance to the public, usually in matters unrelated to crime.

service style Style of policing in which officers cater to citizens' desire for favorable treatment and sensitivity to individual situations by using discretion to handle minor matters in ways that seek to avoid embarrassment or punishment.

sheriff Top law enforcement official in county government who was exceptionally important police official during the country's westward expansion and continues to bear primary responsibility for many local jails.

shock probation A sentence in which the offender is released after a short incarceration and resentenced to probation.

slave patrols Distinctively American form of law enforcement in southern states that sought to catch and control slaves through patrol groups that stopped and questioned African Americans on the roads and elsewhere in public places.

social conflict theories Theories that view crime as the result of conflict in society, such as conflict between economic classes caused by elites using law as a means to maintain power.

social process theories Theories that see criminality as normal behavior. Everyone has the potential to become a criminal, depending on (1) the influences that impel one toward or away from crime and (2) how one is regarded by others.

social structure theories Theories that blame crime on the existence of a powerless lower class that lives with poverty and deprivation and often turns to crime in response.

socialization The process by which the rules, symbols, and values of a group or subculture are learned by its members.

sociological explanations Explanations of crime that emphasize as causes of criminal behavior the social conditions that bear on the individual.

special units Units within local police departments that deploy officers, often in plainclothes if not assigned to the traffic unit, who are dedicated to a specific task, such as investigation, or type of crime, such as narcotics enforcement.

specific deterrence Punishment inflicted on criminals to discourage them from committing future crimes.

state attorney general Chief legal officer of a state, responsible for both civil and criminal matters.

status offense Any act committed by a juvenile that is considered unacceptable for a child, such as truancy or running away from home, but that would not be a crime if it were committed by an adult.

stop Government officials' interference with an individual's freedom of movement for a duration that typically lasts less than one hour and only rarely extends for as long as several hours.

stop-and-frisk search Limited search approved by the Supreme Court in *Terry v. Ohio* that permits police officers to pat down the clothing of people on the street if there is reasonable suspicion of dangerous criminal activity.

subculture The symbols, beliefs, values, and attitudes shared by members of a subgroup of the larger society.

substantive criminal law Law that defines acts that are subject to punishment and specifies the punishments for such offenses.

sworn officers Police employees who have taken an oath and been given powers by the state to make arrests and to use necessary force, in accordance with their duties.

system A complex whole consisting of interdependent parts whose actions are directed toward goals and are influenced by the environment within which they function.

technical violation The probationer's failure to abide by the rules and conditions of probation (specified by the judge), resulting in revocation of probation.

Tennessee v. Garner **(1985)** Deadly force may not be used against an unarmed and fleeing suspect unless necessary to prevent the escape and unless the officer has probable cause to believe that the suspect poses a significant threat of death or serious injury to the officers or others.

Terry v. Ohio **(1968)** Supreme Court decision endorsing police officers' authority to stop and frisk suspects on the streets when there is

reasonable suspicion that they are armed and involved in criminal activity.

testimony Oral evidence provided by a legally competent witness.

theory of differential association The theory that people become criminals because they encounter more influences that view criminal behavior as normal and acceptable than they do influences that are hostile to criminal behavior.

totality of circumstances Flexible test established by the Supreme Court for identifying whether probable cause exists that permits the judge to determine whether the available evidence is both sufficient and reliable enough to issue warrant.

trial courts of general jurisdiction Criminal courts with jurisdiction over all offenses, including felonies. In some states, these courts also hear appeals.

trial courts of limited jurisdiction Criminal courts with trial jurisdiction over misdemeanor cases and preliminary matters in felony cases. Sometimes these courts hold felony trials that may result in penalties below a specific limit.

U.S. Border Patrol Federal law enforcement agency with responsibility for border security by patrolling national land borders and coastal waters to prevent smuggling, drug trafficking, and illegal entry, including entry by potential terrorists.

U.S. marshals Federal law enforcement officials appointed to handle duties in western territories and today bear responsibility for federal court security and apprehending fugitives.

Uniform Crime Reports (UCR) An annually published statistical summary of crimes reported to the police, based on voluntary reports to the FBI by local, state, and federal law enforcement agencies.

United States attorneys Officials responsible for the prosecution of crimes that violate the laws of the United States. Appointed by the president and assigned to a U.S. district court jurisdiction.

United States v. Drayton **(2002)** Judicial decision declaring that police officers are not required to inform people of their right to decline to be searched when police ask for consent to search.

United States v. Leon **(1984)** Supreme Court decision announcing the "good faith" exception to the exclusionary rule.

United States v. Salerno and Cafero **(1987)** Preventive detention provisions of the Bail Reform Act of 1984 are upheld as a legitimate use of government power designed to prevent people from committing crimes while on bail.

USA PATRIOT Act A federal statute passed in the aftermath of the terrorist attacks of September 11, 2001, that broadens government authority to conduct searches and wiretaps and that expands the definitions of crimes involving terrorism.

victimless crimes Offenses involving a willing and private exchange of illegal goods or services that are in strong demand. Participants

do not feel they are being harmed, but these crimes are prosecuted on the ground that society as a whole is being injured.

victimology A field of criminology that examines the role the victim plays in precipitating a criminal incident and also examines the impact of crimes on victims.

visible crime An offense against persons or property, committed primarily by members of the lower class. Often referred to as "street crime" or "ordinary crime," this type of offense is the one most upsetting to the public.

voir dire A questioning of prospective jurors to screen out people the attorneys think might be biased or otherwise incapable of delivering a fair verdict.

waiver Procedure by which the juvenile court waives its jurisdiction and transfers a juvenile case to the adult criminal court.

warrant A court order authorizing police officers to take certain actions, for example, to arrest suspects or to search premises.

watch system Practice of assigning individuals to night observation duty to warn the public of fires and crime that was first introduced to the American colonies in Boston and that later evolved into a system of paid, uniformed police.

watchman style Style of policing that emphasizes order maintenance and tolerates minor violations of law as officers use discretion to handle small infractions informally but make arrests for major violations.

Weeks v. United States **(1914)** Supreme Court decision applying the exclusionary rule as the remedy for improper searches by federal law enforcement officials.

Williams v. Florida **(1970)** Juries of fewer than 12 members are constitutional.

Witherspoon v. Illinois **(1968)** Potential jurors who object to the death penalty cannot be automatically excluded from service; however, during voir dire, those who feel so strongly about capital punishment that they could not give an impartial verdict may be excluded.

Wolf v. Colorado **(1949)** Supreme Court decision in which the Fourth Amendment was applied against searches by state and local police officers, but the exclusionary rule was not imposed as the remedy for violations of the Fourth Amendment by these officials.

Wolff v. McDonnell **(1974)** Basic elements of procedural due process must be present when decisions are made about imposing significant punishments on prisoners for violating institutional rules.

work and educational release The daytime release of inmates from correctional institutions so they can work or attend school.

workgroup A collection of individuals who interact in the workplace on a continuing basis, share goals, develop norms regarding how activities should be carried out, and eventually establish a network of roles, which differentiates the group from others, and facilitates cooperation.

working personality A set of emotional and behavioral characteristics developed by members of an occupational group in response to the work situation and environmental influences.

References

Abbe, O. G., and P. S. Herrnson. 2002. "How Judicial Election Campaigns Have Changed." *Judicature* 85:286–95.

Abrams, D. 2011. "Is Pleading Really a Bargain?" *Journal of Empirical Legal Studies* 8:200–21.

Abrams, J. 2008. "House Sets Standards for Juvenile Boot Camps." Associated Press, June 25. http://www.ap.org.

Abwender, D. A., and K. Hough. 2001. "Interactive Effects of Characteristics of Defendant and Mock Juror on U.S. Participants' Judgment and Sentencing Recommendations." *Journal of Social Psychology* 141:603–16.

Acker, J. R. 2007. "Impose an Immediate Moratorium on Executions." *Criminology & Public Policy* 6:641–50.

Acoca, L. 1997. "Hearts on the Ground: Violent Victimization and Other Themes in the Lives of Women Prisoners." *Corrections Management Quarterly* 1 (Spring): 44–55.

Adams, B., and S. Addie. 2011. "Delinquency Cases Waived to Criminal Court, 2008." Office of Juvenile Justice and Delinquency Programs. Washington, DC: U.S. Government Printing Office.

Adams, G. 2006. "Sex Offenders' Killer Studied States' Lists." http://www.boston.com.

Adams, K. 1992. "Adjusting to Prison Life." In *Crime and Justice: A Review of Research*, vol. 16, ed. M. Tonry. Chicago: University of Chicago Press, 275–359.

———. 1999. "What We Know about Police Use of Force." In *Use of Force by Police: Overview of National and Local Data*. Washington, DC: U.S. Government Printing Office.

Adang, O. M. J., and J. Mensink. 2004. "Pepper Spray: An Unreasonable Response to Suspect Verbal Resistance." *Policing* 27:206–19.

Aden, H., and C. Koper. 2011. "The Challenges of Hot Spots Policing." *Translational Criminology* (Summer), 6–7.

Adler, F. 1975. *Sisters in Crime: The Rise of the New Female Criminal*. New York: McGraw-Hill.

Adler, S. J. 1994. *The Jury: Disorder in the Court*. New York: Doubleday.

Agnew, R., N. L. Piquero, and F. T. Cullen. 2009. "General Strain Theory and White-Collar Crime," in *The Criminology of White-Collar Crime*, ed. Sally Simpson and David Weisburd. New York: Springer, 35–60.

Ahmadi, S. 2011. "The Erosion of Civil Rights: Exploring the Effects of the Patriot Act on Muslims in America." *Rutgers Race and the Law Journal* 12:1–55.

Alarcon, A. L. 2007. "Remedies for California's Death Row Gridlock." *Southern California Law Review* 80:697–52.

Alarid, L., and C. Montemayor. 2010. "Legal and Extralegal Factors in Attorney Recommendations of Pretrial Diversion." *Criminal Justice Studies* 23:239–52.

Alexander, K. 2011. "Fresno Co. Juvenile Justice Campus Hit by Budget Woes." *Fresno Bee*, April 25. http://www.fresnobee.com.

Alexander, M. 2011. "The New Jim Crow." *Ohio State Journal of Criminal Law* 9:7–26.

Alpert, G. 2007. "Eliminate Race as the Only Reason for Police–Citizen Encounters." *Criminology & Public Policy* 6:671–678.

Alvarez, L., and T. Williams. 2011. "Anthony Is Sentenced to 4-Year Term for Lying." *New York Times*, July 7. www.nytimes.com.

Amar, A. R. 1997. *The Constitution and Criminal Procedure: First Principles*. New Haven, CT: Yale University Press.

Amar, V. 2008. "An Enigmatic Court? Examining the Roberts Court as It Begins Year Three: Criminal Justice." *Pepperdine Law Review* 35: 523–31.

American Bar Association. 2010. *National Database on Judicial Diversity in State Courts*. http://apps.americanbar.org /abanet/jd/display/national.cfm.

Amnesty International. 1999. "Annual General Meeting Highlights USA Campaign." Anglen, R. 2008. "Judge Rules for Taser in Cause-of-Death Decisions." *Arizona Republic*, May 2. http://www.azcentral.com.

Anderson, G., R. Litzenberger, and D. Plecas. 2002. "Physical Evidence of Police Officer Stress." *Policing* 25:399–420.

Anderson, T. L. 2003. "Issues in the Availability of Healthcare for Women in Prison." In *The Incarcerated Woman: Rehabilitative Programming in Women's Prisons*, ed. S. F. Sharp and R. Muraskin. Upper Saddle River, NJ: Prentice Hall, 49–60.

Andrews, D. A., and J. Bonta. 1994. *The Psychology of Criminal Behavior*. Cincinnati, OH: Anderson.

Andrews, D. A., I. Zinger, R. D. Hoge, J. Bonta, P. Gendreau, and F. T.

Cullen. 1990. "Does Correctional Treatment Work? A Clinically Relevant and Psychologically Informed Meta-Analysis." *Criminology* 28:369–404.

Antonovics, K., and B. G. Knight. 2009. "A New Look at Racial Profiling: Evidence from the Boston Police Department." *Review of Economics and Statistics* 91:163–77.

Antonuccio, R. 2008. "Prisons for Profit: Do the Social and Political Problems Have a Legal Solution?" *Journal of Corporation Law* 33:577–92.

Applebome, P. 2012. "Death Penalty Repeal Goes to Connecticut Governor." *New York Times*, April 12. www.nytimes.com.

Applegate, B. K., R. K. Davis, and F. T. Cullen. 2009. "Reconsidering Child Saving: The Extent and Correlates of Public Support for Excluding Youths from the Juvenile Court." *Crime & Delinquency* 55(1): 51–77.

Archbold, C., and K. Hassell. 2009. "Paying a Marriage Tax: An Examination of Barriers to the Promotion of Female Officers." *Policing: An International Journal of Policing Strategies and Management* 32:56–74.

Arena, K., and K. Bohn. 2008. "Rape Victim Pushes for Expanded DNA Database." CNN.com, May 12. http://www.cnn.com.

Armour, M. 2008. "Dazed and Confused: The Need for a Legislative Solution to the Constitutional Problem of Juror Comprehension." *Temple Political and Civil Rights Law Review* 17:641–73.

Armstrong, G. S., and D. L. MacKenzie. 2003. "Private versus Public Juvenile Facilities: Do Differences in Environmental Quality Exist?" *Crime & Delinquency* 49 (October): 542–63.

Armstrong, J. 2008. "Perdue Signs DNA Bill, Expanding Use in Crimes; It Allows Comparisons from Suspects, Not Just Those Already Convicted." *Florida Times Union*, May 8. http:// jacksonville.com.

Armstrong, K., and S. Mills. 1999. "Death Row Justice Derailed." *Chicago Tribune*, November 14 and 15, p. 1.

Arnold, N. 2008. "Madison Murder Prompts Look at 911 Procedures." WBAY-TV.com, May 5. http://www .wbay.com.

Arterton, J.B. 2008. "Unconscious Bias and the Impartial Jury." *Connecticut Law Review* 40:1023–33.

Arthur, M., J. D. Hawkins, E. Brown, J. Briney, S. Oesterle, and R. Abbott. 2010. "Implementation of the Communities That Care Prevention System by Coalitions in the Community Youth Development Study." *Journal of Community Psychology* 38:245–58.

Associated Press, 2012a. "Judge: Pa. Boy, 11, Killed Dad's Pregnant Fiancé." *USA Today*, April 13.

———. Associated Press. 2012b. "Roche Warns of Counterfeit Avastin in U.S." *USA Today*, February 14. www.usatoday.com.

Association of Certified Fraud Examiners. 2004. *Report to the Nation on Occupational Fraud and Abuse*. Austin, TX: Association of Certified Fraud Examiners.

Auerhahn, K. 1999. "Selective Incapacitation and the Problem of Prediction." *Criminology* 37:703–34.

Austin, J. 2001. "Prisoner Reentry: Current Trends, Practices, and Issues." *Crime and Delinquency* 47 (July): 314–33.

Austin, J., K. D. Johnson, and M. Gregoriou. 2000. Juveniles in Adult Prisons and Jails. Bureau of Justice Assistance Monograph. Washington, DC: U.S. Department of Justice.

Axtman, K. 2005. "A New Motion to Make Jury Service More Attractive." *Christian Science Monitor*, May 23, pp. 2–3.

Bagnato, C. F. 2010. "Change Is Needed: How Latinos Are Affected by the Process of Jury Selection." *Chicana/o-Latina/o Law Review* 29:59–67.

Bai, M. 2012. "Scott Ritter's Other War." *New York Times*, October 27. www.nytimes.com.

Baker, A. 2008. "11 Years of Police Gunfire, in Painstaking Detail." *New York Times*, May 8. www .nytimes.com.

———. 2010 "New York Minorities More Likely to Be Frisked." *New York Times*, May 12. www .nytimes.com.

Baker, A., and W. K. Rashbaum. 2010. "Police Find Car Bomb in Times Square." *New York Times*, May 1. www.nytimes.com.

Baker, P. 2010. "Obama Signs Law Narrowing Cocaine Sentencing Disparities." *New York Times*, August 3. www.nytimes.com.

Baldus, D. C., G. Woodworth, and C. A. Pulaski. 1994. *Equal Justice and the Death Penalty: A Legal and Empirical Analysis*. Boston: Northeastern University Press.

Balmert, J. 2011. "Budget Cuts Could Send More Local

Offenders to Prison Instead of Rehab." *Mansfield News-Journal*, March 7. http://mansfieldnewsjournal.com.

Bandy, D. 1991. "$1.2 Million to Be Paid in Stray-Bullet Death." *Akron Beacon Journal*, December 3, p. B6.

Bartels, L., and A. Gaffney. 2011. Good Practices in Women's Prisons: A Literature Review. Canberra, Australia: Australian Institute of Criminology.

Basemore, G., and M. S. Umbreit. 1994. Foreword to *Balanced and Restorative Justice: Program Summary*. Washington, DC: Office of Juvenile Justice and Delinquency Prevention, U.S. Government Printing Office.

Bass, P. 2012. "CompStat Ramps Up." *New Haven Independent*, January 31. www.newhavenindependent.org.

Baumgartner, B., S. Linn, and A. Boydstun. 2010. "The Decline of the Death Penalty: How Media Framing Changed Capital Punishment in America." In *Winning with Words: The Origins and Impact of Framing*, ed. B. Schaffner and P. Sellers. New York: Routledge, 159–84.

Baxter, C. 2011. "N.J. Police Dispatches Troopers to Camden to Help Quell Homicide Spree." NJ.COM, December 12. http://blog.nj.com.

Baxter, S. 2011. "Santa Cruz County Sheriff's Office Hires San Jose Police Officers Poised for Layoffs." *San Jose Mercury News*, May 16. www.mercurynews.com.

Beck, A. J., and P. M. Harrison. 2001. "Prisoners in 2000." Bureau of Justice Statistics *Bulletin*. Washington, DC: U.S. Department of Justice.

Beck, A. J., J. C. Karberg, and P. M. Harrison. 2002. "Prison and Jail Inmates at Mid-Year 2001." Bureau of Justice Statistics *Bulletin*, April.

Becker, H. S. 1963. *Outsiders: Studies in the Sociology of Deviance*. New York: Free Press.

Beckett, K., K. Nyrop, and L. Pfingst. 2006. "Race, Drugs, and Policing: Understanding Disparities in Drug Delivery Arrests." *Criminology* 44:105–37.

Beichner, D., and C. Spohn. 2012. "Modeling the Effects of Victim Behavior and Moral Character on Prosecutors' Charging Decisions in Sexual Assault Cases." *Violence and Victims* 27:3–24.

Bell, D. 1967. *The End of Ideology*. 2nd rev. ed. New York: Collier.

Belluck, P. 2001. "Desperate for Prison Guards, Some States Even Rob Cradles." *New York Times*, April 21, p. A1.

Berestein, L. 2008. "Lawsuits Raise Questions about Private Prisons." *San Diego Union-Tribune*, May 4. http://www.signonsandiego.com/uniontrib/20080504/news_1n4detain.html.

Berkheiser, M. 2011. "Death Is Not So Different after All: *Graham v.*

Florida and the Court's 'Kids Are Different' Eighth Amendment Jurisprudence." *Vermont Law Review* 36(1): 1–62.

Bisbee, J. 2010. "Oklahoma Indigent Defense System Struggles to Survive Cuts." *The Oklahoman*, April 14. http://newsok.com.

Bjelopera, J., and K. Finklea. 2012. *Organized Crime: An Evolving Challenge for U.S. Law Enforcement*. Congressional Research Service Report to Congress, January 6. http://www.fas.org/sgp/crs/misc/R41547.pdf.

BJS (Bureau of Justice Statistics). 2000a. *Bulletin*, August.

———. 2000b. *Correctional Populations in the United States, 1997*. Washington, DC: U.S. Government Printing Office.

———. 2003. *Census of State and Federal Correctional Facilities, 2000*. Washington, DC: U.S. Government Printing Office.

———. 2005. *Bulletin*, December.

———. 2007. Adapted from FBI Supplemental Homicide Reports, 1976–2005. Washington, DC: U.S. Department of Justice.

———. 2008. "Survey Methodology for Criminal Victimization in the United States." Washington, DC: U.S. Department of Justice.

———. 2010. *Criminal Victimization in the United States, 2007 Statistical Tables*. Washington, DC: U.S. Department of Justice.

———. 2011a. *Crime in the United States, 2010* (Uniform Crime Reports). www.fbi.gov.

———. 2011b. Sourcebook of Criminal Justice Statistics. http://www.albany.edu/sourcebook/.

———. 2012. "Tribal Law Enforcement." BJS.gov website. http://bjs.ojp.usdoj.gov/index.cfm?ty=tp&tid=75.

Blair, J. 2000. "Ideas and Trends; Boot Camps: An Idea Whose Time Came and Went." *New York Times*, January 2. http://nytimes.com.

Blitz, C. L., N. Wolff, and J. Shi. 2008. "Physical Victimization in Prison: The Role of Mental Illness." *International Journal of Law and Psychiatry* 31(5): 385–393.

Bluestein, G. 2011. "State Budget Cuts Clog Criminal Justice System." *Seattle Post Intelligencer*, October 26. www.seattlepi.com.

Blumstein, A. 2002. "Youth, Guns, and Violent Crime." The Future of Children, Volume 12 (Number 2). Los Altos, CA: The David and Lucille Packard Foundation.

Blumstein, A., and A. Beck. 2005. "Reentry as a Transient State between Liberty and Recommitment" (with Allen J. Beck). In *Prisoner Reentry and Crime in America*, ed. Jeremy Travis and Christy Visher. New York: Cambridge University Press, 55–79.

Blumstein, J. F., M. A. Cohen, and S. Seth. 2008. "Do Government

Agencies Respond to Market Pressures? Evidence from Private Prisons." *Virginia Journal of Social Policy and Law* 15:446–69.

Bogdanich, W. 2008. "Heparin Find May Point to Chinese Counterfeiting." *New York Times*, March 20. http://www.nytimes.com.

Boland, B., E. Brady, H. Tyson, and J. Bassler. 1983. *The Prosecution of Felony Arrests*. Washington, DC: Bureau of Justice Statistics, U.S. Government Printing Office.

Bohmert, M. B., and G. Duwe. 2011. "Minnesota's Affordable Homes Program: Evaluating the Effects of a Prison Work Program on Recidivism, Employment and Cost Avoidance." Criminal Justice Policy Review (online).

Bontrager, S., W. Bales, and T. Chiricos. 2005. "Race, Ethnicity, Threat and the Labeling of Convicted. Felons." *Criminology* 43:589–622.

Bornstein, B., and E. Green. 2011. "Jury Decision Making: Implications For and From Psychology." *Current Directions in Psychological Science* 20:63–67.

Bourque, B. B., M. Han, and S. M. Hill. 1996. "A National Survey of Aftercare Provisions for Boot Camp Graduates." In *Research in Brief*. Washington, DC: National Institute of Justice, U.S. Government Printing Office.

Bousquet, S. 2012a. "Plan to Close Prison Re-Entry Centers Angers Lawmakers." *Tampa Bay Times*, March 2. www.tampabay.com.

———. 2012b. "Prison System Will Keep Re-Entry Centers Open." *Tampa Bay Times*, March 7. www.tampabay.com.

Bowen, D. M. 2009. "Calling Your Bluff: How Prosecutors and Defense Attorneys Adapt Plea Bargaining Strategies to Increased Formalization." *Justice Quarterly* 26:2–29.

Bowen, J. 2008. "Punishing the Innocent." *University of Pennsylvania Law Review* 156:1117–

Bowers, J. 2010. "Legal Guilt, Normative Innocence, and the Equitable Decision Not to Prosecute." *Columbia Law Review* 110:1655–1726.

Bowker, L. H. 1982. "Victimizers and Victims in American Correctional Institutions." In *Pains of Imprisonment*, ed. R. Johnson and H. Toch. Beverly Hills, CA: Sage.

Boyd, T. 2011. "Domestic Violence Court—55th District Court." *Michigan Bar Journal* 90:42–43.

Bradley, C. 1992. "Reforming the Criminal Trial." *Indiana Law Journal* 68:659–64.

Bradley, Craig M. 2010. "Reconceiving the Fourth Amendment and the Exclusionary Rule." *Law and Contemporary Problems* 73:211–38.

Braithwaite, J. 2007. "Encourage Restorative Justice." *Criminology & Public Policy* 6:689–96.

Braithwaite, L., H. M. Treadwell, K. R. J. Arriola. 2005. "Health

Disparities and Incarcerated Women: A Population Ignored." *American Journal of Public Health* 95, 1679–1681.

Bray, K. 1992. "Reaching the Final Chapter in the Story of Peremptory Challenges." *U.C.L.A. Law Review* 40:517–55.

Brennan, P. A., S. A. Mednick, and J. Volavka. 1995. "Biomedical Factors in Crime." In *Crime*, ed. J. Q. Wilson and J. Petersilia. San Francisco: ICS Press.

Breslin, D. M. 2010. "Judicial Merit-Retention Elections in Pennsylvania." *Duquesne Law Review* 48:891–907.

Britt, C. 2000. "Social Context and Racial Disparities in Punishment Decisions." *Justice Quarterly* 17:707–32.

Bronsteen, J. 2010. "Retribution's Role." *Indiana Law Journal* 84:1129–1156.

Brown, D. M. 2009. "Calling Your Bluff: How Prosecutors and Defense Attorney Adapt Plea Bargaining Strategies to Increased Formalization." *Justice Quarterly* 26:2–29.

Brown, H. 2005. "Liberty University: 6 Still Hospitalized after Crash Involving Lacrosse Players." *Roanoke Times*, March 16. www.roanoke.com.

Browne, A., A. Cambier, and S. Agha. 2011. "Prisons Within Prisons: The Use of Segregation in the United States." *Federal Sentencing Reporter* 24:46–49.

Bruce, M. 2003. "Contextual Complexity and Violent Delinquency among Black and White Males." *Journal of Black Studies* 35:65–98.

Brunson, R. 2007. " 'Police Don't Like Black People': African American Young Men's Accumulated Police Experiences." *Criminology & Public Policy* 6:71–102.

Bulman, P. 2010. "Police Use of Force: The Impact of Less-Lethal Weapons and Tactics." *National Institute of Justice Journal* 267: 4–10.

Bundy, T. 2011. "At Critical Time, Budget Ax Falls on Parole Courts." *The Bay Citizen*, October 8. www.baycitizen.org.

———. 2012. "Trying to Prepare for the Toughest of Jobs." *New York Times*, March 29. www.nytimes.com

Bureau of Labor Statistics. 2009. Occupational Employment Statistics, 2010. Washington, DC: Bureau of Labor Statistics.

Bureau of Prisons. 2012. "Quick Facts About Bureau of Prisons." February 25. www.bop.gov/about/facts.jsp.

Burgess-Proctor, Amanda. 2006. "Intersections of Race, Class, Gender, and Crime: Future Directions for Feminist Criminology." *Feminist Criminology* 1(1): 1–27.

Burns, A. C. 2007. "*Beard v. Banks*: Restricted Reading, Rehabilitation, and Prisoners'

First Amendment Rights." *Journal of Law and Policy* 15:1225–70.

Burns, S. 2010. "The Role of Problem-Solving Courts: Inside the Courts and Beyond." *University of Maryland Journal of Race, Religion, Gender, and Class* 10:73–87.

Buruma, I. 2005. "What Teaching a College-Level Class at a Maximum Security Correctional Facility Did for the Inmates—and for Me." *The New York Times Magazine*, February 20, pp. 36–41.

Business Wire. 2001. "WorldNet Technologies, Creators of a State of the Art Weapons Detection System, Signs Consulting Deal with NuQuest." November 27. http://findarticles.com/p/articles /mi_m0EIN/is_2001_Nov_27 /ai_80345651/.

Butler, P. 2010. "One Hundred Years of Race and Crime." *Journal of Criminal Law and Criminology* 100:1043–1060.

Butterfield, F. 2004a. "Repaving the Long Road Out of Prison." *New York Times*, May 4. http:// www.nytimes.com.

———. 2004b. "Study Tracks Boom in Prisons and Notes Impact on Counties." *New York Times*, April 30, p. A15.

Bykowicz, J. 2008. "Juvenile Center Home to Despair." *Baltimore Sun*, May 25. http:// baltimoresun.com.

Bynum, T., and S. Varano. 2002. "The Anti-Gang Initiative in Detroit: An Aggressive Enforcement Approach to Gangs." In *Policing Gangs and Youth Violence*, ed. S. H. Decker. Belmont, CA: Wadsworth, 214–38.

Byrne, J. M. 2008. "The Best Laid Plans: An Assessment of the Varied Consequences of New Technologies for Crime and Social Control." *Federal Probation* 72 (3): 10–21.

Byrne, J. M., and D. Hummer. 2007. "Myths and Realities of Prison Violence: A Review of the Evidence." *Victims and Offenders* 2:77–90.

Cadigan, T. 2009. "Implementing Evidence-Based Practices in Federal Pretrial Services." *Federal Probation* 73:30–32.

Cady, M.S., and J. R. Phelps. 2008. "Preserving the Delicate Balance Between Judicial Accountability and Independence: Merit Selection in the Post-White World." *Cornell Journal of Law and Public Policy* 17:343–81.

Cahill, M. T. 2007a. "Attempt, Reckless Homicide, and the Design of Criminal Law." *University of Colorado Law Review* 78:879–956.

———. 2007b. "Retributive Justice in the Real World." *Washington University Law Quarterly* 85:815–70.

Calhoun, F. 1990. *The Lawmen*. Washington, DC: Smithsonian Institution.

California Department of Corrections and Rehabilitation, 2010.

"Correctional Officer Training." State of California. http://www .cdcr.ca.gov/career_opportunities /por/cotraining.html.

"California's Prison Realignment Has Perils, Potential." *Modesto Bee*, November 19. www.modbee.com.

Cammack, M. "The Exclusionary Rule: The Rise and Fall of the Constitutional Exclusionary Rule in the United States." *American Journal of Comparative Law* 58:631–58.

Camp, C. G. 2003. *Corrections Yearbook, 2002*. Middletown, CT: Criminal Justice Institute.

Camp, S. D., and G. G. Gales. 2002. "Growth and Quality of U.S. Private Prisons: Evidence from a National Survey." *Criminology & Public Policy* 1:427–50.

Campbell, J. 2011. "State Unions Brace for Impact of Layoffs." *The Press & Sun Bulletin*, May 22. http://www.pressconnects.com.

———. 2012. "Budget Cuts Could Gut Probation Officers." FOX 13 News online, March 2. www .myfoxtampabay.com.

Cancino, J. M., and R. Enriquez. 2004. "A Qualitative Analysis of Officer Peer Retaliation: Preserving the Police Culture." *Policing: International Journal of Police Strategies and Management* 27:320–40.

Canning, A., and M. Burbank. 2010. "Jordan Brown Murder Case Takes Emotional Toll." *ABC News/Nightline*, April 28.

Canto, M. 1998. "Federal Government Investigates Use of Stun Belt." *Lansing* (MI) *State Journal*, August 7, p. 4A.

Caputo, M., and C. M. Miller. 2006. "In Wake of Death, Juvenile Boot Camp System is Scrapped." *Miami Herald*, April 27. http:// www.miami.com/miamiherald /14438114.htm.

Carlisle, N. 2012. "Drug Raid Charges: Did Army Vet Ambush Ogden Cops?" *Salt Lake City Tribune*, January 14. www.sltrib.com.

Carlon, A. 2007. "Entrapment, Punishment, and the Sadistic State." *Virginia Law Review* 93:1081–1134.

Carodine, M. 2010. "Keeping It Real: Reform of the 'Untried Conviction' Impeachment Rule." *Maryland Law Review* 69:501–586.

Carr, P. J., L. Napolitano, and J. Keating. 2007. "We Never Call the Cops and Here's Why: A Qualitative Examination of Legal Cyncism in Three Philadelphia Neighborhoods." *Criminology* 45:445–80.

Carroll, L. 1974. *Hacks, Blacks, and Cons: Race Relations in a Maximum Security Prison*. Lexington, MA: Lexington Books.

Carroll-Ferrary, 2006. "Incarcerated Men and Women, the Equal Protection Clause, and the Requirement of 'Similarly Situated.'" *New York Law School Law Review* 51:594–617.

Cauffman, E. L., L. Steinberg, and A. R. Piquero. 2005. "Psychological,

Neuropsychological, and Physiological Correlates of Serious Antisocial Behavior in Adolescence: The Role of Self-Control." *Criminology* 43:133–76.

CBS Chicago, 2011. "Alvarez, Preckwinkle Spar Over Budget Cuts, CBS Chicago.com, February 8. www.chicago.cbslocal.com.

Chacon, J. M. 2010. "Border Exceptionalism in the Era of Moving Borders." *Fordham Urban Law Journal* 38:129–52.

Chaddock, G. R. 2002. "Sniper Revives Prospects for Gun-Tracking Moves." *Christian Science Monitor*, October 17, p. 1.

Champion, D. J. 1989. "Private Counsels and Public Defenders: A Look at Weak Cases, Prior Records, and Leniency in Plea Bargaining." *Journal of Criminal Justice* 17:253–63.

Chapman, S. G. 1970. *Police Patrol Readings*. 2nd ed. Springfield, IL: Thomas.

Chapper, J. A., and R. A. Hanson. 1989. *Understanding Reversible Error in Criminal Appeals*. Williamsburg, VA: National Center for State Courts.

"Charging Common Criminals under Terrorism Laws Doesn't Fit in America's Justice Values." 2003. *Asheville Citizen-Times*, July 23. http://www.citizentimes.com.

Chavez, P. 2005. "Shooting Raises Racial Tension in L.A." *Sacramento Union*, February 21. http://www.sacunion.com.

Cheng, E. 2005. "Mitochondrial DNA: Emerging Legal Issues." *Journal of Law and Policy* 13:99–118.

Chermak, S., and E. McGarrell. 2004. "Problem-Solving Approaches to Homicide: An Evaluation of Indianapolis Violence Reduction Partnership." *Criminal Justice Policy Review* 15:161–92.

Chesney-Lind, M. 2006. "Patriarchy, Crime, and Justice." *Feminist Criminology* 1:6–26.

Chiaramida, A. 2009. "New Hampshire House Approves Death Penalty Appeal." *Newburyport Daily News*, March 26. http:// www.newburyportnews.com.

Chiricos, T., K. Padgett, and M. Gertz. 2000. "Fear, TV News, and the Reality of Crime." *Criminology* 38:755–85.

Chiricos, T., K. Barrick, W. Bales, and S. Bontrager. 2007. "The Labeling of Convicted Felons and its Consequences for Recidivism." *Criminology* 45:547–81.

Christopher, R. L. 1994. "Mistake of Fact in the Objective Theory of Justification." *Journal of Criminal Law and Criminology* 85:295–332.

Church, T. W. 1985. "Examining Local Legal Culture." *American Bar Foundation Research Journal* 1985 (Summer): 449.

Cieply, M. 2011. "Mel Gibson to Plead Guilty in Abuse of Former Girlfriend." *New York Times*, March 10. www.nytimes.com.

Cisco Systems. 2002. *Law Enforcement Solution-Company Profile:*

Seal Beach Police Department. http://pronetsystemsonline.com /sealb_cp.pdf.

Clark, M. 2011. "States Beginning to Rethink Indigent Defense Systems.: Stateline: State Politics & Policy website (Pew Center on the States), December 1. http:// stateline.org.

Clear, T. R. 1994. *Harm in American Penology*. Albany: State University of New York Press.

Clear, T. R., G. F. Cole, and M. D. Reisig. 2009. *American Corrections*, 8th ed. Belmont, Calif.: Cengage/Wadsworth.

Clear, T. R., and D. R. Karp. 1999. *Community Justice: Preventing Crime and Achieving Justice*. New York: Westview Press.

Clisura, A. 2010. "None of Their Business: The Need for Another Alternative to New York's Bail Bond Business." *Journal of Law and Policy* 19:307–351.

CNN. 2004a. "Boston Police Accept 'Full Responsibility' in Death of Red Sox Fan." October 22. http://www.cnn.com.

———. 2004b. "Police Review Policy after Tasers Used on Kids." November 14. http://www.cnn.com

Cochran, J., and P. Warren. 2012. "Racial, Ethnic, and Gender Differences in Perceptions of the Police: The Salience of Officer Race Within the Context of Racial Profiling." *Journal of Contemporary Criminal Justice* (forthcoming).

Coffin, K. G. 2010. "Double Take: Evaluating Double Jeopardy Reform." *Notre Dame Law Review* 85:771–808.

Cohen, T. H., and T. Kyckelhahn. 2010. "Felony Defendants in Large Urban Counties, 2006." Bureau of Justice Statistics *Bulletin*, May. NCJ 228944.

Coleman, K. 2011. "The Mob Goes Green." National Public Radio. http://www.npr.org/blogs/thetwo -way/2011/12/07/143271128 /the-mob-goes-green-organized- crime-profits-with-new-jersey- recycling.

Coleman, T., and D. Cotton. 2010. "Reducing Risk and Improving Outcomes of Police Interactions with People with Mental Illness." *Journal of Police Crisis Negotiations* 10:39–57.

Collins, J. 2005. *Preventing Identity Theft in Your Business: How to Protect Your Business, Customers, and Employees*. New York: Wiley.

Conte, M. 2012. "Former Belleville Man Charged As Member of Credit Card Forgery Ring." *The Jersey Journal*, February 23. www.nj.com

Conway, P. 2001. "The 2001 Electronic Monitoring Survey." *Journal of Electronic Monitoring* 14 (Winter–Spring): 7–9.

Cook, N. 2010. "How the Recession Hurts Private Prisons." *Newsweek*, June 29. http:// www.thedailybeast.com/news- week/2010/06/30/how-the-reces- sion-hurts-private-prisons.html.

Cook, P. J., and J. Laub. 2002. "After the Epidemic: Recent Trends in Youth Violence in the United States." *Crime and Justice: A Review of Research* 29:1–37.

Cooney, M. 1994. "Evidence as Partisanship." *Law & Society Review* 28:833–58.

Cooper, A. and E. L. Smith. 2011. *Homicide Trends in the United States: Annual Rates for 2009 and 2010.* Washington, DC: U.S. Department of Justice.

Cooper, C. 2009. "Yes Virginia, There is a Police Code of Silence: Prosecuting Police Officers and the Police Subculture." *Criminal Law Bulletin* 45:277–282.

Copes, H., G. E. Higgins, R. Tewksbury, and D. Dabney. 2010. "Participation in the Prison Economy and Likelihood of Physical Victimization." *Victims & Offenders* 6(1):1–18.

Cordner, G., and E. P. Biebel. 2005. "Problem-Oriented Policing in Practice." *Criminology & Public Policy* 4:155–80.

Cornwell, E., and V. Hans. 2011. "Representation through Participation: A Multilevel Analysis of Jury Deliberations." *Law & Society Review* 45:667–698.

Corrections Reporter. 2011. "CDCR Forced to Cut Rehab Programs." *Corrections Reporter,* April 19th. http://correctionsreporter.com.

Corsaro, N., R. Brunson, and E. McGarrell. 2012. "Problem-Oriented Policing and Open-Air Drug Markets: Examining the Rockford Pulling Levers Deterrence Strategy." *Crime and Delinquency* (forthcoming).

Costanzo, M. 1997. *Just Revenge.* New York: St. Martin's Press.

Covey, R. D. 2011. "Longitudinal Guilt: Repeat Offenders, Plea Bargaining, and the Variable Standard of Proof." *Florida Law Review* 63:431–455.

Coyle, M. 2009. "New Report Shows Sharp Rise in Prison Time for Federal Offenders." *National Law Journal* February 12. www.law.com

Cratty, C. 2011. "Report: 173 Law Enforcement Officers Killed on Duty in 2011." CNN.com, December 28. www.cnn.com.

Crawford, C. 2000. "Gender, Race, and Habitual Offender Sentencing in Florida." *Criminology* 38:263–80.

Crawford, C., T. Chiricos, and G. Kleck. 1998. "Race, Racial Threat, and Sentencing of Habitual Offenders." *Criminology* 36 (August): 481–512.

Cristani, A. S., and B. C. Frueh. 2011. "Risk of Trauma Exposure among Persons with Mental Illness in Jails and Prisons: What Do We Really Know?" *Current Opinion in Psychiatry* 24(5): 431–35.

Crummy, K. 2009. "Colorado Criminals Owe State's Victims Nearly $778 Million." *Denver Post,* September 24. www.denverpost.com.

Cullen, F. T. 2007. "Make Rehabilitation Corrections' Guiding Paradigm." *Criminology & Public Policy* 6:717–28.

Cullen, F. T., T. Leming, B. Link, and J. Wozniak. 1985. "The Impact of Social Supports in Police Stress." *Criminology* 23:503–22.

Cunningham, W. C., J. J. Strauchs, and C. W. Van Meter. 1990. *Private Security Trends, 1970 to the Year 2000.* Boston: Butterworth-Heinemann.

Daftary-Kapur, T., R. Dumas, and S. D. Penrod. 2010. "Jury Decision-Making Biases and Methods to Counter Them." *Legal and Criminological Psychology* 15:133–154.

Dansky, K. 2008. "Understanding California Sentencing." *University of San Francisco Law Review* 43:45–86.

Dantzker, M., and J. McCoy. 2006. "Psychological Screening of Police Recruits: A Texas Perspective." *Journal of Police and Criminal Psychology* 21 (2006): 23–32.

Davey, J. D. 1998. *The Politics of Prison Expansion: Winning Elections by Waging War on Crime.* Westport, CT: Praeger.

Davey, M. 2011. "Blagojevich Sentenced to 14 Years in Prison." *New York Times,* December 7. www.nytimes.com.

Davis, A. 2008. *Arbitrary Justice: The Power of the American Prosecutor.* New York: Oxford University Press.

Davis, M., R. Lundman, and R. Martinez Jr. 1991. "Private Corporate Justice: Store Police, Shoplifters, and Civil Recovery." *Social Problems* 38:395–408.

Davis, R. C., C. S. O'Sullivan, D. J. Farole, and M. Rempel. 2008. "A Comparison of Two Prosecution Policies in Cases of Intimate Partner Violence: Mandatory Case Filing Versus Following the Victim's Lead." *Criminology & Public Policy* 7:633–62.

Davis, S. 2012. "Ionia Site Targeted in Budget Proposal." *Lansing State Journal,* April 7. www.lsj.com.

Davitz, T. 1998. "The Gangs Behind Bars." *Insight on the News,* September 28.

Dawson, M., and R. Dinovitzer. 2001. "Victim Cooperation and the Prosecution of Domestic Violence in a Specialized Court." *Justice Quarterly* 18:593–622.

Death Penalty Information Center. 2011. *The Death Penalty in 2011: Year End Report* (December). www.deathpenaltyinfo.org.

Dedel, K. 2010. "Fifth Monitor's Report for the Baltimore City Juvenile Justice Center (BCJJC) for the Period of July 1, 2009 through December 31, 2009." http://www.djs.state.md.us.

DeFrances, C. J., and J. Litras. 2000. "Indigent Defense Services in Large Counties, 1999." Bureau of Justice Statistics *Bulletin,* November.

DeJong, C., S. Mastrofski, and R. Parks. 2001. "Patrol Officers and Problem Solving: An Application of Expectancy Theory." *Justice Quarterly* 18:31–61.

DeJong, C., and E. S. Merrill. 2000. "Getting 'Tough on Crime': Juvenile Waiver and the Criminal Court." *Ohio Northern University Law Review* 27:175–96.

Demare, C. 2011. "Ritter Gets Prison Time." *Albany Times-Union,* October 26. www.timesunion.com.

Deng, X. 2012. "Prison Population Continues to Drop." *Daily Tribune,* April 1. www.dailytribune.com.

Dery, G. 2011. "Do You Believe in *Miranda?* The Supreme Court Reveals Its Doubts in *Berghuis v. Thompkins* by Paradoxically Ruling That Suspects Can Only Invoke Their Right to Remain Silent by Speaking." *George Mason University Civil Rights Law Journal* 21:407–40.

Dewan, S. 2007. "An SOS for 911 Systems in Age of High-Tech." *New York Times,* April 6. http://www.nytimes.com.

———. 2009. "Prosecutors Block Access to DNA Testing for Inmates." *New York Times,* May 18. http://www.nytimes.com.

Diamond, S., D. Peery, F. Dolan, and E. Dolan. 2009. "Achieving Diversity on the Jury: Jury Size and the Peremptory Challenge." *Journal of Empirical Legal Studies* 6:425–449.

Dickerson, B.E. 2008. "Hard Lemonade, Hard Price." *Detroit Free Press,* April 28. http://www.freep.com.

Dickson, J. 2011. "Habitat for Humanity, Michigan Prisoner Re-Entry Initiative Team Up to Rehab Ypsilanti Home." *Ann Arbor News,* January 17. www.annarbor.com.

DiIulio, J. J., Jr. 1987. *Governing Prisons.* New York: Free Press.

———. 1991. *No Escape: The Future of American Corrections.* New York: Basic Books.

———. 1993. "Rethinking the Criminal Justice System: Toward a New Paradigm." In *Performance Measures for the Criminal Justice System.* Washington, DC: Bureau of Justice Statistics, U.S. Government Printing Office.

Disha, I., J. C. Cavendish, and R. D. King. 2011. "Historical Events and Spaces of Hate: Hate Crimes against Arabs and Muslims in America." *Social Problems* 58(1): 21–46.

Doerner, J. K., and S. Demuth. 2010. "The Independent and Joint Effects of Race/Ethnicity, Gender, and Age on Sentencing Outcomes in U.S. Federal Courts." *Justice Quarterly* 27:1–27.

Domash, S. F. 2008. "Nassau System Will Pinpoint Gunfire Sites." *New York Times,* July 27. http://www.nytimes.com.

Doney, E. 2010. "State Cuts Sex Offender Rehab." KFOR News, March 11th. http://www.kfor.com.

Donziger, S. R., ed. 1996. *The Real War on Crime: The Report of the National Criminal Justice Commission.* New York: HarperCollins.

Dorell, O. 2011. "Casey Anthony Verdict Could Haunt Jurors." *USA Today,* July 11. www.usatoday.com.

Dority, B. 2005. "The USA Patriot Act Has Decimated Many Civil Liberties." In *Homeland Security: Current Controversies,* ed. A. Nakaya. Detroit: Thomson /Gale, 130–36.

Dripps, D. 2010. "The 'New' Exclusionary Rule Debate: From 'Still Preoccupied with 1985' to 'Virtual Deterrence,'" *Fordham Urban Law Journal* 37:743–801.

Dubail, J. 2009. "Cuyahoga County Jury Pay Cut to Save Money." May 14. www.cleveland.com.

Duke, A., and T. Rowlands. 2009. "Chris Brown Pleads Guilty in Rihanna Assault Case." CNN.com, June 22. http://www.cnn.com.

Durose, M. R., E. L. Schmitt, and P. Langan. 2005. *Contacts between Police and Public: Findings from the 2002 National Survey.* Washington, DC: Bureau of Justice Statistics, U.S. Government Printing Office, April.

Dyer, B. 2012. "Mayors' Courts Should Be Nuked." *Akron Beacon Journal,* January 24. www.ohio.com.

Dzur, A. 2011. "Restorative Justice and Democracy: Fostering Public Accountability for Criminal Justice." *Contemporary Justice Review,* 14:367–81.

Earley, P. 1992. *The Hot House: Life inside Leavenworth Prison.* New York: Bantam Books.

Eckholm, E. 2008a. "Citing Workload, Public Lawyers Reject New Cases." *New York Times,* November 9. http://www.nytimes.com.

———. 2008b. "U.S. Shifting Prison Focus to Re-entry Into Society." *New York Times,* April 8. http://www.nytimes.com.

———. 2010. "Congress Moves to Narrow Cocaine Sentencing Disparities." *New York Times,* July 28. www.nytimes.com.

Edkins, V. 2011. "Defense Attorney Plea Recommendations and Client Race: Does Zealous Representation Apply Equally to All?" *Law and Human Behavior* 35:413–425.

Eichenwald, K. 2006. "On the Web, Pedophiles Extend Their Reach." *New York Times,* August 21. http://www.nytimes.com.

Eigenberg, H. 2000. "Correctional Officers and Their Perceptions of Homosexuality, Rape, and Prostitution in Male Prisons." *Prison Journal* 80 (December): 415–33.

Eisenberg, T., P. Hannaford-Agor, V. P. Hans, N. L. Mott, G. T. Munsterman, S. J. Schwab, and M. T. Wells. 2005. "Judge-Jury Agreement in Criminal Cases:

A Partial Replication of Kalven and Zeisel's *The American Jury.*" *Journal of Empirical Legal Studies* 2:171–206.

Eisenstein, J., R. B. Flemming, and P. F. Nardulli. 1988. *The Contours of Justice: Communities and Their Courts.* Boston: Little, Brown.

Ellement, J. R., and S. Smalley. 2006. "Six Crime Disclosure Questioned." *Boston Globe*, April 18. http://www.boston.com.

Eligon, J., and T. Kaplan. 2012. "New York State Set to Add All Convict DNA to Its Database." *New York Times*, March 13. www.nytimes.com.

Elliott, D. S., S. S. Ageton, and R. J. Cantor. 1979. "An Integrated Theoretical Perspective on Delinquent Behavior." *Journal of Research in Crime and Delinquency* 16:3–27.

Elliott, J., and B. Murphy. 2005. "Parole, Probation Violators Add to Crowding." *Houston Chronicle*, January 20. http://www.chron.com/ca/CDA/printstory.mpl/metropolitan/3000503.

Emery, S. 2012. "Parolee Arrested in Pimping of 15-Year-Old Girl." *Orange County Register*, February 28. www.ocregister.com.

Emmelman, D. S. 1996. "Trial by Plea Bargain: Case Settlement as a Product of Recursive Decision-making." *Law & Society Review* 30:335–60.

Engber, D. 2005. "Does the FBI Have Your Fingerprints?" *Slate*, April 22. http://www.slate.msn.com/id/2117226.

Engel, R. S., and J. M. Calnon. 2004. "Examining the Influence of Drivers' Characteristics during Traffic Stops with Police: Results from a National Survey." *Justice Quarterly* 21:49–90.

Engel, R. S., J. M. Calnon, and T. J. Bernard. 2002. "Theory and Racial Profiling: Shortcomings and Future Directions in Research." *Justice Quarterly* 19:249–73.

Engen, R. 2009. "Assessing Determinate and Presumptive Sentencing—Making Research Relevant." *Criminology & Public Policy* 8:323–336.

Enion, M.R. 2009. "Constitutional Limits on Private Policing and the State's Allocation of Force." *Duke Law Journal* 59:519–51.

Enriquez, R., and J. W. Clark. 2007. "The Social Psychology of Peremptory Challenges: An Examination of Latino Jurors." *Texas Hispanic Journal of Law and Policy* 13:25–38.

Erhard, S. 2008. "Plea Bargaining and the Death Penalty: An Exploratory Study." *Justice System Journal* 29:313–327.

Fahey, T. 2011. "Tough Decisions Remain Regarding State Budget." *The Union Leader*, May 20. http://www.unionleader.com.

Farole, D. J., and L. Langton. 2010. "County-Based and Local Public Defender Offices, 2007." Bureau of Justice Statistics *Special Report*, September. NCJ 231175.

Fathi, D. C. 2010. "The Challenge of Prison Oversight." *American Criminal Law Review* 47:1453–62.

Faturechi, R. 2011. "Report Details Misconduct by L.A. County Sheriff's Deputies." *Los Angeles Times*, August 5. www.latimes.com.

Favate, S. 2012. "Shrinking State Court Budgets: Not Just A New York Thing." *Wall Street Journal*, January 12. www.wsj.com.

FBI (Federal Bureau of Investigation). 2006. "FBI Cyber Action Teams: Traveling the World to Catch Cyber Criminals." March 6. http://www.fbi.gov.

———. 2007. *Hate Crime Statistics, 2006.* Washington, DC: Federal Bureau of Investigation. http://www.fbi.gov.

———. 2008. "Cyber Solidarity: Five Nations, One Mission." March 18. http://www.fbi.gov.

———. 2011a. *Crime in the United States, 2010* (Uniform Crime Reports). http://www.fbi.gov.

———. 2011b. *Hate Crime Statistics, 2010.* Washington, DC.

———. 2011c. *Preliminary Semiannual Uniform Crime Report*, January–June 2011. Washington, DC.

———. 2012a. "Quick Facts, FBI website. http://www.fbi.gov.

———. 2012b. "Special Agent FAQs." FBI website. https://www.fbijobs.gov/114.asp.

———. 2012c. "UCR General FAQs." FBI website. http://www.fbi.gov/about-us/cjis/ucr/frequently-asked-questions/ucr_faqs.

Feeley, M., and E. Rubin. 1998. *Judicial Policy Making and the Modern State.* New York: Cambridge University Press.

Felch, J. 2003. "How a 'Calm but Aggravated' Teenager Died on East Thrill Place." *Denver Post*, July 11. http://www.denverpost.com.

Felch, J., and M. Dolan. 2008. "DNA Matches Aren't Always a Lock." *Los Angeles Times*, May 4. http://www.latimes.com.

Feld, B. 1999. *Bad Kids: Race and the Transformation of the Juvenile Court.* New York: Oxford University Press.

———. 2003. "The Politics of Race and Juvenile Justice: The 'Due Process Revolution' and the Conservative Reaction." *Justice Quarterly* 20(4): 765–800.

———. 2004. "Editorial Introduction: Juvenile Transfers." *Criminology & Public Policy* 3 (November): 599–603.

———. 2011. "More than 30 Baltimore Police Officers Charged, Suspended in Towing Scheme." *Baltimore Sun*, February 23. www.baltimoresun.com.

Feld, B. C. 1993. "Criminalizing the American Juvenile Court." In *Crime and Justice: A Review of Research*, vol. 17, ed. M. Tonry.

Chicago: University of Chicago Press, 197–280.

Ferguson, J. 2009. "Professional Discretion and the Use of Restorative Justice Programs in Appropriate Domestic Violence Cases: An Effective Innovation. *Criminal Law Brief* 4:3–17.

Ferretti, C. and M. Feighan. 2009. "Teen Dies after Warren Police Use Taser." *Detroit News*, April 11. http://www.detnews.com.

Feuer, A. 2006. "For Ex-F.B.I. Agent Accused in Murders, a Case of What Might Have Been." *New York Times*, April 15. http://www.nytimes.com.

Fields, J., and K. Peveto. 2008. "Local Cop Cars Going Hi-Tech." *Abilene (TX) Reporter News*, December 4. http://www.reporternews.com.

Fields, T. 2011. "How High Is the Cost of Justice in Polk County?" WTSP.com, July 19. www.wtsp.com.

Finn, B., M. Shively, J. McDevitt, W. Lassiter, and T. Rich. 2005. *Comparison of Activities and Lessons Learned among 19 School Resource Officer (SRO) Programs.* Boston: Abt Associates.

Finn, P., and J. McDevitt. 2005. National Assessment of School Resource Officer Programs. Report to the National Institute of Justice. Unpublished.

Fischman, J., and M. Schanzenbach. 2011. "Do Standards of Review Matter? The Case of Federal Criminal Sentencing." *Journal of Legal Studies* 40:405–37.

Fishbein, D. H. 1990. "Biological Perspectives in Criminology." *Criminology* 28:27–72.

Fisher, D. M. 2007. "Striking a Balance: The Need to Temper Judicial Discretion against a Background of Legislative Interest in Federal Sentencing." *Duquesne Law Review* 46:65–97.

Fisman, R. 2008. "Going Down Swingin': What If Three-Strikes Laws Make Criminals Less Likely to Repeat Offend—But More Violent When They Do? Slate.com, March 20. http://www.slate.com.

Flanagan, T. J., ed. 1995. *Long-Term Imprisonment.* Thousand Oaks, CA: Sage.

Flango, V. E. 1994. *Habeas Corpus in State and Federal Courts.* Williamsburg, VA: National Center for State Courts.

Fleisher, M. S., and J. L. Krienert. 2006. The Culture of Prison Sexual Violence. Unpublished.

Flock, E. 2012. "California School Protests: 5 Reasons Students Are Demonstrating." *Washington Post*, March 6. www.washingtonpost.com.

Florencio, D. and C. Herley. 2012. "The Cybercrime Wave That Wasn't." *New York Times*, April 14. www.nytimes.com.

Florida Office of Program Policy Analysis and Government Accountability. 2010.

Intermediate Sanctions for Non-Violent Offenders Could Produce Savings, Report No. 10-27 (March).

Flowers, R. 2010. "The Role of the Defense Attorney: Not Just An Advocate." *Ohio State Journal of Criminal Law* 7:647–52.

Fountain, H. 2009. "Plugging Holes in the Science of Forensics." *New York Times*, May 12. http://www.nytimes.com.

Fox, J. G. 1982. *Organizational and Racial Conflict in Maximum Security Prisons.* Lexington, MA: Lexington Books.

Frantz, S., and R. Borum. 2011. "Crisis Intervention Teams May Prevent Arrests of People with Mental Illnesses." *Police Practice and Research: An International Journal* 12:265–72.

Fridell, L. 1990. "Decision Making of the District Attorney: Diverting or Prosecuting Intrafamilial Child Sexual Abuse Offenders." *Criminal Justice Policy Review* 4:249–67.

Friedman, L. M. 1993. *Crime and Punishment in American History.* New York: Basic Books.

Friedrichs, D. O. 2010. *Trusted Criminals: White Collar Crime in Contemporary Society.* 4th ed. Belmont, CA: Cengage.

Frohmann, L. 1997. "Convictability and Discordant Locales: Reproducing Race, Class, and Gender Ideologies in Prosecutorial Decisionmaking." *Law & Society Review* 31:531–56.

Fujii, A. 2012. "Dozens Protest Proposed Juvenile Jail in Downtown Baltimore." CBS Baltimore (March 12). http://baltimore.cbslocal.com.

Gabbidon, S., and G. Higgins. 2009. "The Role of Race/Ethnicity and Race Relations on Public Opinion Related to the Treatment of Blacks by the Police." *Police Quarterly* 12:102–15.

Gabbidon, S., G. Higgins, and H. Potter. 2011. "Race, Gender, and the Perception of Recently Experiencing Unfair Treatment by the Police: Exploratory Results from an All-Black Sample." *Criminal Justice Review* 36:5–21.

Garcia, M. 2005. "N.Y. Using Terrorism Law to Prosecute Street Gang." *Washington Post*, February 1, p. A3.

Garner, J. H., C. D. Maxwell, and C. G. Heraux. 2002. "Characteristics Associated with the Prevalence and Severity of Force Used by the Police." *Justice Quarterly* 19:705–46.

Gau, J., and R. Brunson. 2010. "Procedural Justice and Order Maintenance Policing: A Study of Inner-City Young Men's Perceptions of Police Legitimacy." *Justice Quarterly* 27:255–79.

Gelman, A., J. Fagan, and A. Kiss. 2007. "An Analysis of the New York City Police Department's 'Stop-and-Frisk' Policy in the Context of Claims of Racial Bias." *Journal of the American Statistical Society* 102:813–23.

Georgiady, B. N. 2008. "An Exceedingly Painful Encounter: The Reasonableness of Pain and De Minimis Injuries for Fourth Amendment Excessive Force Claims." *Syracuse Law Review* 59:123–64.

Gershon, R., B. Barocas, A. Canton, X. Li, and D. Vlahov. 2009. "Mental, Physical, and Behavioral Outcomes Associated with Perceived Work Stress in Police Officers." *Criminal Justice and Behavior* 36:275–89.

Gest, T. 2001. *Crime and Politics: Big Government's Erratic Campaign for Law and Order.* New York: Oxford University Press.

Geyh, C. 2012. "Can the Rule of Law Survive Judicial Politics?" *Cornell Law Review* 97:191–253.

Gezari, V. M. 2008. "Cracking Open." *Washington Post*, June 1. http://www.washingtonpost.com.

Gill, J., and M. Pasquale-Styles. 2009. "Firearm Deaths by Law Enforcement." *Journal of Forensic Sciences* 54:185–88.

Giordano, P. C., M. A. Longmore, R. D. Schroder, and P. Seffrin. 2008. "A Life Course Perspective on Spirituality and Desistance from Crime." *Criminology* 46:99–131.

Girshick, L. B. 1999. *No Safe Haven: Stories of Women in Prison.* Boston: Northeastern University Press.

Glaze, L. 2011. "Correctional Population in the United States, 2010." Bureau of Justice Statistics *Bulletin*, December. NCJ236319.

Glaze, L. E., and T. P. Bonczar. 2010. "Probation and Parole in the United States, 2009." Bureau of Justice Statistics *Bulletin*, December. NCJ 231674.

———. 2011. "Probation and Parole in the United States, 2010." Bureau of Justice Statistics *Bulletin*, November. NCJ 236019.

Glaze, L. E. and L. M. Maruschak. 2008. Parents in Prison and Their Minor Children. Bureau of Justice Statistics *Special Report*. Washington, DC: U.S. Department of Justice.

Glueck, S., and E. Glueck. 1950. *Unraveling Juvenile Delinquency.* New York: Commonwealth Fund.

Goldberg, C. 2010. "In Theory, in Practice: Judging State Jurisdiction in Indian Country." *University of Colorado Law Review* 81:1027–65.

Goldfarb, R. L. 1965. *Ransom: A Critique of the American Bail System.* New York: Harper & Row.

Goldkamp, J. S., and E. R. Vilcica. 2008. "Targeted Enforcement and Adverse System Side Effects: The Generation of Fugitives in Philadelphia." *Criminology* 46:371–409.

Goldstein, H. 1979. "Improving Policing: A Problem-Oriented Approach." *Crime and Delinquency* 25:236–57.

———. 1990. *Problem-Oriented Policing.* New York: McGraw-Hill.

Goode, E. 2012. "Stronger Hand for Judges in the 'Barzaar' of Plea Deals." *New York Times*, March 22. www.nytimes.com.

Goodman, J. 1994. *Stories of Scottsboro.* New York: Random House.

Goodnough, A. 2011. "Pharmacies Besieged by Addicted Thieves." *New York Times*, February 6. www.nytimes.com.

Gordon, J. 2005. "In Patriots' Cradle, the Patriot Act Faces Scrutiny." *New York Times*, April 24. http://www.nytimes.com.

Gordon, M. 2006. "Disgraced Bondsman Candid on Eve of Jail." *New Orleans Times-Picayune* October 27. http://www.nola.com.

Gordon, S. 2010a. "Actor's Ex-Girlfriend Testifies About Attack." *North County Times*, August 31. www.nctimes.com.

———. 2010b. "Jury, DA Question Actor Shelley Malil." *North County Times*, September 13. www.nctimes.com.

Gorenstein, N. 2011. "Family Wins $1.2 Million Settlement in Police Shooting." *Philadelphia Inquirer*, April 7. http://articles.philly.com/2011–04–07/news/29393007_1_settlement-in-police-shooting-police-officers-false-arrest.

Gottfredson, M., and T. Hirschi. 1990. *A General Theory of Crime.* Stanford, CA: Stanford University Press.

Gover, A. R., J. M. MacDonald, and G. P. Alpert. 2003. "Combating Domestic Violence: Findings from an Evaluation of a Local Domestic Violence Court." *Criminology & Public Policy* 3:109–31.

Governor's Office on Drug Control Policy. 2006. *Iowa's Drug Control Strategy, 2006.* http://www.iowa.gov/odcp/images/pdf/Strategy_06.pdf.

Grady, D. 2003. "F.D.A. Outlines Plans to Counter Growing Trade in Counterfeit Pharmaceuticals." *New York Times*, October 3. http://www.nytimes.com.

Grasha, K. 2009a. "Going Paperless." *Lansing (MI) State Journal*, February 9, pp. 1A, 4A.

———. 2009b. "Ingham Co. Jail Inmates May Opt for House Arrest." *Lansing (MI) State Journal*, March 11, p. 1A–2A.

Grattet, R., J. Lin, and J. Petersilia. 2011. "Supervision Regimes, Risk, and Official Reactions to Parolees Deviance." *Criminology* 49:371–400.

Green, A. 2009. "More States Use GPS to Track Abusers." *New York Times*, May 9. http://www.nytimes.com.

Green, F. 2011. "System Allows Federal Prisoners to Send E-Mail." *Richmond Times-Dispatch*, September 6. www2.timesdispatch.com.

Green, R. 2011. "State Puts Gingerich in Facility for Youths." *Ft. Wayne Journal Gazette*, January 15. www.journalgazette.com.

Greenberg, A. 2010. "Full-Body Scan Technology Deployed in Street-Roving Vans." *Forbes*, August 24. www.forbes.com.

Greene, J. A. 1999. "Zero Tolerance: A Case Study of Police Policies and Practices in New York City." *Crime and Delinquency* 45 (April): 171–87.

Greer, K. R. 2000. "The Changing Nature of Interpersonal Relationships in a Women's Prison." *Prison Journal* 80 (December): 442–68.

Griffen, W. 2011. "Judicial Elections, Campaigning, and the First Amendment: Looking Past the Hype and Hysteria to Democracy." *Arkansas Law Review* 64:77–87.

Griffin, A. 2011a. "Lab Tech Pleads Guilty to Killing Yale Student." *Los Angeles Times*, March 18. http://articles.latimes.com/2011/mar/18/nation/la-na-yale-killing-20110318.

———. 2011b. "Suspect in Annie Le Slaying at Yale to Change Plea to Guilty, Lawyer Says." *Hartford Courant*, March 15. www.articles.courant.com.

Griffin, K. 2009. "Criminal Lying, Prosecutorial Power, and Social Meaning." *California Law Review* 97:1515–1568.

Griffin, L. 2010. "Untangling Double Jeopardy in Mixed Verdict Cases." *Southern Methodist University Law Review* 63:1033–68.

Griffin, P. 2011. "National Overviews." State Juvenile Justice Profiles. Pittsburgh: National Center for Juvenile Justice. http://www.ncjj.org/stateprofiles.

———. 1995. "The Politics and Economics of Increased Correctional Discretion over Time Served: A New York Case Study." *Justice Quarterly* 12 (June): 307–23.

Grissom, B. 2011. "Proposals Could Make It Harder to Leave Prison." *New York Times*, March 12. www.nytimes.com.

———. 2012. "More Young Inmates Attack One Another." *New York Times*, February 11. www.nytimes.com.

Gross-Shader, C. 2011. "Partnerships in Evidence-Based Policing." *Translational Criminology* (Summer), 8–9.

Grubman, S. 2011. "Bark with No Bite: How the Inevitable Discovery Rule Is Undermining the Supreme Court's Decision in *Arizona v. Gant.*" *Journal of Criminal Law and Criminology* 101:119–70.

Guerino, P., and A. J. Beck. 2011. *Sexual Victimization Reported by Adult Correctional Authorities, 2007–2008.* Bureau of Justice Statistics *Special Report.* Washington, DC: U.S. Department of Justice.

Guerino, P., P. M. Harrison, and W. J. Sabol. 2011. "Prisoners in 2010." Bureau of Justice Statistics *Bulletin*, December. NCJ 236096.

Guevara, L., D. Herz, and C. Spohn. 2006. "Gender and Juvenile Justice Decision-Making: What Role Does Race Play?" *Feminist Criminology* 1(4): 258–82.

Gunnell, J. J., and S. J. Ceci. 2010. "When Emotionality Trumps Reason: A Study of Individual Processing Style and Juror Bias." *Behavioral Sciences and the Law* 28:850–77.

Haarr, R. N., and M. Morash. 1999. "Gender, Race and Strategies of Coping with Occupational Stress in Policing." *Justice Quarterly* 16:303–36.

Haba, C., R. Sarver, R. Dobbs, and M. Sarver. 2008. "Attitudes of College Students toward Women in Policing." *Women and Criminal Justice* 19:235–50.

Hackett, D. P., and J. M. Violanti, eds. 2003. *Police Suicide: Tactics for Prevention.* Springfield, IL: Thomas.

Hagan, F. E. 1997. *Political Crime: Ideology and Criminality.* Needham Heights, MA: Allyn & Bacon.

Hails, J., and R. Borum. 2003. "Police Training and Specialized Approaches to Respond to People with Mental Illness." *Crime and Delinquency* 49:52–61.

Hall, J. 1947. *General Principles of Criminal Law.* 2nd ed. Indianapolis: Bobbs-Merrill.

Hallinan, J. T. 2001. *Going Up the River: Travels in a Prison Nation.* New York: Random House.

Hambling, D. 2005. "Police Toy with 'Less Lethal' Weapons." April 30. http://www.newscientist.com.

Hamilton, Z. K., C. J. Sullivan, B. M. Veysey, and M. Grillo. 2007. "Diverting Multi-Problem Youth from Juvenile Justice: Investigating the Importance of Community Influence on Placement and Recidivism." *Behavioral Sciences and the Law* 25:137–58.

Handy, R. 2012. "Parolee Arrested in Drug Bust." *Colorado Springs Gazette*, March 9. www.gazette.com.

Hanlon, M. 2007. "Run Away the Ray-Gun Is Coming: We Test U.S. Army's New Secret Weapon." *Daily Mail*, September 18. http://www.dailymail.co.uk.

Hannaford-Agor, P. 2011. "Systematic Negligence in Jury Operations: Why the Definition of Systematic Exclusion in Fair Cross Section Claims Must Be Expanded." *Drake Law Review* 59:762–98.

Hans, V., and N. Vidmar. 2008. "The Verdict on Juries." *Judicature* 91:226–30.

Hanson, R. A., and J. Chapper. 1991. *Indigent Defense Systems.* Williamsburg, VA: National Center for State Courts.

Hanson, R. A., and H. W. K. Daley. 1995. *Challenging the Conditions of Prisons and*

Jails: A Report on Section 1983 Litigation. Washington, DC: Bureau of Justice Statistics, U.S. Government Printing Office.

Harcourt, B. E., and J. Ludwig. 2006. "Broken Windows: New Evidence from New York City and a Five-City Social Experiment." *University of Chicago Law Review* 73:271–320.

Harkin, T. 2005. "Confronting the Meth Crisis." Press release, February 7. http://www.harkin.senate.gov.

Harlow, C. 2000. "Defense Counsel in Criminal Cases." Bureau of Justice Statistics *Bulletin*, November.

Harris Poll. 2009. "Who Are You? *CSI* Answers that Question Each Week and Is America's Favorite TV Show." *Harris Interactive.* April 21. http://www.harrisinteractive.com.

Harris, R. 2011. "Shootings by Police Continue to Decline." *New York Times*, November 22. www.nytimes.com.

Harrison, C. 2011. "Ten Rules for Great Jury Selection: With Some Lessons from Texas Case Law." *Defense Counsel Journal* 78:29–54.

Harrison, M. T. 2006. "True Grit: An Innovative Program for Elderly Inmates." *Corrections Today* 68(7): 46–49.

Hartley, R., S. Maddan, and C. Spohn. 2007. "Prosecutorial Discretion: An Examination of Substantial Assistance Departures in Federal Crack Cocaine and Powder Cocaine Cases." *Justice Quarterly* 24:382–407.

Hassell, K., and S. Brandl. 2009. "An Examination of Workplace Experiences of Police Patrol Officers: The Role of Race, Sex, and Sexual Orientation." *Police Quarterly* 12:408–30.

Hastie, R., S. Penrod, and N. Pennington. 1983. *Inside the Jury.* Cambridge, MA: Harvard University Press.

Hathaway, W. 2002. "A Clue to Antisocial Behavior: Study Finds Gene Marker for Which Abused Children May Become Troubled Adults." *Hartford Courant*, August 2, p. A17.

Hawaii Department of Public Safety, 2012. "Law Enforcement Division." Hawaii Department of Public Safety website. http://hawaii.gov/psd/law-enforcement.

Hawdon, J., and J. Ryan. 2003. "Police–Resident Interactions and Satisfaction with Police: An Empirical Test of Community Policing Assertions." *Criminal Justice Policy Review* 14:55–74.

Hayden, J. 2011. "Stretching Police Dollars—How Badly Are Budget Cuts Putting Citizen Safety in Jeopardy?" *Holland (MI) Sentinel*, November 12. www.hollandsentinel.com.

Hays, T. 2006. "NYC Real Time Crime Center Tracks Suspects." *Washington Post*, May 10. http://www.washingtonpost.com.

Heaphy, W. 2010. "Wayne County's Mental Health Court." *Michigan Bar Journal* 89:36–38.

Heffernan, E. 1972. *Making It in Prison.* New York: Wiley.

Heise, M. 2009. "Federal Criminal Appeals: A Brief Empirical Perspective." *Marquette Law Review* 93:825–43.

Hench, D. 2011. "Gurney Sentence: 60 Years." *Portland Press Herald*, March 17. www.pressherald.com.

Henry, S., and M. M. Lanier. 2006. *The Essential Criminology Reader.* Boulder, CO: Westview.

Hensley, J. J., and M. Wynn. 2009. "Close to Two-Thirds of Photos Taken by Speed Cameras Tossed." *Arizona Republic*, May 15. http://www.azcentral.com.

Herbert, S. 1996. "Morality in Law Enforcement: Chasing 'Bad Guys' with the Los Angeles Police Department." *Law & Society Review* 30:799–818.

Hickman, M., and B. Reaves. 2006. *Local Police Departments, 2003* (NCJ210118). Washington, DC: U.S. Department of Justice, Bureau of Justice Statistics.

Hicks, W. 2003. "Police Vehicular Pursuits: An Overview of Research and Legal Conceptualizations for Police Administrators." *Criminal Justice Policy Review* 14:75–95.

Hinduja, S. 2004. "Perceptions of Local and State Law Enforcement Concerning the Role of Computer Crime Investigative Teams." *Policing* 27:341–57.

———. 2007. "Neutralization Theory and Online Software Piracy: An Empirical Analysis." *Ethics and Information Technology* 9 (3): 187–204.

Hinduja, S., and J. W. Patchin. 2007. "Offline Consequences of Online Victimization: School Violence and Delinquency." *Journal of School Violence* 6(3): 89–112.

———. 2009. *Bullying beyond the Schoolyard: Preventing and Responding to Cyberbullying.* Thousand Oaks, CA: Corwin Press.

Hirsch, A. J. 1992. *The Rise of the Penitentiary.* New Haven, CT: Yale University Press.

Hirsch, M. 2007. "Midnight Run Re-Run: Bail Bondsmen, Bounty Hunters, and the Uniform Criminal Extradition Act." *University of Miami Law Review* 62:59–94.

Hirschel, D., and I. Hutchinson. 2003. "The Voices of Domestic Violence Victims: Predictors of Victim Preference for Arrest and the Relationship between Preference for Arrest and Revictimization." *Crime and Delinquency* 49:313–36.

Hirschi, T. 1969. *Causes of Delinquency.* Berkeley: University of California Press.

Hirschkorn, P. 2011. "WH OKs Military Detention of Terrorism Suspects." CBS News.com, December 14. www.cbsnews.com.

Hoctor, M. 1997. "Domestic Violence as a Crime against the State." *California Law Review* 85 (May): 643–700.

Hoffman, M. 1999. "Abolish Peremptory Challenges." *Judicature* 82:202–4.

Hoge, R. D., N. G. Guerra, and P. Boxer. 2008. *Treating the Juvenile Offender.* New York: Guilford Press.

Holl, J. 2005. "How to Find the Gunman: by Listening for the Gunshot." *New York Times*, August 17. http://www.nytimes.com.

Holleran, D., D. Beichner, and C. Spohn. 2010. "Examining Charging Agreement between Police and Prosecutors in Rape Cases." *Crime and Delinquency* 56:385–413.

Holtfreter, K., and M. Morash. 2003. "The Needs of Women Offenders." *Women & Criminal Justice* 14, 137–60.

Homan, C. 2010. "Michigan Lawmakers to Debate Bringing Good Time Back for Prisoners." *Holland Sentinel*, February 15. www.hollandsentinel.com.

Horne, P. 2006. "Policewomen: Their First Century and the New Era." *The Police Chief* 73 (9): September. http://policechiefmagazine.org.

Howard, J. 1929. *The State of Prisons in England and Wales.* London: J. M. Dent. (Original work published in 1777.)

Howlett, D. 2004. "Chicago Plans Advanced Surveillance." *USA Today*, September 9. http://www.usatoday.com.

Huebner, B. M., and R. Gustafson. 2007. "The Effect of Maternal Incarceration on Adult Offspring Involvement in the Criminal Justice System." *Journal of Criminal Justice* 35:283–96.

Huey, L. 2010. "'I've Seen This On CSI': Criminal Investigators Perceptions about the Management of Public Expectations in the Field." *Crime, Media, Culture* 6: 49–68.

Huff, C. R. 2002. "Wrongful Conviction and Public Policy: The American Society of Criminology, 2001 Presidential Address." *Criminology* 40:1–18.

Humes, K. R., N. A. Jones, and R. R. Ramirez. 2011. "Overview of Race and Hispanic Origin: 2010." *2010 Census Briefs* (March). Washington, DC: U.S. Census Bureau.

Hunt, K. 2010. "GOP Rips Holder on Miranda Rights." January 27. www.politico.com.

Hurdle, J. 2008. "Police Beating of Suspects Is Taped by TV Station in Philadelphia." *New York Times*, May 8. www.nytimes.com.

Hutchinson, B. 2009. "Chris Brown Begins Community Service Sentence for Beating Rihanna with Stable Work in Richmond." *New York Daily News*, September 17. http://nydailynews.com.

Indiana Department of Corrections. 2009. "Press Release: Plainfield Educational Facility Relocates to Indianapolis." December 16. http://www.in.gov/idoc/files/PREF_Relocation_Press_Release.pdf.

"Indiana's Answer to Prison Costs." 2011. *New York Times*, January 17. www.nytimes.com.

Ingold, J. 2011. "Prison Black Market A Steal: Correctional Officers Get Drawn into Contraband Smuggling." *Denver Post*, December 18. www.denverpost.com.

Innocence Project. 2012. "Facts about Post-Conviction DNA Exonerations." Innocence Project website. www.innocenceproject.org

Internet Crime Complaint Center, 2011. "2010 Internet Crime Report." Glen Allen, VA: National White Collar Crime Center.

———. 2010. "2009 Internet Crime Report." Glen Allen, VA: National White Collar Crime Center.

———. 2011. "2010 Internet Crime Report." Glen Allen, VA: National White Collar Crime Center.

Iribarren, C. J., J. H. Markovitz, D. R. Jacobs, P. J. Schreiner, M. Daviglus, and J. R. Hibbeln. 2004. "Dietary Intake of n-3, n-6 Fatty Acids and Fish: Relationship with Hostility in Young Adults—the CARDIA Study." *European Journal of Clinical Nutrition* 58:24–31.

Irwin, J. 1970. *The Felon.* Englewood Cliffs, NJ: Prentice-Hall.

———. 1980. *Prisons in Turmoil.* Boston: Little, Brown.

Irwin, J., and D. Cressey. 1962. "Thieves, Convicts, and the Inmate Culture." *Social Problems* 10:142–55.

Ith, I. 2001. "Taser Fails to Halt Man with Knife; Seattle Officer Kills 23-Year-Old." *Seattle Times*, November 28, p. A1.

Iyengar, R. 2008. "I'd Rather Be Hanged for a Sheep than a Lamb: The Unintended Consequences of 'Three-Strikes' Law." National Bureau of Economic Research Working Paper No. 13784.

Jacob, H. 1973. *Urban Justice.* Boston: Little, Brown.

Jacobs, C., and C. Smith. 2011. "The Influence of Justice John Paul Stevens: Opinion Assignments by the Senior Associate Justice." *Santa Clara Law Review* 51: 743–774.

Jacobs, J. B., and C. Panarella. 1998. "Organized Crime." In *The Handbook of Crime and Punishment*, ed. M. Tonry. New York: Oxford University Press, 159–77.

Jaksic, V. 2007. "Public Defenders, Prosecutors Face Crisis in Funding." *National Law Journal.* March 27. http://www.law.com.

Johnson, A. 2011. "Sentencing Overhaul Would Save State $78 Million." *Columbus Dispatch*, May 5. www.dispatchpolitics.com.

Johnson, B. D. 2006. "The Multilevel Context of Criminal Sentencing: Integrating Judge- and County-Level Influences." *Criminology* 44:259–98.

Johnson, K. 2002. "From Extreme Isolation, Waves of Felons are Freed." *USA Today*, December 12, p. 1A.

———. 2011. "Some States Rethink Felony Property Crimes." *USA Today*, October 30. www .usatoday.com.

Johnson, M., and L. A. Johnson. 2012. "Bail: Reforming Policies to Address Overcrowded Jails, the Impact of Race on Detention, and Community Revival in Harris County, Texas." *North-western Journal of Law and Social Policy* 7:42–87.

Johnson, M. A. 2010. "Already under Fire, Crime Labs Cut to the Bone." MSNBC.com, February 23. www.msnbc.com.

Johnson, R. 2002. *Hard Time: Understanding and Reforming the Prison*. 3rd ed. Belmont, CA: Wadsworth.

———. 2011. "Suspect Mental Disorder and Police Use of Force." *Criminal Justice and Behavior* 38:127–45.

Jordan, J. 2002. "Will Any Woman Do? Police, Gender and Rape Victims." *Policing* 25:319–44.

Jordan, W., L. Fridell, D. Faggianai, and B. Kubu. 2009. "Attracting Females and Racial/Ethnic Minorities to Law Enforcement." *Journal of Criminal Justice* 37:333–41.

JRSA (Justice Research and Statistics Association). 2008. *Status of NIBRS in the States*. http://www.jrsa.org/ibrrc/ background-status/nibrs_states .shtml.

Karmen, A. 2001. *Crime Victims*. 4th ed. Belmont, CA: Wadsworth.

Karnow, C. E. A. 2008. "Setting Bail for Public Safety." *Berkeley Journal of Criminal Law* 13:1–30.

KATC-TV. 2010. "New Prison 'Good Time' Law Frees 463." KATC. com, October 27. www.katc.com.

Kelling, G. L. 1985. "Order Mainte-nance, the Quality of Urban Life, and Police: A Line of Argument." In *Police Leadership in America*, ed. W. A. Geller. New York: Praeger.

Kelling, G. L., and C. M. Coles. 1996. *Fixing Broken Windows: Restoring and Reducing Crime in Our Communities*. New York: Free Press.

Kelling, G. L., T. Pate, D. Dieckman, and C. E. Brown. 1974. *The Kansas City Preventive Patrol Experiments: A Summary Report*. Washington, DC: Police Foundation.

Kenney, D. J., and J. O. Finckenauer. 1995. *Organized Crime in America*. Belmont, CA: Wadsworth.

Kenny, K. 2009. "When Cultural Tradition and Criminal Law Collide: Prosecutorial Discretion in Cross-Cultural Cases." *Judicature* 92:216–19.

Kerley, K. R., A. Hochstetler, and H. Copes. 2009. "Self-Control, Prison Victimization, and Prison Infractions." *Criminal Justice Review*, 34:553–68.

Kerlikowske, R. G. 2004. "The End of Community Policing: Remem-bering the Lessons Learned." *FBI Law Enforcement Bulletin* 73:6–11.

Kilgannon, C., and N. Cohen. 2009. "Cadets Trade the Trenches for Firewalls." *New York Times*, May 11. http://www.nytimes.com.

Kim, K., and M. Denver. 2011. *A Case Study on the Practices of Pretrial Services and Risk Assessment in Three Cities*. Washington, DC: District of Columbia Policy Institute.

Kimber, K. 2008. "Mental Health Courts—Idaho's Best Kept Secret." *Idaho Law Review* 45:249–81.

Kimberly, J. 2003. "House Passes Crime Lab Bill." *Houston Chronicle*, May 2. http://www .houstonchronicle.com.

King, N., F. Cheesman, and B. Ostrom. 2007. *Habeas Litigation in the U.S. District Courts: An Empirical Study of Habeas Corpus Cases Filed By State Prisoners under the Antiterrorism and Effective Death Penalty Act of 1996*. Williamsburg, VA: National Center for State Courts.

King, N., and J. Hoffmann. 2011. *Habeas for the 21st Century*. Chicago: University of Chicago Press.

King, N. J., and S. Sherry. 2008. "Habeas Corpus and Sentencing Reform: A Story of Unintended Consequences." *Duke Law Journal* 58:1–67.

Kingsnorth, R., R. MacIntosh, and S. Sutherland. 2002. "Criminal Charge or Probation Violation? Prosecutorial Discretion and Implications for Research in Criminal Court Processing." *Criminology* 40:553–77.

Kinports, K. 2011. "The Supreme Court's Love-Hate Relationship with *Miranda*." *Journal of Criminal Law and Criminology* 101:375–440.

Klahm, C., and R. Tillyer. 2010. "Understanding Police Use of Force: A Review of the Evidence." *Southwest Journal of Criminal Justice* 7:214–39.

Klain, E. 2012. "President Obama Signed the National Defense Authorization Act—Now What?" *Forbes*, January 2. www.forbes .com.

Kleck, G., B. Sever, S. Li, and M. Gertz. 2005. "The Missing Link in General Deterrence Research." *Criminology* 43 (3): 623–59.

Klein, A. 2008. "D.C. Police to Carry Semiautomatic Rifles on Patrol." *Washington Post*, May 17, p. B1.

Klein, D. 1973. "The Etiology of Female Crime." *Issues in Criminology* 8 (2): 3–30.

Kleinknecht, W. 1996. *The New Ethnic Mobs: The Changing Face of Organized Crime in America*. New York: Free Press.

Kleymeyer, C. 2010. Division of Corrections Training 2010 Annual Report. Kentucky Department of Corrections.

Klingler, D. 2012. "On the Problems and Promise of Research on Legal Police Violence." *Homicide Stud-ies* 16:78–96.

Kloepfer, C. 2012. "Prison Guards Now Equipped with Tasers." WLNS.com. March 2. www.wlns .com.

Klofas, J., and J. Yandrasits. 1989. "'Guilty but Mentally Ill' and the Jury Trial: A Case Study." *Criminal Law Bulletin* 24:423–43.

Knoll, C., and M. Sickmund. 2011. *Delinquency Cases in Juvenile Court, 2008*. Washington, DC: Office of Juvenile Justice and Delinquency Programs.

———. 2010. *Delinquency Cases in Juvenile Court, 2007* (NCJ 230168). Washington, DC: Office of Juvenile Justice and Delinquency Programs.

Kotch, S., and R. Mosteller. 2010. "The Racial Justice Act and the Long Struggle with Race and the Death Penalty in North Carolina." *North Carolina Law Review* 88:2031–128.

Kotlowitz, A. 1994. "Their Crimes Don't Make Them Adults." *New York Times Magazine*, February 13, p. 40.

Kramer, G. P., and D. M. Koenig. 1990. "Do Jurors Understand Criminal Justice Instructions? Analyzing the Results of the Michigan Juror Comprehension Project." *University of Michigan Journal of Law Reform* 23:401–37.

Krautt, P. 2002. "Location, Loca-tion, Location: Interdistrict and Intercircuit Variation in Sentencing Outputs for Federal Drug-Trafficking Offenses." *Jus-tice Quarterly* 19 (December): 633–71.

Kravets, D. 2011. "Wi-Fi-Hacking Neighbor from Hell Sentenced to 18 Years in Prison." WIRED.Com, July 12. http://www.wired.com /threatlevel/2011/07/hacking -neighbor-from-hell/.

Kris, D. 2011. "Law Enforcement as a Counterterrorism Tool." *Journal of National Security Law and Policy* 5:1–79.

Krischke, S. 2010. "Absent Ac-countability: How Prosecuto-rial Impunity Hinders the Fair Administration of Justice in America." *Journal of Law and Policy* 19:395–434.

Kruger, K. 2007. "Pregnancy and Policing: Are They Compatible? Pushing the Legal Limits on Behalf of Equal Employment Opportunity." *Wisconsin Women's Law Journal* 22:61–89.

Kruttschnitt, C. 2010. "The Paradox of Women's Imprisonment." *Daedelus*, 139(3):32–42.

KTKA-TV. 2011. "Shawnee Co. Looks to Cost Cuts with Early Retirement, Jury Pay Cuts." KTKA.com, February 10. www .ktka.com.

Kubrin, C. E., and E. A. Stewart. 2006. "Predicting Who Reof-fends: The Neglected Role of Neighborhood Context in Re-cidivism Studies." *Criminology* 44:165–97.

Kurlychek, M. 2010. "Transforming Attitudinal Change into Behav-ioral Change: The Missing link." *Criminology & Public Policy*. 9:119–26.

Kurlychek, M., and C. Kempinen. 2006. "Beyond Boot Camp: The Impact of Aftercare on Offender Re-Entry." *Criminology & Public Policy* 5:363–88.

Kyckelhahn, T. 2011. *Justice Ex-penditures and Employment, FY 1982–2007—Statistical Tables*. Washington, DC: U.S. Depart-ment of Justice.

Kyckelhahn, T., and T. Cohen. 2008. *Felony Defendants in Large Urban Counties, 2004— Statistical Tables*. Washington, DC: Bureau of Justice Statistics.

Lacey, M. 2011. "Evidence Points to Methodical Planning." *New York Times*, January 9, p. A1.

LaFraniere, S. 2009. "Facing Counterfeiting Crackdown, Beijing Vendors Fight Back." *New York Times*, March 2. http://www.nytimes.com.

Lambert, L. 2011. "States Seek to Escape Rising Prison Costs." Reuters News Service, May 20. www.reuters.com.

Langan, P., and D. Levin. 2002. "Recidivism of Released Prisoners Released in 1994. Bureau of Justice Statistics *Special Report*, June. NCJ 193427.

Langton, L. 2011. "Identity Theft Reported by Households, 2005–2010." Bureau of Justice Statistics *Crime Data Brief*, November. NCJ 236245.

Langton, L., and D. Farole. 2010. "State Public Defender Programs, 2007." Bureau of Justice Statis-tics *Special Report*, September. NCJ 228229.

Lattman, P. 2011. "Galleon Chief Sentenced to 11-Year Term in Insider Case." *New York Times*, October 13. www.nytimes.com.

Laub, J. H., and R. J. Sampson. 2003. *Shared Beginnings, Divergent Lives: Delinquent Boys to Age 70*. Cambridge, MA: Harvard University Press.

Lauritsen, J., and N. White. 2001. "Putting Violence in Its Place: The Influence of Race, Ethnicity, Gender, and Place on the Risk for Violence." *Criminology & Public Policy* 1:37–59.

Lauritsen, J. L., K Heimer, and J. P. Lynch. 2009. "Trends in the Gender Gap in Violent Offending: New Evidence from the National Crime Victimization Survey." *Criminology* 47(2): 361–99.

Lave, T. R. 1998. "Equal before the Law." *Newsweek*, July 13, p. 14.

Lawrence, A. 2009. *Cutting Correc-tions Costs: Earned Time Policies for State Prisoners*. Denver, CO: National Conference of State Legislatures.

Lazarus, D. 2010. "Customer Stuck with Counterfeit Money from Post Office." *Los Angeles Times*, May 25. www.latimes.com.

LeDuff, C. 2011. "Riding along with the Cops in Murdertown, U.S.A." *New York Times*, April 15. www.nytimes.com.

Lee, H., and M. Vaughn. 2010. "Organizational Factors that Contribute to Police Deadly Force Liability." *Journal of Criminal Justice* 38:193–206.

Lee, J. 2009. "Study Questions Whether Cameras Cut Crime." *New York Times*, March 3. http://www.nytimes.com.

Leiber, M. J., and K. Y. Mack. 2003. "The Individual and Joint Effects of Race, Gender, and Family Status on Juvenile Decision-Making." *Journal of Research in Crime & Delinquency* 40(1): 34–70.

Leo, R. A. 1996. "*Miranda's* Revenge: Police Interrogation as a Confidence Game." *Law & Society Review* 30:259–88.

Leonard, J. 2002. "Dropping 'Nonlethal' Beanbags as Too Dangerous." *Los Angeles Times*, June 3, p. 1.

Lersch, K. M. 2002. "Are Citizen Complaints Just Another Measure of Officer Productivity? An Analysis of Citizen Complaints and Officer Activity Measures." *Police Practices and Research* 3:135–47.

Lersch, K. M., and L. Kunzman. 2001. "Misconduct Allegations and Higher Education in a Southern Sheriff's Department." *American Journal of Criminal Justice* 25:161–72.

Levy, M. 2011. "The Mechanics of Federal Appeals: Uniformity and Case Management in Circuit Courts." *Duke Law Journal* 61:315–91.

Lewis, L. 2007. "Rethinking Miranda: Truth, Lies, and Videotapes." *Gonzaga Law Review* 43:199–238.

Lewis, N. A., 2009. "Stimulus Plan Has $1 Billion to Hire More Local Police." *New York Times*, February 6. www.nytimes.com.

Lichtblau, E. 2008. "Senate Approves Bill to Broaden Wiretap Powers." *New York Times*, July 10. www.nytimes.com.

———. 2012. "Police Are Using Tracking as Routine Tool." *New York Times*, March 31. www.nytimes.com.

Lichtblau, E., and J. Risen. 2009. "Officials Say U.S. Wiretaps Exceeded Law." *New York Times*, April 16. http://www.nytimes.com.

Lineberger, K. 2011. "The United States-El Salvador Extradition Treaty: A Dated Obstacle in the Transnational War against Mara Salvatrucha (MS-13)." *Vanderbilt Journal of Transnational Law* 44:187–216.

Liptak, A. 2003. "County Says It's Too Poor to Defend the Poor." *New York Times*, April 15. http://www.nytimes.com.

———. 2008a. "Electrocution Is Banned in Last State to Rely on It." *New York Times*, February 9. http://www.nytimes.com.

———. 2008b. "Illegal Globally, Bail for Profit Remains in U.S." *New York Times*, January 29. http://www.nytimes.com.

———. 2008c. "U.S. Prison Population Dwarfs That of Other Nations." *New York Times*, April 23. www.nytimes.com.

———. 2009. "Supreme Court Steps Closer to Repeal of Evidence Ruling." *New York Times*, January 31. www.nytimes.com.

———. 2011. "Justices, 5–4, Tell California to Cut Prisoner Population." *New York Times*, May 23. www.nytimes.com.

———. 2012. "Justices' Ruling Expands Rights of Accused in Plea Bargains." *New York Times*, March 21. www.nytimes.com.

Liska, A. E., and S. F. Messner. 1999. *Perspectives on Crime and Deviance*. 3rd ed. Upper Saddle River, NJ: Prentice-Hall.

Listwan, S. J., M. Colvin, D. Hanley, and D. Flanner. 2010. "Victimization, Social Support, and Psychological Well-Being: A Study of Recently Released Prisoners." *Criminal Justice and Behavior* 37:1140–59.

Lithwick, D., and J. Turner. 2003. "A Guide to the Patriot Act, Part 4." *Slate*, September 11. http://www.slate.msn.com.

Livsey, S. 2011. Juvenile Delinquency Probation Caseload, 2008. Washington, DC: Office of Juvenile Justice and Delinquency Programs.

Llana, S. M. 2006. "What's at Root of Boston's Rise in Murders?" *Christian Science Monitor*, May 10. http://www.csmonitor.com.

Loewy, A. 2011. "Rethinking Search and Seizure in a Post-9/11 World." *Mississippi Law Journal* 80:1507–21.

Logan, C. 1993. "Criminal Justice Performance Measures in Prisons." In *Performance Measures for the Criminal Justice System*. Washington, DC: Bureau of Justice Statistics, U.S. Government Printing Office, 19–60.

Lombroso, C. 1968. *Crime: Its Causes and Remedies*. Montclair, NJ: Patterson Smith. (Original work published in 1912.)

Lord, V. B., and P. Friday. 2003. "Choosing a Career in Police Work: A Comparative Study between Applications for Employment with a Large Police Department and Public High School Seniors." *Police Practices and Research* 4:63–78.

Loviglio, J. 2002. "Judge Reverses Himself, Will Allow Fingerprint-Analysis Testimony." Associated Press Wire Service, March 13 (available on Lexis-Nexis).

Luginbuhl, J., and M. Burkhead. 1994. "Sources of Bias and Arbitrariness in the Capital Trial." *Journal of Social Issues* 7:103–12.

Lum, C., C. Koper, and C. Telep. 2011. "The Evidence-Based Policing Matrix." *Journal of Experimental Criminology* 7:3–26.

Lumb, R. C., and R. Breazeale. 2003. "Police Officer Attitudes and Community Policing Implementation: Developing Strategies for Durable Organizational Change." *Policing and Society* 13:91–106.

Lundman, R., and R. Kaufman. 2003. "Driving While Black: Effects of Race, Ethnicity, and Gender on Citizen Self-Reports of Traffic Stops and Police Actions." *Criminology* 41:195–220.

Lunney, L. A. 2009. "Has the Fourth Amendment Gone to the Dogs?: Unreasonable Expansion of Canine Sniff Doctrine to Include Sniffs of the Home." *Oregon Law Review* 88:829–903.

Lynch, J. P., and L. A. Addington. 2009. *Understanding Crime Statistics: Revisiting the Divergence of the NCVS and UCR*. New York: Cambridge University Press.

Lynem, J. N. 2002. "Guards Call for Higher Wages, More Training: Industry Faces Annual Staff Turnover Rate of up to 300%." *San Francisco Chronicle*, August 22, p. B3.

Maag, C. 2008. "Police Shooting of Mother and Infant Exposes a City's Racial Tension." *New York Times*, January 30. http://www.nytimes.com.

MacArthur Foundation. 2007a. "The Changing Borders of Juvenile Justice: Transfer of Adolescents to the Adult Criminal Court." MacArthur Foundation Research Network on Adolescent Development and Juvenile Justice, *Issue Brief 5*. http://www.aadj.org/content.

MacArthur Foundation. 2007b. "Creating Turning Points for Serious Adolescent Offenders: Research on Pathways to Desistance." MacArthur Foundation Research Network on Adolescent Development and Juvenile Justice, *Issue Brief 2*. http://www.aadj.org/content.

MacArthur Foundation. 2007c. "Less Guilty by Reason of Adolescence." MacArthur Foundation Research Network on Adolescent Development and Juvenile Justice, *Issue Brief 3*. http://www.aadj.org/content.

MacCormack, J. 2011. "Border Issues Not Confined to the Border." *San Antonio Express-News*, June 8. www.mysanantonio.com.

Magda, L., A. Canton, and R. Gershon. 2010. "Web-Based Weapons of Mass Destruction Training for Transit Police." *Journal of Public Transportation* 13:63–78.

Maguire, E., C. Uchida, and K. Hassell. 2012. "Problem-Oriented Policing in Colorado Springs: A Content Analysis of 753 Cases." *Crime and Delinquency* (forthcoming 2012).

Maher, J. 2011. "Sacramento Police Handcuffed by Budget Cuts." News 10-TV, August 29. www.new10.net.

Maitland, A. S., and R. D. Sluder. 1998. "Victimization and Youthful Prison Inmates: An Empirical Analysis." *Prison Journal* 78:55–73.

Maki, A. 2012. "Crimes Lurk in Memphis Police Department Memos." *Memphis Commercial Appeal*, January 25. www.commercialappeal.com.

Mallory, Stephen L. 2012. *Understanding Organized Crime*. 2nd ed. Sudbury, MA: Jones & Bartlett.

Malone, P. 2012. "Crime Labs Fear Budget Cuts." FOX 10 TV, January 12. www.fox10tv.com.

"Man Acquitted of Concealed Weapon Charge on 'Necessity' Defense." *San Francisco Examiner*, July 10. www.sfexaminer.com.

Mann, D. 2011. "Why the Willingham Case Matters." *Texas Observer*, September 8. www.texasobserver.org.

Manning, A. 2012. "Local Officials Look to State to Pay Indigent-Defense Bills." *Columbus Dispatch*, February 26. www.dispatch.com.

Manning, P. K. 1977. *Police Work*. Cambridge, MA: MIT Press.

Marceau, J. F. 2008. "Un-Incorporating the Bill of Rights: The Tension between the Fourteenth Amendment and the Federalism Concerns of Modern Criminal Procedure Reforms." *Journal of Criminal Law and Criminology* 98:1231–302.

Mardar, N. 2010. Answering Jurors' Questions: Next Steps in Illinois. *Loyola University Chicago Law Journal* 41:727–52.

Markoff, J. 2009. "Tracking Cyberspies through the Web Wilderness." *New York Times*, May 12. http://www.nytimes.com.

Martin, S. E. 1991. "The Effectiveness of Affirmative Action." *Justice Quarterly* 8:489–504.

Martindale, M. 2012. "Audit: Michigan's Prisoner Re-Entry Initiative Harms Public Safety, Fails to Track Ex-Convicts." *Detroit News*, February 8. www.detroitnews.com.

Martinson, R. 1974. "What Works? Questions and Answers about Prison Reform." *Public Interest*, Spring, p. 25.

Maruschak, L. M. 2009. "HIV in Prisons, 2007–2008." Bureau of Justice Statistics *Bulletin*. Washington, DC: U.S. Department of Justice.

Mascaro, L. 2011. "Patriot Act Provisions Extended Just In Time." *Los Angeles Times*, May 27. www.latimes.com.

Maschke, K. J. 1995. "Prosecutors as Crime Creators: The Case of Prenatal Drug Use." *Criminal Justice Review* 20:21–33.

Mastrofski, S. D., M. D. Reisig, and J. D. McCluskey. 2002. "Police

Disrespect toward the Public: An Encounter-Based Analysis." *Criminology* 40:519–52.

Mauer, M. 2011. "Opposing View: Reduce Prison Populations." *USA Today*, May 24. www .usatoday.com.

Mauer, M., and M. Chesney-Lind, eds. 2002. *Invisible Punishment: The Collateral Consequences of Mass Imprisonment*. New York: New Press.

Maxson, C. 2011. *Street Gangs. In Crime and Public Policy*, ed. J. Q. Wilson and J. Petersilia. New York: Oxford University Press.

Maxwell, S. R. 1999. "Examining the Congruence between Predictors of ROR and Failures to Appear." *Journal of Criminal Justice* 27:127–41.

Maxwell, S. R., and C. Maxwell. 2000. "Examining the 'Criminal Careers' of Prostitutes within the Nexus of Drug Use, Drug Selling, and Other Illicit Activities." *Criminology* 38:787–809.

Maxwell, T. 2011. "Now It's Up to Judge to Decide If Gurney Was Sane." *Portland Press Herald*, January 20. www.pressherald .com.

Mayrack, B. 2008. "The Implications of *State ex rel. Thomas v. Schwarz* on Wisconsin Sentencing Policy after Truth-in-Sentencing II." *Wisconsin Law Review* 2008:181–223.

Mazerolle, L. D., D. Rogan, J. Frank, C. Famega, and J. Eck. 2003. "Managing Citizen Calls to the Police: The Impact of Baltimore's 3-1-1 Call System." *Criminology & Public Policy* 2:97–124.

McAuliff, B., and T. Duckworth. 2010. "I Spy with My Little Eye: Jurors' Detection of Internal Validity Threats in Expert Evidence." *Law and Human Behavior* 34:489–500.

McCall, M. A., M. M. McCall, and C. E. Smith. 2008. "Criminal Justice and the U.S. Supreme Court 2007–2008 Term." *Southern University Law Review* 36:33–87.

McCall, M. M., M. A. McCall, and C. Smith. 2010. "Criminal Justice and the U.S. Supreme Court's 2008–2009 Term." *Mississippi College Law Review* 29:1–47.

McCampbell, S. W. 2005. *Gender-Responsive Strategies for Women Offenders*. Washington, DC: National Institute of Corrections.

McCarthy, B. 2012. "Marlon Defillo Is Still Coordinating Police Details for Movie Sets." *New Orleans Times-Picayune*, February 6. www.nola.com.

McCartney, A. 2011. "Mel Gibson Pleads Guilty to Battery Charge of Ex-Girlfriend." *Chicago Sun Times*, March 12. www.suntimes .com.

McCollister, K. E., M. T. French, and H. Fang. 2010. "The Cost of Crime to Society: New Crime Specific Estimates for Policy and Program Evaluation." *Drug and Alcohol Dependency* 108(1–2): 98–109.

McCormick, J. 2000. "Scene of the Crime." *Newsweek*, February 28, p. 60.

McCoy, C. 1993. *Politics and Plea Bargaining: Victims' Rights in California*. Philadelphia: University of Pennsylvania Press.

———. 2007. "Caleb Was Right: Pretrial Detention Mostly Determines Everything." *Berkeley Journal of Criminal Law* 12:135–48.

McFarlane, L. 2009. "Ending Prisoner Rape in Michigan." *Free Press*, July 21.

McGarrell, E., S. Chermak, A. Weiss, and J. Wilson. 2001. "Reducing Firearms Violence through Directed Patrol." *Criminology & Public Policy* 1:119–48.

McKee, T. A. 2007. "Judges as Umpires." *Hofstra Law Review* 35:1709–24.

McKelvey, B. 1977. *American Prisons*. Montclair, NJ: Patterson Smith.

McMahon, P. 2002. "311 Lightens Load for Swamped 911 Centers." *USA Today*, March 5. http:// www.usatoday.com.

McNulty, T. L., and P. E. Bellair. 2003. "Explaining Racial and Ethnic Differences in Adolescent Violence: Structural Disadvantage, Family, Well-Being, and Social Capital." *Justice Quarterly* 20:1–31.

Meade, B., and B. Steiner. 2010. "The Total Effects of Boot Camps that House Juveniles: A Systematic Review of the Evidence." *Journal of Criminal Justice* 38:841–53.

Mears, B. "Nebraska Court Bans the Electric Chair." CNN, February 8. http://www.cnn.com.

Medina, J. 2011. "Jackson's Doctor Is Sentenced to Four Years." *New York Times*, November 29. www.nytimes.com.

Meier, R. F., and T. D. Miethe. 1993. "Understanding Theories of Criminal Victimization." In *Crime and Justice: A Review of Research*, ed. M. Tonry. Chicago: University of Chicago Press.

Meisner, J. 2011. "What Happened to the Elite Officers Charged." *Chicago Tribune*, September 9. www.chicagotribune.com.

Melde, C. 2009. "Lifestyle, Rational Choice, and Adolescent Fear: A Test of a Risk-Assessment Framework." *Criminology* 47:781–812.

Melde, C., F-A. Esbensen, and T. J. Taylor. 2009. "May Piece Be with You: A Typological Examination of the Fear and Victimization Hypothesis of Adolescent Weapon Carrying." *Justice Quarterly* 26:348–76.

Melde, C., T. J. Taylor, and F. Esbensen. 2009. " 'I Got Your Back': An Examination of the Protective Function of Gang Membership in Adolescence." *Criminology* 47:564–94.

Melendez, L. 2011. "BART's Citizen Review Board Questions SFPD Investigation." KGO-TV website, September 19. http://abclocal .go.com/kgo.

Menard, S. 2000. 'The Normality' of Repeat Victimization from Adolescence through Early Adulthood." *Justice Quarterly* 17:543–74.

Mentzer, A. 1996. "Policing in Indian Country: Understanding State Jurisdiction and Authority." *Law and Order* 44 (June): 24–29.

Merton, R. K. 1938. "Social Structure and Anomie." *American Sociological Review* 3:672–82.

Messerschmidt, J. W. 1993. *Masculinities and Crime: Critique and Reconceptualization*. Lanham, MD: Rowman & Littlefield.

Messner, S. F., S. Galea, K. J. Tardiff, and M. Tracy. 2007. "Policing, Drugs, and the Homicide Decline in New York City in the 1990s." *Criminology* 45:385–413.

Messner, S. F., and R. Rosenfeld. 1994. *Crime and the American Dream*. Belmont, CA: Wadsworth.

Michigan Department of Corrections. 2012. "New Employee Training in the MDOC." Lansing, MI. http://www.michigan.gov /corrections.

Miethe, T. D. 1995. "Fear and Withdrawal from Urban Life." *Annals of the American Academy of Political and Social Science* 539 (May): 14–27.

Milhizer, E. 2004. "Justification and Excuse: What They Were, What They Are, and What They Ought to Be." *St. Johns Law Review* 78:725–895.

Mihm, S. 2006. "No Ordinary Counterfeit." *New York Times*, July 23. http://www.nytimes .com.

Miller, M. 2009. "LPD Cars Receive $24K Upgrade." *Lansing (MI) State Journal*, May 14, p. 4B.

Miller, R. 2012. "Hundreds Picket in Effort to Rescue Dwight Prison." March 15, 2012. http:// pantagraph.com.

Minton, T. D. 2011. *Jail Inmates at Mid-year 2010—Statistical Tables*. Washington, DC: U.S. Bureau of Justice Statistics.

Miroff, N. 2008. "Detainee Program Strains Va. Jail." *Washington Post*, April 8, p. A01.

Monkkonen, E. H. 1981. *Police in Urban America, 1869–1920*. Cambridge, England: Cambridge University Press.

Moore, M. 1992. "Problem-Solving and Community Policing." In *Modern Policing*, ed. M. Tonry and N. Morris. Chicago: University of Chicago Press, 99–158.

Moore, S. 2009. "Number of Life Terms Hits Record." *New York Times*, July 22. www.nytimes .com.

Moore, T. 2011. " 'East Coast Rapist' Caught, Officials Say after Man's DNA Linked to Spree of Sex Assaults." *New York Daily News*, March 5. www.dailynews.com.

Moran, R. 2002. *Executioner's Current: Thomas Edison, George Westinghouse, and the Invention of the Electric Chair*. New York: Knopf.

Morash, M., J. K. Ford, J. P. White, and J. G. Boles. 2002. "Directing the Future of Community-Policing Initiatives." In *The Move to Community Policing: Making Change Happen*, ed. M. Morash and J. Ford. Thousand Oaks, CA: Sage, 277–88.

Morash, M., R. N. Haarr, and L. Rucker. 1994. "A Comparison of Programming for Women and Men in the U.S. Prisons in the 1980s." *Crime and Delinquency* 40 (April): 197–221.

Morris, H. 2012. "Europe Cracks Down on Cybercrime." *New York Times*, March 29. www.nytimes .com.

Morris, N., and M. Tonry. 1990. *Between Prison and Probation: Intermediate Punishments in a Rational Sentencing System*. New York: Oxford University Press.

Moses, P. 2005. "Corruption? It Figures: NY Police Department's Crime Stats and the Art of Manipulation." *Village Voice*, March 29. http://www .villagevoice.com.

Mosher, C., T. Miethe, and D. Phillips. 2002. *The Mismeasure of Crime*. Thousand Oaks, CA: Sage.

"The Most Stress Related Occupations." 2006. *Consumer Awareness Journal* (September). http://www.consumer -awareness-journal.com.

Mueller, R. S. 2011a. "Changing Threats in a Changing World: Staying Ahead of Terrorists, Spies, and Hackers." Speech delivered to the Commonwealth Club of California, San Francisco, November 17. http://www.fbi .gov/news/speeches/changing -threats-in-a-changing-world -staying-ahead-of-terrorists-spies -and-hackers.

———. 2011b. "Statement before Senate Committee on Homeland Security and Governmental Affairs." Washington, DC, September 13.

Murphy, K., and N. Riccardi. 2011. "Arizona Rep. Gabrielle Giffords Shot." *Los Angeles Times*, January 8.

Murphy, P. V. 1992. "Organizing for Community Policing." In *Issues in Policing: New Perspectives*, ed. J. W. Bizzack. Lexington, KY: Autumn Press, 113–28.

Murray, J. (2008). "Transforming Juvenile Justice." *Indianapolis Star*, May 27. http://indystar .com.

Muskal, M. 2012. "Officer Killed in Utah Drug Raid." *Los Angeles Times*, January 5. www.latimes .com.

Na, C., and D. C. Gottfredson. 2011. "Police Officers in Schools: Effects on School Crime and the Processing of Offending Behaviors." *Justice Quarterly*, 1–32.

Nagin, D. S., A. R. Piquero, E. S. Scott, and L. Steinberg. 2006. "Public Preferences for Rehabilitation versus Incarceration of Juvenile Offenders: Evidence from a Contingent Valuation Survey." *Criminology & Public Policy* 5(4):301–26.

Nakamura, D. 2012. "Obama Signs Defense Bill, Pledges to Maintain Legal Rights of U.S. Citizens." *Washington Post*, December 31. www.washingtonpost.com.

Nakamura, D., D. Hedgpeth, and S. Horwitz. 2011. "Videos Show Details of Tucson Shooting." *Washington Post*, January 19. www.washingtonpost.com.

Nalla, M. 2002. "Common Practices and Functions of Corporate Security: A Comparison of Chemical, Financial, Manufacturing, Service, and Utility Industries." *Journal of Security Administration* 25:33–46.

National Academy of Sciences. 2009. *Strengthening Forensic Sciences in the United States*. Washington, DC: National Academy of Sciences.

National Association of Women Judges. 2011. "2010 Representation of United States State Court Women Judges." http://www.nawj.org/us_state_court_statistics_2010.asp.

National Public Radio (NPR). 2011. "Nation's Jails Struggle with Mentally Ill Prisoners." *All Things Considered* show website. September 4. www.npr.org.

National Youth Gang Center. 2009. National Youth Gang Survey Analysis. http://www.nationalgangcenter.gov/Survey-Analysis.

Nava, M. 2008. "The Servant of All: Humility, Humanity, and Judicial Diversity." *Golden Gate University Law Review* 38:175–94.

New York State Division of Criminal Justice Services. 2008. *New York State Probation Population: 2007 Profile.* (June).

Nir, S. 2011. "Indictment of 55 in Cybercrime Ring Expected Friday." *New York Times*, December 15. www.nytimes.com.

Noblet, A., J. Rodwell, and A. Allisey. 2009. "Job Stress in the Law Enforcement Sector: Comparing the Linear, Non-Linear, and Interaction Effects of Working Conditions." *Stress and Health* 25:111–20.

Nolasco, C., R. delCarmen, and M. Vaughn. 2011. "What *Herring* Hath Wrought: An Analysis of Post-*Herring* Cases in the Federal Courts." *American Journal of Criminal Law* 38:221–61.

O'Brien, B. 2009. "A Recipe for Bias: An Empirical Look at the Interplay between Institutional Incentives and Bounded Reality in Prosecutorial Decision Making." *Missouri Law Review* 74:999–1048.

O'Harrow, R. 2008. "Centers Tap into Personal Databases." *Washington Post*, April 2. www.washingtonpost.com.

O'Hear, M. M. 2006. "The End of *Bordenkircher*: Extending the Logic of *Apprendi* to Plea Bargaining." *Washington University Law Review* 84:835–49.

O'Keefe, K. 2010. "Two Wrongs Make a Wrong: A Challenge to Plea Bargaining and Collateral Consequence Statutes through Their Integration." *Journal of Criminal Law and Criminology* 100:243–277.

Oklahoma Department of Corrections. 2011. "Facts at a Glance." March 31. www.doc.state.ok.us.

Oppel, R.A. 2011. "Private Prisons Found to Offer Little in Savings." *New York Times*, May 18. www.nytimes.com.

Orr, K. 2009. "S.D. Probation Dept. Seeing Increased Workload, Less Money." KPBS radio website, August 7. www.kpbs.org.

Osborne, J. 2011. "Union Faults Camden County Jail's Elevators." *Philadelphia Inquirer*, April 18. www.philly.com.

Ostermann, M. 2009. "An Analysis of New Jersey's Day Reporting Center and Halfway Back Program: Embracing the Rehabilitative Ideal through Evidence-Based Practices." *Journal of Offender Rehabilitation* 48:139–53.

"Our View: Don't Just Cut Prisoners Loose" [Editorial]. 2011. *USA Today*, May 24. www.usatoday.com.

Owen, B. 1998. *"In the Mix": Struggle and Survival in a Woman's Prison.* Albany: State University of New York Press.

Owen, B., J. Wells, J. Pollock, B. Muscat, and S. Torres. 2008. "Gendered Violence and Safety: A Contextual Approach to Improving Security in Women's Facilities" (Final Report). Unpublished.

Packer, H. L. 1968. *The Limits of the Criminal Sanction.* Stanford, CA: Stanford University Press.

Palmer, B. 2011. "Oklahoma's Female Inmate Population Skyrockets." *Oklahoman*, January 30. http://newsok.com.

Palmer, T. 1992. *The Re-Emergence of Correctional Intervention.* Newbury Park, CA: Sage.

Paoline, E. 2003. "Take Stock: Toward a Richer Understanding of Police Culture." *Journal of Criminal Justice* 31:199–214.

Paoline, E., and W. Terrill. 2007. "Police Education, Experience, and the Use of Force." *Criminal Justice and Behavior* 34:179–196.

Papparozzi, M., and G. Hinzman. 2005. "Caseload Size in Probation and Parole." *Perspectives* 29 (Spring): 23–25.

Parent, D. 2003. *Correctional Boot Camps: Lessons from a Decade of Research.* Washington, DC: National Institute of Justice.

Patchin, J. W., and S. Hinduja. 2012. *Cyberbullying Prevention and Response: Expert Perspectives.* New York: Routledge.

Peart, N. 2011. "Why Is the N.Y.P.D. after Me?" *New York Times*, December 17. www.nytimes.com.

Peralta, E. 2011. "In Report, ACLU Claims Chicago's Surveillance Cameras Violate Privacy." National Public Radio, February 8. www.npr.org.

Perez, D. M., A. R. Gover, K. M. Tennyson, and S. Santos. 2009. "Individual and Institutional Characteristics Related to Inmate Victimization." *International Journal of Offender Therapy and Comparative Criminology* 54:378–94.

Perin, M. 2009. "Hazswat Changed?: Combining Hazmat and SWAT Training for Tactical Operations." *Law Enforcement Technology* 36:20–25.

Perrine, J., V. Speirs, and J. Horwitz. 2010. "Fusion Centers and the Fourth Amendment." *Capital University Law Review* 38:721–87.

Petersilia, J. 1990. "When Probation Becomes More Dreaded Than Prison." *Federal Probation*, March, p. 24.

———. 2003. *When Prisoners Come Home: Parole and Prisoner Reentry.* New York: Oxford University Press.

———. 2009. *When Prisoners Come Home: Parole and Prisoner Reentry.* New York: Oxford University Press.

Peterson, J. L., and M. J. Hickman. 2005. "Census of Publicly Funded Forensic Crime Laboratories, 2002." Bureau of Justice Statistics *Bulletin*, February, p. 1.

Petteruti, A., and N. Walsh. 2008. *Jailing Communities: The Impact of Jail Expansion and Effective Public Safety Strategies.* Washington, DC: Justice Policy Institute.

Pew Center on the States. 2007. "What Works in Community Corrections: An Interview with Dr. Joan Petersilia." *Public Safety Performance Project*, No. 2. November.

———. 2008. One in 100: Behind Bars in America 2008. Washington, DC: Pew Center on the States.

———. 2009. *One in 31: The Long Reach of American Corrections.* Washington, DC: Pew Charitable Trusts.

———. 2010. "Prison Count 2010: State Population Declines for the First Time in 38 Years." *Issue Brief.* April 2010.

———. 2011. *State of Recidivism: The Revolving Door of America's Prisons.* Washington, DC: Pew Charitable Trusts.

Phelps, M. S. 2011. "Rehabilitation in the Punitive Era: The Gap Between Rhetoric and Reality in U.S. Prison Programs." *Law & Society Review* 45, 33–68.

Phillips, M. 2011. *Commercial Bail Bonds in New York City: Characteristics and Implications.* New York: New York City Criminal Justice Agency.

Phillips, S. 1977. *No Heroes, No Villains.* New York: Random House.

Pisciotta, A. W. 1994. *Benevolent Repression: Social Control and the American Reformatory-Prison Movement.* New York: New York University Press.

Pizarro, J. M., and R. E. Narag. 2008. "Supermax Prisons: What We Know, What We Do Not Know,

and Where We Are Going." *Prison Journal* 88:23–42.

Platt, A. 1977. *The Child Savers.* 2nd ed. Chicago: University of Chicago Press.

Pochna, P. 2002. "N.J. Police Linking with National Data Network." *Baltimore Sun*, April 2. http://articles.baltimoresun.com/2002-04-02/news/0204020041_1_jersey-state-police-bergen-county-computer-center.

Podgor, E. 2010. "The Tainted Federal Prosecutor in an Overcriminalized Justice System." *Washington and Lee Law Review* 67:1569–85.

Podlas, K. 2006. "The 'CSI Effect' and Other Forensic Fictions." *Loyola of Los Angeles Entertainment Law Review* 27:87–125.

Poole, 2011. "Brown's Attorneys to Meet with Judge." *Beaver County Times*, May 7.

Porter, R. 2011. *Choosing Performance Indicators for Your Community Prosecution Initiative.* Washington, DC: Association of Prosecuting Attorneys.

Porter, R., S. Lee, and M. Lutz. 2002. *Balancing Punishment and Treatment: Alternatives to Incarceration in New York City.* New York: Vera Institute of Justice.

Post, L. 2004. "ABA Wants to Transform Way Jurors Do Their Jobs." *New Jersey Law Journal* August 16:1.

Poston, B. 2011. "Racial Gap Found in Traffic Stops in Milwaukee." *Milwaukee Journal Sentinel*, December 3. www.jsonline.com.

PR Newswire. 2001. "Ion Track Instruments Unveils New Technology to Aid in Fight against Terrorism and Drug Trafficking." March 22 (available on Lexis-Nexis).

Pratt, J. 2011. "Are We Being Fair to Our Judges and the Perception of Justice in Alabama by Having Partisan Elections for Judicial Office?" *Alabama Lawyer* 72:443–44.

Preston, J. 2005. "Rape Victims' Eyes Were Covered, but a Key Clue Survived." *New York Times*, April 28. http://www.nytimes.com.

Price, M. 2009. "Performing Discretion or Performing Discrimination: Race, Ritual, and Peremptory Challenges in Capital Jury Selection." *Michigan Journal of Race and Law* 15:57–107.

"Private Jails: Locking in the Best Price." 2007. *Economist*, January 25. http://www.economist.com/node/8599146.

Propper, A. 1982. "Make Believe Families and Homosexuality among Imprisoned Girls." *Criminology* 20:127–39.

Protess, B. 2009. "The DNA Debacle: How the Federal Government Botched the DNA Backlog Crisis." ProPublica.com, May 5. http://www.propublica.org

Provine, D. M. 1996. "Courts in the Political Process in France." In *Courts, Law, and Politics in Comparative Perspective,* ed. H. Jacob, E. Blankenburg, H. Kritzer, D. M. Provine, and J. Sanders. New Haven, CT: Yale University Press, 177–248.

Prussel, D., and K. Lonsway. 2001. "Recruiting Women Police Officers." *Law and Order* 49 (July): 91–96.

Public Opinion Strategies. 2010. *National Research of Public Attitudes on Crime and Punishment* (September). Washington, DC: Pew Center on the States.

Puzzanchera, C., B. Adams, and M. Sickmund. 2011. *Juvenile Court Statistics, 2008.* Pittsburg: National Center for Juvenile Justice.

Puzzanchera, C., and W. Kang. 2011. "Easy Access to the FBI's Supplementary Homicide Reports: 1980–2009." http://www.ojjdp.gov/ojstatbb/ezashr/.

Rabe-Hemp, C. 2008. "Female Officers and the Ethic of Care: Does Officer Gender Impact Police Behaviors?" *Journal of Criminal Justice* 36:426–34.

Radelet, M. L. 2004. "Post-*Furman* Botched Executions." http://www.deathpenaltyinfor.org/article.php?scid=8&did=478.

Rafter, N. H. 1983. "Prisons for Women, 1790–1980." In *Crime and Justice*, 5th ed., ed. M. Tonry and N. Morris. Chicago: University of Chicago Press.

Rainville, G., and S. Smith. 2003. "Juvenile Felony Defendants in Criminal Courts." Bureau of Justice Statistics *Special Report*, May. NCJ 197961.

Rand, M. 2010. *Criminal Victimization, 2009.* Washington, DC: Bureau of Justice Statistics.

Randolph, E. D. 2001. "Inland Police Like New Weaponry." *Riverside* (CA) *Press-Enterprise*, November 24, p. B4.

Rashbaum, W. K., and A. Baker. 2010. "Smoking Car to an Arrest in 53 Hours." *New York Times*, May 4. www.nytimes.com.

Rashbaum, W. K., M. Mazzetti, and P. Baker. 2010. "Arrest Made in Times Square Bomb Case." *New York Times*, May 3. www.nytimes.com.

Ratcliffe, J. 2010. "Crime Mapping: Spatial and Temporal Challenges." *Handbook of Quantitative Criminology* 1: 5–24.

Ratcliffe, J., T. Taniguchi, E. Groff, and J. Wood. 2011. "The Philadelphia Foot Patrol Experiment: A Randomized Controlled Trial of Police Patrol Effectiveness in Violent Crime Hotspots." *Criminology* 49:795–831.

Ravitz, J. 2009. "Scanners Take 'Naked' Pics, Groups Says." CNN.com, May 18. www.cnn.com.

Reaves, B. 2006. "Violent Felons in Large Urban Counties." Bureau of Justice Statistics *Special Report*, July. NCJ 205289.

Reaves, B. 2010. *Local Police Departments, 2007.* Washington, DC: U.S. Bureau of Justice Statistics.

———. 2011. "Census of State and Local Law Enforcement Agencies, 2008." Bureau of Justice Statistics *Bulletin*, July. NCJ233982.

Regoli, R. M., and J. D. Hewitt. 1994. *Criminal Justice.* Englewood Cliffs, NJ: Prentice-Hall.

Reid, T. R. 2004. "Rape Case against Bryant Is Dropped." *Washington Post*, September 2. http://www.washingtonpost.com.

Reid, T. V. 2000. "The Politicization of Judicial Retention Elections: The Defeat of Justices Lamphier and White." In *Research on Judicial Selection 1999.* Chicago: American Judicature Society, 45–72.

Reilly, R. 2011. "Mueller: House GOP 2011 Budget Would 'Undermine' FBI." TPM.com, March 16. http://tpmmuckraker.talkingpointsmemo.com/.

Reisig, M. D. 2010. "Community and Problem-Oriented Policing." *Crime and Justice* 39:2–53.

Reisig, M. D., J. D. McCluskey, S. D. Mastrofski, and W. Terrill. 2004. "Suspect Disrespect toward the Police." *Justice Quarterly* 21:241–68.

Reiss, A. J., Jr. 1992. "Police Organization in the Twentieth Century." In *Crime and Justice: A Review of Research*, vol. 15, ed. M. Tonry and N. Morris. Chicago: University of Chicago Press, 51–97.

Rempel, M., J. Zweig, C. Lindquist, J. Roman, S. Rossman, and D. Krastein. 2012. "Multi-Site Evaluation Demonstrates Effectiveness of Adult Drug Courts." *Judicature* 95:154–57.

Renzema, M., and E. Mayo-Wilson. 2005. "Can Electronic Monitoring Reduce Crime for Moderate to High-Risk Offenders?" *Journal of Experimental Criminology* 1:215–37.

Reuland, M. 2010. "Tailoring the Police Response to People with Mental Illness to Community Characteristics in the USA." *Police Practice and Research: An International Journal* 11:315–29.

Rhodes, K., M. Dichter, C. Kothari, S. Marcus, and C. Cerulli. 2011. "The Impact of Children in Legal Actions Taken by Women Victims of Intimate Partner Violence." *Journal of Family Violence* 26:355–64.

Riccardi, N. 2009. "Cash-Strapped States Revise Laws to Get Inmates Out." *Los Angeles Times*, September 5. www.latimes.com.

Rich, J., S. E. Wakeman, and S. L. Dickman. 2011. "Medicine and the Epidemic of Incarceration in the United States." *New England Journal of Medicine* 364:2081–83.

Richburg, K. B. 2007. "N.J. Approves Abolition of Death Penalty; Corzine to Sign." *Washington Post*, December 14, p. A3.

Richey, W. 2006. "US Creates Terrorist Fingerprint Database." *Christian Science Monitor*, December 27, pp. 1, 4.

Richmond, K. M. 2012. "The Impact of Federal Prison Industries Employment on the Recidivism Outcomes of Female Inmates." *Justice Quarterly* (forthcoming).

Richtel, M. 2002. "Credit Card Theft Thrives Online as Global Market." *New York Times*, May 13. http://www.nytimes.com.

Richter, E., and A. Humke. 2011. "Demonstrative Evidence: Evidence and Technology in the Courtroom." In *Handbook of Trial Consulting*, ed. Richard L. Wiener and Brian H. Bornstein. New York: Springer, 187–201.

Ring, W. 2005. "Backlogs in Labs Undercut DNA's Crime-Solving Value." *Lansing* (MI) *State Journal*, April 28, p. A3.

Roane, K. R., and D. Morrison. 2005. "The CSI Effect." *U.S. News and World Report*, April 25. http://www.usnews.com.

Robbins, L. 2011. "A Fateful Stop for Candy for a Helper to So Many." *New York Times*, November 1. www.nytimes.com.

Roberts, D. E. 2004. "The Social and Moral Costs of Mass Incarceration in African-American Communities." *Stanford Law Review* 56 1271–1305.

Robinson, P. H., and M. D. Dubber. 2007. "The American Model Penal Code: A Brief Overview." *New Criminal Law Review* 10:319–41.

Rockwell, F. G. 2008. "The Chesterfield/Colonial Heights Drug Court: A Partnership between the Criminal Justice System and the Treatment Community." *University of Richmond Law Review* 43:5–17.

Rogers, R., J. Rogstad, J. Steadham, and E. Drogin. 2011. "In Plain English: Avoiding Recognized Problems with *Miranda* Miscomprehension." *Psychology, Public Policy, and Law* 17:264–85.

Rose, D. 2009. "North Korea's Dollar Store." *Vanity Fair*, August 5. www.vanityfair.com.

Rosen, L. 1995. "The Creation of the Uniform Crime Report: The Role of Social Science." *Social Science History* 19 (Summer): 215–38.

Rosenberg, T. 2012. "Out of Jail, and Into a Job." *New York Times*, March 28. www.nytimes.com.

Rosenfeld, R., R. Fornango, and E. Baumer. 2005. "Did *Ceasefire, Compstat,* and *Exile* Reduce Homicide?" *Criminology & Public Policy* 4:419–50.

Rosenfeld, R., R. Fornango, and A. F. Rengifo. 2007. "The Impact of Order-Maintenance Policing on New York City Homicide and Robbery Rates: 1988–2001." *Criminology* 45:355–83.

Rosenmerkel, S., M. Durose, and D. Farole. 2009. "Felony Sentences in State Courts, 2006—Statistical Tables." Bureau of Justice Statistics *Statistical Tables* (December). http://bjs.ojp.usdoj.gov/.

Rosenthal, J. A. 2008. "For-Profit Terrorism: The Rise of Armed Entrepreneurs." *Studies in Conflict & Terrorism* 31(6): 481–98.

Rossi, P. H., and R. A. Berk. 1997. *Just Punishments: Federal Guidelines and Public Views Compared.* New York: Aldine DeGruyter.

Rothman, D. J. 1971. *The Discovery of the Asylum: Social Order and Disorder in the New Republic.* Boston: Little, Brown.

Rotman, E. 1995. "The Failure of Reform." In *Oxford History of the Prison*, ed. N. Morris and D. J. Rothman. New York: Oxford University Press.

Rousey, D. C. 1984. "Cops and Guns: Police Use of Deadly Force in Nineteenth-Century New Orleans." *American Journal of Legal History* 28:41–66.

Rudolph, J. 2012. "Police Layoffs Ripple through Key Swing State of Florida." *Huffington Post*, January 31. http://www.huffingtonpost.com/2012/01/31/police-layoffs-florida_n_1244364.html.

Rydberg, J., and W. Terrill. 2010. "The Effect of Higher Education on Police Behavior." *Police Quarterly* 13:92–120.

Saad, L. 2010. "Nearly 4 in 10 Americans still fear walking alone at night." Gallup.com, November 5. http://www.gallup.com/poll/144272/Nearly-Americans-FearWalking-Alone-Night.aspx.

Sabo, D., T. A. Kupers, and W. London. 2001. "Gender and the Politics of Punishment." In *Prison Masculinities*, ed. D. Sabo, T. A. Kupers, and W. London. Philadelphia: Temple University Press.

Sack, K. 2011. "Executions in Doubt in Fallout over Drug." *New York Times*, March 16. www.nytimes.com.

Samaha, J. 2011. *Criminal Law*, 10th ed. Belmont, CA: Cengage.

Sampson, R. J., and J. H. Laub. 1990. "Crime and Deviance over the Life Course: The Salience of Adult Social Bonds." *American Sociological Review* 55:609–27.

———. 1993. *Crime in the Making: Pathways and Turning Points through Life.* Cambridge, MA: Harvard University Press.

Sampson, R. J., and W. J. Wilson. 1995. "Toward a Theory of Race, Crime and Urban Inequality." In *Crime and Inequality*, ed. J. Hagan and R. Peterson. Palo Alto, CA: Stanford University Press.

Sanchez, C. E, and M. Giordano. 2008. "Gang Activity in Suburbs Acknowledged." *Nashville Tennessean*, April 28. http://tennessean.com.

Sanger, D. E., and E. Lichtblau. 2006. "Administration Starts Weeklong Blitz in Defense of Eavesdropping Program." *New York Times*, January 24. http://www.nytimes.com.

Santos, F. 2007. "'CSI Effect'; Evidence From Bite Marks, It Turns Out, Is Not So Elementary." *New York Times*, January 28. http://www.nytimes.com.

———. 2008. "Plan to Close Prisons Stirs Anxiety in Rural Towns."

New York Times, January 27. www.nytimes.com.

Santos, M. 2004. *About Prison*. Belmont, CA: Wadsworth.

Saphire, R. B., and P. Moke. 2008. "The Ideologies of Judicial Selection: Empiricism and the Transformation of the Judicial Selection Debate." *University of Toledo Law Review* 39:551–90.

Sarche, J. 2005. "Kobe Case Settled." *Pasadena Star-News*, March 2. http://www .pasadenastarnews.com.

Savage, C. 2011. "Trend to Lighten Harsh Sentences Catches on in Conservative States." *New York Times*, August 12. www.nytimes .com.

Scalia, J. 2002. "Prisoners Petitions Filed in U.S. District Courts, 2000, with Trends 1980–2000." Bureau of Justice Statistics *Special Report*, January.

Schaible, L., and V. Gecas. 2010. "The Impact of Emotional Labor and Value Dissonance on Burnout among Police Officers." *Police Quarterly* 13:316–41.

Schlanger, M. 2008. "Jail Strip-Search Cases: Patterns and Participants." *Law and Contemporary Problems* 71:65–88.

Schlesinger, T. 2011. "The Failure of Race Neutral Policies: How Mandatory Terms and Sentencing Enhancements Contribute to Mass Incarceration." *Crime and Delinquency* 57:56–81.

Schlosser, L. Z., D. A. Safran, and C. A. Sbaratta. 2010. "Reasons for Choosing a Correction Officer Career." *Psychological Services* 7(1), 34–43.

Schofield, D. 2011. "Playing with Evidence: Using Video Games in the Courtroom." *Entertainment Computing* 2: 47–58.

Schultz, D. 2000. "No Joy in Mudville Tonight: The Impact of Three Strikes' Laws on State and Federal Corrections Policy, Resources, and Crime Control." *Cornell Journal of Law and Public Policy* 9:557–83.

Schwartz, J. 2009. "Mistrial by iPhone: Juries' Web Research Upends Trials." *New York Times*, March 18. http://www.nytimes .com.

Schwartz, J., and E. G. Fitzsimmons. 2011. "Illinois Governor Signs Capital Punishment Ban." *New York Times*, March 9. www.nytimes.com.

Scott, A. 2011. "Prison for ex-U.N. Official Scott Ritter in Monroe Sex Sting Case." *Pocono Record*, October 27. www.poconorecord .com.

Secret, M. 2010. "N.Y.C. Misdemeanor Defendants Lack Bail Money." *New York Times*, December 2. www.nytimes.com.

Segal, D. 2009. "Financial Fraud Is Focus of Attack by Prosecutors." *New York Times*, March 12. http://www.nytimes.com.

Segal, L., B. Ngugi, and J. Mana. 2011. "Credit Card Fraud: A New Perspective on Tackling an Intransigent Problem." *Fordham Journal of Corporate and Financial Law* 16: 743–81.

Shane, J. 2010. "Organizational Stressors and Police Performance." *Journal of Criminal Justice* 38:807–18.

Shapiro, B. 1997. "Sleeping Lawyer Syndrome." *Nation*, April 7, pp. 27–29.

Sharkey, J. 2008. "Mistakes on Terrorist Watch List Affect Even Children." *New York Times*, September 9. http://www .nytimes.com.

Sharp, D. 2011. "Judge Rejects Insanity Defense in Maine Decapitation Case." *Boston Globe*, February 5. www.boston .com.

Shay, G. 2009. "What We Can Learn about Appeals from Mr. Tillman's Case: More Lessons from Another DNA Exoneration." *University of Cincinnati Law Review* 77:1499–553.

Sherman, J. L. 2009. "Boy, 11, Charged in Slaying of Father's Girlfriend." *Pittsburgh Post-Gazette*, February 22.

Sherman, L. W. 1998. "Police." In *Handbook of Crime and Punishment*, ed. M. Tonry. New York: Oxford University Press, 429–56.

Sherman, L. W., and D. A. Weisburd. 1995. "General Deterrent Effects of Police Patrol in Crime 'Hot Spots': A Randomized Controlled Trial." *Justice Quarterly* 12 (December): 625–48.

Shermer, L., and B. D. Johnson. 2010. "Criminal Prosecutions: Examining Prosecutorial Discretion and Charging Decisions in U.S. Federal District Courts" *Justice Quarterly* 27:394–430.

Sickmund, M., A. Sladky, and W. Kang. 2012. "Easy Access to Juvenile Court Statistics: 1985–2009." http://www.ojjdp .gov/ojstatbb/ezajcs/.

Sickmund, M., A. Sladky, and W. Kang. 2011. "Easy Access to Juvenile Court Statistics: 1985–2008." http://www.ojjdp .gov/ojstatbb/ezajcs/.

Silverman, E. 1999. *NYPD Battles Crime*. Boston: Northeastern University Press.

Simmons, A., and B. Rankin. 2010. "Gwinnett Cuts Pay Rate for Defending Indigent." *Atlanta Journal Constitution*, February 1. www.ajc.com.

Simon, R. 1975. *Women and Crime*. Lexington, MA: D.C. Heath.

Simonoff, J., C. Restropo, R. Zimmerman, Z. Naphtali, and H. Willis. 2011. "Resource Allocation, Emergency Response Capability, and Infrastructure Concentration around Vulnerable Sites." *Journal of Risk Research* 5:597–613.

Simons, K. W. 2008. "Self-Defense: Reasonable Belief or Reasonable Self-Control?" *New Criminal Law Review* 11:51–90.

Simons, M. 2010. "Prosecutorial Discretion in the Shadow of Advisory Guidelines and Mandatory Minimums." *Temple Political and Civil Rights Law Review* 19:377–87.

Sims, B., B. Yost, and C. Abbott. 2005. "Use and Nonuse of Victim Services Programs: Implications from a Statewide Survey of Crime Victims." *Criminology & Public Policy* 4:361–84.

Singer, N. 2008. "Budget Cuts Force King County Charging Process to Change." *Seattle Times*, September 25. http:// seattletimes.nwsource.com.

Skogan, W. G. 1995. "Crime and Racial Fears of White Americans." *Annals of the American Academy of Political and Social Science* 539 (May): 59–71.

Skogan, W. G., S. M. Hartnett, N. Bump, and J. Dubois. 2008. Evaluation of CeaseFire-Chicago. Unpublished Report (March 20).

Skolnick, J. H. 1966. *Justice without Trial: Law Enforcement in a Democratic Society*. New York: Wiley.

Skolnick, J. H., and D. H. Bayley. 1986. *The New Blue Line*. New York: Free Press.

Skolnick, J. H., and J. J. Fyfe. 1993. *Above the Law: Police and Excessive Use of Force*. New York: Free Press.

Slater, H. P., and M. Reiser. 1988. "A Comparative Study of Factors Influencing Police Recruitment." *Journal of Police Science and Administration* 16:160–75.

Smith, C. E. 1990. *United States Magistrates in the Federal Courts: Subordinate Judges*. New York: Praeger.

———. 1995b. "Federal Habeas Corpus Reform: The State's Perspective." *Justice System Journal* 18:1–11.

———. 1997. *Courts, Politics, and the Judicial Process*. 2nd ed. Belmont, CA: Wadsworth.

———. 1999. "Criminal Justice and the 1997–98 U.S. Supreme Court Term." *Southern Illinois University Law Review* 23:443–67.

———. 2000a. "The Governance of Corrections: Implications of the Changing Interface of Courts and Corrections." In *Boundary Changes in Criminal Justice Organizations*. Vol. 2 of *Criminal Justice 2000*. Washington, DC: National Institute of Justice, 113–66.

———. 2000b. *Law and Contemporary Corrections*. Belmont, CA: Wadsworth.

———. 2003. *Criminal Procedure*. Belmont, CA: Wadsworth.

———. 2004. *Constitutional Rights: Myths and Realities*. Belmont, CA: Wadsworth.

———. 2007. "Prisoners' Rights and the Rehnquist Court Era." *Prison Journal* 87:457–76.

———. 2010a. "Justice John Paul Stevens and Capital Punishment." *Berkeley Journal of Criminal Law* 15:205–60.

———. 2010b. "Justice John Paul Stevens: Staunch Defender of Miranda Rights." *DePaul Law Review* 60:99–140.

Smith, C. E., C. DeJong, and M. McCall. 2011. *The Rehnquist Court and Criminal Justice*. Lanham, MD: Lexington Books.

Smith, C. E., and H. Feldman. 2001. "Burdens on the Bench: State Supreme Courts' Non-Judicial Tasks." *Judicature* 84:304–9.

Smith, C. E., M. A. McCall, and M. M. McCall. 2009. "The Roberts Court and Criminal Justice at the Dawn of the 2008 Term." *Charleston Law Review* 3:265–87.

Smith, C. E., M. McCall, and C. Perez McCluskey. 2005. *Law and Criminal Justice: Emerging Issues in the Twenty-First Century*. New York: Peter Lang.

Smith, C. E., and R. Ochoa. 1996. "The Peremptory Challenge in the Eyes of the Trial Judge." *Judicature* 79:185–89.

Smith, L. 2012. "Wyoming City Council Adopts Zoning Limits on Where Parolees May Live." Michigan Public Radio. January 16. http:// michiganradio.org.

Snyder, H. N. 2011. Arrest in the United States, 1980–2009. Bureau of Justice Statistics *Patterns and Trends*. Washington, DC: U.S. Department of Justice.

Snyder, H. N., and M. Sickmund. 2006. *Juvenile Offenders and Victims: 2006 National Report*. Washington, DC: U.S. Office of Juvenile Justice and Delinquency Prevention.

Sommers, S. 2009. "On the Obstacles to Jury Diversity." *Jury Expert* 21:1–10.

Sorensen, J. R., and D. H. Wallace. 1999. "Prosecutorial Discretion in Seeking Death: An Analysis of Racial Disparity in the Pretrial Stages of Case Processing in a Midwestern County." *Justice Quarterly* 16:561–78.

Spagat, E. 2010. "'40-Year-Old Virgin' Actor Gets Life in Stabbing." Today.com, December 12. http://today.msnbc.com.

Spangenberg Group. 2007. "Rates of Compensation Paid to Court-Appointed Counsel in Non-Capital Felony Cases at Trial: A State-by-State Overview." *American Bar Association Information Program*, June. http://www .abanet.org.

Spangenberg, R. L., and M. L. Beeman. 1995. "Indigent Defense Systems in the United States." *Law and Contemporary Problems* 58:31–49.

Sparrow, M. K., M. H. Moore, and D. M. Kennedy. 1990. *Beyond 911: A New Era for Policing*. New York: Basic Books.

Spears, J. W., and C. C. Spohn. 1997. "The Effect of Evidence Factors and Victim Characteristics on Prosecutors' Charging Decisions in Sexual Assault Cases." *Justice Quarterly* 14:501–24.

Spencer, C. 2000. "Nonlethal Weapons Aid Lawmen: Police

Turn to Beanbag Guns, Pepper Spray to Save Lives of Defiant Suspects." *Arkansas Democrat-Gazette*, November 6, p. B1.

Spencer, M. 2009. "The Wrong Stephen Morgan's Photo Posted Online in Wesleyan Student's Death." *Hartford Courant*, May 8. http://www.courant.com.

Spitzer, S. 1975. "Toward a Marxian Theory of Deviance." *Social Problems* 22:638–51.

Spohn, C. 2011. "Unwarranted Disparity in the Wake of the *Booker/Fanfan* Decision: Implications for Research and Policy." *Criminology & Public Policy* 10(4):1119–27.

Spohn, C., and D. Holleran. 2000. "The Imprisonment Penalty Paid by Young, Unemployed Black and Hispanic Male Offenders." *Criminology* 38:281–306.

———. 2001. "Prosecuting Sexual Assault: A Comparison of Charging Decisions in Sexual Assault Cases Involving Strangers, Acquaintances, and Intimate Partners." *Justice Quarterly* 18:651–85.

Staba, D. 2007. "Killer of 3 Women in Buffalo Area Is Given a Life Term." *New York Times*, August 15. http://www.nytimes.com.

St. Clair, S. 2008. "R. Kelly Verdict: Not Guilty." *Chicago Tribune*, June 13. http://www.chicagotribune.com.

St. Clair, S., and K. Ataiyero. 2008. "R. Kelly Defense Rests Case after 2 Days of Testimony." *Chicago Tribune*, June 10. http://articles.chicagotribune.com.

Stafford, M. C., and M. Warr. 1993. "A Reconceptualization of General and Specific Deterrence." *Journal of Research in Crime and Delinquency* 30 (May): 123–35.

Stahl, A. 2008. "Drug Offense Cases in Juvenile Courts." 1985–2004. Washington, DC: U.S. Department of Justice.

Stahlkopf, C., M. Males, and D. Macallair. 2010. "Testing Incapacitation Theory: Youth Crime and Incarceration in California." *Crime and Delinquency* 56:253–68.

Stanko, E. 1988. "The Impact of Victim Assessment on Prosecutors' Screening Decisions: The Case of the New York District Attorney's Office." In *Criminal Justice: Law and Politics*, 5th ed., ed. G. F. Cole. Pacific Grove, CA: Brooks/Cole.

Stanley, K. 2011. "Florida Crime Keeps Falling, and Experts and Law Enforcement Search for Why." *St. Petersburg Times*, November 17. http://www.tampabay.com/news/public-safety/crime/article1203703.ece.

Stanley, T. 2011. "Nancy Grace Says 'the Devil Is Dancing at Casey Anthony Verdict.'" *Los Angeles Times*, July 5. www.latimes.com.

State of Florida Correctional Medical Authority. 2010. Aging and Older Inmates in the Florida Department of Corrections. http://www.doh.state.fl.us/cma/meetings.

Stecklow, S., J. Singer, and A. O. Patrick. 2005. "Watch on the Thames." *Wall Street Journal*, July 8. http://www.wsj.com.

Steden, R., and R. Sarre. 2007. "The Growth of Private Security: Trends in the European Union." *Security Journal* 20:222–35.

Steen, S., R. Engen, and R. Gainey. 2005. "Images of Danger and Culpability: Racial Stereotyping, Case Processing, and Criminal Sentencing." *Criminology* 43:435–68.

Steffensmeier, D., B. Feldmeyer, C. T. Harris, and J. T. Ulmer. 2011. "Reassessing Trends in Black Violent Crime 1980–2008: Sorting out the 'Hispanic Effect' in Uniform Crime Reports Arrests, National Crime Victimization Survey Offender Estimates, and U.S. Prisoner Counts." *Criminology* 49:197–252.

Steffensmeier, D., J. Kramer, and C. Streifel. 1993. "Gender and Imprisonment Decisions." *Criminology* 31:411–46.

Steffensmeier, D., J. Ulmer, and J. Kramer. 1998. "The Interaction of Race, Gender, and Age in Criminal Sentencing: The Punishment Cost of Being Young, Black, and Male." *Criminology* 36:763–97.

Steinberg, J. 1999. "The Coming Crime Wave Is Washed Up." *New York Times*, January 3, p. 4WK.

Steiner, B., C. Hemmens, and V. Bell. 2006. "Legislative Waiver Reconsidered: General Deterrent Effects of Statutory Exclusion Laws Enacted Post-1979." *Justice Quarterly* 23(1): 34–59.

Steiner, B., M. Makarios, L. Travis, and B. Meade. 2012. "Examining the Effects of Community-Based Sanctions on Offender Recidivism." *Justice Quarterly* 29:229–55.

Steiner, B., and E. Wright. 2006. "Assessing the Relative Effects of State Direct File Waiver Laws on Violent Juvenile Crime: Deterrence or Irrelevance?" *Journal of Criminal Law and Criminology* 96:1451–77.

Stensland, J. 2011. "Island County Sheriff, Prosecutor Struggle with Cuts." *Whidbey (WA) News Times*, January 25. www.whidbeynewstimes.com.

Stephan, J. 2008. *Census of State and Federal Correctional Facilities, 2005*, October. NCJ 222182.

Stephan, J., and J. Karberg. 2003. *Census of State and Federal Correctional Facilities, 2000*. (August) Washington, DC: Bureau of Justice Statistics.

Stephens, M. 2008. "Ignoring Justice: Prosecutorial Discretion and the Ethics of Charging." *Northern Kentucky Law Review* 35:53–65.

Stephens, S. 2007. "The True Effect of Crime Scene Television on the Justice System: The "CSI Effect" on Real Crime Labs." *New England Law Review* 41:591–607.

Steward, D., and M. Totman. 2005. *Racial Profiling: Don't Mind If I Take a Look, Do Ya? An Examination of Consent Searches and Contraband Hits at Texas Traffic Stops*. Austin: Texas Justice Coalition.

Stewart, E., E. Baumer, R. Brunson, and R. Simons. 2009. "Neighborhood Racial Context and Perceptions of Police-Based Racial Discrimination Among Black Youth." *Criminology* 47:847–87.

Stickels, J. W., B. J. Michelsen, and A. Del Carmen. 2007. "Elected Texas District and County Attorneys' Perceptions of Crime Victim Involvement in Prosecution." *Texas Wesleyan Law Review* 14:1–25.

Stoddard, E. R. 1968. "The Informal 'Code' of Police Deviancy: A Group Approach to Blue-Coat Crime." *Journal of Criminal Law, Criminology, and Police Science* 59:204–11.

Stojkovic, S. 1990. "Accounts of Prison Work: Corrections Officers' Portrayals of Their Work Worlds." *Perspectives on Social Problems* 2:211–30.

Stolzenberg, L., and S. J. D'Alessio. 1994. "Sentencing and Unwarranted Disparity: An Empirical Assessment of the Long-Term Impact of Sentencing Guidelines in Minnesota." *Criminology* 32:301–10.

Streib, V. 2010. "Innocence: Intentional Wrongful Conviction of Children." *Chicago-Kent Law Review* 85:163–77.

Streitfeld, D. 2008. R. Kelly Is Acquitted in Child Pornography Case." *New York Times*, June 14. www.nytimes.com.

Strickland, C. 2011. "Regulation without Agency: A Practical Response to Private Policing in *United States v. Day*." *North Carolina Law Review* 89:1338–62.

Strodtbeck, F., R. James, and G. Hawkins. 1957. "Social Status in Jury Deliberations." *American Sociological Review* 22:713–19.

Strom, K., M. Berzofsky, B. Shook-Sa, K. Barrick, C. Daye, N. Horstmann, and S. Kinsey. 2010. *The Private Security Industry: A Review of the Definitions, Available Data Sources, and Paths Moving Forward*, report prepared for U.S. Bureau of Justice Statistics (December), https://www.ncjrs.gov/pdffiles1/bjs/grants/232781.pdf.

Strom, K. J., and J. M. MacDonald. 2007. "The Influence of Social and Economic Disadvantage on Racial Patterns in Youth Homicide over Time." *Homicide Studies* 11(1):50–69.

Stroshine, M. S. 2005. "Information Technology Innovations in Policing." In *Critical Issues in Policing*, 5th ed., ed. R. G. Dunham and G. P. Alpert. Long Grove, IL: Waveland Press, 172–83.

Sullivan, J. 2009. "New Statewide Database Tracks Sex Offenders." *Seattle Times*, March 10. www.seattletimes.com.

Sullivan, K. M. 2003. "Under a Watchful Eye: Incursions on Personal Privacy." In *The War on Our Freedoms: Civil Liberties in an Age of Terrorism*, ed. R. C. Leone and G. Anrig Jr. New York: Public Affairs, 128–46.

Summers, A., R. D. Hayward, and M. Miller. 2010. "Death Qualification as Systematic Exclusion of Jurors with Certain Religious and Other Characteristics." *Journal of Applied Social Psychology* 40:3218–34.

Sundby, S. 2010. "War and Peace in the Jury Room: How Capital Juries Reach Unanimity." *Hastings Law Journal* 62:103–54.

Sutherland, E. H. 1947. *Criminology*. 4th ed. Philadelphia: Lippincott.

Swarns, R. L. 2004. "Senator? Terrorist? A Watch List Stops Kennedy at Airport." *New York Times*, August 20. http://www.nytimes.com.

Swarz, J. 2004. "Inmates vs. Outsourcing." *USA Today*, July 6, p. 1.

Sykes, G. M. 1958. *The Society of Captives*. Princeton, NJ: Princeton University Press.

Taifa, N. 2002. Testimony on Behalf of American Civil Liberties Union of the National Capital Area Concerning Proposed Use of Surveillance Cameras, before the Joint Public Oversight Hearing Committee on the Judiciary, Council of the District of Columbia, June 13. http://www.dcwatch.com.

Tashima, A. W. 2008. "The War on Terror and the Rule of Law." *Asian American Law Journal* 15:245–65.

Taslitz, A. E. 2010. "Fourth Amendment Federalism and the Silencing of the American Poor." *Chicago-Kent Law Review* 85:277–312.

———. 2012. "High Expectations and Some Wounded Hopes: The Policy and Politics of a Uniform Statute on Videotaping Custodial Interrogations." *Northwestern Journal of Law and Social Policy* (forthcoming).

Tavernise, S. 2011. "Ohio County Losing Its Young to Painkillers' Grip." *New York Times*, April 19. www.nytimes.com.

Taylor, M. 2009. *Achieving Better Outcomes for Adult Probation*. Sacramento: Legislative Analyst's Office (May).

Teeters, N. K., and J. D. Shearer. 1957. *The Prison at Philadelphia's Cherry Hill*. New York: Columbia University Press.

Terrill, W. 2005. "Police Use of Force: A Transactional Approach." *Justice Quarterly* 22:107–38.

Terrill, W., and E. Paoline. 2012. "Conducted Energy Devices (CEDs) and Citizen Injuries: The Shocking Empirical Reality." *Justice Quarterly* 29: 153–82.

Texas Board of Pardons and Parole. 2012. *Parole in Texas: Answers to Common Questions*. Austin, TX: Texas Department of Criminal Justice.

Third Branch. 2008a. "Economics of CJA Regulations Costly to Attorneys." Administrative Office of the U.S. Courts. Vol. 40 (4), April. http://www.uscourts.gov.

———. 2008b. "National Summits Help Federal Courts Prepare for Sentence Reduction Requests." Administrative Office of the U.S. Courts. Vol. 40 (2), February, pp. 1–3, 6. http://www.uscourts.gov.

Thompson, G. 2009. "Couple's Capital Ties Said to Veil Spying for Cuba." *New York Times*, June 18. http://www.nytimes.com.

Thurman, Q., J. Zhao, and A. Giacomazzi. 2001. *Community Policing in a Community Era*. Los Angeles: Roxbury.

Tillman, Z. 2012. "D.C. Judicial Applicants, Complaints Up in 2011." *The Blog of the Legal Times*, February 24. http://legaltimes.typepad.com/blt/2012/02/dc-judicial-applicants-complaints-up-in-2011.html.

Toch, H. 1976. *Peacekeeping: Police, Prisons, and Violence*. Lexington, MA: Lexington Books.

Tonry, M. 1993. "Sentencing Commissions and Their Guidelines." In *Crime and Justice*, vol. 17, ed. M. Tonry. Chicago: University of Chicago Press.

———. 1995. *Malign Neglect: Race, Crime, and Punishment in America*. New York: Oxford University Press.

———. 2008. "Learning from the Limitations of Deterrence Research." *Crime and Justice* 37:279–307.

Tonry, M., and M. Lynch. 1996. "Intermediate Sanctions." In *Crime and Justice*, vol. 20, ed. M. Tonry. Chicago: University of Chicago Press, 99–144.

Toobin, J. 2007. "The CSI Effect." *New Yorker*, May 7. http://www.newyorker.com.

Toscano, P. 2011. "The Dangerous World of Counterfeit Prescription Drugs." *USA Today*. October 7. www.usatoday.com.

Travis, J. 2002. "Invisible Punishment: An Instrument of Social Exclusion." In *Invisible Punishment: The Collateral Consequences of Mass Imprisonment*, ed. M. Bauer and M. Chesney-Lind. New York: New Press, 15–36.

Travis, J., and J. Petersilia. 2001. "Reentry Reconsidered: A New Look at an Old Question." *Crime and Delinquency* 47 (July): 291–313.

Trulson, C. R. 2005. "Victims' Rights and Services: Eligibility, Exclusion, and Victim Worth." *Criminology & Public Policy* 4:399–414.

Truman, J. 2011. *Criminal Victimization, 2010*. Washington, DC: Bureau of Justice Statistics.

Truman, J., and M. Rand. 2010. "Criminal Victimization 2009." Bureau of Justice Statistics *Bulletin*, October. NCJ 231327.

Tyler, K. A., and M. R. Beal. 2010. "The High-Risk Environment of Homeless Young Adults: Consequences for Physical and Sexual Victimization." *Violence and Victims* 25:101–15.

Uchida, C. 2005. "The Development of the American Police: An Historical Overview." In *Critical Issues in Policing*, ed. R. G. Dunham and G. P. Alpert. Long Grove, IL: Waveland Press, 20–40.

Uchida, C., and T. Bynum. 1991. "Search Warrants, Motions to Suppress and 'Lost Cases': The Effects of the Exclusionary Rule in Seven Jurisdictions." *Journal of Criminal Law and Criminology* 81:1034–66.

Ullman, S. 2007. "A 10-Year Update of 'Review and Critique of Empirical Studies of Rape Avoidance.'" *Criminal Justice and Behavior* 34:411–29.

Ulmer, J. T., J. Eisenstein, and B. Johnson. 2010. "Trial Penalties in Federal Sentencing: Extra-Guidelines Factors and District Variation." *Justice Quarterly* 27:560–92.

Ulmer, J. T., M. T. Light, and J. H. Kramer. 2011. "Racial Disparity in the Wake of the *Booker/Fanfan* Decision." *Criminology & Public Policy* 10(4):1077–118.

Unah, I. 2010. "Choosing Who Will Die: The Effect of Race, Gender, and Law in Prosecutorial Decisions to Seek the Death Penalty in Durham County, North Carolina." *Michigan Journal of Race and Law* 15:135–79.

Unnever, J. D. 2008. "Two Worlds Far Apart: Black-White Differences in Beliefs about Why African-American Men Are Disproportionately Imprisoned." *Criminology* 46:511–38.

Urbina, I. 2009. "Citing Cost, States Consider End to Death Penalty." *New York Times*, February 25. http://www.nytimes.com.

Urbina, I., and S. D. Hamill. 2009. "Judges Plead Guilty in Scheme to Jail Youths for Profit." *New York Times*, February 13, p. A1.

U.S. Department of Health and Human Services. 2007. "Illicit Drug Use, by Race/Ethnicity, in Metropolitan and Non-Metropolitan Counties: 2004 and 2005." *NSDUH Report* (National Survey on Drug Use and Health), June 21.

U.S. Department of Justice, 2011. "Department of Justice Disrupts International Cyber Crime Rings Distributing Scareware." *FBI National Press Releases*, June 22. www.fbi.gov.

———. 2012. "Justice Department Charges Leaders of Megaupload with Widespread Online Copyright Infringement." *FBI National Press Releases*, January 19. www.fbi.gov.

U.S. Government Accountability Office. 2011. Bureau *of Prisons: Evaluating the Impact of Protective Equipment Could Help Enhance Officer Safety*. April. GAO-11–410.

U.S. Marshals Service, 2011. "Facts and Figures." U.S. Marshals Service website. www.usmarshals.gov.

U.S. President's Commission on Law Enforcement and Administration of Justice. 1967. *The Challenge of Crime in a Free Society*. Washington, DC: U.S. Government Printing Office.

U.S. Sentencing Commission. 2006. *Final Report on the Impact of* United States v. Booker *On Federal Sentencing* (Washington, DC: U.S. Sentencing Commission).

University of Pittsburgh Medical Center. 2005. "Lead in Environment Causes Violent Crime, Reports University of Pittsburgh Researcher at AAAS." *UPMC News Release*, February 18. http://newsbureau.upmc.com.

Utz, P. 1978. *Settling the Facts*. Lexington, MA: Lexington Books.

Valenzuela, B. 2012. "Parolee Arrested after Attacking Former Girlfriend." *Victorville Daily Press*, March 14. www.vvdailypress.com.

Van Stelle, K., and J. Goodrich. 2009. *The 2008/2009 Study of Probation and Parole Revocation*. Madison: University of Wisconsin Population Health Institute (June).

Varano, S. P., J. D. McCluskey, J. W. Patchin, and T. S. Bynum. 2004. "Exploring the Drug–Homicide Connection." *Journal of Contemporary Criminal Justice* 20:369–92.

Vaughn, M. S. 2001. "Assessing the Legal Liabilities in Law Enforcement: Chiefs' Views." *Crime and Delinquency* 47:3–27.

Vermont Parole Board. 2010. *Vermont Parole Board Manual*. http://www.doc.state.vt.us/about/parole-board/pb-manual.

Vidmar, N., and V. P. Hans. 2007. *American Juries: The Verdict*. New York: Prometheus Books.

Vila, B., and D. J. Kenney. 2002. "Tired Cops: The Prevalence and Potential Consequences of Police Fatigue." *National Institute of Justice Journal* 248:16–21.

Visher, C., S. Debus-Sherrill, and J. Yahner. 2011. "Employment after Prison: A Longitudinal Study of Former Prisoners." *Justice Quarterly* 28:698–718.

Vitiello, M. 2008. "Punishing Sex Offenders: When Good Intentions Go Bad." *Arizona State Law Journal* 40:651–90.

Vives, R., and A. Blankstein. 2009. "A Mixed Reaction to a Use of Force." *Los Angeles Times*, May 15. http://www.latimes.com.

von Hirsch, A. 1976. *Doing Justice*. New York: Hill and Wang.

Wade, N. 2006. "Wider Use of DNA Lists Is Urged in Fighting Crime." *New York Times*, May 12. http://www.nytimes.com.

Wagner, J. 2009. "O'Malley Set to Move on as Death Penalty Repeal Sinks." *Washington Post*, March 5, p. B1.

Waldman, E. 2007. "Restorative Justice and the Pre-Condition for Grace: Taking Victims' Needs Seriously." *Cardozo Journal of Conflict Resolution* 9:91–108.

Walker, R. N. 2006. "How the Malfunctioning Death Penalty Challenges the Criminal Justice System." *Judicature* 89 (5): 265–69.

Walker, S. 1984. "'Broken Windows' and Fractured History: The Use and Misuse of History in Recent Police Patrol Analysis." *Justice Quarterly* 1 (March): 88.

———. 1999. *The Police in America*. 3rd ed. New York: McGraw-Hill.

———. 2001. *Sense and Nonsense about Crime and Drugs: A Policy Guide*. 5th ed. Belmont, CA: Wadsworth.

Walker, S., C. Spohn, and M. DeLeone. 2007. *The Color of Justice: Race, Ethnicity, and Crime in America*, 4th ed. Belmont, CA: Wadsworth.

———. 2011. *The Color of Justice: Race, Ethnicity and Crime in America*, 5th ed. Belmont, CA: Cengage Wadsworth.

Walker, S., and B. Wright. 1995. "Citizen Review of the Police, 1994: A National Survey." In *Fresh Perspectives*. Washington, DC: Police Executive Research Forum.

Ward, S. 2011. "Tweeting Jurors to Face Jail Time with New California Law." *American Bar Association Journal*, August 8. www.abajournal.com.

Warren, J. 2011. "What Blagojevich's Sentence Says about Corruption and Greed." *New York Times*, December 8. www.nytimes.com.

Warren, P., D. Tomaskovic-Devey, W. Smith, M. Zingraff, and M. Mason. 2006. "Driving while Black: Bias Processes and Racial Disparity in Police Stops." *Criminology* 44: 709–38.

Warren, R. 2007. "Evidence-Based Practices and State Sentencing Policy: Ten Policy Initiatives to Reduce Recidivism." *Indiana Law Journal* 82:1307–17.

Washburn, K. K. 2008. "Restoring the Grand Jury." *Fordham Law Review* 76:2333–88.

Wasserman, D. T. 1990. *A Sword for the Convicted: Representing Indigent Defendants on Appeal.* New York: Greenwood Press.

Wehrman, M., and J. DeAngelis. 2011. "Citizen Willingness to Participate in Police–Community Partnerships: Exploring the Influence of Race and Neighborhood Context." *Police Quarterly* 14:48–69.

Weinstein, H. 2001. "Georgia High Court Relegates Electric Chair to History." *Los Angeles Times*, October 6. http://www.latimes.com.

Weisberg, R. 2010. "The Not-So-Golden State of Sentencing and Corrections: Calfornia's Lessons for the Nation." *Justice Research and Policy* 12:133–68.

Weisburd, D. 2011. "The Evidence for Place-Based Policing." *Translational Criminology* (Summer), 10–11, 16.

Weisburd, D., S. D. Mastrofski, A. M. McNally, R. Greenspan, and J. J. Willis. 2003. "Reforming to Preserve: Compstat and Strategic Problem Solving in American Policing." *Criminology & Public Policy* 2:421–56.

Weisburd, D., C. Telep, J. Hinkle, and J. Eck. 2010. "Is Problem-Oriented Policing Effective in Reducing Crime and Disorder?" *Criminology & Public Policy* 9:139–72.

Weiser, B. 2008. "Police in Gun Searches Face Disbelief in Court." *New York Times*, May 12, p. 1.

———. 2011. "A New York Prosecutor with Worldwide Reach." *New York Times*, March 27. www.nytimes.com.

Weiss, D. C. 2008. "New DOJ Rule Expands FBI Database to Include Arrestee DNA." *American Bar Association Journal*, December 12. http://abajournal.com.

———. 2009a. "Calif. DA Dismisses Misdemeanor and Drug Charges in Exchange for DNA." *American Bar Association Journal*, April 15. http://abajournal.com.

———. 2009b. "Fear of Financial Ruin Has More Potential Jurors Claiming Hardship." *American Bar Association Journal*, September 2. www.abajournal.com.

Weisselberg, C. 2011. "Selected Criminal Law Cases in the United States Supreme Court and a Look Ahead." *Court Review* 47:52–62.

Weisselberg, C. D. 2008. "Mourning *Miranda*." *California Law Review* 96:1519–600.

Weitzer, R. 2002. "Incidents of Police Misconduct and Public Opinion." *Journal of Criminal Justice* 30:397–408.

Welch, M. 1994. "Jail Overcrowding: Social Sanitation and the Warehousing of the Urban Underclass." In *Critical Issues in Crime and Justice*, ed. A. Roberts. Thousand Oaks, CA: Sage, 249–74.

Wells, J., and M. Keasler. 2011. "Criminal Procedure: Confessions, Searches, and Seizures." *Southern Methodist University Law Review* 64:199–220.

West, H. C., W. J. Sabol, and S. J. Greenman. 2010. "Prisoners in 2009." Bureau of Justice Statistics *Bulletin, December.* NCJ 231675.

White, J. 2004. *Defending the Homeland.* Belmont, CA: Thomson/Wadsworth.

White, M. D., J. Fyfe, S. Campbell, and J. Goldkamp. 2003. "The Police Role in Preventing Homicide: Considering the Impact of Problem-oriented Policing on the Prevalence of Murder." *Journal of Research in Crime and Delinquency* 40:194–225.

White, M. S. 1995. "The Nonverbal Behaviors in Jury Selection." *Criminal Law Bulletin* 31:414–45.

White, T., and E. Baik. 2010. "Venire Reform: Assessing the State and Federal Efforts to Attain Fair, Cross-Sectional Representation in Jury Pools." *Journal of Social Sciences* 6:113–18.

Widom, C. S. 1995. "Victims of Childhood Sexual Abuse—Later Criminal Consequences." National Institute of Justice *Research in Brief*, March. NCJ 151525.

Williams, C. J. 2010. "Weighed Down by Recession Woes, Jurors Are Becoming Disgruntled." *Los Angeles Times*, February 15. www.latimes.com.

Williams, H., and P. V. Murphy. 1990. "The Evolving Strategy of Police: A Minority View." In *Perspectives on Policing*, 13. Washington, DC: National Institute of Justice, U.S. Government Printing Office.

Williams, M. R., S. Demuth, and J. E. Holcomb. 2007. "Understanding the Influence of Victim Gender in Death Penalty Cases: The Importance of Victim Race, Sex-Related Victimization, and Jury Decision Making." *Criminology* 45:865–91.

Williams, T. 2012. "Brutal Crimes Grip an Indian Reservation." *New York Times*, February 2. www.nytimes.com.

Williams, V., and M. Fish. 1974. *Convicts, Codes, and Contraband.* Cambridge, MA: Ballinger.

Willis, J. J., S. D. Mastrofski, and D. Weisbrud. 2004. "Compstat and Bureaucracy: A Case Study of Challenges and Opportunities for Change." *Justice Quarterly* 21:463–96.

Willis, J., S. Mastrofski, and T. Kochel. 2010. "Recommendations for Integrating Compstat and Community Policing." *Policing: A Journal of Policy and Practice* 4:182–93.

Wilson, J. Q. 1968. *Varieties of Police Behavior.* Cambridge, MA: Harvard University Press.

Wilson, J. Q., and R. Herrnstein. 1985. *Crime and Human Nature.* New York: Simon & Schuster.

Wilson, J. Q., and G. L. Kelling. 1982. "Broken Windows: The Police and Neighborhood Safety." *Atlantic Monthly*, March, pp. 29–38.

Wilson, M. 2010. "Life in Prison for Would-Be Times Square Bomber." *New York Times*, October 5. www.nytimes.com.

Winkeljohn, M. 2002. "A Random Act of Hate: Duckett's Attack Linked to Racism." *Atlanta Journal and Constitution*, August 4, p. E1.

Winterdyk, J., and R. Ruddell. 2010. "Managing Prison Gangs: Results from a Survey of U.S. Prison Systems." *Journal of Criminal Justice* 38:730–36.

Wiseman, S. 2009. "Discrimination, Coercion, and the Bail Reform Act of 1984." *Fordham Urban Law Journal* 26:121–57.

Witt, H. 2009. "Highway Robbery? Texas Police Seize Black Motorists' Cash, Cars." *Chicago Tribune*, March 10. www.chicagotribune.com.

Wodahl, E. J., B. Garland, S. E. Culhane, and William P. McCarty. 2011. "Utilizing Behavioral Interventions to Improve Supervision Outcomes in Community-Based Corrections." *Criminal Justice and Behavior* 38:386–405.

Wolf, A., B. E. Bloom, and B. A. Krisberg. 2008. "The Incarceration of Women in California." *University of San Francisco Law Review* 43:139–70.

Wooldredge, J. 2012. "Distinguishing Race Effects in Pre-Trial Release and Sentencing Decisions." *Justice Quarterly* 29:41–75.

Wooley, B. 2011. "Inside the Montana Women's Prison: Preparing for Reentry." KAJ18 News, November 4. www.kaj18.com.

Worden, A. P. 1993. "The Attitudes of Women and Men in Policing: Testing Conventional and Contemporary Wisdom." *Criminology* 31 (May): 203–24.

———. 1995. "The Judge's Role in Plea Bargaining: An Analysis of Judges' Agreement with Prosecutors' Sentencing Recommendations." *Justice Quarterly* 12:257–78.

Worth, R. F. 2001. "73 Tied to Genovese Family Are Indicted, Officials Say." *New York Times*, December 6, p. A27.

Wright, K., and J. Rosky, 2011. "Too Early Is Too Soon: Lessons from the Montana Department of Corrections Early Release Program." *Criminology & Public Policy* 10:881–908.

Wu, J., and C. Spohn. 2010. "Interdistrict Disparity in Sentencing in Three U.S. District Courts." *Crime and Delinquency* 56:290–322.

Yardley, W. 2006. "DNA Samples Link 4 Murders in Connecticut." *New York Times*, June 8. http://www.nytimes.com.

Zagaris, B. 1998. "U.S. International Cooperation against Transnational Organized Crime." *Wayne Law Review* 44 (Fall): 1401–64.

Zaitz, L. 2011. "Oregon Taxpayers Pay Spiraling Cost of Prison Health Care with No Solution in Sight." June 18, 2011. http://oregonlive.com.

Zalman, M., and B. W. Smith. 2007. "The Attitudes of Police Executives toward *Miranda* and Interrogation Policies." *Journal of Criminal Law and Criminology* 97:873–942.

Zedlewski, E. 2010. "Alternatives to Custodial Supervision: The Day Fine." National Institute of Justice Discussion Paper, April. NCJ 230401. https://www.ncjrs.gov/pdffiles1/nij/grants/230401.pdf.

Zedner, L. 1995. "Wayward Sisters." In *The Oxford History of Prisons*, ed. N. Morris and D. J. Rothman. New York: Oxford University Press, 329–61.

Zerwas, K. 2011. "No Strict Scrutiny—The Court's Deferential Position on Material Support to Terrorism in *Holder v. Humanitarian Law Project*." *William Mitchell Law Review* 37:5337–58.

Zhao, J., C. Gibson, N. Lovrich, and M. Gaffney. 2002. "Participation in Community Crime Prevention: Are Volunteers More or Less Fearful of Crime?" *Journal of Crime & Justice* 25:41–61.

Zhao, J. S., N. P. He, N. Loverich, and J. Cancino. 2003. "Marital Status and Police Occupational Stress." *Journal of Crime & Justice* 26:23–46.

Zimmerman, E. 2011. "The Federal Sentencing Guidelines: A Misplaced Trust." *University of Michigan Journal of Law Reform* 43:841–70.

Zimring, F. E. 2007. *The Great American Crime Decline.* New York: Oxford University Press.

———. 2007. "Protect Individual Punishment Decisions from Mandatory Penalties." *Criminology & Public Policy* 6:881–86.

Name Index

Abbe, O. G., 219
Abbott, C., 58
Abrams, D., 258
Abwender, D. A., 267
Acker, J. R., 291
Acoca, L., 366
Adams, B., 476, 479, 489
Adams, G., 420
Adams, J., 240
Adams, K., 146, 361
Adang, O. M., 147
Addams, J., 473
Addie, S., 476
Addington, L. A., 49
Aden, H., 159
Adler, F., 67
Adler, S. J., 267
Ageton, S. S., 66
Agha, S., 374
Agnew, R., 64
Ahmadi, S., 169
Alarcon, A. L., 269
Alarid, L., 245
Albrecht, H-J., 390
Alexander, K., 490
Alito, S., 202, 213, 477, 478
Allisey, A., 128
Alpert, G., 28
Alpert, G. P., 214
Alvarez, L., 4
Amar, A. R., 261
Amar, V., 182
Amos, M., 376
Anderson, G., 128
Anderson, M., 396
Anderson, T. L., 366
Andrews, D. A., 368, 369
Anthony, C., 3, 4
Antonovics, K., 94
Antonuccio, R., 322, 323
Applebome, P., 293
Applegate, B. K., 369, 476
Archbold, C., 125
Arena, K., 447
Armour, M., 267
Armstrong, G. S., 323
Armstrong, J., 447
Armstrong, K., 292
Arnold, N., 441
Arriola, K. R. J., 366
Arterton, J. B., 263
Arthur, M. J., 164
Ataiyero, K., 266
Atkins, D., 290
Auerhahn, K., 280
Austin, J., 421, 471, 485
Axtman, K., 262

Bagnato, C. F., 263
Bai, M., 429, 430, 435

Baik, E., 96
Baker, A., 136, 141, 142, 165
Baker, P., 142, 284
Baldus, D. C., 290
Baldwin, L., 124
Bales, W., 30
Balmert, J., 404
Bandy, D., 80
Barrick, K., 175
Bartels, L., 365
Basemore, G., 281
Bass, P., 152
Baumer, E., 152
Baumgartner, B., 286
Baxter, C., 115, 122
Bayley, D. H., 160
Beal, M. R., 53
Beccaria, C., 60
Beck, A. J., 253, 333, 355, 374, 402, 422
Becker, H., 64
Beckett, K., 28
Beebe, K., 243
Beeman, M., 236
Beichner, D., 227
Bell, D., 42, 402
Bell, V., 485
Bellair, P. E., 28
Belluck, P., 448
Berk, R., 301
Berkheiser, M., 476
Bernard, T. J., 28
Bernstein, G., 417
Berzofsky, M., 175
Beto, G., 375
Biebel, E. P., 160
Bisbee, J., 235
Bjelopera, J., 436
Blagojevich, R., 42, 222, 276, 278, 282
Blair, J., 490
Blankstein, A., 452
Blitz, C. L., 372
Bloom, B. E., 321
Bluestein, G., 10, 13, 246
Blumstein, A., 402, 469
Blumstein, J. F., 324
Bogdanich, W., 439
Bohmert, M. B., 368
Bohn, K., 447
Boland, B., 227
Boles, J. G., 160
Bonczar, T. P., 333, 337, 382, 387, 398, 406, 414, 416
Bonta, J., 368
Bontrager, S., 30
Bornstein, B., 267, 268
Borum, R., 162
Boston, B., 29
Bourque, B. B., 396

Bousquet, S., 403, 406
Bout, V., 8
Bowen, D. M., 257
Bowen, J., 258
Bowker, L. H., 375
Boyd, T., 214
Boydstun, A., 286
Bradley, C., 198, 199, 266
Braithwaite, J., 281
Braithwaite, L., 366
Brand, G., 36
Brandl, S., 125
Bray, K., 263
Breazeale, R., 129
Brennan, P. A., 61
Breslin, D. M., 220
Breyer, S., 202, 213
Bridge, M., 47
Britt, C., 30
Brockway, Z., 315, 407
Bronstad, A., 240
Bronsteen, J., 277
Brown, C., 379–380, 395
Brown, D. K., 235
Brown, D. M., 256
Brown, F., 34–37
Brown, H., 73
Brown, J., 467
Brown, R., 461
Browne, A., 374
Bruce, M., 28
Brunson, R., 26, 160
Bulman, P., 454
Bundy, T., 423, 443
Burbank, M., 467
Burger, W., 93, 199
Burgess-Proctor, A., 67
Burkhead, M., 293
Burns, A. C., 328
Burns, S., 214, 218
Bursztajn, H., 74
Buruma, I., 368
Bush, G. W., 75, 101, 184, 462
Butler, P., 223
Butterfield, F., 281, 339
Bykowicz, J/, 484
Bynum, T., 159, 199
Byrd, J., Jr., 45
Byrne, J. M., 375, 462, 463, 464

Cadigan, T., 249
Cady, M. S., 220
Cahill, M. T., 79, 277
Cairns, V., 36
Calhoun, F., 111
Callahan, L. A., 88
Calnon, J. M., 28, 29
Cambier, A., 374
Cammack, M., 200

Camp, C. G., 353
Camp, S. D., 324
Campbell, J., 382, 490
Cancino, J. M., 148
Canning, A., 467
Canto, M., 460
Canton, A., 167
Cantor, R. J., 66
Caputo, M., 396
Carlisle, N., 107, 108
Carlon, A., 85
Carodine, M., 217
Carr, P. J., 163
Carrell, S., 243
Carroll, L., 359
Carta, M., 108
Cauffman, E. L., 61
Cavendish, J. C., 45
Cebull, R., 240
Ceci, S. J., 267
Chacon, J. M., 186
Chaddock, G. R., 445
Champion, D. J., 256
Chapman, S. G., 154
Chapper, J., 237, 269
Chaves, P., 146
Cheesman, F., 270
Cheney, D., 222
Cheng, E., 264
Chermak, S., 160
Chesney-Lind, M., 65, 420
Chiaramida, A., 293
Chiricos, T., 30, 58, 67, 302
Christenson, T., 37
Christopher, R. L., 85
Churchill, S., 74
Ciavarella, M., 256
Cieply, M., 244
Clark, J. W., 263
Clark, M., 236
Clark, R., III, 209–210
Clear, T. R., 252, 280
Clementi, T., 304
Clisura, A., 249, 251
Cochran, J., 124
Coffin, K. G., 94
Cohen, M. A., 324
Cohen, N., 443
Cohen, T., 251, 253, 267
Cohen, T. H., 25, 246, 248, 249, 259
Coke, C., 8
Cole, G. F., 252
Cole, R., 74
Cole, S., 265
Coleman, C., 30
Coleman, K., 42
Coleman, T., 162
Coles, C., 41, 114
Collins, J., 434, 443

Conahan, M., 256
Conte, M., 435
Conway, P., 392
Cook, N., 323
Cook, P. J., 468
Cooney, M., 256
Cooper, A., 55
Cooper, C., 127, 148
Cooper, S. K., 281
Copes, H., 362, 371, 372
Cordner, G., 160
Cornwell, E., 262, 267
Corsaro, N., 160
Costanzo, M., 293
Cotton, D., 162
Couch, W., 329
Couture, H., 333
Covey, R. D., 245
Craig, L., 229
Cramer, J., 278
Cratty, C., 108
Crawford, C., 284, 302
Cressey, D., 359
Cristani, A. S., 372
Crofton, W., 407
Crummy, K., 391
Cullen, F. T., 64, 129, 281, 369, 476
Cunningham, R., 391
Cunningham, W. C., 171

Daftary-Kapur, T., 267
Daily, K., 302
D'Alessio, S. J., 301
Daley, H. W. K., 270
Dansky, K., 283
Dantzker, M., 121
Davenport, C., 45
Davey, J. D., 338
Davey, M., 276
Davis, A., 245
Davis, M., 173
Davis, R. C., 144
Davis, R. K., 476
Davis, S., 418
Davitz, T., 373
Dawson, M., 58, 226
Daye, C., 175
DeAngelis, J., 164
Debus-Sherrill, S., 403
Decker, S., 493
Dedel, K., 484
DeFrances, C. J., 236
DeJong, C., 101, 160, 485
Del Carmen, A., 226
delCarmen, R., 201
DeLeone, M., 26, 27, 30, 163, 223
Demare, C., 430
Demuth, S., 30, 290
Deng, X., 403
Denver, M., 251
Dery, G., 195
Dewan, S., 83, 441, 449
Diamond, S., 261
Dickerson, B. E., 86
Dickman, S. L., 372
Dickson, J., 402

Diggs, T., 45
Dilulio, J. J., Jr., 5, 352, 375
Dinovitzer, R., 58, 226
Dioso-Villa, R., 265
Disha, I., 45
Doerner, J. K., 30
Dolan, J., 461
Dolan, M., 162, 447, 449
Domash, S. F., 443
Doney, E., 404
Donziger, S. R., 286
Dorell, O., 3
Dority, B., 169
Dougherty, J., 83
Doyle, B., 430
Doyle, R., 334
Dripps, D., 199
Drummond, E., 86
Dubail, J., 262
Dubber, M. D., 77
Duckett, T. J., 84
Duckworth, T., 264
Duggan, P., 393
Duke, A., 379
Dumas, R., 267
Durose, M., 29, 285, 298, 388, 446
Duwe, G., 368
Dyer, B., 214, 215
Dzur, A., 281

Earley, P., 361, 372
Eckholm, E., 30, 236, 281, 303
Edkins, V., 229
Edwards, J., 23
Egelko, B., 271
Eichenwald, K., 435
Eigenberg, H., 373
Eisenberg, T., 268
Eisenstein, J., 257, 258
Eisley, M., 95
Elias, H., 244
Eligon, J., 445, 447
Ellement, J. R., 459
Elliott, D. S., 66
Elliott, J., 337
Ellis, R., 299
Ellis, R. G., 360
Elmore, E. L., 288
Emmelman, D. S., 256
Engber, D., 444
Engel, R. S., 28, 29
Engen, R., 283, 302
Enion, M. R., 173
Enriquez, R., 148, 263
Erhard, S., 257
Eriksson, L., 390
Esbensen, F-A., 470, 493
Escobedo, D., 194

Fagan, J., 165
Fahey, T., 490
Fang, H., 57
Farnham, E., 316
Farole, D., Jr., 232, 236, 298, 388
Fasano, R., 209–210
Faturechi, R., 145

Favate, S., 214
Feeley, M., 314
Feighan, M., 454
Felch, J., 162, 447, 449
Feld, B. C., 475, 485
Feldman, H., 217
Feltner, E., 297
Ferguson, J., 225
Ferretti, C., 454
Feuer, A., 19, 136
Fielding, H., 109
Fielding, J., 109
Fields, J., 441
Fields, T., 430
Finckenauer, J. O., 42
Finklea, K., 436
Finn, B., 156
Finn, P., 481
Fischman, J., 301
Fish, M., 361
Fishbein, D. H., 61
Fisher, B. S., 369
Fisher, D. M., 283
Fisman, R., 284
Fitzgerald, P., 222
Fitzsimmons, E. G., 293
Flanagan, T. J., 358
Flango, V. E., 269
Fleisher, M. S., 365
Flemming, R. B., 257
Florencio, D., 435
Flower, L., 473
Flowers, R., 231
Ford, J. K., 160
Fornango, R., 152, 159
Fosdick, R., 112
Fountain, H., 433
Fox, J. G., 364, 365
Franks, B., 62
Frantz, S., 162
French, M. T., 57
Freud, S., 62
Friday, P., 125
Fridell, L., 226
Friedman, L. M., 314, 315, 407, 472
Friedrichs, D. O., 42
Frohmann, L., 223
Frueh, B. C., 372
Fry, E. G., 316
Fujii, A., 484
Fuld, L., 112
Fyfe, J. J., 145

Gabbidon, S., 163
Gaffney, A., 365
Gainey, R., 302
Galea, S., 159
Gales, G. G., 324
Gant, K., 179–180
Garcia, M., 169
Garner, J. H., 146
Gecas, V., 128
Gelman, A., 164, 165
Georgiady, B. N., 183
Gershon, R., 128, 167
Gertz, M., 58, 279, 485
Gest, T., 123

Geyh, C., 216, 218, 220
Gezari, V. M., 284, 303
Giacomazzi, A., 160
Gibson, C., 164
Gibson, M., 244
Giffords, G., 39, 40, 59
Gilbert, D., 34, 35
Gill, J., 146
Ginsburg, R. B., 101, 202, 213
Giordano, M., 470
Giordano, P. C., 66
Girshick, L. B., 364
Glaze, L., 16, 25, 333, 337, 356, 366, 380, 382, 387, 398, 406, 416
Glueck, E., 66
Goff, E., 168
Goldfarb, R. L., 251
Goldkamp, J. S., 159
Goldstein, H., 114, 160
Goode, E., 258
Goodin, R. E., 390
Goodman, J., 92
Goodnough, A., 28
Goodrich, J., 386
Gordon, J., 170
Gordon, M., 249
Gordon, S., 243, 244
Gorenstein, N., 150
Gottfredson, D. C., 481
Gottfredson, M., 64
Gover, A. R., 214
Grace, N., 3
Grady, D., 439
Granack, T. T., 360
Grasha, K., 165, 455, 460
Grattet, R., 422
Green, A., 460
Green, E., 267, 268
Green, F., 346
Green, R., 82
Greenberg, A., 452
Greene, D., 97
Greene, J. A., 159
Greene, J. R., 154
Greenman, S. J., 321
Greer, K., 364
Gregoriou, M., 485
Griffen, W., 218
Griffin, A., 210
Griffin, K., 225
Griffin, L., 94
Griffin, P., 480, 485
Grissom, B., 402, 492, 494
Grogan, S., 107
Gross-Shader, C., 151
Grubman, S., 200
Guerino, P., 333, 336, 337, 338, 355, 356, 362, 363, 374
Guevara, L., 489
Gunnell, J. J., 267
Gurney, C., 73–74, 87
Gustafson, R., 366
Gustafson, S., 222

Haarr, R. N., 128, 365
Haba, C., 125
Hackett, D. P., 129

Hagan, F. E., 43
Hails, J., 162
Hall, J., 80
Hallinan, J. T., 373
Hambling, D., 454
Hamill, S. D., 324
Han, M., 396
Handy, R., 401
Hanlon, M., 454
Hannaford-Agor, P., 262
Hans, V., 96, 262, 267, 268
Hansen, M., 231
Hanson, R. A., 237, 269, 270
Harcourt, B. E., 160
Harden, J., 303
Harkin, T., 28
Harlow, C., 232
Harlow, C. W., 325, 356
Harris, E., 45
Harris, M. B., 316
Harris, R., 146, 147
Harrison, C., 262
Harrison, M. T., 355
Harrison, P. M., 253, 325, 333, 336, 337, 338, 355, 356, 362, 363
Hartley, R., 30
Hartney, C., 279
Hassell, K., 125, 160
Hastie, R., 267
Hathaway, W., 62
Hawdon, J., 127
Hawkins, G., 267
Hay, C., 485
Hayden, J., 132
Hayward, R. D., 292
He, N. P., 128, 160
Heaphy, W., 213
Hedgpeth, D., 39
Hefferman, E., 316
Heimer, K., 67
Heise, M., 268
Hemmens, C., 485
Hench, D., 74
Henry, S., 66
Hensley, J. J., 165, 451
Heraux, C. G., 146
Herbert, S., 127
Herley, C., 435
Hernson, P. S., 219
Herrnstein, R., 61
Herz, D., 489
Hewitt, J. D., 62
Hickman, M., 159
Hickman, M. J., 448
Hicks, W., 135
Higgins, G., 163
Higgins, K. J., 436
Hill, S. M., 396
Hillard, G., 136
Hinckley, J., 88
Hinduja, S., 434, 443, 494
Hinzman, G., 385
Hirsch, A. J., 311
Hirsch, M., 249
Hirschel, D., 144
Hirschi, T., 64
Hirschkorn, P., 184

Hochstetler, A., 371, 372
Hoctor, M., 144
Hodge, W. T., 299
Hoffman, M., 263
Hoffmann, J., 269
Holcomb, J. E., 290
Holl, J., 443
Holleran, D., 227, 245, 302
Holtfreter, K., 366
Holwell, R., 275
Homan, C., 285
Hoover, J. E., 116
Horne, P., 124
Horstmann, N., 175
Horwitz, J., 167
Horwitz, S., 39
Hough, K., 267
Hough, M., 369
Houk, K., 468
Houston, O., 11
Howard, J., 312, 316
Howie, C., 390
Howlett, D., 451
Huebner, B. M., 366
Huether, K., 188
Huey, L., 458
Huff, C. R., 244, 303
Hughes, T. A., 422
Humes, K. R., 216
Humke, A., 455
Hummer, D., 375
Hunt, K., 184
Hurdle, J., 146
Hutchinson, B., 379
Hutchinson, I., 144
Hutt, A. V., 82

Ingold, J., 351
Iribarren, C. J., 62
Irwin, J., 359, 490
Ith, I., 454
Iyengar, R., 284

Jabail-Nash, N., 45
Jackson, M., 22, 260, 276
Jacobs, J. B., 42
Jaksic, V., 236
James, R., 267
Janoski, D., 340
Jenkins, M., 384
Johnson, A., 310
Johnson, B., 258
Johnson, B. D., 30, 296
Johnson, K., 28, 77, 246
Johnson, K. D., 485
Johnson, L. A., 250, 252
Johnson, M., 250, 252
Johnson, M. A., 445, 446, 448
Jones, C., 21, 34–37, 412–413
Jones, N. A., 216
Jordan, J., 125
Jordan, W. L., 123

Kagan, E., 101, 291
Kang, W., 51, 469, 483, 484, 485, 489
Kanka, M., 420
Kaplan, T., 445, 447

Karberg, J., 253, 354, 373, 374
Karmen, A., 53, 389
Karnow, C. E. A., 247
Karp, D. R., 281
Kaufman, R., 26
Keasler, M., 181
Keating, J., 163
Kelling, G. L., 41, 113, 114, 158
Kelly, R., 172, 229, 266
Kemmler, W., 432
Kempinen, C., 491
Kennedy, A., 101, 202, 213
Kennedy, D. M., 114
Kennedy, E., 444
Kenney, D. J., 42, 129
Kenny, K., 223
Kerley, K. R., 371, 372
Kerlikowske, R. G., 115
Kilgannon, C., 443
Kim, J., 438
Kim, K., 251
Kimber, K., 214
Kimberly, J., 448
King, N. J., 269, 270, 284
King, R., 45, 94
Kingsley, J., 35–37
Kingsnorth, R., 246
Kinports, K., 195
Kinsey, S., 175
Kiss, A., 165
Klaas, P., 420
Klahm, C., 146
Klain, E., 169
Kleck, G., 279, 302
Klein, A., 431
Klein, D., 66
Kleinknecht, W., 42
Kleymeyer, C., 353
Klingler, D., 147
Klockars, C. B., 154
Kloepfer, C., 460
Klofas, J., 88
Knight, B. G., 94
Knoll, C., 468, 486
Kochel, T., 152
Koenig, D. M., 266
Koper, C., 151, 159
Kopp, J., 43
Kotch, S., 223
Kotlowitz, A., 475
Kramer, G. P., 266
Kramer, J., 25, 298, 302
Krautt, P., 301
Kravets, D., 44, 434
Kravets, L., 393
Krienert, J. L., 365
Kris, D., 167
Krisberg, B., 471
Krisberg, B. A., 321, 347
Krischke, S., 223
Kruger, K., 124, 125
Kruttschnitt, C., 366
Kubrin, C. E., 67–68
Kunzman, L., 123
Kupers, T. A., 359
Kupferberg, N., 29
Kurlychek, M., 396, 491

Kyckelhahn, T., 25, 57, 246, 248, 249, 251, 253, 259, 267

Lacey, M., 39, 40
LaFraniere, S., 439
Lambert, L., 335
Landau, D., 292
Langan, P. A., 29, 285, 355
Langton, L., 232, 234, 236, 435
Lanier, M. M., 66
Lathrop, J., 473
Laub, J. H., 65–66, 67, 468
Lauritsen, J., 55, 67
Lave, T. R., 232
Lawrence, A., 285
Lawson, B., 31
Lazarus, D., 437
Le, A., 209, 210
LeDuff, C., 10, 115, 161
Lee, H., 147
Lee, J., 452
Lee, S., 394
Leiber, M. J., 489
Leming, T., 129
Leo, R. A., 196
Leonard, J., 453
Lersch, K. M., 123, 153
Levin, D., 355
Levy, M., 217
Lewis, L., 196
Lewis, N. A., 114
Li, S., 279
Lichtblau, E., 169, 452, 462
Lien, I-L., 493
Light, M. T., 25
Lin, C. J., 69
Lin, J., 422
Lineberger, K., 167
Linn, S., 286
Liptak, A., 201, 249, 258, 291, 309, 371
Liska, A. E., 63
Listwan, S. J., 372
Lithwick, D., 170
Litras, J., 236
Litsky, P., 471
Litzenberger, R., 128
Livsey, S., 489
Llana, S. M., 68
Loewy, A., 186
Logan, C., 347, 348
Loggins, K., 484
Lombroso, C., 61
London, W., 359
Londoño, E., 45
Lonsway, K., 125
Lopez, J., 209
Lopofsky, S., 384
Lord, V. B., 125
Loughner, J., 39, 40
Loviglio, J., 440
Ludwig, J., 160
Luginbuhl, J., 293
Lum, C., 151
Lumb, R. C., 129
Lundman, R., 26, 173
Lunney, L. A., 93
Lutz, M., 394

Lynch, J. P., 49, 67
Lynch, M., 397
Lynds, E., 314
Lynem, J. N., 174

Maag, C., 163
Macallair, D., 280
MacCormack, J., 187
MacDonald, J. M., 214, 469
MacIntosh, R., 246
Mack, K. Y., 489
MacKenzie, D. L., 323
Maconochie, A., 406, 407
Maddan, S., 30
Magda, L., 167
Maguire, E., 160
Maher, J., 135
Maitland, A. S., 371
Maki, A., 47
Maldonado, D., 243
Males, M., 280
Malil, S., 243, 244
Mallory, S. L., 42
Malone, P., 446
Mana, J., 436
Mancini, C., 485
Mann, D., 289
Manning, A., 234
Manning, P. K., 109
Marceau, J. F., 92
Marchese, L., 74
Marchionna, S., 279, 347
Mardar, N., 268
Markoff, J., 443
Martin, B., 229
Martindale, M., 407
Martinez, J., 67
Martinez, R., Jr., 173
Martinson, R., 269, 281, 317
Maruschak, L. M., 356,
    357, 366
Mascaro, L., 170
Maschke, K. J., 225
Mastrofski, S., 154, 160
Mastrofski, S. D., 127, 152
Mauer, M., 409, 420
Maxson, C., 470
Maxson, C. L., 493
Maxwell, C., 65, 146
Maxwell, S. R., 65, 251
Maxwell, T., 74, 87
Mayo-Wilson, E., 392
Mayrack, B., 286
Mayweather, F., Jr., 11, 31
Mazerolle, L. D., 151
Mazzetti, M., 142
McAuliff, B., 264
McCall, M., 101, 163
McCall, M. A., 95, 101,
    180, 201
McCall, M. M., 95, 101,
    180, 201
McCampbell, S. W., 365
McCarthy, B., 172
McCartney, A., 244
McCleskey, W., 290
McCluskey, C. P., 163
McCluskey, J. D., 127

McCollister, K. E., 57
McCormick, J., 402, 457
McCoy, C., 253, 255
McCoy, J., 121
McDevitt, J., 481
McDonnell, R., 292
McFarlane, L., 365
McGarrell, E., 159, 160
McKee, T. A., 215
McKelvey, B., 315
McKinley, W., 118
McMahon, P., 441
McNichol, T., 461
McNulty, T. L., 28
McVeigh, T., 43
Meade, B., 396
Mears, B., 433
Mears, D., 485
Mednick, S. A., 61
Meier, B., 83
Meier, R. F., 53, 55
Meisner, J., 147
Melde, C., 54, 470, 493
Melendez, L., 149
Menard, S., 52
Mensink, J., 147
Mentzer, A., 118
Menzel, I., 45
Merkin, B., 209
Merrill, E. S., 485
Merton, R., 63
Messerschmidt, J. W., 67
Messner, S. F., 59, 63, 159
Michelsen, B. J., 226
Miethe, T., 49, 53, 55, 57
Mihm, S., 438
Milhizer, E., 81
Miller, C. M., 396
Miller, M., 292, 441
Miller, R., 366
Mills, S., 292
Minton, T. D., 213, 325
Miroff, N., 324
M'Naghten, D., 86
Moke, P., 218
Monkkonen, E. H., 111
Montemayor, C., 245
Moore, M., 160
Moore, M. H., 114
Moore, S., 83, 335, 433, 448
Moore, T., 447
Moran, R., 432
Morash, M., 128, 160, 365, 366
Morgan, S., 85, 433
Morris, D. S., 45
Morris, H., 434
Morris, N., 286, 388
Morrison, D., 449
Moses, P., 47
Mosher, C., 49
Mosteller, R., 223
Mueller, R., 9, 166
Mueller, R. S., 9
Murphy, B., 337
Murphy, K., 39
Murphy, P. V., 110, 160
Murray, C., 22, 260, 276
Murray, L., 450

Muskal, M., 108
Myers, D. L., 281
Myers, E., 281

Na, C., 481
Nagin, D. S., 481
Nakamura, D., 39, 169
Nalla, M., 172
Napolitano, L., 163
Narag, R. E., 254, 320, 321
Nardulli, P. F., 257
Nesbitt, E., 291
Newport, F., 293, 339
Ngugi, B., 436
Nigam, H., 171
Nir, S., 434
Noblet, A., 128
Nolasco, C., 201
Nyrop, K., 28

Obama, B., 42, 45, 101,
    184, 240, 276, 461
O'Brien, B., 223
Ochoa, R., 263
O'Connor, A., 83
O'Connor, S. D., 218
O'Harrow, R., 167
O'Hear, M. M., 258
O'Keefe, K., 258
Oldfather, C., 97
Oppel, R. A., 323, 324
Orr, K., 385
Osborne, J., 326
Ostermann, M., 394
Ostrom, B., 270
Owen, B., 364, 365

Packer, H., 23, 24
Padgett, K., 58
Palmer, B., 321
Palmer, K., 45
Palmer, T., 369
Panarella, C., 42
Paoline, E., 123, 126, 454
Papparozzi, M., 385
Parascandola, R., 45
Parent, D., 396
Parks, R., 160
Pasquale-Styles, M., 146
Patchin, J. W., 434, 494
Pate, T., 158
Patrick, A. O., 451
Pealer, J. A., 369
Peart, N., 26
Peel, R., 86, 109
Pennington, N., 267
Penrod, S., 267
Pepey, T., 393
Peralta, E., 451
Perez, D. M., 375
Perin, M., 168
Perrine, J., 167
Petersilia, J., 402, 403,
    407, 417, 422
Peterson, D., 493
Peterson, J. L., 448
Peterson, M., 11, 121
Petteruti, A., 325

Peveto, K., 441
Pfingst, L., 28
Phelps, J. R., 220
Phelps, M., 370, 468
Phillips, D., 49
Phillips, M., 249
Phillips, S., 266
Piquero, A. R., 61
Piquero, N. L., 64
Pisciotta, A. W., 315
Pittman, C., 85, 86
Pizarro, J. M., 320, 321
Platt, A., 472
Plecas, D., 128
Pochna, P., 442
Podgor, E., 223
Podlas, K., 458
Poole, E., 468
Porter, R., 227, 394
Porter, T. N., 31
Post, L., 268
Poston, B., 25, 28
Potter, H., 163
Pratt, J., 218
Preston, J., 448
Price, M., 263
Propper, A., 364
Protess, B., 447
Provine, D. M., 218
Prussel, D., 125
Pugmire, L., 31
Pulaski, C. A., 290
Puzzanchera, C., 51, 479,
    483, 489

Quinn, P., 294

Rabe-Hemp, C., 125
Radelet, M. L., 291
Rafter, N. H., 316
Rainville, G., 25
Rajaratnam, R., 275, 278
Ramirez, R. R., 216
Rand, M., 14, 45, 56, 144
Randolph, E. D., 454
Rankin, B., 234
Rashbaum, W. K., 141, 142
Ratcliffe, J., 159, 443
Ravi, D., 304
Ravitz, J., 452
Reagan, R., 88
Reaves, B. A., 15, 16, 25, 116,
    118, 119, 122, 123, 124, 156,
    159, 441, 442, 443
Regoli, R. M., 62
Reid, T. R., 19
Reid, T. V., 220
Reilly, R., 10
Reiser, M., 120
Reisig, M. D., 127, 160, 252
Reiss, A. J., Jr., 113
Rempel, M., 213
Rengifo, A. F., 159
Renzema, M., 392
Reuland, M., 162
Rhodes, K., 226
Riccardi, N., 39, 284, 286
Rich, J., 372

...hey, W., 102, 340, 445
...chmond, K. M., 369
Richtel, M., 436
Richter, E., 455
Rihanna, 379
Ring, W., 448
Risen, J., 462
Ritter, S., 430
Roane, K. R., 449
Robbins, L., 77
Roberts, D. E., 366
Roberts, J., 101, 190, 202, 213, 369
Roberts, M., 243
Robinson, P. H., 77
Robinson, R., 216
Rockwell, F. G., 213
Rodriguez, M., 291
Rodwell, J., 128
Rogers, R., 196
Rosales, R., 405
Rose, D., 438
Rosen, L., 46
Rosenberg, T., 423
Rosenfeld, R., 59, 152, 159
Rosenmerkel, S., 298, 388
Rosenthal, J. A., 43
Rosky, J., 408, 409
Rossi, P., 301
Rothman, D. J., 311
Rotman, E., 314
Rousey, D. C., 111
Rowlands, T., 379
Rubin, E., 314
Rucker, L., 365
Ruddell, R., 373
Rudolph, E., 43
Rudolph, J., 151
Ryan, G., 294
Ryan, J., 127
Rydberg, J., 123

Saad, L., 58
Sabo, D., 359
Sabol, W. J., 321, 325, 333, 336, 337, 338, 355, 356, 362, 363
Sack, K., 291
Safran, D. A., 353
Salazar, R., 69
Samaha, J., 81
Sampson, R., 63, 65–66, 67
Samuel, J., 101
Sanchez, C. E., 470
Sanger, D. E., 462
Santana, S. A., 369
Santos, F., 339, 433
Santos, M., 344, 362
Santos, M. G., 345, 346
Saphire, R. B., 218
Sarche, J., 19
Sarnacki, Z., 74
Sarre, R., 171
Savage, C., 409, 452, 463
Sbaratta, C. A., 353
Scalia, A., 101, 202, 213, 478
Scalia, J., 270
Schaible, L., 128

Schanzenbach, M., 301
Schauer, F., 29
Schlanger, M., 253
Schlesinger, T., 302
Schlosser, L. Z., 353
Schmitt, E. L., 29
Schreck, C., 97
Schultz, D., 284
Schwartz, I. M., 471
Schwartz, J., 293, 457
Scott, A., 430
Secret, M., 247, 248
Segal, D., 225
Segal, L., 436
Semukhina, O. B., 97
Seth, S., 324
Sever, B., 279
Severson, K., 461
Shane, J., 129
Shapiro, B., 237
Sharkey, J., 444
Sharp, D., 73
Shay, G., 269
Shearer, J. D., 313
Sheldon, C. H., 66
Shelton, D. E., 265
Shepard, M., 45
Sherman, J. L., 467
Sherman, L. W., 152, 158
Shermer, L., 30
Sherry, S., 284
Shi, J., 372
Sickmund, M., 468, 469, 475, 479, 484, 485, 486, 489, 490, 491
Silverman, E., 152
Simmons, A., 234
Simon, R., 67
Simonoff, J., 172
Simons, K. W., 84
Simons, M., 226
Sims, B., 58
Singer, J., 451
Singer, N., 221
Skogan, W. G., 54, 470
Skolnick, J. H., 126, 145, 160
Skook-Sa, B., 175
Sladky, A., 469, 484, 485, 489
Slater, H. P., 120
Slepian, B., 43
Sluder, R. D., 371
Smalley, S., 459
Smith, A., 69
Smith, B., 112
Smith, B. W., 195
Smith, C. E., 95, 96, 98, 101, 163, 180, 194, 201, 217, 237, 252, 263, 268, 270, 287, 327, 330, 331, 412
Smith, E. L., 55
Smith, J., 264
Smith, L., 418
Smith, S., 25
Snipes, W., 299
Snyder, H. N., 468, 475, 490, 491
Sommers, S., 262
Sorensen, J. R., 223

Sotomayor, S., 101, 213, 291, 477
Souter, D., 202
Sowell, A., 62
Spagat, E., 244
Spangenberg, R., 236
Sparrow, M. K., 114
Spears, J. W., 227
Speirs, V., 167
Spencer, C., 453
Spencer, M., 433
Spitzer, S., 65
Spohn, C., 25, 26, 27, 30, 163, 223, 227, 245, 301, 302, 489
St. Clair, S., 229, 266
Staba, D., 448
Stafford, M. C., 278
Stahl, A., 469
Stahlkopf, C., 280
Stanko, E., 227
Stanley, K., 51
Stanley, T., 3
Stecklow, S., 451
Steden, R., 171
Steen, S., 302
Steffensmeier, D., 28, 298, 302
Stein, A., 299
Steinberg, J., 51
Steinberg, L., 61
Steiner, B., 396, 422, 485
Stensland, J., 225
Stephan, J., 353, 354, 368, 369, 373, 374, 418
Stephens, M., 225
Stephens, S., 155, 458
Stevens, J. P., 202
Stewart, E., 163
Stewart, E. A., 67–68
Stewart, M. D., 107
Stewart, P., 255
Stickels, J. W., 226
Stoddard, E. R., 148
Stojkovic, S., 351
Stolzenberg, L., 301
Stone, C., 29
Strauchs, J. J., 171
Streib, V., 244
Streifel, C., 298
Streitfeld, D., 266
Strickland, C., 173
Strodtbeck, F., 267
Strollo, D., 210
Strom, K., 171, 174, 175, 469
Stroshine, M. S., 443
Sullivan, J., 420
Sullivan, K. M., 170
Sullivan, T., 393
Summers, A., 292
Sundby, S, 267
Sutherland, E., 64
Sutherland, S., 246
Swarns, R. L., 444
Swarz, J., 369
Sykes, G. M., 359

Taifa, N., 451
Tashima, A. W., 247
Taslitz, A. E., 93, 451

Tauber, J., 423
Tavernise, S., 28
Taylor, M., 381, 386
Taylor, T. J., 470, 493
Teeters, N. K., 313
Telep, C., 151, 160
Terrill, W., 123, 146, 454
Terry, C., 104, 206, 306, 426
Thomas, C., 45, 184, 202, 213
Thompson, G., 43
Thurman, Q., 160
Thurston, H., 473
Tillman, Z., 215
Tillyer, R., 146
Toch, H., 373
Tonry, M., 31, 279, 286, 300, 388, 397
Toobin, J., 458
Toscano, P., 439
Travis, J., 402, 403, 420
Treadwell, H. M., 366
Trulson, C. R., 58
Truman, J., 14, 47, 51, 49, 50, 56, 144
Turner, J., 170
Tyler, K. A., 53
Tyler, T., 199

Uchida, C., 110, 114, 115, 160, 199
Ulmer, J., 25, 258, 302
Umbreit, M. S., 281
Unah, I., 223
Unnever, J. D., 29
Urbina, I., 293, 324
Utz, P., 257

Valenzuela, B., 401
van Gemert, F., 493
Van Meter, C. W., 171
Van Stelle, K., 386
Varano, S., 159
Varano, S. P., 53
Vaughn, M., 147, 150, 201
Vick, M., 229
Vidmar, N., 96, 268
Vila, B., 129
Vilcica, E. R., 159
Violanti, J. M., 129
Visher, C., 403
Vitiello, M., 280
Vives, R., 452
Volavka, J., 61
Vollmer, A., 112
von Hirsch, A., 277

Wade, N., 447
Wagner, J., 293
Wakeman, S. E., 372
Waldman, E., 281
Walker, R. N., 290
Walker, S., 22, 26, 27, 30, 110, 114, 149, 151, 163, 199, 223
Wallace, D. H., 223
Walsh, N., 325
Ward, S., 458
Ward, S. F., 231, 271
Warr, M., 278

Warren, E., 92, 93, 98, 198
Warren, J., 278
Warren, P., 28, 124
Warren, R., 286
Washburn, K. K., 95
Wasserman, D. T., 269
Watanabe, K., 244
Weerman, F. M., 493
Wehrman, M., 164
Wehrwein, , K., 393
Weinstein, H., 433
Weisberg, R., 246
Weisburd, D., 152, 158,
   159, 160
Weiser, B., 8, 188
Weiss, D. C., 262, 447
Weisselberg, C. D., 195, 196
Weitzer, R., 145
Welch, M., 252
Wells, J., 181

West, C., 31
West, H. C., 321
Whichard, J., 393
White, J., 160, 167
White, M. D., 160
White, M. S., 263
White, N., 55
White, T., 96
Widom, C. S., 67
Williams, C., 313
Williams, C. J., 262
Williams, H., 110
Williams, J., 229
Williams, M. R., 290
Williams, T., 4, 119
Williams, V., 361
Willis, J. J., 152
Wilson, D. J., 422
Wilson, J. Q., 61, 113, 114, 135
Wilson, M., 132, 142

Wilson, O. W., 112
Wilson, W. J., 63
Winkeljohn, M., 84
Winterdyk, J., 373
Wiseman, S., 247, 252
Witt, H., 391
Wodahl, E. J., 395
Wolf, A., 321
Wolff, N., 372
Woodworth, G., 290
Wooldredge, J., 248
Wooley, B., 401, 404
Worden, A. P., 125, 239
Worth, R. F., 42
Worthy, K., 222
Wright, B., 149
Wright, E., 485
Wright, K., 408, 409
Wu, J., 301
Wynn, M., 451

Yahner, J., 403
Yandrasits, J., 88
Yardley, W., 446, 448
Yellen, L., 136
Yokom, S., 322
Yost, B., 58

Zagaris, B., 43
Zaitz, L., 371
Zalman, M., 195
Zedlewski, E., 389, 390
Zedner, L., 316
Zernike, K., 304
Zerwas, K., 170
Zhao, J., 128, 160, 164
Zimmer, L., 370
Zimmerman, E., 301
Zimring, F. E., 283

Subject Index

Abortion, 43

About Prison (Santos), 346

Accelerated release of offenders, 410

Accusatory process, 228

Accused, whether to stand trial, 265

Actual time served, 284–286, 338, 414

Actus reus, 80

Adams v. Williams, 189, 192

Adjudication, 16

Adversarial process, 211

Affidavit, 183

African Americans. *See* Race and ethnicity

Age, 51, 54. *See also* Juvenile justice

Aggravated assault, 78

Aggressive patrol, 157, 159–160

AIDS, prisoners with, 357

Air guns, 453

Anomie, 63

Anticontract Law of 1887, 315

Antisocial personality, 62

Antiterrorism and Effective Death Penalty Act, 270

Antiterrorism task force, 156

Appeal, 21, 268

Appellate courts, 212, 213

Appellate process, 268–270

Apprehension process, 155–156

Argersinger v. Hamlin, 233

Arizona v. Gant, 189

Arraignment, 20, 245

Arrest, 19, 183, 206

Arson, 78

Assigned counsel, 234, 235

Atkins v. Virginia, 290

Auburn plan, 313–314

Austin v. United States, 98

Automobile search, 191–192

Auxiliary police officers, 136

Backscatter X-rays, 452

Bail, 98, 247–250

Bail agent, 249

Bail bondsman, 249

Bail fund, 251

Bail guidelines, 251

Bail Reform Act of 1984, 252

Ban on plea bargaining, 255

Batson v. Kentucky, 263

Baze v. Rees, 291

Beanbags, 453

Beard v. Banks, 328

Bell v. Wolfish, 329

Bench trial, 259

Berghuis v. Thompkins, 194

Bicycle patrol, 159

Bill of Rights, 89

Biological explanations, 61–62, 68

Blackledge v. Allison, 255

Blakely v. Washington, 301

Blameworthiness, 298

Board of Education v. Earls, 475

"Bobbies," 109

Body of Proof, 265

Bones, 265

Booking, 19–20, 206, 244

Boot camp, 395–396, 490

Bordenkircher v. Hayes, 258

Border and Transportation Security, 9

Border Patrol, 167

Border patrol analyst, 188

Border stops, 186

Bounty hunters, 249

Bow Street Runners, 109

Boykin v. Alabama, 257

Brady v. Maryland, 224

Breaking or entering, 78

Breed v. Jones, 474

Brendlin v. California, 182

Brewer v. Williams, 200

Brigham City, Utah v. Stuart, 190

Brink's, 174

"Broken Windows: The Police and Neighborhood Safety" (Wilson/Kelling), 113

Broken windows theory, 159, 160

Bronx Freedom Fund, 251

Brown v. Mississippi, 194

Brown v. Plata, 330, 371, 409

Budget cuts
defense attorneys, 234
juvenile justice, 490
policing, 115, 132, 135
prisoner release, 403–404, 423

Bumper v. North Carolina, 190, 192

Burch v. Louisiana, 261

Bureau of Alcohol, Tobacco, Firearms, and Explosives (ATF), 117

Bureau of Prisons, 319

Burger Court, 93, 95

Burglary, 78, 79

Burns, 174

CALEA, 149

California v. Acevedo, 191, 192

"Call to Oneness," 6

Capital punishment. *See* Death penalty

Careers in Criminal Justice
border patrol analyst, 188
clinical director, 370
crime analyst, 47
criminal defense attorney, 82
district associate judge, 302
forensic DNA analyst, 450
intake referee, 484
intelligence analyst, 168
police officer, 121
probation officer assistant, 384
prosecuting attorney, 222
reentry specialist, 405
resident unit supervisor, 322

Carroll v. United States, 191, 192

CAT, 437

Catching a suspect, 155

Causation, 80

Causes of crime, 59–69. *See also* Theories of criminality

CCA, 323

CEDs, 454

Cell phones
jurors, 457–458
prison, in, 461

Chain of command, 133

Challenge for cause, 263

Chandler v. Miller, 475

Charging, 20

Child savers, 472

Chimel v. California, 189, 192

Cincinnati Declaration of Principles, 315, 316

Circuit court, 214

Circuit courts of appeals, 213

Circumstantial evidence, 264

CIT, 162

Citation, 250–251

Citizen crime-watch groups, 164

City of Indianapolis v. Edmond, 187, 192

City police departments, 119

Civic accountability, 148–150

Civil infractions, 76

Civil law, 75

Civil liability lawsuits, 150

Civil service laws, 332

Civilian review board, 149

Clark v. Arizona, 86

Classical criminology, 60

Classification, 367–368

Clearance rate, 153

Clinical director, 370

Close Up boxes
cell phones in prison, 461
criminal intent and appropriateness of punishment, 83
free exercise of religion inside prison, 329
Herring v. United States, 202–203
home confinement, 393
J.D.B. v. North Carolina, 477–478
life in prison, 345–346
living under suspicion, 164–165
parole process, 412–413
prisoners, survival tips, 360
prosecutors, accountability, 224
scientific evidence (*CSI* effect), 265
sentencing, 299
volunteers in law enforcement, 136

Closing arguments, 266

Coast Guard, 9

CODIS, 446, 447

Coercion, 84–85

Commission on Accreditation for Law Enforcement Agencies (CALEA), 149

Commonwealth attorney, 221

Community-based correctional facilities, 417–418

Community corrections, 319, 335–336
assumptions, 380–381
defined, 317
future of, 398
intermediate sanctions. *See* Intermediate sanctions
least restrictive alternative, 381
parole. *See* Parole
probation. *See* Probation
technological advancements, 463

Community crime prevention, 163–164

Community model, 316–317

Community policing, 114, 115, 160

Community policing era (1970–present), 113–114

Community prosecution, 227

Community service, 392–394

"Comparative International Rates of Incarceration" (Mauer), 334

Comparative Perspectives
  exclusionary rule
    (Canada), 199
  exclusionary rule (Europe),
    199
  exclusionary rule
    (Germany), 199
  fines (Europe), 389, 390
  incarceration rates, 334
  pretrial detention
    (Philippines), 254
  procedural criminal law
    (Russia), 97
Comprehensive Crime
  Control Act, 87, 368
CompStat, 152
Computer crime, 434–437
Computer hackers, 44, 436
Computer predators, 435
Concurrence, 80
Conditions of release, 415
Conducted energy devices
  (CEDs), 454
Confession, 196
Congregate system, 313
Connick v. Thompson, 224
Conscience, 62
Consent search, 190–191
Constitution of the United
    States. *See* Constitutional
    rights of prisoners;
    Procedural criminal law
Constitutional rights of
    parolees, 331–332
Constitutional rights of
    prisoners, 327–331
  due process (discipline), 330
  Eighth Amendment,
    329–330
  equal protection, 330–331
  First Amendment, 328
  Fourteenth Amendment,
    330
  Fourth Amendment,
    328–329
  freedom of speech/religion,
    328
  Myth & Reality, 328
  search and seizure, 328–329
Constitutional rights of
    probationers, 331–332,
    386–387
Continuance, 238
Contract counsel, 234, 236
Contract labor system, 314
Contractual security
    services, 174
Control theories, 64, 66
Coolidge v. New Hampshire,
    181
Cooper v. Pate, 327
Copping a plea. *See* Plea
    bargaining
COPS Office, 114
Correctional costs, 335
Correctional officers, 352–354
  body armor, 459
  civil service laws, 332

female officers, 353, 354
force, use of, 354
less-lethal weapons, 460
liability, 332
race/ethnic composition, 354
recruitment, 353–354
role, 352–353
sexual misconduct, 365, 374
Corrections, 16–17, 21,
    333–339
  community. *See*
    Community corrections
  defined, 310
  employees. *See*
    Correctional officers
  federal system, 319
  hands-off policy, 327
  historical overview,
    310–318
  jail, 324–326
  juveniles, 488–492
  prison. *See* Prison
  prisoner rights. *See*
    Constitutional rights of
    prisoners
  private prisons, 322–324
  state system, 319–321
  statistics, 333
  technology, 459–460, 463
  women, and, 319, 321
Corrections Corporation of
    America (CCA), 323
Costs of crime, 56–57
Couch v. Jabe, 329
Count, 226
Counterfeit consumer
    products, 438–439
Counterfeit medications, 439
Counterfeiting, 437–439
County attorney, 221
County law enforcement
    agencies, 118
Courts and administration,
    16, 209–241
  defense attorney. *See*
    Defense attorney
  dispute processing, 212
  felony courts, 297
  functions of courts, 211–212
  informality of lower
    courts, 214
  judge. *See* Judge
  local legal culture, 237–238
  misdemeanor courts, 297
  norm enforcement function,
    212
  policy making, 212
  problem-solving courts,
    213, 218
  prosecutorial system. *See*
    Prosecutorial system
  structure of courts, 212–214
  Supreme Court. *See*
    Supreme Court
  technological advance-
    ments, 455–458, 463
  workgroup, 238–239
Courts of appeals, 213

Credit card fraud, 435, 436
Crime
  causation. *See* Theories of
    criminality
  classification, 41
  costs, 56–57
  cyber, 44, 434–437
  elements, 79
  fear of, 57–58
  hate, 45
  occupational, 42
  organized, 42–43
  political, 43–44
  trends, 50–51
  types, 41–45
  victimless, 43
  visible, 41
  white-collar, 63–64
Crime analyst, 47
Crime and Human Nature
    (Wilson/Herrnstein), 61
Crime control, 6
Crime control model
  corrections, 317–318
  criminal justice system,
    23–24
Crime control period (1980–
    2005), 471, 475
Crime mapping, 443
Crime prevention, 6–7
Crime rate, 337
Crime statistics, 45–50
  CompStat, 152
  dark figure of crime, 46
  NCVS, 49–50
  NIBRS, 49
  UCR, 46–49, 50
Crime Stoppers Program, 164
Crime trends, 50–51
Crime victimization
  acquaintances and
    strangers, 55–56
  experience of victims, 58
  low-income city dwellers, 55
  role of victims in crime, 59
  who is victimized?, 52–55
  women, youths, nonwhites,
    54–55
Criminal defense attorney, 82.
    See also Defense attorney
Criminal homicide, 77, 78
Criminal intent and
    appropriateness of
    punishment, 83
Criminal justice database,
    443–445
Criminal justice process
  appellate process, 268–270
  corrections. *See* Corrections
  flowchart, 18
  Michigan vs. Jones, 34–37
  overview, 19–21
  plea bargaining. *See* Plea
    bargaining
  pretrial process. *See*
    Pretrial process
  punishment. *See* Punish-
    ment and sentencing

release. *See* Release into the
    community
  Terry, Chuck, 206–207,
    306–307
  trial, 259–260. *See also* Jury
    trial
Criminal justice system, 3–37
  careers. *See* Careers in
    Criminal Justice
  corrections, 16–17
  courts, 16. *See also* Courts
    and administration
  decision-making process,
    17–21, 34–37
  discretion, 12–13
  federal government
    involvement, 7–10
  filtering, 14–15
  goals, 5–7
  local government
    involvement, 10
  police, 15–16. *See also*
    Police
  police bureaucracy, and,
    134–135
  public opinion, 27
  racial bias, 28–30
  resource dependence, 13
  sequential tasks, 14
  system perspective, 11
  technology. *See* Technology
    and criminal justice
  wedding cake model, 22–23
Criminal justice wedding
    cake, 22–23
Criminal law
  civil law, contrasted, 75
  procedural law. *See*
    Procedural criminal law
  seven principles, 80–81
  substantive law, 75, 76–88
Criminal sanctions. *See* Pun-
    ishment and sentencing
Criminogenic, 61
Crisis intervention team
    (CIT), 162
Critical criminology, 64–65, 68
Cross-cultural differences.
    See Comparative
    Perspectives
Cross-examination, 265–266
Cruel and unusual
    punishment, 98–99
*CSI: Crime Scene Investiga-
    tion*, 155, 265, 433, 458
CSI effect, 265, 458
Cupp v. Murphy, 190, 192
Customs and Border
    Protection, 118
Cyber action team (CAT), 437
Cyber bullying, 494
Cyber crime, 44, 434–437

Dakota v. Opperman, 192
Dark figure of crime, 46
Databases, 443–445
Day fine, 389, 390
Day reporting center, 394

Death penalty, 287–294
    death-qualified juries,
        292–293
    effectiveness of counsel, 292
    mentally ill defendants, 292
    pros/cons, 294
    public opinion, 293
    statistics, 288, 289
    Supreme Court cases,
        289–291
Death-qualified juries,
    292–293
Decision-making process,
    17–21, 34–37. *See also*
    Criminal justice process
Defense against criminal
    charges, 81–85
    duress, 84–85
    entrapment, 85
    infancy, 85
    insanity, 86–88
    intoxication, 86
    mistake of fact, 85–86
    necessity, 84
    self-defense, 84
Defense attorney, 229–237
    assigned counsel, 235
    attorney effectiveness and
        competence, 236–237
    contract system, 236
    defined, 229
    indigent defendants,
        232–236
    pretrial proceedings, 245
    public defender, 231,
        232, 236
    realities of the job, 230, 231
    role, 229–230
    state-run system/county-
        run systems, 234
    typical actions, 230
    up-close profile, 82
Delaware v. Prouse, 187
Delinquent children, 479. *See
    also* Juvenile justice
Demonstrative evidence, 263
Department complaint
    procedures, 149
Department contract model,
    172–173
Department of Homeland
    Security (DHS), 9, 166
Department of Justice, 117
Dependent child, 480
Detectives, 155
Detention hearing, 484
Determinate sentence, 283
Deterrence, 277–279, 282
DHS, 9, 166
Dickerson v. United States, 194
Differential response, 151
Direct evidence, 264
Discovery, 226
Discretion, 12–13
    police, 143–145
    prosecutor, 225–226, 245
Discretionary release, 409,
    414–415

Discrimination, 27
Disorganized criminal, 361
Disparity, 26
District associate judge, 302
District attorney, 221
*District Attorney's Office v.
    Osborne*, 303, 449
District court, 214
*District of Columbia v.
    Heller*, 91
Diversion, 483
DNA analysis, 445–449
DNA exonerations, 449
DNA technology, 303
Doing justice, 5–6
Doing time, 360
Domestic violence, 144
Domestic violence court, 214
Double jeopardy, 90, 94
Douglas v. California, 233
Dropping the charges, 245
Drug courts, 213
Drug dealing, 42
Drug Enforcement Adminis-
    tration (DEA), 117
Drug law enforcement, 157
Drunken driving, 462
Drunkenness, 86
Dual court system, 16
Due process. *See* Procedural
    criminal law
Due process model, 23, 24
Due process revolution,
    92–93
Duress, 84–85
Durham Rule, 87

Earned time, 285
Eastern State Penitentiary, 313
Eddings v. Oklahoma, 474
Eighth Amendment, 92,
    97–99, 247
Elderly prisoners, 355–357
Electric chair, 432–433
Electronic file management,
    455
Electronic monitoring, 392,
    393, 460
Elements of a crime, 79
Elmira Reformatory, 315
Emergency Preparedness and
    Response (DHS), 9
English roots of American
    police, 108–109
Enlightenment, 310
Entrapment, 85
Equal Employment
    Opportunity Act, 123
Escobedo v. Illinois, 194
*Essay on Crimes and
    Punishment, An*
    (Beccaria), 60
Evidence, 263–266
Evidence-based policing,
    151, 159
Ex-felons' gun ownership
    rights, 91
Ex post facto laws, 80

Excessive fines, 98
Excessive use of force, 145
Exchange, 11, 12
Exclusionary rule, 197–201
    defined, 197
    good faith exception,
        199–200
    inevitable discovery
        exception, 200
    international differences,
        199
    Supreme Court cases, 200
Excuse defenses, 84–88
Exigent circumstances,
    189–190
Expiration release, 408
External stress, 129

Fairness. *See* Procedural
    criminal law
FBI
    cyber crime, 436–437
    DNA analysis, 448
    federal agency, 7
    legal attaches (legats), 166
    Myth & Reality, 116
    priorities, 117
    terrorism, 9, 166
Fear of crime, 57–58
Federal Bureau of
    Investigation. *See* FBI
Federal Bureau of Prisons, 319
Federal corrections system, 319
Federal court system, 214
Federal law enforcement
    agencies, 8, 116–118
Federal Law Enforcement
    Training Center
    (FLETC), 122
Federal marshals, 117. *See
    also* U.S. marshals
Federal Probation and Pretrial
    Services System, 319
Federal special agents, 155
Federalism, 7
Felony, 22, 76
Felony cases, 246
Felony courts, 297
Feminist theories, 65
Fifteenth Amendment, 92
Fifth Amendment, 90–91,
    94–95, 193
Filtering, 14–15
Filtering process, 14
Fine, 98, 388, 389
Fingerprint database, 444
Fingerprint evidence, 440,
    444–445
Fixing Broken Windows
    (Kelling/Coles), 114
FLETC training centers, 122
Florida v. J. L., 189
Florida v. Powell, 194
Foot patrol, 159
Force, use of
    correctional officers, 354
    police, 146–148, 182–183
    search and seizure, 182–183

Forcible rape, 78
Ford v. Wainwright, 292
Forensic DNA analyst, 450
Forensic science laboratories,
    446
Forfeiture, 391
Fourteenth Amendment, 92
Fourth Amendment, 90,
    93–94
Frankpledge, 108
Fraternal Order of Police
    (FOP), 113
Free exercise of religion,
    328, 329
*Freedom and Death inside the
    City Jail* (Narag), 254
Freedom of speech, 328
Frisk search, 187–189
From arrest to trial. *See*
    Criminal justice process
Fundamental fairness, 92
Furlough, 418
Furman v. Georgia, 290
Fusion center, 167

Gangs
    MS-13, 167
    prison, 373
    youth, 469–470, 492–493
Gender gap, 66
General deterrence, 278
GEO Group, 323
Geographic information
    system (GIS), 443
Georgia v. Randolph, 191
Geriatric prison, 355
Gideon v. Wainwright, 95, 233
GIS, 443
Gleaning, 360
Glover v. Johnson, 330
Going rate, 238, 257
Good faith exception,
    199–200
Good time, 284
Gragnon v. Scarpelli, 332
Graham v. Connor, 183
Graham v. Florida, 99,
    474, 476
Grand jury, 20, 94, 228
"Grass eaters," 147
Gregg v. Georgia, 290
Griffin v. Wisconsin, 331
GRYD program, 470
Guilty plea, 228, 257, 258

Habeas corpus, 269–270
Hackers, 44, 436
Halfway house, 418–419
Hamdi v. Rumsfeld, 75, 169
Hands-off policy, 327
Hard/soft technology,
    462, 463
Harm, 80
Hate crime, 45
Heath v. Alabama, 94
Heroin addiction, 104–105
Herring v. United States, 201,
    202–203

Hispanics. *See* Race and ethnicity
Historical overview
  Cincinnati Declaration of Principles, 315, 316
  colonial era/early republic, 110
  community model, 316–317
  community policing era (1970–present), 113–114
  corrections, 310–318
  crime control model, 317–318
  English roots of American police, 108–109
  juvenile justice, 470–478
  lease system, 314
  medical model, 317
  New York system, 313–314
  parole, 406–407
  Pennsylvania system, 312–313, 314
  policing, 108–114
  political era (1840–1920), 110–111
  prisons, 344
  probation, 382–383
  professional model era (1920–1970), 112–113
  reformatory movement, 315
  rehabilitation model, 316–317
HIV-positive inmates, 357
Home confinement, 391–392, 393, 460
Homeland security, 9, 166–170, 172
Homicide, 78
Hot spots, 158–159
House, 458
House arrest, 391–392, 393
House of Refuge of New York, 472
Hudson v. Palmer, 328
Human-trafficking task force, 156
Hung jury, 267

Id, 62
Identity theft, 434, 435
Ignition interlock system, 462
Illinois v. Caballes, 93
Illinois v. Gates, 185
Illinois v. Lidster, 187
Illinois v. Rodriguez, 191
Illinois v. Wardlow, 189, 192
Immaturity, 85
Implicit plea bargaining, 257
Imprisoned mothers, 366
In re Gault, 473, 474
In re Kemmler, 432
In re Winship, 474
In the Name of the Father (film), 193
Incapacitation, 279–280, 282
Incarceration, 283–286
  custodial model, 347

determinate sentence, 283
  goals, 347
  indeterminate sentence, 283
  mandatory sentence, 283–284
  rate of, 334, 336, 337, 339
  rehabilitation model, 347
  reintegration model, 347
  sentence *vs.* actual time served, 284–286, 338
  three-strikes law, 284
  tougher sentencing policies, 338
  truth in sentencing, 286
Incarceration rate, 334, 336, 337, 339
Inchoate offense, 79
Incident-driven policing, 151
Incomplete offense, 79
Incorporation, 92, 93
Indefinite sentence, 283
Indeterminate sentence, 283
Index offenses, 48
Indiana v. Edwards, 95
Indianapolis Re-entry Education Facility, 404–405
Indictment, 20, 228
Indigent defendants, 232–236
Inevitable discovery exception, 200
Infancy, 85
Information, 20
Information Analysis and Infrastructure Protection (DHS), 9
Initial appearance, 20, 244–245
Inmate code, 359, 374
Inmate rights. *See* Constitutional rights of prisoners
Inner cities, 55
Innocence Project, 449
Inquisitorial process, 211
Insanity defense, 86–88
Inside: Life behind Bars in America (Santos), 346
Inside the Criminal Justice System
  arrest, booking, etc., 206–207
  coming home, 427
  heroin addiction, 104–105
  Michigan vs. Jones, 34–37
  prison, 426–427
  prosecution, adjudication, and sentencing, 306–307
  reflections, 496–497
Institutional diversion, 394
Institutional reentry preparation programs, 404–406
Intake hearing, 483
Intake referee, 484
Integrated Automated Fingerprint Identification System (IAFIS), 444
Integrated theories, 66

Intelligence analyst, 168
Intelligence information, 167
Intensive supervision probation (ISP), 394–395
Intermediate appellate courts, 213
Intermediate sanctions, 21, 286, 388–397
  boot camp, 395–396
  community service, 392–394
  continuum of sanctions, 389
  day reporting center, 394
  electronic monitoring, 392, 393, 460
  fine, 388, 389
  forfeiture, 391
  home confinement, 391–392, 393, 460
  implementation, 396–397
  ISP, 394–395
  juveniles, 489
  new widening, 397
  restitution, 389–391
Internal affairs unit, 149
Internal Revenue Service (IRS), 117
International Association of Chiefs of Police (IACP), 113
International comparisons. *See* Comparative Perspectives
Internet Crime Complaint Center (IC3), 44, 436
Interpol, 166
Interrogation, 193–196
Intoxication, 86
Inventory search, 192
Investigation, 19, 155
Investigative tools, 440–463. *See also* Technology and criminal justice
"Invisible punishment," 420
Iowa's Drug Control Strategy, 30
Irizarry v. United States, 301
Irresistible impulse test, 87
ISP, 394–395
Italian American Mafia, 42

J. D. B. v. North Carolina, 194, 476, 477–478
Jail, 324–326
Jailing, 360
Jaywalking, 76
Job stress, 128–129
Johnson v. California, 330
Johnson v. Zerbst, 233
Judge, 215–220
  actions of trial court judge, 217
  adjudicator, as, 216
  administrator, as, 217
  election campaigns, 218–219
  functions, 216–218
  gender, 216

loose administrative ship, 239
  methods of selection, 219
  negotiator, as, 217
  problem solver, as, 218
  prosecutors, and, 227
  public opinion, 220
  race and ethnicity, 216
  selection of, 218–220
  sentencing, and, 297–298, 299
  tight control over process, 239
  up-close profile, 302
Judge's instructions to jury, 260
Judicial selection, 218–220
Jurisdiction, 211
Juror compensation, 262
Jury, 259
Jury deliberation, 267
Jury pool, 261
Jury selection, 261–263
Jury size, 261
Jury trial, 260–268
  accused's constitutional right, 96
  challenges, 263
  closing arguments, 266
  CSI effect, 265
  death-qualified juries, 292–293
  evaluating the system, 267–268
  evidence, 263–266
  functions of the jury, 260
  judge's instructions to jury, 260
  juror compensation, 262
  jury deliberation, 267
  jury selection, 261–263
  jury size, 261
  opening statements, 263
  prosecution's presentation of evidence, 263–265
  sequestering the jury, 267
  standard of proof, 266
  technology, 457–458
  verdict, 267
  voir dire, 262
  whether accused will take the stand, 265
Just deserts or deserved punishment, 277
Justice for All Act, 58, 447
Justifiable homicides, 78
Justification defenses, 84
Juvenile court period (1899–1960), 471, 472–473
Juvenile justice, 467–495
  adjudication, 486–488
  adult system, compared, 487
  aftercare, 491
  age, 479
  budget cuts, 490
  community treatment, 491–492

Juvenile justice (*continued*)
constitutional rights, 475, 487
corrections, 488–492
crime control period (1980–2005), 471, 475
custodial care, 489–490
cyber bullying, 494
detention hearing, 484
disposition, 488
drug use, 469
future directions, 494
gangs, 469–470, 492–493
historical overview, 470–478
institutional programs, 490–491
intake hearing, 483
intermediate sanctions, 489
jurisdiction criteria, 479–480
juvenile court period (1899–1960), 471, 472–473
juvenile rights period (1960–1980), 471, 473–475
"Kids Are Different" (2005–present), 471, 475–478
LWOP sentences, 476
overview (flowchart), 482
police interface, 481–483
pretrial procedures, 484–485
probation, 489
public opinion, 485, 490
Puritan period (1646–1824), 471, 472
refuge period (1824–1899), 471, 472
status offense, 475, 480
Supreme Court cases, 474
theories of causation, 66, 468–469
transfer (waiver) to adult court, 476, 480, 485, 486, 490
types of crime, 469
Juvenile Justice and Delinquency Prevention Act, 475
Juvenile rights period (1960–1980), 471, 473–475
Juvenile waiver, 476, 480, 485, 486, 490

Kansas City Preventive Patrol Experiment, 158
Kansas v. Hendricks, 420
Kennedy v. Louisiana, 291
Kent v. United States, 473, 474
Kentucky v. King, 190
Keystroke-logging device, 452
"Kids Are Different" (2005–present), 471, 475–478
Kinship-based DNA searching, 447
Knowles v. Iowa, 191, 192
Kyllo v. United States, 452

Labeling theories, 64
"Ladder of social mobility," 42

Lafler v. Cooper, 257
Latent fingerprint, 445
Law enforcement, 129–130
Law enforcement agencies, 116–119
county agencies, 118
FBI. *See* FBI
federal agencies, 116–118
municipal agencies, 119
special jurisdiction agencies, 119
state agencies, 118
tribal police, 118–119
Law enforcement certification, 122
Law enforcement intelligence, 167
Learning theories, 64
Lease system, 314
Lee v. Washington, 330
Legal attaches (legats), 166
Legal responsibility, 75
Legalistic style, 136
Less-lethal weapons, 453–455, 460
Lewis v. United States, 96
Liability of correctional personnel, 332
Lie detector, 440
Life course theories, 65–66, 68
Lifestyle-exposure model, 54–56
Local detectives, 155
Local legal culture, 237–238
Local police officers, 116, 119
Lockhart v. McCree, 292
Lockyer v. Andrade, 99
Long-term prisoners, 358
Low-income city dwellers, 55
Lower courts, 297
Lyman School for Boys, 472

Machismo, 372
Magna Carta, 108
Mala in se, 5
Mala prohibita, 5
Mandatory cocaine sentencing laws, 284
Mandatory minimum sentence, 283
Mandatory release, 408
Mandatory sentence, 283–284
Manslaughter, 78
Mapp v. Ohio, 198, 200
Mark system, 315
Marxist criminologists, 65
Maryland v. Wilson, 191, 192
Massiah v. United States, 194
Maximum-security prison, 320–321
McCleskey v. Kemp, 290
McDonald v. Chicago, 91, 213
McKeiver v. Pennsylvania, 474
"Meat eaters," 147
Medical model, 317
Medicare/medicaid fraud, 118
Medium-security prison, 321

Melendez-Diaz v. Massachusetts, 449
Mens rea, 81–83
Mental health courts, 213
Mentally ill persons
death penalty, 292
insanity defense, 86–88
prisoners, 357–358, 372
Mere suspicion, 184
Merit selection, 219, 220
Merton's anomie theory, 63
Metropolitan Police Act, 109
Michigan Department of State Police v. Sitz, 187, 192
Michigan Reformatory, 322
Michigan v. Long, 191
Miller v. Alabama, 476
Minimum-security prison, 321
Minority police officers, 124
Miranda v. Arizona, 193, 233
Miranda warnings, 193–195
Misdemeanor courts, 297
Misdmeanor, 23, 76
Missouri v. Frye, 257
Missouri v. Seibert, 196
Mistake of fact, 85–86
M'Naghten Case, 86
M'Naghten Rule, 86
Model Penal Code, 77, 87
Monell v. Department of Social Services of the City of New York, 150, 332
Money laundering, 42
Monitoring and surveillance, 451–453
Montana v. Egelhoff, 86
Morrissey v. Brewer, 331, 421
Motions, 245
Motor vehicle theft, 78
Motorized patrol, 159
MS-13 gang, 167
Multiagency task force, 156
Multiple-offense indictment, 256
Multiracial feminism, 67
Municipal law enforcement agencies, 119
Murder, 78
Murder in the first degree (Delaware), 78–79
Murray v. Giarratano, 233
Myth & Reality
community service, 394
constitutional rights of juveniles, 475
constitutional rights of prisoners, 328
correctional officers, 350
deterrence, 280
FBI, 116
patrol officers and the crime rate, 152
plea bargaining, 239, 255
probable cause to search, 191
rape, 56
reentry into the community, 420
right to trial by jury, 96

scientific testing of evidence, 433
tough on crime, 15

National Crime Victimization Surveys (NCVS), 49–50
National Defense Authorization Act, 169
National Incident-Based Reporting System (NIBRS), 49
National Parks Service, 118
Native American Tribal Police, 118–119
NCIS, 458
NCVS, 49–50
Necessity, 84
Neglected child, 480
Negotiating a settlement, 255. *See also* Plea bargaining
Neoclassical criminology, 60
New generation prison, 375
New widening, 397
New York v. Class, 191, 192
New York v. Quarles, 194
New York system, 313–314
NIBRS, 49
NIMBY attitude, 418
911 system, 151, 911
Nix v. Williams, 200
Nolle prosequi, 226
Nonnegligent manslaughter, 78
Nonpartisan election, 218
North Carolina v. Alford, 258
Northern Correctional Facility, 320

"Oath or affirmation," 183
"Objective reasonableness," 182
Occupational crime, 42
Off-duty employment of police officers, 172–173
Offender tracking information system (OTIS), 459
Offenses
inchoate/incomplete, 79
misdemeanor/felony, 76
status, 475
UCR definitions, 78
Office of Community Oriented Policing Services (COPS Office), 114
Officer contract model, 173
Officer-prisoner violence, 374–375
Oklahoma Publishing Co. v. District Court, 474
One man's journey. *See* Inside the Criminal Justice System
Opening statements, 263
Operational stress, 129
Operational units, 134
Order maintenance, 129
Ordinary crime, 41
Organizational chart (Odessa, Texas police dept), 133

Organizational stress, 129
Organized crime, 42–43
Other conditional release, 408
OTIS, 459

Paid Detail Unit, 172
Parens patriae, 470, 473
Parole, 335–336, 409–419
  author's personal
    experience, 412–413
  bureaucratic environment,
    419
  conditions of release, 415
  constitutional rights of
    parolees, 331–332
  defined, 406
  hearing, 411–413
  historical overview, 406–407
  officer, 418–419
  parolees, 416
  revocation, 421, 422
  underlying concepts, 406
Parole board, 409
Parole board process, 409–413
Parole bureaucracy, 419
Parole hearing, 411–413
Parole officer, 418–419
Parole revocation, 421, 422
Parole violations, 336, 337
Part I (index) offenses, 48
Part II offenses, 48
Partisan election, 218
PATRIOT Act, 169–170, 452
Patrol-car technology, 441–443
Patrol function, 154–155,
    158–161
  aggressive patrol, 159–160
  assignment of officers,
    158–160
  community policing, 160
  directed patrol, 159
  foot *vs.* motorized patrol, 159
  future of patrol, 161
  hot spots, 158–159
  patrol-car technology,
    441–443
  preventive patrol, 158
  time allocation (Wilmington,
    Delaware), 154
Patrol units, 133
Pelican Bay, 320
Penal code, 75
Penitentiary, 312
*Pennsylvania Board of
    Pardons and Parole v.
    Scott*, 331
Pennsylvania system,
    312–313, 314
Pepper v. United States, 301
PepperBalls, 453
Percentage bail, 251
Peremptory challenge, 263
Personal stress, 129
Petty offenses, 76, 96
PINS, 479
Place-based policing, 159
Plain view doctrine, 181
Plea bargain, 11

Plea bargaining, 20, 255–257
  criticisms of, 257
  defense tactics, 257
  exchange relationships, 256
  implicit, 257
  legal issues, 257–258
  multiple-offense
    indictment, 256
  Myth & Reality, 239, 255
  pleas without bargaining,
    257
  prosecution's tactics,
    256–257
Police, 15–16, 107–139. *See
    also* Law enforcement
    agencies; Policing
  accreditation, 149–150
  authority, 127
  bureaucratic elements,
    132–134
  certification, 122
  chain and unity of
    command, 133–134
  citizens, and, 143
  civic accountability,
    148–150
  civil liability, 150
  Close-Up profile, 121
  corruption, 147–148
  crime-fighter image, 131
  discretion, 143–145
  division of labor, 132–133
  duties, 16
  educational requirements,
    123
  force, use of, 146–148,
    182–183
  functions, 130–132
  gateway to justice
    system, 134
  historical overview,
    108–114
  juveniles, and, 481–483
  minority officers, 124
  morality, 127–128
  off-duty employment,
    172–173
  operational units, 134
  organizational chart, 133
  private employment,
    172–173
  private law enforcement,
    and, 173
  productivity, 152–153
  prosecuting attorney,
    and, 226
  public opinion, 26, 128,
    143, 153
  questioning suspects,
    193–196
  recruitment, 120–123
  response to calls for
    service, 151–152
  salary, 122, 123
  stress, 128–129
  superior-subordinate
    relationship, 134
  training, 122, 125–126

  volunteers, 136
  women officers, 124–125
  working personality,
    126–127
Police abuse of power, 145–148
Police academy, 122
Police accountability, 148–150
Police accreditation, 149–150
Police agency. *See* Law
    enforcement agencies
Police auxiliary units, 136
Police brutality, 145
Police bureaucracy, 132
Police corruption, 147–148
Police departments, 119
Police discretion, 143–145
Police functions, 130–132
Police interrogation, 193–196
Police isolation, 128
Police morality, 127–128
Police policy, 135–137
Police productivity, 152–153
Police response, 151–152
Police shootings, 146, 147
Police subculture, 126–129
Policing. *See also* Police
  apprehension, 155, 156
  budget cuts, 115, 132, 135
  changing priorities, 114–115
  community, 114, 160
  community crime
    prevention, 163–164
  danger, 127
  drug law enforcement, 157
  evidence-based, 151
  implementing the mandate,
    131–132
  incident-driven, 151
  investigation, 155
  law enforcement, 129–130
  legalistic style, 136
  multicultural society,
    in, 162–163
  order maintenance, 129
  problem-oriented, 114, 160
  service, 131
  service style, 136–137
  special operations, 156–157
  special populations, 162
  standards, 149–150
  traffic regulation, 157
  vice, 157
  watchman style, 135–136
Policy Debate
  accelerated release of
    offenders, 410
  death penalty, 294
  ex-felons' gun ownership
    rights, 91
  juvenile waiver, 486
  terrorism suspects/Bill of
    Rights, 184–185
  tough crime-control
    policies, 52–53
Political crime, 43–44
Political era (1840–1920),
    110–111
Polygraph, 440

Positivist criminology, 60–61
Posse comitatus, 111
Powell v. Alabama, 92, 233
Precinct-level accountability
    for crime reduction, 152
Predispositional report, 488
Preliminary hearing, 20
Prerelease facilities, 404–406
Presentence report, 298–299
Presumptive sentence, 283
Pretrial detention,
    252–253, 254
Pretrial process, 244–253
  arraignment, 245
  booking, 244
  initial appearance, 244–245
  motions, 245
  pretrial detention,
    252–253, 254
  pretrial release. *See* Pretrial
    release
  preventive detention,
    251–252
Pretrial release
  bail, 247–250
  bail fund, 251
  citation, 250–251
  percentage bail, 251
  release on recognizance, 251
Preventive detention,
    251–252
Preventive patrol, 154, 158
Prison, 320–321, 343–377
  cell phones, 461
  cigarettes, 362
  classification of prisoners,
    367–368
  constitutional rights. *See*
    Constitutional rights of
    prisoners
  defects of total power, 350
  disorganized criminal, 361
  doing time, 360
  economic transactions,
    361–362
  educational programs, 368
  elderly prisoners, 355–357
  exchange relationships, 351
  family assistance programs,
    366–367
  gangs, 373
  gleaning, 360
  historical overview,
    310–318, 344
  HIV/AIDS, 357
  industrial programs, 369
  inmate code, 359, 374
  inmate leadership, 351–352
  jailing, 360
  level of security, 320–321
  long-term prisoners, 358
  medical services, 366,
    370–371
  mentally ill prisoners,
    357–358, 372
  Myth & Reality, 350
  organizational chart, 349
  population growth, 336, 337

Prison (*continued*)
  private, 322–324
  protective custody, 374
  public opinion, 347, 403
  race/ethnicity, 356, 372
  rape, 365, 373–374
  rehabilitative programs,
    369–370
  rewards and punishments,
    350–351
  state politics, 339
  survival tips for
    beginners, 360
  vignette, 345–346, 426–427
  violence. *See* Violence in
    prison
  vocational education, 368
  women. *See* Women in
    prison
Prison construction, 338
Prison currency, 362
Prison economy, 361
Prison gangs, 373
Prison industries, 369
Prison Litigation Reform
  Act, 409
Prison organization, 348–349
Prison programs, 367–371
Prison rape, 373–374
Prison Rape Elimination Act,
  365, 373
Prison siting, 339
Prison violence. *See* Violence
  in prison
Prison vocational
  programs, 368
Prisoner-officer violence, 374
Prisoner-prisoner violence,
  373–374
Prisoner reentry. *See* Reentry
  into the community
Prisoner rights. *See*
  Constitutional rights
  of prisoners
Prisoner's rights
  movement, 331
Private employment of public
  police, 172–173
Private policing. *See* Security
  management and private
  policing
Private prisons, 322–324
Proactive strategies, 151, 152
Probable cause, 183–185, 191
Probation, 21, 287, 335,
  381–388
  assessing, 387–388
  constitutional rights of
    probationers, 331–332,
    386–387
  electronic monitoring, 392
  historical overview, 382–383
  intermediate sanctions, 396
  ISP, 394–395
  job description, 384
  juveniles, 489
  organization, 383
  revocation, 385–387

risk classification, 385
shock, 287
termination of, 387
violations, 385–386
volunteers, 385
Probation diversion, 394
Probation officer assistant, 384
Probation revocation,
  385–387
Probation services, 384–385
Probation violations, 385–386
Problem-oriented policing,
  114, 160
Problem-solving courts,
  213, 218
Procedural criminal law,
  88–99
  Bill of Rights, 89
  cruel and unusual
    punishment, 98–99
  defined, 75
  double jeopardy, 94
  due process revolution,
    92–93
  Eighth Amendment, 92,
    97–99
  excessive fines, 98
  Fifth Amendment, 90–91,
    94–95
  Fourteenth Amendment, 92
  Fourth Amendment, 90,
    93–94
  overview (figure), 99
  release on bail, 98
  right to counsel, 95
  right to impartial jury, 96
  right to speedy and
    public trial, 96
  Russia, in, 97
  self-incrimination, 94
  Sixth Amendment, 92,
    95–96
  unreasonable search and
    seizure, 93–94. *See also*
    Search and seizure
Procunier v. Martinez, 328
Professional model era
  (1920–1970), 112–113
Progressive movement, 112
Project Safe Neighborhoods,
  164
Projectile weapons, 453
Property crime, 41
Prosection complex, 223
Prosecuting attorney, 221, 222
Prosecutorial discretion, 223,
  225–226
Prosecutorial system,
  221–228
  accountability of
    prosecutors, 224
  close-up profile of
    prosecuting attorney, 222
  community, and, 227
  community prosecution,
    227
  decision-making policies,
    227–228

discretion of prosecutor,
  225–226, 245
discrimination, 233, 245
dropping the charges, 245
exchange relationships, 12
judges/courts, and, 227
plea bargaining, 256–257
police, and, 226
politics and prosecution,
  221–223
power of prosecuting
  attorney, 223
prosection complex, 223
roles of prosecutor,
  223–225
types of prosecutors, 221
typical actions of
  prosecution, 228
victims/witnesses, and,
  226–227
Prosecutor's bias, 223
Protective custody, 374
Psychoanalysis, 62
Psychological explanations,
  62–63, 68
Psychopath, 62
Public defender, 231, 232, 236
Public opinion. *See* Myth &
  Reality; What Americans
  Think
Public-order crime, 41
Public safety exception, 195
Punishment and sentencing,
  275–307
  death. *See* Death penalty
  deterrence, 277–279, 282
  goals, 277–282
  incapacitation, 279–280, 282
  incarceration, 283–286
  intermediate sanctions,
    286. *See also*
    Intermediate sanctions
  overview, 295
  probation, 287. *See also*
    Probation
  rehabilitation, 280–281, 282
  retribution, 277, 282
  sentencing. *See* Sentencing
  truth in sentencing, 286
Puritan period (1646–1824),
  471, 472

Quantifying police work, 152
Questioning suspects,
  193–196

R. v. Grant, 199
Race and ethnicity
  aggressive patrol, 160
  confidence in justice
    system, 27
  confidence in police, 26
  correctional officers, 354
  disparity and discrimina-
    tion, 25–30, 113
  explanations for disparities,
    27–30
  hate crime, 45

jail, 325
judges, 216
jurors, 146–147
mandatory sentences, 284
multiracial feminism, 67
organized crime, 42
parolees, 416
police officers, 124
policing, 162–163
prison, 330, 356, 372
racial profiling, 28, 29,
  164–165
sentencing, 301–303
stop-and-frisk searches,
  164, 165
tribal police, 118–119
use of force, 146–147
victimization, 54–55
Racial profiling, 28, 29,
  164–165
Rape, 56, 78
Reactive, 151, 155
Real evidence, 263
Reasonable doubt, 266
Reasonable expectation of
  privacy, 181
Reasonable suspicion, 182
Recidivism, 381, 404
Red Hook Youth Court, 483
Reentry courts, 423
Reentry into the community,
  401–427
  adjustment to life outside
    prison, 419–421, 459–460
  budget cuts, 403–404, 423
  community programs
    following release, 416–418
  furlough, 418
  future directions, 422–423
  halfway house, 418–419
  Myth & Reality, 420
  parole. *See* Parole
  Policy Debate, 410
  prerelease facilities,
    404–406
  reentry courts, 423
  reentry preparation
    programs, 404–406
  reentry problem, 402–403
  release mechanisms,
    407–409, 414–415
  work and educational
    release, 417
Reentry preparation
  programs, 404–406
Reentry specialist, 405
Reform school, 472
Reformatory, 315
Reformatory movement, 315
Refuge period (1824–1899),
  471, 472
Rehabilitation, 280–281, 282
Rehabilitation model,
  316–317, 347
Reintegration model, 347
Release into the community, 21
Release mechanisms,
  407–409, 414–415

Release on bail, 98
Release on recognizance
    (ROR), 20, 251
Religious Land Use and
    Institutional Persons Act
    (RLUIPA), 329
Remote-controlled stun
    belt, 460
Resident unit supervisor, 322
Resource dependence, 13
Resource scarcity, 246
Response to calls for service,
    151–152
Restitution, 389–391
Restorative justice, 483
Retribution, 277, 282
Revocation
    parole, 421, 422
    probation, 385–387
Ricketts v. Adamson, 258
Right to counsel, 95, 233
Right to impartial jury, 96
Right to public trial, 96
Right to speedy and
    public trial, 96
RLUIPA, 329
Robbery, 78
Roberts Court, 101
Robinson v. California, 80
Roper v. Simmons, 291,
    474, 475, 494
ROR, 20, 251
Ross v. Moffitt, 95, 233
Rothgery v. Gillespie, 95
Rubber bullets, 453

Safford Unified School District
    #1 v. Redding, 475
Samson v. California, 331
Santobello v. New York,
    255, 258
Scanners, 452
Scareware, 436
Schall v. Martin, 474, 475
School resource officer
    (SRO), 156, 481
Science and Technology
    (DHS), 9
Scientific evidence, 264, 265
Scientific testing of
    evidence, 433
Search, 181
Search and seizure, 93–94,
    181–192
    automobile search, 191–192
    consent search, 190–191
    definitions, 181, 182
    exigent circumstances,
        189–190
    plain view doctrine, 181
    prisons, 328–329
    probable cause, 183–185, 191
    reasonable expectation of
        privacy, 181
    search incident to arrest, 189
    special needs, 186–187
    stop-and-frisk search, 164,
        165, 187–189

Supreme Court cases,
    192, 200
    warrantless search, 186–192
Search incident to arrest, 189
Second Amendment, 89–90
Secret Service, 9, 118
Section 1983 lawsuits, 150,
    327, 332
Security management and
        private policing, 170–175
    functions, 171–172
    homeland security, 172
    licensing requirements, 175
    private employment of
        public police, 172–173
    private-public interface, 173
    recruitment and training,
        173–175
Security manager, 171
Security officers, 174, 175
Security threat groups, 373
Seizure, 181
Selective incapacitation, 280
Self-defense, 84
Self-incrimination, 90, 94, 193
Sentence vs. actual time
    served, 284–286, 338
Sentencing, 21, 296–303
    felony courts, 297
    guidelines, 299–301
    judges, 297–298, 299
    misdemeanor courts, 297
    presentence report,
        298–299
    racial disparities, 301–303
    wrongful convictions, 303
Sentencing guidelines,
    299–301
Separate confinement, 313
Sequestering the jury, 267
Service, 131
Service style, 136–137
Seven principles of criminal
    law, 80–81
Sex offender registry, 459
Sex workers, 43
Sexual assault, 56
Sexual offender notification
    laws, 420, 421
Sheriff, 111, 118
Shock incarceration, 395
Shock probation, 287
Sisters in Crime (Adler), 67
Sixth Amendment, 92, 95–96
Skinner v. Oklahoma, 61
Slave patrols, 110
Smith v. Daily Mail
    Publishing Co., 474
Sobriety checkpoint, 187
Social learning theory, 66
Social process theories, 64, 68
"Social sanitation," 252
Social structure theories,
    63–64, 68
Socialist feminists, 65
Socialization, 125, 127
Sociopath, 62
Soft/hard technology, 462, 463

Software piracy, 438–439
Special agents, 155
Special jurisdiction
    agencies, 119
Special operations, 156–157
Special populations, 162
Special units, 134
Specific deterrence, 278
"Spit and acquit" program, 447
Split probation, 287
SRO, 156, 481
Staff-on-inmate violence, 374
Standard of proof, 266
Stanford v. Kentucky, 474
State attorney general, 221
State corrections system,
    319–321
State court system, 214
State law enforcement
    agencies, 118
State of Michigan versus
    Christopher Jones, 34–37
State of Prisons in England
    and Wales, The
    (Howard), 312
State of Recidivism: The
    Revolving Door of
    America's Prisons, 404
State prison system, 320–321
State supreme court, 213
State's attorney, 221
Status offense, 475, 480
Statute of Winchester, 109
Stop, 182
Stop-and-frisk search, 164,
    165, 187–189
Strain theory, 66
"Stranger-in-the-bushes"
    stereotype of rape, 56
Street crime, 41
Stress, 128–129
Strickland v. Washington,
    233, 292
Strict liability offenses, 81
Student loan fraud, 118
Styles of policing, 135–137
Subculture, 126
Substantial capacity test, 87
Substantive criminal law, 75,
    76–88
Super predators, 468
Superego, 62
Superior court, 214
Supreme Court, 213. See also
    Constitutional rights of
    prisoners; Procedural
    criminal law
    breadth of police powers,
        100–101
    current composition of
        court (2012), 213
    death penalty, 289–291
    due process for
        probationers, 331–332,
        386–387
    due process revolution,
        92–93, 198
    exclusionary rule, 200

forensic evidence, 449
    juvenile justice, 474
    new police technologies, 452
    peremptory challenge, 263
    right to counsel, 233
    warrantless searches, 192
Surveillance and
    identification, 450–452
Surveillance cameras, 451
Survey of Youth in
    Residential Placement
    (SYRP), 490
Sworn officers, 154
System, 11

Taser, 454
Task force, 156, 157
Technical violation, 385
Technology and criminal
    justice, 429–465
    civil liberties, 462–463
    corrections, 459–460, 463
    counterfeiting, 437–439
    courts, 455–458, 463
    cyber crime, 434–437
    databases, 443–445
    DNA analysis, 445–449
    effectiveness of technol-
        ogy in preventing
        crime, 464
    hard/soft technology,
        462, 463
    overview, 463
    patrol-car technology,
        441–443
    police, 440–455, 463
    surveillance and
        identification, 450–452
    weapons technology,
        453–455
Technology-based crimes, 8.
    See also Cyber crime
Ten percent cash bail, 251
Tennessee v. Garner, 182
Terrorism
    fingerprints, 444–445
    homeland security, 9,
        166–170, 172
    new laws and
        controversies, 169–170
    organized crime, 43
    PATRIOT Act, 169–170
    Policy Debate, 184–185
    political crime, 43–44
    preparing for threats,
        166–168
    public opinion, 194, 231
Terrorist-oriented policing, 115
Terry v. Ohio, 164, 187, 192
Testimony, 263
Texas Board of Pardons
    and Paroles, 409
"The chain," 426
"The mix," 364
Theories of criminality, 59–69
    biological explanations,
        61–62, 68
    classical school, 60

Theories of criminality
    (*continued*)
    critical theories, 64–65, 68
    feminist theories, 65
    integrated theories, 66
    life course theories,
        65–66, 68
    limitations of theories, 67–69
    neoclassicism, 60
    overview (table), 68
    positivism, 60–61
    psychological explanations,
        62–63, 68
    social process theories,
        64, 68
    social structure theories,
        63–64, 68
    women and crime, 66–67
Theory of differential
    association, 64
"Thief-takers," 109
Thirteenth Amendment, 92
Thompson v. Oklahoma, 474
Three-strikes law, 284
311 system, 151, 411
"Ticket" (citation), 250–251
Time served, 284–286,
    338, 414
Tithings, 108
Torture, 78
Totality of circumstances
    test, 185
Tough crime-control policies,
    15, 52–53
Tougher sentencing
    practices, 338
Traffic regulation, 157
Traffic stops, 191
Transnational criminal
    groups, 42–43
Transportation of
    prisoners, 460
Transportation Security
    Administration (TSA),
    9–10, 118
Trends in crime, 50–51
Trial, 21, 259–260.
    See also Jury trial
Trial courts of general
    jurisdiction, 212
Trial courts of limited
    jurisdiction, 212, 213
Trop v. Dulles, 98
True bill, 20
True Grit Senior Structured
    Living Program, 355

Truth in sentencing, 286
Turner v. Safley, 328

UCR, 46–49, 50
Uniform Crime Reports
    (UCR), 46–49, 50
Union brokerage model, 173
United States v. Bajakajian, 98
United States v. Booker, 301
United States v. Brawner, 87
United States v. Drayton,
    190, 192
United States v. Jacobson, 85
United States v. Jones, 452
United States v. Leon,
    199, 200
United States v. Robinson,
    189, 192
*United States v. Salerno and
    Cafero*, 98, 252
United States v. Wade, 233
United States attorney, 221
Unreasonable search and
    seizure, 93–94. *See also*
    Search and seizure
U.S. Border Patrol, 167
U.S. Constitution. *See*
    Constitutional rights of
    prisoners; Procedural
    criminal law
U.S. marshals, 111, 117, 250
U.S. Supreme Court. *See*
    Supreme Court
USA PATRIOT Act, 169–170,
    452
Use of force. *See* Force, use of

Vagrancy laws, 65
Vehicle stop, 187, 191–192
Verdict, 267
*Vernonia School District v.
    Acton*, 475
Vice work, 157
Victimless crime, 43
Victimology, 52
Victims' assistance laws, 58
Victims' rights statutes, 58
Vignettes. *See* Inside the
    Criminal Justice System
Violence in prison, 371–376
    age, 372
    architectural design, 375
    gangs, 373
    officer-prisoner violence,
        374–375
    prison management, 375

    prisoner-officer violence, 374
    protective custody, 374
    race, 372
    rape, 373–374
Violence interrupters, 470
Violent crime, 41, 51
Virginia v. Black, 45
Virginia v. Moore, 189
Visible crime, 41
Voir dire, 262
Volunteer police officers, 136

Wackenhut, 174
Waiver, 476, 480, 485, 486, 490
Walnut Street Jail, 312
War on drugs, 43, 338–339
Warden v. Hayden, 189, 192
Warrant, 19
Warrantless search, 186–192.
    See also Search and
    seizure
Warren Court, 92–93,
    98–99, 198
Watch system, 110
Watchman style, 135–136
Weapons technology, 453–455
Wedding cake model, 22–23
Weeks v. United States, 197,
    198
Wethersfield Prison for
    Women, 316
What Americans Think
    attorney-client privilege, 95
    crime, 46
    criminal justice system, 27
    cyber crime, 436
    death penalty, 293
    fear of crime, 57
    judges, 220
    jury, 261
    juvenile justice, 485, 490
    marijuana, legalization
        of, 339
    monitoring and
        surveillance, 451, 452
    police, 26, 128, 143, 153
    police brutality, 146
    prison, 347, 403
    racial profiling, 163
    recidivism, 279
    rehabilitative programs, 369
    release from prison, 381
    rights of criminals, 89
    terrorism, 194, 231
    torture/suspected
        terrorists, 194

White-collar crime, 63–64
Wiggins v. Smith, 292
Williams v. Florida, 261
Wilson v. Seiter, 329
Wisconsin v. Mitchell, 45
Witherspoon excludables, 292
Witherspoon v. Illinois, 292
Wolf v. Colorado, 198
Wolff v. McDonnell, 330
Women. *See also* Women
    in prison
    correctional officers,
        353, 354
    crime, and, 66–67
    domestic violence, 144
    jail inmates, 325
    judges, 216
    parolees, 416
    police officers, 124–125
    victims, as, 54
Women and Crime (Simon), 67
Women in prison, 321, 356,
    362–367
    educational/vocational
        training, 365–366
    equal protection, 330–331
    future of women's correc-
        tional institutions, 367
    historical overview, 316
    male prisons, compared,
        364–365
    medical services, 366
    mother and their children,
        366–367
    race/ethnicity, 356
    rape, 365, 374
    "the mix," 364
Women's Prison
    Association, 316
Work and educational
    release, 417
Workgroup, 238–239
Working personality, 126–127
Writ of habeas corpus,
    269–270
Wrongful convictions, 303
Wyoming v. Houghton, 191

Young Men's Christian
    Association (YMCA), 17
Youth crime. *See* Juvenile
    justice
Youth gangs, 469–470,
    492–493

Zero-tolerance policing, 159